Party ideology and popular politics
at the accession of
George III

ALWAYS READY · IN A · GOOD CAUSE

CAMBRIDGE UNIVERSITY PRESS

CAMBRIDGE

LONDON · NEW YORK · MELBOURNE

JUSTICE SANS PITIE.

Party ideology and popular politics at the accession of George III

JOHN BREWER

ASSISTANT LECTURER IN HISTORY
UNIVERSITY OF CAMBRIDGE

Published by the Syndics of the Cambridge University Press
The Pitt Building, Trumpington Street, Cambridge CB2 1RP
Bentley House, 200 Euston Road, London NW1 2DB
32 East 57th Street, New York, NY 10022, USA
296 Beaconsfield Parade, Middle Park, Melbourne 3206, Australia

ISBN: 0 521 21049 6

First published 1976

Printed in Great Britain
at the
University Printing House, Cambridge
(Euan Phillips, University Printer)

The broadsides on pp. ii–iii ('Arms of Liberty and Slavery') and
pp. 192–3 ('The Times') are reproduced by permission of the
Guildhall Library, City of London.

Contents

v

Contents

Preface

This book began life as a Cambridge Ph.D. thesis with the title 'Political Argument and Propaganda in England, 1760–1770'. Since then it has changed somewhat. I have become increasingly less preoccupied with the issues of parliamentary politics, and ever more fascinated by political and social life beyond Westminster. I would not, however, wish to write a book that did not in some way bring together the worlds of parliamentary politics and of popular political culture.

During the course of my work I have used a number of archives and record deposits, the owners of which have treated me with unfailing kindness.

I have to acknowledge the gracious permission of Her Majesty the Queen to make use of the papers of George III in the Royal Archives at Windsor.

I have also to thank the Marquis of Bute, the Marquis of Salisbury, the Duke of Devonshire, the Duke of Bedford, the Earl Fitzwilliam and the Fitzwilliam Estates Company, Lord Denbigh and Lord Rayleigh for permission to use their collections.

I would also like to express my appreciation to the archivists and librarians at the national and university libraries as well as those in the local records offices for their cheerful help and cooperation. And I owe a special debt to Miss Catharine Armet, the archivist at Mount Stuart, for the loan of transcripts of the Bute–Campbell correspondence, and for her prompt help with my all too frequent inquiries.

My thesis was supervised by Professor Bernard Bailyn of Harvard University, Professor Christie of the University of London, and Professor Jack Plumb. I have to thank them all; each offered guidance, encouragement and criticism in his own inimitable way. I owe special thanks to Jack Plumb: my intellectual debt to him should be clear to any reader of this book, but I also have to thank him for his kindness and personal support. Derek Beales of Sidney Sussex College has read my work continuously, has proof-read it, and provided a great many helpful suggestions together with some really tough criticism. All of our conversations have contributed to my understanding of the period. I have also to thank John Murrin for his comments and suggestions; Edward Thompson for his helpful remarks on the chapter on Wilkes; and Harry Dickinson for his thoughts on the Introduction. Quentin Skinner made helpful criticisms on the chapter on Pitt, and has been a constant source of inspiration. Others who have helped me during the rather long gestation of this book include Tom Pickard, Valerie Brewer, Dick Roberts, Nick Rogers, Susan Hewitt (who helped with the diagrams and map), and Charles Warren who scrutinised the typescript.

Nowadays scholarship is a luxury good of ever-growing expense. Fortunately I have received financial aid from the Henry Fund and the Fulbright Fund (both for work undertaken in the USA); from Sidney Sussex College, my *alma mater*, to cover research expenses and to keep body and soul together as a research fellow; from Washington University during a year's fascinating teaching there; and from the Huntington Library, that oasis of learning in Southern California. All of these institutions not only funded me but treated me with great kindness and hospitality; I am grateful to them all.

A book represents a chunk of its author's living experience. I would never have finished this work without the help of my friends, nor without support from students and colleagues. More especially this book could never have been written without the support, both financial and moral, of my parents. To be brought up in a household crammed with antiques, and to hear regularly of the superiority of candle-power over the electric light certainly served to increase my historical curiosity, just as the many visits to museums and galleries awakened my interest in the past. For these and many other reasons I dedicate this book to my parents.

J.B.

A note to the reader

This book is intended for an undergraduate audience as well as being addressed to experts in the field. One of its purposes is to raise certain general questions about how we should study the political society of eighteenth-century England, and about the role of ideology or argument in politics. The introduction is intended as a synopsis of the arguments advanced in the rest of the book, and does not contain the sort of detailed annotation that some students find highly indigestible; the subject matter of the other chapters is, I think, made clear by their titles. Those interested in the perennial problems of Georgian 'high' politics will find chapters 3 to 7 and chapter 12 most to their liking (or, at least, most to their interest). Those who prefer extra-parliamentary politics should read chapters 8 to 11; addicts of the study of crowd behaviour might also find chapter 9 of interest. Those interested in ideology will find that nearly all of the discussion of parliamentary politics concerns itself with politics *as argument*, and that chapter 10 offers yet another link between political ideology in England and America in this period.

Readers will notice that I refer to the followers of Rockingham and Newcastle in this period in a number of ways: as the Newcastle connection, the Newcastle–Rockingham connection, the Rockingham–Newcastle connection, and finally as the Rockingham whigs. This is intended to give some indication of the point in time at which the group is being discussed in any particular context. Newcastle connection is used for the period up until 1763; 1763–5 is the period of the Newcastle–Rockingham connection; thereafter, and until Newcastle formally consigned party leadership to Rockingham in January 1768 (*sic*), the party is called the Rockingham–Newcastle connection. From 1768 the connection is designated the Rockingham whigs.

Part I

Introduction

1. Hanoverian politics and
the 1760s

The people of Japan had been long divided between two inveterate parties known by the names of Shit-tilk-ums-heit, and She-it-kums-hi-til, the first signifying *more fool than knave*; and the other *more knave than fool*. Each had predominated in its turn, by securing a majority in the assemblies of the people; for the majority had always interest to force themselves into the administration: because the constitution being partly democratic, the Daire was still obliged to truckle to the prevailing faction. To obtain this majority, each side had employed every art of corruption, calumny, insinuation, and priestcraft; for nothing is such an effectual ferment in all popular commotions as religious fanaticism. No sooner one party accomplished its aim, than it reprobated the other, branding it with the epithets of traitors to their prince; while the minority retorted upon them the charge of corruption, rapaciousness, and abject servility. In short, both parties were equally abusive, rancorous, uncandid and illiberal. (Tobias Smollett, 'The History and Adventures of an Atom' in Smollett, *Works* (12 vols., 1901) XII, 374–5)

If we were bold enough to try to schematise eighteenth-century British politics we might well employ a threefold division of such a politically complex century. 1675 to 1725, as Professor Plumb has so ably argued, were the years which saw the emergence of the stable political order which most historians deem characteristic of eighteenth-century politics. If stability emerged in these years, then the period of whig hegemony, and especially the years 1725 to 1754, marked the consolidation of a system designed to ensure political equilibrium and equanimity. These were the halcyon days of oligarchical politics, disturbed only by the occasional if sometimes violent political storm. From 1754 until the spectre of the French revolution was to change fundamentally the nature of politics, a further stage can be observed: the gradual disintegration and fragmentation, slow but inexorable, of a previously stable political order. It is with the early years of this third period, especially the decade of the 1760s, that this study is concerned.

The system of political stability, the situation that pertained during most of the early years of Hanoverian government, was contingent upon a set of peculiar circumstances. It was dependent, in the first instance, upon single-party government; secondly, upon the control

3

or grip (never total but ever-tightening after 1725) on the legislature by the executive; thirdly, upon what Plumb has called 'a sense of common identity' amongst those who wielded power[1] – which meant, of course, that if, as Namier argued, the king was *primus inter pares*, he and the political class from which he drew his government must act on a set of common political presuppositions; and finally, it rested upon the exclusion of a substantial part of the nation from the institutionalised political process. The importance of the 1760s to the historian lies in the fact that all of these prerequisites of political stability were in some way challenged, modified or altered during that stormy decade.

From the 1720s, at least until 1754, and in a sense until 1762, Britain had single-party government. That party may not have been prone to clear ideological definition (though it certainly proceeded on certain political axioms), it may well have been a coalition of whig groups, and its strength and unity were probably contingent upon its skilled leadership and its ability to monopolise the corridors of power. But, with all these reservations, it was a single party, and sought with remarkable success to exclude all those who did not accept its basic tenets. Fundamental to its successful continued existence was the party's ability to convince the monarch that single-party, whig rule was the only viable sort of Hanoverian government. Under George I and George II, with a strong, though admittedly diminishing, Jacobite threat this was not too difficult a task. Both of the first two Georges were implacably anti-tory, seeing them at worst as crypto-Jacobites (which some undoubtedly were), and at best as men who were to be much watched and little trusted. This produced a kind of whig consensus of which the monarch was a part. Whig politicians might quarrel over the spoils that their political hegemony made available to them, but they all, even the elder Pitt, realised that their strength lay in placing themselves as a barrier between the Crown, and the tories and independents. Only such an alliance, a union of monarch and those who were politically proscribed for so long, could present a sufficiently strong alternative to whig aristocratic dominance and undermine whig solidarity. No such alliance materialised under the first two Georges, not because they were held in thrall (though frequently the constraints upon their actions were considerable if largely self-imposed), but primarily because the monarch accepted the basic premise of the Venetian oligarchy, namely that single-party rule was the only feasible form of government. George I and George II were court whigs; they accepted that party divisions were real divisions, and that tories were politically *personae non gratae*. Both, in other words, accepted the basic premise of political stability. Thus single-party government and the

4

existence of 'a sense of common identity' were mutually reinforcing and dependent; conversely, the collapse of one threatened the demise of the other.

The ideological convergence of court and treasury under the umbrella of Walpolean whiggery made doubly effective the patronage which had so much increased in the years 1675 to 1725. Treasury appointments proliferated under the financial and administrative pressures of war; appointments in the armed forces were increasingly politicised; the diplomatic service, colonial administration and the church were all harnessed to the whig gravy-train.[2] Walpole became a spider at the centre of an elaborate web of patronage which extended to every walk of administrative, political and social life. And the very fact that it was one large web, and that there were not competing centres of power, strengthened whig government and enabled it to control the legislature. Admittedly patronage was never enough; it was, as John Owen puts it, a necessary but not a sufficient condition of securing power.[3] Its limitations were, for example, well brought out in Walpole's fall, and in the difficulties that Newcastle experienced after Henry Pelham's death in 1754.[4] But, although political acumen and brilliance in debate were important assets, one cannot escape from the fact that patronage was the bedrock of politics, and the foundation stone of political stability.

By 1760 its importance in politics was as great as it ever had been, and was greater than it ever would be again. In 1761 there were more placemen and those linked to government through patronage (260 in all) in the House of Commons than ever before.[5] In part this was because there were two royal households: that of the late Prince of Wales, now George III, which continued under the supervision of his mother, and the body attached to George in his regal capacity. No doubt the numbers were also swollen by the immediate pressures of the Seven Years War, and more substantially by the coalition government's need to satisfy its almost ubiquitous supporters. 1760 was the climacteric of parliamentary patronage, the last occasion on which broad-based political unity rested firmly on the podium of the Walpolean political edifice. For patronage *per se* never procured stability, only patronage harnessed to single-party hegemony, and after 1761 this ceased to be a feature of the political landscape.

Patronage, single-party rule, and the consensus that it created helped exclude many from the political process. Nowhere is this clearer than in the activities – or more accurately the absence of them – of the eighteenth-century electorate. Both Plumb and Speck have been at pains to demonstrate the vigorous and independent behaviour of the electorate between 1689 and 1715.[6] Political passions ran high, elections were frequent, contests regular, and voters independent. This situation, however, did not persist in the years of political stability. The Septennial Act of 1716 cut the frequency of general elections by more than a half. At the same time the number of actual electoral contests dropped.[7] Thus in 1705 65% of the counties, generally the most populous seats, went to the poll; in 1747 only 7·5% were the scene of a contest.[8] Increased electoral costs, partly the product of increased political controversy at the beginning of the century, but also the result of making a parliamentary seat a seven- and not a three-year investment, encouraged formal compromises, and helped obtain continuity of representation: men of substance sat for the same seat for years. This trend towards political oligarchy was reinforced and strengthened by the consolidation of land holdings:[9] 'aristocratisation' proceeded apace in Britain, as in other European countries.

The electorate was not just frozen; in some cases it was shrunk. The aggregate number of those able to vote in the counties of Bedfordshire, Buckinghamshire, Northamptonshire, Suffolk and Wiltshire was less in 1761 than it had been under Queen Anne. A similar situation obtained in London, Southwark, Bedford, Reading, Cambridge, most of the Cornish boroughs, Plymouth, Hereford, Hertford, Wigan, Stamford and Shrewsbury.[10] Even where electorates grew they became an increasingly smaller percentage of the population. Liverpool's total electorate expanded from 860 to 2,000 between 1715 and 1760, but the proportion of the population entitled to vote fell from 20% to 8%.[11] Overall, between 1715 and 1754 the national population increased by approximately 18%; the total electorate by a mere 8%.[12] Members of parliament helped reinforce this trend: on the occasions when they had to determine the franchise they tended to find for the smaller electorate. Thus, although copyholders' votes were allowed in the famous Oxfordshire election of 1754, thereafter they were specifically excluded by a statute brought in under the auspices of Blackstone.[13]

Yet, even as the arteries of the formal body politic were hardening, the political nation at large was flexing new muscles. While institutionalised politics stagnated, other means of political expression and new sources of political information became available to a public eager for the chance to express its (admittedly fairly unsophisticated) political views.[14] Much of this informal political activity centred on the nation's capital. London, the home of one person in ten, the workplace of one adult male in six,[15] was the ideal breeding-ground of political consciousness. Not only was it the national political forum, the venue of court and parliament; it also enjoyed its own relatively democratic

civic politics which invited a high degree of local participation.[16] Even
by twentieth-century standards a remarkably large number of people
were literate.[17] A half-hour walk from St Paul's Churchyard, down
Fleet Street, through Temple Bar, up into the stews of Covent Garden
and then on into the Strand would have enabled the eighteenth-century
Londoner to visit a sizeable majority of the city's pamphlet-shops and
political print-sellers.[18] *En route* he could have purchased a ballad from
a hawker, or listened to a ballad-singer proclaim the latest political song
from a street corner. If he had felt so inclined, he might have entered
one of the city's coffee houses (there were 550 of them in 1740),[19]
scrutinised a wide selection of newspapers – four different dailies and
five or six tri-weeklies in 1760[20] – and thumbed through pamphlets.
Doubtless he belonged to a club (it would be distinctly unusual if he
did not), perhaps one of the many 'free and easy' groups, or to a
masonic or pseudo-masonic society. Here politics and conviviality were
combined. The Robin-Hood Society, an open debating forum rather
than a club, provided the opportunity for public political discussion.
Anyone, as so many of its visitors complained, could express his views.[21]
The London theatre was also an important vehicle of political expression. For a small sum Londoners could see Walpole or other ministers
lampooned and satirised, could shout and cheer, and make their own
political allusions.[22] The enduring success of Gay's *Beggar's Opera* (it
was performed thirty-two times in three different London theatres in
the years 1767–70)[23] is, I am sure, attributable to the ease with which
it lent itself to this type of topical political reference and comment.
Theatre, press and club, all provided an indigenous popular political
culture that flourished in the metropolis even while the forces of
political constraint were at their height.

   This phenomenon was by no means confined to England's first city.
A growth in the existing communications network, in turnpikes, inland
waterways, public transport and post roads, facilitated the widespread
dissemination of political information. More specifically, the improvement and development of the postal services in the first half of the
century, largely thanks to the efforts of that typical eighteenth-century
entrepreneur, Ralph Allen,[24] together with a concomitant growth of
the provincial newspaper, made available in almost every regional
centre the sort of political intelligence and debate that flourished in
the metropolis. The dissemination of news was more reliable and was
achieved with much greater rapidity. By the mid-century there were
at least nine coffee houses in Bristol (almost certainly more), six in both
Liverpool and Chester, two in Northampton, and at least one in most
substantial market towns.[25] These, like their London counterparts,
contained clubs, supplied newspapers and were the home of debating

societies. In Liverpool, for example, the Conversation Club met at the George; the Ely Pamphlet Club convened at the Red Lion Inn.[26] Further political information was usually available from the circulating libraries which grew so rapidly after 1740.[27] Though their shelves were predominantly stocked with histories, travel literature and some novels, many contained more topical political literature or runs of current newspapers.

The problem that this indigenous political culture faced was one of *focus*. Provided that there was a unity of purpose among the nation's political leaders, it was extremely difficult for those who were excluded from the formal political process to impinge directly upon national politics. Burgesses might combine to attack a local corporation oligarchy, newspapers might advance a view of politics that by parliamentary standards was radical, and issues might be debated in local societies in a way that was inconceivable in the House of Commons; but only occasionally, and on specific issues, did such activities have focussed impact upon the deliberations at Westminster. Such events as the Excise Crisis (1733), the Gin Act (1736), the attempt to provide a Jewish Naturalisation Bill (1753), and the support of William Pitt in 1756–7, all demonstrated that popular political mobilisation could be achieved, but they also exhibited a lack of political organisation and, in the majority of cases, a blithe disregard for any concrete, long-term political aspirations. And it would be foolish of us to assume any homogeneity of political opinion, or agreement on political principles among those 'out-of-doors'. Their politics, to a remarkable degree, was the politics of the excluded: it might take the form of Jacobitism as readily as republican whiggery.

Prior to the mid-eighteenth century, then, there were, as Professor Plumb has put it, 'two political nations in England, one growing, the other shrinking, with little contact between them'.[28] Such a situation was bound to create political tensions. Indeed, I would wish to argue that in the 1760s these tensions had become sufficiently great to produce sizeable fissures, even permanent faults in the old political order.

No doubt there are some who would wish to antedate this development. It is argued, for instance, that 1754 saw the beginning of a major deterioration in political stability, despite the respite provided by the coalition of 1757–61. Supporters of this view maintain that it was the absence of strong ministerial leadership in the House of Commons that produced political disequilibrium, and that it began with the death of Henry Pelham. The intention here is to deny that there was any significant, qualitative change in politics in 1760, and to maintain that the political instability of the subsequent decade is attributable to a similar absence of strong leadership in the lower house.[29] Such a view betrays a strong preoccupation with the workings of Westminster and a singularly narrow view of politics.

Alternatively it could be pointed out that these years saw the emergence of a more radical political journalism, notably in the paper sponsored by Beckford, the *Monitor,* which advocated substantive measures of parliamentary reform designed to undermine oligarchy, and which did not confine itself to the old shibboleths of country-party ideology.[30] Equally significant was the way in which, for the first time in Hanoverian politics, a paper defending government, the *Con-Test,* used anti-party, patriot rhetoric, employing arguments that had formerly been characteristic of country-party *opposition* thought.

It would appear, therefore, that the period 1754–7 saw the adumbration of a number of features that were to become a familar part of the political landscape of the 1760s: parliamentary instability, an extra-parliamentary radicalism particularly associated with the press, and a reconfiguring of attitudes towards party. Clearly there is some plausibility to this case, but in the 1760s both in the spheres of extra-parliamentary politics and political infighting at Westminster a qualitative change can be observed. To equate the parliamentary instability of 1754–7 with the instability of the 1760s is to fail to make a distinction that was quite apparent to contemporaries. They saw the quarrels of 1754–7 as a battle amongst the politicians for leadership (possibly even control) of the dominant group in politics, the Old Corps of whigs. Pitt and Fox were fighting for the right to lead a long pecking order that gave access to a very substantial slice of the political cake.[31] This phenomenon had its disturbing aspects, but it was a *familiar* phenomenon and certainly did not threaten any *structural* change in party politics. After 1760, however, and appropriately enough in a situation in which the monarch had changed his political allegiance and the Old Corps had finally atomised, it was widely held by contemporaries of every political view that the situation had substantially changed. Similarly, extra-parliamentary radicalism of the 1760s was of a different order from the activity out-of-doors in the preceding decade. It was not only ideologically more coherent, but succeeded in providing itself with organisation and leadership separate from the main parliamentary groups.

What, then, is the evidence or the argument for treating the 1760s as a crucial decade in Hanoverian political history? The first area in which major change can be observed is that of party alignments and party ideology. These are the subject of the first sections of this book. I will simply sketch out here the chief lines of argument that are developed and substantiated in more detail in chapters 3 to 5.

Introduction

Broadly, perhaps rather crudely summarised, this section can be seen as an analysis of the debate that produced a crack-up in the political elite.

By 1760 nearly all politicians recognised that single-party rule was based on the whig ability to convince the monarch of the validity of party distinctions, and of the authenticity of the tory threat. Members of the Old Corps as well as followers of the future George III all knew this to be an axiom of whig court politics. They also knew that it was a premise that George III, unlike his grandfather, refused to accept. Such a non-party, or rather anti-party king who combined this ideological antipathy to organised politics with a very strong personal resentment of the Old Corps obviously threatened its very existence. Freed from the constraints of court whiggery as much as from court whigs, George was in a position to create a new political alliance that would break Old Corps dominance of patronage, power and the legislature. It is hard for us (for some historians it has been impossible) to appreciate the momentousness of this threat. It was rather as if a member of the Kennedy family had decided to try to occupy the White House as a Republican. The panic, there is almost no other term for it, with which the Old Corps whigs greeted the new reign is therefore perfectly explicable. They, as much as George, knew that the hour of reckoning had come.[32] Although it was not until 1762 that George and his supporters effected any substantial political change, from the first hours of the reign the atmosphere at court was completely transformed. Able tories and independents such as Dashwood and Morton now felt that they had a reasonable prospect of a political career, just as the hardy perennials of the Old Corps feared that their days were numbered.

Under these pressures the Old Corps crumbled. It had, of course, always been an uneasy alliance of groups. Prior to 1760, however, one vital consideration had held it together, namely a common investment in a single-party system that gave most of their followers a share in the spoils and perquisites of power. Not all whigs, it is true, were totally committed to this view. Pitt had tried to escape from the ideology of single-party politics, but even in 1756–7 tories were not given national political office nor received at court. His move towards the tories was flattering but without much political substance. Besides it was very difficult to admit more to the Elysian fields of patronage. By the 1750s the pastures of preferment were overstocked; a sort of saturation point had been reached which, it might be argued, was then conducive to the renewal of political conflict. Yet these minor indications of impending change in single-party politics dwindle into relative insignificance when compared with the impact of George III's accession. For above all else it was the desertion from the Old Corps of whigs of its most important member, the monarch, that produced disintegration. Hegemony and unity, with his departure, were no longer a reality, and every man had to fend for himself.

In fact there were three chief responses to the crisis in confidence between the king and the old politicians. Some, such as George Grenville (for a while) and Lord North, stuck to their task as helmsmen of the nation. They were men who by predilection or experience were administrators and royal servants, loath to surrender the responsibilities and perquisites of power. Although, as George Grenville showed in 1765 and Lord North in 1783, they still retained many of the party ideas and practices of Old Corps whiggery, they regarded the Crown, the court and the executive as a more powerful and attractive object of allegiance than their party. Their chief problem in the 1760s was not the task of stomaching George's anti-party politics, but of accepting his personal infatuation (admittedly ever-waning throughout the decade) with Lord Bute. The favourite was politically inexperienced, diplomatically maladroit, unpopular, and a disturbing influence in any administration as he offered a competing source of power and influence to the incumbent minister. He was therefore both unconducive to good efficient government (a notion to which the likes of George Grenville was very strongly committed), and a threat to the personal power of the whigs who stayed with the Crown. We find, therefore, as is discussed in chapter 7, that hostility to Bute, and the evolution of a coherent political case against him is the one common characteristic of Old Corps politicians, regardless of whether or not they agreed on other matters of policy.

A second response to the political changes of 1760 came from Pitt and those who were loosely attached to him. As is all too frequently forgotten, Pitt was just as vulnerable as Newcastle to the threat posed by George III. It is perfectly true that his professions of patriotism and independency, together with his hostility to party, accorded with the views of the new monarch. But a patriot king threatened to replace a patriot minister, especially when the monarch offered peace, retrenchment and independency, a far more attractive prospect to the bucolic, tax-paying squirearchy than the expensive bellicose foreign policy promoted by Pitt. Besides, George still resented Pitt's conduct in 1756–7 as much as he condemned Newcastle's behaviour in 1744 and 1746. The king was at first reluctant to deal with the politician whom he felt had deserted him, and Pitt himself could not afford to lose his maverick status. It is often remarked that Pitt's wayward conduct during the 1760s was one of the causes of instability,[33] but it was only by acting in this way that he could retain his separate

11

political identity. Caught in the cross-fire between the king and the most party-minded members of the Old Corps, he could not afford to join either camp: he had perforce to avoid absorption by either court or party politicians. In chapters 5 and 6 we can see how Pitt tried to deal with this dilemma. His tenuous *rapprochement* with the Old Corps between 1762 and 1765, and his attempt to woo the young men of their party from Newcastle and Rockingham are discussed, as well as the problems that he faced when he moved in 1766 towards the court and away from the Rockinghamites. One of Pitt's reactions to his difficulties was to attempt to retire with the honours that befitted the heroic conception that he and his followers entertained of him. Yet this, as can be seen in chapter 6, enabled Pitt's opponents to blacken his reputation. Attempts to feather the Pitt family's nest were seized upon as totally irreconcilable with Pitt's professed patriot ideology. The extremely venomous infighting that ensued prevented Pitt from retiring. Despite ill-health and a genuine reluctance to work in the political climate of the new reign, Pitt could not bear to retire from politics in an atmosphere of acrimony and anti-climax. Cast in the heroic mould he intended to leave politics with a bang not a whimper. To some extent, therefore, Pitt is a twilight figure in the 1760s, appearing very infrequently in parliament, wracked with gout, and eventually succumbing to total breakdown. Only when he took part in the flourishing Wilkite opposition of the last two years of the decade was there any recovery in his political powers.

A third reaction to the changed state of Hanoverian politics can be seen in the complex response of the Newcastle–Rockingham whigs. These men were above all else party politicians, but their political experience stemmed from their activities in office, not in opposition. This meant that the position that they occupied after 1762 was peculiarly incongruous. Those who went into opposition in that year, and again in 1766, were unfamiliar with the tactics and unused to the ideology of opposition. They regarded themselves as natural rulers, a sort of patrician elite with a presumptive right to rule (forgetting, of course, that they had received this privilege at the hands of a Norfolk gentleman). The party's adaptation to opposition was therefore a difficult and painful one. Their first problem was the question of how the party was to alter its old political practices – most notably that of procuring party unity and cohesiveness of action – to serve the opposition's purposes in its battle with the king and his adherents. This forms the subject matter of chapter 5. This examines the process by which the corpulent, gross figure of the Old Corps was slimmed to the gaunt form of the Rockingham whigs. This changed state of the party is partly attributable to the altered political scene. Newcastle lost the allegiance of the perennial officeholders to the Crown, Bute and Grenville, just as he failed to keep the support of the hot young men of the party who preferred Pitt's more charismatic leadership. But the process by which the Newcastle connection became the snug chaste corps attached to Rockingham was also the result of an altered *conception* of politics. Newcastle, the Old Corps man *par excellence*, wanted to recreate the old Pelhamite Broadbottom, a loose coalition of whig groups, in order to fight the Crown and Bute. He was even prepared, as was apparent in the all-important negotiation of July 1767, to ally himself with Bedford and George Grenville, despite their desertion of him at the beginning of the reign. On the other hand, Rockingham, who only reached political maturity in the 1760s, was much more concerned to emphasise the differences between the Rockinghams and the other proprietary groups. As he showed in December 1766, July 1767 (and, for that matter, in June 1780), he preferred ideological purity to the kind of compromise that would have obtained office and power. Newcastle's politics reflected his desire to recreate the old single-party milieu; Rockingham, on the other hand, was working towards a politics that recognised the political differences of the whig groups and which accepted the prospect of an enduring party struggle. Thus the Marquis emphasised consistency and policy, hammering out party principles in an attempt (both appropriate and necessary for those in opposition) to win the support of the 'Publick' – by which he meant the parliamentary classes.

This narrower view of party, what I call 'little-endianism', was espoused by the party's greatest ideologue, Edmund Burke. He, more than any other Rockinghamite, was responsible for distinguishing the party from its allies and opponents. His *Observations on the Late State of the Nation* (1769) was a scathing attack on the entire fiscal and imperial policy of George Grenville, just as the *Thoughts on the Cause of the Present Discontents* (1770) showed the differences between Rockingham and Chatham, and rejected conciliation with extra-parliamentary radicals.

Little-endianism brought its problems. The party was not only committed to preserving its ideological purity, but to the notion of removing 'secret influence', personified by Bute and epitomised by the King's Friends, from government. Unfortunately this was only a serious possibility if the party allied with those other groups whose political views it had publicly opposed. Paradoxically, the achievement of one of the party's chief political aspirations was only possible at the expense of other vital elements in its creed. The solution to this problem that Rockingham reached in 1767, that Burke expressed in his pamphlets of 1769 and 1770, and which the party later adopted in 1782 and 1783 was to accept the idea of a coalition against the Crown *provided that* sufficient guarantees could be built into the agreement to ensure Rockinghamite hegemony.

The process of acquiring ideological definition, which was necessary if the Rockinghams were to win public and parliamentary support, and successfully to override the competing claims for allegiance made by the other opposition groups, produced an entirely new party strategy. But this desire to create a Rockingham-controlled coalition (whether in opposition or in office) was only one facet of the general problem of political organisation. The other major issue that confronted the party was that of how to legitimate 'formed opposition' to the king's ministers.

This problem can be fully understood only by examining the interrelationships between the different concepts of party: party as proprietary party, as opposition, and in the sense of whig and tory. It is only if we distinguish these three varieties of party – an enterprise to which much of chapters 3 to 5 of this book is devoted – that we can begin to understand both the significance of the reconfiguration of party politics in the 1760s, and the special contribution that the Rockingham whigs made to the legitimation of party.

Prior to 1760 all the arguments used to justify opposition, even those employed by the country-party ideologues, condemned party in the same breath that they condoned opposition. Either they maintained that the purpose of opposition (even 'formed opposition', though they never described it as such) was to destroy party – both by annihilating whig/tory distinctions and eradicating proprietary parties and oligarchy – or they argued that the consideration of 'measures not men' (an anti-party notion if ever there was one) legitimised opposition to the Crown. The former of these arguments is perfectly understandable given the political circumstances under the first two Georges. Whig administrations maintained their power through party (oligarchical) unity and by convincing the Crown that the distinction between whig and tory was a valid one. An opposition numerically dominated by tories but led, as often as not, by disgruntled whigs could only hope to succeed – indeed, could only achieve a modicum of unity – by maintaining that whig/tory distinctions were spurious, and that oligarchy must be broken. In other words, under George II oppositions were anti-party, and administrations favoured party divisions.

Under George III this position was very largely reversed. The new king's assault on party in general, and the Old Corps in particular, forced into opposition those whose political *raison d'être* had been bound up with the (supposed) presence of genuine party conflict. Of all the former members of the Old Corps the Rockinghamites were the most adamant in their assertion that a whig/tory struggle still existed – reconfigured, it is true, into an opposition/government rather than a government/opposition battle. Familiar with the strengths to be derived from proprietary party unity and committed to the idea of a whig/tory struggle, it is scarcely surprising that the Rockinghams should see notions of party and opposition as mutually reinforcing.

This determination to defend party in all its forms is one of the features that distinguishes the Rockinghamites' greatest apologia, Burke's *Thoughts on the Cause of the Present Discontents*. Burke's opposition is an opposition to defend not destroy party. Thus Burke, unlike his predecessors, was prepared to argue that party – in the sense of principled 'honourable connections' – ought to be a persistent and enduring feature of politics. Out of the conflicts of the 1760s emerged a new view of party which went beyond the old clichés of the country-party view. This was just one instance of the way in which the ideological hegemony of the old country-party views was broken down in the decade.

These developments, and especially the escalation of political conflict, naturally had ramifications beyond Westminster. Local political conflicts – between rival gentry, or gentry and aristocracy in the counties, and between corporations and burgesses in the boroughs – had previously been contained (though never totally suppressed) by the stranglehold of whig hegemony. Now local protagonists were able to exploit national political divisions, and opposition politicians – most notably Portland – were able to tip the balance in constituency conflicts. Simultaneously a press war of very considerable ferocity broke out – far more sustained than that of the 1740s and far more vitriolic than that of 1756–7. The indigenous popular political culture that had lacked focus before 1760 slowly acquired definition. The issues of Wilkes, America and parliamentary reform provided points of concentration for a previously all too amorphous group. This did not mean that the old Walpolean system of political exclusion was overcome so much as circumvented. The impact of organised public opinion and the emergence of an incipient radicalism were not felt as forcibly in parliamentary elections – except in the metropolis – as in the field of extra-parliamentary political organisation and in the organs of the press. Indeed, to understand these developments we have to understand the 'other' political nation, the circumstances of those who were excluded from participation. Ideally this would involve very detailed studies of informal, non-parliamentary political and social activity for almost every region in Britain. Clearly such a task is beyond the scope of this book. As an alternative strategy, however, I have undertaken to examine during and prior to the 1760s what I have termed an 'alternative structure of politics', namely the press. This is the substance of chapter 8.

Undoubtedly the press was the single most important factor in obtaining any degree of *national* political consciousness, in dispelling ignorance (such as it was), and in providing a congeries of political grievances with a common focus. In this respect the growth of a press *network* in the period *c.* 1720 to 1760 was crucial. The circulation of a typical newspaper or pamphlet was not very different at the accession of George III from what it had been in 1720. The difference lay in the overall increase in the number of papers and materials in circulation, and in the rapid growth of new sorts of journalism, most notably the provincial newspaper, the periodical magazine and the review journal.

Let us take the provincial press first. By 1735, making the most charitable estimate possible, there were twenty-five provincial papers. In 1760 there were fifteen towns, including Coventry, Birmingham, Cambridge, Oxford, Leicester, Hull, Liverpool, Halifax, Exeter and Sheffield, which had acquired papers since 1735, and the total number of provincial papers was thirty-five.[34] A somewhat scattered regional distribution had been transformed into fairly comprehensive coverage of England.

The successful and sustained establishment of the *Gentleman's Magazine*, the *London Magazine*, and of the *Monthly* and *Critical Reviews* was symptomatic of the growing maturity of the press in these years. Taken together they represent the growth of what I term a press infrastructure, an interlocking, overlapping complex of publications, engaging in frequent and blatant plagiarism, and generating controversy and polemic.

It might be thought that, despite the growth and development of this alternative structure of politics, it had little impact on the politics of Westminster. Chapter 11 shows that such was not the case. The press activities of three political groups – Bute and his followers, the Rockinghamites, and the supporters of George Grenville – show just how widespread was concern about a party's public image, and demonstrate the significance attached to press propaganda as a political weapon. All three groups – and they were deliberately chosen as being *less* likely than others, such as the city radicals or Chathamites, to involve themselves in press activites – subsidised and employed writers, provided their authors with information, and kept an ever-watchful eye on the press, in an effort to counteract the polemical works of their opponents. These men were not only the leaders of the political nation; they were also an important part of our alternative structure of politics. Naturally this is not to attribute to them a conception of the press as a 'fourth estate', nor to equate their necessary acceptance of political journalism with wholesale approval. By and large the leading political groups, even those in opposition, were concerned to limit political participation, except on the few occasions when it was thought expedient to drum up popular support. An understanding of the politicians' view of the press is contingent upon an understanding of their views on the public, and these, as the widespread acceptance of the notion of virtual representation demonstrates, placed the people not on the apron but in the wings of the political stage. Parliamentary whiggery might pay lip-service to the notion that power emanated from the people and might use popular discontent for its own purposes, but it expected that the public would be willing to be led by the nose. Political initiative and all the star roles were to be reserved for a political elite. This produced a highly ambivalent attitude towards the public, especially among whig opposition politicians. They wanted *limited* popular support, based on their (rather narrow) conception of the significant political issues, and mediated by their leadership. At the same time they feared any independent political initiative, or any attempt to raise issues outside the parameters of parliamentary debate.

Yet this is what they had to contend with in the 1760s. An amorphous, incipient, popular political culture was given shape and direction by the issues of John Wilkes and, to a lesser extent, of America. The circumstances of the 1760s were highly propitious for the emergence of this 'focussed radicalism'. The economy, for instance, was not in a good state. Only 1761 and 1764 were years of economic buoyancy. There was a sharp economic slump in 1762 and, although 1764 saw an improvement, thereafter the decade was characterised by depression. Droughts in 1762 and 1766, deteriorating harvests from 1764, and low meat production between 1766 and 1768 helped the squeeze. The prices of meat, dairy produce and grain all rose.[35] The end of the war (1763) brought its own problems. Significant numbers of ex-servicemen were brought onto a low-demand labour market. A number of industries, notably hardware, textiles, coal-mining and ship-building, suffered a recession with the removal of the economic stimulus of war.[36] Other trades, most notably silk-weaving, were penalised by the end of war-time protection. The textile trade (which had its own difficulties) and the English merchant community, together with a great many manufacturers, also suffered after 1765 from the non-importation agreements imposed (1765–6, 1769) by American traders because of the British government's tax policies.[37] In these circumstances popular protest was widespread. As was usually the case after a war, crime was on the increase.[38] There were strikes, machine-breaking and crowd activity among silk-weavers (1763, 1765, 1768–71), pitmen (1765), sailors, coal-heavers, watermen, coopers, hatters, glass-grinders, sawyers and tailors (all *c.* 1768–70).[39] Rural price fixing – of bread, grain and foodstuffs – was increasingly prevalent, reaching a peak in 1766: Rudé records some sixty incidents of riot in that year.[40]

The precise relationship of this social protest to the political de-velopments of these years is far from clear. It can be asserted with confidence, however, that there was considerable overlap between an incipient political radicalism and the manifestations of social discon-tent. It is no mere coincidence that London coal-heavers were or-ganised by a group of forty-five men who modelled their organisation on a Wilkite club.[41] Nor is it fortuitous that weavers were prominent among Wilkes's supporters. Wilkes's greatest enemies – Bute and the king – were also those responsible for the peace that had contributed to the weavers' penury and destitution. Equally important was the way in which social protest contributed to the growing sense of crisis at the end of the decade. It provided additional fuel for the radicals' critique of government, and amplified the apprehensions of both administra-tion and opposition. As we see in chapter 12, it helped make the issue of discontent *the* political issue of 1768–70, provoking a debate that ranged beyond the parliamentary classes and the portals of St James's.

Two other circumstances were vital in ensuring the growth of focussed radicalism. The first was the fragmentation of the political elite. As we have seen, monopolistic, monolithic whiggery was severely weakened by the political quarrel at the beginning of the reign. By the end of the decade political divisions were sufficiently well formed to ensure that extra-parliamentary protest had adequate protection (though this should not be confused with support) from within the House of Commons. Secondly, the press was sufficiently well devel-oped to be able not merely to sustain a political campaign for a period of three years or more on a *national* scale, but also to make a considerable contribution to the campaign itself.

Up to this point I have deliberately dodged the difficult question of what we should understand by the focussed radicalism that I go on to discuss in chapters 9 and 10. The nettle must now be grasped. There can be no doubt that our understanding of eighteenth-century radicalism has been severely hampered by our knowledge of early nineteenth-century and Victorian reform movements. Too often, in precisely the same way that Burke and Rockingham have been seen as precursors of Victorian parliamentary government, Wilkes and the early reformers (the very term 'early' reveals the perspective) are portrayed as unfocussed adumbrations, thumb-nail sketches of an immanent radical political consciousness which was to manifest itself in demands for comprehensive parliamentary reform, and in on-going class conflict. Even when this rather crude teleological approach is eschewed, there is always a tendency to try to see how far a set of mid-eighteenth-century demands approximates to a later platform for reform. Yet what is radical is not what approximates to some notional political scheme, but any position which, if fulfilled, would undermine or overturn *existing* political authority. It has, in other words, to be defined contextually, and particularly with regard to the ideology and institutions that support prevailing authority.

If we try to use this approach we can understand rather better the precise nature of eighteenth-century radicalism. It may surprise some historians, but we can perfectly legitimately describe the country-party platform of frequent elections (annual or triennial) and the removal of placemen from Lords and Commons as a species of radicalism – perhaps the only Hanoverian species before *c.* 1750. Its radicalism stemmed from the fact that, if enacted, it would have completely removed two of the most vital props supporting the edifice of political stability. As the ideology of the excluded – whether they were disgruntled tory backbenchers or those who were enfranchised but rarely had the chance to vote – these views were eminently sensible. Together with the other, less frequently cited shibboleth of a 'more equal representation' (by which was usually meant an increase in the number of county seats) they promised, if acted upon, to change politics fundamentally. Certainly it has to be conceded that these views were frequently employed both cynically and unscrupulously by opposition MPs, and that there was no organised body of extra-parliamentary opinion committed to their implementation; yet radical they were.

The 1760s, as chapters 9 and 10 show, saw two new developments in eighteenth-century radicalism. The first was ideological. Between 1765 and *c.* 1774 radical demands for reform were extended to include both a redistribution of seats (with emphasis on the enfranchisement of urban areas) and a wider suffrage. No very satisfactory explanation of this development has ever been offered. Although historians have pointed to growing urbanisation and an increasing middle class as necessary elements in the emergence of this kind of reform, they have not accounted for the *form* that radical demands assumed, nor the arguments that were used in their favour. This is all the more remarkable because the demands of the 1760s mark a qualitative shift in the argument about reform almost comparable to the move from property to persons as the basis for the franchise. Before 1760, reform – frequent elections, no placemen, equal representation – had been designed to obtain a pure House of Commons.

It had only rarely touched upon the enfranchisement of new men and the representation of new interests. After 1760, though the concern with a pristine lower house remained, this new aspiration became an enduring feature of reform.

In effecting this qualitative leap the American debate about taxation and its relationship to representation was crucial. As chapter 10 demonstrates, it was the American critique of virtual representation – the sole justification for the current, incongruous electoral system – that provided a growing number of British reformers with their case for the enfranchisement of new, unincorporated but populous and wealthy towns. The debate about taxes helped highlight the incongruity of keeping towns unenfranchised when they made such a substantial contribution to national revenue. At the same time the American emphasis on 'no taxation without representation' was transformed in an English context into the realisation that there were a great many who suffered the burdens of taxation without the requisite right to vote. This could be used as a very radical argument indeed. It was pointed out by a number of advocates for reform, including those writing in the 1760s as well as Burgh, Cartwright and Wilkes in his famous speech in 1776, that every man paid taxes, including the poor and impecunious.[42] Direct taxation might be confined to land, but indirect taxes on such necessities as beer, leather, candles and soap affected the entire population. Such levies were directly analogous to the Stamp Tax that had originally provoked colonial resistance. The American claim for immunity, therefore, was used to justify the case not only for redistribution, but for a widespread franchise increase. It could even be used, as Cartwright showed in *Take Your Choice!*, to sneak in universal male suffrage though the back door.[43] If all men paid taxes, i.e. handed a part of their property over to the government, all men should be enfranchised; otherwise they were not free. The American contribution, therefore, was to help to alter the parameters of debate about parliamentary reform, and to go beyond traditional country-party ideology. In arguing this, I am not claiming that the Americans were the first to employ such arguments, and were therefore causally responsible for the breakthrough in debate. They were not. They did, however, make these arguments *familiar* and helped increase their availability. Before the Stamp Act debate the connection between taxation and parliamentary reform was unfamiliar and only dimly perceived; thereafter, the link was obvious to any protagonist in the discussion about electoral distribution and the franchise.

The second important development in radicalism during the 1760s occurred in its organisation. It is one of the nicer ironies of British history that the first extra-parliamentary organisation devoted to a programme of reform should have started life in an attempt to pay off the accumulated debts (incurred more through riotous living than political commitment) of a mercurial elusive rake, John Wilkes. Chapter 9 is devoted to the extremely complex movement that developed around his political career. To obtain any clear sense of Wilkes's significance we have to look beyond the immediate activities of the Society of Supporters of the Bill of Rights (hereafter SSBR). It was the conception of politics that Wilkes sought to project that made him so important. Although there is little doubt that he was a cynical political manipulator, intent upon assuring himself a comfortable niche in the pantheon of English liberty, he also (quite possibly because his politics were both malleable and sceptical) grasped the importance of style and technique in developing a broadly-based political movement. This is made clear in the examination in chapter 9 of Wilkite propaganda. Skilled marketing techniques, the advocacy of political participation and the highly effective use of wit and humour all demonstrate how Wilkes commercialised politics and developed, as a consequence, the notion of politics as a form of entertainment. These ideas were far from completely novel, but they had never previously been used on the same scale. And naturally because they encouraged, and even promised to achieve, a high level of political participation, they threatened the enclosed world of institutionalised politics.

This threat can be seen in the issues that Wilkes chose, or to some extent had forced on him, in his battle with the Crown and its ministers. Freedom of election, freedom of the press, the extension of subjects' liberties in the face of attack by an overweening executive, and emphasis on the accountability of both ministers and parliament were all part and parcel of a more open, public conception of politics. They were also issues with which those who had embraced the politics of the excluded before *c.* 1750 were fully familiar. One, comparatively insignificant example demonstrates this continuity. The Wilkite colour – as it appeared on banners, buttons, snuff-boxes and ribbons or favours – was *blue*. Under the early Hanoverians this same colour had been that of the London tories.

Wilkes, therefore, should be seen in the context and tradition of an on-going attack on the whig system of political stability. But what of the Wilkites? In a study that concentrates on political argument and ideology it might be felt that the humble supporters of Wilkes – as opposed to the affluent merchants, businessmen and country-gentlemen who manned the SSBR – would play little or no part. Such an assumption is, however, erroneous. Throughout this book I am concerned with the problem of legitimation: how, in what ways and with what objects in view did those involved in politics seek to justify their actions? Obtaining legitimacy, the strength and comfort of moral sanction was never the prerogative of the mandarins of Westminster. As Edward Thompson has persuasively argued, it can be observed as an enduring characteristic of eighteenth-century crowd behaviour.[44] Legitimation and the expression of political belief do not have to assume the form of the printed or even the spoken word. Ritualised conduct, the employment of symbols, or engagement in symbolic action can all be used to convey a political creed. Ritual and symbol therefore take up a large part of the discussion of the Wilkites. Riots, demonstrations, gift-giving, banquets and celebrations are all discussed within this framework. The results reveal the extent to which much of the protest associated with Wilkes was traditional. Traditional in that it was frequently licensed; traditional in that it was festive; and traditional in that it was cathartic.

The disparate elements involved in the Wilkite movement ensure that it was the most complex of phenomena. Wilkes's peculiar 'open' brand of politics and traditional legitimised social protest went hand-in-hand with the fully-fledged platform for parliamentary reform adopted by the members of the SSBR. All three facets of the movement were a threat to the existing political order. Wilkes's politics of participation threatened the politics of oligarchy. At the same time Wilkite social protest undermined the social order. Finally the radicals of the SSBR promised to recreate institutionalised politics in a form that would have readmitted those who had been excluded for the past generation, and would newly admit an emergent social group based on mercantile and entrepreneurial wealth which wanted power commensurate with its financial status.

The extent to which all three were a threat can be seen in the parliamentary debates and pamphlet discussion of the last years of the 1760s. By 1770 the 'present discontents' were well nigh an obsession. Government, opposition and radicals all addressed themselves to the problem of disorder, and each produced its own distinctive explanation of growing licentiousness, attributing and proportioning blame in their own respective ways. These form the subject matter of my final chapter and serve, by way of conclusion, to bring together the different strands of argument discussed in the earlier part of the book. Undoubtedly it is in this debate that we can see how the different lines of allegiance were drawn, and the extent to which political argument in the 1760s broke out of the straightjacket of country-party ideology.

There were two explanations of the present discontents advanced by the political protagonists: one adopted by the opposition, the other by administration. They should not be seen as explanations *tout court*; rather they were evaluative descriptions designed to make causal attributions of blame for what all agreed was an unfortunate political situation. Starting from a common normative framework – that of the mixed, balanced constitution – each side sought, within the context of this constitutional paradigm, to fix responsibility on the other. The government blamed factious opposition designed to foment anarchy; the opposition condemned administrative tyranny intended to sap the foundations of free government. This not unsurprising division can be further refined when we examine the *cures* offered by all parties. The government saw the re-establishment of public confidence, the termination of faction and the reassertion of strong government as solutions to the crisis. The opposition was more divided. On the one hand, the radicals and the SSBR and most of the London press advocated a *structural* change in politics. Their point of departure (as the final section discussing the historical bases of political argument demonstrates) was not the decade of 1760–70, but the commencement of whig hegemony.[45] The first ten years of George III's reign were only the most conspicuous example of an enduring perversion, or to use the correct contemporary term, corruption of the political system. A change of men was not enough; what was needed was an alteration (restoration) of the fabric of the constitution. No doubt the much vaunted and widely publicised efforts of George and Bute to introduce the reign of virtue, and its subsequent collapse when Henry Fox stepped in to convert it into yet another species of jobbery, helped accentuate a disillusionment comparable with that after 1742, and convinced many that virtuous men were not capable of curing the nation's ills. Such republicans as Thomas Hollis had been favourably disposed towards George III at his accession because they thought he might destroy the whig political machine; that, after all, is what his apologists had claimed he would do.[46] George only succeeded, how-ever, in opening up substantial antagonisms within the political elite, and in the quarrel that ensued, he was forced to employ the same weapons as his opponents, because they were his most effective armoury. For the radicals and for those who had been politically dispossessed under the first two Georges the middle years of the decade were deeply disillusioning. As far as they were concerned, these years hinted at a continuity, fully demonstrated between 1765 and 1770, with the system of the Old Corps. From the standpoint of Westminster the political climate may have changed considerably, but for those who wanted to see a change in the nature of politics the same sombre atmosphere prevailed. Historically, then, reformers dated their ills back to the perversion of 1688 or, in the case of the radical minority, even earlier. As far as they were concerned both George III and Rockingham were tinkering with the *ancien régime.*

Such an analysis provoked loud protestations from the supporters of the second opposition view, that of the Rockingham whigs. Seeing themselves, as indeed they were, a vestigial part of the Old Corps tradition, they could hardly condemn the politics of Walpole and Pelham. Their misfortunes (and, by implication, those of the nation) had begun with the new reign, not in the halcyon days of whig hegemony. Appropriately enough, therefore, their remedy for the nation's ills was the replacement of malevolently by beneficently intended men. Rockinghamites were to succeed the incumbent administration because it was not the political system *per se* that was at fault but the men who managed it. Rejecting the platform of parliamentary reform as a speculative chimera, they pursued a party policy designed to help them vault back into the chariot of power.

Both radical and Rockingham arguments went beyond the old constraints of country-party ideology, and it is one of the purposes of this book to explain how and why this was achieved. Prior to the 1760s the only inroads on country-party ideology had been made by apologists for the whig hegemony. They had argued, in remarkably pragmatic, utilitarian terms, that so-called corruption could only be described as legitimate influence, which was necessary to the workings of stable government, and thereby to the preservation of liberty. Increased liberty was contingent upon increased stability, therefore Englishmen now enjoyed more liberty than ever before. Ironically this attempt to legitimate existing political arrangements on the grounds of their practical necessity, and its concomitant rejection of the notion of a perfectly balanced constitution located at some indeterminate date in the past, has been largely neglected by historians in favour of the opposition ideas of Bolingbroke and his compatriots.[47] Scholars have plumped for the familiar and, in so doing, have rejected the novel.

The emergence in the 1760s of an opposition view that legitimised party in all its disparate forms, and of a radicalism that, although it did not reject the old assumptions of the country-party platform for reform, went beyond them in seeking changes in representation and suffrage, is not only symptomatic of the gradual demise of country-party ideology, but of a change in the nature of politics. Country-party ideology derived its *raison d'être*, both as an opposition and a radical critique, from the single-party hegemony of Walpole and the Pelhams. It ceased to have its former force with those in opposition who were committed to party politics, and it was only partially relevant to those radicals who were concerned to invest power in social groups over and beyond the country gentlemen. The old whig machine and country-party ideology lived in a peculiar relationship of symbiosis; as the one declined, so did the other. Naturally both were an unconscionable time a-dying, and it would be foolish to underestimate their resilience to decay. During the 1760s, however, it became very apparent that both had contracted ailments which, if not fatal, were at least the first signs of serious debilitation.

2. Historiography and method

That certain Kings reigned, and certain battles were fought,
we can depend upon as true; but all the colouring, all the
philosophy, of history is conjecture. (R. W. Chapman (ed.),
Boswell's Life of Johnson (Oxford, 1970), 628)

If the early years of George III's reign have given birth to a flourishing
body of historical work, they have also engendered a historiographical
controversy which has affected almost every historian of modern
British politics. I do not propose, in this brief discussion of previous
historiography, to explore in any great depth the body of work which
began well within George III's own lifetime and has continued, in a
somewhat prolix and tedious form, to the present day.[1] The more
flippant or facetious historian might well argue (and there would be
more than a grain of truth in the observation) that, for all the archival
exploration and exhibition of historical expertise, the polemic over the
politics of George's reign has advanced little beyond the contemporary
controversy that was found in speech, pamphlet, letter and newspaper.
(It is interesting to speculate on the place which historians might have
occupied if they had sat in the eighteenth-century House of Commons:
Namier and Butterfield facing each other across the dispatch box as
Pitts and Foxes had done before them.) Yet the historiography
demands attention: a large intractable body of literature whose very
description and classification has sparked off further debate.

In discussing approaches to the politics of George III's reign I have
opted to use Occam's razor; no doubt some historians will feel that,
in doing so, I have cut my own throat. But by employing a comparatively simple classification of the historiography a great many of the
blind alleys of the controversy can be avoided, and the most salient
features be given appropriate emphasis. This may lead to charges of
simplification, abridgement and even distortion, but it is a risk that
has to be taken. The discussion begins with two stereotypes or idea-
types of 'whig' and 'tory' historiography which are necessarily rather
crude, and proceeds to refine them in the light of recent historical
writing. It concludes by seeking to explain how the approach employed
in this book differs from previous methods adopted.

There are three main areas of difference between the traditional
whig interpretation and the views put forward by its critics, most

notably Sir Lewis Namier. The first lies in the interpretation of eighteenth-century constitutional theory; the second (and this follows logically from the first) in the evaluation of certain political practices both from the point of view of constitutional propriety and practical importance; and the third in the explanation and evaluation of the conduct of the chief political actors. Attention has been focussed in all three cases on the central issues of the political powers of the monarch and the legitimacy and political significance of party.

The differences between the whig and tory commentators are immediately apparent when we examine their interpretations of the eighteenth-century constitution. Almost every whig account – and this includes the full-blown views of Erskine May as well as the more subtle (and recent) writings of Fryer and Cannon – has emphasised the constitutional correctness of the convention of ministerial responsibility, and has stressed the degree to which it was accepted that the Crown's powers were constrained not only by law, but also by constitutional propriety.[2] Certain personal acts of the king – maintaining a minister in power while apparently incompetent and unpopular (Bute), or without a majority in the House of Commons (the younger Pitt) – were clear breaches of the rules, or so it was argued, even though such contraventions were not dealt with by statute.[3] Such conduct was, moreover, recognised by contemporaries as constitutionally improper. Whig historians have not been slow to point to an abundance of contemporary material culled from varied and disparate sources that reprobated the king's (illicit) employment of the personal powers of the monarchy.

Tory historians, on the other hand, have categorically denied the existence in the mid-eighteenth century of anything that resembled 'the full doctrine of responsible Parliamentary Government'.[4] They have emphasised the personal powers of the Crown and the degree to which they were recognised as both constitutionally legitimate and politically necessary. The monarchy was not above politics, but an active participant in the political process. The king's legal right of ministerial appointment was recognised by nearly all contemporaries, even those who sought practically to constrain his choice of ministers. In maintaining either Bute or the younger Pitt in office, the king was in no way acting unconstitutionally, though he might have been behaving imprudently.[5]

The implications of this disagreement over the constitutionally recognised powers of the Crown are considerable. If the whig view is correct then opposition to the king's government was legitimate. Opponents of the Crown could distinguish between opposition to the king's person (treason) and opposition to his ministers who were politically responsible for the government's policies and actions. At least a semblance of constitutional monarchy (in the modern sense of the term) could be said to exist. *Per contra*, if the tory view of the king's personal powers can be sustained, then opposition, or at least organised opposition, might lack any formal justification. Opposing the administration was tantamount to opposing the Crown, and this action, naturally enough, was tainted with treason. So the interpretation of the constitutional conventions that governed the conduct of the monarch has obvious ramifications in the assessment of organised political parties. In committing himself to a view of monarchy, the historian is also revealing an attitude towards the propriety of party.

The difference in interpretation between the whig and tory views can perhaps best be put this way: whig commentators, notably Dicey, have tended to equate the constitutional conventions of 1760 with those of the nineteenth century,[6] while tory historians have been concerned to differentiate mid-eighteenth-century constitutional ideas from those of their own day.[7] In their more extreme form these two views are antithetical but as often as not they merely represent points or areas of emphasis. Thus whig historians will concede that the Crown had personal powers, and tories accept that there were some constraints upon monarchy, but each will then go on to maintain that their overall view is not altered by such a concession. To a certain extent, therefore, the argument between tory and whig historians (just like the argument between eighteenth-century politicians) is not just a question of the efficacy of certain constitutional conventions or rules, but a quarrel about which rule of two or several applies in a particular instance. A whig historian, for example, might construe a politician's conduct as a legitimate recognition of the idea of ministerial responsibility, while a tory might see it as an unconstitutional constraint on the Crown. Conversely, an instance of what a tory historian would call the legitimate exercise of royal prerogative might be seen through whig eyes as an abuse of the personal powers of the Crown.

This leads us to the second area of disagreement in the historiography – the constitutional evaluation of certain political actions or practices and the assessment of their practical political importance. Clearly, it is extremely difficult to distinguish this area of disagreement from the one which has already been discussed. Perhaps the best way to understand the points at issue here is to begin with the different interpretations of eighteenth-century politics generally, and of the 1760s in particular. Whig historians have all, admittedly with varying degrees of emphasis, seen eighteenth-century politics in terms of party politics. In its classical forms whig historiography construed politics as a continuous struggle between whigs and tories. 'The annals of party', May boldly declared, 'embrace a large portion of the history of England.'[8] This view, as applied to the eighteenth century, received strong endorsement from both G. O. and G. M. Trevelyan, is clearly expressed in, for instance, Macaulay's *Essay on Chatham*, and was more subtly delineated in Winstanley's works on the whig opposition in the 1760s, and in Guttridge's analysis of whiggism in the American revolutionary period.[9] It represents the other face of a conception of politics that accepts the idea of ministerial responsibility. If you have ministerial responsibility you may also have legitimate political parties and these, traditionally, have been the great parties of whig and tory.

This view has received short shrift from tory historians. Votes and divisions in the House of Commons, they have pointed out, are far more intelligible in terms of a struggle between 'ins' and 'outs' or 'court' and 'country'; they certainly do not correspond to any clear-cut whig–tory dichotomy. Besides, two substantial groups in the lower house, a large proportion of what Namier called the 'Court and Administration Party', and most of the country-gentlemen, were at pains to disavow party allegiance or they demonstrated through their political conduct that allegiance to the Crown or constitution superseded attachment to party.[10] This is scarcely surprising if one accepts the other premise of tory historiography, namely that there was no view of responsible government. In such circumstances one would expect allegiance to the Crown to override support of party. The tory conception of eighteenth-century politics is altogether more atomistic and complex than its whig counterpart; equally, it is at one with the views of the constitution advanced by its proponents.

The third area of difference is again intimately connected with the first two. With their respective sets of constitutional conventions, and individual scenarios of politics, it is scarcely surprising that whig and tory historians have so strongly differed in their assessment of the conduct of the chief political actors. The whigs see 1760 as something of a watershed: the date which heralds the imminent demise of the whig party and a return of tory principles to government. Party conflict, according to this view, was revived. The king, allied with tories and whig apostates, adopted a plan to increase prerogative, influence and the personal powers of the monarch over and against the party politicians. Whether with malevolent intentions (as the nineteenth-century whigs claimed), or because of a misapprehension of the conventional and constitutional limitations on monarchy, George, it is argued, acted in a manner contrary to the customs of his time. The portrait that emerges is one of a young, obstinate king fighting party battles against an entrenched body of whigs who clung to the orthodoxy of constitutionalism and counterattacked with the weapons of party and ministerial responsibility.[11]

This condemnation of George III and its parallel glorification of Burke, Rockingham, Fox and the elder Pitt has been very effectively attacked by its tory opponents. Namier and Sedgwick have between them shown that George III's political *intentions* had constitutional warrant: 'he talked', said Namier, 'flapdoodle of the most innocent kind'.[12] Certainly there is no evidence of the royal plot so beloved of whig historiography. This is not especially surprising, tory historians maintain, because the political conduct and ideas of George III did not fundamentally differ from those of his grandfather. Both kings entertained a personal view of monarchy, but such a view was constitutionally respectable. The crucial variable of the 1760s was the political situation. George II's difficulties in 1746 stemmed from a peculiar concatenation of circumstances; George III enjoyed the advantages of youth and a highly factionalised political elite which enabled him to choose his ministers more freely than had been possible fifteen years before.[13] This produced cries of protest from some of the political factions that were not chosen to assume power and led them to try to justify opposition, but it would be a serious error to elevate such complaints into an historical interpretation of the new reign.

Underpinning these two very different versions of the 1760s are two different conceptions of political behaviour. The former, whig view of politics has an epic quality about it. Politics is envisaged as a struggle between conflicting principles which are not only professed but believed. The forces of progress battle with the forces of reaction. The political actors have coherent intentions and seek rational ends. When we observe men disputing matters of principle we are able to see what politics is about. The pursuit of sincerely held beliefs is a strong motive force in politics.[14] Tory historians' views tend, however, in a diametrically opposite direction. They start from the premise that politics is about power – its acquisition, exercise and retention. Professions of principle are secondary; they merely serve the purpose of providing basic political instincts with an air of legitimacy. They act, in other words, as a species of *ex post facto* rationalisation: as Namier put it, 'what matters most [in politics] is the underlying emotions, the music, to which ideas are a mere libretto, often of a very inferior quality'.[15] It follows from this that talk about the constitution or political ideas is frequently cosmetic and has little or no effect on the course of politics; the only occasions on which such ideologies might affect political actions is when the agent credulously believes what he says and acts because he genuinely holds that belief.

Both these whig and tory views of the relationship between ideology and action accept that an ideology or principle can *only* affect an action when it is a *motive*.[16] The only difference, therefore, between these two formulations of the problem of ideology and action is that whigs stress the degree to which people believe what they say and act on their beliefs, while tory historians stress that most of the political agents of the period utilised ideology for their own ends and interests. Both of these views raise problems. In the case of the whig formulation, although it is correct to assert that reference to a belief is needed to explain an action if the belief is a motive, it is very far from clear that this situation was as common as its protagonists claim. The tory case, in turn, assumes that *if* it can be shown that professions of principle are not believed, then they are merely *ex post facto* rationalisations and no weight can be placed on them when we explain or try to understand the disbelieving agent's action. Both of these assumptions are criticised in chapter 6 which is, in part, designed to show that a professed principle *can* affect an action even when it is not a motive.

Here, then, are the two main interpretative frameworks for the politics of the 1760s. Naturally not all discussions of the period fit neatly into either of these categories. In recent years there has been a fair amount of convergence between the two views. Christie, for example, is willing to accept, in a way that Namier would probably not have done, that ideas, political 'myths' as he calls them, may well be an important part of political reality.[17] Equally none of the 'new' whigs, i.e. those writing in the post-Namier period, have attempted to argue that George III cherished a design to subvert the constitution and establish an arbitrary or absolutist government, nor have they tried to impose a simple-minded whig–tory typology on politics. Yet, despite this growing *détente*, the whig and tory views remain the chief modes of interpretation. To some extent it seems as if the historiography has reached a terminus or, at least, degenerated into nothing more than an interminable game of historical badminton in which the shuttlecock is struck back and forth between whig and tory protagonists.

Can we move beyond or outside these two typologies? One approach, as I have mentioned, is to look at the ways in which principles might affect actions even when they are not motives. But we can go even further than this by looking at other mutual weaknesses of the whig and tory cases. In the realm of constitutional theory, for example, they both suffer from the same inadequacies. Each has the problem, as we can see in chapter 3, that, having decided what is constitutionally correct, it has to explain away or ignore a large number of statements and assertions that directly conflict with its own conception of constitutional propriety, or which apply constitutional conventions in a way

31

that it would consider improper. A variety of tactics have been used to resolve this problem. Quite often, and this is especially noticeable in Namier's discussion of political responsibility,[18] contrary views of constitutionality have simply been ignored. A second and equally popular stratagem has been to concede the existence of views that conflict with the historian's interpretation of constitutional propriety, but to deny their correctness or applicability.[19] They may be found among contemporaries, but they are simply wrong or inappropriate. A third tactic, most frequently associated with the tory interpretation, is to write off opposition views by designating them spurious *ex post facto* rationalisations.[20]

None of these ways of dealing with the problem is very satisfactory. The first, the omission of any discussion or explanation of what is, after all, a concrete historical phenomenon, is plainly partial and inadequate. The second and third tactics, although they actually consider differing political views or arguments, again fail to explain both their presence and the particular form that they assume. Neither of these problems is solved by the contentions that a view is incorrect or a mere rationalisation. For, even if a political argument is an erroneous rationalisation, its employment and articulation are not arbitrary. It has, perforce, to make reference to conventions, norms and modes of legitimation if it is to make any sense at all. If, therefore, we ask the question, 'why *this* particular view?' – an important question for the historian who is concerned with what is characteristic or peculiar about any particular historical period – we have to move beyond a concern for the truth and status of an argument and consider its use and appropriateness in the context of a set of conventions or rules.

There is a further difficulty shared by the whig and tory cases. The existence in the 1760s of conflicting views about the appropriate application of constitutional rules raises an awkward question: how do we, as historians, decide on the criteria by which to determine when rules have been correctly applied? Presumably the answer given by whig and tory historians is dependent upon the assumption that there is some contemporary consensual basis for the application of conventions to specific instances of political behaviour. Yet clearly, as can be seen in chapter 7, this is not the case. The presence during the 1760s of so many conflicting views about how we ought to interpret political conduct is, thanks to the combined efforts of whig and tory historiography, one of the most conspicuous features of the decade. Conflict not consensus appears to dominate. Whether that conflict be one of lofty principles (as in the traditional whig interpretation) or between two different varieties of rationalisation (as tory historians would argue), the fact remains that, as Richard Pares pointed out, such a conflict did exist and must be explained if we are to begin to understand the politics of the 1760s.

If we are to escape the Scylla of the whig interpretaion and the Charybdis of tory revisionism we must pose new questions. Rather than asking, 'is this contemporary view constitutionally correct?' – and this is a question that I have scrupulously tried to avoid in the subsequent discussion – we should ask, 'why is it that certain contemporaries put forward a particular view, and to what purpose?' Put another way, 'what were they trying to *do* in articulating a particular line or mode of argument?' Two points should be emphasised about formulating the problem in this way. First, it enables us to deal with the particularity of individual arguments, and secondly, it does not pass a constitutional judgement upon the argument being discussed; it merely seeks to explain the argument and its use and development as a discrete historical phenomenon.[21]

In the subsequent chapters of this book, this type of approach is applied to all the major constitutional issues of the period. The question of the efficacy and application of constitutional conventions, the problem of the viability and existence of party divisions – an issue that divided politicians throughout George's reign – and the contentious question of the propriety of individuals' conduct, are all discussed as debates and arguments whose form and content needs explanation rather than normative evaluation.

Similarly I have not, on the whole, asked whether a particular view of politics is empirically true. This may seem an odd omission, especially as one of the most distinguished historians of the period has argued (and others have concurred in his view) that it is the historian's prime task 'to unravel the truth of the situation as distinct from the myth that is current about it'.[22] Clearly, I do not wish to argue that political arguments or the so-called 'myths' under discussion should be taken at face value. But they should also not be treated as myths that arise as a result of 'sheer ignorance of fact' or from 'misinterpreting the facts'.[23] One has to concede that it is perfectly legitimate to take other (usually whig) historians to task for assuming that contemporary political arguments were (accurate) descriptions of political 'reality'. But this is a separate issue from that of whether or not political arguments were *intended* as an objective historical description of so-called reality. Critics of whig naïvety, by and large, retain the original whig assumption that arguments are such descriptions; the only point of difference is whether or not they are correct.

The problem here is that the shared assumption is very often a false one, for it serves as a misdescription of what many politicians are *doing*

33

in putting forward a political argument. *Prima facie* one would not expect politicians to spend their time trying to provide an historically accurate account of political reality, and, when one investigates their intentions, one finds, not unsurprisingly, that this is customarily not the case. Rather we discover that they seek to legitimate certain courses of political action in the context of a set of political norms or values, or that they seek to attribute blame to their opponents for political misfortunes or deeds that can be construed as politically reprehensible. This may entail the use of certain types of description known, somewhat clumsily, to philosophers as 'evaluative descriptions', but their employment or articulation has little to do with an attempt to describe a particular situation objectively or historically. We should not expect eighteenth-century politicians to be historians any more than (despite, it is true, the tenor of much of the historiography of this period) we should expect historians to be politicians. To criticise eighteenth-century politicians for misdescribing historical reality is a trifle ridiculous, for it is to blame them for something that they did not intend to do.

There is, moreover, a further weakness to this case. 'Myths', misdescriptions of reality, are explained as misapprehensions of reality. The reason, therefore, why a myth emerges is because of the ignorance and folly of its protagonists. Clearly, however, if the argument ('myth') is not intended as a description of reality, then this explanation put forward for its emergence also collapses. Quite apart from this, the objections that I have already discussed to the view of argument or 'myth' as erroneous *ex post facto* rationalisation also apply here. An explanation of the particularity of the 'myth', its specific form and the ways in which it is developed, is not possible if we simply account for it as misapprehension. Some alternative and more appropriate model of explanation is evidently required.

Such an account or explanation will have to be, first of all, both *instrumental* and *dynamic*. It must, in other words, set out to show how, why and with what purposes in mind a particular view or argument was presented or expressed. Changes or developments in the argument can be explained as a sort of problem-solving process in the light of a set of norms and conventions as well as in the face of new difficulties or shifts in perspective. This is intended to avoid a difficulty that those who write about ideas find hard to circumvent. By asking what an argument *does*, rather than what it *is*, we breathe life into it; it is not a fly in amber, but a living, developing phenomenon.[24] It is for this reason that I employ the terms argument or ideology rather than idea(s). Not only does this give the impression of a continuous activity, but it also serves to distinguish the cut and thrust of political debate from 'political philosophy' or formulations of politics elaborated in the scholar's study.

A much more sophisticated case, with philosophical backing, can be made for a similar methodology to the one here advocated. It would seem, however, gratuitous to rehearse a case that has been more fully expressed elsewhere.[25] Instead my contention that political argument illuminates our understanding of the politics of the 1760s stands or falls by the evidence and views presented in chapters 3 to 7 and in chapters 10 and 12 of this book. If the reader is convinced that we cannot account for the changes in party politics without reference to ideas about party; if he accepts the view that the vagaries of the elder Pitt are inexplicable without recourse to the ideology of patriotism; if he comes to share with me the belief that the struggle between the Crown and the politicians can only be satisfactorily understood by referring to the debate about ministerial responsibility and the powers of the Crown, than one of the main purposes of this book will have been achieved.

One final point needs to be made. Political argument in eighteenth-century England was never the exclusive preserve of the parliamentary classes. It could be found expressed in pamphlets, in the columns of almost every provincial paper and, in ideographic form, in political cartoons and caricatures. Much of the ritual behaviour of crowds during political demonstrations was ordered by their view of politics. Ballads, verse, periodicals and squibs, all, with varying degrees of sophistication, touched upon the chief political issues of the day. For this reason I have used a wide range of sources. As much attention is deliberately devoted to the examination and use of pamphlets, handbills and cartoons, as to the manuscript collections of the great. (Hence the inclusion in the bibliography of a detailed locational analysis of the pamphlets of the 1760s.) The printed materials, which are often difficult to trace and are less likely to survive the ravages of time, provide as much information – often more information – about political attitudes as do the diaries and political correspondence of the nation's leaders. For, although considerable efforts were made by the nation's chief politicians to exclude others from debate, and although this elite (like so many) were concerned to emphasise the arcane nature of their craft, the political nation of the 1760s was never co-terminous with the parliamentary classes. Political argument – disseminated in a whole variety of ways as chapters 8 and 9 demonstrate – bound together, whether the elite liked it or not, the two political nations of those who were excluded from institutionalised politics, and those who dominated its formal structures. Men might not be entitled to vote, and might not exercise political power, but they could not be prevented from developing political attitudes, engaging in political argument, and giving forceful expression to their views.

Part II

The reconfiguration of politics

3. Whig and tory

I am sensible that Party-Names are below the Dignity of
History, and I have affected to avoid them, but in some Cases
they are unavoidable. (J. Oldmixon, *The History of England
during the reigns of William and Mary, Anne and George I*
(London, 1735), 15)

The study of party in the eighteenth century has been dominated by
those concerned to illuminate the process by which Britain acquired
the much-praised institution of constitutional monarchy. When, in
what way, or by whose agency was the transition effected from mixed
to parliamentary government? It was this question that united those
as far apart as Namier and Trevelyan, even though they proffered
different solutions to the problem.[1]

To pose such a question is, as its historical pedigree implies, a
perfectly respectable enterprise, but there are certain pitfalls which
such an approach does not easily avoid. Certain, primarily whig
historians have shown a propensity to attribute special prescience to
certain eighteenth-century politicians whom they regard as having
contributed more substantially than others to the development of the
ideal party system. Burke, Rockingham and Fox are the names that
they usually have in mind. There is a tendency, in other words, to
assume that because some, though by no means all, of the political
practices advocated by these 'party' whigs approximated to nineteenth-
century conventions, therefore such men 'forecast parliamentary
government'.[2] The result is the faintly ludicrous picture of a group
of politicians *intending* to drag eighteenth-century political practice
kicking and screaming into the nineteenth century.[3]

A rather different, though related difficulty can be observed when
tory historians compare eighteenth-century party with the two-party
ideal. As we have seen in the preceding section,[4] tory historiography
has been concerned to emphasise the difference between eighteenth-
century and modern political practice. Indeed, it has not proved
difficult for them to show that a rigid, regular two-party situation did
not pertain under George III. But occasionally this has led tory
historians to assume that, because the idealised (nineteenth-century)
case for party did not apply, party can be banished from the historical
landscape altogether. This, indeed, is a view that Namier subscribed

39

to when he remarked that 'the political life of the period could be fully described without ever using a party denomination'.[5] Of course Namier never actually tried to do this. All his writings employ party labels, however modified, and doubtless the remark was something of a *jeu d'esprit* directed against a prevailing whig historiography. Nevertheless such a blanket statement highlights the dangers immanent in employing an anachronistic view to examine eighteenth-century party.

A further difficulty of this approach is that these whig and tory approaches have a common failing: both all too often tend to treat all forms of eighteenth-century political organisation in a similar manner, or at least judge them by the same criteria. This is something that contemporaries did not do. There was no 'eighteenth-century attitude' towards party. Rather there were attitudes, different views that could be held by the same man, and which varied according to the type of political organisation that he chose to discuss or defend. This is not to deny that there was some consensus on the question of party. Nearly all men agreed that 'in all governments which are in any degree popular, faction must make as necessarily and unavoidably a part, as trumps do in the game of whisk[*sic*]'. They also assumed that it therefore followed that 'as our own country is blessed with the greatest share of liberty, so it is the more subject to civil dissensions than any other nation in Europe'.[6] In addition political divisions were generally condemned. But attitudes towards the existence and legitimacy of the various forms of dissension varied considerably.

The term 'party', moreover, was never a specific designation, but a broad generic term used variously to describe whigs and tories, oppositions, and proprietary parties such as the Bedford or Rockingham whigs. Thus, when the Duke of Newcastle and Lord John Cavendish talked of 'the party' in the summer of 1766, they were referring to that small band of the faithful, the Rockinghamites,[7] though the same term had been used two years earlier by Horace Walpole to describe the whole opposition,[8] and was frequently employed by pamphleteers as if the only parties were whig and tory.[9] Even on a purely hypothetical level the definitions of party varied. Dr Johnson, for instance, revealed his good tory pedigree by failing to distinguish between a party and a faction. Conversely, Burke, in his *Thoughts on the Cause of the Present Discontents*, was at pains to differentiate the two on the grounds that the intentions and aspirations of those in the former were far more virtuous than those of the latter.[10]

Thus to talk of Hanoverian party or parties is to talk of widely differing phenomena which should be distinguished not simply by locating or tabulating their different individual members – though naturally this is a central means of identifying parties – nor by the modern criterion of the two-party model or party government, but by ascertaining their different political purposes and means of legitimation. It is on this area of the study of political organisation that the following assessment of party in the 1760s focusses.

THE HISTORY OF PARTY

The history of the two parties under the Hanoverians was well known to contemporaries, and their basic account of the fate of whigs and tories has remained remarkably unaltered by modern scholarship. The ebb of the old tories and the flow of a Hanoverian whig party that exploited to the full the political advantages gained at the accession of George I was much too obtrusive a development to escape even the less acute Georgian commentators. Recent writing has, however, brought a blurred historical image into focus, sharpening the profiles of both parties with the aid of statistical techniques. On the demise of the tory party the figures speak for themselves: in the last parliament under Anne there were 358 tories and 200 whigs; after the election of 1715 the numbers were 217 and 341 respectively.[11] Thereafter, except for a brief and inconsequential revival at the 1734 election, the tory party went into continuous decline: in 1742 136 of them sat in the lower house; in 1747 there were 117, and by 1761 this number had been further reduced to 113.[12] By the 1780s there were practically no old tories left.[13]

The Hanoverian succession, the taint of Jacobitism, and the establishment of whig hegemony under the brilliant political management of Sir Robert Walpole had ensured the tory party's gradual demise. Before the 1750s tories had only three alternatives open to them. If they saw the occupation of office as their first concern they could trim their sails to the wind and gradually transform themselves into whigs (or, as John Owen puts it, cease to be tories);[14] they could give their toryism greater point by following the Pretender; or, because of their proscription from office, they could resign themselves to the role of backbench country-gentlemen.[15] Hence Horace Walpole's famous aphorism: 'In truth, all sensible Tories I ever knew were either Jacobites or became Whigs; those that remained Tories remained fools.'[16]

The demise of the old tory party was not without its consequences for the whigs. During the reigns of the first two Hanoverians, as whig enveloped tory, it was increasingly likely that the unqualified epithet 'whig' would become meaningless through its universality. Thus contemporaries like the hard-headed[17] Earl Waldegrave came to see the whigs not as a party 'united in one body, under one general, like a regular and well-disciplined army', but as 'an alliance of different clans, fighting in the same cause, professing the same principles, but influenced and guided by their different chieftains'.[18] It was increasingly otiose to describe a man simply as 'whig'; rather he was a 'Newcastle whig', a 'Bedford whig', a 'Chathamite' or an 'independent whig'.[19]

The changing fortunes of the parties also altered their political complexion. Gradually the more extreme wings of both parties went into decline. One pamphleteer, echoing the sentiments of many others, commented that,

The Tories are not *now* Jacobites, any more than the Whigs are *now* Republicans. A long humiliation and loss of their object at last, has quite extinguished the high tory party. The very term *Jacobite* is *obliviated* with the person whose name and cause were signified by that term, (and I have not yet heard of any Charlobites); and as to the Whigs, their propensity to *republicanism* is also lost for want of use; for since the revolution they have had no occasion to exert such kind of principles; they have enjoyed in a kind of aristocracy, all the power they could wish for, not under indeed, but rather over our respective monarchs, almost since 1688.[20]

Contemporaries were faced with the seemingly incongruous situation of finding the party traditionally associated with prerogative firmly relegated to the role of opposition, and by the equally anomalous circumstance of finding the party of liberty acting as the agent of the court. Such a development, immanent as it had been since the days of William and Anne, seemed to render the principles of whigs and tories interchangeable. The two parties, in a process accurately if invidiously described by Macaulay as 'a wonderful metamorphosis' between 'a human form and a serpent',[21] had

blended together, separated again, coaxed and abused each other; and even changed their very nature and essence according to their particular interests and necessities, and as they have been in or out of power. Thus have we seen the Whigs, in support of their administration, acting upon Tory principles; and the Tories in opposition, act upon the broad bottom of liberty and sound original whiggism.[22]

In these circumstances it was increasingly difficult to identify a distinct set of principles that comprised a 'whig' or 'tory' creed. All three of the developments discussed – the gradual acceptance by the tories of the Hanoverian succession, and therefore their assumption of the titles of 'whig' or 'country-gentleman', the transformation of the whig party as a party of power, and the apparent interchangeability of political principles – helped create an almost ubiquitous form of whiggism which made constant, if vague reference to 'the principles

42

of 1688' or 'revolution principles' and embraced almost all except those at the political extremities. Thus when that rather eccentric member of the lower house, Nicholson Calvert, declared 'I am neither a Jacobite, [n]or Republican, nor Tory, thank God. [*sic*] but an admirer of this constitution' (and therefore, if only by default, a whig) he expressed the ideologically inchoate view of most of his colleagues.[23] They knew what they were not, but it is not unfair to say that they knew not what they were.

These trends made the problem of party identification, the accurate attachment of a party label to a particular individual, increasingly more intractable. Henry Fielding in his parody of political society in *Jonathan Wild* might have been able to distinguish 'those who wore their hats *fiercely* cocked' and were known as '*cavaliers* and *tory rory ranter boys*' from those who preferred 'the *nab*, or trencher-hat with the brim flapping over their eyes' and were called '*wags, roundheads, shakeboys,* [and] oldnolls',[24] but neither his contemporaries nor the historians who have followed them have found it so easy to classify politicians in this way. For, although party labels were widely used descriptively as well as *in pejorem sensum*, there was an increasing number of political figures, especially independents and country-gentlemen, who either denied both of the party labels, or who occupied an ever-growing penumbra between those who were palpably whig or obviously tory. Particular personalities all too often failed to fit snugly into a party cocoon: Sir Francis Dashwood, for example, was variously described as 'tory', 'independent tory', 'Jacobite' and 'opposition whig', while Sir Francis Knollys could be classed by Bute, admittedly not the most knowledgeable of politicians, as 'tory', 'old-whig' and 'Walpolean'.[25]

The fate of the parties in the 1760s served to compound an already confused situation. Before 1757 one could be reasonably sure of finding an opposition dominated, at least numerically speaking, by the tories, and a government that was almost exclusively whig.[26] Despite the occasional exception to this rule – most notably the forty tories who followed Gower in support of the Pelhamite Broadbottom in 1744[27] – such a party configuration obtains until the great war coalition between Pitt and Newcastle. Thereafter tory prospects brightened. They co-operated with Pitt who declined to proscribe them, gave them more posts in the county commissions, and enabled them to re-establish contact with their old whig rivals in the officers' messes of the militia. With the accession of George III they came jubilantly to court and, for once, were not turned away. Some switched allegiance from Pitt to the king; some joined the proprietary parties; others found it harder to shed the habits of a lifetime, and remained as one of the many species of independent.[28] All felt that they were leaving the political wilderness.

These changes, which marked the break-up of the old tory party, were conspicuous, and much remarked upon. When Chase Price drew up a memorandum on the changing state of the parties between 1760 and 1762 for the young Duke of Portland, he laid more stress on the shifting allegiance of tories and independents than on any other single development.[29]

He might also have added that the disintegration of the tories was paralleled by a disintegration of the Old Corps of whigs. Internal divisions were made explicit at the prospect of peace, and were exacerbated by the attitudes of the new king. The Old Corps was already ailing when it was dispatched at the so-called 'Massacre of the Pelhamite Innocents'. This wholesale removal of Newcastle's supporters from office – the cleanest sweep since the Hanoverian succession – completed the process by which a new political configuration had emerged. Party politics was now a matter of an elaborate patchwork of groups and factions, dominated by neither of the two great parties. The political nation, to steal a phrase from Burke, was like a 'tessellated pavement'.

The pulverisation of party into factions, of whig and tory into proprietary groups, quickly became a common topic of political conversation. Horace Walpole, the era's greatest gossip, was soon circulating the current political *bon mot*. Plagiarising a parliamentary speech of Bamber Gascoigne, Walpole claimed it as his own: 'I have a maxim, that *the extinction of party is the origin of faction.*'[30] This development was greeted with considerable anxiety, and many came to attribute the instability of the 1760s to the absence of a traditional binary political division.[31] Reluctantly, contemporaries came to accept factionalised politics as an inevitable, if highly unpalatable fact of political life.[32]

But even while this political atomisation continued, far-reaching changes were taking place in the alignment of politics. The issues raised by the conduct of the king, by Wilkes and the situation in North America divided the politicians on new lines which over the next twenty-five years were to fix the pattern of politics. Regardless of whether one chooses to label this new configuration whig and tory, or court and country, there is no doubt that, both in ideology and personnel, it was different from both whig and tory or court and country in the generation before the 1760s.

Whig and tory

Yet what is of more immediate concern to us than the changing fate of the parties are the attitudes towards this changing fate. For contentions about the existence or absence of a true whig/tory schism, views bolstered by an often highly coloured history of the parties since the Revolution, were an essential component of the different political arguments of the period. Indeed, one can almost say that party alignments were taken up on the basis of attitudes towards party.

Thus after the Hanoverian succession and before *c.* 1757–60 two distinct views of party *qua* whig and tory were upheld. On the one hand there were those who argued that the changes in party creed and the decline of party excesses indicated that any genuine whig/tory distinction was at an end:

Every Body knows that, for near a *Century* past, this Kingdom hath been almost continually agitated with Contentions; occasion'd by the mutual Jealousies and Uneasiness between the *Prince* and the *People*, for *Liberty* on one side, and *Prerogative* on the other; in which also Religion has been not a little concern'd. These Disputes, which have divided the Nation into two great Factions, and brought about several wonderful Revolutions in our Government, seem, at present, to be in great Measure terminated by the firm Establishment of the *Protestant Succession*, against all attempts to defeat it; and by the genuine affection of the People to his Majesty's Person, Family and Government.[33]

Hence, it was argued, any attempt to retain the old party divisions was factious, an attempt to sow the seeds of division in the commonwealth, and to produce an exclusive, proscriptive administration. The sole criterion by which the acts of government and the conduct of individuals ought to be judged was their adherence to the constitution and, if there were to be parties, they too should be assessed by the extent to which they maintained the settlement of 1688. Men should abandon the obsolescent names of whig and tory, terms no longer needed because all accepted the political reality of Hanoverian rule, and unite in a concern for just government and British liberty.[34] It was in this vein that the *Craftsman*, the most successful exponent of this view, urged its readers to

act like wise Men; and remember that *Liberty* is the same divine Blessing, whether it be dispensed to us under a *Whig* or a *Tory* Administration; and that *arbitrary Power*, or any Degree of it, cannot alter its Nature; but is equally destructive of the *British* Constitution, by whatsoever Hands or under whatsoever Shapes, it shall be imposed on us.[35]

The attempt to dissolve the distinction between whigs and tories, to contend that such a distinction was no longer real, was a crucial plank in the country-party platform of the 1730s, 1740s and early 1750s. It was also an aspiration of the passionate supporters of Broadbottom, which was advocated with the specific purpose of rendering the old party divisions unnecessary.[36] The enthusiasm with which such a view was taken up by politicians outside administration is not difficult to explain. As a loose coalition of tories and disgruntled whigs,[37] branded by the government as Jacobite and therefore carrying the political mark of Cain, the country-party opposition needed, if it were to be politically effective, to play down its association (putative or otherwise) with the Pretender and to minimise differences within their own ranks.[38] Thus Bolingbroke, the leading exponent of the country-party case, expended considerable ink and intellectual energy in an attempt to 'explode our former distinctions, and unite men of all denominations'.[39]

Yet this was something that his opponents, who interpreted party history in a somewhat different light, refused to do. It was an axiom of the politics of Walpole and the Pelhams that the difference between whig and tory was, despite the vagaries of party history, still a valid one.[40] Indeed, the governmental whigs were able to sustain their case for as long as the Jacobite movement, though weak and riven with treachery, appeared as a possible threat to the house of Brunswick. While the spectre lingered, the whig/tory distinction could be plausibly maintained, the opposition stigmatised as the allies of the Pretender (or at least the enemies of the king), and the lucrative perquisites of power kept in the hands of the faithful.[41] Hence the very frequent complaints from those who were excluded from office of the way in which government apologists ensured their proscription by painting contemporary politics in the most lurid party colours:

it is every day publickly denounced [sic] by the ministerial writers that the country party is at an end, and that there is no distinction now but Courtiers and Jacobites; the context of which maxim is that all men will be treated as rebels, who will not be the creatures of the ministry.[42]

Thus, on the one hand, the government maintained that the whig/tory distinction was a valid one and proved its own case by proscribing tories from government, while on the other, the opposition continued to urge that any difference between the parties was chimerical. No one denied the reality of political strife but the protagonists entertained conflicting interpretations of its outline. Government supporters saw the battle as one between whigs and tories; most members of the opposition saw the struggle in constitutional terms, or in those of court versus country.

In the late 1750s this argument fell effectively into abeyance. The absence of political strife, and the extraordinary success of Pitt in uniting country-gentlemen and courtiers behind the war coalition, meant that for once in the eighteenth century, and if only because of the begrudging silence of the Old Corps of whigs, it seemed to be agreed that political divisions and distinctions no longer existed. In the words of one of Bute's supporters: 'the moment that the right honourable gentleman [i.e. Pitt] and his friends came into power, I mean directive power, all distinctions were abolished, and court and country became the same'.[43]

George III, succeeding to the throne in such auspicious circumstances, clearly sought to conserve this situation. Indeed, he seems to have regarded himself as the creator of non-party government, going to great lengths to emphasise his own lack of party bias. Thus when looking back on his accession he wrote:

the only difference of conduct [from my predecessor] I adopted was to put an end to those unhappy distinctions of party called Whigs and Torys by declaring I would countenance every Man that supported my Administration & concurred in that form of Government which had been so wisely established by the Revolution.[44]

He intended in other words to be 'monarch of the *British Islands*, not King of a despicable party'.[45] In order to make this change in political climate quite apparent both to the parliamentary classes and the political public, George introduced a number of innovations whose symbolic importance was immediately obvious to all. He and Bute, admittedly at Pitt's instigation,[46] appointed a number of tories to the Royal Household,[47] and asked Harley, a tory, to second the Address in November 1762

in order to shew that what they [the opposition] thought an Imputation was by H.M. & his Servants thought a Virtue, & that Torys and Whigs should in every thing according to their Merits be employ'd indiscriminately.[48]

Simultaneously, and in part because of the propagandist efforts of Bute, the newspapers were filled with material underlining George's determination 'to be Sovereign of the Hearts of All his Subjects'.[49] Prince Frederick's paper, promising 'his intention to abolish for the future all Distinctions of Party', and which he had read to a meeting of tories in 1747, was also put into print, as were exhortations 'to make a noble stand under the auspice of your beloved monarch, against *Faction, Arbitrary Power,* and *Corruption*'.[50] Lord Bute, the Favourite, who was seen by many as the architect of this non-party stance, was extolled because

He is steady in council, an alien to party, and an enemy to faction: he recommends men of real merit, paying no distinction to locality of birth: he unites the jarring interests of prerogative and patriotism, and sacrifices his private ease to public labours.[51]

Such propaganda clearly had some effect. Lord Bute was gratified to learn from one of his coffee-house spies that the chief reason why members of London's Half Moon Club held him in esteem was because

they think it was your [Bute's] advice, His Majesty has not confined his Loyal [*sic*] Favour to a club of people, who call themselves Whigs, and Confined everything amongst themselves, by which his Majesty is father of all his people.[52]

Yet, despite these genuine and vigorous efforts by the new king and his Favourite, the revival of party strife was a widespread topic of debate and conversation within a year of the accession. George's non-party stance had only succeeded in reviving party contentions. Commentators in the press and from every political faction agreed with an author in the *London Magazine* who remarked, in a tone of considerable disappointment, that 'the spirit of party, which seemed to have been quite smothered, or rather to have existed no more, [has] burst forth in a blaze'.[53] Murphy, writing in the *Auditor*, Almon, under the *nom de plume* of 'Independent Whigg', and unaligned journalists such as 'W. M. PRYNNE' in *St James's Chronicle*, together with the author of the *Political Balance*, agreed with Pitt, Bute, the Duke of Devonshire and a host of other politicians in asserting that 'the state is divided into two parties'.[54] Indeed, such was the degree of contention, that George's reign was readily compared to the last four years of the reign of Queen Anne.[55]

Renewed political strife heralded the return of the old quarrel about the nature of political contention, about the existence or absence of a whig/tory schism. This debate was dominated by those who, whether in or out of power, argued that the onus for the revival of party divisions must fall firmly on the shoulders of the young king, or to be more precise, on those of his *éminence grise*, Lord Bute. Their case was perhaps most explicitly stated in a *Review of Lord Bute's Administration*:

They [Bute's followers] made a loud cry about the *independency* and the prerogative of the crown. They rooted up the musty names of whig and tory; the latter they reserved for themselves, and with the former they distinguished their opponents. Before this cry was raised, many people had perceived a revival of *tory maxims*; and now they were confirmed in what they before only suspected...The sensible and honest part of the nation were extremely sorry to see the old and exploded distinctions of whig and tory revived.[56]

An alliance, it was argued, had been formed between a Favourite who needed to invoke tory ideas of personal monarchy to maintain his position, and the party which, not content with seeing an end to the proscription imposed upon it by the last king, now wished to become the dominant group in government. The king and his Favourite had moved from a position in which they had ended the proscription of the tories to one in which they openly supported 'the Doctrines of Toryism and Slavery'.[57]

This development was evidently one which such moderate whig leaders as the Duke of Devonshire had feared from the start of the reign. He had gone to some lengths to warn Bute against proceeding too hastily in support of the formerly proscribed tories. In his political journal Devonshire recorded a conversation with Bute in which he tried to make clear the whig position:

he asked me if I wou'd have him proscribe any Set of Men & quarrell with all the Tories, I said no I was against any proscription what ever, that it was perfectly right to take in men of Character and Abilities from among them, but that if he attempted to take in the whole party, he wou'd by that means lose two thirds of the Nation.[58]

Within two years of this warning, whigs like Devonshire felt that their original apprehensions had been more than confirmed. George's supposedly new conception of monarchy, the resignations of Pitt and Newcastle, the abrupt dismissal of Devonshire himself, and the subsequent massacre of the Pelhamite Innocents may not have alienated two thirds of the nation, but all of these events were taken as indications of a hostility to traditional whiggery and as symptoms of a new toryism in politics which – and this was seen as especially portentous – was focussed on government and the court. What was emerging in the 1760s, it was argued, was a toryism dedicated to the notion of personal royal government and which refused to countenance the idea of political responsibility. This differed from the recent 'toryism' of the Jacobites and country-gentlemen; its creed was much more akin to the principles of the tory party under the Stuarts, now transferred for the first time to a Hanoverian monarch.[59] According to his whig opponents the king, urged on by Bute, had constructed an alliance with the tories who had come to court 'with all their old prejudices. They abjured their ancient master, but retained their principles.'[60] It was this situation that led Henry Bilson Legge to tell Newcastle that

He was not now afraid of Jacobitism; He really believed, It was pretty well over; But he was afraid of Toryism, Tory arbitrary Principles, to fling every Thing into the Power of the Crown, which he seem'd to think was the present danger, & the present object.[61]

The threat that had to be faced was of a new type of tory who was bent on 'endeavouring to restore the Principles & Cause, tho' not the Family'.[62]

The reconfiguration of politics

Indeed, because this was a toryism of principle as much as one of pedigree, and because those who argued that toryism was rampant in government had the uncomfortable task of explaining why so many men with impeccable whig pedigrees supported administration, it became increasingly common amongst those who opposed the king's ministers in the 1760s to call an apostate whig a tory. Bute, it was argued, could only command the support of 'Tories, Scotchmen, & fellows *who call themselves Whigs* & are just as saleable as ginger-bread men at a Country Fair'. The Grenville administration with its authoritarian (though perfectly orthodox) position on Wilkes, General Warrants and America was denounced as a 'detested tory Administration'. Even Pitt, who had previously denied the existence of whig/tory divisions, condemned his brother-in-law's ministry be-cause it 'was not founded on true Revolution principles...it was a Tory Administration'.[63] An old whig with new tory principles was con-demned outright as a rank tory. Thus at the end of the decade when a whig like Grafton was at the Treasury, one of his opponents could write: 'I have strong reasons for suspecting, that your G - - - is a rank Tory yourself; for by your arbitrary and unconstitutional measures, you seem to have adopted the very principles of Toryism.'[64]

This situation prompted constant complaints about the desertion of those who sported a whig pedigree or who had supported the Old Corps. It was especially humiliating to find that the most conspicuous whig apostates had often been important members of the old New-castle following. 'Would to God!' declaimed Sir George Yonge, in a tone that conveys much of the hand-wringing desperation of New-castle's faithful followers, that 'All that wear the *Name* of *Whig*, adhered to the *Principles* of one.'[65] Pitt was especially sarcastic about these desertions. Newcastle informed Devonshire that:

Mr. Pitt...in the Presence of Lord Temple, Lord Lincoln and Jemmy Grenville had a good Deal of Raillery, about the Name of *Whig*; That that was now out of the Question; that One Hundred and Fifty of Mr. Fox's Whigs had deserted me, and supported Lord Bute & his Peace. That he would make use of the words, Revolution Principles, & not Whigs...

He said that he was a Whig; but for the Substance of Whiggism, *the Constitution, & the Liberty of the Subject*: That such Whigs, as would give up these points to humour the Court; and to extend the Power of the Crown, to the Diminution of the Liberty of the Subject, He should never call whigs.[66]

The tactic of calling bad whigs tories enabled the opponents of the Crown, particularly during the opposition activity of 1762–5 and between 1768 and 1771, to portray the struggle between government and opposition as a contest between tory and whig. While the mob cried 'Whigs for ever, No Jacobites',[67] many opposition politicians proclaimed their belief that the administration was tory and the opposition whig. It was therefore clear to George Onslow that the purpose of opposition was 'the Re-establishment of the Whigs in this Country, & consequently of the Cause of Liberty'.[68] In the same spirit Pitt and Charles Townshend refused to accede to what they called a tory administration, and declined to come into power without the whigs.[69] Indeed almost every statement made during these years by such self-conscious whigs as Newcastle and Rockingham was coloured by the assumption that, except when they themselves briefly occupied power, and perhaps during the first six months of the Chatham administration, government and opposition corresponded to the traditional division of tory and whig.[70] Much of the contemporary pamphlet literature reinforced this assumption. A typical item was 'A Battle of the Whigs and Tories' which appeared in the *Oxford Magazine*:

I was highly entertained last night with a military belligerous vision. Methought I was in the balcony window of the lower Packhorse, upon Turnham-Green, when two formidable bodies marched into the field, armed cap-a-pee: the Whigs, headed by the redoubtable Chatham – the Tories, by the rough, boisterous Lord North. The numbers of the last were much superior to the first, which surprised me the more, when I found the illustrious Chatham for the people, and the ministerial Phalanx under Lord North, against them. The arms of the Patriots bore the motto Vox Populi Vox Dei; and those of the Royalists, Pro Semper Rege.[71]

The situation, as envisaged by the whigs, was well summarised by one of the most radical journalists of the day, the author of the *Parliamentary Spy*: 'the royal ear is engrossed by Tories, the Whigs are frowned upon'.[72]

This interpretation of the conflict between government and opposition was vigorously attacked by the apologists of administration. They pointed out that neither Bute nor the triumvirate of Grenville, Halifax and Egremont which followed him could have been responsible for raising party strife, because they had deliberately tried to mollify those from every political camp. What some tendentiously construed as a battle between whigs and tories was, in reality, one 'between the prerogative of his [George's] crown, appointed by the wisdom of the constitution, and the intrigues of precipitate ambition, joined with the arrogance of family, and led on by a spirit that delighteth in blood'. A factious opposition had deliberately and maliciously raised the cry of party that the king and his Favourite had sought to bury. In a characteristic piece of political manoeuvring, the politically discontented and ambitious had 'assumed to themselves, as most honourable, the no-longer existing title of whigs; they have given

us, the country-gentlemen, as most ignominious, the no-longer existing name of tories'.[73]

There were a few government apologists who, once the old war-cries
had been raised, were prepared to accept the label of tory and do battle
with the old weapons.[74] These defenders of government were more
numerous and more prominent than many historians have been
prepared to admit, although it has to be conceded that they were the
bane of the many apologists who defended government from an
anti-party stance. Several authors complained bitterly of the way in
which

He [Bute] has been accused of an intention to form a tory administration, and
the opposition has assumed to itself the name of whigs. Now nothing was more
easy than to contradict this assertion by referring to the Court Calendar, and,
desiring mankind to consider the character of those in high office, and their
known denomination; and then setting the opposition in its true light, shew
it to be only a small cabal of disappointed faction. But our apologists chose
to admit the charge, and as if in fact the tories were in administration, and
the whigs in opposition, they do in the name of the tories, 'intreat the whigs
not to act from mere caprice and prejudice, nor to draw any arguments from
popular murmuring and discontent, unless they can prove, in a parliamentary
way, after the tory example, that such murmuring and discontent have their
foundation in reason, and are justified by wicked and unconstitutional
measures adopted by the administration'. *Risum teneatis amici?*[75]

The anti-party line was more effective and less controversial than its
'tory' equivalent and was used, on occasion, with deadly effect. The
opposition's idea of a genuine, portentous party struggle of epic
proportions could be contrasted with their mean and petty aspirations.
Equally, their bold views could be used to ironic effect, and their true
(malevolent) intentions exposed to public view. One example fully
illustrates the political advantages to be derived from such tactics. In
a brilliant parody of the opposition's views – so effective, indeed, that
historians have always taken the irony at face value[76] – a government
apologist masquerading as Wilkes laid bare the opposition's tactics:

First then, by representing the members of the Club at WILDMAN's, as warm
expousers of Revolution-Principles, you will pretty plainly insinuate, that the
present proceedings of the court are in point-blank opposition to those
principles: And although nothing can be less true than such an insinuation,
yet it will be of infinite service to your party.[77]

The tactic, in other words, was to lay exclusive claim to properly
constitutional conduct and 'Revolution Principles'. This, as many
recognised, was a more recent version of the old dodge of branding
one's opponents as Jacobite. The very same pamphlet goes on to make
precisely this point:

Since then we can no longer accuse those, whom we call Tories, of disaffection and Jacobitism, let us turn the tables, and charge them with too servile an adherence to the Crown: If we cannot prove them guilty of fomenting tumults, and exciting rebellions, let us tax them with being enemies to liberty, bred up in the slavish doctrines of passive obedience and non-resistance.[78]

This perceptive remark provides us with a clue as to how, and in what ways, the configuration of the argument about whig and tory had changed since the days of Walpole and Pelham. As we have seen, before 1760, or perhaps more precisely before the great coalition of 1757, successive whig governments had insisted on the validity of a whig/tory schism and of the approximate correspondence of that division to one of government and opposition. This is not to say that governments did not take in the occasional tory – though this was very much on whig terms – but it is to urge the contrast between a government that exploited political divisions to such good effect and an opposition which sought to end the whig/tory division. By the 1760s, however, the position had almost completely changed. Government apologists – with the exception of those of the Rockingham administration – were the deprecators, not the defenders of party divisions; they made no attempt to stigmatise the opposition as tory, and denied the existence of a schism on old party lines. The oppositions of 1762–5 and 1766–70, on the other hand, were emphatic that whig and tory were a political reality and that the contests of the period were genuine party battles.

The explanation of this ideological volte-face is not difficult to find. The years 1757–62 saw the triumph of country-party (i.e. non-party) ideology: the Jacobite threat was clearly no longer a reality; the elder Pitt had shown how country-party principles could be taken into government and only marginally debased; and, most significant of all, in 1760 the proscriptive whig party, the branch of the whigs who exploited whig/tory divisions, lost their most important member with the death of George II and acquired a country-party opponent in George III. Non-party politics became a part of both government *and* court policy. This, indeed, provides us with one of the reasons why the Old Corps Whigs who went into opposition complained so bitterly of the desertion of the king; he had abandoned one of the cardinal points of the whig governmental creed: that whig and tory were a reality, and that those seen as tories must be kept from power. After 1762, because George combined a theoretical hostility to party with personal enmity towards Newcastle and his followers, the Old Corps, those executive politicians *par excellence*, had either to share the cake with those whom they had previously excluded from the political table, or else accept the crumbs of opposition.

The reconfiguration of politics

It is hardly surprising, therefore, that there were those who deserted Newcastle for the king. But many of those who before 1757 had exploited the putative whig/tory division went with Newcastle and Rockingham into opposition. Once there they had recourse to a new variation on the familiar theme of party conflict. In this respect, as in others, there is a clear continuity between the ideas of Pelham and the contentions of Rockingham. Both they and their followers persistently argued, not simply as all whigs did, that they were the only true whigs, but that they were locked in mortal combat with toryism whether it be in opposition or at the seat of government.

The fact that during the 1760s the party that most strongly espoused the idea of a genuine whig/tory battle was usually in opposition may, at first sight, appear unremarkable. But, as we shall see as we turn to proprietary parties and opposition, the marriage between attempts to legitimate opposition and the contention that a true party struggle was in progress was to prove a fruitful one, yielding important innovations in contemporary political argument.

4. Opposition and the proprietary parties

They [opposition] leave no means unattempted to draw your m - - - - - -'s faithful subjects into factions and cabals, and to engage them in schemes prejudicial to the public good; they endeavour to clog the wheels of government; they would rather see their country in ruins, *than in other hands beside their own faction.* (To the K - - g. BELISARIUS, *London Evening Post,* 17 February 1770)

Opposition, in parliament, to the measures of government, is so far from being in itself an evil, that it has been often productive of good to the state. It may arise from principles that are highly commendable; and even when the motive has been thought indefensible, prudent and well-timed opposition has frequently been of benefit to the community, as well as to the party. The fault lies not in the thing itself, but in the perversion of it to a sinistrous [*sic*] purpose; for as there can be no ministry without errors, it is highly expedient, that there should be some political Argus's, who, either from principle, or selfish views, may watch over the conduct of the servants of the Crown, and check their encroachments upon the civil rights of the people. (CREON, *Gazetteer,* 30 January 1770)

Perhaps the greatest problem that confronted those who formed an opposition or proprietary party was the overwhelming hostility of those who prided themselves on their personal independence and integrity, or upon their paramount allegiance to the Crown. Courtiers or independents with such varied backgrounds as Sir Nathaniel Curzon (a one-time tory made a peer by George III); George Pitt who declaimed 'I am of no club, no party and dare avow the most cordial attachment to your Majesty's person, independent of every factious connection'; Charles Bunbury, who married George's first *amour* and was one of the founders of the Derby; and the strait-laced Lord Barrington who 'detested faction equally in and out of court; and would never have anything to do with it'; or James Oswald who wanted his Treasury appointment directly from the king: all had available to them a veritable barrage of arguments against the formation or existence of any sort of political connection.[1]

A party, any party, was by definition partial; it had particular aims and ends and therefore could hardly sit comfortably with what Professor Bailyn has called the 'ideal of an organic polity whose parts, operating independently within their assigned spheres, fitted together harmoniously'.[2] This was the strongest, and the most frequently reiterated objection to any political grouping: 'Private Views and separate interests chill and destroy all social Duties, and none but large and disinterested Minds can take in those Objects that relate to the Interest of the Whole.'[3] The pursuit of private as opposed to public ends, of the particular instead of the general good, meant that there was a *prima facie* case that, regardless of how well intended party men were when they began their political activities, they would soon sink into corruption and the ways of faction.[4] The ways of party led down the path of unreason; they promoted blind hostility and unfettered antipathy. Individual conscience, that most necessary and humane critical tool, gave way to base and primitive passions. In the words of 'Anti-Sejanus', men fell victim of 'that hideous monster PARTY... [that] horrid, shapeless, unwieldy creature, without either eyes or understanding; falling upon every thing that comes in its way, with blind and undistinguished fury'.[5] Party men, especially those in opposition, lost their capacity for deliberation and sobriety of judgement. As Kinnoull put it:

Whoever is convinced that the greatest & most essential Service He can do his Country, is to procure the Removal of those to whom the Government is entrusted, will be justified in using Means that may be conducive to that End, of which He would not otherwise abstractly approve, because the lesser Evil in Political Considerations must always be preferred to the Greater. And it is this Principle which leads wise and Good Men, who once enter into Opposition, from One step to Another, till they become actually reconciled to Measures, which at first would perhaps have startled them. Opposition, in order to achieve its Object, which is the Removal of the ministers must take in the Aid of popular Clamour, and consequently must pay a greater Regard to popular Prejudices than is strictly consistent with the true Principles of Government. That Object becomes so much the ruling Principle of Action, and the Criterion of judging upon every Measure, that it weakens every other Principle in the Minds even of wise and good Men. The Opposition in order to attack and get the better of Ministers often affects Government itself with lasting Prejudice, Opposition, as it grows more intent upon its Object, grows more and more violent, till it acquires such a Degree of Impetuosity as cannot be checked or restrained by the wisdom & temper of the best, the greatest, and the ablest Men, not even by a Lord Hardwicke.[6]

Party conflict, moreover, was invariably used by the malevolently intended to delude honest men, who were recruited in a cause they thought genuine but which frequently proved to be a stepping-stone for the avaricious and power-hungry.[7] As Arthur Onslow, who had plenty of opportunity to observe party conduct during his many years in the Speaker's chair, remarked:

there is nothing more certain than that by some fatal darkness of understanding or imbecility of heart many persons otherwise of great probity and honour have suffered themselves to be made instruments and supports of these factions, and have been brought to believe, what is in truth the common bond of all party unions, and only justifiable where the Constitution is really in danger, from the settled plan of an Administration for that purpose that they might very honestly act against their conscience in particulars, in order in general to pull down one man they did not like, and to set up another they did, nay to make it a point of honour and fidelity to their friends so to do.[8]

The problem for any potential supporter of party was, therefore, to distinguish between the spirit of faction which would lead him into error, and the spirit of liberty which might support legitimate party activity.[9] For, although parties might have ostensibly good purposes, and although they occasionally contained honest (if deluded) men, they were nevertheless as often as not intended to overthrow government and undermine the constitution.

When party was condemned in these ways as 'a destructive political disease', 'the pest of society', 'the greatest evil of this poor country' and 'the madness of many for the gain of a few'[10] contemporaries were almost invariably applying these criticisms to oppositions or proprietary parties; only occasionally did they refer to party *qua* whig and tory in this way.

Opposition, indeed, had a further objection to contend with. To oppose the king's ministers, to attempt their removal, to 'storm the King's closet' was to constrain the powers of the Crown, preventing the king from exercising his full prerogatives of ministerial appointment and dismissal. If the king was fettered in this way, forced to concede the demands of those who sought power, patronage and office, he would become a cipher, unable to retain 'the Liberty that his poorest subject enjoys, of choosing his own menial servants'.[11] The balance of the constitution would be subverted by those who had created political disorder and dissent to effect their private, factious ends.

These ideological objections to party cannot be underestimated; they formed large and numerous conceptual barriers which had to be leapt or circumvented in order to sustain a case for the formation of party. At the same time it would be foolish to omit or overlook the many practical difficulties that party politicians faced. Naturally, to contrast the practical and ideological problems is to set up something of a false antithesis; attitudes, especially hostile attitudes, towards party presented one of the chief obstacles to party organisation. Pride in independence of mind and means, and hostility to the idea that one

3-2

might become a puppet of party managers meant that even those who acted with a party – for example Sir George Savile with the Rockinghams and Alexander Forrester with the Bedfords – required that their independent sensibilities were pampered and that they were consulted with assiduity and care.[12] Typical was the attitude of Torrington who signed his letters to Portland 'Squire':

If you shall Really desire to find my Appearance in the House can be of any Service to the Good Cause, I am both ready & willing to attend with this *Proviso*, That you shall only send me word *when* and *wherefore* & not let me be made the *Jack* to be called for at all Times & as the Majority is at Present so great I flatter myself It will be rarely I shall Receve yr. Commands & when you do do that You will Absolutely Divest yrself of the Great Man & Minister & Vouch that as an *Independent Country Gentleman* you really think that the Scheme on foot is *Pro Patria*. Under this Restriction I am yr most Obedient, so tell the *Great*, But know otherwise, as to my Wishes...One More thing I should add, Keep me not too much in the Dark.[13]

On the periphery of every party there were those whose fine sensibilities meant that their tenuous allegiance to any political group was difficult to discern. Even the industrious Newcastle or, in a later period, that assiduous party organiser, John Robinson, were unable to compile accurate party lists.[14] They never quite knew how to label that body of men, numerous though diminishing, which refused to be dragooned into the lobbies of the House of Commons.

Parliamentary politics was, moreover, only a part of the life-style (the term is scarcely an anachronism in the eighteenth century) of the average politician. It was almost impossible, as every political organiser knew, to discuss major matters of policy or business in the House before Christmas and after Easter because of the difficulties of securing the attendance of the country gentlemen. As Denbigh, a man who knew the foibles of the independents as well as any peer, wrote to Rochford: 'you may be assur'd that the Country Gent, which compose our best Phalanx in the H. of Commons will not be brought up so soon as Novr unless they think we are at the Eve of War.'[15] Even well-organised political parties found it hard to secure the attendance of their supporters except in the first four months of the year. In the summer of 1768, for instance, Rockingham did not bother to summon his followers to town, despite the possibility of important business, because he knew they would not come.[16] Even the most active politician found much to keep him in the country. At his family seat he was a big fish in a small pond; in London he might feel, as many did, that he would be eaten by the parliamentary sharks. In the country he could concentrate on those pursuits that gave pleasure and were appropriate to his class. Almost every MP seems to have had his own distinctive hobby or recreation: botany, antiquarianism, history, the cultivation of fruit or of the rarer classics. Many more shared the passions of the ruling elite: house-building, emparking, agricultural improvement, the local bench, horse-racing and, above all, hunting. The many varied articles in the *Gentleman's Magazine* – from home medicine to road-building – attest the strength and variety of a bucolic patrician culture that attracted some gentlemen far more than the sins and pleasures of the metropolis.

Thus even political leaders like Rockingham or Richmond had to be badgered and cajoled from their country seats, and forced to travel the bumpy, muddy and dangerous road to Westminster. Not un-characteristic was the conduct of Richmond in 1768. Newcastle wrote to him

Lord Rockingham told Me, that you were very unwilling to leave your Hunting, to come to Town, to consider with our Friends the Plan of Conduct to be held by them, any considerable Time before the Meeting. Your Grace must forgive Me, if I press you very strongly, upon that Subject and I have a Right to do it, from the Respect and Affection which I have for you, and the Cause; and from My Knowledge of your right way of Thinking upon the Subject, and of the Ability with which you support your Opinion, which made so much impression, upon Charles Yorke. For God's sake, My Dear Lord, Don't let it be said that upon Points of this Infinite Consequence to this Nation, Your Grace has suffer'd Your Fox Hunting to deprive the Cause, and your Friends, of the Advantage of your Assistance, and most Material Support, and for the sake of a Fox Chace.[17]

Once in London, the MP was subject to many other distractions. The theatre, the gaming-table, clubs, the pleasures of sexual dalliance and of 'society' all offered more immediate gratification than weary hours on the hard benches of the lower House. The advent of a Newmarket meeting could play havoc with party politics. In April 1764, for example, Onslow was unable to provide Newcastle with any political information because of the races: 'Newmarket has so thinn'd the Town that tho' I call'd last night at Wildman's & at Betty's, I could see not a Soul, nor pick up a word of News.'[18] And in 1757 consideration of the case of Admiral Byng was put off because it clashed with a Newmarket meeting.[19] Such was the exodus on these occasions that in 1765 government and opposition actually carried on major political negotiations in the Suffolk town.[20]

Both hostility to party, and the many social demands that could be made on an MP's time helped impede the development of any sophisticated party organisation. When it came to elections, or to the days immediately before the House was in session, both oppositions and proprietary parties were usually poorly organised. Before the

59

coordinating efforts of Adam and Portland in the election of 1790,[21] there was little system to party electoral activities. Each patron merely looked to his own local and regional interests, and few tried to develop their electoral base, or increase the number of seats that they could influence if not control. Portland, however, was very active in the election of 1768. This was the first general election after the collapse of the Old Corps, and the young duke, undoubtedly one of the most enthusiastic of the Newcastle–Rockingham whigs, made deliberate attempts to increase his interest or establish it anew in Cumberland, Westmorland, Carlisle, Wigan, Callington and Radnorshire. He and William Meredith were responsible for establishing a party subscription to pay off electoral and legal costs incurred during the Wigan contest.[22] Overall, however, the prominence of Portland's work, far more the result of youthful enthusiasm than party organisation, only serves to highlight the absence of system in opposition electoral activity.

When the House was in session, party organisation was little better. The Newcastle–Rockingham whigs, it is true, held regular party *conciliabula*, as well as less formal party dinners to discuss party strategy, propaganda and tactics. Such a meeting was held, for instance, at Claremont, the Duke of Newcastle's seat, in June 1765, when the party leaders voted twelve to six to take office without Pitt.[23] But this sort of organisation rarely extended to the opposition as a whole, which was a party by virtue of being an opposition, not an opposition by virtue of being a party. Even in the most propitious circumstances it was difficult to weld together the disparate proprietary groups. Only when an opposition was in full cry could cooperation be anywhere near complete, or a united phalanx present itself to government and the public. On 9 January 1770, the day that the ministers held their own Cockpit meeting, leaders of the entire opposition assembled at London's Thatched House Tavern.[24] A tottering administration, the flaming issue of Wilkes, the desertion of the Chathamite enclave from Grafton's ministry: no moment could have been more favourable to opposition. Yet, within a few months, they had resumed their old internecine squabbles. On the occasions when a party caucus did manage to formulate some broad plan of action, there was still no regular means by which its intentions could be passed on to other party followers. Individuals simply undertook to write to friends and colleagues requesting attendance for a particular session or, less frequently, for a specific division. Even the Rockingham whips did not emerge until the 1770s.[25]

Undoubtedly the most successful attempt at opposition organisation in the period was Wildman's Club in Albemarle Street. This dining society, led by the younger members of the Newcastle whigs and supported by the followers of Pitt, emerged between December 1763 and January 1764. It had a membership of approximately 150, a set of rules governing payment and attendance, and by the summer of 1764 was holding weekly dinners. Available at the club, if we are to believe one government pamphleteer, were newspapers, pamphlets and broadsheets.[26] Contacts with the press were intimate: John Almon, publisher, author and friend of Earl Temple, seems to have acted as the club's press agent.[27] And Wildman's seems to have been envisaged, by at least some of its members, as the focal point of a more carefully organised and aggressive opposition. Charles Townshend, for example, in the most far-reaching and comprehensive plan of attack on the government drawn up in the 1760s, urged Newcastle and the members of the club to act in every direction:

To gain upon the minds of the people, a daily paper, upon the plan of the Prints, should be set up and circulated diligently, tho' quietly, and two good pens should be employed to write, from material suggested by men of knowledge and subject to their inspection. Some leading men in each Town through the several counties should be admitted to confidence, and be persuaded to give their clubs and districts the tone of conversation directed from hence.

A Committee should be desired to consider and prepare heads of business for next winter, and, in one word, the kingdom should be kept warm, and the chiefs active and laborious during the recess. Sir W. Baker should be desir'd to put the City in Motion, both as an example to other Counties, and as the Attack, nearest Home.[28]

The club and its tactics were, however, hampered by the ambivalent attitude of the Duke of Newcastle and the more overt hostility of such senior whigs as Kinnoull. Newcastle was at first out of sympathy with the club but, as it gained more and more support, he characteristically changed his mind, providing venison for the members' dinners and even, on at least one occasion, actually attending the club in person. Devonshire underwent a similar shift in attitude. His patrician caution and natural inclination towards compromise led him to look askance at the young bloods of Wildman's. But as the temperature of politics rose over the General Warrants affair, and especially after the dismissal of Conway, which he regarded as particularly reprehensible, Devonshire became an active club member. Yet, at exactly the time when the old guard of the party were beginning to overcome their reluctance for such overt acts of opposition, a patronage quarrel broke out over Dr Hay's appointment to the Dean of Arches and created a new rift within the whig society. The appointment itself was of little consequence, but to the younger members of Wildman's and their city friends, those who wanted a wholehearted opposition centred on the club itself, it represented the moderate, pragmatic (and, by implication, ineffectual) politics which rested on the leadership of a few (ageing) whig magnates. The patronage quarrel clarified Newcastle's attitude to the club, and stiffened his resolve: 'The Boys of Wildmans', he determined, will 'not be the Whig party'. Rent by these schisms, the club went into a decline which was accelerated as the issue of General Warrants became less prominent.[29]

The history of Wildman's illustrates a number of points. First and foremost, it demonstrates the fragility of opposition organisation. When the government had committed what appeared to be a conspicuous transgression, and on the occasions when the nuisance-value of opposition was obviously high, opposition organisations could spring up in almost mushroom-like fashion. Yet they could die with equal celerity. Before the 1780s, perhaps before the 1790s, there was never any institutionalised party framework, or even party organs, that were capable of enduring when the opposition's prospects were gloomy or almost totally dark.

Secondly, such evanescent organisations as Wildman's illustrate the extent to which an opposition was dependent upon issues. To have any hope of success, indeed to have the chance of simply retaining its numbers, an opposition had to be active; there could be no half-measures. Thus Newcastle, though in practice as dilatory as ever, quickly grasped the dilemma he faced after his resignation in May 1762. Though reluctant to go into opposition, he knew full well that 'if I was to declare absolutely *the contrary*, my Lord Bute's next levee would be twice as full as any he has yet had'.[30] Any sign that the ageing duke would not lead his cohorts back into the promised land would have been the signal for mass desertion. But, although an opposition had perforce to be active, it had to be active in the right kind of way. Indiscriminate opposition was counter-productive. To maintain one's credibility one had to choose the right issues, and ensure that divisions revealed a genuine party strength. As Newcastle again commented: 'I am inclin'd to think an Opposition, not properly headed, or sufficiently supported, – may rather expose us, & do Hurt, than otherwise.'[31] Yet without an issue, without what Devonshire called 'facts and grounds to go upon',[32] which could generate broadly-based support and inflate a minority, any opposition was bound to be weak. Hence Newcastle's desperate efforts to find an issue behind which he could unite his followers and win independent support in the lower House. The idea of Bute as sole Scotch minister, the dismissal of the Duke of Devonshire, the preliminaries to peace of 1762, and the massacre of the Pelhamite Innocents were all tried (and found wanting) as grounds for successful opposition.[33] Until 1765, when the Rockingham party had hammered out a rudimentary party creed, it was the constant complaint that there were no worthwhile grounds, with the exception of General Warrants, on which to attack the government. As Newcastle wrote to Charles Townshend in sentiments that were echoed by Bessborough within the year, 'Our Friends are, Every Day, calling out for a *point*. The great Difficulty is to find a good One.'[34]

Vital to the success of an opposition was its ability to demonstrate that the administration had in some way infringed the political and constitutional conventions of the time. It was necessary to find or even manufacture an appropriate issue. Regardless of whether those in opposition believed the accusations that they hurled at government, they could not do without them. For it was *only if* they were able to advance such arguments that they could obviate the traditional objections to opposition and proprietary party, and stand some chance of winning the independent and uncommitted. Thus it was no coincidence that the most successful oppositions of the 1760s were centred on two issues, General Warrants and the rights of electors, that raised major constitutional questions and which appealed to the political sensitivities both of the parliamentary independents and of the political nation at large.

The presence of a major issue also helped overcome the bugbear of opposition disunity. By agreeing on what they did not want, the members of the opposition could overlook their disagreement on what they did want. The task of obtaining unity was made a little lighter, though it rarely enjoyed much success. The frequency with which the leaders of opposition appealed for unity is indicative of how hard it was for the ministers' opponents to close their ranks.[35] Yet it was only by acting with concert and unanimity that any opposition could hope for success. As Lord Jersey rather optimistically put it:

If our friends will cooperate without jealousy, and with animated unanimity, we cannot be resisted – Every question (and some should be daily moved, and without the form of Notice to the Ministry) ought to be made a common cause without reserve, refinement, or Delicacy – Your Grace cannot forget the Spirit, and cohesion of the Opposition to Sr Robert Walpole, and without which it could not have prevailed.[36]

Jersey's political memory was short, and he had obviously forgotten how, as the events of 1742–3 amply demonstrated, the opponents of Walpole had only been united in their implacable determination to oust that overmighty subject.

Opposition unity was equally fragile in the 1760s. The opposition to Bute and Grenville (1762–5) is a case in point. Newcastle's following was divided by a quarrel between the old magnates and the young Turks. Newcastle himself was at odds with Pitt, who had not forgiven him for his betrayal in 1761. Pitt was also extremely hostile to the Yorke family, gave only sporadic support to opposition, and was bent on pursuing his own rather convoluted course of political action.[37] A semblance of unity was only obtained because of the controversial issue of General Warrants. Temple, writing to Wilkes, summarised the situation thus: 'There is no union, to be sure, betwixt the D[uke]. of N[ewcastle]. and us; but if there be a union of sentiments concerning public matters, there must follow an union of conduct.'[38]

After 1766 the situation was scarcely any better. The tenuous unity of the opposition to Chatham was fully revealed in the abortive negotiation of July 1767. The Rockinghams, Bedfords, and Grenvilles had no real basis for agreement, and were divided over the issue of America.[39] Commenting on the failed negotiation, Lord Denbigh, a government supporter, could hardly restrain his delight: 'I foretold the D. of Grafton that Oil & Vinegar could as soon mix as the three parties in Opposition agree either about Offices or Measures',[40] and Lord Chancellor Camden touched the nub of the matter when he said 'the difference of the Opposition was clear as It was impossible for *Stamp Men & No Stamp Men* ever to agree'.[41] By the end of 1767, Bedford's original optimism had been replaced by a much more cautious, almost gloomy view. Informing George Grenville that 'a further coalition of what would be advisable to be done in the future, will be impracticable', he concluded that, 'I am readier to pull down than set up; that is owing to the unhappy circumstances of the times'.[42] This very guarded attitude proved justified; on the opening day of the new parliamentary session, 24 November 1767, Grenville and the Rockinghamites were involved in a furious public quarrel which made apparent the depth of the schism within opposition.[43]

Similarly, and despite the issue of the Middlesex election, the alliance of 1769–70 between the Rockinghams and the so-called 'Faction of Cousins' – Chatham, Temple and Grenville – had only the slenderest of bases. Rockingham outlined his party's strategy in a letter to Dowdeswell:

we ought to avail ourselves of other parties now in opposition, in order to effectuate good purposes; and we should be cautious not even to throw the appearance of leading into hands, whose principles we have no reason to think similar to our own, and whose honour we have no reason to confide in.[44]

These sentiments were reciprocated by the other parties in opposition. Burke reported to his party chief that

He [Temple] said, and he repeated it, that to be sure, there was no Treaty expressed or implied to bind the Parties in honour, to one another, or to any measure, except the establishment of the Rights of Freeholders [to see their elected candidate Wilkes sit in the House of Commons]. In Every thing else we were both free.[45]

Horace Walpole, therefore, was not far wrong when he wrote of the opposition in 1770: 'the several factions hated each other more than they did their common enemies...Discord and interest...tore in pieces the opposition'.[46]

Clearly there were a great many difficulties faced by those who wished to organise themselves either as an opposition or as a proprietary party in the eighteenth century: the cards were stacked against them. This did not mean, however, that the exponents of party immediately threw in their hands. They were playing for high stakes and knew that finesse, intelligence and bluff could more than compensate for their lack of court cards. What was needed to overcome the inherent difficulties of party were persuasive arguments against those who opposed political organisation, and cogent grounds for immediate organised action. Three expositions designed to legitimate opposition or proprietary party stand out in the period: the country-party argument with its related idea of Broadbottom; the conception of 'measures not men'; and the view that received its clearest articulation in the 1760s, which I shall dub 'honourable connections'.

The country-party argument was one of elegant simplicity. Its broad premise was that, although it might be conceded that all or almost all parties were illegitimate because they entailed the pursuit of particular ends and the corruption of the constitution, this was not the case with the country party. It was an exception to the general rule because its purpose as a group or combination was to guard against and work for the removal of whatever evils might exist in government, and these might include the evils of oligarchy, party monopoly, or the confinement of the king by his advisers.[47] Thus, although it would be inaccurate to say that country-party supporters were *plus royaliste que le roi*,[48] they certainly claimed to be *plus royaliste que ses ministres*. They argued that the touchstone of political affiliation was loyalty (or disloyalty) to the constitution, not whig or tory party membership, and that the country party embodied the true principles of the constitution, pursuing the common good. [49] Faction and conduct subversive of the delicate edifice that preserved British liberty could be found just as readily in government as in opposition:

There may be conspiracies against liberty, as well as against prerogative. Private interest may screen or defend a bad administration, as well as attack or undermine a good one. In short, conspiring against any one part of the constitution in favour of another, or perverting, to the support of national grievances, the very means which were instituted to redress them, are destructive of the whole framework of such a government, and are the proper characteristics of faction.[50]

In such circumstances one had not only the opportunity but an obligation to oppose government:

whenever the fundamentals of a free government are attacked, or any other schemes, ruinous to the general interest of the nation, are pursued; the best service that can be done to such a nation, and even to the prince, is to commence an early and vigorous opposition to them; for the event will always show...that those who form an opposition in this manner, are the truest friends to both, however they may be stigmatised at first with odious names, which belong more properly to those who throw the dirt at them.

If the opposition begin late, or be carried on more faintly, than the exigency requires, the evil will grow; nay it will grow more by such an opposition, till it becomes at length too inveterate for the ordinary methods of cure; and whenever that happens; whenever usurpations on natural liberty are grown too strong to be checked by these ordinary methods, the people are reduced to this alternative: they must either submit to slavery and beggary, the worst of all political evils; or they must endeavour to prevent the impending mischief by open force and resistance, which is an evil but one degree less eligible than the other.[51]

Thus the country-party was a remedial or, at least, a conservative party whose existence as a legitimate body was contingent upon the presence of abuses of the constitution. This, as Foord has pointed out, was an eschatological view of party: the success of the country party ensured its own destruction.[52] Moreover as a party to destroy abuses, a party to destroy parties in their whig and tory and proprietary forms (and therefore almost a meta-party), it was not properly a party at all, in the sense of being partial. As Bolingbroke put it:

A country party must be authorized by the voice of the country. It must be formed on principles of common interest. It cannot be united and maintained on the particular prejudices, any more than it can, or ought to be, directed to the particular interests of any set of men whatsoever. A party, thus constituted, is improperly called party. It is the nation speaking and acting in the discourse and conduct of particular men.[53]

Thus, and this cannot be sufficiently emphasised, although the country-party argument was a common means of legitimating opposition to government, it was *not* a means of legitimating party in its whig and tory or proprietary forms. Indeed the country party was self-consciously hostile to all forms of political organisation except that of a constitutionally remedial opposition.

These arguments were developed with great sophistication by Bolingbroke, whose work dominated country-party ideology from the 1720s to 1740s. He did not, it is true, retain exclusive rights over the country-party platform which is to be found expressed, time and again, in the polemical writings of the opposition to Walpole and the Pelhams, and which was taken up in modified form by some of the opposition in the 1760s. But Bolingbroke was especially responsible for the contention that, if the country party was to fulfil its proper aim of preserving the constitution, it should not simply act as a constitutional goalkeeper, but as an active attacker in the political game. 'Every Administration is a system of conduct,' he argued, 'opposition therefore should be a system of conduct likewise; an opposite but not dependent system.'[54] In other words formed opposition (though Bolingbroke would never have called it that) was legitimate.

The country party, in its efforts to remove those who were holding the king in thrall and subverting the constitution, was therefore entitled to storm the closet, thrusting wicked men from power as the only means of restoring constitutional equalibrium. This meant, in effect, that even the all-important prerogative of the Crown, the appointment and dismissal of the king's ministers, could be overruled because of the paramount importance of preserving the constitution.

Closely akin to the country-party argument was the idea that was a visual satirist's joy, the notion of Broadbottom. So close were the two concepts that at least one contemporary's definition of the term Broadbottom could easily be taken for an adumbration of country-party ideology:

an Association of all honest Men to abolish all Party-Distinctions, to free it from every Yoke, to disencumber it of every Load, to labour jointly, one and all, whether in Power, or out, to restore the broken Constitution of Old *England*.[55]

But Broadbottom, at its inception at least, was a Bolingbrokian innovation, for it implied a 'clean sweep': the removal of all wicked men from power by an organised opposition and their complete replacement by those endowed with virtue. The Broadbottom opposition would be transformed into a Broadbottom administration, which would accommodate all those, regardless of party distinctions in the old sense of whig and tory, who supported the constitution. Since oligarchy was equally rooted in factious and proprietary parties, these too would be excluded from any Broadbottom administration. Men would be taken in as unfettered individuals, or not at all.[56] As an *opposition* argument then, Broadbottom, like country-party ideology, was pro-opposition but anti-party. It refused to countenance either the traditional two-party schism or the small proprietary groups.

Yet, as Foord has pointed out, the Pelhams rather tendentiously appropriated the term Broadbottom to describe the coalition of groups, not individuals, that emerged after 1746; and, in consequence, the idea of Broadbottom as an anti-party coalition was gradually submerged by the successful and ever-growing all-party (in the sense of proprietary party) coalition of Pelham and Newcastle. The notion did not revive in its original sense until after 1757 when, in the hands of first Pitt and then George III, it became virtually indistinguishable from the concept of 'measures not men'.[57]

The view that it should be 'measures not men' that determined one's political conduct was frequently invoked to legitimate opposition.[58] By emphasising consideration of every measure according to its merits, and by elevating the idea of personal conscience, it sought to avoid the criticism that

an opposition. . .is bound to oppose every government plan of supplies, right or wrong. . .[and] controvert every thing advanced by an administration in the gross, and without exception. . .[being] governed by no other principle but that of enriching and agrandising themselves by the ruin of those they oppose.[59]

Moreover, by solely opposing the minister's *measures* and not attacking the minister himself, an opposition based on 'measures not men', it was argued, avoided placing itself in the invidious position of forcing the king. Of course, in practical terms, as the backbench opponents of Lord North found in 1782,[60] it was extremely difficult, if not well nigh impossible, to maintain such a distinction. It was a virtually unavoidable step from the (successful) opposition to a minister's most important measures, to the position that the minister, unable to enact his policies, must leave the service of the Crown. Nevertheless 'measures not men' was one of the most popular justifications for opposition, and was even regarded as an intrinsic part of the Revolutionary Settlement:

I hope you will consider, that an opposition to measures, when those measures are contrary to the general sense of the nation, is most intimately interwoven with our civil constitution, and most strongly blended with those principles on which that glorious revolution is founded, that happily bequeathed to use the illustrious [royal] family.[61]

Furthermore opposition on the basis of 'measures not men', i.e. not a 'formed opposition', was thought, provided it produced only the occasional vote against government, to confer an agreed immunity from retribution on those who might normally vote with the administration or even those who held office. It was used as a kind of 'conscience clause' designed to permit a degree of elasticity in government support. This view was certainly put by Jeremiah Dyson to Lord Rockingham when the former opposed government on the repeal of the Stamp Act,[62] and was bitterly invoked by the opposition in 1764 when Henry Seymour Conway was dismissed from both Household office and regiment because of his votes with them over General Warrants.[63]

But, because of its emphasis on individual conscience and personal freedom of action, 'measures not men' could be employed just as easily to thwart as to further opposition. Thus, when Waldegrave wished to steer clear of the opposition to the preliminaries to peace at the end of 1762, he wrote: 'I may oppose measures which I think wrong but shall never enter into engagement with any Factious opposers who presume to dictate to the Crown merely to gratify their Ambition or their Resentment.'[64] It is therefore no surprise to find the most independent and wayward of eighteenth-century political figures, the elder Pitt, constantly employing the notion of 'measures not men' to preserve his freedom of action. In 1764, for instance, Newcastle was trying desperately hard to organise opposition, but Pitt kept him at arm's length, frequently repeating 'that for one, He never would force Himself upon the King; that however, He would oppose all Measures, He thought wrong, whoever were Ministers; And let George Grenville do right, He would support Him'.[65]

Indeed, although 'measures not men' may have legitimated *opposition*, it could also be used, as one would expect from the offspring of country-party ideology, as an anti-party argument. Opposition, whigs and tories, proprietary parties, all could be stigmatised on this basis. So that, when those arch exponents of 'measures not men', Pitt and George III, reached a *modus vivendi* in 1766, they attempted to create an administration that was anti-party in several senses: as an *omnium gatherum* it sought to provide no excuse for opposition and to disregard party *qua* whig and tory, and by taking in men as individuals it implicitly sought the end of the proprietary party.[66]

Thus these three arguments employed to legitimate opposition before 1760 were anti-party arguments, except in as much as they justified opposition. And although country-party and Broadbottom were invoked to secure an *organised* opposition, 'measures not men' did not even obtain that, for its emphasis was upon individuals and individual conscience, not upon group or political organisation.

It is not difficult to explain why these legitimations of opposition denied other forms of political organisation. The arguments marked, after all, only an early stage in the legitimation of group political activity. In an era when party was generally frowned upon, it was highly provocative and therefore potentially counterproductive to legitimise all parties. In a sense there was no need or necessity for such a justification. We can go further than this, however. Before 1757, the defenders of opposition had good reasons for maintaining that there was only one legitimate sort of political combination. They were intractably opposed to the whig oligarchy whose power, as we have seen, was partly, perhaps largely maintained by associating whiggery with government and toryism with opposition, and by branding tories as crypto-Jacobites. Denial of these distinctions was essential to opposition for an emphasis on party labels threatened to divide their members, brand them as unfaithful to the Crown or at least to the current dynasty, and alienate them from the affections of the king. In sum the perpetuation of party divisions helped preserve the whig oligarchy in power. Hostility to party, therefore, was a natural opposition tactic in the struggle between administration and those who were politically excluded.

Those who supported 'measures not men' were fiercely opposed by those who maintained 'that public men are so closely connected with public transactions, that it is utterly impossible to give our opinion about the latter, without, in some measure, including the former'.[67] This view, that men and measures were inextricably intertwined, was used to argue that there were certain forms of party – 'honourable connections' – that were politically and constitutionally legitimate. The contention that there were such connections only received full articulation after 1760. Thereafter the adoption, by the king and his supporters, of the view that '*all* political connections are in their nature factious, and as such ought to be destroyed'[68] forced those who had taken party for granted to attempt a general defence of their position. Thus, to a very large extent, the explicit avowal of 'honourable connections' was a response to a king who refused to bring into power or negotiate with politicians *qua* group leaders, and who maintained that both proprietary parties and fully-fledged oppositions forced the hand of the Crown.

At first sight the idea of 'honourable connections' seems to be an appeal to the political facts of life, an attempt to secure the recognition of political groups as not only necessary but beneficial. Lord Hardwicke, for instance, in a statement of characteristic probity and pragmatism, put his position to Lord Egremont thus:

in this country there were such things as honourable connections, which some might represent under the odious name of faction, but might really be only necessary engagements in order to carry on and effectuate right and necessary measures; that by breaking through such honourable connections, (if supposed practicable), individuals might be gained, but they would come naked and be rendered unable to serve either the king or themselves.[69]

Honourable connections are necessary to stable politics; whether in power or out protagonists of this view recognised that, because men and measures cannot be distinguished and because effective political action requires unity, only a firmly allied body of men can make a real contribution to politics. Thus Burke, in his paean to connection made in the House of Commons in February 1769, argued:

The maxim of '*not men but measures*' is an insignificant maxim. If I see any set of men acting systematically wrong, and consider their intentions towards the public are evil, in that case I declare that no acts of such men ought to be supported. Low as I am, I do say that it is wrong; I do say that it is dangerous; I do say it is unparliamentary. If you support these men for a year in doing wrong acts, it is confirming their power to do wrong always, merely because they may, now and then, do a good act. I am connected; I glory in such connection. I ever shall do so... When I find good men, I will cling to them, adhere to them, follow them in and out, wash the very feet they stand on. I will wash their feet and be subservient, not from interest, but from principle; it shall be my glory.[70]

In discussing 'honourable connections', however, neither Burke nor his colleagues argued that every connection should be so dubbed. They were always careful to distinguish groups that had 'a narrow, bigoted, and proscriptive spirit', and were therefore likely to 'sink the idea of the general good in this partial and circumscribed interest', from an honourable connection whose members pursued principle and the public good.[71] As Lord John Cavendish put it:

With regard to party connexions, it is easy to imagine a body of individuals associated with the worst designs; but men of honour will never unite together for unworthy purposes. The country can never be well governed, but by persons united in principle, concurring in sentiment, and bound together by affection.[72]

This is the distinction made by Burke in the most sophisticated of the 'honourable connections' arguments, his *Thoughts on the Cause of the Present Discontents: party,* 'a body of men united for promoting by their joint endeavours *the national interest* upon some particular principle in which they are all agreed', could be contrasted with *faction* which was a body of men pursuing their own private interests at the expense of the national good.[73]

At first sight Burke's attempt, or for that matter that of his colleagues, to distinguish honourable connections from illicit forms of combination does not appear unduly novel. The argument seems analogous to that, for instance, which contrasts country party with faction. Moreover, distinctions between party and faction had frequently been drawn by previous exponents of organised opposition, particularly by those who had replied to Lord Egmont's famous pamphlet *Faction Detected by the Evidence of Facts* (1743). No Rockinghamite, nor any apologist for opposition, more explicitly stated this position than the author of *The Detector Detected* (1743):

71

A *Party* is, when a great Number of Men join together *in Professing a Principle*, or Set of Principles, which they take to be for the *Publick Good*, and therefore endeavour to have them established and universally professed among their own countrymen. *Faction* again is, when a Number of Men unite *for their own private Advantage*, in order to force themselves into Power, or to continue themselves in Power after they have once got it.[74]

The argument of the Rockinghams as expressed in Burke's *Thoughts* was, however, novel in two important respects. First, in talking of party, i.e. legitimate political organisation, Burke was referring not simply, as those who had written in the 1740s had done, to an opposition, but to a proprietary party and one of the great parties – the Whigs. He may even have been referring to both great parties. He once remarked in the House of Commons, 'I highly respect the principles of a Whig, and also the principles of Tories; because I respect men who have any principles at all.'[75] Indeed, what is so important about Burke's argument is that, unlike previous apologias for opposition, he defends an opposition to *preserve*, not to destroy party. Given that, as we have seen, Burke and his colleagues argued that the quarrel between the government and opposition was, in fact, a struggle between tory and whig, the opposition's first purpose was to preserve the whig party from an incipient governmental toryism, and the proprietary Rockingham group from the insidious policy of *divide et impera*. Hence the plea in the *Thoughts* for party unity in the face of a common tory threat, for an alliance like that of the whigs under Queen Anne.[76] Of course such exhortations begged a great many questions about the precise nature and location of the whig party in the 1760s, questions that perplexed the Rockingham whigs for the entire decade;[77] but Burke's plea for unity was substantially different from those of his predecessors precisely because he sought an alliance to prevent, not procure, the disintegration of a great party.

Secondly – and this follows from the way in which Burke employed the term party to refer to a proprietary party and to the whigs as well as an opposition – party would not cease to exist, as would, for example, Bolingbroke's country party, with the triumph of opposition. Once in office, as Burke remarked, the party should not

suffer themselves to be led, or to be controlled, or to be overbalanced, in office or in council, by those who contradict the very fundamental principles on which their party is formed, and even those upon which every fair connection must stand.[78]

This was an important departure in as much as it affirmed the idea of party dominance of government, something the Rockinghams tried to achieve in 1765–6, in the negotiation of 1767, and again in 1782. And, although Burke did not go so far as to argue that party should be co-terminous with government, i.e. he did not defend what we should think of as 'party government', nevertheless his conception of politics is one that envisages party as an enduring feature of politics.

The precise nature of Burke's position can be seen in the way in which he sought to legitimate party. Burke did not argue, despite his obviously strong belief in the virtues of political connection, that every political group or organisation was legitimate. He did not, in other words, believe in a party system. Indeed in the context of the late 1760s his *Thoughts* were explicitly designed to show

the ground upon which the [Rockingham] Party stands; and how different its constitution, as well as the persons who compose it are from the Bedfords, and Grenvilles and other knots, who are combined for no publick purpose; but only as a means of furthering with joint strength, their private and individual advantage.[79]

But neither did Burke argue, as earlier apologists had done, that all parties were *prima facie* constitutionally subversive, although exceptions could be found to this general rule in special circumstances and for certain specific reasons. Rather his overriding case was an inversion of this argument: he maintained that parties were inherently beneficial to the body politic, but admitted that they could be perverted and suborned by the malevolently intended:

Every profession, not excepting the glorious one of soldier, or the sacred one of a priest, is liable to its own particular vices; which, however, form no argument against those ways of life; nor are the vices themselves inevitable to every individual in those professions. Of such a nature are connexions in politics; essentially necessary for the full performance of our public duty, accidentally liable to degenerate into faction. Commonwealths are made of families, free commonwealths of parties also; and we may as well affirm, that our natural regards and ties of blood tend inevitably to make men bad citizens, as that the bonds of our party weaken those by which we are held to our country.[80]

Unsullied connections, in other words, ought to be a permanent feature of politics. They are not or ought not to be simply the product of peculiar circumstance but an inherent part of a stable political order.

After all, according to Burke and his colleagues, the instability of the 1760s was the product of an attack on party, and, because party was or ought to be a permanent feature of that somnolent constitutional balance that was considered so politically desirable, the attack on party was an attack on the constitution. So if the king, Bute and their supporters were not branded as constitutionally subversive tories, intent on reviving the forgotten powers of the Crown, they could still be stigmatised for their destruction of a political balance and stability which, according to Burke, was the outcome of party solidarity.

Thus Burke and his allies had a fundamentally different conception of politics from that espoused by earlier apologists for opposition: they saw party as a regular and desirable feature of politics, not as a cancer on the body politic which ought to be removed as swiftly as possible. The emergence, during the 1760s, of such an opposition group as the Rockingham whigs, who saw the court and country struggle in whig/tory terms, marked the convergence of the justification of a genuine party struggle and the legitimation of opposition. And because the Rockingham party was simultaneously becoming more conscious of its own special identity as a proprietary group, the party and its doctrine of 'honourable connections' mark the first occasion in the eighteenth century when party was defended in all three of its chief forms.[81]

All three of the arguments discussed – the country-party argument, 'measures not men', and 'honourable connections' – contributed to a further, more radical case for parliamentary opposition. This saw the opposition's central function as that of preserving responsible government. Political contention, it was argued, was not simply an inherent part of free government; party, especially an opposition party, helped preserve the freedom and liberties that were intrinsic to the British mixed constitution:

Parties are what we can't expect, nor should we if we could, wish to have them subside. They are the Props of our *Freedom*; it has been supported by them for many Ages; and whenever *Parties* are no more, we may look upon our *Liberties* as absorb'd by the Regal Power. Where would our *Liberties* have been now, if there had been no *Party* but the Court of Minister's, during the late Administration?[82]

Opposition itself became an important component in the constitution, acting as one of the agencies preserving political equilibrium. It was

the weight which keeps the machine together and makes it go. If it be steady and uniform, government will either be maintained in the same proportion of steadiness, uniformity and strength, or there will be a change of hands. If it be light weak and desultory; if there be no fixed general principles of opposition, experience shows that government will soon sink down to the same level of weakness, uncertainty and disunion.[83]

In other words, apologists for opposition were appropriating the function of the legislature as the guardian of political responsibility, and claiming that opposition was the true guarantor of responsible government. It was this view of opposition that led Douglas to criticise the political unanimity that immediately preceded George III's accession: 'the Extinction of factious Opposition', he remarked, 'hath deprived those who direct the Cabinet, of all such Parliamentary

Instruction, as their Predecessors in Power used to receive'.[84] Opposition guaranteed a modicum of political constraint upon the actions of those in power.

It was but a short step from this argument to the view, which was admittedly only occasionally expressed, that 'Opposition is of use in this country whether upon good or bad motives'.[85] This obviously represents a quite radical departure from the conventions about opposition. Nearly all politicians emphasised the importance of *intentions* in assessing the political virtue and constitutional propriety of opposition. To argue, therefore, that opposition, *regardless of the intentions of those who oppose*, was both necessary and valuable was to move the debate onto another plane. Here was a pragmatic, utilitarian justification that legitimated opposition in functional rather than normative terms. Opposition served a useful purpose:

The attachments established between individuals from adhering to some party, have a favourable effect on the genius of a nation; and tend to keep alive some of those nobler passions that are apt to languish in a life of insipid ease and luxury. The art which must be used to get possession of office, will contribute to conduct it, when obtained, with ability. What is vulgarly, but justly called patriotism, in parliament, is serving a kind of apprenticeship, without which, no parts can qualify a man to guide the affairs of the nation with propriety and dispatch.[86]

This kind of exposition, unlike the three arguments for opposition discussed earlier, does not seem to have been associated with any particular political group. It was only very rarely employed by parliamentary politicians, although the Chathamite Barré seems to have been fond of the idea.[87] Newspapers and pamphleteers were its chief advocates, especially at times when the opposition was in full cry. We find it receiving its fullest expression, therefore, during the contentious years of 1768–71.

The idea that opposition can be justified as useful is a fascinating one, for it represents the convergence of, or accommodation between, two types of argument. On the one hand there is the normative case based on the notion of constitutional equilibrium, and, on the other, there is the practical business of obtaining stable politics. In the age of Walpole these two aspirations were frequently, indeed customarily seen as conflicting: the price you paid for political equanimity was a loss of political virtue. Some of Walpole's apologists had tried to argue that the two were compatible and, in order to maintain their case, had used highly pragmatic arguments. It was their opponents who contrasted stability with a loss of moral sanctity. Throughout the second half of the eighteenth century, however, the willingness to accept the pragmatic case for political institutions or practices seems to have

75

increased. On these grounds alone the case for opposition was bound to be strengthened. Besides, the practical and normative views *did* converge. It simply was the case that the opposition came, more and more frequently, to act as a responsible check on administration, and that it could therefore be described as the chief agency of political responsibility.

This gradual, if intangible acceptance of opposition was paralleled by a greater toleration on the part of oppositions of the pillars of government power. Though economical reform sought to remove placemen, its supporters were careful to insist that this did not mean *all* placemen (hence Dunning's motion that 'the influence of the Crown has increased, is increasing, and ought to be *diminished*', not, let it be noted, altogether removed). Provided that the opportunities for royal abuse of power were kept to a minimum, the Rockinghamite whigs were prepared to tolerate (and even defend) a modicum of administrative influence and power. In this sense, as in so many others, they still retained at least some of the residual characteristics of Pelhamite whiggery.

This *détente* between opposition and government was, it has to be conceded, still very much a thing of the future in the 1760s. Nevertheless, as we have seen, inklings, and more, of its development are observable by 1770. Doubtless the presence in opposition of those whose experience had been derived from office and power facilitated this trend, and it is to these men and their difficulties that we must turn if we are to complete the complex pattern of party in this crucial decade.

5. From Old Corps to Rockinghamite whigs: the emergence of a party

I will attend to measures not men, but wish to see those measures conducted by [the] Butes and Grenville connection, rather than by Rockinghams, etc. I have reason to think the former wishes to extirpate party distinctions, as I know the latter wants to establish 'em. (Sir Armine Wodehouse to Lord Townshend, 9 August 1767. Norfolk RO Townshend Mss.)

Two closely related problems dominated the thinking of the Newcastle and Rockingham whigs after the political disasters of 1762. The first of these was the question of the fate of the whig party. Because the Rockinghams saw the battle between government and opposition as a struggle between tory and whig, it was not difficult for them to agree with others in opposition who urged that the whig party ought to be united against the threat of a (putative) new toryism. This, after all, was merely the application, in opposition, of a tried and well-worn tactic which the whig alliance had used when it had dominated officeholding. But, throughout the first decade of George III's reign, there was very considerable disagreement amongst those who self-consciously opposed the 'new toryism', about both the ideological complexion of the whig party and the composition of its leadership. Tensions that had usually, though by no means invariably, remained covert before 1761 were now, in the adverse circumstance of opposition, made quite explicit. In essence, there developed a continuous and often highly acrimonious struggle between, on the one hand, the elder Pitt and a coterie of his followers, and, on the other, the Newcastle–Rockingham connection. Pitt wanted a party based on his own leadership and held together in a loose-knit alliance by the doctrine of 'measures not men'; Newcastle and Rockingham wanted a whiggism of 'honourable connections' led by the great patrician whig families. This quarrel coloured a great many of the activities of both groups, and an appreciation of its gravity is essential to an understanding of whig conduct.

77

The second difficulty that Newcastle and Rockingham faced was that of determining the degree to which their political activities should be constrained by their public professions and their party creed. Their political effectiveness was clearly dependent, at least in part, upon their political credibility; but their concern for credibility could equally limit their effectiveness. Should the party be prepared to ally themselves with tories, apostate whigs, or even the followers of Lord Bute in order to achieve or retain political power? Or should they honour their party creed and accept the consolation that they acted with virtue and consistency? Time and again the party had to choose between an alliance with those whose political ideas they abhorred, and the preservation of the party's ideological purity; between a compromise that made them politically effective, and a strait-laced scrupulousness that reduced their scope for political action.

These two problems are central to an understanding of the way in which the chaste snug corps of the Rockingham whigs emerged from the old Newcastle connection, and of the process by which the Newcastle tactic of trying to recreate a Broadbottom coalition amongst equals was slowly replaced by Rockingham's formula of a coalition dominated by the Rockingham corps.

In their position of adversity after 1762, the whigs naturally appealed to one another for party unity in order to fight Bute's supposed policy of *divide et impera*. In fact attempts to close the serried ranks of the 1757 coalition had been made even earlier, during the first few days of the new reign.[1] Concern quickened, however, after 1762. In October 1763 Pitt advocated an alliance on 'revolution principles' (he preferred this terminology because there were so many whigs who had deserted to Bute and the King)[2] and by the following year Hardwicke was regretting the disunity of the whig party in the face of a new tory phalanx.[3] Newcastle spoke for the entire opposition when he wrote fancifully in June 1765:

All that I wish, with Regard to Publick Affairs, is, to see Such an Administration settled, as may support the Whigs & carry on the King's Business, & that of the Publick with Ease, Honour, & Success, which I think, cannot be done, without Mr. Pitt, & the Great, & Little Whigs, I mean the Whole Whig Party. There is my Heart; and there shall be my Wish.[4]

Although the administration of July failed to live up to this ideal, Newcastle, firm in his belief in the virtues of coalition, was soon rehearsing his favourite theme. Urged on by West, and prompted by the administration's triumphant repeal of the Stamp Act, the Duke exhorted Rockingham to capitalise on his victory, arguing that 'This is the Time to fix a compleat Whig administration'.[5] Even after Newcastle's death whigs continued to pay lip-service – and more – to the idea of a united whig party. Richmond and Chatham, the former believing that the only solution to the nation's problems 'was to reunite in Party, to hold steady together, and by acting upon true whig principles, to recover the weight and Party of the whigs',[6] exhorted each other to cement a true whig union, while Grafton, when making his fateful offer of the Lord Chancellorship to Charles Yorke, professed to want a comprehensive administration which he believed 'could only be brought about by the re-union of the Whigs'.[7]

Despite these frequent and sometimes deeply-felt professions, the Newcastle–Rockingham connection, like the other whig groups, found it difficult to recreate a whig alliance which, for many of them, had been epitomised by the coalition of 1757–61. The situation was not helped by the steady flow of desertions from the Old Corps of whigs leadership to the king and Bute, and later to the administration of Grenville. But, quite apart from these desertions to a government branded as 'tory', there was the problem of the party's relations with Pitt. No whig party would be complete (or safe) without the man who claimed himself to be 'the Oldest Whig in England',[8] yet no party could recruit a more independently minded member. When it suited him to do so Pitt would act the party man. This was certainly the case in the negotiation at the end of August 1763 when, according to George Grenville, Pitt stipulated that 'he and his friends could never come into Government but as a party'.[9] But usually the 'Great Commoner's' brand of whiggism was hostile towards connection and, as the Newcastle–Rockingham group were soon to realise, Pitt was only prepared to contemplate a whig party union of individuals, not groups, for this was the only way in which he could hope to obtain party leadership.

There were, moreover, other reasons why a Pitt–Newcastle *entente* was difficult. When he resigned in October 1761 and thereby ended the great coalition, Pitt had good reason to feel ill-disposed towards the leadership of the Old Corps. He felt, with some justification, that Newcastle, who had sought an understanding with Bute,[10] had united with the Favourite and sabotaged his war policy. Newcastle and Hardwicke, after all, had been (perhaps unwillingly) instrumental in bringing Bute into office in March 1761 behind Pitt's back,[11] and had certainly joined with the Favourite in the cabinet to defeat Pitt's proposals over Spain.[12] When the two groups found themselves together in opposition, their antipathy was compounded by an important patronage quarrel. Newcastle was committed to supporting Charles Yorke, his closest friend's son, as a potential Lord Chancellor in any future administration in which the party participated. Pitt, on the other hand, was highly suspicious of Yorke's halting support for government over General Warrants, and had his own candidate as Lord Chancellor in Sir Charles Pratt, the future Lord Camden.[13] Throughout these years Pitt's suspicion of Newcastle seems to have grown, and it was probably for this reason that he refused, when negotiating with the Rockingham administration in January 1766, to come into office if Newcastle remained in power.[14]

So, despite his cooperation with the whig corps in August 1763 when he attempted to force the closet, Pitt, who knew perfectly well that his best chance of leading a government was to retain his independence and freedom of action, refused to cement a whig opposition union and moved gradually away from those who had been his colleagues at the beginning of the decade. To some extent this is to be explained by the lessons that Pitt learnt from the negotiation in August. He professed to have decided that 'Nothing can be done by *Opposition* in Parliament', and that there was no hope of success 'except the King was convinced of the Necessity of an Alteration, & his Favourite also'.[15] Parliamentary opposition simply seemed counterproductive.

This naturally reduced the potency of Newcastle's opposition as his followers included no speaker who could match Pitt's remarkable rhetorical powers. It also had the much more serious consequence of provoking a division within the Newcastle–Rockingham connection on their attitude towards Pitt. Although this division was not made fully explicit before June 1765, it began as early as December 1762.[16] The party mandarinate – Newcastle, Kinnoull, Bessborough, Devonshire, Hardwicke and Cumberland – were willing to cooperate with Pitt but wanted to pursue a somewhat muted opposition; the young Turks of the party, men like Thomas Walpole, George Onslow and Tommy Townshend Junior, were altogether more extreme: they wanted a vigorous prosecution of the fight against government centred upon Wildman's club and, despite his recently acquired indifference, also wished Pitt to be *the party's leader*.[17]

This schism became clear in June 1765, when, after an extremely complex series of negotiations which had produced deadlock between Pitt and the Crown,[18] the Newcastle–Rockingham connection was offered power. A meeting was held on the 30th at Newcastle House to decide whether or not the party should assume office without the Great Commoner; twelve of those attending – Portland, Rockingham, Albemarle, Bessborough, Lords George, John and Frederick Cavendish, Grantham, Conway, Fitzroy, Walsingham and Newcastle – were prepared to undertake a narrow-bottomed, traditionally-led whig administration, but Ashburnham, Villiers, George Onslow, Thomas Walpole, and the two Charles Townshends were strongly opposed to any administration without Pitt.[19] It seems probable that final agreement on the decision was only reached because it was understood that the party 'came forward with the full declaration of our desire to receive Mr. Pitt at our head, *whenever* he should see the situation of affairs to be such as to allow him to take that part.'[20]

The weakness of the Newcastle–Rockingham connection in office ensured that the question of party leadership remained to the fore. As early as November 1765 the King and his ministers agreed, because of the death of Cumberland, to approach Pitt.[21] In part because of the attitude of George, nothing seems to have come of this negotiation, nor of the tentative suggestions put out by Onslow in December.[22] Instead the party tried to undermine Pitt's support by offering places to two of his most prominent followers, Shelburne and Barré. The strategy was totally without success.[23] But in January 1766, with the threat of Grafton's resignation if Pitt was not brought in, the administration finally managed to elicit the Great Commoner's terms.[24] These constituted a demand for the leadership of a united whig administration: they stipulated that Newcastle should go out (for 'there could be but *One Minister*'),[25] and that Temple, at least in the first instance, should be offered the Treasury. Although Newcastle, as he indicated in a minute presented to the king,[26] was prepared to stand down to cement the coalition, neither Rockingham nor the king would approve the terms which Grafton and Conway, Pitt's strongest supporters, were ready to accept:

Ld. Rockingham tells me, [wrote Newcastle,] in the handsomest Manner, That the King & his Lordship look upon this Declaration of Mr Pitt, to imply a Total Change of the Administration, & My Ld. Rm. thinks so much so Himself, & that his own Honour requires Him not remaining One Moment in his Employment, If this is consented to; & therefore he is determined to quit. The Duke of Grafton, & Mr. Conway are of a different Mind; They suppose, Mr. Pitt must depart from his Unjustifiable Declaration against me; But those two are for Taking Him in, in all Events, & upon his own Terms.[27]

In fact the king's refusal to see Pitt unless he dropped his two conditions, and Pitt's refusal to negotiate with anyone but the king, ensured the breakdown of negotiations.[28] Rockingham made one last-ditch attempt to win over Pitt. During February 1766, in secret discussions which he did not reveal even to his cabinet colleagues, Rockingham offered titular headship of the administration to Pitt provided that the Rockingham–Newcastle connection was not 'broke in pieces'.[29] Pitt, typically, refused to deal with anyone but the king and declined anything less than full power. He held all the cards, and he knew it; he had merely to wait a propitious moment to play his full hand.

The moment was not long in coming. Grafton's resignation in May and the refusal of the Rockingham's to come to an accommodation with the King's Friends seem to have convinced the king that his administration was no more than a caretaker government.[30] In July, when all was ready, he sent for Pitt. The establishment of the Chatham administration and the events of the next six months revealed the extent to which the choice of either Chatham or Rockingham and Newcastle as the whig party's leaders entailed the adoption of very different conceptions of the whig party itself. Chatham, as he told all and sundry,[31] was determined to establish an administration "formed of the best and ablest men, – without any regard to parties, distinctions, or *connections*".[32] He planned an *omnium gatherum* which the king, at least, hoped would 'aid towards destroying all party distinctions'.[33] The only sop that the newly created earl could offer the Newcastle–Rockingham corps, the connection *par excellence*, was that 'as he despair'd of being able to bring that [non-party administration] about, the Whig party must be the *basis* or *foundation*, and consequently the present administration'.[34]

In these circumstances the Rockingham–Newcastle leadership, apprehensive at the possible disintegration of their following, could only try to minimise their losses. They therefore elected to pursue a plan that had first been intimated by Rockingham the previous spring.[35] The party was to maintain a substantial enclave of support inside the administration, but at the same time act as a corps under Rockingham and Newcastle's direction. The idea, therefore, was to dominate the administration by instruction from outside the government's ranks. As Brooke argues, there is a certain naïvety about Rockingham's assumption that his followers would place allegiance to him and the party before allegiance to the Crown;[36] nevertheless, the very fact that he could make such an assumption is indicative of the extent to which Rockingham thought in group and party terms. Indeed, if he was to try to retain his group following intact, there was little else that Rockingham could have done; packing the *omnium gatherum* might just have retained whig corps leadership for the marquis and the ageing duke.

But, as the next few months were to show, Chatham had no truck with a party enclave in his 'measures not men' administration. Instead he tried (not altogether successfully, it is true) to construct an administration of individuals. The more heterogeneous the administration, the harder it would be for the party enclave to achieve domination, and the easier for him to ensure his personal hegemony.[37] Newcastle touched the heart of the matter when he wrote to Onslow,

I take it for granted, that My Ld Chatham, after having gratified Mr. Mackenzie, & made My Ld Northumberland a *Duke*, is determined to get the Duke of Bedford's Party, at any Rate, to enable Him to use the Friends of the last Administration, & the zealous Whigs, as Ill as he pleases; and thereby, (which is His Chief View, & has always been so,) to destroy the Whig party; & make way for his Comprehensive Scheme *of His Creatures only.*[38]

It was this clash between the non-party attitude of Chatham and the pro-party views of Newcastle and Rockingham that made the Edgcumbe affair[39] more than a simple quarrel about places. What was at stake was not merely the dismissal of a Rockingham supporter, but the status of the Rockingham enclave in the administration. Edgcumbe's dismissal was tantamount to a refusal to treat the Rockinghams as a party. For some time the connection had suspected Chatham of trying to destroy their solidarity and they therefore decided to use the incident to test Chatham's attitude towards them. This explains the stridency of the party's demands once the quarrel was under way, and the reason why they did not accept the compromise formulated by Bessborough and Conway. Portland's formulation of the party's case brings out their position well:

I constantly insist upon immediate reparation to Lord Edgcumbe, absolute security to all the party, & assurances of respect support countenance & favor & that they shall be treated with as a Party & as a party only.[40]

When Brooke dismisses the Edgcumbe affair as a matter of patronage unconcerned with any substantive issue, he therefore misapprehends the true nature of the quarrel.[41] The party resignations (admittedly not as numerous as Rockingham had hoped)[42] in the wake of Edgcumbe's dismissal signified the Rockingham–Newcastle connection's recognition that Chatham would not accept them as a group or party. Indeed, repeated statements by the whig leaders,[43] views which Brooke sees fit to ignore, indicate how clearly the withdrawal of Rockinghamite support marked an open schism between those who wanted a party administration and those who sought a government of 'measures not men'. The attitudes of someone like Portland, whose political views are crystallised in the remark, 'I consider myself as a Servant of Party & shall always think it my duty to act in the manner that is most conducive to its support',[44] were totally inappropriate in an administration such as Chatham sought to create. It is therefore unsurprising to find that by Christmas 1766 the schism between the two groups was complete. The whig party had divided once again on both measures and men, and in consequence the Rockingham–Newcastle corps had suffered a further loss of strength.

The situation of the Rockingham–Newcastle party at the end of 1766 was very different from that of the Newcastle corps in 1762. The opposition that started out in 1762 contained many who, though their original political connections had been with the Old Corps, were hesitant, perhaps because of Newcastle's age and because of Pitt's success during the war coalition, to accept the party leadership of the whig grandees. This lack of confidence in the old party leadership became more and more apparent between 1762 and 1766, and was made quite explicit by those who refused to leave Chatham at the end of 1766 and nail their colours to the Rockingham mast. For, apart from those who had come in with Rockingham in 1765 and, like George Brudenell, subsequently became perennial placemen,[45] there were a group of young men centred on Grafton and Charles Townshend who either accepted Chatham's distinctive brand of whiggery, or regarded him as the party's rightful leader, or simply felt that his administration was honest or politically attractive enough to support. Henry Bridgeman, B. Burton, John Calvert, Hon. Charles Fitzroy, William Fitzherbert, George Jennings, Hugo Meynell, George Onslow, Robert Pratt, Henry Penton, Edward Popham, Viscount Howe, Lord Villiers, Henry Seymour Conway, Hon. Thomas Robinson, C. Fitzroy-Scudamore, Thomas Walpole, Spanish Charles Townshend, his namesake and Tommy Townshend Junior, all added their names to the list of those who rejected the old whig leadership.[46] This process of desertion gained momentum after 1765. Charles Townshend, for instance, refused office in July 1765 when the Rockingham administration was first established. Others, like Charles Fitzroy, left the administration when Grafton resigned. The majority, however, demonstrated their loyalty to Chatham in the quarrel of December 1766.

These desertions completed the transformation that had begun when those whose political mentality was dominated by officeholding had left Newcastle for Fox and Bute. By the end of 1766 the corpulent, rotund figure of the Old Corps had been slimmed to the sylph-like form of the Rockingham whigs. Until 1766 the Rockingham corps, still very much dominated by Newcastle, had sought to recreate a broad-based whig party centred on the Old Corps; they had, in other words, tried to resurrect the Pelhamite type of Broadbottom, or a group modelled on the grand coalition of 1757–61. At the same time a number of forces – the Massacre of the Pelhamite Innocents, the waning confidence of the young men of the party in its leadership, and especially the conduct of Pitt – had made such a strategy increasingly less practicable. Political circumstances favoured a group, the 'little endians', who gradually began to emerge as the dominant force in the Rockingham–Newcastle party in these years. Brought up on the political lessons of the early 1760s and not those of an earlier Broadbottom, they were more conscious of the differences between themselves and other proprietary groups than they were of the need for coalition; in consequence they were less willing to compromise the party's ideological stance which had, after all, been formulated on the basis of issues raised since 1760. As the practical possibility of a whig reunion receded, so the 'little endians' gained in strength. But they won no easy, nor, for that matter, a complete victory over those who advocated coalition. The battle over the extent to which the party should make ideological compromises to become politically effective was a prolonged struggle which had its roots in the opposition to Bute and Grenville but which was still problematic at the end of the decade.

Perhaps the first occasion on which the Newcastle–Rockingham corps faced this dilemma was in October 1764, when the cider county tories, through the offices of Sir George Yonge, offered to make an alliance with the party over the repeal of the cider tax and on other common constitutional points.[47] Newcastle, ever eager to consolidate the party's support, was by no means averse to this acquisition of strength.[48] He had, after all, responded to Francis's *Letter from the Cocoa Tree*, which he believed was 'calculated to prevent the Tories from joining us', by planning to issue a declaration stating that he and his followers did not proscribe them.[49] But even in the dire circumstances of 1764 the other whig leaders, especially Cumberland, Grafton, Rockingham and Portland, were unwilling to ally themselves with those whom they regarded as their traditional enemies. The project was therefore dropped.[50]

There was only one other potential ally whom the Rockinghams regarded with greater distaste than the tories, and that was Lord Bute. Seen as the beneficiary of the new 'toryism' and, together with Henry Fox, as the instigator of the Massacre of the Pelhamite Innocents, he was anathematised by nearly all members of the party, even though he represented what was probably the greatest single source of political power. Admittedly Charles Townshend adopted the bold expedient in April 1764 of suggesting an alliance with Bute and Holland, but he was quickly slapped down by the party leaders.[51] Besides, in 1764 Townshend's plan was far removed from political possibility. Yet two years later, when the party was back in power, it had to face the unpalatable choice of either staying in office by allying with the man (or, at least, his supporters) whom they genuinely abhorred, or facing yet another period in the political wilderness. Weakened by Grafton's resignation, and urged on by an enthusiastic king, the Rockingham–Newcastle connection in May 1766 reluctantly began negotiations with the rump of Lord Bute's following, the King's Friends. On 1 May the party held a meeting at the Lord Chancellor's house where they discussed with Lord Egmont, who acted as the king's informant as well as on behalf of the King's Friends, the terms that might be reached.[52] Rockingham and Newcastle were especially determined to ensure that there was not even the *appearance* of a reassertion of Bute's power. Any such development would undermine their credibility, as they had insisted when they came into office that Bute should absolutely be excluded.[53] In consequence they were only prepared to make a gesture towards the King's Friends: they would restore Bute's brother, Mackenzie, who had been axed by Grenville in June 1765, but they would not grant the King's Friends the substance of power. As Egmont reported to the king:

As the Conversation became by degrees more open, It was directly asked whether Lord Butes Friends or Party (as they called them) would join and exert themselves fairly if they were kept in their Places – and they hinted farther that they might even Consent so far as to Suffer Mr. Mackenzie to hold a Lucrative Post – General Conway was explicit for this – Lord Rockingham rather reluctantly consenting – Lord Winchelsea well inclined, but the Duke of Newcastle with great difficulty yielding to this Measure – Indeed all of them agreeing that this was the *Ne plus ultra* of the Condescension possibly to be made.[54]

The King's Friends, however, were determined on the substance of power as well as its shadow, and would treat only as a party.[55] But the Rockinghams would not budge from their position and, although the King's Friends continued the negotiation at Egmont's request in order to give the king time and room for manoeuvre,[56] the transaction was effectively closed. Richmond's efforts to revive the negotiation in June foundered, in part because, as a new boy in the cabinet, he does not seem to have understood that the honorific places he wanted to see offered to the King's Friends would have been refused.[57] The party leaders who, earlier in the same year, had declined to hand over party leadership to Pitt, now repudiated an alliance with those whom they regarded as the agents of the 'new toryism'. Concern for the party's appearance to the public and a determination to stand by its professions, and beliefs had triumphed over a mere desire for power. At the same time, the party had confirmed its self-consciousness through a refusal to cooperate with its political opponents.

It was not, of course, that difficult for the party to agree to impose a proscription of Lord Bute and his friends. In 1766 most members of the party had been implacably hostile to Bute, and even those, such as Richmond, who wanted a degree of cooperation with the King's Friends, nevertheless wished to exact a price for their collaboration.[58] The attitude towards the followers of the Duke of Bedford and George Grenville was, however, altogether more ambiguous. Though they had been the apostates of the first years of the reign, and despite their opposition to the Rockingham administration's American policy, they were still regarded by the Rockingham–Newcastle connection as former comrades and possible future compatriots. The abortive alliance between Rockingham, Grenville and Bedford, and the negotiations with the Chatham administration in July 1767 on which it foundered, reveal more clearly than any other incident in the 1760s the difficulties and paradoxes that the Rockingham–Newcastle connection faced, and the struggle between the 'big' and 'little endians' within the party.

As soon as there was a possibility of an alliance between the followers of Rockingham and Newcastle and the other opponents of Chatham, the tensions and ambiguities within the party became apparent. In December 1766, when Chatham had failed to win Bedford and had therefore made concessions to the King's Friends which appeared like a sell-out to Bute, the question of a new opposition alliance was discussed. Portland, and even Albemarle who was later to be the strongest advocate of a Bedford alliance, were both cautious about such a union. Portland, probably the most party conscious of the whig politicians, felt that the party's image of disinterestedness would be undermined by association with Bedford and would certainly suffer from any connection with Grenville, the greatest whig apostate of them all.[59] But against such apprehensions had to be set the overwhelming advantage of a broadly-based opposition coalition: that it would effectively destroy the influence of the supposedly ubiquitous Favourite, Lord Bute. As Portland saw it, there could be only one true purpose of such a coalition: ' I mean a *solemn determination & unalterable resolution totally to annihilate the influence of Lord Bute in the Closet.*'[60] And it was on this ground that the Duke of Bedford and Newcastle, who claimed to know 'from a Knowledge of this Country of above half a century'[61] that only a coalition could bring stability, came to an understanding in April 1767:

We Both agreed, that the only Thing to be done for the Publick, effectually to put an End to the present Administration, & to prevent any Secret Influence hereafter, from defeating, or Supplanting a Solid Able Administration to be substituted in the Room of the Present, was to establish a Solid, Cordial Agreement, & Union with his Grace, & his Friends, & My Lord Rockingham & his Friends.[62]

It was this aspect of the plan of union that made it so attractive to such party members as Lord Bessborough, Albemarle, Sir William Meredith and Frederick Montagu,[63] and which led Rockingham, as he told Conway and, in rather different terms the king, to embrace the idea of a comprehensive administration in July 1767.[64] And, when the opposition coalition started to fall apart, the strongest argument that Newcastle could muster for its preservation was that *only* a united front could keep out the influence of the Favourite:

I will venture to give it, as My Opinion, That Neither the Duke of Bedford, & His Friends, nor (If you will give Me Leave to say so,) Your Lordship, and your Friends, can, without Each Other, form such an Administration, as can last, & do the Business of the Publick, without absolutely depending upon My Lord Bute, for Its Success, and Duration; And that, I am persuaded, Neither the Duke of Bedford, nor your Lordship will ever consent to.[65]

But for many within the party, and especially for Rockingham, there was much more to the party's creed than the (admittedly important) consideration of the exclusion of Bute. For, as Rockingham made clear to Lord Lyttelton as early as January 1767 – and here one detects an invocation of the achievements of the party set out by Burke in his *Short Account of a late Short Administration* (1766) – he regarded hostility to Grenville and his political creed as an essential plank in the Rockinghamite platform. On the question of supporting Grenville if he came into office, Rockingham said,

That I did not think Mr. G[eorge]: G[renville]: *personally* was quite in the same Light as Lord Temple, but that making Mr. Grenville *Minister*, would be the most inconsistent Act for us, that could be thought of, & that of Course We who were determined to act consistently, would never join in such a Plan.

That our Credit has rose with the Publick by opposing Mr. G:['s] Measures – when he was *Minister* – & that we had confirmed our Credit – by reversing his Measures, when we were in administration.[66]

This was a theme to which Rockingham was to return time and again in the ensuing months. It was on these grounds (*pace* Brooke) that he was generally ill-disposed to the idea of a united opposition, and they explain his readiness to break with Bedford and Grenville when it came to concrete terms.[67] For Rockingham, although eager to see an alliance to remove Bute's putative secret influence, and although aware that this could only be achieved through a broad coalition, would accept nothing less than alliance led and dominated by the Rockingham party. For the Marquis was just as eager to ensure (primarily through the distribution of places) that the influence of Temple and Grenville was negligible in any new administration as he was to exclude the allies of Bute. This he made clear to Bedford at a very early stage in the growth of the opposition alliance, and certainly before the administration's offer in July. In March he wrote to Newcastle of having told the Bedfords

that all our Strength depends upon *Publick Opinion* & that it is entirely owing to our having & *meaning to persist in Acting* a Consistent Part. The Proof of our Consistency turns upon Two Points – the one Ld. B[ute]: the other G[eorge]: G[renville]: – & the Conduct towards the One & the Other – decides our Character.[68]

By the end of the month the schism that was eventually to emerge between the 'little-endian' Rockingham and the 'big-endian' Newcastle had already begun. Rockingham's terms, the duke complained, were far too stringent:

Lord Rockingham has three Points upon which he will insist, – To have a Majority of Friends in the Cabinet, – To give the whole Care of the West Indies, & North America, to My Lord Dartmouth, with the Seals as Third Secretary of State. – To insist, that Mr. Grenville should have Nothing to do with North America.[69]

No doubt Rockingham's determination to prevent Grenville or any of his principles from intruding into the opposition alliance explains the Marquis's uncharacteristic sensitivity during the meetings of 20 and 21 July 1767 to decide on what terms the Bedfords and Rockinghams would unite in administration. On both those occasions it was apparent that the marquis, once he had seen the correspondence that had passed between Grenville and Bedford's agent Rigby, suspected that the former was up to no good. Hence the quarrel, eventually resolved, over the attitude towards America of the various parties involved, and the final breakdown of the negotiations over the question of Conway's continuation as Secretary of State.[70] Rockingham felt that if Conway did not remain as the leader of the lower house, Grenville would become the chief spokesman of the new coalition, something that, as the Marquis had all along insisted, he was not prepared to contemplate. Bedford on the other hand was adamant about Conway's removal:

he thought Mr. Conway a very improper civil Minister in the House of Commons, that His Grace had never approved his conduct there as such, and that he never would consent to Mr. Conway's having the conduct of the House of Commons.[71]

This rock on which the negotiation foundered was one that the Duke of Newcastle clearly felt could have been avoided. In this respect he differed fundamentally from Rockingham. Indeed, as by far the strongest advocate of coalition within the Rockingham group,[72] the duke became highly critical of the marquis's stance, refusing to accept that the principle of Grenville's exclusion was as important as that of Bute, and disbelieving that Grenville could not be trusted. Even after the failure to form an administration in July, the ageing duke urged the continuation of a coalition. On 11 September 1767 he produced a full-scale critique of Rockingham's policy:

It is my firm Opinion, That this *Bute* Administration must last; and will grow too strong for you all, if there is not, from this Moment, the most Cordial, Unlimited, and Unreserved Connection between the Duke of Bedford, and All His Friends, & your Lordship, & all your Friends, and I don't think, any one can be a Sincere Friend to either Party, That does not think, & act upon That Principle...

I entirely agree with your Lordship, that Nothing will give the Parties concerned so much Credit, & Character, with the Publick, & entitle them, to have Weight and Consideration in this Country, so much as a Strict Adherence to Professions & Principles, so often, so publickly, & so invariably laid down by us; which I take to have been, not, in any Measure, to act with, or countenance, or support that influence of Lord B[ute]., which is, & has been so justly lamented, and dreaded by the whole Kingdom. And It is upon that Principle only, That I think, All Connection with the present Administration, or any Part of it, formed entirely by Him, would be directly contrary to those Professions and Declarations.

As to Mr. George Grenville, I never put My Lord Bute, & Him, upon the same Foot; Except, when Mr. George Grenville acted Entirely under His Lordship, How soon This may happen again, I know not; But, whenever It does, I shall think of them Both, as I did before. My present View is, If possible, to prevent it: But I am afraid, It will not be in my Power...

My Wishes, Principles, and Actions, are all guided by the same View; and I did, and do think, That the getting Mr. Grenville, by the Duke of Bedford's Means, to acquiesce, would have been a great Strengthening to the Then intended System, and Coalition; And, by that Means, preventing His Joining My Lord Bute, & My Lord Chatham.[73]

But, despite the support that Newcastle claimed for his views from the Duke of Portland, Sir Charles Saunders, Lord Albemarle and Lord Bessborough,[74] and despite Richmond's apprehensions,[75] Rockingham – strongly backed by the Cavendishes,[76] Dowdeswell and Burke – was determined not to shift his position nor to compromise with Bedford. In reply to Newcastle's criticisms he reiterated once again the importance he attached to the party's *two* principles:

I must beg to lay Stress on Principles in the plural Number – because I think the Publick are very near equally interested in our Adherence to the same Line of Conduct which we have always held against the Power of Lord Bute, & also in the prevention of the return of Power into the Hands of one [i.e. George Grenville] who when Minister, had his Measures opposed by us, & when we were Ministers – those Measures were corrected much to the Publick Security & Advantage.[77]

As he complained to Dowdeswell,

I have had a long letter from the D[uke]: of N[ewcastle]: whose Hurries & Impatience & Want of Steadiness to adhere Strictly to what in my Judgement appears to be *one* of the Fundamental Principles on which we have acted – perplexes me very much.[78]

Rockingham stuck to his guns until the new parliamentary session. Grenville's opening speech hammered home the last nail in the coalition's coffin. His scathing attack on Rockingham's American policy, which no Bedfordite could bring himself to defend, revealed the depth of the fissures within opposition. It also convinced Rockingham himself that his suspicions of Grenville had been soundly based.[79]

Throughout 1767 the Rockingham–Newcastle whigs, or perhaps more precisely their leader, had to face a basic paradox: that the party could only achieve its professed aim of removing Bute's supposed secret influence by forming a Broadbottom coalition. This entailed cooperation if not an accommodation with Grenville, the very man that the party – at least in Rockingham's eyes – was determined to oppose. Given this situation Rockingham pursued the only potentially effective solution to the problem. He set out to create a coalition, but one that had guarantees built into it to ensure Rockinghamite hegemony and the exclusion of any Grenville influence. Hence the insistence that Rockingham himself take the Treasury, that a Rockinghamite – Conway – lead the House of Commons, and that the party have a majority in the Cabinet.[80] Clearly Rockingham, unlike some of his colleagues, felt that in the final analysis the guarantees of Grenvillite exclusion were insufficient; he therefore ended the negotiation.

The events of 1767 saw the triumph of the 'little endians' within the party. Rockingham was successful in preventing Newcastle from forming a reincarnated Pelhamite Broadbottom which, as the marquis, Burke and the Cavendishes all believed, would have sacrificed policy for power and would have been a breach of the party's much-vaunted consistency. Just as the vicissitudes of the Rockingham administration and the confrontation over the Edgcumbe affair had helped define the Rockingham group *vis-à-vis* Bute and Chatham, so the self-conscious process of definition had been continued during the July negotiation. Throughout, whether dealing with the Crown and Grafton, or seeking terms with Bedford and Grenville, Rockingham had insisted that his followers be treated as a party; a party, moreover, that was conscious of its obligations to the public, and thereby felt duty-bound to preserve its consistency even if this entailed relegation into the political wilderness.

It might be argued that, despite this growing party consciousness, the willingness of Rockingham actually to consider a comprehensive administration in July, the resurrection of the idea by Dowdeswell in his important memorandum at the end of the month, and the reluctance of the party to come in on its own bottom imply at least a non-party, if not an anti-party, view of politics.[81] This, however, would be to equate the comprehensive administration proposed by Rockingham with the *omnium gatherum* of Chatham and the king, an error analogous to equating the Pelhamite idea of Broadbottom with the country-party notion of a broad-based administration of men taken in *as individuals*. For what Rockingham insisted upon was not an administration of individuals but one of allied groups *dominated by a single party*. This he made clear in the negotiations, was stated explicitly in the Dowdeswell memorandum,[82] and it became a pillar of the Rockingham fabric thereafter, appearing in both Burke's *Observations on the Present State of the Nation* and his *Thoughts*.[83] The Rockinghamite comprehensive plan was, as George III recognised, designed as a 'clean sweep' to force, capture and hold the closet, and it only failed because of the king's hostility, and because, in practice, no solid party phalanx could be formed on such a broad front. The purpose of the coalition was not to dissipate but to increase party strength; and not to dilute but to concentrate party ideology.

Moreover, for precisely these reasons, the party's refusal to come into power on their own should not be seen as a non-party step. A narrow-bottomed assumption of power would have prevented the Rockinghams from carrying out their avowed policy of excluding Bute and his secret influence; it would have been a fruitless act that would have opened the party to charges of self-interestedness.[84] As Sir George Savile complained (and he might have been speaking of some historians of the period as well as of certain contemporaries)

There are such numbers of People that can not even comprehend that there is any sense in anything but pulling down, coming in, &c.; without considering what footing they must come in upon or how long they could last, or whether they would have it in their power to do any one good thing.[85]

Admittedly, the inability of the party to obtain union behind a set of principles or policy on anything but a narrow front is indicative of the contemporary limitations of party; it also highlights the essential paradox that the Rockinghams never resolved in the 1760s: that, in order to obtain their party ends from the Crown and to force the closet, they had to appeal to those outside the party and with whom they often differed on other political matters. The answer of the 1760s – that other parties should subordinate themselves to a Rockingham-led opposition or administration – was clearly not a very palatable prospect for those such as Chatham, Bedford and Grenville, particularly as what the Rockinghams offered with one hand – coalition – they took away with the other by emphasising the uniqueness of their own party and the errors of their potential allies. In short, the Rockingham answer was not a practical possibility.

Yet, such was the level of party consciousness, that in 1767 the Rockinghams persisted in the idea of a party-dominated coalition while simultaneously vaunting the party's particular virtues. In particular Burke's two important pamphlets, his *Observations* and his *Thoughts*, pressed home this theme. One of their prime concerns was to draw the line between the Rockinghams and the other proprietary parties. The *Observations*, with its blistering attack on Grenville's financial policy both at home and in the empire, made abundantly clear the differences that had been implicit in the abortive coalition of 1767,[86] whilst the *Thoughts*, casually rejecting any radical remedies,[87] spelt out the contrast between a Rockinghamite whiggery based on 'honourable connections' and the 'light and portable' Chathamite principle of '*Not men but measures*'.[88] Indeed when Burke scorned those who, acting on Chatham's precepts, "never differed from a certain set of men until they lost their power, and who never agreed with them in a single instance afterwards", he was fighting again the battles of 1766–7.[89]

In drawing these contrasts, Burke's writings reflected the way in which, after the fiasco of 1767, the party's connections with other groups became deliberately tenuous. Despite the highly advantageous situation of the opposition between 1768 and 1771 the Rockinghams were extremely cautious in their treatment of their opposition allies. Always at the back of their minds lay the thought that their colleagues did 'not mean to raise the same kind of edifice out of the ruins that we do'.[90]

This led to accusations that the party was conducted on an 'exclusive and proscriptive spirit',[91] but it did not prevent its chief protagonist from urging the need for union – to stop secret influence and the piecemeal taking-in of different opposition groups – in the same breath that he condemned the other proprietary parties. But, as the party's opponents had come to expect, Burke once again was advocating a union led by the Rockinghams on strictly Rockinghamite terms.[92] The *Observations* gives the fullest exposition of this argument, although it was repeated again in the *Thoughts*. The Rockinghamites, Burke says,

will be charged..with a dangerous spirit of exclusion and proscription, for being unwilling to mix in schemes of administration, which have no bond of union, or principle of confidence. That charge...they must suffer with patience. If the reason of the thing had not spoken loudly enough, the miserable examples of the several administrations constructed upon the idea of systematic discord would be enough to frighten them from such monstrous and ruinous conjunctions. It is however false, that the idea of a united administration carries with it that of a proscription of any other party. It does indeed imply the necessity of having the great strong-holds of government in well-united hands, in order to secure the predominance of right and uniform principles; of having the capital offices of deliberation and execution of those who can deliberate with mutual confidence, and who will execute what is resolved with firmness and fidelity. If this system cannot be rigorously adhered to in practice, (and what system can be so?) it ought to be the constant aim of good men to approach as nearly to it as possible. No system of that kind can be formed, which will not leave room fully sufficient for healing coalitions: but no coalitions, which under the specious name of independency, carries in its bosom the unreconciled principles of the original discord of parties, ever was, or will be, an healing coalition. Nor will the mind of our sovereign ever know repose, his kingdom settlement, or his business order, efficiency, or grace with his people, until things are established upon the basis of some set of men, who are trusted by the public, and who can trust one another.[93]

By the time that Burke had written his great synthesis of the Rockinghamites' creed, the party had already come of age. Although the original opposition that had set out in 1762 had, in Richmond's words, been 'glean'd of some rotten Limbs',[94] the party was still some eighty strong and was far better organised than any other group in the lower House.[95] By the end of the decade those characteristics which the party was to retain for the next fifteen years had already been formed. As Brooke points out, the lessons of the negotiation of 1767 were to dominate party thinking thereafter.[96] Rockingham's conduct during the abortive negotiation of 1780, and again at the foundation of the Rockingham administration of 1782, was dominated by the desire to ensure party hegemony within any new ministry. The same ideas informed party policy during the cementing of the Fox–North coalition.[97] But, as the coalition showed, the old problem of balancing public credibility against acquiring the capacity to force the Crown was a very delicate and difficult one; the election results of 1784 attest the way in which politicians could miscalculate this intricate political equation.

The determination of party tactics was accompanied by the emergence of a party creed. What began as a vigorous *ad hominem* attack on Bute developed, as the conflict with the Crown and its ministers grew, into a general resolve to strain the personal powers of the Crown. In this respect, the struggles of the 1760s were, in embryo, the struggles between the king and the Fox–North coalition.[98] Parallel with this desire to curb the powers of the Crown was a concern for the propertied and personal rights of the subject. Doubtless such support was occasionally expedient, as in the case of Wilkes, or transparently self-interested, as in the *Nullum Tempus* bill; but support was enduring, and was emphasised as one of the party's more creditable attributes. It was, after all, rather long after the event (and with the complicity of the new Rockingham administration) that Wilkes finally had the resolutions on the Middlesex election expunged from the Commons' Journal. It could also be justifiably maintained that the party managed, despite the occasional tottering, to maintain its knife-edge policy over the American colonies. Though much has been made of the vagaries of Rockinghamite policy, its difference from that of

94

Grenville and Bedford, on the one hand, and Chatham, on the other, was always quite clear. The emphasis was always upon a pragmatic flexibility that laid great stress on the importance of British trade and manufactures, and which was underpinned by a determined unwillingness to use force to keep the North Americans within the empire. A similar, more direct continuity can be seen in Dowdeswell's proposals of 1769 to disenfranchise revenue officers;[99] here we see laid the first plank of what was to become a full platform of economical reform.

By the 1770s the Rockinghamite whigs had a rudimentary political creed to which, for better or for worse (in the view of most tory historians, for worse), they were committed. The political exigencies of the 1760s had brought them a long way from the Newcastle connection of 1762 that had been forced to search out promising issues with which to berate the government. This shift could only have been achieved as the party rejected the old tactics of a Broadbottom coalition, that favourite project of the Duke of Newcastle, and deliberately adopted a 'little-endian' stance on the basis of the issues and quarrels that arose after the accession of George III. As the transition was effected, so Rockingham grew to dominate the party. The quarrel with Newcastle in July 1767 revealed that, even at this late stage, the marquis had to defer to the duke. Only after the collapse of those negotiations, and the recognition that the re-creation of a coalition like those of old was now impossible, did Rockingham come to enjoy total hegemony. Yet, even after Newcastle's death, his tactics could not totally be rejected. For an opposition politician like Rockingham shared with a ministerialist like Newcastle the common concern of party politicians with imposing their will on the king. This could only be achieved through the use of a broad party phalanx. The emergent Rockinghamite whigs, therefore, were a Janus-faced party: they looked to the future, but they had an eye on the past.

6. Pitt and patriotism: a case study in political argument

The popular Cry by *Whigs* and *Tories, Jacobites* and *Revolutionists* is PATRIOTISM, but by what little I see, at this vast distance I am from the *Great World*, the bottom of them All, in *Church* as well as *State*; (like Hell and the Grave, 'Give, Give!') is SELF. Give them but a *Place, Pension, Government-Contract*, or *Mitre*, and farewell *Patriotism*! ('*The MINISTRY in the Suds*' (1774), 15)

Throughout his checkered career William Pitt, subsequently Earl of Chatham, cast himself in the role of patriot. He played the part with immense panache (one of the reasons why the theatrical metaphor is so appropriate) and exploited its political advantages to the full. Unfortunately, however, neither Pitt's political position nor his political intentions during the 1760s could be as readily accommodated to this patriot ideal as they had been earlier in his political career. After the accession of the new king, and as the configuration of politics changed, so the patriot stereotype became as much a liability as a political advantage. Pitt's problem was quite simply that certain of his actions, and here the obvious instances were his acceptance of a pension in 1761 and a peerage in 1766, could easily be construed or attacked as incompatible with the tenets of true patriotism. In these years Pitt was hoist with his own petard. Having professed for so long to being motivated by the patriot ideal, he proved an easy target for his enemies and opponents once he acted in defiance of the stereotype; *because* Pitt chose to legitimate his actions by the notion of patriotism, he made himself doubly vulnerable to attack.

This had not been a problem for him at the beginning of his political career. Almost immediately after his election to the lower house, he launched a series of trenchant and rhetorically brilliant attacks on administration. Within a year he had been acclaimed as a patriot martyr when Walpole tried to silence him by dismissing him from his cornetcy.[1] As Dr Douglas subsequently remarked, epitomising what was to become part of the Pittite legend, he was not 'tutored in the school of corruption, but listed from...[his] earliest Years, under the Banner of Patriotism'.[2] From the first, Pitt's rhetoric evinced his commitment to the patriot cause and camp. In his speeches and public pronouncements he constantly emphasised the way in which he and others ought to place country before self, and liberty and national honour before the profits of office and fruits of corruption; even his private correspondence abounds with such references.[3] By the early 1740s Pitt's reputation had risen to such heights that French agents could describe him as 'the famous Mr. William Pitt, so well known for his patriotic zeal'.[4] Not even his assumption in 1746 of the office of Paymaster of the Forces, a post customarily and rightly regarded as the most corrupt plum of them all, could diminish his patriotic reputation. He refused to accept the Paymaster's advance of £100,000 or to exploit this money and other revenues for his own gain.[5] As far as his admirers were concerned, his time in office merely served to confirm that Pitt was capable of what was regarded as almost impossible, namely 'joining the Patriot to the Courtier'.[6]

During the 1750s, despite his changing and ambiguous attitudes towards Hanover and the continental war, the Great Commoner was able to enhance his patriot reputation even further. Whether in opposition or in power, his high-flown rhetoric emphasised his patriot ideals. For a while, when he came into office with Newcastle and began to support Hanoverian measures, he was strongly attacked for acting at odds with his professions; but the voices of those who doubted Pitt's integrity were soon drowned by the praises for his war ministry, especially during the *annus mirabilis* of 1759. Again, and if only by the skin of his teeth, Pitt had preserved his credit as both 'the True Patriot' and 'the Patriot Minister'.[7] His unique success in this respect was much commented upon:

In that assembly where the public good is so much talked of, and private Interest only pursued, he set out with acting the Patriot, and performed that part so ably that he was adopted by the Publick their Chief, or rather their only unsuspected Champion. The Weight of his popularity and Universally acknowledged abilitys obtruded him upon King George 2nd to whom he was personally obnoxious. He was made Secretary of State. In this difficult and delicate situation which one would have thought must have reduced either the patriot, or the Minister to a decisive option, he managed with such ability, that while he served the King in his most unwarrantable Electoral [*sic*] View⁑...He still preserved all his credit and popularity with the Publick.[8]

Indeed, so thoroughly typecast was Pitt that his chief apologist during the Pitt–Devonshire ministry, the author of the *Con-Test*, could indulge in the most uncharacteristic but highly successful gambit of defending a minister and attacking the opposition by using patriot rhetoric.[9] It can, therefore, be confidently asserted that by 1760 Pitt was regarded as the English patriot *par excellence*. For what was so impressive about him was not the consistency of his actions, but the consistency with which he appealed to the patriot stereotype, or employed the rhetoric of patriotism to justify his actions.

Why should Pitt choose to adopt or at least choose to accept the role of patriot, and what advantages did he gain by it? This raises a number of difficult questions about his motives. It seems plausible to suggest that when Pitt embarked upon his political career he may well have believed that the mainspring of a man's actions ought to be the patriot ideal. The political environment in which he was nurtured, brought up in association with Cobham's Cubs, made this an easy belief in his earlier years. He was never really confronted with the problem of whether or not he was willing to stick to his principles. Put crudely, ideology and interest worked in harmony.

Subsequently, however, Pitt dropped aspects of the patriot programme as and when it was necessary. If he retained a belief in its efficacy he also submitted to the prudential necessities of politics, which usually triumphed over such scruples as he might retain. Thus he played a relatively quiescent role between 1746 and 1754 as a passenger on the whig gravy-train, and abandoned his opposition to Hanoverian connections in 1757 when it finally seemed as if he would obtain the power he had always courted. One is left with the distinct impression that Pitt, having adopted the patriot role, was lumbered with it, whether he liked it or not. On occasion, and especially when Newcastle and George II declined to put him in the place of the recently deceased Henry Pelham as leader of the House of Commons, it proved singularly in tune with Pitt's intentions; on other occasions, and especially after 1757, it was much more of a liability.

Yet Pitt never abandoned the entire framework of patriotism as a justification for his actions, even when there *might* have been an opportunity to do so. This would seem to evince a strong political belief in patriotism, but I think it would be much more appropriately characterised as a strong attachment to patriotism because it served Pitt's purposes so well. For instance, as a mode of justification, patriotism had many advantages. To be able to show that the spring of one's actions was patriotism was to demonstrate that one acted from motives which, judged by contemporary conceptions of the constitution and political virtue, were the most desirable and laudable. A patriot was one who affirmed the ideology of England's Glorious Revolution; he acted, as Pitt himself always put it, on 'revolution principles'. His political purpose was to preserve the delicate constitutional balance of mixed government that was said to have been achieved in 1688, and which every politician ought selflessly to pursue.

This might appear to be a cliché. Very few politicians at all denied that the principles of 1688 were the governing precepts of the constitution. But patriots were especially stringent in their criteria of what constituted conformity to the ideology of the Glorious Revolution. More specifically they were at pains to point out that there were many, especially in the ranks of the whig oligarchical administration, who only paid lip-service to these principles, and whose actions belied their public professions of faith.

The patriot was no such hypocrite:

such a Man will attach himself neither to the *Regal,* nor to the *Popular Power.* – He will fix his Attention solely to maintain the true Ballance of this Government. – He will neither be moved by Disappointment from the Crown, nor by Abuses from the People. – He will act resolutely with *either,* when they are *right.* – He will oppose *both* vigorously, in their Turns, when they are *wrong.* – His sole View in Power, or out of Power, will be the good of his Country. – His Study will be, to support the Crown, without flattering the Prince. – And he will consider more the *real Service* of the People, than their *giddy Approbation.* – He will neither be fettered by general Maxims, nor tied to any chimerical System, but will be governed by Times and Circumstances, of which he will endeavour faithfully to make the best Advantage for the Publick. – Such a Man is a true Patriot.[10]

This required support of the national or common interest at the expense of all others. In order to fulfil his task of preserving the mixed balanced constitution, a patriot had to be 'regulated by one single motive, the love of his country'.[11] Patriotism, therefore, was regarded as both anti-party and anti-corruption. No true patriot could place allegiance to his party leaders above that to his nation, nor could he selfishly regard the acquisition of power and the fruits of office as more important than the national good. The emphasis, therefore, was on personal autonomy and individual virtue. Patriotism was incompatible with the blinkered pursuit of party ends or the retention of a government place or sinecure. Both of them placed constraints on the individual's unfettered conscience which, if uncorrupted, would lead him to pursue the path of virtue and the national good.[12]

Pitt was hardly the first politician to appropriate this ideology for his own use. Throughout the Hanoverian period oppositions sought to clothe their attacks on administration in patriot garb. By the 1720s the term 'patriot' had become virtually synonymous with that of 'member of the opposition'. During the 1730s, patriotism, in the hands of Lord Bolingbroke, became not only one of the chief means of legitimating opposition, but also a programme if it should win power. His *Letter on the Spirit of Patriotism* (1736) and *The Idea of a Patriot King* (1738) combined patriot ideas with the justification of opposition, the aspirations of the Prince of Wales, and the pious, if somewhat distant vision of a reign of virtue once the patriots won office. But the sanctity of this political arcadia-to-be was violated, and the possibility of its realisation pushed even further into the future, by the conduct of the opposition in 1742. When Pulteney and his whig colleagues abandoned their allies for the perquisites of office, failing to achieve either a 'clean sweep' or changes in policy, scepticism of patriot professions reached its peak. It became apparent that the dissident whigs had been cynically using the ideology of patriotism in order to cajole the government into conceding place and fortune. What many had regarded as a political crusade now appeared as an act with the most secular and venal motives. This is one of the reasons why Egmont's pamphlet, *Faction Detected by the Evidence of Facts*, caused such a stir. By its explicit denial of one of the central tenets of patriot ideology, namely that party distinctions were unreal, it seemed to uncover the true intentions of those who compromised with the Old Corps.

Yet, despite growing scepticism about those who professed to be patriots, Pitt's reputation remained relatively untarnished (he had broken with Pulteney in 1742), and he was able to continue to put patriot ideology to good use. Pitt had never been a good party man. He was aloof, unfriendly and socially awkward. He was also ambitious and, to some extent, unstable. Emphasis, therefore, on the patriotic idea of political independence, especially in its characteristic Pittite form of 'measures not men',[13] helped provide Pitt with the personal scope and political freedom which he needed. While in opposition he could vote with government and vice versa, and he could always free himself from the encumbrance of party ties.[14] Indeed, such an ideology was particularly appropriate for a man whose political credentials were based on personal ability and not on the landed acres and party allegiance that so frequently constituted a politician's sole claim to consideration. In this respect, if in few others, Pitt was always in a stronger position than the other political leaders of the day. If he wished to come into power his demands for places were few because of his small following, and he could therefore be more easily accommodated in administration. Moreover this ideology helped him to play the part of the 'grand man'. He constantly emphasised how he could brook no superior but the king, and used patriotism as a justification for maximising his political influence both in office and opposition.

Quite apart from these advantages, Pitt was able to build up his political support through his patriot professions. Patriot rhetoric appealed to the country-gentleman, the parliamentary back-bencher, the tory (because rejection of party entailed rejection of tory proscription), and the political nation out-of-doors. Pitt solicited and gained their support precisely because he promised to fulfil their conception of political virtue: to rule without corruption, and oppose without faction. His political strength was, therefore, not built on party or patronage, but on his ability to act as the nation's patriot leader. This made him vulnerable, for he had little political substance to fall back on; but it also had its advantages: he was more independent than party politicians and was therefore freer to pursue his own course of action.

Prior to 1760 or, at least, 1757, Pitt had relatively little difficulty in reconciling his conduct and intentions with his patriot creed. After the accession of the new king, however, Pitt's situation changed and, in consequence, so did his aspirations: he found it increasingly hard to square them with the patriot ideal by which he had asked others to judge him.

Under George III Pitt's political position was very considerably weakened. Having finally managed to win the support of the old king by a vigorous prosecution of the war in the last years of the reign, Pitt once again found himself in the familiar situation of being without royal favour. This was very largely because George bitterly resented the way in which Pitt had failed to provide patronage and consultation for the Leicester House interest between 1758 and 1760,[15] despite their important part in helping him achieve power. Less than six months before the accession George contemptuously described Pitt (whom he saw as his former ally) as 'the most ungrateful and in my mind most dishonourable of men' and 'the blackest of hearts'.[16] This attitude persisted in the new reign. When Pitt resigned in October 1761 many of the administration were fearful and wanted to keep him in. George, however, was overjoyed to see the back of him.[17]

From the first days of the new reign the Great Commoner faced the threat of isolation in the cabinet over his all-important war policy. He now not only had to contend with Newcastle's criticisms of the war on financial grounds, but had to face the anti-Germanism of Bute and the king who had described the war in the first draft of his opening proclamation as 'bloody and expensive'.[18] This was always a danger to Pitt in the first year of the reign, and one which was eventually realised in the union of Bute and Newcastle against Pitt's determination for a Spanish war.

Far more serious than either of these threats to Pitt's position was, however, the way in which George and Bute contrived to undermine Pitt's political support. As the much-vaunted and long-awaited 'patriot king', George's political appeal and stance was directed at precisely the same segment of the political nation that Pitt had so successfully wooed. In the previous reign the Prince of Wales had been unable to compete with the Great Commoner. But after his accession George and Bute could offer a great deal more than Pitt to the politically independent and politically dispossessed. By refusing to adopt a party stance, the king gave Pitt's tories both the opportunity to support the administration *and* to enjoy the favour of the court, and by promising to introduce a reign of virtue and 'oeconomy' he rendered the patriot minister virtually obsolete. Moreover Pitt's appeal as a patriot minister was, as the nation grew more war-weary, more than countermanded by his complete commitment to a long and expensive war with continental connections. The king and Bute, on the other hand, not only offered patriot rule, but an end to hostilities and to that traditional bugbear of the tories and independents, Hanoverian connections.

The king, Bute and later Fox all attempted with considerable success to acquire the allegiance of those – especially tories and independents – who had formerly been supporters of Pitt. The king's opening speech to parliament with its famous phrase, 'I glory in the name of Britain' was clearly designed to appeal to them.[19] Members of the Cocoa Tree Club were shepherded by Lord Talbot to the royal leveés where they were conspicuously marked out for royal attention.[20] Backbenchers were consulted over finance, summoned to the Cockpit before parliamentary sessions, and a tory was even chosen to second the address in November 1762.[21]

These efforts were not without effect. George Grenville told Hardwicke in October 1761 that

He did not imagine that Mr. Pitt would have any great Following of the Tories, that Ald. Beckford and Sir John Phillips pretended to answer for them but could not; and that Sir Charles Mordaunt & the sober part of them were sick of Mr. P---'s Measures of War, more especially continental, & of the immense Expence. That Lord Bute had gained my Lord Lichfield & Lord Oxford & Lord Bruce who had great Credit with the Party; & in short had made a great In road amongst them.[22]

Indeed by the following December – notably in the debate on the motion for Spanish papers – Pitt's fortunes had reached their nadir. As Fox wrote enthusiastically to the Duke of Devonshire:

Never did Man make a more miserable figure than Mr. Pitt. He found, He felt, He own'd He had hardly one Friend in the House of Commons...Death to Mr. Pitt. & Mr. Pitt look'd dying. So that two bon mots of Sellwins [*sic*] were really just. Of Barré & Him, 'There (says He) is *Gladiator pugnans*, & there is *Gladiator moriens*'. The other is, 'I thought Pitt spoke very ill & yet I wonder I Dislik'd Him, for I generally like a dying Speech and Confession'.[23] Such it really was, & had it been the prelude to his natural not political Death, He could not have look'd otherwise than He did.[24]

As men like Lord Denbigh (who had even offered to resign in October 1761)[25] deserted him for Bute, Pitt became more and more apprehensive. In November 1762 he complained to Thomas Walpole that 'being out Toried by Lord Bute & out Whigged by [the] D[uke] of N[ewcastle] he had nobody to converse with but the Clerk of the H[ouse]. of Commons', and two months later he expressed to Newcastle 'the apprehension, that now, as *His Tories* have flung themselves all into My Lord Bute, He shall be forced to depend entirely on us [the Old Corps]'.[26] So that when an issue arose like the cider tax which might have rallied some of his old supporters to his standard. Pitt played it for all it was worth.[27] But he only achieved a limited success and was reduced to hectoring the tories and backbenchers, vowing that once they returned to their senses they would see how much they needed his support.[28]

Pitt's dilemma in the early years of the reign was a cruel one. His career had reached a peak by 1760: he was the war hero and he had the confidence of the king and his colleagues. His patriotism had even induced the tories, in an almost unprecedented way, to support the war coalition. Once George succeeded, however, Pitt's problems multiplied. His commitment to the war effort was total, yet Bute, and especially the king, opposed it. Pitt was unwilling to compromise his political views in any way ('my sentiments in politicks like my religion are my own, I cant change them', he told Gilbert Elliot),[29] yet recognised that this courted political disaster. For a while he tried to bluff and bluster his way through the crisis: he combined powerful threats and big words with the occasional suggestion that he resign and leave Bute and Newcastle to finish the war, a prospect that neither of them relished. But when Newcastle and Bute ganged up on Pitt to defeat his Spanish proposals it became clear that his role of *generalissimo* was over, and he resigned.

Pitt's withdrawal from administration was more than resignation, it was the announcement of his political retirement. He had made it clear to Bute in April and October 1760 that he would have nothing to do with the Favourite's supremacy, but that he would not go into opposition, as he was both too old and too infirm.[30] He had also hinted strongly that he would like some public mark of gratitude to ease his withdrawal from politics. (It is an interesting reflection of the psychology of the two men, that Pitt should do this, but that Newcastle should be surprised when offered a reward, and should absolutely refuse it.) On numerous occasions in the first year of the reign Pitt had spoken of retirement. As early as March 1761, Bute was confidently telling Newcastle that 'Mr. Pitt would never go into Opposition, But in all Events would retire, with some honourable provision' – as if he and the Great Commoner had already come to some kind of agreement.[31] When Pitt did resign in October Devonshire certainly thought that he might quit the Commons, and by 1762 Temple was writing as if the Great Commoner had already withdrawn from politics permanently.[32] Indeed, when Pitt accepted a pension of £3,000 per annum for three lives and a peerage for his wife, it seems likely that he had determined to retire.

It was only the political developments of the next two years that brought him back into politics. One of the most important of these was the public reaction to the announcement of Pitt's pension, and the way in which this revulsion was used by Bute, the Yorkes and, to a lesser extent, Newcastle to destroy Pitt's political credit.[33] The publication of Pitt's pension, deliberately released by Bute in the *Gazette*, was greeted first with incredulity, and then with hostility and disillusionment. Horace Walpole's immediate reaction was typical:

Am not I an old fool? at my years to be a dupe to virtue and patriotism; I, who have seen all the virtue of England sold six times over!..I adored Mr. Pitt, as if I was just come from school and reading Livy's lies of Brutus and Camillus, and Fabius; and romance knows whom. Alack! alack! Mr. Pitt loves an estate as well as my Lord Bath![34]

For a few days the City of London was up in arms against its old hero. It looked as if they would carry out their threat (made when a pension was rumoured) that 'If Mr. Pitt did not oppose, and act with vigour out, but Accepted any Thing from the King He would be resigned, and treated like my Ld. Bath'.[35] At the same time a tremendous press campaign, appearing in verses, pamphlets, magazines and newspaper letters, was launched by Bute against the Great Commoner.[36] Not until he published a letter of apology and explanation was Pitt able to curb the onslaught, and not until the following month did he begin to reestablish his position in the City. Despite his recovery, the popular outcry and propaganda had had its effect. For someone as politically naïve as Conway, the press revealed the true motives for Pitt's actions:

The good care he has taken of himself shows his dear country was not the first Object with him, if it had he shou'd have left himself Free & not tied up his hands by the acceptance of Emoluments which will make opposition a sort of ingratitude & the affected caracter [sic] of Patriot in my opinion even ridiculous.[37]

Moreover the incident sowed the first seeds of doubt about Pitt's professions, seeds that were to bear fruit when he was granted his peerage in 1766.

Why did accepting a pension do Pitt so much political damage, and why was it chosen by his enemies as the major issue on which to attack him? The answer is quite simple: in taking a pension Pitt acted in a way that could be most readily construed as directly contrary to the ideology by which he had justified his every act. As the author of *The Right Hon. Annuitant Vindicated* pointed out: 'to retire with a PENSION, was to retire with ignominy and disgrace, in direct contradiction to the principles, which he [Pitt] has all along so openly avowed and professed'.[38] Pitt was therefore charged with being a 'mock patriot' whose vagaries were comparable to those of such figures as Pulteney, Lord Bath, the patriot apostate of 1742. He was revealed never to have been a patriot in the sense of 'One whose ruling passion is the love of his country',[39] but a supporter of 'the new mode of patriotism' which, 'like the weathercock changing with every wind, knows how to veer and turn, and is ready to adapt itself to times and their seasons, things and their circumstances – In or out – for or against – just as their convenience suits, or occasion requires'.[40] In order to achieve his own particular ends Pitt, it was alleged, had obscured his true intentions behind a mask of patriotic virtue:

Public Virtue, or at least the Appearance of it, is essential to the Schemes of political Ambition; for without a Mask she would appear so horrid hideous and despicable, that no body could possibly countenance her. He, therefore, who has formed Designs of aggrandizing himself, is obliged to disguise his real Sentiments, that he might more easily take Advantage of the short-sighted, ignorant, and weak Part of Mankind, who are but too often abused by a Specious Affectation of Public Spirit, and a sham Disregard of Power and Riches, that old, trite, stale Pretext, by which artful and conspiring Men have often gained such Credit as has enabled them to attain to the highest Degree of Wealth and Power; which, without it, they could not have attained; and which, in the End, we have never failed to find that they have had in View, however much they affected to despise them.[41]

Pitt's hypocrisy, it was maintained, had now clearly been revealed. With this fact established to their satisfaction, his critics turned to his past career, unearthing yet more evidence of earlier unpatriotic conduct.[42] The entire indictment was then assembled to prove that Pitt, like Pulteney before him, had been responsible for the debasement of the 'Name of Patriotism' into 'a Term of Mockery and Ridicule'.[43]

Although Pitt's friends and apologists recognised his opponents' tactics and tried to counter them,[44] there can be little doubt that his acceptance of rewards from the Crown contributed towards the decline of his support amongst the groups that Bute and the king were trying to win from him.

In many ways this attack on Pitt was a serious error of political judgement on the part of his opponents. His pride had been hurt, and resentments nurtured. Doubtless Pitt had not been worried about the public reaction to his pension because he saw himself as politically *hors de combat*, and therefore immune from criticism. But the vituperative attack on him guaranteed that his retirement was only of the most temporary kind, and led him to change his political tactics.

He began, in a rather desultory way, to try to get back into politics. His first plan was to attempt to divide the Old Corps rump, to win over the young men of the party, and to build up a new political following to replace the one he was losing to the king and Bute. His attempts to do this have been discussed in the last chapter.[45] Suffice it to say that this seems to explain his stringent conditions in August–September 1763 when he was negotiating with the Crown. He was prepared to ally himself with the followers of Newcastle and impose them on the king in order to annex some of their support for himself. In the event, the negotiation failed and Pitt realised that party tactics would not work with the king because they would not obtain royal confidence.[46] This made him even more reluctant to work constructively with the Newcastle–Rockingham connection, though he continued to try to win over members of the corps throughout 1765 and 1766, attempting to atomise the party in order to increase his own political clout. The tactic had only limited success, however, and Pitt had to content himself with the acquisition of some new, but not especially trustworthy followers.

The failure to gain any serious political advantage from the Newcastle–Rockingham connection undoubtedly brought home to Pitt just how politically weak he had become. Pre-empted of patriotism, he could not make any headway with party. Where could he turn? In 1765, and despite his refusal to form an administration in June of that year (perhaps he thought that Newcastle and Rockingham would not come in, and the king would then have had to give him *carte blanche*), Pitt started to move back towards the other chief pole of political support, the court power associated with the king and the former followers of Bute.

The task that Pitt had set himself was one of considerable delicacy. Although he needed to win back his old supporters and conciliate the king, he could ill afford to be connected in any way with Lord Bute who, as the royal Scottish Favourite and the epitome of prerogative politics, was anathema to the nation at large and especially the City of London. He therefore trod with great care. During the negotiations with the Crown in 1765 he made clear that he could not contemplate Bute in office. Nevertheless, as an act of conciliation he offered to restore Stuart Mackenzie – who had been removed in compliance with one of the absolute conditions imposed on the king by George Grenville – to a suitable, if not responsible post.[47] The process of conciliation continued throughout 1766. In his famous speech of 14 January, Pitt carefully pointed out that his objections to Bute were purely political and not based on either national (chauvinist) or personal considerations.[48] By February Fox, of all people, was urging Bute to bring in Pitt:

he will not be that commanding that Termigant Pitt He was a Month ago nor come link'd with your inveterate and malicious Enemy Ld Temple. He will gladly go into the H. of Lords, which will supply what is wanting for the Ministry there. The first thing He will do will be to restore Mr. Mackenzie, that is the K[ing]'s Honour, & the whole World will applaud it without one dissentient voice. He declares that the Earl of Bute ought to have that Situation at Court, that his Rank and Favour entitles Him to. He will restore Ld Despenser, shew regard, & if I mistake not take a Pride in shewing regard to your Friends, which he declares it is mean cowardice, & absurd Fear in the Present Ministers to be so averse to.[49]

On 4 March Pitt made his most conciliatory move yet, making a speech in the lower house that convinced many observers that he was about to make a deal with Bute and the king to come into power:

he prais'd my Ld Bute and said tho' he did not wish to see him minister yet it was shameful to proscribe his relations and his friends, and said that he had said as much to his sovereign, and that he would avow that advice and meet the enraged citizens and support him to their faces, and that the displacing the noble lord's brother was an insult upon the King provided the office did not lead to ministerial influence.[50]

The king's employment of Pitt in July was, therefore, the natural and successful culmination of the great commoner's strategy over the previous twelve months. His refusal to support the Rockingham administration, and his total reluctance to deal with anyone but the king, and then only if he was given *carte blanche*, had finally paid dividends. The king gave him total control over the new administration; he was *generalissimo* once more.

Yet, as in 1761, Pitt's plans went badly awry. His acceptance of a peerage, an act of quite appalling political folly, was immediately unpopular. Moreover, his apparently increasing dependence on the friends of Lord Bute, culminating in the appointment of a number of King's Friends in the first week of December, increased antipathy towards 'the great commoner dwindled into a Peer'.[51] As before, hostility was greatest in the City of London where Pitt's elevation to the upper House was said to be inextricably bound up with the agreement that he had perfidiously made with Bute.[52] Coals were heaped on the fire by Temple, who had been dissatisfied in the negotiations of 1765 and 1766 with the part offered him in the ministry. He published his own account of the discussions that led to the new administration, placing great emphasis on Pitt's newly acquired 'Butism'.[53] Again there was an avalanche of anti-Pittite propaganda: cartoons,[54] songs, squibs, newspaper essays and pamphlets, all united in reprobating the triumph of Bute in obtaining the fall of Pitt:

> Mourn, ALBION mourn, the wretched Change deplore;
> In CHATHAM buried, WILLIAM PITT's no more!
> B---, thou arch foe to Freedom and her Friends,
> At Length thy subtle Craft has gain'd its Ends.[55]

The strain of the propaganda was precisely that used when Pitt had accepted a pension. But now its effect was even more devastating, as it appeared to demonstrate that the apprehensions of 1761 were correct, and that Pitt had been intriguing with Bute for almost the entire reign. For how else could a man who claimed to be a true patriot accept yet another reward from government, and simultaneously ally himself with the man widely regarded as responsible for all the nation's current ills? The contrast between Pitt's patriot professions and his actual course of conduct, it was argued, reinforced the evidence of 1761. On that occasion Pitt had only briefly revealed his true character; now he had 'thrown down the mask' and exposed himself completely.[56] Hence the appearance of newspaper advertisements such as the following:

Lost supposed to be Stolen by a SCOTCHMAN. A PATRIOTIC MASK, decorated with many fine flowers of Rhetoric, and set round with Tropes, long sounding Words and Similes. Whoever shall find it and bring it undamaged, to a quondam *Great* Commoner, so that he may wear it again, shall receive a Gouty Shoe and an old pair of Crutches for his Pains.[57]

So far had Pitt's standing fallen between 1760 and 1766 that he was now no longer the exemplar of patriot purity, but epitomised the 'patriot unmask'd'.

Chatham was evidently deeply wounded by the way in which his former allies turned on him in 1766, and he said as much at the time.[58] Yet it was difficult for him to construct an adequate defence, although some efforts were made to prove that a peer and a patriot were not necessarily different persons.[59] His only hope of redemption lay in emulating the success of the ministry of 1757–61, and this he was not to achieve. His collapse in 1767, when he became incapable of handling public business, was the culmination of his failure as both patriot and patriot minister in the 1760s.

Even when Pitt returned to politics in July 1769, and assumed the somewhat more ideologically comfortable role of the opposition guardian of the constitution against a tyrannical ministry, the patriot bugbear remained with him. Despite what was effectively a public recantation in his House of Lords speech of March 1770, when he admitted that he had been beguiled by Bute in 1766,[60] his opponents in government used his record of mock-patriotism to brand him as, in Dr Johnson's words, a 'factious disturber of the government'.[61] For, although it was by no means a recent innovation, a second, pejorative definition of patriot and patriotism was more and more frequently used during the 1760s alongside its more complimentary counterpart.[62] Thus, in the first edition of his *Dictionary* (1755) Dr Johnson included the definition of patriot as 'One whose ruling passion is the love of his country', but by the fourth edition of 1773 the pejorative sense of the term had become sufficiently commonplace also to be included. There can be little doubt that, just as the frequency of the appearance of this latter definition in the early 1740s can be directly linked to the apparently flagrant denial of true patriot principles by Pulteney, so its use in the 1760s was connected with the conduct of Chatham. Distinctions were drawn between 'true' and 'false', 'real' and 'mock' patriots, and ancient, virtuous patriotism was contrasted with the modern practice which

requires but little Art, & no Genius: You have only to humour the popular Prejudices of the Times, insult your S-v--n, embarras [*sic*] his Government, slight his Authority, oppose *all* the Measures of his Ministers, *right* or *wrong*; foment Divisions at *home*, and expose our weakness *abroad*.[63]

Unfortunately for Chatham, as his opponents persisted in pointing out, his patriotism much more closely resembled the latter definition than the former.

Pitt's conduct during the 1760s has usually been explained in terms of a growing megalomania or, if that seems to put the case too strongly, of an ever-increasing self-obsession.[64] His refusal to cooperate with others, or to come into office on anything except the very best terms, is certainly attributable in part to this Olympian self-conception. But it also made more political sense than historians have been prepared to recognise. Doubtless Chatham, as Namier emphasised,[65] made his contribution to the parliamentary instability of the 1760s but, if he was to remain an important political figure, he had, as he was well aware, to plough a solitary furrow. The king had destroyed his old base of support, the party politicians would only unite with him if they could make him into a top party hack. He could not go over to Grenville in 1765 because it would have looked like too great an act of political apostasy. He was therefore forced to try to undermine the solidarity of other groups in order to remain politically effective.

What has this to do with the ideology of patriotism? First of all, Pitt's dilemmas in the 1760s illustrate very strongly the way in which his patriot professions acted as a constraint upon his actions, or affected the choices open to him. One of the reasons why Pitt was so badly hit by the accession of George III was that he justified his conduct through patriot rhetoric. It made him especially vulnerable to the alternative political appeal of the new monarch, and was doubtless a factor in deciding him to retire. Moreover, although his putative commitment to patriotism did not stop Pitt from taking first a pension and then a peerage, it ensured that when he did do so he was sorely embarrassed, precisely because his action could so easily be shown to conflict with the patriot ideal. If Pitt decided to act, or was forced to act in ways which were incongruent with his patriotism, he was bound to be in trouble. Pitt's problem was that both in 1761 and 1766 he wanted recognition of his status as a political hero; unfortunately, however, this necessarily entailed an act in breach of patriot ethics which, by virtue of that fact, inevitably reduced his heroic stature.

We can go further than this in discussing Pitt's breaches of patriot convention. Without a study of the rhetoric and ideology of patriotism it would not be possible to explain why Pitt was so vulnerable on the particular issues mentioned, and why those issues rather than any others were chosen to attack him. No doubt Pitt would have come under fire anyway after his resignation in 1761 and during the formation of his administration in 1766. But to explain why he was attacked so aggressively and most successfully for accepting first a pension and then a peerage, one must have recourse to the ideology of patriotism. It was *because* these two actions could be most successfully construed as breaches of the patriot ideal, and *a fortiori* of the constitutional principles which every virtuous man ought to pursue, that they were the actions which his opponents attacked. If one had the object of discrediting Pitt with the political nation and especially with those who had been his previous supporters – and this was clearly the aim of his enemies in 1761 and 1766 – then these were the issues that one would naturally choose. The ideology is a necessary component in any such explanation.

Pitt, it would seem, was less than totally committed to patriot ideology after 1757. The tenuousness of this allegiance had previously been concealed by the ease with which Pitt could harmonise his actions with his mode of legitimation, but after the formation of the war coalition and with the accession of the new king, this was no longer possible, and Pitt was exposed. Therefore, even though we can say that allegiance to the ideology of patriotism was *not* the motive for many of the actions that he performed in his later career, nevertheless we can see that the ideology affected that conduct. It constrained his actions, and was a factor in the political calculations that he made. Even when he chose to disregard those constraints, he found himself vulnerable *because* he was not acting as a patriot should. Pitt's political fortunes therefore have to be explained and understood in terms of his ideology. It is when we look at that ideology as a living active argument rather than as a static entity that we can see its importance for the understanding of political history.

7. Ministerial responsibility and the powers of the Crown

The friends of Lord B[ute] and of the ministry, which succeeded, were for preserving to the crown the full exercise of a right, of which none disputed the validity, that of appointing his own servants. Those of the opposition did not deny this power of the crown, but they contended that the spirit of the constitution required, that the crown should be directed to the exercise of this public duty by public motives, and not by private liking and friendship. That great talents, great and eminent services to the nation, confidence amongst the nobility, and influence amongst the landed and mercantile interests, were the directions, which the crown ought to observe in the exercise of its right in nominating officers of state. The observation of this rule would, and, they were of opinion, nothing else could, in any degree, counterballance that immense power, which the crown has acquired by the gift of such an infinite number of places. (*Annual Register* (1763), 41)

Nearly all eighteenth-century political commentators saw the relations between the king and his ministers in terms of the two concepts of ministerial responsibility and the royal prerogative. Not surprisingly, therefore, these notions provided the ideological framework for the notorious struggle between George III and the politicians. This conflict is incomprehensible without a working knowledge of what contemporaries understood by these two loosely defined, generic categories, and without a rigorous examination of the way in which they were employed. One question in particular, that of why, regardless of the facts of the matter, George III was subject to accusations which had not been levelled at the earlier Georges, can never be resolved without an understanding of the norms and conventions by which royal and ministerial conduct were judged in Hanoverian England.

Put in its baldest form, the notion of ministerial responsibility, as it was generally understood in the eighteenth century, was that the king's ministers were responsible for the general conduct of government, including the exercise of many powers legally vested in the monarch. This responsibility they bore to parliament, or more specifically to the elected representatives of the House of Commons. This is not to say that ministers were not deemed responsible to the king. In law they were ministers by virtue of royal appointment, and ceased to hold office when they were removed by the Crown. But, as far as almost every writer on the eighteenth-century constitution was concerned, ministerial responsibility was inextricably bound up with the notion of responsible government. To say that the minister was responsible for a measure or measures was tacitly to admit that he was responsible to parliament or the legislature, not, as perhaps we might expect, to the king.

This interpretation will naturally come as a surprise to those historians who regard the concepts of responsible government and party government as inextricably intertwined. This view, which received its most forceful and lucid articulation in the works of Namier, is, however, anachronistic. Eighteenth-century polemicists and political theoreticians all understood responsible government to mean responsibility of ministers to parliament, and although, as Namier points out, this does not preclude active participation of the king in government, it nevertheless was a constitutional constraint on the executive. As in the case of party, Namier's concern to demonstrate the ahistorical assumptions of whig historiography led him to emphasise what responsibility in the eighteenth-century was not, rather than inducing him to examine what it was. Political and ministerial responsibility in the eighteenth century was not the same as in the nineteenth, but that certainly does not mean that it had no existence at all.[1]

In fact, contemporaries saw the advantages of ministerial responsibility as twofold. First, it preserved the lustre of monarchy untarnished. It helped affirm the elevated and important status of the king and his prerogatives. To achieve this a political fiction was employed: it was assumed that in political, as in legal matters, 'the king could do no wrong'. This did not mean that the government, administration or executive was necessarily impeccable, but that the king could not be blamed for such errors as occurred. Instead, his ministers were deemed culpable. In other words, a convention was observed whereby, regardless of the facts of the matter, the king was assumed to have acted through and on the advice of his ministers and Privy Councillors who thereby assumed responsibility for those acts. 'A sovereign of Britain is not,' wrote one commentator

by our constitution to perform any high acts of power, but by and with the advice of his privy council. Hence arises his sacredness of character, and the safety of the royal person. A King can do no wrong, because he acts only by the advice of his counsellors. So that if wrong acts are done by him in his regal capacity, they are supposed to have been influenced by the advices of evil counsellors, and those counsellors are to be answerable to the nation for such proceedings.[2]

Ministerial responsibility preserved the aura of monarchy, but it achieved much more. The distinction between the king and his ministers also provided the opportunity for redress for the subject if government policies were unfair, and acted as a check upon the power of the executive. This preserved the all-important equilibrium which was one of the British constitution's most vaunted virtues. As Dowdeswell put it:

It is good policy to presume that great powers *will be abused*, where-ever they may be placed. The excellence of our constitution is, that there is a check on every power existing in it: and the probability of its continuance depends upon constantly maintaining those checks in their full effect and vigour. This cannot be done, unless there is a *constant* jealousy, and apprehension of abuse.

It is a maxim in our constitution, *that the King can do no wrong*. But the same law which holds this language on the *power of the King*, looks to the *security of the subject*, and provides that, where wrong *is done* on the part of the Crown, the Minister who advised the measure, and the Officer who executed it, shall be answerable for the evil.[3]

This mechanism of redress, which was, in effect, a legitimation of opposition to the measures of the king's ministers, was seen as one of the pillars of a free constitution. Above all it prevented those in authority from engaging in arbitrary acts. As long as there was some formal constraint on executive powers, free government based on law could be preserved. Once the idea of responsibility was lost, however, the British government would become as corrupt as the tyrannies of the East: 'If no Minister is ever to be called to an account till he is given up by the Crown, the people of Turkey have as just pretence of *Liberty*, as the People of England could pretend to.'[4] The existence of a means of legally constraining the executive was seen as one of the chief defining characteristics of the British constitution. It was a guarantee of liberty unknown in arbitrary states, but intrinsic to one governed by the rule of law.

This idea of public accountability was scarcely new. In its somewhat cumbersome form of impeachment, and in the more flexible practice of addressing the Crown, it had been frequently employed in the constitutional battles of the seventeenth century.[5] By the mid-eighteenth century the broad constitutional principle had become accepted dogma. George III, for example, gave it implicit recognition when he warned Bute that 'if my friend should keep out of Ministry, the voice of envy will call him the Favourite'. Bute himself similarly argued at a later date that he had assumed responsible office in order to be accountable for measures that were obviously his.[6] This was a view that one King's Friend, Gilbert Elliot, wholeheartedly endorsed;[7] and even that arch-tory Dr Johnson accepted the idea of ministerial responsibility, though naturally he preferred to emphasise the fact that the king could do no wrong.[8] There appeared, therefore, to be broad agreement on the need to observe the convention of ministerial responsibility in the context of a free constitution such as that of Britain.

A similar consensus appears to have existed about the royal prerogative of ministerial appointment. It was universally recognised that, as one opposition pamphlet put it, 'To appoint his Servants is the undoubted Right of the King.'[9] Indeed, as Namier was at great pains to point out, even those who were the government's most strident critics denied that they could or would in any way infringe the king's right to choose his own ministers. Pitt, for example, was adamant in 1764 that he would never 'force' George to accept him in office, while Newcastle, even when still in power, insisted that he had no intention of 'governing' or developing a hold over the young king.[10] Similarly it was generally accepted that no one should infringe the king's independency – i.e. neither constrain him in his choice of ministers, nor limit his powers during the conduct of an actual administration.

The relations between the king and his ministers, therefore, appeared to be perfectly clear: he appointed and dismissed them, and while in office they were responsible for the government's actions. In this way, it was maintained, the royal prerogative and the idea of ministerial responsibility complemented each other; they were 'like different movements in one piece of mechanism',[11] compatible facets of a system designed to secure constitutional equilibrium.

Yet the agreement that existed over the relationship between ministerial responsibility and the royal prerogative was primarily abstract and theoretical, confined to tomes of constitutional theory or to the most general utterances. When particular cases were considered, and the specific application of the conventions was discussed, the situation became altogether more complex. It was, for instance, not at all clear what action could be taken by the House of Commons against the king's minister(s) to ensure responsible rule. Could redress only be achieved through the legal, though almost obsolete procedure of impeachment, through an address to the Crown, or by a motion that made clear that the house no longer supported the administration? Indeed on what grounds could parliament act against ministers? On the basis of a breach of law, or simply because they were condemned by common fame?[12] And how far could opposition to the king's servants go in order to obtain redress? All of these questions were unanswered or, at least, admitted of a plurality of answers. Similarly it was unclear what obligations responsible ministers incurred. There was the problem of ascertaining who was responsible for any individual act – the cabinet, the departmental minister, or the first minister[13] – and therefore might justly claim to have a say in its formulation. And there was no hard and fast rule to determine how much say ministers might have over general policy or control of patronage. A similar situation pertained for the king. There were no specific guidelines to tell him what considerations should govern his appointment of ministers. Was he obliged to appoint the politically experienced, or did his footman or best friend have equal title to high office? The scope of his personal rule – the *amount* of control he could retain over policy and patronage – was equally ill-defined.

The absence of any adequate definition of the relations between king, ministers and parliament – despite the hypothetical compatibility of prerogative and ministerial responsibility – left great scope for argument when the king and ministers clashed as they did in the 1760s. The quarrel between George III and the politicians on this matter was prolonged and confused. Nevertheless, when we examine the debate, there emerge two clearly different attitudes towards the nature of royal power and the constraints upon it.

The first of these, which I shall call the royal or court case, was the constant theme of George and Bute, as well as of a substantial number of courtiers and politicians. Proceeding from the assumption that the chief royal prerogative was 'that the King names, creates, constitutes, and removes all the great Officers of the Government',[14] the royal view went on to assert that

Tho' a subject had connexions with all the greatest families in England, and had as much property as all of them put together, yet he can have no natural pretension to be minister. That appointment is personal to the King, and to the King only.[15]

Ministers were ministers by virtue of royal appointment and could not expect to be ministers on any other grounds. Ministerial appointment, moreover, was a matter of the *personal* choice of the king. Using an analogy that was to be repeated throughout the decade, the royalist view emphasised that the king's liberty or prerogative was the same as 'the liberty his poorest subject enjoys, of choosing his own menial servants'.[16] Thus Henry Fox, Lord Holland, told Horace Walpole that the king could make his page minister if he so wished, while court pamphleteers and the likes of Lord Denbigh echoed the view that a royal minister was like a nobleman's servant.[17] Ministers were the executors of the royal wishes; they were, in George's own words, his 'tools' or 'instruments'.[18] No recognition was accorded to the un-constitutional post of 'Minister' or 'Prime Minister'; rather

Great Britain knows no first minister, no grand vizier, unless the K--- be such, who is intrusted by the constitution, with the whole executive power of government; and in this respect may be said to be the first minister, or if you will, grand vizier, of a free people.[19]

The king was *primus inter pares* and acted as his own first minister.[20]

Because of this emphasis on the unconstrained exertion of the royal prerogative, it was natural for the royalist case to give little weight to the role of the people in government. Clearly, if ministers only held office by virtue of royal appointment, the people could have little or no say in the selection of their rulers. Moreover, it was a pillar of the court argument that, if the people were to have any say in the rejection or dismissal of the king's ministers, this could only be achieved through their representatives in parliament, not through the collective voice of the people, and that if they wished to obtain redress they should employ the legal means of impeachment.[21]

It was on the basis of this view of his relations with his ministers that George sought to exert his prerogative unfettered by the constraints which the politicians might seek to impose upon him. In Dodington's words he sought 'to recover Monarchy from the inveterate Usurpation of Oligarchy'.[22] It was the constant theme of the king and his followers that George was trying to 'preserve his independency', attempting both to maintain his prerogative of ministerial choice and to protect the power of the Crown in administration.[23] Therefore those who endeavoured to oppose the king's ministers and acquire power were seen as attempting to curb the king's prerogative and undermine his independency.[24] Similarly, if the ministers in power tried to make terms, or exact conditions from the king, they also were held responsible for constraining him. Thus the royalist argument condemned any conduct on the part of politicians, both in and out of power, which could be construed as curbing the powers of the Crown as head of the executive. In such circumstances the king, it was maintained, would be reduced 'to the state of a *humble Doge of Venice*; all pageantry and outward show';[25] he would become a king in 'leading-strings', a puppet monarch, a 'cypher', a king of 'threads and patches' forced 'to bend the knee' to every man.[26]

It was on these grounds, for instance, that Pitt's demand in 1761 that he should 'guide' measures was seen as tantamount to the creation of a 'chess-board King'.[27] The same complaint was voiced against the Great Commoner in the abortive negotiation of August–September 1763 when George demanded of the Newcastle whigs: 'what do they mean? Do they mean to put a Tyrant over me and themselves too?'[28] Similarly, in 1762 and 1767, it was maintained that the Newcastle and Rockingham whigs had a plan to 'give the Law to the best of Kings' by making George a prisoner in the royal closet.[29] Such were George's apprehensions about constraints of this kind that it became the avowed purpose of ministerial appointments to preserve the royal independency. This was the reason given for Henry Fox's promotion to the leadership of the House of Commons in 1762, for the formation of the Grenville administration in 1763, and, ironically, for the creation of the Rockingham and Chatham ministries:[30] all were designed to prevent the king from being forced.

The royal or court case, which accused politicians of undermining the powers of the Crown, did not go unanswered. If to oppose the king's minister was, as the court view claimed, effectively to undermine the king's independence, then no distinction could be observed between a ruler and his servant.[31] 'The doctrine', that every future attack on the *measures* of the *ministry*, which have received the royal approbation, is ALSO an insult upon the king', made opposition to government opposition to the king, and therefore tantamount to an illegal or treasonable activity.[32] It also ensured that there was no check upon the executive and therefore encouraged the abuse of power. In other words, to employ the language of the royal independency was, if only implicitly, to reject the idea of responsible government.

The same arguments pertained in the opposition's criticism of the view that the king should be his own minister. A completely independent monarch, it was said, constituted unlimited monarchy, for again there were no constraints on the executive power.[33] As one critic put it:

The King is his own Minister. That is, the whole executive power and administration of the State is to be placed in hands superior to controul; too strong for ordinary resistance, and too sacred as is supposed for punishment. In effect therefore, whenever people can be subdued to the practice of such theory, this principle amounts to perfect and complete despotism.[34]

If the king really was *primus inter pares*, then responsible government was not possible.

Moreover, even if the court was willing to concede these points, there were other, equally serious objections to its case. Ministers, it was argued, were as much the servants of the nation as they were of the king, and it was therefore completely inappropriate to compare them to a private subject's servants.[35] Indeed, it was on the grounds that ministers were public servants that the critics of the royal case went on to argue that the wishes of the people should be consulted in the dismissal and sometimes even the appointment of the Crown's ministers. 'John Bull' put this view in the following manner:

Ministerial responsibility

There is a wide difference between a Sovereign's servants and his ministers. His servants have the care of the palace only: but his ministers have that of the kingdom: in the choice of the latter, therefore, the inclinations of the people ought always to be consulted. Ministers are, by our constitution, considered as the servants of the commonwealth, as well as of the crown, and must be as much answerable to the former as to the latter for their conduct in office. It may be quite indifferent to the people who wear the feathers of state; but it cannot be so with regard to those who have the dispositions of their properties, lives and privileges in their hands. In trusts, therefore, of such kinds, their passions become interested. It is fit they should be so: and it is fit also, in such matters, that their inclinations should be consulted.[36]

An anonymous writer in the radical *Political Register* was prepared to go even further:

Absolute monarchs choose their ministers as they govern their kingdoms; that is, for themselves, and their own pleasure; but the Kings of England reign for their people. Though the ministers of state are named by the Crown; they are the servants of the public. The King wears the crown for the public service...It is most absurd to draw a parallel between the crown's appointment of ministers and private persons choosing their domestics. The King's power of nomination no-body disputes; but it should never be forgot, that even this part of the prerogative is liable to a constitutional controul; and it will always be most wisely exercised, when a just regard is shewn to the inclinations of the people. Parliament has not only a power to punish bad ministers, but without going so far as that, it has a constitutional and an effectual power to remove, from the King's presence and counsels for ever, those of whom they do not approve: And the incorrupt proceedings of parliament will always depend chiefly on the sense of the nation.[37]

The argument, therefore, was that if the king had a due regard for constitutional properties he ought to appoint a popular man, one of weight and credit in the nation, to be his minister, and that if he failed to do so, the voice of the people could remove him not simply through impeachment but on the grounds that he was unpopular.[38] This put into normative, constitutional terms the practical point that Devonshire had made to Fox in 1762:

You may fancy what you please about the power of the Crown, but believe me you will find yourself mistaken. If a King of England employs those People for his Ministers that the Nation have a good opinion of, he will make a great figure, but if he chuses them merely thro' personal favour, it will never do, and he will be unhappy.[39]

There is no doubt that this view received full and explicit articulation in the 1760s because of the political conspicuousness of Bute. Virtually monopolising royal favour in the early years of the reign (even Devonshire, the Lord Chamberlain and therefore the most intimate of the personal servants of the Crown, had to communicate with George via the Favourite), he seemed to his critics to epitomise all of the worst facets of personal, royal rule. As 'a person known to be regarded with so partial an eye by his sovereign',[40] he enjoyed the special status and power of the 'overmighty subject'. His extraordinary preponderance, and the fact that it was derived from the personal favour of the king rather than from a natural influence in society at large, made him appear unaccountable to others, and thereby threatening to the balance of the constitution.[41] Like all favourites he would, it was assumed, abuse his power, excite the envy of others, and with his 'sycophants and parasytes' come to monopolise the affections of the Crown.[42] This, in turn, would divert patronage from the public to Bute's private ends.[43] Such a system abnegated political responsibility, for it enabled the Favourite to isolate the king from his subjects and, simultaneously, to mislead an uninformed monarch.[44] This naturally would excite the envy of other politicians and provoke the hostility of those 'out of doors'.[45]

Such, indeed, was Bute's fate. Politicians might disagree on almost every matter, but they were united in their determination to exclude Bute from the processes of government. The mobbing of the Favourite, the expressions of hostility in the localities, the vituperative press attack on his personal and public character, all helped affirm the existence of a system of favouritism.[46] This was intrinsically undesirable, but its offensiveness was compounded by two further problems. Unpopular ministers, especially favourites, brought the king into disrepute and created political instability.[47] Moreover, their very unpopularity made them an even greater threat to the constitutional equilibrium of the nation: 'An unpopular minister has not the principal thing necessary towards his stability in a free country, the *confidence of the people.* He has not the motives, which popular men have, to guard the public liberty, and administer *constitutional* advice to the Crown.'[48] If an escalating situation like this arose, the king, it was argued, ought to put aside his personal feelings and remove his minister; otherwise instability would naturally ensue and government suffer accordingly.

Underpinning these arguments against the royal view was a specific interpretation of the idea of ministerial responsibility which was employed by politicians both in as well as out of power. It was agreed, they argued, that in order to preserve the idea of accountability it had to be assumed that in all matters of government the king did not act *personally* but on the advice of his ministers, that the king did

nothing of himself, but every thing by the advice of his council and ministers. The speeches from the throne; treaties of peace and war; the application of public revenue; appointments to offices in the state; the direction of crown prosecutions; and, in a word, every other act of government must be always debated, questioned, and blamed as the act of the minister.[49]

This view entailed a distinction between the king's acts in his official capacity and those undertaken at his personal whim or inclination:

by the wisdom of *this* constitution, no act of the *kingly office*, whether *oral* or *graphical*, is considered as the *personal* act of the *Sovereign*; nor is or can be imputed to his Majesty *personally* or *individually*. All *regal* acts of *whatever kind* are the acts of the *ministers* of the Crown, by whose advice the King is *constitutionally* bound to act, and only can act *legally*; and they are *personally* and *individually* responsible for them... The King, as well as other men, has his *natural* person; but he has a *political* one too: and in the exercise of the *royal functions* the latter absorbs the *former*. The King's *natural* person the *constitution* hardly knows; insomuch, that the *King* never dies, though the *Sovereign*, as well as the subject, obeys the law of *mortality*. To the king's *political* person *only* all *regal* acts are ascribed; and the ministers of the crown compose that political person, much in the same manner, and to the same effects, that the individual members of the *corporation* make up the political person of *it*... It is as a necessary consequence of this principle of the constitution, that the well known (but perhaps very generally misunderstood) *adage*, has been received, *That the King can do no wrong.*[50]

This distinction was used by the king's opponents to sustain an interpretation of ministerial responsibility that threatened to eliminate all the personal powers of the Crown. By maintaining that, both theoretically and *in practice*, the king could only act in government in his political or official capacity, and by defining that capacity in terms of the occasions on which the king had actually consulted and acted upon the wishes of his ministers, the king's opponents would erase his personal powers. For the argument refused to admit that the king could be 'a party in a natural character in any... kinds of disputes',[51] or, indeed, that he could have political views independent of his own servants.

Pushed to its extreme, this case could obviously place very serious limitations on the actions of the king. Indeed, this proved to be the case when Grenville constrained the king in 1765, and again in 1782–3 when the Fox–North coalition stormed and captured the closet. But it was just as common to use this view defensively, against what were considered to be unjustifiable instances of royal intrusion into areas previously dominated by politicians. Thus Newcastle, while still in power in 1761, bemoaned the way in which George himself undertook to supervise certain areas of patronage, and Wilkes complained of the king's personal involvement in the prosecution of the *North Briton*. Similarly in October 1763, after the King's abortive negotiation with Pitt, it was regretted 'that His Majesty's Name has been so openly, and by Anonymous Letters, so universally made use of, by the King's

Ministers to support. . . [their] Representations against Mr. Pitt'.[52] But perhaps the most important occasion on which this complaint was voiced was in February 1766. The king had told Lord Strange on the 10th of that month that, contrary to the policies of his ministers, he preferred modification of the Stamp Act to its repeal. The party bitterly remonstrated with the king and it became the prime example in Rockinghamite historiography of the king's avowed purpose to engage in personal rule.[53] The Rockinghams were not, however, the only group who felt themselves so slighted. By the end of the decade it was a cause for parliamentary complaint that the king's name had been so frequently invoked to support his ministers' measures.[54]

But the foremost grievance that the politicians bore against the use of the personal powers of the Crown was the presence of a royal Favourite. Particularly offensive was George's remark to the Duke of Argyll that 'whoever speaks against My Lord Bute, I shall think speaks against Me'.[55] For George seemed explicitly to have disavowed the distinction between king and minister which was fundamental to the idea of ministerial responsibility. Moreover, because the Crown's opponents were determined to observe this distinction, they were impelled to argue that it was Bute, not the king, who was responsible for the perpetuation of a system of government that disregarded the precepts of political responsibility. In this way, and regardless of the facts of the case, Bute became a political scapegoat, forced to suffer because of the conflict between the king and the nation's political leaders.[56]

It is, for instance, very noticeable how the disparate claims made by the politicians on the Crown were so frequently directly connected with problems that arose out of Bute's political career. Perhaps the most conspicuous example of this was the frequently reiterated demand that the king should consult only those in office, and even only those who were members of the incumbent cabinet. Otherwise, it was argued, ministers would be in the invidious position of bearing responsibility for decisions which they had neither formulated nor sanctioned. For most of the 1760s this demand was tantamount to demanding the continued exclusion of Bute or those, like Jenkinson, who were thought to act as intermediaries between George and the Favourite. Hence the extraordinary, and very largely unjustified, obsession with Bute and his political influence after his retirement in 1763. For three years before his resignation, the politicians – whether in office or opposition – had had ample opportunity to observe the extraordinary influence that Bute exercised over the king. Confronted with so much evidence, it was hard for them to believe that the Favourite had really retired. Besides, because of their apprehensions of 'secret influence', they took the snippets of evidence available to them, and constructed a plausible account of covert, conspiratorial politicking against them. The visits of both George and Bute to the Princess Dowager at Carlton House or Kew; the occasional and fumbling interventions that the Favourite made in politics in August 1763, March–April 1765, February 1766 and June 1767; and the emergence of a party composed chiefly of Bute's former associates, the King's Friends: all these events helped confirm Bute's opponents' view that he was still illicitly active in government.[57] Hence the frequent references to the disjunction between the favour and authority of the Crown, and the contention that government had become a dual system with 'real' and 'apparent' ministers.[58] Before 1763 it had been possible for contemporaries to explain the breakdown of confidence between George and the politicians by the malevolent advice of Bute. After 1763, however, when the Favourite no longer held responsible office, an *entente* between the king and the politicians ought to have emerged; but it failed to materialise, and the possibility of Bute's secret influence was used to explain the absence of royal cordiality. Bute, it was argued, had created a system of government that flouted a basic constitutional convention, and prevented the politicians from establishing any adequate *rapport* with their master.

Though Bute was the chief cause of complaint, there were other demands that the politicians put to the king, regularly endorsing them by appeals to the convention of ministerial responsibility. It was pointed out, for example, that because politicians ought to be responsible ministers, answerable for men and measures, they ought also to have a full say in matters of government; hence the right of politicians to make conditions when negotiating for admission to office, and even after they had been appointed the king's ministers. Thus, when Bute's resolution wavered in the summer of 1762, and feelers were put out for the possible return of Newcastle or his followers to office, the duke was adamant that he would only return on two specific conditions. He insisted that the government support the German war while it lasted and that there be an alliance with either Prussia or Russia regardless of whether Britain was at war or peace. As Hardwicke put it:

He [Newcastle], & his Friends, adher'd to the two grand points, upon wch the great Difference had broken out viz: the Support of the German War, & the preserving of the Connection with the King of Prussia, united, as He is, with the Emperor of Russia, & England's availing itself of both those Powers in War & in Peace. That the way to satisfy His Grace would be to satisfy Him upon these national points.[59]

These conditions, completely unmentioned in Namier's account of these months, were often repeated by Newcastle in his correspondence and were actually put to the king in an interview that the duke had with George on 3 September.[60]

The demand for the retention of a continental alliance was not confined to Newcastle. Pitt made it during the abortive negotiation at the end of August 1763 and again in June 1765; and it was tacitly understood, when the Rockinghams came into office in the same year, that this condition still pertained.[61]

During 1765 there was practically no group of politicians who did not attempt to make terms with the king. In May (in an action that was heartily applauded by Newcastle)[62] Bedford, Grenville and their followers presented George with five absolute conditions, refusing to continue in office unless their demands, which included the exclusion of Bute, Stuart Mackenzie the Favourite's brother, and Lord Holland, were complied with.[63] During the same month Pitt had stipulated to the Duke of Cumberland, who acted as the king's intermediary throughout the negotiations between May and July, that he made acceptance of office contingent upon five conditions:

First, on the Restoration of all the Officers of the Army as well as many others as had been displaced for their opposition. *Secondly*, on ample justice and Favour being shewn Lord Chief Justice *Pratt*: – *Thirdly* on a Necessity of making Men's Minds easy about the *Warrant* as well as amending the unpopular Clauses of the Cyder Bill: *Fourthly*, a Necessity of restoring the Relaxations got into both the Navy & Army, & preferring the Officers for their Services, & not for dancing-Attendance: as also *Fifthly*, on a foreign Sistem [*sic*] of Affairs, which he feared had been greatly neglected, avowing himself still in Prussian sentiments, which, he feared, would not render the Closet more favourable to him.[64]

Lord Temple, in turn, endorsed those three conditions that dealt with the restoration of officers, general warrants and a foreign alliance.[65] Within a few days the Newcastle–Rockingham connection included the same terms in a paper drawn up for presentation to the Duke of Cumberland if he opened negotiations with them. They also added a further stipulation of their own:

That some Effectual Means should be taken, to convince the Publick that Neither His Majesty, nor his Ministers should have any Thing to do with My Lord Bute, directly or indirectly, in the Conduct of Administration, & the Management of Publick Affairs.

And that, neither my Lord Bute, nor his brother Mr. Mackenzie, should concern themselves, or have anything to do in the Administration of Affairs in Scotland.

And, as a Proof of this, that some Persons, known to depend entirely upon My Lord Bute, & to be in His Lordship's Confidence, should with others of the present Administration, be immediately removed from their Employments.[66]

As it transpired this paper was never presented, for negotiations were broken off shortly afterwards. Indeed, it is not altogether clear whether the king agreed to these stipulations when the Rockinghams finally came into office in July. George, however, did agree to one of the terms. Cumberland wrote to Newcastle in July:

I am to acquaint you, that His Majesty has declared to Me, That It is not his Intention, that the Earl of Bute should, either publickly or privately, interfere in the Management of Publick Affairs, either at Home, or Abroad; Or, recommend to any Employments either in England, or Scotland.

And I am also to acquaint you, that I took the Liberty to let His Majesty know, that, if any Thing of that Kind should appear, you, and the other Ministers, who should now come into His Majesty's Service, would find yourselves obliged, immediately to resign your Employments, And, that I could not dissuade you from it.[67]

But of the other stipulations there is no mention. It appears most probable that the party in fact made three conditions: those for a continental alliance, for action over the illegality of general warrants, and for the exclusion of Bute.[68] The king accepted the last but, it would appear, made no reference to the other two, for in a draft of a letter, probably intended for Cumberland but in fact never sent, Newcastle wrote:

That I was very sorry, to find that His Majesty had not been pleased to declare His Intention upon the two Points, which I made, as well as all the Company, If I may presume to say, the Conditions, sine qua non, without which we all unanimously thought, we could not enter into the King's Service, consistently with his Majesty's Interest, and our own.[69]

Whether Newcastle insisted upon these stipulations or not, or whether the king gave some informal kind of undertaking, we do not know. Certainly Cumberland, the all-important intermediary in the negotiation, and the effective leader of the administration in its early months,[70] did not support the exaction of any such conditions. Quite possibly he cushioned the king against the party politicians, or ensured that the question was left in a sufficiently ambiguous state to satisfy both George and his new ministers.[71]

It is noticeable that many of the stipulations made by the leaders of the various political groups were conditions about persons. Thus the exclusion of Bute in 1765 was agreed to by all parties, and in 1766 Pitt insisted that Newcastle be kept out of any ministry that he might form.[72] These seem like characteristic squabbles over place and patronage, but there was much more to them than this. For the exaction of conditions, whether about measures or men, was frequently employed as one way of trying either to ensure or to test royal confidence. The claim, once again made on the basis of the idea of ministerial responsibility, was that the king's ministers should not simply enjoy the semblance of royal power, but the full and complete confidence of the king. This could, of course, be tantamount to a demand for ministerial control of the powers of the Crown (George certainly interpreted Pitt's conduct in September and October 1761 in this light); and, at the very least, it meant that the monarch was required to give full consultation to his ministers and take no advice from another.

The issue of confidence frequently recurred during the first decade of George's reign. Throughout 1761 and until his resignation in 1762, Newcastle, for example, constantly bemoaned the way in which Bute monopolised royal favour and failed to consult him.[73] No doubt he was excessively sensitive in these matters (he even complained of lack of confidence during the Rockingham administration);[74] yet his psychological predisposition to feel shunned and excluded should not conceal the substance in Newcastle's accusations. Others, as well as he, remarked upon the way in which Bute and the other members of the government failed to give him full confidence.[75] A memorandum he drew up in July 1761 epitomised his situation:

> Never consulted
> hardly informed
> Difficulties about common Things in my own Office.[76]

It was his constant complaint that the other ministers under the control of Bute and the king arranged business behind his back and presented him with a *fait accompli*. Thus Newcastle only learnt of the break with Spain in December 1761 after it had been decided upon:

> I was summoned, the next Day but one, to the Meeting of the Lords. When I came to St. James's, the Two Secretaries [of State] were with the King. When they came out, Neither of Them said One Word to Me, by way of Consultation; Every Thing had been settled before.[77]

The other ministers even altered one of Newcastle's own Treasury minutes without informing him. As he pointed out, 'I cannot consent to have my Name – put to a Thing, I don't understand; Much less when I am to have the Interpretation of it, and the Execution in Consequence.'[78] When Newcastle finally resigned in May, it was again over an issue of confidence: Bute and his allies had been instructing those in the Treasury who, unbeknown to Newcastle, had formulated proposals which conflicted with those of the Duke.[79] If the Treasury was to formulate policy at odds with the First Lord, clearly he had little choice but to resign.

George Grenville's term as First Lord of the Treasury was equally fraught with problems of confidence. Grenville's troubles began in the summer and autumn of 1763. In August the king, perhaps on the advice of Bute and certainly with his aid, began negotiations with Pitt behind the backs of his ministers.[80] Not until the negotiation was virtually public did Grenville learn of George's surreptitious activities.[81] To the ministers this appeared as a flagrant breach of confidence and, as a result, Bute's offer to go into political exile was taken up by Grenville and his colleagues and converted into a *sine qua non* for staying in office.[82] Only with the actual physical removal of the Favourite did the ministers feel that they stood the remotest chance of enjoying full royal support.

As Grenville learnt the details of the autumn negotiation he became increasingly apprehensive that the king would continue to consult others. His discovery that the king had opened negotiations with Pitt *before* the death of Egremont, which might have been taken as an occasion which justified George in opening negotiations with the opposition, particularly alarmed him.[83] This increased the existing tension between the king and his first minister, and pushed an ever-more insecure Grenville into seeking conspicuous and public signs of royal confidence. He even tried to interfere in an appointment in the Royal Household, an area of patronage customarily sacrosanct to the Crown, because he feared that the promotion of a friend of Bute, Sir William Breton, would be construed as evidence of the Favourite's continued influence.[84] By 1764 the first minister was regularly asking the king to confirm his faith in his ministers, and he requested, as signs of personal royal favour, the use of a royal house, the gift of a royal portrait and the donation of places to his young children.[85] His fears, exacerbated by quarrels amongst the ministers, meant that Grenville became ever more sensitive about patronage. He quarrelled violently with Stuart Mackenzie, Bute's brother, who still controlled Scottish places, and frequently remonstrated with the king over appointments.[86] By the time of the Regency Crisis of April 1765 it was clear that the situation which the over-sensitive first minister had sought to avoid was now a reality: the king no longer had confidence in his 'instruments'.[87]

Yet, as it transpired, circumstances favoured Grenville. George was unable to form a new administration and the First Lord of the Treasury was therefore in a position to make the terms he had wanted to impose during the previous two years. The resulting five conditions, exacted *sine qua non*, removed all vestiges of Bute's 'influence' from the administration and gave Grenville control over patronage.[88] Ironically, for he had been brought in to protect the king's independency, Grenville more effectively shackled the king than at any other time until the Fox–North coalition. But he still did not win the confidence that he felt it was his right to claim. The king's behaviour at court was obvious to all; Grenville was to go out as soon as George could make alternative arrangements.[89]

Yet when the king had established a new administration, its members were as eager as their predecessors to ensure royal confidence and favour. Their passionate pursuit of this end was intensified by the Lord Strange affair, and by the very conspicuous division within government between the incumbent ministers and the King's Friends over American policy. The political events of January to May 1766 made it appear as if the king's government was divided between the king's personal servants, privy to George's wishes, and a group of ministers who merely held ostensible power. This unfortunate impression was heightened by a disagreement between George and his ministers over the payment of the establishment to the king's brothers. Faced with this prospect, Rockingham asked for signs of royal confidence; he wanted Dyson, the most intractable of the King' Friends, dismissed, and a number of new peers created.[90] George flatly refused to do either. Instead he responded to Rockingham's demands by giving a number of places and appointments to his brothers, without consulting or mentioning them to the ministers.[91] This, of course, publicly conveyed George's feelings about the ministers' handling of the princes' establishment, and the party naturally saw it as a sign of diminishing royal confidence. At a meeting held on 27 June they therefore decided to ask the king for a public statement of support. Some members of the party even wished to tell the king that if it was not forthcoming they would immediately resign:

It was proposed..that we should lay before the King the necessity of His Majesty's giving some publick demonstration of his resolution to support his present administration. That this should be introduced by, and chiefly founded upon, an intercepted letter from M. Gross, Minister here from the Empress of Russia; wherein this M. Gross advises Her Imperial Majesty not to conclude, at present, the treaty now depending with Russia; as it is generally thought that the present administration cannot last long as they have not the confidence of the King, their master.

This was thought, as it certainly is, a very proper foundation to speak to the King upon, and to insist with His Majesty that some demonstration should be given by him to contradict these reports, or otherwise his affairs, both at home and abroad, must suffer; and particularly that that demonstration should be given by immediately removing Mr. Dyson and my Lord Eglintoun.

It was also proposed, chiefly by the Duke of Richmond, that in case His Majesty should not agree to what should thus be proposed to him, that the administration should declare that they could no longer continue in his service.[92]

The king contrived to avoid meeting the party's demands but he was clearly ready for another change.[93] Perhaps he feared a situation like that of May 1765, when he had no alternative but to keep the incumbent ministry in on their own terms, or perhaps he wanted to pre-empt a mass resignation. At all events, within two weeks George sent for Pitt and asked him to form a new administration.[94]

The demand for royal confidence received its most extreme expression during ministerial negotiations. On two occasions in the 1760s, during Pitt's negotiation with the administration in January 1766, and Rockingham's discussions with Grafton in July 1767, the opposition politicians demanded that the incumbent administration be dissolved before an agreement was concluded.[95] This was demanding, in effect, that royal confidence be transferred from the king's ministers to the men with whom the Crown was negotiating, before they had actually been admitted to power. It also constituted, and indeed was intended as an effective means of excluding royal influence during the negotiation. The power of the monarch would be hostage to the (possible) incoming ministers. This, of course, was placing constraints on the Crown, though it was never admitted by its practitioners as such. Rather they maintained that, if men were to be the king's ministers, he should show them that he was prepared to give them his confidence.

During the 1760s, therefore, there were current two opposed views of the relations between the king and his ministers, each of which was used to support a claim about courses of political action. The first of these, the royal view, emphasised the importance of the royal prerogative and maintained that the king had a considerable personal role in politics which he was entitled to exert to the full. It was opposed by what, for want of a better title, we might call the 'ministerial case' which stressed the public accountability of royal servants, and the way in which, if this accountability was to be retained, the king would not be able to play an active personal part in government. Indeed the claims made on behalf of the ministerial argument – that politicians could make terms with the king, that he should not consult others but only act through his ministers, that he should give them complete confidence, and consign large areas of patronage to them – threatened to erode the king's personal character in politics completely.

Thus – and this cannot be sufficiently stressed – identical incidents were very differently construed by the different parties involved. When George Grenville imposed his conditions on the king in May 1765 he maintained that he was trying to obtain the confidence to which he felt fully entitled, but according to George III he was 'giving the law to the best of Kings'. In each case the protagonists were applying one of two different constitutional rules or conventions, both of which were recognised by the opposing side as constitutionally legitimate.

The question at issue, therefore, was not the constitutional status of the respective rules, but their applicability and scope in a particular situation. If no conflict had existed between the king and his ministers, this question would not have arisen. The constitutional mechanisms would have complemented one another as they were ideally supposed to do. But the quarrel between the Crown and the politicians raised the question of what criteria should be used for the application of the conventions of prerogative and ministerial responsibility. This, in turn, raised the question of who should determine the criteria. Each view, royal and ministerial, recognised that implicit in the other was a different conception of politics. The royalist view had, finally, to fall back on the ultimate power of the Crown; the ministerial case, on the other hand, rested on a view of the people, *as represented in the Commons*, as the final source of legitimate authority. The precise ramifications of this conflict were not, needless to say, worked out in the 1760s. It was a slow and laborious task, especially for an instinctively conservative political elite, to recognise the implications of the dispute. Yet by 1770 we can observe the two distinct views of the relations between the king and his ministers.

In practical terms the extent to which either of the two views could be successfully acted upon was a matter of immediate political circumstance. Thus, in many ways, George's exertion of his personal powers at the beginning of the reign, especially in the appointment of Bute, was a reflection of the extremely auspicious circumstances of his succession; similarly, his 'enslavement' by Grenville in 1765 showed the lack of choice of ministers available to him at that time. Party unity such as that employed by the Rockinghams in 1767, the limiting of the king's choice through common agreement, and control of the House of Commons were all used by the politicians to constrain the king. He, in turn, opposed them with his personal will power, his powers of influence and patronage, his prerogative and support in the nation at large. On any particular occasion the strength or weakness of either side was the result of these conflicting forces. Thus George III defeated the Fox–North coalition and delayed Catholic Emancipation because, in both cases, the Commons could be seen not to represent the public, while the Crown had the support of the Lords. *Per contra*, George II was defeated by the Pelhams in 1746 partly because he had no real base of support. The City, the public at large, and parliament preferred the Old Corps to the Hanoverian politics of Pulteney and Carteret. As these cases show, the fiction of the mixed, balanced constitution acquired some reality during these crises; one element in the mechanism could not easily overthrow the combined power of the others. In this way some sort of equilibrium was maintained.

But these political circumstances do not explain why George III was subject to accusations that were never levelled against his grandfather. No one ever accused George II of 'raising the standard of prerogative', nor of creating an old-style tory monarchy in flat contradiction of constitutional convention. Yet George III was so pelted that much of the mud still sticks. Why?

It might be argued that politicians in the 1760s made such accusations against George because they wished to lay claim to areas of power previously within the royal demesne. Yet this case cannot be sustained. The events of 1744 to 1746 have been too well discussed by John Owen to bear detailed reiteration, but they amply demonstrate that the claims of Pitt, Newcastle, Rockingham and Grenville had all been anticipated by the Pelhams.[96] The issue of royal confidence, of control over policy and patronage, of making terms with the king, and of the principle that 'they who dictate in private should be employed in public',[97] were all rehearsed during the crises of those years. Indeed the Pelhams were able to enforce their demands with unparalleled rigour, engineering a resignation *en bloc* in February 1746, eventually exacting a promise of royal support from George, and thereby becoming ministers in substance as well as form.[98]

Could it be, perhaps, that it was not the claims of the politicians but the conduct of George III that produced new accusations against the monarchy? At first sight this would appear unlikely. As John Owen has recently so skilfully argued,[99] George II's attitudes and conduct look as if they were formed in the same school as those of his grandson. The Army, the Royal Household and peerage appointments were as much under his sway as they were under George III. In day-to-day matters of policy neither king was especially more active than the other. If George III confided in Bute, his grandfather consulted both Bath and Carteret (Granville) when they were without responsible office. In addition George II failed to give the Pelhams his full confidence between 1744 and 1746, and Pitt his support in 1756–7.[100] He even actively intrigued against his ministers, playing off the Pelhams against Bath and Granville, and offering Harrington *carte blanche* in 1745 if he would only rid him of the brothers. During the Pitt–Devonshire coalition he negotiated with Newcastle and Fox behind Pitt's back.[101] He was also, like his grandson, very sensitive about being 'forced'. In 1744–5 he complained bitterly of being 'confined', and it was on this occasion that he made his famous ironic remark that 'Ministers are the Kings in this Country'.[102] Indeed, George was prepared, when he felt it necessary, to go to great lengths to preserve his prerogative of ministerial appointment. In 1746 he tried to set up a ministry which had no support in parliament or in the nation at large rather than accept the Pelhams' terms, and in 1757 there was a ten-week interministerium while the king unsuccessfully attempted to keep Pitt from power.[103]

Owen is correct, therefore, in emphasising the similarities between the two monarchs, and in correcting the traditional picture of George II as a huffing and puffing monarch impotently letting the politicians have the run of the court. But, although Owen's account is salutary, it appears to overlook a number of important differences, not in the circumstances of the two kings, but in their political conduct, and the way in which it was justified.

George II never appointed to high office someone like Bute whose *sole* claim to a position of public responsibility was the *personal* favour of the king. When Bute became a Privy Councillor at the accession he was neither a member of the House of Commons nor the House of Lords. His political power and experience were negligible. His appointment could only be justified as a personal act of the king. It might be said that Bute's position was little different from that of the favourites of the first two Georges. There are obvious parallels, for instance, between Bute and Carteret, George II's confidant. Doubtless Carteret was a drunk (appearing at cabinet meetings in a state of considerable intoxication) and a madcap; but he was also a brilliant linguist – this was one of the reasons for George II's attachment to him – and was as well versed in European affairs as any contemporary politician. Many thought him brilliant, if unstable, and he had considerable status in the political nation apart from that provided by the king's favour. In sum, he was the Charles Townshend of his generation: volatile, no respector of persons, clever and erratic. But he was not, like Bute, politically inexperienced, a virtual nonentity, solely dependent on the king for his power and status.

Secondly, George III, unlike his predecessor, was both anti-whig (or more accurately anti-Old Corps) and not anti-tory. George knew what had happened to his grandfather in 1744–6 and had seen Newcastle and Pitt impose their will on the king in 1757. This was something he was determined to avoid – indeed, was determined to revenge. The politicians were well aware of this. Some, like Horace Walpole and Richmond, recognised that the successes of the Pelhams and the Old Corps had contributed towards George's hostility,[104] and all saw that the king's intentions were very different from his grandfather's. They were different because George III directed his view of personal monarchy against a particular party, the Old Corps, and because that view complemented his determination to end party distinctions, and to remove party from politics altogether.[105] It was this combination of the defence of personal monarchy and an anti-party view of politics that enabled

George's opponents to stigmatise the king, or more especially his followers, as a new species of tory. For the reconfiguration of politics, for which George was at least in part responsible, created a situation in which recent 'country-gentleman/tory' views which were anti-party, anti-Hanover and anti-Old Corps rubbed shoulders with the old-style toryism of personal monarchy and prerogative.

Just as important as George's political conduct was the way in which he and his followers justified or sought to legitimise their political actions. This can be seen in the case of Bute. When George refused to countenance the distinction between the king and his minister and said, 'whoever speaks against My Lord Bute, I shall think speaks against me', Hardwicke commented:

I am sorry to hear of the Language – *whoever speaks against my Lord Bute, speaks against me.* How can this come out of the School of Opposition? It is the very thing wch. the grand opposition roared against Sir Robert Walpole's Ministry; and yet the late King never condescended to use such a Language, nay would have been very angry had any body imputed it to Him.[106]

George III certainly used, permitted to be used, or at least tolerated the use of his name to support persons and policies in a way which his grandfather never countenanced.

At the same time his apologists developed a number of arguments, notably that the king was and ought to be his own first minister, and that the appointment of his ministers should be completely free from public considerations, that were not, to my knowledge, used to defend the actions of George II. During the 1760s, in line with George's conception of his role as monarch, the argument from the premise of an unconstrained royal prerogative was invoked to legitimate a number of royal actions, most notably the elevation of Bute, which the king saw as his personal actions and wished to justify as such.

The explanation of this new use of the old and familiar argument of 'royal independency' is not difficult to find. The king and his followers needed an argument both to counter opposition and to preserve the king's power against his ministers in the closet. Since George rejected the idea of party divisions, it was no longer possible to attack the opposition on the grounds that it was tory and therefore, by implication, Jacobite. Indeed such an argument would look doubly foolish against an opposition usually dominated by the former members of the Old Corps, i.e. those who had pressed the distinction between whig and tory in the previous reign. But an argument against opposition based on the notion of royal independency made eminent sense when directed against those who (or so it appeared) had confined the Crown for a generation.

This, however, created a new situation. Under George II it had been the opposition, not the administration, that had talked disapprovingly of the confinement of the king. But in the 1760s *royal apologists*, including many who held office, employed the notion of the king's independency, using it to ward off not only opposition, but, when the occasion demanded, politicians in power. For the first time the king's prerogatives were defended against threats both from within administration and from the ranks of opposition. The royal case dealt neatly with both contingencies, but it also proved a liability. With the union of the claims of prerogative with the claims of the court, it was easy for George's opponents to indict him of toryism and arbitrary intentions.

Such arguments had not been used by the defenders of the Crown and administration under George II for several reasons. First there was a sense in which they had no need of any such argument. They were able to deal with the opposition simply by the strategy of stigmatising it as tory/jacobite. Secondly, even if this had not been the case, apologists of the Old Corps were not eager to base their defence on the prerogative, precisely because they themselves were concerned to keep the king on a tight rein. If those in power were to have an ideological bargaining card to play against George II, they needed the notion of responsible government to legitimise their position. They were therefore at pains not to deny that conception when employed by the opponents of administration. Thus that identification between administration and defence of the royal prerogative and independency was not made under the aegis of Old Corps rule.

The success of the Pelhams was intimately bound up with George II's uncritical acceptance of the premises of Old Corps whig politics. As Owen has suggested, George *confined himself* by his acceptance of the view that a real party struggle was in progress and that the Jacobite threat was genuine. In accepting these tenets he conceded the political necessity for whig rule. No doubt George II did not choose to be a party king, but this was his understanding of British politics; and although he might have wanted to be even less constrained than was actually the case, he never realised that this could only be fully achieved by rejecting the party distinctions that so many whigs maintained, and by encouraging the dissolution of Old Corps organisation. In other words it was as much George II's *view of politics* as his personality that explains why he did not successfully assert himself against the whig politicians. Indeed, to have succeeded he would have had to adopt the assumptions and determination of his grandson. If, for example, he had stood by the 'Forty-Eight-Hour Ministry' of February 1746 he would have had to turn to the tories for support.

If (and I admit that this would have been unlikely) they had been willing to cooperate with him, whig historiography would be very different, and George II would have been transformed into an arbitrary monarch. For, in order to achieve his ends, George would have had to deny the reality of party distinctions, and employ court apologists to argue in favour of the royal independency. It was precisely these actions that led to George III's condemnation as a tory supporter and a whig apostate by the Old Corps. But George II did not have the attitudes for such business. He was a 'court' whig in exactly the same way that his grandson was a 'country' whig.

As such, George III wholeheartedly rejected governmental whig values. His attitudes towards the monarchy and to party threatened to corrode completely the existing configuration of politics. In many ways the effect was shattering: it destroyed all the confidence that the politicians might have had in the young king, for it demonstrated to them that he, in turn, had no confidence in them, and questioned the very ideas and practices on which their power was based.[107] This led certain politicians – and until 1763 these included Pitt as well as Newcastle – to want to constrain the king all the more, and it made every ministerial office-holder more sensitive than he might have been about royal confidence. Even those politicians like George Grenville who subscribed to the idea of the king's independence could not accept the idea of a truly personal monarchy. The politicians therefore fell back on the tactics and arguments that had served so well under George II. Yet, in so doing, they confirmed George III's greatest apprehensions, and increased his distrust and contempt for the political class.

Thus, as in the case of party, the struggles of the 1760s foreshadowed those of the 1780s: Grenville, Rockingham and, to a lesser extent, Chatham, fought on a more limited scale the war that Fox and North waged against the king between 1782 and 1784. No one in this period was ever as outspoken as Fox, nor was any party, with the possible exception of the Grenvilles in 1765, ever in as strong a position as the Fox–North coalition in 1783. But the basic case against royal interference, putative or otherwise, had been made and, very largely because of the example of Bute, had gained much wider currency. The intensity of the quarrel in the 1780s cannot be fully understood without reference to the highly acrimonious debate of the 1760s.

At the same time the limits of the ministerial view of responsibility should not be forgotten. The politicians, despite comparatively sophisticated notions of political confidence and ministerial responsibility, had yet to develop any clear idea of collective responsibility. Ministers openly differed with one another in parliament, and even opposed the administration's policy; Conway and Charles Townshend, for instance, both dissented from the government's East India measures in 1767. On the other hand some sense of corporate responsibility is apparent in the convention that those who were present at a cabinet, or signed the cabinet minute (which was, after all, the criterion for responsibility in the case of impeachment) were all responsible for the decisions taken. Hence the attempts of Devonshire (over the peace) and Camden in 1768 (over Wilkes) to avoid attendance or expressions of opinion on matters in hand. This rather nebulous, corporate feeling did not, however, manifest itself in a formal tender of collective advice to the king, which was only to emerge with the formation of the second Rockingham administration in 1782.[108] Naturally it was difficult to obtain a collective opinion when nearly all administrations were coalitions. Even the Rockingham whigs, the most party-minded group, aspired only to a majority in the cabinet, and not to total control.[109]

In some of the more extreme and polarised situations of the 1760s, such as May 1765, collective responsibility might briefly have been achieved. Yet this did not so much demonstrate a commitment to a collective ideal as manifest a widely-held belief that ministerial responsibility entitled ministers to confidence. It also shows that Richard Pares' adage, that 'there was a conflict between a more and less personal conception of the constitutional monarch',[110] was as true for the 1760s as for any of the eventful decades of George III's reign.

Part III

An alternative structure of politics

8. The press in the 1760s

The first thing we lay our hands on in the morning is a libel; the last thing we lay out of our hands in the evening is a libel. Our eyes open upon libels; our eyes close upon libels. In short, libels, lampoons and satires, constitute all the writing, printing, and reading, of our time. (Lord North, *Parliamentary History* XVI, 1165–6)

We may suppose that the press, and the print-shops will swarm with productions both grave and comic: That venal rhetorick, will turn prostitute in the service of disappointed ambition; and that buffonry [*sic*], capped like an ideot [*sic*], will ring her bells, to tickle vulgar ears, with the silly chimes of ridicule. (*Con-Test* XXXI, 18 June 1757)

Almost every discussion of the controversy that contemporaries believed was the dominant feature of the politics of the 1760s ascribed an important role to the press in the growth of contention. For nearly all eighteenth-century Englishmen believed that England's position as a nation that enjoyed a free constitution, a free press, liberty, leisure and wealth enabled its citizens to enjoy a greater depth of political knowledge and extent of political information than was possible in any other country. The British constitution was credited with the encouragement of the press, political knowledge and polemic:

In unlimited monarchies, men have neither inclination, ability, nor spirit to write; but in a well-constituted free State, the possession of property, the love of liberty, the cultivation of science, will necessarily produce freedom of inquiry, and maintenance of rights: Hence must result literary contentions, and the various opinions of different parties.[1]

But, although it was recognised that free constitutions produced political strife and that the protagonists would naturally employ 'political Prize fighters'[2] to exchange blows in the press, opinion was far from unanimous in praising what one commentator called this 'epidemic Frenzy of reading News-papers'.[3] Admittedly some maintained that the press helped secure responsible government and reflected public opinion, providing an accurate assessment of the feelings and misgivings of the political nation;[4] but many more saw the press as 'a *political* way of trade'[5] with a strong vested interest in writing 'a whole nation into broils'.[6] They felt that the newspaper proprietor was often too willing that 'a nation...be ruined, that a newspaper may sell'.[7]

Both of these views – which were usually put forward by opposition and government respectively – concurred, however, on one cardinal point: the press, whether malevolent or beneficial, played an important part in the political education of those 'out-of-doors'. Thus writings in support of government in the period make frequent reference to the satirically portrayed 'humble reader'. Invariably he appears as a man who wished to ape his superiors and rise above his natural station; of lowly origin, he is perhaps a barber, a breeches-maker, a cheesemonger,[8] or simply a 'sage, snuff-taking coffee-house politician, with a consequential gravity, and significant distention of nostril',[9] who has the temerity to involve himself in the wasteful activities of politics and poring over newspapers 'which employ three Parts of [people's] ...Time, and the whole of their Attention seven Days in every Week'.[10] Indeed, if government satirists are to be believed, there were few men in England, and certainly not a citizen of London, who did not feel competent to pronounce on the problems of the nation. As one commentator sarcastically put it:

at this fortunate period, there is not a citizen, within the bills of mortality, but what [sic] is capable of filling the first offices of government, – the veriest drudge, who now wears a leathern apron, can tell how far a secretary of state's power ought to extend; and expatiate on the illegality of General Warrants with the perspicuity of a *Camden*. – The liberty of discussing the principles of Magna Charta is no longer confined to the limits of St. Stephens. – On the contrary the neighbourhood of St. Giles's now possesses a right of debating on the formation of our laws, and is so well instructed in the business of the state, that it is utterly impossible for a bad minister to pass any injurious law without being immediately liable to detection.[11]

It is, therefore, not surprising that the term politician was not applied exclusively to the parliamentary classes but was used equally of 'a Prime Minister or a Scribbler, a Frequenter of a Coffee-House, or one of the Privy Council, a Member of Parliament, or a member of the Robin-Hood Society'.[12]

To most observers there was an inexorably forged link between the humble politician and a thriving press:

in this land of liberty, of general wealth, curiosity, and idleness, where there is scarce a human creature so poor that it cannot afford to buy or hire a Paper or a Pamphlet, or so busy that it cannot find leisure to read it; where every man, woman, and child, is, by instinct, birth and inheritance a politician; where the ordinary subjects of common conversation turn not, as in most countries, upon the impertinent trivial occurrences of the week or the day, nor on the small concerns, offices, and duties of private and social life; but on the greater and more important subjects of war, negociations, peace, laws, and the public and general weal; where men are more solicitous about the integrity and abilities of a lord commissioner of the treasury, or a secretary of state, than the fidelity of their own wives, the chastity of their own daughters, their sons, or their own honour and virtue; and where, like the virtuous citizens of Rome and Sparta, they reluctantly offer up all the slenderer ties of blood, the endearments of love, the connections of friendship, and the obligations of private gratitude, daily sacrifices and victims of the commonwealth; in such a country the dullest Pamphlet may have a fair chance of gaining some readers provided it be a political Pamphlet.[13]

The picture that emerges from these comments is perhaps one that historians have not led us to expect. Even if we are to concede that there were some contemporaries, as there indubitably were, who disparagingly referred to the ignorant and illiterate populace, we are still left with the problem of explaining why so many politicians and pamphleteers spoke of such an all-embracing 'political nation'. It might, of course, be argued that the impression of politically conscious middle and lower orders was the fiction of government satire: a rhetorical device to brand one's opponents as socially and morally inferior; but if this were the case one would expect opposition apologists to deny the existence of such followers, a tactic which they never employed.[14] Indeed, one is left with the impression that those who scorned the humble politician were satirising a phenomenon which, for all their disapproval, they were powerless to change.

We would seem, therefore, to have good grounds for at least re-opening the question of who comprised the political nation in the 1760s. Should it really be limited to the parliamentary classes, or should it be extended to include those of much humbler origin who were either literate or politically interested? A reinvestigation of the press in the decade should give us some indication of what political information was available, and how extensively it was distributed.

Admittedly, even this relatively modest ambition is extremely difficult to realise. It is natural that, when we turn to the question of the extent to which the press was instrumental in disseminating political information, we should start with the related problems of literacy, circulation and readership. Clearly the impact of the press on politics at this level must in some way be related to the capacity to read, but a real problem arises not simply in trying to solve the tricky quantitative question of measuring literacy or readership, but in deciding what concepts are most useful in talking about those who read or were able to read the political literature available. The trouble with the concept of literacy, as Schofield has pointed out, is that for the specific questions that the historian of the press and politics wishes to ask, it remains too vague.[15] The criterion employed to assess literacy in most pre-industrial societies, namely the capacity to sign one's name, is one that covers a multitude of political sins. On the basis of information gleaned from marriage registers after Hardwicke's Marriage Act of 1754,[16] we know that between 1754 and 1762 64% of married couples in the East Riding of Yorkshire, 48% in the West Midlands, 66% in Bristol, 62% in King's Lynn and 60% in Halifax signed their names in the register.[17] But how many had access to political journalism? How many could obtain, or read and understand Burke or, for that matter, the less sober offerings of John Wilkes? Clearly literacy as it is at present measured cannot answer the sort of questions we would like to ask. Indeed nowhere is this more apparent than in the eighteenth century. Given the considerable limitations of the available statistics, it has been argued that 'so far as the middling classes of town and countryside were concerned...by about 1675 they had reached a literacy plateau of between 75 and 85% where they remained for a century'.[18] But in that same period (1675–1775) there is overwhelming evidence for a burgeoning growth of the press. All that the available information on literacy provides us with, therefore, is a safety-net in which to catch an (improbable) maximum potential number of readers. In sum, it is insufficiently specific, and it would therefore seem unlikely that we could reconstruct an accurate picture of the political reading public, or test Burke's estimate that this comprised a group of 400,000 by the 1790s.[19]

Much more precise is the evidence for the circulation of the press in the 1760s. We know that in 1750 7·3 million newspaper stamps were issued, 9·4 million in 1760, and by 1775 the figure was 12·6 million, i.e. 34,700 a day.[20] Not only was there an increase in the aggregate number of papers, but an increase in the number of individual newspapers, advertisers and journals. In 1760 London had four dailies, and five or six tri-weekly evening papers which were circulated in the country on the three main post days; in all there were eighty-nine papers paying advertising revenue in the metropolis.[21] By 1770 the main papers had been joined by three more tri-weeklies, the *Middlesex Journal*, the *Morning Chronicle* and the *London Packet*,[22] and throughout the 1760s political controversy gave birth to innumerable evanescent weekly, fortnightly, and monthly publications, many of which were unstamped. The *North Briton*, the *Briton*, the *Auditor*, the *Citizen*, the *Constitutional Guardian*, the *Contrast*, the *Free Enquirer*, the *Parliamentary Spy*, the *Whisperer*, the *Plain Dealer*, the *Weekly Amusement*, the *Political Register*, *Freeholder's Magazine* and many others all contributed to the current political debate.

A similar growth in the number of publications can be seen in the provinces: between 1714 and 1725 twenty-two provincial papers had emerged; by 1753 there were thirty-two, and by 1760 either thirty-five or thirty-seven papers which, it is estimated, supplied about one fifth of all papers published.[23] By 1782 there were approximately fifty provincial papers altogether.[24] As early as the 1760s Newcastle enjoyed three newspapers and its own monthly magazine, the *Newcastle General Magazine*,[25] while the Midlands were served by three thriving local papers, the *Northampton Mercury, Jopson's Coventry Mercury* and *Aris's Birmingham Gazette*.[26]

Although it is not hard to see from these figures the secular increase in the importance of the press in the period, it is difficult to gauge the precise significance or the scale of the growth until the circulation of specific papers or items of intelligence is examined. Unfortunately it is precisely here that evidence is so scattered and fragmentary. For the London papers, for example, Lutnick has made a number of estimates for the period of the American war ranging from the *Independent Chronicle* with a circulation of 1500 to the *Public Advertiser* with that of 3000,[27] and Haig in his history of the *Gazetteer* has plausibly argued that the paper was selling about 5000 copies by the early 1770s.[28]

The only truly reliable evidence, however, is to be found in the accounts of the *Public Advertiser* from 1765 to 1771 (graph, p. 144).[29] A number of interesting trends can be observed here. First, there is a marked fluctuation in sales within the calendar year which corresponds with the London season. Sales reached a peak in February or March, just before parliament, as often as not, ended its business for the year; they did not really pick up again until the new parliamentary session in late October or early November. This seasonal trend is corroborated by an examination of the number of published pamphlets reviewed in the *Monthly Review*. December to March was the most popular time of year for reviewing (and, by inference) for publication, while precious few pamphlets at all were discussed between July and October (diagram, p. 145). Secondly, the sales of the *Public Advertiser* gradually grew throughout the period. In the six years for which we have figures average circulation rose by approximately 1000 per issue, a growth of about 50%. After 1770 sales figures never dropped below 3000. Junius's Letter to the king does not seem to have affected the secular trend, though it briefly disturbed the otherwise fairly constant relationship between maximum and minimum sales.

Unfortunately the figures do not cover a sufficiently long timespan to enable us to draw any firm general conclusions. They indicate the strength of the paper, but the gradual growth in sales may be explicable merely in terms of the very high degree of political controversy generated in the late 1760s. Our conclusions, therefore, necessarily have to be highly tentative.

In the case of the provincial press, information about the circulation

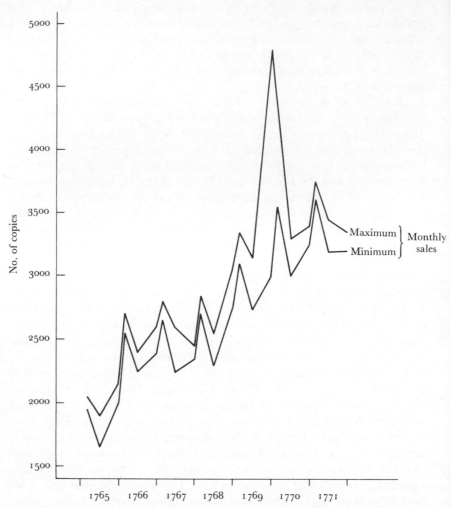

Public Advertiser sales 1765–71. Source: BM Add. Mss 38, 169.

of particular papers is even more scanty. It would appear probable that, in the 1720s, the circulation of most provincial papers was between 250 and 400 copies a week. By the 1760s and 1770s, however, this figure had substantially increased for a number of popular papers; the *York Chronicle*, for instance, had a sale of about 2000, one comparable to, if not better than, some London papers.[30] In the absence of detailed circulation figures some idea of the growing importance and size of the provincial press can be obtained by plotting the distribution centres for individual papers, though the

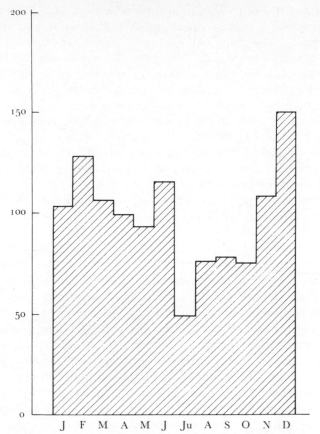

Average number of pamphlets reviewed per month, 1752–70.
Source: *Monthly Review* 1752–70.

method must be used with caution; one of the agents of the *Leicester and Nottingham Journal*, for example, received only twenty-five copies of each issue.[31] Nevertheless the general trends can clearly be seen from this information. As early as 1739 the *Newcastle Journal* cited agents from forty-two towns and villages going as far north as Berwick and as far west as Whitehaven.[32] By 1758 the *Cambridge Chronicle* claimed that it circulated in 'Cambridgeshire, Huntingdonshire, Bedfordshire, Hertfordshire; Northamptonshire, Lincolnshire, Leicestershire, Rutlandshire, Nottinghamshire, Derbyshire, and some parts of Norfolk, Suffolk and Essex'.[33] During the 1760s claims to cover such a wide area were increasingly common: Aris in his *Birmingham Gazette* listed his agencies in London, Shrewsbury, Bridgnorth, Worcester, Wolverhampton, Newcastle-under-Lyme, Lichfield, Tamworth, Stafford, Dudley, Walsall and Stratford-on-Avon,[34] while the *Leeds Mercury* had a similar organisation that extended to Halifax, Bradford, Elland, Huddersfield, Rochdale, Wakefield, Barnsley, Pontefract, Doncaster, Harewood, Wetherby, Knaresborough, Harrowgate, Skipton, Gisburn, Malton, Grassington, Pateley Bridge, Settle, Colne and Keighley.[35] Local shopkeepers, publicans and innkeepers who sold a provincial paper, or took in requests for advertisements which were to appear on its pages, were linked by a system of hawkers and carriers to the editor in his provincial centre. As communications improved, and as the commercial value of using the provincial press became apparent, an increasingly complex, regional network of distribution was developed. Even if we are unsure of the precise numbers of papers distributed, we can be confident that, as the century proceeded, the provincial newspaper was spreading further and further afield.

Thanks to the punctilious accounting of Bowyer and Strahan it is somewhat easier to be specific about the sales of that other vital organ of journalism, the political pamphlet. From their ledgers it is apparent that the average number of copies printed for a single impression or edition of a pamphlet was five hundred. This seems to have been a consistent and regular practice unless the publisher and printer had very good reasons for supposing that the edition would command a much larger audience.[36] A great many of the pamphlets that appeared in the shops in the Strand and were advertised in the columns of the local newspapers therefore never sold more than a mere five hundred. The works that were more successful were usually party manifestoes, recognised as being the chief statement or the main attempt to put forward a particular point of view. Thus Douglas's *Seasonable Hints from an Honest Man* (1761), widely regarded as an authoritative statement of the new court's attitude, sold 2000 in a first edition, as did the government's two later manifestoes, Francis's *Letter from the Cocoa Tree to the Country Gentlemen* (1762), and Richardson's *Letter to a Gentleman in the City* (1762). Similarly Burke's *Thoughts on the Cause of the Present Discontents* (1770), the Rockinghams' political testament, sold 3250 copies and Mauduit's famous critique of the government's German policy *Considerations on the present German War* (1760) went through five editions in three months with a total printing of 5750.[37]

The general pattern that emerges for pamphlet sales is therefore clear enough: a standard edition was 500, the more successful writings sold between 1500 and 3000 copies and, if a work was a spectacular success, it might even run to a sale of 5000.

One of the chief forms of publicity that a pamphlet could obtain was to be reprinted, abstracted or reviewed in the periodical press. For most readers the first contact with a new pamphlet publication would be in this form. The *Gentleman's Magazine*, the *London Magazine*, the *Town and Country Magazine*, the *Monthly Review* and the *Critical Review* all enjoyed a far greater circulation than all but the most successful pamphlets, and all were widely distributed in the provinces. Cave's *Gentleman's Magazine* exemplifies this type of journalism: rich in material, varied in content, and practical in presentation. Whether it be extraordinary events, the art of good husbandry, or the latest political scandal, the *Gentleman's Magazine* provided easily digestible, synoptic coverage. Johnson, in one of his more charitable moments, estimated that Cave sold 10,000 copies of his magazine per issue. No other periodical could match this, but Dodsley's *Annual Register* and the whiggish *Monthly Review* both achieved sales in excess of 3000.[38] With circulations such as these, the magazines naturally attracted political polemicists who knew that a larger and more varied audience could be reached through the periodicals than by means of the usual shilling or one and six-penny pamphlet.

When we move from the well illuminated realm of newspapers, pamphlets, and periodicals to the publishers' twilight zone of printed ephemera – squibs, handbills, songs, *affiches* – and to the political cartoon, even fewer circulation figures survive. Contemporary authorities, whose testimony is admittedly not very reliable, claimed that Wilkes circulated 40,000 handbills at the first Middlesex election of 1768,[39] and we know that one political cartoon 'The Repeal or the Funereal Procession of Miss Americ-Stamp' eventually sold about 16,000 copies.[40] But the most reliable evidence that survives for the circulation of this kind of ephemera is to be found in the printing accounts of electoral contestants. The court party in the Westminister election of 1749 issued no fewer than 227,500 electoral letters, advertisements and broadsheets.[41] This, of course, was an exceptional election in an exceptional constituency. More characteristic, perhaps, was the election of 1768 in Essex. There one of the candidates, standing for a seat that had 6000 voters, managed to circulate 33,700 pamphlets, broadsides, squibs and songs.[42] Local issues, as in the case of the Westminster election, were touched upon; but so too were those of national import: Lord Bute and the peace of 1763, the Land Tax, the Cider Tax, the Stamp Act and the Window Tax all feature prominently in the material.[43] Contested elections (and even those that were not contested, such as that at Buckingham in 1779 when the Grenville family produced over 6500 handbills)[44] certainly generated a considerable body of literature; but it would be wrong to assume that handbills and broadsheets were *only* produced on these occasions. There is abundant qualitative evidence to show that leafleting was endemic in London, and was a fairly common practice in the provincial towns; sadly, however, quantitative information does not survive.

It might well be argued that the overall circulation figures for the period are not that impressive. A printing of 500 pamphlets, after all, meant that there was not a copy for every member of the House of Commons, and the sales of a newspaper were no better, if not perhaps a little worse than those of a scholarly tome today. But in the eighteenth century circulation figures were *not* readership figures, and it is almost certain that for every copy of a pamphlet or newspaper produced there were a great many readers, or a great many to whom the press was read. This was an assumption made by nearly all authors and publishers whose estimates of readers per copy varied from twenty (the figure given in the *Spectator*) to as high as fifty.[45]

Although the last figure is undoubtedly optimistic, it was not unrealistic for the political journalist to expect a copy of his pamphlet, journal or newspaper to pass through many hands. The press was publicly available: anyone who frequented, as nearly all citizens did, coffee houses, inns, taverns and tearooms could usually obtain several papers or peruse the latest pamphlets. In London, in 1739, there were 551 coffee houses, 207 inns and 447 taverns.[46] Not all, it is true, stocked 'the public prints' as well as coffee, cocoa, liquor and ale; but a great many did, largely because it enhanced their beverage trade. Customers liked to pour over the papers while supping their ale or sipping their coffee.

This was a well-established custom: there had been coffee houses under Charles II, and by Queen Anne's reign it was common knowledge that, 'You may go into a coffee house and see a table of half an acre's length covered with nothing but tobacco, pipes and pamphlets, and all the seats full of mortals leaning on their elbows, licking in tobacco, lies and laced coffee, and studying for arguments to revile one another.'[47] If contemporaries are to be believed, the situation had grown worse by the 1760s; as one coffee-house politician put it:

Tired with the fatigue of reading the morning and evening papers, which I think amounted at least to ten in number, one night at the coffee-house, I could not avoid entering into the train of following reflections, when I laid down the last paper, on the raging thirst for news, which is excited by the very multiplication of the means of satiating us with occurrences, within memory of old persons now alive, no newspaper was printed excepting the Gazette; all other intelligence being circulated from hand to hand by casual information in coffee house conversation, which I think must have furnished more social amusement than we now find, when every one who can seize a paper sits sullenly poring over it in silence, while the rest are eagerly gaping for the first that is laid down, without knowing what to do with themselves in the interim.[48]

The coffee house was a centre of political news open to all those, including tradesmen, apprentices and mechanics, who could afford the beverages offered.[49] They were centres of political communication where someone like Boswell could amuse himself by breakfasting, reading the papers, chatting with the citizens or listening to them discuss such political issues as Lord Bute's peace.[50] They could even be used as a base and accommodation address from which to solicit patronage.[51] Above all, the tavern and coffee house combined politics with conviviality. Many of them were the meeting-places of the innumerable clubs and societies that flourished in London. Clubs of rakes and of masons, neither of which might appear to be political but which often formed the basis of political organisation, together with the 'free and easy' clubs which were found all over London, met in the upper rooms of taverns or used their drinking and dining facilities. The Horn Tavern in Doctors' Commons, for instance, served as the meeting-place for a 'free and easy' of nearly a thousand members, and as the home of the Ancient French Lodge and the Lodge of Harmony; it was also the favourite tavern of members of the Joiners Company.[52] The Mitre Coffee House in Fleet Street, where papers could be read, was the venue of the West Indian and American Lodge, and the Lodge of Freedom; Wilkes dined there with the Common Councilmen of his aldermanic Ward of Farringdon Without, and the Society of Antiquaries and the Royal Society Club, together with a club of which Boswell was a member, all used the house as a meeting-place.[53] Coffee houses such as Peele's and St James's were famous for their comprehensive runs of newspapers.[54] Wildman's, admittedly a club rather than an open coffee-house society, kept votes of the House of Commons, 'along with the Two Volumes of the North Briton, the *Royal Register* and Gazetteer' for the personal use of its members.[55]

For party politicians the two most important London coffee houses were Arthur's, a whig stronghold, and the Cocoa Tree, the home of the country-gentlemen and tories. Both were a fund of gossip and information. It was natural, therefore, that when Bute wanted to assess the hostility of the Newcastle whigs to his peace preliminaries in 1762, Sir Harry Erskine should pass on news of the rumours circulating at Arthur's.[56] Similarly, when the whig factions wanted to know of the activities of other proprietary groups, they came here. It was in this way, for instance, that Rockingham learnt of the failure of the negotiations between Chatham and Bedford in December 1766.[57] The news at Arthur's, in other words, was a good guide to the current state of whiggery; hence Newcastle's alarm in 1763 when he learnt that the Massacre of the Pelhamite Innocents had stopped all criticism of the administration from being voiced in the main coffee room.[58]

The Cocoa Tree, where Gibbon dined in 1762, commenting on the members' old principles and their newly acquired offices,[59] was a similar establishment to Arthur's. Within its portals members 'Violated their Sobriety...by Drinking felicity to his Majesty in pint Bumpers' after the first royal speech from the throne in the new reign.[60] Tory peers used it as a forwarding address, and whenever they arrived in town, solid country-gentlemen like Sir Roger Newdigate 'immediately marched to Cocoa [Tree] to Breakfast to learn News'.[61] Newdigate, a highly active parliamentary backbencher, was a great frequenter of the coffee house; during the month of November 1761,[62] for instance, he visited it on no less than thirteen separate occasions. When in town, he made a habit of spending part of his Sunday at the club, conversing with friends and reading the latest political pamphlets.[63] By the end of the decade, if not earlier, he was a member of the Cocoa Tree Board, its chief political body.[64] The detailed information provided by Newdigate's meticulous diaries demonstrates how club life and newspaper and pamphlet reading were intrinsic to the political experience of the ordinary MP.

Press facilities and club life were not confined to London. Again and again, as we examine the social life of the large provincial towns, we find the same indigenous political culture, centred upon a few taverns or coffee houses. By 1757 there was a coffee house in Winchester that claimed to take 'the *Votes*, Kings Speech and Addresses, the *Gazette*, *Daily Advertiser*, *General Evening Post*, *Evening Advertiser*, and *London Chronicle*, Weekly Journals, Monthly Magazine, the Sessions Papers, and Dying Speeches'.[65] Of Liverpool's six coffee houses, George's was the most important. Sales and public meetings took place there; it was the venue of the Conversation Club which debated such issues as the ballot and the rights and wrongs of taxing the unrepresented; the Wilkite group in the town used it for rallies and meetings. London and Irish papers could be consulted there, and at the Salopian Coffee House nearby.[66] The four leading coffee houses in Newcastle, Nelly's, the Exchange, Katy's and the Custom House, provided committee rooms for the local supporters of Wilkes to organise a subscription in his favour; across the Tyne, in Gateshead, similar clubs existed at the King's Head, the Cappadocian, Mr Cowling's and Mr Byerley's.[67]

Even as small a town as Knaresborough had its coffee room that took the four main London papers.[68] Growing communities like Birmingham, whose taverns and clubs were so important in developing local political consciousness, offered far superior facilities. Overton's Coffee House claimed, by the 1770s, to stock the *London Gazette*, *Lloyd's Evening Post*, *London Packet*, *General Evening Post*, *St James's Chronicle*, the *London Evening Post*, the *Morning Post*, *Morning Chronicle*, *Public*

Advertiser and *Gazetteer* along with Commons division lists, sessions papers, bills of entry, Lloyd's lists and Irish and provincial papers with the *Utrecht Gazette*.[69] Its local rival, Freeth's Coffee House, professed to offer similar facilities.[70] Most of the current political journalism was available at these local centres, and the clubs and debating societies created an environment which was strongly conducive to political conversation and argument. Within this milieu, there were considerable social pressures on the provincial newsreader to remain politically informed and interested. For those who pursued knowledge in the hope of eventually acquiring local political power, the tavern, inn or coffee house served as nursery school and university; it gave access to the arcane science of politics.

If not read in coffee houses, newspapers and pamphlets could be obtained elsewhere. A quarterly or annual sum paid to one of the circulating libraries, so frowned upon by Sir Antony Absolute,[71] could obtain access to at least some political literature shelved among the novels, histories, travel books and ephemeral literature that were so popular. There had been few such libraries before the 1740s.[72] London, it is true, had had its reading rooms, and individual entrepreneurs had been remarkably successful; George Barton, for instance, established three libraries, at St Ives, St Neots and Peterborough.[73] But from the mid-century circulating libraries grew apace. Paul Kaufman estimates that by 1800, 112 had been established in London and 268 in the provinces.[74] Competition was so fierce that proprietors resorted to cunning stratagems to keep up custom. One London library offered a spurious version of Wilkes's *Essay on Woman* to boost its subscriptions.[75] At Bath one of the most famous circulating libraries, vividly described in Smollett's picaresque *Humphrey Clinker*, stocked thirteen London and twenty-two provincial newspapers.[76] The holdings of such libraries were considerable; the Bristol Library Society, for example, lent over nine hundred titles in the years 1773–84.[77]

These circulating libraries were not cheap; their subscriptions placed them beyond the pocket of all but the gentle and professional or merchant classes. Rather less expensive were pamphlet clubs which concentrated on buying current political and commercial literature. At Ely, for example, a subscription of ten shillings per annum gave access to over six hundred titles.[78] For the poorer still there were a whole series of expedients that could be employed to obtain literature on the cheap. Clubbing together to buy a paper or pamphlet was common, as was hiring a paper from one of the many newspaper hawkers.[79] Those who were curious enough seem to have found ways to circumvent the problem of obtaining such literature without too much difficulty. The result was a wide readership for many pamphlets and papers.

Printed ephemera, however, seem to have enjoyed even wider currency. The print shops like those of Darly in the Strand or Dicey in Northampton[80] displayed their wares for any passer-by who, if he wished, could see ministers and politicians 'libelled in their persons by a million scandalous caricatures hung up for the gaping multitude'.[81] Nor did those who gathered at the print-shop window have to be literate; they could easily understand the simple pictographic messages of Bute's supposed intrigues with the Princess Dowager, Pitt's patriotism, or of parliamentary bribery and corruption.

Similarly handbills were available to all in the City. Widely circulated, they could be read aloud, put up on walls, or passed from hand to hand. During the crises over General Warrants and the Middlesex election they were issued on a large scale by Wilkes. As Beaumont Hotham complained: 'Hand Bills are circulated to every house, and almost to the lowest Cobler, containing the Warrants, Speeches, &c. I can't pass along the Streets without having them crammed down my throat, by every Black guard that I meet, who is employed to distribute them.'[82] The handbill, however, was equally likely to be a weapon of government propaganda. Before the debate on the peace preliminaries in December 1762, for instance, the administration were assiduous in their distribution of printed sheets and squibs:

printed bills have been handed about for the best part of the present week, signifying that an address from this great city to - - - -, in commendation of the glorious *preliminaries*, would sound well in the *north*, and be extremely acceptable to the children of *Boreas*, who would immediately put on their blustering countenances, and convey the happy tidings to every part of the globe.
Other bills have likewise, with great assiduity, been popt into the hands of the public, positively affirming, that the advancing of the price of *strong beer*, was not owing to the present m - - - - - -, and intimating that this, together with the act, touching the additional duty upon window-lights, shall immediately be expunged.[83]

Within a few days government lackeys were at work again. It was reported that '*Printed Copies of the following* extraordinary Paper *were distributed gratis, in the* Court of Requests, *and at the* Doors of both Houses of Parliament, *on the 9th, when the* Preliminaries of Peace were to be debated upon'.[84] The paper in question, 'Sentiments d'un Francois', purported to be the views of an irate Frenchman who believed that his government had failed to make a satisfactory peace with the English.

In addition to handbills and cartoons there were also a great many *affiches* on display: posters, often with treasonous, brief and pithy messages. Bute was a particular victim of this form of propaganda throughout the decade.[85] During the crisis of 1768–70 such papers became more frequent and daring. Indeed the proximate cause of the 'St George's Fields Massacre' was a quarrel between demonstrators and the magistrates about the removal of such a sheet from the walls of the King's Bench prison.[86] Some of these papers penetrated the portals of the royal palace itself. Thus in May 1768 'a most audacious and treasonable paper was found stuck up with wafers on the walls of St. James's Palace; and also the same night a letter was found on the back stairs, of the same atrocious tendency'.[87] A year later similar papers appeared on the doors of Buckingham House, the king's new residence. And in the following April not only were 'several places in St. James's Park, and on the walls in the neighbourhood of the Parliament House' covered 'in letters near a foot long' declaring 'Impeach the - - - - -s mother – Impeach the D - - - - - r – Impeach her!', but the wall of St James's palace was inscribed with the following lines:

> A Prophesy.
> A cold winter
> A mild spring
> A bloody summer
> A dead - - - - - - -.[88]

Even the House of Commons was attacked in this way. Colonel Onslow apprehended one Thornton, a milkseller, who had stuck up a paper on the corner of Bond Street containing Oliver Cromwell's speech at dissolving the Long Parliament, a clear call for the dissolution of a corrupt assembly.[89]

As expressions of a rather rudimentary demotic political consciousness, these papers and graffiti never conveyed a particularly subtle or sophisticated message. In form and style of expression they resemble the many anonymous and threatening letters which the government published in the *Gazette* in the vain hope of apprehending their authors. *Affiches*, however, were *public* expressions of protest, displayed on walls for all to see; and in this sense they were more explicitly political than the threatening letter. Their intention was not merely to frighten those against whom the slogan was directed, but to obtain support from others who might have good reason to resent the conduct of the king, a particular politician or the House of Commons. Each copy of a paper, each chalked slogan was designed to be read by as large an audience as was possible.

Clearly, at all levels, from the highly sophisticated political tract to the epigramatically phrased handbill, there were many more readers than there were copies in circulation. In sum, circulation and readership were in no way coextensive.

6-2

The complex relationship between circulation and readership is further compounded for the historian by the very frequent eighteenth-century practice of publishing a particular item of political journalism and propaganda in a variety of places. In an age when a shilling pamphlet made the same demands on a man's income as a month's supply of candles,[90] some of the more expensive works, especially pamphlets, would only be available to many in condensed and reviewed forms. These however were considerable in number. Anyone who has tried to wend his way through the labyrinths of the eighteenth-century press is familiar with the way in which a piece of political journalism, especially a successful piece, was likely to appear in all manner of newspapers, reviews and journals. The weeklies of 1762–3, for example, the *Monitor, North Briton, Briton* and *Auditor*, apart from being papers in their own right, were republished in the *Political Controversy*, appeared in the periodicals, the *Gentleman's Magazine, Universal Magazine, London Magazine, Weekly Amusement*,[91] and were printed in such papers as the *St James's Chronicle, Lloyd's Evening Post,* the *London Chronicle* and the *Gazetteer*.[92] In addition vignettes were published in *The True Flower of Brimstone* (1763) and *Collection of all the remarkable passages* (1766).

Similarly Burke's *Thoughts*, apart from the 3000 copies it sold in the space of six weeks,[93] appeared either in review or extract in five London papers – the *Independent Chronicle, Public Advertiser, Gazetteer, General Evening Post, London Chronicle*[94] – which, if Lutnick's figures are correct, had an aggregate sale of 11,000.[95] It was also reviewed and given extensive quotation in the *Gentleman's Magazine* as well as in the rival *London Magazine* and four other monthly periodicals.[96] The *Monthly* and *Critical Reviews*, whose joint sales must have been about 5000, both discussed the work, as did such provincial papers as the *Cambridge Chronicle* and the *Norwich Mercury*.[97] Thus, even if we exclude consideration of the two pamphlet replies to the *Thoughts*, the work was still available in one form or another in between twenty and thirty thousand items.

Only someone as controversial as Junius could hope to match such a wide circulation. One contemporary commentator remarked that the famous letters had 'been as extensively published as any modern piece whatsoever – being copied into five or six newspapers – some of the Magazines and also dispersed as a sixpenny pamphlet'.[98] There were two collected editions of the letters within a year of their appearance.[99] Individual letters were featured in the columns of the *Universal Magazine, Freeholder's Magazine, Gentleman's Magazine, Political Register* and *London Museum*, as well as forming part of the *Repository or Treasury of Politics and Literature* (2 vols., 1770–1),[100] and they were also published in the Newcastle periodical, the *Literary Register*.[101] Such London papers as the *London Evening Post, Independent Chronicle, St James's Chronicle* and the *Gazetteer*[102] as well as the provincial *Cambridge Chronicle*, and *Leeds Mercury* reproduced the letters.[103] Indeed, it is an indication of how widely the letters were circulated that it was thought discriminatory to plan to prosecute only six of Junius's printers.

Thus, apart from the difficulty of having to multiply circulation figures perhaps as many as twenty times in order to ascertain readership, we also face the problem of finding individual items of journalism duplicated and reproduced in other publications. Naturally this multiplication would have produced a certain amount of overlap, as some readers would doubtless have access to several of the publications that carried such writings as the *North Briton*, Burke's *Thoughts*, or *Junius's Letters*. But the evidence would still seem to indicate that the readership of a publication like Burke's *Thoughts* in its original and condensed forms might have been over 100,000, and that the readership of the *North Briton* and Junius might have been even greater.

Moreover there may well have been those who, although they could not read, were acquainted or familiar with the different materials of political propaganda. There is ample evidence, as Schofield has pointed out, that in pre-industrial, partially literate societies such as eighteenth-century England, a process known as 'bridging' was likely to occur. Bridging is the transmission of printed information in traditional oral forms: the establishment of a link between the literate and non-literate.[104] Perhaps the most obvious example of this kind of link was the ballad, a song printed on a single sheet which was sold by balladmongers who regaled passers-by with renderings of their wares. Ballads might appear a rather crude form of political propaganda but they were taken seriously by contemporaries. In the volatile year of 1769, for example, efforts were made to keep balladsingers off the streets. The *London Magazine* regarded ballads as one of the most important forms of propaganda:

Ballads, or popular songs, have in every nation had the greatest influence...We remember how Mr. Glover's ballad of the Hosier's Ghost roused us against Sir Robert Walpole. Dr. Smollett's Mourn, hapless Caledonia, made every tender-hearted Whig feel himself for a moment a Jacobite. And Mr. Garrick's Hearts of Oak warmed our seamen with the love of glory, made them look upon the French as beings utterly contemptible, and persuaded them that they were all voluntiers, when perhaps, half the crew of many ships had been pressed...

Such being the influence which ballads may have, I wonder that no administration in this country for their own good, or no worthy magistrates for the public good, have been at pains to have ballads of a proper tendency circulated among the people. I am sure money could not be better employed, and I am certain that no placemen, or pensioners, can be of so much service as a set of well chosen ballad singers might be. We might have the discontented and turbulent populace sung into quietness and good humour, as froward children are by their nurses.[105]

In practice ballads, as in the case of so many forms of propaganda, were a predominantly opposition weapon, and on occasion they were used with deadly effect. When one pamphleteer observed in 1757 that 'If I am not mistaken, the Clamour was begun against the Admiral [Byng], by the Hawkers and Ballad-singers; every one must remember *Sing Tantarara Hang Byng*',[106] he was not far from the mark. One hundred ballad singers paraded through the streets of Westminster singing 'To the block with Newcastle and the Yard Arm with Byng', and a great many other songs with such ominous titles as 'An ADDRESS FROM the Regions Below to A - - - - -l B - - - -g' and 'A RUEFUL STORY, ADMIRAL B - - -G's GLORY; OR WHO run away First' were also popular.[107] In the 1760s opposition writers were equally prolific in composing 'the foolish ballads and papers that are sung and cried about the streets'.[108] Henry Howard produced a whole series of anti-court ballads and songs at the beginning of the reign including *The K - - -s A - -* (1762), *The Masquerade* (1762) and *The Pe**e Soup-Makers* (1762).[109] In the cider counties a ballad was distributed 'alluding to the Case of Charles 1st',[110] whilst at the end of the decade the Princess Dowager, a favourite victim of the song writers, was libelled in a ballad 'the cow has left her calf'.[111]

Wilkite and anti-Bute ballads were especially in demand. The author of the *North Briton* no. 45 was the subject of many laudatory ballads, including 'The Sound of Fame', 'True Blue will never Stain, or WILKES for ever', 'Wilkes and Glyn', 'Wilks and Libity' (*sic*), 'Wilkes and Liberty in honour of no. 45', 'Wilkes and Loyalty', 'HEARTS OF OAK... For the Worthy Liverymen of LONDON', 'WILKES and the LIVERY', and 'WILKES and our COUNTRY'.[112] These songs were matched in popularity only by such anti-Scottish ballads as 'Our nation by sawney has quite been undone', and 'Sawney turn'd Barber' which, according to Boswell was 'as popular as Wilkes himself'.[113]

There were, of course, other ways in which this bridging effect could be achieved. The public reading of the newspapers and political propaganda on display in coffee houses and other places of public resort meant that even the illiterate could enjoy the excitement of political polemic. Indeed, by the end of the century when middle-class and artisan politicians had realised the importance of political education, public reading had become an organised activity.[114]

The theatre was also used to purvey political ideas to a non-literate public. In 1764, for example, that most enduring of political satires, Gay's *Beggar's Opera*, was used to brand Lord Sandwich as 'Jemmy

Twitcher', after he had hypocritically attacked Wilkes in the House of Lords for his *Essay on Woman*.[115] A similar incident occurred when George III went to see a play by Murphy, a government pamphleteer and playwright. In Horace Walpole's words: 'the last time the King was at Drury Lane, the play given out for the next night was *All in the Wrong*: the galleries clapped, and cried out, 'Let *us* be all in the right! Wilkes and Liberty!''[116] Such allusions were, it has to be admitted, as much the responsibility of the spectators as of the play itself, for the theatre audience regarded political *manifestations* as their traditional prerogative. But there were also self-conscious attempts to produce political propaganda, among them a tragedy by Mallet attacking Wilkes and the *North Briton*, and a play by Foote praising the young king.[117] Such performances, however, did not include such published offerings as *The Three Conjurers*, *The Fall of Mortimer*, and *The Favourite, an Historical Tragedy* which were too explicit in their criticisms, scandal and sexual innuendo for even the eighteenth-century stage.[118]

Bridging, the extensive multiplication of materials, and the substantial number of readers per copy, all indicate how inadequate circulation figures can be if taken on their own as a guide to readership, or political awareness. Two examples illustrate this. We concluded that Burke's *Thoughts* was probably available in some twenty or thirty thousand items. If we assume that only five different people read each item (and this conservative estimate should deal with the problem of overlap), then it had a projected readership of about 100,000. Given that the population was approximately six and a half million, one person in sixty-five may have had contact with the *Thoughts*. Similarly, if a newspaper sold 3000 copies and had a readership of about twenty persons per issue, it might have been read by one person in a hundred. The figure for the proportion of adult males rather than the proportion of the total population in contact with pamphlet or newspaper would, naturally, be considerably higher.

These figures must be treated with the greatest caution; they are probably optimistic, and are only intended to convey a general impression of the availability and extent of the press in the period. Nevertheless they serve to underscore the way in which the press had grown since the beginning of the century. This development can easily be overlooked. Individual sales of newspapers, periodicals and pamphlets had not substantially increased since the reign of Anne. The *Post Boy*, the *Evening Post* and the *Post Man*, for instance, all maintained circulations comparable to the newspapers of the 1760s.[119] Similarly the *Craftsman* of the late 1720s and early 1730s sold as well as, if not better than the weeklies of the Wilkite controversy.[120] There were, however, three important differences between the press at the beginning of the century and in the 1760s. First, although the sale of individual items – and therefore the scale of business – was still much the same, the aggregate press sale had increased. Secondly, the press had developed a complicated 'infrastructure', a tangled web of connections that ensured the multiplication of items on a wide scale and which very largely accounts for the impressive final figures for readership. At the beginning of the century there were few provincial papers to duplicate London items, nor were there the many magazines and reviews. The *Gentleman's Magazine* was not started until 1731; the *London Magazine*, its main rival, was founded in 1732. The *Universal Magazine*, the *Annual Register*, and *London Museum* appeared in 1747, 1758 and 1770 respectively. The *Monthly* and *Critical Reviews*, which are such a fund of information on contemporary literature, were not operative until 1749 and 1756. It was, in other words, not until mid-century and perhaps even later that the phenomenon of duplication had developed to its full extent. The 1760s and 1770s were the heyday of this development. Thereafter the organisation and, to an extent, the scale of individual enterprises began to grow; the eighteenth-century press developed even further.[121]

Moreover press coverage was more extensive for the provinces. Many of the magazines, journals and reviews were designed to cater to a provincial market, intended to provide potted versions of the culture and politics of the metropolis. New London tri-weekly papers helped the development of the provincial press by providing more of the basic information that had to fill its pages. The new commercial and manufacturing towns such as Halifax, Birmingham, Liverpool, Sheffield and Leicester all acquired papers after 1735. The amount of political information available in the provinces in 1760 was incomparably greater than it had been a generation before.

This information explosion must be seen in the context of two developments. First, the period 1720–60 saw an enormous improvement in communications, especially of the sort that facilitated the distribution of news. Before 1720, turnpike roads were confined, by and large, to the chief arterial routes in the vicinity of London. After that date turnpiking proceeded apace, first on the outlying stretches of the chief routes (thirteen in all) between London and the main provincial regions, and then, during the 'turnpike mania' of the 1750s and 1760s, within the regions themselves. 'By 1750', the historian of the turnpike system concludes, 'most of the main roads between London and the provincial centres, as well as a number of important inter-provincial routes, had been almost completely turnpiked, and by the mid-1770s an interconnected and fairly comprehensive network of improved roads had been formed.'[122]

Parallel with this development, and undoubtedly helped by it, was the growth of the postal service. This was crucial: the post brought news from the metropolis and was an important, though by no means the only way in which the provincial paper was distributed within the locality. Between 1720 and 1762 Ralph Allen transformed the postal service; he removed corruption, increased efficiency so that letters were much less frequently lost and, most significantly of all, radically expanded the area covered by the Post Office. Improvement was effected by increasing the frequency of existing services, and by developing the cross-country posts between provincial towns. In 1741 Allen set up new 'every day' posts between London and the West (via Bath, Bristol and Gloucester), and between London and East Anglia (through Cambridge, Lynn, Norwich and Yarmouth). Similar new services were established in 1748 and 1755 to the south-west and north-west of the country. In 1760 the system of daily posts was extended further to the West Riding of Yorkshire, to Tyne and Teesside, and to Cumberland.[123] During the same year Allen also began a series of new 'cross posts' designed 'for quickening the Correspondence between all the trading parts of Yorkshire, to those of Staffordshire, Shropshire, North Wales, Lancaster, Westmorland and Cumberland'.[124] This and other cross posts in the same year marked the virtual completion of a nationwide cross posts network developed by Allen between 1735 and 1760. By the accession of George III most of the major towns in the country were linked both with London and each other by an efficient, frequently daily service. This sort of facility made a local paper feasible. It was not fortuitous that a Cambridge paper started immediately after Allen had implemented his East Anglian 'every day' post which passed through the university city.[125] Provincial papers had to have a lifeline to the metropolis, and it was Allen who threw it to them.

Improvements in communication undermined the parochialism of the provincial town, yet simultaneously helped develop an indigenous culture that mimicked (*sotto voce*) the consumerism and client economy of the metropolis. The growth of the provincial press and the efflorescence of a local coffee-house culture have to be seen in this context. The social centre of many provincial towns was either, as in the case of Northampton, the chief inns of the town – the George, the Red Lion and the Peacock[126] – or a similar group of coffee houses. In such hostelries the local magistrates met for either quarter or petty sessions, book auctions were held, floral exhibits displayed, and balls and assemblies arranged for the local gentry, pseudo-gentry and professional classes. Innkeepers and coffee-house proprietors, aware of the profits that could be made for the leisure activities of others, built larger public rooms, arranged concerts and invested in theatrical productions.[127] Thus Sloswick Carr, landlord of the Red Lion in Northampton, set up a coffee room and newsroom at his inn in 1748 to cater to the political curiosity of the local gentlemen.[128] In Birmingham, John Freeth, proprietor of the Leicester Arms Tavern in Bell Street (known locally as Freeth's Coffee House), encouraged book clubs and debating societies on his premises, wrote ballads and poems with such titles as 'Ode on Wilkes's Enlargement', and helped organise the political campaigning of Sir Watkin Lewes (a member of the SSBR) for the borough of Worcester.[129]

There was profit to be made from leisure, and politics or, at least, an interest in politics was one of the requisite accomplishments of the leisured man. There was, therefore, an element of social emulation in the efforts of coffee-house habitués to learn of the political contests of the metropolis and to engage in political debate. Such aspirations, long prominent in the City of London, were nurtured and catered to by those who realised that politics, so long regarded as a luxury good, was beginning to transform itself into yet another mass marketable commodity.

In consequence, the difference between the political sophistication of London and that of a provincial town was considerably diminished. More people had access to political information, and more were interested in politics. The problem was that many of these men lacked a focus for their political activity. Though numerous, they were frequently excluded from the processes of institutionalised politics or felt unsympathetic to the alternatives offered within the existing political structure. This substantial political nation, far larger than the parliamentary classes, needed such issues as Wilkes and America to give it even a semblance of national coherence, and an opportunity to have any kind of impact upon organised party politics. So when the Wilkes affair became the predominant issue in politics it had a ready-made political organisation and culture to fall back on. Coffee houses, taverns, debating clubs, local papers and political societies, all took up Wilkes because he presented those who used such facilities with a golden opportunity to give point to their somewhat inchoate political aspirations. The Wilkite phenomenon would not have been possible without a strong provincial press and thriving indigenous political culture. Equally the impact of this substantial and ever-growing 'alternative' political nation upon the institutionalised political process would not have been so great, if it had not been for the opportunism of Wilkes. He and his radical followers were to unite, if only for a short while, the disparate political forces outside the parliamentary classes, thereby revealing both the strengths and the weaknesses of an alternative structure of politics.

Part IV

Focussed radicalism

9. Personality, propaganda and ritual: Wilkes and the Wilkites

❧❦❧

In the even read several political papers called the 'North Briton', which are wrote by John Wilkes, Esq., member for Ailsbery [*sic*] in Bucks, for the writing of which he has been committed to the Tower, and procured his release by a writ of Harbus Corpus' [*sic*]. I really think they breath forth such a spirit of liberty, that it is an extreme good paper. (F. M. Turner (ed.), *The Diary of Thomas Turner of East Hoathley 1754–65* (1925), 77–8)

The Father of his country; the English David; the beloved Patriot; the heroic Champion; the Martyr of Liberty. (Charlotte Forman to John Wilkes (describing him), 28 October 1769, Add. Mss 30870 f. 216)

John Wilkes is remembered as much for his startling personality as for the political issues that were raised during his controversial career. At first sight, as all those who have seen Hogarth's wicked caricature would concede, he was a most unprepossessing figure. Of no great stature and, by all contemporary accounts, of quite startling ugliness, his portrait in etchings and cartoons more closely resembles that of an inbred Habsburg than the British '*God of liberty*'.[1] Yet, despite these disadvantages – or perhaps because of them – Wilkes possessed what can only be called style. His public manner – epitomised by the way in which he picked his teeth, and hummed and hawed while the Court of Common Pleas deliberated on his fate in May 1763 – together with his flamboyant dress, won him the immediate admiration of all those who would have loved to flout authority. Type-cast as an anti-hero, he played the part with immense panache. There was always a highly theatrical element in his conduct. As Wraxall remarked: 'He seemed to consider human life itself as a mere comedy';[2] and, one might add, he envisaged politics as the most outrageous scene in the farce of life. He appeared determined to play the malicious jester at the court of George III. To most historians this facet of Wilkes's career has seemed inconsequential and unworthy of elaboration: significant only as a source of anecdote to relieve the tedium of scholarly investigation. Yet it was Wilkes's social skills, his wit and his irreverence which were crucial in his recruitment of popular support. It is not just that we should not underestimate his beguiling charm (who else, with such insubordinate views, could have won over the crotchety Dr Johnson?). He used his personal talents to political effect, and it was this projection of his personality (as well as the importance of the issues that he raised) that made the Wilkite movement peculiarly dependent on its eponymous leader. No one would deny Wilkes his political inadequacies, nor his delightful personal vices, but, as is apparent when one examines Wilkite propaganda as well as the conduct of those who supported their squinting hero, it was the outrageous behaviour of the man that endeared him to an increasingly politically-aware public.

This is not to say, however, that the issues that Wilkes raised can be regarded as trivial. Taken together they constituted a frontal assault on the politics of oligarchy, and thereby threatened the political *status quo*. Wilkes's counterattack after his arrest on a general warrant as the author of the *North Briton* no. 45 resulted in a number of legal decisions that reduced the powers that the executive could employ against political journalists.[3] In this way the freedom of the press was extended.

Even more significant was his election for Middlesex in 1768, and the subsequent battle that took place between an electorate, determined to ensure that Wilkes, the candidate with the most votes, should sit in the House of Commons, and the majority of MPs who were equally resolved to exclude this convicted felon.

Wilkes portrayed his repeated expulsions as a deliberate attempt by the government to prevent the freeholders of the county from exercising their right of election. Here was a typical example of the oligarchical process by which politics had become confined to the few. Just as the lower House had decided on so many previous occasions for a smaller electorate, or had determined disputed elections in favour of the interest of the parliamentary majority,[4] so now it sought to deprive Englishmen of their fundamental right – 'the first principle of our constitution',[5] Wilkes called it – the freedom of election. Every burgess who had fought the stranglehold of a borough corporation, every freeholder who had opposed the county magnates, and every rightfully elected candidate who had been unseated on a petition in the lower House was immediately familiar with and sympathetic towards Wilkes's cause. The Middlesex election raised *nationally* issues that had long been in contention in the localities. Real whigs, with their long memories, might compare the case with the arbitrary actions of the Stuarts; but politicians of whatever political persuasion, including tories, recalled more readily the skilled process of exclusion developed under Walpole.

The Middlesex election, undoubtedly the most important incident in Wilkes's career, was a challenge to oligarchical politics; it questioned the very basis on which a system of political stability had been built. It did so because it questioned the grounds on which exclusion was justified, and because Wilkes and his supporters were adamant in their insistence that political power emanated from the *people*, and not from the oligarchical House of Commons. Indeed Wilkes extended this principle into metropolitan politics. When he stood as the Aldermanic candidate in the Ward of Farringdon Without he enunciated a political creed that was equally applicable to the election of members of the national lower house. 'Mr Wilkes', his manifesto went,

does not wish to be CREATED Alderman of your Ward by the MANDATE of your Common Council: he hopes to be chosen by the free Voices of a Majority of that BODY, in whom the Law has vested the Right of Election. [There follows a description of how, in the past, the Alderman has been chosen at a private meeting of the Common Council]...they have but too often been successful in obtruding *their Decision*, in a Matter which ought to be determined by the general Sense of the WHOLE WARD. – Thus *your Stewards, your own Creatures*, have had the Insolence to create themselves into your DICTATORS! but you are ALL now awake to the calls of Liberty. And it is not doubted that the worthy Inhabitants of the Ward will unite with the *worthy Freeholders* of MIDDLESEX in manifesting their Detestation of CHAMBER ELECTIONS.
A Man who thus solicits a Seat in the court of Aldermen, is not likely to desert his Constituents...He abhors the Idea of an ARISTOCRACY. He will assert the Consequence of every Individual, and the Interest and Freedom of the Whole.[6]

This conception of politics, it almost goes without saying, was incompatible with a view of virtual representation as held by most politicians, and it very strongly reinforced the notion (accepted and openly canvassed by Wilkes) that politicians should be subject to instructions from their constituents. Political power was to emanate from below, not percolate down from above.

The final issue with which Wilkes was concerned in this period, that of the publication of parliamentary debates, reflects a similar attitude towards politics. His defence of the printers and publishers of parliamentary proceedings meant that although the lower House could still exclude strangers (including reporters) from their debates, they could no longer effectively prosecute those who succeeded in publishing accounts of their deliberations.[7] This was an important victory in principle as well as in practice. For again it exemplified an anti-aristocratic, anti-oligarchical conception of politics which emphasised the importance of the accountability of the people's representatives to their public, and underlined the necessity for open political discussion.[8]

All three of these issues were very much the personal creation of Wilkes himself. How, then, did he manage to achieve such extraordinary notoriety, and what was the key to his success? It is tempting, in view of the crowd activity that surrounds his career, to look on Wilkes as a mob orator. But, as Horace Walpole remarked,[9] he was a very poor public speaker. His public pronouncements, such as his famous speech in Westminster Hall on 6 May 1763,[10] were always carefully prepared, and when he spoke extemporaneously he fumbled over his words. He never made his mark as a parliamentary debater, nor did he ever exert the kind of rhetorical power over large audiences that men who subsequently cast themselves in his mould – one thinks of Burdett and Orator Hunt – achieved in their long perorations in favour of parliamentary reform.

Rather, the popularity and political support that Wilkes won was gained through the power of the pen. There is, indeed, no clearer indication of the organisation, potency and sophistication of the press in the 1760s than its paramount importance in Wilkes's career. Wilkes was a propagandist whose skills fell little short of genius: he knew the value of publicity; he judged exactly how to make his public appeal; and, to ensure as wide an audience as was possible, he exploited every available political medium.

Wilkes used publicity in two main ways: to counteract the very considerable powers of constituted authority, and to keep his own political pot constantly on the boil. The former tactic was one which he used from the first. Immediately after he had been arrested on a general warrant in April 1763, arraigned before the Secretaries of State and imprisoned in the Tower, Wilkes went onto the attack. He published an account of the events of his arrest, his accusations against those who had confined him and, in what was considered an appalling breach of political etiquette, had the correspondence between the Secretaries of State and himself printed on a flysheet and dispersed throughout London.[11] By creating a major public issue out of a fairly commonplace occurrence, namely the arrest of a putative libeller, Wilkes transformed what was essentially a minor political feud into a matter of general concern. He quickly defined not only the terms of the dispute but the context of the debate, one in which the public was perforce to be involved. This recruitment of popular support was deliberate and self-conscious; it sought to mobilise opinion as a counterweight to the powerful forces of administration. Wilkes knew perfectly well that as long as he could keep his cause in the public eye, out in the political market-place and away from the smoke-filled rooms of Westminster and St James's he stood a chance of survival, even of success.

Wilkes had, therefore, to sustain interest in his cause, and the only means that he had at his disposal to achieve this was the press. When he wanted to return from exile in 1768 he faced a difficult problem. In his absence interest in him had naturally waned. Two brief returns from exile in 1766 had failed to procure a pardon, or very much public support. The only tangible benefit was some surreptitious bribes from the Rockingham whigs to remove him from the sensitive political scene. Taking stock of his difficulties, Wilkes realised that he was defeating his own ends by trying to return to England as discreetly as possible. Only if he returned with a fanfare of publicity would he be able to extricate himself from his political and financial difficulties. He therefore set out to prepare the ground for his return by launching a private press campaign on his own behalf. His opening salvo, his *Letter to his Grace the Duke of Grafton*, was perhaps his most effective. It contained new and (characteristically for Wilkes) entertaining revelations about the general warrants affair, and castigated Chatham for his recent desertion from the patriot cause. The letter was so acerbic that Almon originally published it in what he called a 'castrated version'. This Wilkes followed by a series of newspaper letters, and a number of items that were published in Almon's *Political Register*; all of them strongly hinted at his impending return and candidacy at the forthcoming general election.[12]

Once again Wilkes had created a 'Wilkite' situation: one in which he was the centre of controversy and attention. His deliberately provocative journalism created the right climate for an end to his self-imposed exile, and provided the perfect prologue for an equally well-publicised return.

In a similar manner Wilkes succeeded in sustaining a high level of interest during the Middlesex election. Throughout this protracted affair he kept his followers informed of every turn of events, as well as urging them to continue their support of his cause, through a constant stream of printed addresses. These were ostensibly for circulation within his constituency, and were addressed to 'The Gentlemen, Clergy and Freeholders of the County of Middlesex'.[13] Addresses in this form were not, of course, uncommon eighteenth-century electoral practice. But Wilkes had more than this audience in mind. While henchmen distributed them in handbill form through the streets of London and the lanes of Middlesex, they were also reprinted in almost every metropolitan and provincial newspaper, as well as being issued in book form.[14] Appearing with increasing frequency – eight were issued between March and December 1768, and in the first four months of 1769 no fewer than ten were printed – they reached a national audience. As a result of Wilkes's propagandist efforts there was absolutely no reason why those from every part of the country, who were politically interested, should not have had a working knowledge of the issues raised by the Middlesex election. Indeed for many the Middlesex election was a newspaper phenomenon. Wilkes's published writings helped first to create, and then to sustain his cause.

A further crucial element in Wilkes's success as a propagandist was the way in which he expressed his appeal to the public. Only Junius matched his unerring polemical accuracy and rhetorical skill. In the early days of the *North Briton* Wilkes concentrated on arousing chauvinist, anti-Scottish feeling, on maligning the personalities of the chief actors in politics, and on sustaining a high level of irreverent invective and effortless sarcasm.[15] As he himself put it: 'no political paper, tho' writ in the most masterly manner, wou'd be relish'd by the public, unless well season'd with personal satire'.[16] But as Wilkes came to reap the none-too-palatable fruits of his attack on government, personal satire was superseded by increasingly frequent appeals to lofty general principles. He was especially concerned to dispel the notion that his quarrel with the government was a question of 'Wilkes versus the administration'. This conflict was not *personal*, he argued, but a clash between the forces guarding liberty and those working in favour of arbitrary power. Wilkes's speech in the Court of Common Pleas on 6 May 1763 marked the first rehearsal of what was subsequently to become a very familiar theme:

The LIBERTY of all peers and gentlemen, and, what touches me more sensibly, of all the middling and inferior class of the people, which stands most in need of protection, is in my case this day to be finally decided upon: a question of such importance as to determine at once, whether ENGLISH LIBERTY be a reality or a shadow.[17]

These words were not idly chosen: they were to reappear on Wilkite handbills which laid special emphasis on the liberties of *ordinary people*. Appropriately enough it was on the occasion of this speech that the battle-cry 'Wilkes and Liberty' was first publicly heard.

Wilkes never feared that his followers would tire of this theme. He remorselessly reiterated his determination to fight to the very last on the side of law and liberty. This view dominated his Addresses during the Middlesex election, and was the first subject he pronounced upon when he was released from the King's Bench prison in April 1770. 'I will go on', he boldly declared, 'with the same spirit, in the cause of a brave and free people. To this service, to the defence of laws, and to the preservation of the religious and civil liberties of the whole British empire, the remainder of my life shall be dedicated.'[18]

This uncharacteristically pompous utterance naturally invites a certain amount of scepticism. After all, the ideological nature of Wilkes's appeal was scarcely novel. A call to defend the ancient liberties enjoyed by every British citizen had been employed in such previous agitations as those against Walpole's Excise, the Gin Act of 1736, the Jewish Naturalisation Bill of 1753 and Bute's Cider Tax. It would be not altogether unfair to call the argument an opposition cliché. Wherein, therefore, lay Wilkes's special appeal and his novelty?

It lay first of all in the way in which he so closely associated his own person with the abstract notion of liberty. As John Almon put it, 'the words Wilkes and Liberty became synonymous terms'.[19] The abstract and, to most of the public, somewhat vague concept of liberty acquired both specificity and meaning in the person of John Wilkes. He became the emblem of liberty or, at least, its personification. This is particularly noticeable in the broadsides and cartoons which appeared on his behalf. Britannia, with her staff of maintenance and cap of liberty, was given a secondary place to the portrait of the patriot hero himself.

Placed in the foreground, Wilkes's dapper if rather ugly figure was often schematically and antithetically contrasted with those of his opponents. A typical example was the broadside *Arms of Liberty and Slavery* (see pp. ii–iii). (The engraving on this single sheet was also produced as a transfer and put on the side of punch-bowls.) It consists of two coats of arms. The first shows Wilkes, complete with lion passant, cap of liberty and cornucopia; the second portrays Lord Mansfield (though the figure could just as easily have been Lord Bute), surrounded by a serpent, and a garniture that includes chains, a hydra, thorns and Scottish thistles.[20] In almost every Wilkite cartoon, broadside and ballad, the person of Wilkes was designed to epitomise a political order based on the principle of liberty and devoted to the removal of all forms of arbitrary oppression. There is no doubt that this association made the political issues involved that much more *tangible* and *intelligible* to the public. 'Personal' politics could be used just as effectively to open up political issues as to contain them.

The association of the person of Wilkes with the notion of liberty highlights the second way in which he developed his approach to the public. Throughout his contentious career Wilkes emphasised that his quarrel with the government was a matter of the ordinary, honest citizen struggling with the ever-increasing powers of the Crown and its servants. His dilemma was everyone's problem; the misfortunes that he suffered could be inflicted upon anyone. In this way he associated

himself with 'the middling and inferior class of people',[21] attempting
to dissolve the barriers or distinctions that might have existed between
him and his constituents or followers. Thus, when Justice Pratt
released him in 1763 because of his parliamentary privilege, Wilkes
claimed that he should have been freed because the general warrant
was illegal and a violation of subjects' rights. He did not wish to plead
parliamentary privilege, but to rest his case on the liberty enjoyed by
every British subject.[22]

Such tactics were highly effective. Here was a man of political
consequence talking to his constituents and the public at large in a way
that implied that their opinions mattered. His appeal was totally
without condescension and was therefore extremely flattering. It is
instructive, in this context, to contrast Wilkes's Addresses with those
of Sir Beauchamp Proctor, the unsuccessful candidate for Middlesex
in 1768. Proctor's statements creak under the burden of a ponderous
paternalism. Such propaganda squibs as his letter from 'A Freeholder
of Wapping' portray the humble as forelock-tugging simpletons of
embarrassing worthiness and malleability.[23] Nothing could be further
from Wilkes's freeholder who was eulogised as politically sophisticated,
well-informed and independent. The simple tactic of attributing
to one's followers the most rudimentary political virtues inevitably
engaged many to the Wilkite cause.

The success of this strategy is well illustrated by the way in which
Wilkes was discussed by artisans and publicans in the city of London's
taverns,[24] and by the familiarity with which his humble correspondents
addressed him. A young girl from Durham, a Norfolk draper, and
a farmer from Lincolnshire all wrote to him in the most familiar terms
while affirming their support for his cause.[25] A Manchester merchant
with whom he was not acquainted felt quite at ease in asking him to
spend the summer at his house after he was released from the King's
Bench prison.[26] There is no evidence to show that any of Wilkes's
supporters felt that their leader was a remote or aloof figure; as a
friend to liberty he was also a friend of theirs – someone for whom
they had a natural and heartfelt sympathy.

Moreover, by emphasising that he was no different from his supporters, Wilkes encouraged his followers to think of themselves not
only as the defenders of liberty and the persecuted, but as participating
vicariously in his well-publicised nose-thumbing antics against the
government and civil authority. Wilkes's appeal was such that, when
he mocked constituted authority, outwitted officials, and brazened his
way to success, every Middlesex elector, disgruntled city merchant, or
provincial newsreader could share in the real pleasure of asserting his
personal integrity and political independence. Wilkes, of course,

invited and encouraged this vicarious pleasure; indeed, it was an important part of his appeal to the electors of the Ward of Farringdon Without in the Aldermanic election of 1769.[27] He knew perfectly well that it was a vital part of his popular appeal, and one that distinguished him from others who had solicited public support, that he was not simply the passive victim of authority that he portrayed himself to be, but the mischievous, belligerent scourge of all those who presumed to stand for overweaning power. This was why Wilkes himself, Wilkes as a prince of misrule, was personally so important to the Wilkite movement. A more sober politician, even one who held similar or more radical views, could only have failed where Wilkes sailed to success. It was an intrinsic part of his appeal – and one that clearly infuriated such ideological fellow-travellers as Alderman Beckford – that he was a wit, a rake and a man of extraordinary boldness and unbounded temerity. No doubt he was helped by the fact that when he returned to England he was an outlaw: he had nothing to lose, and having failed (in the phrase of the day) to fling himself at the feet of the king, he could risk the heroic gesture, and fling himself at the feet of a delighted public.

If the uncommitted were not won over by these tactics they might have been attracted to Wilkes for a further reason. His cause, Wilkes maintained, was the cause of every honest citizen. It therefore followed that all who felt for persecuted liberty ought to act as her defenders. They had a responsibility to participate in the battle with corruption and arbitrary power. For this reason Wilkes solicited, exhorted and endorsed, as no other contemporary politician had done, the active involvement of his supporters in his cause. He was constantly at pains to emphasise that responsibility for the success or failure of the movement lay, not merely with him, but with his followers. They stood at the centre of the political stage: 'In proving yourselves enemies to ministerial persecution, the eyes of the whole world are upon you, as the first and firmest defenders of public liberty.'[28] Wilkes thrust the initiative into his supporters' hands, maintaining that, 'my steady purpose is to concert with you, and other true friends of this country... I hold myself accountable to you for every action of my life, which respects the public.'[29] One politician, at least, seemed to recognise that power emanated from the people.

The tone and tenor of Wilkes's appeal, what Almon called his 'singular merit of writing to, and for, the people',[30] was amplified by his and his allies' extraordinary skill in producing propaganda in almost every shape, form and size. Pamphlets, periodicals, newspaper letters, handbills, ballads, verses and political cartoons were all marshalled in the Wilkite cause.[31] There was a superabundance of material and, though much of it may be regarded as printed ephemera, its impact, while short-lived, was powerful. Moreover, if Wilkites missed specific items, they could always obtain them subsequently in the many collected editions of Wilkes's life and works which the patriot produced himself, usually prefacing them (such was his modesty) with a laudatory account of his own virtues.[32]

This material is not only remarkable for its sheer volume, but for the way in which it was carefully tailored to appeal to widely differing audiences. In Wilkite propaganda we can observe a deliberate, self-conscious attempt to capture the attentions of the humble as well as the middling-sort-of-people, the poor purchaser of chapbooks as well as the prosperous bookbuyer. Wilkes's collected works are a case in point. Some editions, such as the two-volume folio *English Liberty* that Isaac Hitchcock of Stafford so painstakingly annotated, were both highly elaborate and expensively printed, priced well beyond the pocket of the humble reader.[33] But Wilkes's works also appeared in a much smaller octavo edition, also entitled *English Liberty*, which was distributed as a serial publication. This two-volume work was a highly organised commercial enterprise. Each part of the book could be purchased, a few pages at a time, for a price that was certainly no higher than a halfpenny, and may have been less. The first volume was divided, appropriately enough, into forty-five such sections, which could be bought throughout the country as they were circulated with the London tri-weekly papers. Purchasers were encouraged to continue their subscriptions until the final issue by the offer of a free engraving of John Wilkes in the last number. They could also obtain back numbers by ordering them from their local hawker. Complete sets of the 378 pages of volume one, stitched in blue paper, were also available at the cut price of 1s. 6d.[34] A similar octavo serial publication, 522 pages in length, was produced in Birmingham. It used the type of John Baskerville, the famous japanner, printer, free-thinker and personal friend of Wilkes.[35] Subscriptions could be taken up in London or in seventeen different locations in the Midlands.[36]

A similar variety of materials can be found in Wilkite handbills and single sheets. Some were black-letter, crudely produced and without subtlety or sophisticated ideological appeal. *No 45. A Comic Song* is a fairly typical example. It is a simple, mildly bawdy tale of an inhabitant of Spitalfields and his wife, whose sexual behaviour involves permutations on the number 45.[37] This is merely political entertainment. It is far removed from such single sheets as *English Liberty Established*, its companion broadside which begins with a ballad – *Number Forty-Five a New Ballad* – but which also incorporates several of Wilkes's speeches, or the elaborate italic version of one of Wilkes's Addresses.[38] All three of these sheets contain portraits of Wilkes which appear to have been produced by the same engraver. In the case of the italic address the portrayal is deliberately miniaturised so that 'the *Portrait of Mr. Wilkes*, cut round the circle', may serve 'for a Watch Paper'. As significant as the visual appeal of these sheets is their printed content. *English Liberty Established*, and *Number Forty-Five* both incorporate Wilkes's Address of 29 March 1768 and his speech in the court of King's Bench in April of that year. The former also contains an extract from Wilkes's *Letter to his Grace the Duke of Grafton*, together with his speech made in the court of Common Pleas in April 1763; the latter, by way of variation, includes his letter to the king asking for clemency, and also his speech to the livery of London after unsuccessfully contesting a City seat. A survey of the main incidents of Wilkes's career and the ideology underpinning the Wilkite movement were both encapsulated in these two broadsheets. *English Liberty Established*, according to its distributors, was 'Printed on fine Paper, fit for Framing'. They also claimed, in a fit of disingenuous magnanimity, that despite its advertised price of 6*d.*, it 'would not, according to the usual Custom of the Trade, be fixed at less than a Shilling, but the price is put low, so that every one who has a Regard for Mr. Wilkes may purchase it'.[39] It could be displayed in the home, or lent out to friends to scrutinize and admire.

One of the most successful pieces of Wilkite propaganda was a blasphemous rendition of the creed which went through at least nine editions in a single year, was published on both sides of the Atlantic, spawned a rather feeble imitation, and was still being sold and sung in the streets in 1770.[40] It is one of the best examples of the way in which Wilkite publications were adapted for different markets and to cater for audiences from every rank of society. The original work was an octavo piece, badly printed and only eight pages in length. Its format and the paper on which it was produced meant that it could easily have been mistaken for another of the chap-books with which the eighteenth century abounded. Such was the popularity of this *New Form of Prayer and Thanksgiving for the Happy Deliverance of John Wilkes, Esq.* that quarto and folio editions soon appeared, printed and priced to amuse a much more affluent audience. Wilkes's marketing techniques, in other words, would have excited the admiration of Josiah Wedgwood.

Quite apart from the skilful way in which materials were designed for specific audiences and markets, Wilkites made full use of all the available channels of political communication. Such a policy benefited both Wilkes's cause and the pockets of the newsmen. There were strong commercial as well as political reasons for developing close cooperation between radicals and the gentlemen of the press. Wilkes himself, of course, was the friend of many of London's leading pressmen, including John Almon, John Williams, Roger Thompson of the *Gazetteer*, Cuthbert Shaw of the *Middlesex Journal*, and Woodfall of the *Public Advertiser*.[41] Familiar with the complex infrastructure of the press, personally known to its devils and printers, it was not difficult for him to construct an elaborate web of Wilkite propaganda. He would insert items in magazines, have handbills republished in a format appropriate to journals, *précis* pamphlets and prepare copy for the newspapers.[42] Although this produced a great deal of duplication, it also ensured that the available market was saturated with Wilkite products. In this way Wilkes and his followers engaged in a process which constituted, in effect, a commercialisation of politics. No technique could have been more appropriate. In attempting to give the urban and commercial classes a more central place in the political arena (and thereby reinforcing their own political position), the Wilkites were using techniques that they had learnt from precisely those groups which they sought to emancipate. To a very large extent this helps us explain Wilkes's success. By using commercial techniques he was able to open up a national market for his propaganda, and to make his cause a national issue.

To some extent this is a contentious assertion. Even George Rudé, who has done more than any other modern historian to locate the different pockets of Wilkite support, is cautious about the extent of Wilkes's following.[43] But it seems to me perfectly clear that the phenomenon of Wilkes was one of nationwide scope. And if this can be shown to be true, then it can be maintained with equal validity that the (admittedly traditional) issues with which he was associated also received a national airing for, as we have already seen, the person of Wilkes and the cause of liberty were virtually indistinguishable. In fact three sorts of evidence point strongly to national interest in and enthusiasm for Wilkes. They are the preoccupation of the provincial press with Wilkes, the disparate locations from which he received presents during his confinement in the King's Bench prison, and the ubiquitous celebrations in April 1770 when he was released. (See map.)

Prior to the 1760s there had often not been much in the way of political comment and even political information in the local press. Such information as there was usually consisted of such 'safe' items as diplomatic, foreign and military intelligence culled from that unimpeachable source, the official *London Gazette*. Besides, there were good reasons why a provincial editor fought shy of explicit political comment. His paper was usually highly dependent upon advertising revenue (indeed, it often *was* an advertiser) and could ill afford to

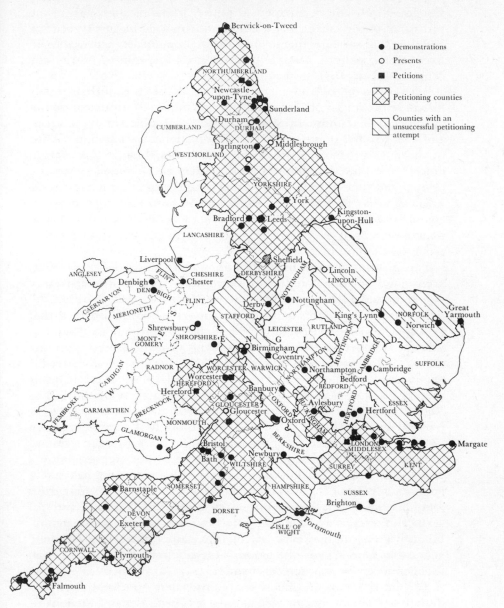

Support for John Wilkes 1768–71.

alienate potential or actual customers. If he took up a particular political stance he might encourage a party rival in a town capable of sustaining only one newspaper. Moreover, the delicate health of the provincial paper meant that it could not run the risk of prosecution and the expensive fines that so often dogged a politically active editor.[44] Even when politics obtruded, therefore, the editors were self-consciously impartial.[45]

But politics did obtrude. The rebellion of 1745 meant that for the first time provincial papers could provide important information not available to the London press. The South Sea Bubble, the excise crisis, and the Jew Bill of 1753, all created a demand for comment. Most of those who produced provincial papers ran them as commercial enterprises; they were businessmen, traders and booksellers seeking to augment their profits.[46] They now found that it no longer made financial sense to exclude political opinion, and they turned to the columns of London papers for information and comment. Trade papers such as *Williamson's Liverpool Advertiser* began to steal essays from the London press.[47]

This growing interest in politics on the part of the local press was accelerated by Wilkes. Indeed this criterion – a far more satisfactory one than the formal, institutional yardstick of election results[48] – demonstrates the degree of penetration into the English provinces that Wilkes achieved. I have yet to find a single provincial newspaper that was not crammed with information about the patriot hero. His life, details of the various Middlesex elections, personal anecdotes, his expulsions from the House of Commons, the legal issues raised by his career, his speeches, the activities of the Supporters of the Bill of Rights, all appear in the columns of the provincial papers devoted to political information. The newspaper editors took comments from London papers, wrote letters themselves, or published the opinions of their correspondents. The issues of parliamentary representation, political corruption, and even that of the ballot were all rehearsed in considerable detail,[49] just as they were discussed by the debating clubs and societies of the larger provincial towns. Such a high level of political interest may have been a passing or transient phenomenon, but its presence in the years 1768 to 1770 cannot be doubted. In these years, thanks to Wilkes, the organs of local opinion acted both in an independent, and in a radical manner.

The information and comment conveyed in the local press was doubtless partially responsible for the exuberant manifestations of Wilkite support throughout the country. One of the favourite forms that this assumed was the sending of presents to the great protector of liberty during his confinement in the King's Bench prison. The inhabitants of Plymouth, Newcastle and Gloucester sent him salmon, one of which was reputed to have weighed 45 lb.[50] Some of the citizens of Norwich gave him 45 lb of tea, and kept him supplied with turkeys.[51] Richmond in Yorkshire donated a barrel of strong beer; friends from Shrewsbury sent brawn; and Stockton, making many of the other generous gifts seem paltry, presented Wilkes with forty-five hams, forty-five tongues, and forty-five dozen of ale.[52] One, Captain Cole of Dartmouth, presented Wilkes with a 45 lb Cheshire cheese, and a hogshead of Devonshire cider.[53] Articles of clothing were sent as well as food. A Durham girl whose father led a local Wilkite club sent him ruffles (which doubtless pandered to the patriot's vanity); Birmingham manufacturers, in turn, contributed '100 Groce [sic] of Coat and Waistcoat Buttons, most elegantly edged and silvered with an Olive Branch in the Center; with Directions to distribute them amongst the Sons of Liberty'.[54] Another Midlands present was a gift of 45 gross of clay pipes presented by the gentlemen of Broseley.[55]

Not all the presents were so magnificent. A Lincolnshire gentleman sent Wilkes a dozen teal, and a humble Norfolk draper could only afford a single hare.[56] But the value of the gifts accumulated. Donations from abroad contributed their share. The South Carolina lower House, in what was to prove a highly controversial decision in the coming years, voted to donate £1500 sterling to the Society of Supporters of the Bill of Rights.[57] Boston's Sons of Liberty sent turtles to Wilkes, and a group of Maryland planters contributed forty-five hogsheads of tobacco.[58] An admirer from Hamburg even enclosed forty-five bottles of stone wine.[59] One newspaper estimated that by November 1769 Wilkes had received more than seven thousand pounds' worth of gifts.[60]

Wilkes's gifts were conveyed with remarkably little self-consciousness, and with an intimacy that strongly underscores the success of his *personal* propaganda campaign. Donors clearly felt like friends and, by implication, equals. Of course they may have had less exalted motives. It might well have been true that, in Goldsmith's words, 'They give to get esteem'.[61] The press was assiduous in its reporting of Wilkite donations and a gift almost guaranteed publicity. (In this way the attention paid by the newspapers to Wilkes's presents encouraged and stimulated the munificence of Wilkite supporters.) At the same time the symbolic import of the presents was obviously considerable. No doubt the many gastronomic delights that Wilkes received pleased him greatly, but it can hardly be said that they were vital to his sustenance. Rather, as the many puns and plays on the number 45 further emphasise, their donation symbolised the solidarity that

Wilkes's supporters felt with him: they were a token of their esteem, and an act of commitment to the cause of 'Wilkes and Liberty'.

There were of course other ways in which Wilkites could manifest their support for the cause. Public demonstrations, for instance, were both frequent and widespread. In November 1768 there was public rejoicing on Wilkes's birthday not only in London, but in Hertford, Ware and Nottingham.[62] But undoubtedly the most important occasion on which such demonstrations occurred was in April 1770 when Wilkes was released from the King's Bench prison. (It was rumoured that he left at exactly 5.45 in the afternoon.)[63] The prisoners of Newgate lit up their windows in Wilkes's honour, and the papers commented on how in the City 'Many Courts, Lanes and Alleys were illuminated...as well as the Principal Streets, which is quite unusual.'[64] The humble, poor, and those without status or liberty were paying their respects to their hero. The environs of London soon caught the festive spirit. Brentford and Isleworth, both Wilkite strongholds, and the inhabitants of Kingston, Hampton and Greenwich all arranged lavish demonstrations.[65] In the last town

several select pieces of music were performed in the principal streets for about an hour, the town was greatly illuminated, particularly the Greyhound Inn, which was lighted with upwards of 300 wax tapers, displaying the words *Wilkes and Liberty*; in the market place, a grand fire work was displayed, sky rockets were thrown up every 45 seconds from nine to ten o'clock, and 45 pieces of artillery discharged.[66]

Soon the celebrations spread to Great Marlow and East Grinstead.[67] Other demonstrations were held in the south-east at Redbourne in Hertfordshire, and at Rochester, Chatham, Brompton, Sheerness and Queenborough.[68] The towns of Whitney, Portsmouth, Gosport and Bristol either illuminated their streets or held banquets.[69] Similar celebrations were held in Stroud, Fairford (Gloucestershire), Bath, Castle Cary, Bradford (Somerset), Sherborne, Honiton, Plymouth, Cerne (Dorset), Falmouth, Barnstaple, Liskeard, Penzance, St Michael's Mount, Probus, Banbury, and Bruton.[70] In Derby 'four sheep were roasted whole in the public streets and given to the populace', while at Tewkesbury the Abbey's bells were rung and guns fired.[71] Celebratory dinners were held in Birmingham, Bridgnorth and Worcester.[72] In Northampton a ball was held after a public concert, 'when 45 couples concluded the ball with the favourite country dance of Wilkes's wriggle'.[73] In Newcastle, after public feasting, a subscription was taken up to pay off Wilkes's debts, while across the Tyne at Gateshead a local pipe manufacturer distributed his wares as gifts at the four local Wilkite clubs.[74] Other demonstrations were held in Alnwick, Shields, Durham, Darlington, Bedale, Leeds, Hull, Sunderland, Morpeth, Bradford, Hexham, Tadcaster, Chester, Wakefield and Halifax.[75] At York there were windows illuminated by forty-five candles displaying the words 'no. 45, *Magna Charta* and *Bill of Rights*'.[76] The inhabitants of Yarmouth celebrated with a bonfire and fireworks. In King's Lynn and Swaffham in Norfolk bells were rung, forty-five cannon discharged, and local gentlemen provided entertainment. In the latter town the celebrations were completed when 'a JACK BOOT, filled with combustibles, after being suspended for some time upon a gibbet, was blown up amidst the universal acclamations of the populace'.[77] Textile workers in Norwich arranged their own distinctive demonstration:

At Noon a Company of Woolcombers preceded by a Band of Music, and 45 of them dressed in Holland Shirts, with Caps (representing the Cap of Liberty) made of Wool of various Colours on their Heads, walked in Procession thro' the Market and principal Streets of this City; they were joined by several Societies of Weavers, and behaved themselves in a quiet and decent Manner.[78]

North Americans in South Carolina and Boston celebrated in a similar fashion,[79] as did Englishmen in Rotterdam. The only untoward event on this day of national rejoicing was the ducking of an over-enthusiastic Wilkite who had chosen to celebrate the patriot's release in the town of Berwick-on-Tweed.[80]

All three of these extra-institutional sources of evidence – the local press, presents and demonstrations – help to show that the remarkable number of signatures achieved on the Wilkite petitions of 1769, 55,000 in all,[81] tends to underestimate rather than exaggerate Wilkite support. Besides, quite apart from the fifteen counties and dozen boroughs which actually presented petitions, there were many other localities which went some way towards drawing up a petition or collecting signatures. Inevitably the issues involved over Wilkes and the Middlesex elections were discussed on these occasions. In Lincolnshire, Norfolk, Northamptonshire, Hampshire, Oxfordshire, Kent, Essex, Warwick and Staffordshire petitions were mooted, and some action taken.[82] Frequently, as in Essex, those who were eager in the Wilkite cause were unable to overcome the power of local men who supported government. But the fact that Wilkite sentiment did not eventually manifest itself in the form of a petition does not mean that it was not there at all.

Indeed, there can be very little doubt that in the years 1768 to 1770 a very high level of political interest was being shown not only in Britain's capital, but in its provinces. In these years were planted the seeds of a political sensibility that was to flower in the 1780s and 1790s, manifesting itself in strains of thought that were both anti-aristocratic and reformist. Doubtless the period of political quiescence before and during the early years of the American war can convey the impression that such ideas lacked support outside the metropolis. But this was not the case.

Admittedly a distinction has to be drawn between two separate sources of Wilkite support. The country-gentlemen, those who approximated to the bucolic Squire Western, Squire Bramble stereotype, found that there was much about Wilkes that they could not stomach. They looked askance at his personal licentiousness, and feared the radicalism of the Supporters of the Bill of Rights. They wanted to fit Wilkes and his followers into the classical republican framework of traditional country-party ideology. These men could not sit comfortably with the shopkeepers, tavern proprietors, wine-merchants, free-thinkers, booksellers, and budding entrepreneurs who were to be found in small, but ever-expanding groups in almost every market-town in the country,[83] and in large numbers in the metropolis. This urban element instinctively understood Wilkes's special, commercial brand of politics; they also knew that it would be the way for them to win political power. Both groups worked together in the heat of political crisis, just as they cooperated with the aristos for whom they had so little respect. All three interests could unite behind the traditional cry of 'the constitution, and liberty in danger' but, as the ramifications of the Wilkes affair extended, so Wilkite support waned. The Parliamentary politicians and the country element were not prepared to go beyond traditional diagnoses and traditional panaceas. They disliked Wilkes's political style, and loathed his supporters' radical ideology. In the towns support for Wilkes persisted, but those who thought they had got their foot in the door that opened into institutionalised politics were to be disappointed. The allies that they needed left them. This meant that radicalism lost its focus, its capacity to impinge directly upon the institutionalised political process; but its informal manifestations persisted.

Although greater attention needs to be paid to the provincial supporters of Wilkes, there is no doubt that the bulk of his support came from the metropolis. Here overt acts of Wilkite solidarity were most conspicuous. From 1768 to 1771 there were frequent manifestations of crowd support for Wilkes which assumed a variety of forms. Much of this behaviour has been scrutinised by George Rudé, and one hesitates to invade territory that has been so ably and so thoroughly investigated. But Rudé's prime concern in examining Wilkite crowds was to ascertain the social origins and status of their participants. (One can see that he wished to show that the members of the 'mob' were not the despised members of the lumpenproletariat, but respectable wage-earners and working men.)[84] In doing so he tended, however, to simplify the actual *forms* of crowd behaviour, and neglected to examine what exactly the crowd was *doing*. This has led him to omit discussion of what Natalie Zemon Davis has called the 'social meaning' of Wilkite collective behaviour.[85] But the question, 'what is the crowd doing?', is especially pertinent in the case of the Wilkites.

Rudé emphasises, indeed claims as typical the crowd which consists of 'itinerant bands, marching (or running) through Shoreditch, the City of London, Westminster, or Southwark, getting fresh forces on the way' but composed of 'local men who were perfectly recognizable to publicans and other local witnesses'.[86] No one would deny that such crowd activity took place, especially in the two days after the first occasion on which Wilkes was elected for Middlesex: windows were certainly smashed; citizens were forced to illuminate their houses. But there were also a great many other occasions, more appropriately described as demonstrations than riots, which were either organised by the electoral supporters of Wilkes and took place on the three different occasions on which the county of Middlesex re-elected him; or were held under the aegis of one of the London trades – chimney-sweeps were particularly active in this sphere;[87] or were organised around the many tavern clubs, societies and masonic lodges that were a central part of the city's flourishing social life. A typical demonstration of this sort occurred in April 1769 on the third occasion of Wilkes's re-election at Brentford. Three parties of Wilkites from different parts of the city converged on the county town:

At a little after ten o'clock 200 of Mr. Wilkes's friends, preceded by music, and a flag with the words – FREEDOM. LIBERTY! entered Brentford. This procession was closed by Mr. John Swan, carrying a white wand. Five minutes after this came a coach and six, the horses sumptuously adorned with blue ribbons; and persons were on the roof, bearing flags, inscribed BILL OF RIGHTS. MAGNA CHARTA. At half past ten 300 sons of liberty entered Brentford on horseback, preceded by six French horns, and four silk flags, with the above inscription in letters of gold... Many ladies (freeholders) were among the friends of freedom, and [were] distinguished by breastknots of blue and silver, with the motto abovementioned.[88]

These demonstrations were not confined to the capital. Crisp Moly-neux and Thomas Walpole, Supporters of the Bill of Rights, together with one Mr James Fysh, 'an eminent wine merchant', seem to have been chiefly responsible for the extremely elaborate illuminations, ceremonials and bellringing that occurred in King's Lynn to celebrate the reversal of Wilkes's outlawry.[89]

All of these demonstrations are characterised by a wealth of cere-monial and ritualised behaviour, as well as by the overt employment of a variety of political symbols.[90] It is to these rites that I wish to devote particular attention. Perhaps this needs some justification. The forms and shape, symbol and ritual of social protest are, after all, very frequently either neglected, or condensed (in a rather vulgar, reductionist way) to particular manifestations of economic discontent.[91] Yet they are precisely the clues that enable us to decode what is happening when protest occurs. As Hobsbawm has remarked, 'in primitive movements, as in Gothic cathedrals, an entire universe of symbolism and allegory may exist, each piece corresponding to, and indeed 'being', a specific piece small or large, of the entire ideology and movement'.[92] Ritual and symbol, in other words, are the crowd's 'belief system' made concrete.

This realisation was not lost on those in authority. They were peculiarly obsessed (the term is not, I think, an exaggeration) by acts of protest or dissent which were most conspicuously symbolic in form, or by the symbols of protest themselves. This is well illustrated by the treatment, for example, of the rebel standards captured after the Battle of Culloden. Normally an enemy's flags were an object of respect, but the Jacobite standards were carried by the chief hangman of Edinburgh and by chimney-sweeps, laid in the dust, and then consigned to fire.[93] This was ritual humiliation and symbolic contempt.

Magistrates in the 1760s adopted a similar attitude to the symbols of Wilkite protest and of industrial unrest. By far the most savage sentence meted out to a Wilkite political demonstrator was that of two years' imprisonment, imposed on John Percival, a pewterer. This was not for assault, or inflicting damage on property; it was for marking a magistrate with the number 45.[94] During the Mansion House riots of 9 May 1768 the Lord Mayor, Thomas Harley, was more concerned with seizing the crowd's gibbet with its boot and petticoat – the symbols of Bute and the Princess Dowager – than he was with quelling the riot. At one stage in the proceedings the scrimmage outside the Mansion House resolved itself into a tug-of-war between Wilkites and the Lord Mayor's servants for the possession of the offending object. On this occasion, at least, the forces of authority were victorious.[95] When London magistrates met in the Guildhall two days later they resolved to obtain the seizure of the striking sailors' and coalheavers' flags, banners and drums.[96] One is reminded that the Peterloo massacre was started by the order to the yeomanry of 'Have at their Flags', and that it was those who carried banners, placards and flags who suffered most at the hands of the military.[97]

Those who carried them were singled out for special treatment not because they were ringleaders (though they might have been), but because they were considered, with some justification, to be those whose actions were the most flagrant breach of constituted authority. This is not really so surprising. Every society is steeped in ritual, and every government or ruling group attempts the symbolic enforcement of order and authority.[98] Eighteenth-century England was no exception. Most subjects, especially the inhabitants of London who had the opportunity to observe such occasions personally, were familiar with the rituals of monarchy. Coronations, state openings of parliament, court levées and entertainments, royal birthdays and funerals all served to emphasise the special status of the Crown and its government. These public spectacles were invariably reported in the newspapers and magazines; no detail was omitted, nor any ritual overlooked. For these occasions each town planned its own special celebrations. In Newcastle, for instance, George III's coronation was commemorated in high fashion. There was a gun salute and a parade of local Volunteers. A city fountain was made to flow with wine; gentlemen threw money to the populace from the windows of coffee-houses, and the town was illuminated. A concert and a ball were held. The day's celebrations were completed when the Master and Brethren of Trinity-House burnt a boat on the river to the accompanying illumination of 200 candles.[99]

Similarly the working apparatus of the law was bedecked with symbolic paraphernalia: legal costume emphasising the different status of those privileged in the interpretation of the law, the other symbols of judicial authority, and the pageantry of the assize. The rites of punishment were no different. Tyburn fair (note the immediate festive connotations of its name) was a spectacle in its own right. The grizzly ritual accorded to traitors, the grinning heads festering on Temple Bar, and the concern of the government that unusual or especially heinous offenders (such as strikers) should be executed in a special locality, or near the scene of the crime, are all indicative of the awesome, exemplary scene that the theatre of the macabre was intended to set. In this way legal sanctions and moral disapproval were more intimately connected.

The rituals of government and of the law were complemented by many others. Every parishioner could witness ecclesiastical ritual; every borough had its civic ceremonial. The whole of society was marked, ordered and differentiated, yet held together by a complex set of symbols of status. As Adam Ferguson observed with his astute, sociological eye:

the object of every rank is precedency, and every order may display its advantages to their full extent. The sovereign himself owes a great part of his authority to the sounding titles and dazzling equipage which he exhibits in public. The subordinate ranks lay claim to importance by a like exhibition, and for that purpose carry in every instant the ensigns of their birth, or the ornaments of their fortune. What else could mark out to the individual the relation in which he stands to his fellow-subjects, or distinguish the numberless ranks that fill up the interval between the state of the sovereign and that of the peasant? Or what else could, in States of a great extent, preserve any appearance of order, among members disunited by ambition and interest, and destined to form a community, without the sense of any common concern?[100]

In a society such as this, dominant symbols and the rituals of authority obviously would be threatened by alternative rites – hence the marked reaction of those in power.

The confrontation between authority and protest is immediately apparent in one of the commonest modes of behaviour adopted by Wilkite crowds, namely one in which they took over the role of constituted authority. The participants in protest, in other words, set out by means of direct action to show (*demonstrate*) to the magistrate or civil authority how he ought to act if he were truly fulfilling the crowd's conception of his office and, *a fortiori*, the higher dictates of social morality. This will be a familiar mode of conduct to those acquainted with the activities of food crowds in eighteenth-century England and France. Just as bread and grain rioters took over the role of the assize of bread, the regulation of markets, or the *entrave* (preventing the removal of grain from the locality), so political demonstrations acted out their conception of the duties of the just judge.[101] Thus, on April Fool's day 1771, effigies of the Princess Dowager, Lord Bute, the Speaker of the House of Commons and the two Fox brothers were placed in two carts preceded by a hearse, and taken through the streets of London to the properly constituted execution place of all traitors, Tower Hill, where they were decapitated by a chimney-sweep who also doubled as the officiating minister; they were then ceremoniously burnt. A similar ceremony was carried out four days later with the effigies of Lord Halifax, Lord Barrington, Alderman Harley, Colonel Luttrell, Lord Sandwich, Colonel Onslow, and William De Grey, the Attorney General.[102] Here was ritual retribution on a parallel with that actually exacted during the Revolution in France. Notice how carefully the crowd observed the proper forms and customs of an official public execution: the ritual of authority became the rites of the mob. This imitation, a deliberate act of mimesis, was what gave meaning to their action.

Acting in the place of authority is just one instance of the Wilkite use of the ritual and symbols of authority. Other examples are to be found in the treatment accorded Wilkes by his followers. As I have already remarked, Wilkes was not a mob orator. The role he played in the crowd was, in fact, much more akin to that of a flag, a badge or a symbol. Dapperly dressed in his fancy waistcoat, dragged through the streets in his unharnessed coach, or huzzahed by the crowd as he stood on the balcony of a coffee house or at his prison window, he literally provided a rallying-point for his supporters on the streets. Wilkite propaganda, as we have seen, frequently portrayed Wilkes as a symbol of and synonym for liberty; the same phenomenon can be observed in the extraordinary number of artifacts that bore the image of his ungainly features. Thirty-one different engraved portraits, coffee and tea pots, spoons, jugs, figurines, snuff-boxes, pipes, tobacco papers, buttons, and twenty-six different coins and medals could all be purchased, used or displayed as an act of ideological solidarity with the squinting patriot hero.[103]

As the eponymous, symbolic head of the movement, Wilkes was accorded the highest honours possible. Plagiarising the distinctions employed by legitimate authority, his followers treated him as their monarch and ruler. London streets reverberated to the refrain, 'God save great Wilkes our King', and handbills were pasted on church walls and doors urging the clergy to pray not for the monarch but for the well-being of 'Wilkes and Liberty'.[104] The handbill hose removal from the walls of the King's Bench prison started the violence that ended in the St George's Fields massacre again reflects the crowd's assumption that, as far as they were concerned, Wilkes was their legitimate ruler:

> Venal judges & ministers combine
> Wilkes and Liberty to confine,
> Yet in true English hearts secure their fame is,
> Nor are such crowded levies at St. James's.
> While thus in Prison envy dooms their stay,
> Here, O grateful Britons, your daily homage pay.[105]

Royal and loyal toasts were drunk to him, as 'the King over the water' had been toasted in earlier days. His birthday, like that of the monarch, was the occasion for popular celebration and public rejoicing.[106] Just as the rulers, members of the royal family and 'loyal' popular heroes gave their name and figures to public houses, so Wilkites tried to name taverns after their leader. A publican at Rotherhithe had a licence refused for his intended 'Wilkes Head', though there seems to have been a tavern of that name in Shoreditch. There were also inns called the 'Wilkes Head' in Leek in Staffordshire, and in St Ives. In addition Wilkes, together with Horne Tooke and Glynn, was portrayed on the sign 'The Three Johns' based on Richard Houston's painting of the three heroes. Four London taverns were so named. Coats of arms ascribed to him and to John Glynn were also hung up at the Phoenix Tavern in Isleworth. No doubt this was an intentional reference to Wilkes's determination to be elected again and again.[107]

Just as the Wilkites took up and appropriated for their own use the distinctions and ranks of everyday society, so they employed the celebratory rituals of popular jubilation. Thus one of the favourite Wilkite devices was illumination, the lighting up of one's house in celebration of victory. This could be carried to extraordinary lengths. In April 1770 'a gentleman in the Strand' arranged an illumination which consisted of 'a transparent painting of a patriot, supported by Freedom and Britannia pointing to the Temple of Fame'.[108] Customarily, however, illumination simply consisted of lighting a few candles and displaying them in an unshuttered window. This tradition became a hallmark of Wilkite success. Just as it was usual to illuminate one's windows after a national military victory, or at the coronation, or on any day of national festivity,[109] so the Wilkites celebrated the victories of their hero. Thus, after the first Middlesex election, the crowds ran through the streets forcing householders to recognise Wilkes's triumph by lighting their houses, pushing innocent by-standers into a situation where their actions (if not their sentiments) condoned Wilkite rule.[110] Similarly Wilkes's release, as we have seen, was the occasion for the exhibition of all the paraphernalia of national victory: bonfires, illuminations, fireworks, music, gunshot salutes, the pealing of bells and general public festivity. There could scarcely have been more popular rejoicing at the time of Pitt's greatest victories during the Seven Years War.

All of the Wilkite rituals and ceremonies employed the only symbol that was more common than Wilkes himself, the number 45. In many ways it was the perfect symbol: simple to execute, recognisable even to the illiterate, it was rich with irony in view of its associations with Jacobitism and yet, by virtue of that fact, was also a badge of revolt. Amongst Wilkites it assumed an obsessive, almost magical or mystical significance. Chalked on every door from Temple Bar to Hyde Park, and found on almost every house from London to Southampton, it was blazoned on blue Wilkite cockades. The Patriotic Club in Newbury, Berkshire elected forty-five members; Nottingham's Sherwood Youths rang peals on the number 45 at their annual feast; a Wilkite publican hired the hackney coach no. 45 to attend the London City poll, and the number 45 was even chalked on the soles of the outraged Austrian ambassador's shoes.[111] The newspapers and the many joke-books that appeared on Wilkes's behalf were filled with tales involving humorous plays upon and references to the ubiquitous number. One of the mock lessons from the parody of the creed,

Britannia's Intercession, summed up the situation in its suitably pseudo-Biblical prose:

the people...made great noises together; and many got themselves chalk which was white, for to make a mark on every man, yea, and on every chariot that passed, thus, 45. And this mark was put upon the coverings of all the Wilkites, and Buteites, the Houseites, and Mobites, and of all the Commonites who passed this way or that way, in honour of their great idols Wilkes and Liberty.[112]

And in what was probably the most elaborate play on the number of all, chimney-sweeps in Brentford invited forty-five of their number, with forty-five attendants, to eat 45 lb of beef, 45 lb of ham (the latter stuck with a flag with the number 45 painted on it), together with forty-five pots of porter and 45 oz of bread.[113]

What purpose, what use did these symbols and rituals serve? First, and perhaps most obviously, they were a *demonstration* of political feeling. One cannot but be struck by the deliberate theatricality of much of the crowd's behaviour. Formalised conduct of the sort associated with rituals, and the frequent reappearance of a standard set of symbols indubitably served to heighten the element of spectacle. This sort of politics manifestly could not take place in a smoke-filled room; the more public, the more visually impressive the demonstration, the greater the possibility of raising support, and the higher the probability of those in authority taking notice of the crowd, if not its grievances.

Secondly, the employment of different rites and symbols served to *legitimate* much crowd activity. The use of the rituals of authority conferred upon the crowd's deeds a status that went beyond their mere instrumentality, imbuing them with legitimacy. When Wilkite crowds ceremonially 'executed' effigies of their political enemies, observers could recognise through the ritual that there was a socially appropriate role or function being performed, even if it was not being carried out by normal authority. Besides, eighteenth-century England was a society in which crowd behaviour as a regulatory mechanism, acting as both guardian and repository of the community conscience – perhaps punishing scolds or methodists, regulating prices, or closing bawdy houses – was frequently either openly condoned, tacitly approved, or surreptitiously winked at by those in authority.[114] Thus one source of legitimation – the powers that be, or were – sometimes reinforced a second source, that of popular or community sanction. This, in turn, had its traditional rites and ceremonies – illumination being an example – which could be appropriated by the crowd and used as a means of justification. Frequently these two sources of legitimation were polar opposites, or represented conflicting ideologies, but they might also exist in uneasy apposition, or in a position of mutual reinforcement. Whatever the case, rituals from both were employed by Wilkites.

A third way in which rites were of consequence in crowd behaviour was as a means of *differentiation*. Here we must distinguish difference at two levels. There were a number of symbolic actions to be found in Wilkite crowds and during the industrial unrest that surrounded them which can be regarded as virtually universal signs of the peculiar and the special circumstances of the crowd situation. Turning one's coat inside out, blackening faces, wearing eccentric apparel, dressing in a way inappropriate to your social group or in the clothing of the opposite sex are all not only a fairly effective means of disguise, but an indication, found in almost all crowds, of the peculiar circumstances of collective protest, one in which many customary social rules and conventions cease to apply.[115] To anthropologists these are familiar, so-called liminal figures: those who have ceased, in peculiar circumstances, to be quite what they were, but who are socially transient, not having yet acquired a new status, role or identity separate from the existing social order from which they are temporarily displaced or parted.[116]

These symbols of separation have to be distinguished from the blue cockades and favours, and the number 45 itself which served to differentiate those who accepted and supported Wilkes from those who stood on the side of authority. These signs are specifically, historically located, and served a number of related functions. They were also symbols of *solidarity and identity*. To sport a blue favour, chalk 45 on a chariot, wear Wilkite buttons, or purchase a Wilkite mug was in itself an act of political commitment, though admittedly not necessarily of a particularly consequential kind. To perform such acts was, nevertheless, to announce one's allegiance to an alternative Wilkite moral order, one which emphasised liberty and independence, and rejected tyranny and over-weaning authority. Even the imitation of the rituals of authority was in some sense an act of differentiation. There was always an element of parody on those occasions which meant, paradoxically, that the rites were insulting as well as obliquely affirmatory of the existing order.

When employed by the crowd symbols of differentiation were frequently also acts of symbolic *appropriation*. Elias Canetti has remarked on the way in which the crowd occupies and seizes both individuals, objects and space.[117] Symbols record this acquisition. To mark oneself, a piece of property such as a coach or dwelling, or another person, with the all-important number 45 was to initiate a process by which property and persons were removed from one realm (the term is deliberately chosen) to another. Thus we find Wilkites mapping out their territory, marking their routes from the City of London to Brentford. In a similar way a Wilkite seized a magistrate by the collar and cried, '"Damn you, I'll mark you"; and accordingly he did mark him with large figures no. 45 on the cape of his Coat'.[118] It was as if the rioter believed that, in some magical way, the power of the magistrate would be destroyed or dispelled by the badge of Wilkite authority.

This process of acquisition can also be seen in the many jokes that were retailed in the newspapers, periodicals and special joke-books that were full of puns, anecdotes and anti-authoritarian sallies of wit. Time and again jokes were told in which an opponent of the Wilkite regime unwittingly contributed to, or created a Wilkite situation. We are told how Lord Sandwich, 'Jemmy Twitcher', attending a meeting of the elder Brethren of Trinity-House, Deptford, was the forty-fifth person to arrive, and was suitably discomfited by having contributed to the Wilkite jest. A man in a tavern curses Wilkes; on the forty-fifth occasion he is brought to book by Wilkites drinking there.[119] These and analogous stories were considered amusing because they were occasions on which the process of transference from constituted to Wilkite order was achieved through the offices of one who was a firm supporter of established authority.

A final function of the symbols and rituals of the Wilkite crowd was that of facilitating *organisation* and good order. The rites of authority and popular tradition did not have to be learnt; they were an indigenous part of the nation's political culture. The Wilkites who helped decapitate effigies on Tower Hill might well have been present at Lord Lovat's demise; the guests at the elaborate Wilkite feasts that were held on the streets or in London's taverns could model their ceremonial on the annual Lord Mayor's Banquet; the men who led a child dressed as Liberty through the streets of the city could copy the insignia portrayed in almost every Wilkite cartoon.[120] Though they might develop rituals based on the number 45 which had no outside source of origin, there was no need for them to do so. There were an abundance of readily available practices sanctioned by both tradition and authority.

Although – and I have been at pains to emphasise this – Wilkite crowd behaviour was orderly and very rich in its forms of expression, it nevertheless seems to betray relative ideological immaturity. It is true that many in the crowds outside the Mansion House in March 1770 had tickets in their hats with the motto, 'Annual Parliaments. Equal Representation. Place and Pension Bill';[121] but on the whole there is very little evidence to show that the street supporters of Wilkes – as opposed to the determined body of more affluent radicals who were eventually to split the Supporters of the Bill of Rights – went any further in their political beliefs than desiring the recovery and maintenance of traditional rights, defining what Edward Thompson has called 'the *limits* beyond which the Englishman was not prepared to be pushed around'.[122] And the movement – despite the occasional cry such as, 'No Wilkes. No King. . . This is the most glorious opportunity for a Revolution that ever offered',[123] was remarkably loyalist. Almost every Wilkite ballad maintained, in a way that we perhaps would regard as incongruous, the compatibility of ardent support for the Crown with allegiance to 'Wilkes and Liberty'.[124]

Indeed, what strikes one about the order of the Wilkite crowd is how, as an alternative 'order', it resembles disorder and misrule, rather than offering a competing value system. No doubt it was extremely disturbing, and was regarded so, to see the servant ignoring the influence of his master, the apprentice defying his employer, the humble rejecting the advice of the great; but so much Wilkite activity seems, to employ a distinction made by Pauline Maier, to be extra-institutional as much as anti-institutional.[125] Wilkite demonstrations, even when quite orderly, seem to have been occasions of licence, characterised by such festive activities as drinking – lists of Wilkite toasts abound[126] – feasting and joke-playing. The beard-growing competition which was to terminate when Wilkes finally took his seat is typical of this sort of spirit.[127] There is an almost cathartic atmosphere about the escape from customary constraints to be found in the movement, and the festive element serves to enforce this impression.[128]

In this jocose context, it is a not altogether implausible notion to see Wilkes both as a court jester and a lord of misrule. (In Britain, unlike the Continent, there seems to have been remarkably little differentiation between the two.)[129] He certainly had all the appropriate characteristics. He was, if not physically deformed, at least extremely ugly, having a horrible squint and, in late life, precious few teeth. Physical affliction was traditionally associated with extreme sexual potency, again a characteristic of fools, which Wilkes was eager to claim for himself, and which his enemies constantly attacked him for.[130] He certainly saw himself, like the court fool, as a specially licensed critic and, to his followers at least, he seemed gifted with the acute perception often attributed to the simpleton, madman or oddity.[131] His success was explicable by another 'foolish' characteristic, the persistent violation of propriety. Wilkes performed what Welsford calls 'one of the perennial functions of the fool, the power of melting the solidity of the world'.[132] He also played the part of fool as 'delight maker',[133] as so many stories about him attest. Though scarcely packed full of sparkling wit, such joke-books as *The Battle of the Quills, Wilkes's Jest Book*, and the *Patriotic Miscellany* all indicate how Wilkes set out to make politics entertaining. Besides, contemporaries actually referred to Wilkes as a political jester. He became a regular character at masques, complete with motley, and erratic behaviour to match. When Wilkes himself appeared at a masque in May 1770 shortly after his release from prison, he was accompanied by 'a man dressed like him, with a visor, in imitation of his squint, and a cap of liberty on a poll'.[134] This so-called political Bedlamite had two rivals. Another man appeared as a squinting Alderman, and a third dressed as 'The Times', with half of his dress in Wilkite guise, the other half in the Scottish manner.[135] Such portrayals were reproduced in political cartoons (see over).[136]

Wilkes, then, not only made politics commercial; he made it entertaining and sociable. This politics of pleasure had its serious side. Indeed, there can be no more foolish error than to be beguiled by Wilkes's flamboyant hedonism into thinking that he lacked skills as a political organiser. A more accurate judgement would be the one made by a commentator after Wilkes's death:

With all his wit and pleasantry, he was in many respects a man of *method*, particularly in his *political lines*, the management of which he understood better than any man of his time. He was the first who introduced the practice of a candidate's sending a card of thanks to his voter in an hour's time after giving him that vote; a circumstance which in the proportion that it flatters individual vanity, sets it at work to repay the flatterer by fresh exertions in his cause.

He likewise kept a book wherein he carefully and alphabetically arranged the names of all those who either voted for him, or whom he knew, or thought wished well to him, or who had written any thing in favour of his party. An instance of this occurred to a Gentleman who had called upon him one day about particular business, and who imagined himself totally unknown to him; but Wilkes let him know the contrary, by politely telling him he believed he had the honour of his acquaintance; and then turning to a port folio, he showed the Gentleman his name, the place of his abode, with the title of a pamphlet he had written some years before on a political subject.[137]

This was the Wilkes who, within hours of the death of the Alderman of Farringdon Without in January 1769, had handbills on the street announcing his forthcoming candidature for the vacated office.[138] Naturally he was aided by his followers, especially the indefatigable Horne Tooke, who was chiefly responsible for the high level of organisation operating during the various Middlesex elections. Handbills were distributed, carriages arranged, banners paid for, and a certain amount of formalised control was exercised over the crowds of supporters.[139] Similarly political organisation was not lacking in the Wilkite build-up of political support in the City. The infiltration of the

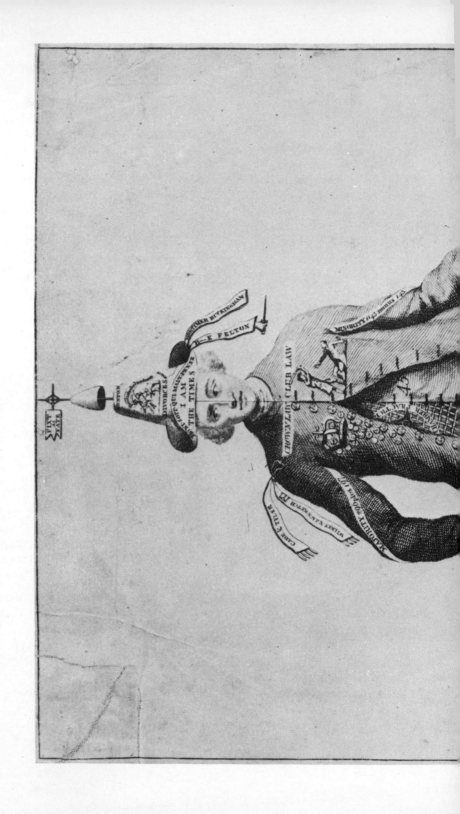

liverymen's ranks, followed by a concerted campaign in December 1769 to elect sympathetic Common Councilmen made Wilkes a force in the City as well as in metropolitan politics.[140]

Again, although it is very difficult to ascertain the precise personal role that Wilkes played in its activities, the SSBR had its organisational successes. It organised petitioning in the Metropolis, Middlesex, Surrey and parts of the West Country, and circulated a national appeal for funds. Admittedly the attempt to establish a nationwide network of corresponding societies was much less fruitful, and the political pledge that the society attempted to exact from parliamentary candidates only obtained twelve followers in the 1774 parliament. The divisions that produced an open schism in 1771 robbed the society of much of its political momentum, and it is true that Wilkes bears a considerable responsibility for that breach. But the SSBR, though it never became the focus of a successful national political organization, was extremely successful in a propagandist capacity; it always managed to keep Wilkes's cause in the public eye.

This hard-nosed politicking was not, of course, incompatible with conviviality. Indeed the two were complementary and mutually reinforcing. We can best see this by looking at Wilkes's tavern and club connections. During his confinement in the King's Bench prison Wilkes was elected to a great many societies. He was appointed a member of the Ancient and Honourable Order of Freemasons, which met at the Jerusalem Tavern in Clerkenwell, and of the Ancient Order of Hiccobites of the Mermaid, in Doctor's Commons. A similar honour was conferred on him by the Union Grand Lodge of the Three Tuns in Spitalfields. (When the crowd seized his coach in April 1768, they took him to this tavern, and he addressed them from its balcony, before surrendering himself at the King's Bench prison.) He was also admitted into the Society of Old Souls, and the Society of Bucks, both of whose officers staged their elaborate rituals of induction in the prison itself. Two other societies, the Antigallicans and the Ancient Family of Leeches, elected him to be their chief officer.[141]

There is an observable pattern to these club and tavern connections. The most prominent area of Wilkite supporters was in the City, immediately around St Paul's. The Sun, in St Paul's Churchyard itself, was the venue of a club that elected Wilkes as its forty-fifth member. It was almost immediately adjacent to the Queen's Arms (also known as the King's Arms) which was the home of the Leeches, and of West India and American Lodge, the centre of resistance to Grenville's American policies in the middle years of the decade, a favourite dining place of Wilkes, and the local club of such London printers as Henry Baldwin, an American sympathiser and friend of Wilkes. A stone's throw distant and both in the Doctor's Commons were the Mermaid, the home of the Hiccobites, and the Horn Tavern, which was a popular meeting place for members of the Joiners Company, including Wilkes; it also accommodated three masonic lodges and a 'free and easy' club. Nearby were the Paul's Head in Cateaton Street where Wilkes and SSBR members used to dine, the London Tavern in Bishopsgate Street in which the SSBR conducted all its serious business, and the famous Half-Moon Tavern in Cheapside which was also frequented by our patriot hero.[142]

A number of Fleet Street and Strand Taverns were also Wilkite. Wilkes's personal favourite was the Globe in Fleet Street which was run by Thomas Thorpe, a Common Councilman from the Ward of Farringdon Without. This hostelry should not be confused with the Globe in the Strand. Here one of the thirteen Lodges of Bucks, in this case the Euphrates, regularly convened. It was this lodge, including in its number the famous William Hickey, which elevated Wilkes into their fraternity. On the same, north side of Fleet Street stood the Mitre where Wilkes entertained the Common Councillors of Farringdon Without, and which became, after the Queen's Arms, the home and venue of the West Indian and American Lodge.[143]

This cluster of Wilkite support is complemented by a similar one in Westminister. Here the more socially elevated supporters of Wilkes met. Two taverns were regularly used for Wilkite rallies, and for meetings to boost morale and prepare electoral work. They were the Swan in Bridge Street, which was conveniently near Westminister Bridge and therefore the closest Westminister tavern to the King's Bench prison, and the Prince of Orange Tavern in Jermyn Street, used as a starting point for marches to Brentford. Between the two and close to the House of Commons was Appleby's in Parliament Street. Here was established a new political society, the Liberty Beefsteak Club (so-called no doubt to distinguish it from its namesake that met near the stews of Covent Garden) which, on Wilkes's release, staged a banquet with the hero and forty-four chosen members. SSBR members also liked to dine at the Parliament Coffee House in the adjacent Old Palace Yard.[144]

The precise significance of these connections is difficult to assess. We do know, however, that almost all of the taverns mentioned were distribution points for the Wilkite newspaper, the *Middlesex Journal*.[145] Moreover, the clubs and lodges to which Wilkes belonged contributed to his electoral organisation. Their flags and banners were prominent, for instance, amongst those carried by the Wilkites to Brentford in April 1769.[146] The Greyhound at Greenwich, the meeting place of the AntiGallicans, was also the scene of one of the most extravagant celebrations on Wilkes's release in April 1770.[147] We are also able to distinguish the taverns that were used as rallying places – the Swan, the London Tavern and the Prince of Orange – from the dining places that Wilkes and a few friends used to frequent quite regularly, and which would doubtless be full of sympathisers.

The latter were also the homes of the lodges. Wilkes's masonic connections seem to have been pretty indiscriminate. Despite the great schism between Ancients and Moderns that had occurred in 1751, he belonged to both lodges, though he seems, as far as one can tell, to have been favoured by, or to have preferred the former which, despite its name, was the more recent foundation.[148] Masons were supposed to be politically neutral, at least in their masonic activities. Often, however, this was simply not the case. The Great Lodge at Swaffham in Norfolk, for example, was simply a club consisting of all the political leaders of the local independent whigs.[149] Similarly, the Jerusalem Sols, admittedly regarded by some masons as a pseudo-masonic institution, had strong political overtones. Its members included Horne Tooke and the SSBR member Sir Watkin Lewes who subsequently became Lord Mayor of London.[150] Naturally the masons who admitted Wilkes into their fraternity were also acting in a political way. Indeed, the making, passing and raising of a mason in a prison was especially controversial as only a *free man* could be inducted.[151] The political implications of Wilkes's admission were obvious.

Masons looked askance at such clubs as the Bucks, Leeches and Hiccobites. These clubs seem to have been much less sober, and considerably less orderly than the masons. Masonic rules included the punishment of blasphemers; the Bucks and their companion clubs, on the other hand, seem to have been the spiritual inheritors of a hell-fire tradition. In the 1750s they were notorious for their 'Frolicks' and, although it is generally felt that they had sobered somewhat by the time of Wilkes's notoriety, they were still, as William Hickey's *Memoirs* attest, an extremely lively, if not licentious group.[152] Such organizations as these obviously relished Wilkes's displays of wit and sexual notoriety as much as his politics. They were willing, indeed eager to place at his disposal the resources that they could command for the encouragement of spectacles, festivity and licence.

Wilkes often appears as a rather incongruous figure for an eighteenth-century radical. He seems to have much closer affinities to a seventeenth-century rake than to the sober Reverend Christopher Wyvill. But although this image of unbridled roué may have cost him the support of some of the more sober sort, it also secured the admiring allegiance of the young bloods of the city. Wilkes was quite prepared to use their purchasing power and popularity in particular inns, coffee houses or taverns to pressure publicans into supporting his cause; failure to do so could result in boycott.[153] Taverns and club connections, then, consolidated Wilkite support, facilitated organisation, and provided centres of recruitment. They also ensured that politics and pleasure went in tandem.

The areas of support that Wilkes obtained were highly disparate, and an explanation of why he recruited such a varied following must necessarily be rather complex. In the case of the urban radicals an answer is not too difficult to find. Sawbridge, Beckford, Horne Tooke, Townshend and Oliver, and the corresponding radicals such as Crisp Molyneux and Gardiner in provincial towns like Norwich and King's Lynn, had already committed themselves to the idea of political reform – sometimes, it is true, of a rather nebulous kind – long before the meteoric rise of Wilkes. Their attitude towards him was always highly ambiguous. They needed his journalistic talents and his political theatricality to reach the nooks and crannies of the English provinces and to penetrate deep into the alleyways and taverns of the city; only through him could they be sure of obtaining the widespread dissemination of political ideas that he himself had never seriously countenanced. At the same time they were aware of his limitations. As Lucy Sutherland has emphasised, Wilkes's political creed does not seem to have extended far beyond the furtherance of his own immediate political interests.[154] His adoption of a reformist platform was largely the result of competitive pressures from the radicals themselves. They wanted to immerse, perhaps even bury the personality of Wilkes beneath the cause of radicalism. They needed Wilkes's help, but were determined to exact a price for their support. In return for espousing his cause, attempting the near impossible task of making him solvent, and giving him a place in city politics, they wanted to take over Wilkite political organisation and utilise Wilkes's popularity for their own ends.

In this sense, therefore, and despite the fact that their political views were very different, they had affinities with the parliamentary politicians who leapt onto the Wilkite bandwagon. Rockingham, Grenville, Shelburne and Chatham had little personal sympathy for Wilkes, no truck with Wilkite crowds, and feared the SSBR's radical aspirations. They merely wished to use the political furore of those years to gain political power.

The social composition of Wilkes's other supporters and their political purposes are somewhat harder to ascertain. We know that Wilkes's city supporters were chiefly small merchants, manufacturers and craftsmen: the members of the City's Common Hall and, to a lesser extent, of the Common Council.[155] A not altogether different picture can be observed, as Rudé has shown, in the Wilkite Middlesex electors. It was the merchants, tradesmen and manufacturers of the Middlesex out-parishes that provided the backbone of Wilkes's support.[156] Similarly, although only the most impressionistic picture can be formed, Wilkes's supporters in the provinces seem to have been local merchants, manufacturers and entrepreneurs. Wilkite crowds, as one would expect, were of a rather different composition. Although the occasional man of substance or even gentleman, like Matthew Christian who led a Wilkite crowd in March 1768, was observed in their number,[157] by and large they were wage-earners: journeymen, apprentices, weavers, domestic servants and labourers.

These groups were those who were most attracted by the radical aspects of Wilkes's view of politics. Wilkes may not have had radical political aspirations, but his *methods* and their ramifications were radical. First of all, he was one of the first, if not *the* first political entrepreneur. He made a business of politics, especially of political journalism. Of course every opposition politician, and a great many on the government's side, had set out on previous occasions to organise press campaigns, or attempt some broad-based political appeal. Wilkes had simply organised more efficiently, more intelligently, and with a greater sensitivity to the conditions of the political market. The Wilkite movement was a large-scale enterprise, and substantial profits were to be made. Thus printers and publishers sold more copy, brewers (who usually cut their prices during a Wilkite election)[158] sold more ale, and manufacturers developed new lines of Wilkite artifacts.

Large-scale political organisation was not, of course, new to the metropolis. As Nick Rogers has recently demonstrated, the arts of cajoling, coercing, wooing and persuading a large urban electorate were well known in the constituency of Westminster.[159] But the *scale* of Wilkes's activities was greater than before. They included the metropolis as a whole and, as far as the propaganda was concerned, the even wider ambit of the whole kingdom. This commercialisation of politics undoubtedly appealed to Wilkes's merchant and manufacturing supporters. Based on notions that they thought important and really understood, it was their kind of politics, promising them greater political power and leverage.

Wilkes's ideological solution to his personal dilemma was all of a piece with his entrepreneurial view of politics. By equating himself with liberty, and at the same time identifying himself with his followers, he not only made politics more real to them, he also produced the most persuasive of arguments in favour of humble support for his cause.

The artisan, wage-earner, small employer and craftsman were naturally predisposed towards Wilkes because he gave them status and consequence that no one had ever offered them before. There had, it must be confessed, been many, many occasions in the past when an appeal had been made to the spirit of liberty and independence in the populace at large. But this had never been so vividly personified in the career and actions of one man, nor had anyone been so irreverent, so eager to ensure that his followers shared the vicarious pleasure of tormenting, teasing and goading the great. The entertainment that Wilkes offered was quite unlike the customary pleasures of electoral treating (though he and his followers were not parsimonious in their distribution of alcohol and viands). Treating was licensed pleasure, condoned and usually financed by the great. The pleasure that Wilkes offered was at the expense of the powerful, but in a very different sense. Their defeat, humiliation, their ridiculousness in the face of Wilkes's provocative conduct was the source of his supporters' enjoyment.

These were the characteristics that made Wilkes different; they were also those that gave him such extensive support. In trying to depersonalise the Wilkite movement the city radicals were, whether they liked it or not, inevitably throwing the baby out with the bath water. The schism that developed in the SSBR in 1771 was one between those who were radical in method (Wilkite), and those who were radical in ideology and purpose (Horne Tooke, Sawbridge *et al.*). The two groups had much in common. They were both determined to emancipate themselves from the leading parliamentary groups, and to take independent political initiatives. They were not above trying to manipulate the parties into supporting policies and positions that they did not really uphold,[160] and they dealt with the party leaders as equal participants in an agreement based on political expediency. They never went cap-in-hand to their superiors. Both groups were also determined to broaden the political forum, to increase the level of participation. Beckford, Sawbridge and their allies, however, were much more cautious about their supporters than was Wilkes. They feared the crowd and resented Wilkes's popularity. Wilkes was prepared to countenance the allegiance of anyone who supported Wilkes; the reforming radicals wanted commitment to a political platform which would still have excluded many from the political process.

Wilkes in some ways created a 'pre-political' situation in English politics. He was unconcerned with political education as such or with long-term organisation, except in as much as it served his own immediate purposes. The radicals, on the other hand, wanted to build on a traditional base, set up a standing political organisation and go beyond 'Wilkes and Liberty' to the notion of 'Wilkes and Reform'. Unfortunately for them John Wilkes was still thinking very much more in terms of 'Wilkes and Licence'.

This is perhaps the most epigrammatic way in which the complexity of the Wilkite movement can be expressed. The Wilkite movement must be seen as a *focus* for a disparate collection of grievances, most of which stemmed from the successful operation of an oligarchical and enclosed system of politics. Only the radicals, Horne Tooke *et al.*, had new remedies for the old disease; only they looked beyond a set of political contingencies and to any qualitative change in political society. Yet, ironically, they were nowhere near as innovative as Wilkes in the sphere of method, which is what makes him appear such a modern figure. Contemporary manipulators of the sort studied by Vance Packard could have taught Wilkes precious little. The public whom he exploited was more open to commercialisation than radicalisation. The political tradition that they had available to them was potent, and, to some, seemed to provide both diagnosis and remedy of their political ills. Others, however, were moving away from the old panaceas, and trying new cures. Their radicalism, fertilised by the ideas of the dissident colonists, developed new, hybrid strains of thought, nurtured in the soil of country-party ideology but burgeoning into new and unfamiliar blooms.

10. American ideology and British radicalism; the case for parliamentary reform

~~~

> The inequalities in the representation of one country are no
> reason for rejecting the representation of another...we are not
> to reason from defect to defect, thereby making the political
> system still more and more defective. ([W. Bollan], *Succinct View
> of the Origin of our Colonies* (1766), 25)

The decade of the 1760s saw the emergence of a number of new political issues which were to clarify, even to harden, the new political lines that had been drawn at the beginning of George III's reign. Of these new issues, undoubtedly one of the most important was the imperial problem posed by the North American colonies.

The American question can be, and indeed was approached in a variety of ways. It could, for example, be seen in geo-political, strategic terms. During the prolonged and occasionally extremely acrimonious discussions that surrounded the peace negotiations at the end of the Seven Years War, the thirteen colonies were discussed in precisely this way. The government's decision to plump for hegemony on the North American continent by retaining the whole of Canada, and to content itself with a holding operation in the West Indies, placed the Americans at the very centre of the British imperial design.[1]

Yet this momentous geo-political decision raised other questions about America which were of an administrative and financial nature. The acquisition of very considerable new territories had only been achieved after major military and naval operations; with peace the ambit of imperial administration had inevitably been extended. All of this cost money. The problem of revenue from taxation was a thorn in the side of every eighteenth-century minister. High levels of taxation, especially in peace time, undermined a government's parliamentary support; the land tax, particularly, antagonised the bucolic backbencher.

One solution to the sensitive fiscal problem of the costs of empire, George Grenville's (not altogether novel) idea that the colonists themselves should pay for the benefits of imperial trade and military protection, was calculated to pacify domestic critics. Indeed, the subsequently notorious Stamp Act was passed both with the plaudits of country-gentlemen and against precious little opposition.[2] In the colonies, however, it stirred up a hornet's nest. Moreover, the legislation imparted yet another perspective to American affairs: the colonial battle-cry of 'no taxation without representation' raised questions that were explicitly political, constitutional and ideological. It is with these questions that this chapter is concerned.

The attitudes of the different parliamentary groups and parties to the question of colonial taxation are considerably more complicated than might at first appear. We can, however, observe a spectrum of views ranging from the ardent determination of George Grenville and his followers to assert parliament's right to tax the colonies, to the (more constitutionally dubious) radical and Pittite position that denied not merely the practical wisdom of colonial taxation, but even its constitutional propriety.[3] The Rockinghamites occupied a position between these two views. They never denied parliamentary supremacy over North America but, on the whole, they were reluctant to see this enforced. In fact this general position, manifested by their simultaneous repeal of the Stamp Act and introduction of the Declaratory Act, concealed a variety of views on colonial policy within the party. The opinions of some, such as Charles Yorke and, to a lesser extent, Dowdeswell, approached the views of Grenville, while there were those, notably Newcastle, whose attitudes betrayed a Pittite hue.[4]

But, rather than attempting to distinguish the various opinions on the pragmatic necessity or legality of colonial taxation, examining what were, in effect, different formulations and appraisals of British colonial policy, I wish to raise the equally complex question of the impact of American political argument upon the British political scene.

Even the most perfunctory examination of the evidence indicates that the debate in the thirteen colonies and the major issues of British politics cannot be treated as encapsulated entities. Take, for example, the amount of polemical literature that was disseminated on both sides of the Atlantic. Of the eighty-four pamphlets which explored the issue of the relations between the colonies and the mother country and were published in America between 1764 and 1770, thirty-seven were reprinted in England. Similarly, we find many of the major English pamphlets, not to mention newspaper comment, reproduced in the colonies.[5]

A great deal of information was passed back and forth between the two continents by the merchants who traded from one or other side of the Atlantic, or by those who had business or familial ties across the ocean. American merchants in London, such as the Virginian R. H. Lee and his trading partner Stephen Sayre, or those in Liverpool like Charles Steuart, together with such Englishmen as George Hayley of London, Richard Champion of Bristol and Charles Goore of Liverpool, all sought to ensure that political as well as commercial intelligence was conveyed to both trading communities.[6]

Throughout the decade there was a strong lobby of English merchants trading with America, which was centred upon one of the most radical taverns in London, the Queen's Arms, in St Paul's Churchyard. Although the members of that particular society were highly conscious of the political implications of the government's policy towards the thirteen colonies, most merchants were reluctant to raise the constitutional issues involved in colonial policy. Though sometimes supported for political as well as commercial reasons, the highly organised campaign of 1765–6, which aimed at procuring the repeal of the Stamp Act, deliberately eschewed issues of principle, and based its arguments on the state of the British domestic economy.[7] But the less politically sensitive merchants trading with America could not avoid hearing the colonists' case, however much they might dislike its bold employment of the language of constitutionalism; nor, for their own sakes, could they afford to neglect the presentation of colonial grievances to parliament and the public.

Besides, they were not the only group that had Anglo-American interests at heart. The colonial agents, spurred on by sharp criticism from the colonies, were much less fastidious in their presentation of the political points at issue. They worked assiduously, especially during the Stamp Act crisis, to present the American case to the British public. The most famous of their number, Benjamin Franklin, apart from arranging for the publication of sympathetic newspaper letters in the London press, devised cards and cartoons, wrote to the papers himself, and persuaded his friend Strahan to print two editions of Dulany's *Considerations on the Propriety of Imposing Taxes on the British Colonies*, together with two of John Dickinson's pamphlets.[8] William Bollan, another colonial agent, supplemented his radical writings on the Middlesex election with pamphlets favourable to the colonial cause. He was one of a number of authors who categorically asserted that there was an intimate connection between British colonial policy and domestic political conflict.[9]

A similar view was held by Arthur Lee, the brother of the Virginian merchant. While a student at the Inns of Court in London, Lee, besides sending home frequent, somewhat gloomy reports on the English political scene to friends and relatives, set out to demonstrate to Englishmen that, in his own words, 'the cause of *America* is the common cause of the realm...both countries have the same complaint, and therefore claim the same friends'.[10] To this end he joined the Society of Supporters of the Bill of Rights, purchased the freedom and livery of the city of London, and 'procured the introduction of the grievances of America into the famous Middlesex petition'.[11] Shortly afterwards he began a series of newspaper letters under the pseudonym 'Junius Americanus'. They had the purpose of 'mixing popular subjects here with that of America',[12] and were sufficiently well received to be produced subsequently in pamphlet form. A successful journalist on both sides of the Atlantic (he was the author of the *Monitor's Letters*, first published in the *Virginia Gazette*), Lee devoted his entire career in London to the furtherance of his own, radical interpretation of the antagonism between the thirteen colonies and the mother country. In so doing, he exercised an important influence on the thinking of Englishman and American alike.

Arthur Lee and his brother were also responsible for disseminating American pamphlet literature in England. They sent presentation copies of what was probably the most successful colonial pamphlet in England, John Dickinson's *Letters from a Farmer in Pennsylvania, to the Inhabitants of the English Colonies*, to Lord Shelburne, Isaac Barré, a number of members of the SSBR, and the famous republican historian, Catharine Macaulay. Those who read the pamphlet, however, were not confined to Real Whig and republican circles. It was a great commercial success, sold well in England, and even appeared in an imprint in French.[13]

The activities of the Lee brothers were matched by the efforts of the man whom Bernard Bailyn has justly characterised as 'that extraordinary one-man propaganda machine in the cause of liberty'.[14] Thomas Hollis, a whig of the old school, was as industrious in promoting the colonial cause in England, as he was in providing his distinguished American correspondents with political intelligence and published material from the empire's metropolis. During the Stamp Act crisis he sent letters to the press, and distributed copies of James Otis's *Considerations on behalf of the Colonists*; he was also personally responsible for the detailed accounts that appeared in the British press of the Boston Massacre of March 1770. Both published correspondence and critical commentaries on government legislation were printed by John Almon at his behest.[15] Hollis, personally convinced of a covert conspiracy to undermine liberty in Old World and New, was categorically committed to his role as radical propagandist. The serried ranks of volumes, tooled and embossed with the emblems of liberty, which were sent to his American allies and have found their resting-place in the Houghton Library, affirm his assiduity and are a physical confirmation of his success in linking the English and American causes. Yet even without the efforts of such committed individuals, intelligence was always available. A cursory glance at any English newspaper, metropolitan or provincial, or at the periodical press reveals comment as well as news from and about the thirteen colonies.[16]

Clearly, the links forged between England and America were many; merchants, politicians, publishers, intellectuals and a coterie of Americans temporarily resident in the nation's chief trading towns all deliberately and self-consciously sought to keep the communities on both sides of the Atlantic informed of each and every political development. Moreover, many of them were dedicated to the proposition that English and American politics were inextricably intertwined. Of this there can be no doubt. But when the historian comes to try to unravel the strands of English and colonial political thinking in order to understand how and why they were first entangled, the problem becomes altogether more intractable.

It can, however, be maintained that the polemical riposte of the American colonies to the English government affected English political argument in at least two ways. First, as a great many English authors were quick to point out, the government's conduct in North America, as interpreted by the colonial dissidents, provided abundant evidence of the court's intention (and, sometimes, that of the government also) to establish a regime that was certainly politically irresponsible, and possibly despotic. Colonial unrest was all grist to the English opposition's mill.[17] A considerable, some might say a vast body of contemporary material deals with this topic. Much of it is highly conjectural, some is plainly risible; but the force and potency of this view should not be underestimated. It need not, however, detain us here, as the questions of conspiracy and discontent are dealt with elsewhere.[18]

Rather concentration will be focussed on the second of the two connections between American and English polemic, that between the colonial debate on taxation and representation which occurred predominantly between 1765 and 1766, and the British demands for parliamentary reform that emerged at the end of the decade. That the two are in any way connected is, in itself, a somewhat contentious claim. It is true that the most recent historian of British parliamentary reform has cautiously conceded, in a single paragraph devoted to the subject, that the debate on representation 'had implications for both countries';[19] but the most distinguished historian of representation in

England and America is not prepared to go even thus far. 'It was not', he argues

> the debating of the issues of representation between the Colonists and the mother country that impelled the new reformist wave in Britain; America had few sympathisers, and the American arguments had little bearing on British political arrangements. What really affected the domestic politics of representation was not American reasoning but American resistance.[20]

Nevertheless, in making such an assertion, Dr Pole skirts round, if he does not avoid, one of the most fascinating and perplexing questions about British domestic politics in the 1760s. The demand for parliamentary reform at the end of the decade is historically important not only as a call for reform *tout court*, but as a call for a different kind of reform. Earlier in the century, advocates of an improved parliament had put forward proposals that were in accord with the tenets of country-party ideology; they sought more frequent elections (i.e. annual or triennial parliaments), and the removal of placemen and pensioners from the House of Commons.[21] Both of these measures were intended to preserve the constitutional purity of the lower house, and thereby to secure the delicate balance between king, Lords and Commons which was deemed so necessary to a healthy state. These traditional aims, it is true, were part of the platform advocated by the Society of Supporters of the Bill of Rights. But, in addition, the society sought 'a more fair and equal representation of the people',[22] by which they meant the representation of new interests, notably those of the manufacturing and mercantile communities. It is this demand, more than any other, that reveals the extent to which country-party arguments, usually associated with the rural backbencher and the squirearchy, had become the stock-in-trade of urban radicals and city reformers. Employing the staple creed that had been espoused by almost every opposition in the Hanoverian era, they added to it their own peculiarly appropriate platform for reform. The attack on the state of representation marked, as it were, the urbanisation of country-party ideology. By this I do not mean that urban, especially metropolitan interests had not previously adopted country-party rhetoric; far from it, this had been a common characteristic of metropolitan and borough opponents of the Walpolean political machine.[23] Prior to the 1760s, however, this rhetoric had not had a distinctive urban component despite its advocacy by merchants, manufacturers, and the inhabitants of unincorporated towns.

If this is the case, then the question arises not merely of why there were demands for reform, but why they should include the issue of representation. It is the contention of what follows that the emergence of this issue was primarily attributable to a process of ideological contamination from the American debate about British attempts to tax the thirteen colonies.

This is not to say that other circumstances were not extremely important. The demand for the representation of mercantile and manufacturing interests could not have occurred without the existence of at least small groups of city men who wanted political power and status commensurate with their wealth. More generally, the impulse for reform was strongly propelled, as John Cannon has emphasised, by the political conflicts that had arisen at the beginning of George III's reign.[24] The king's conduct was readily construed as part of a covert attempt to subvert the constitution and, *a fortiori*, the House of Commons, and was indubitably responsible for the fissures in the political nation that led some politicians to consider, or at least discuss, a mild measure of parliamentary reform. Moreover, the Middlesex election, because it revealed a direct conflict between the House of Commons and a county electorate, compounded the disquiet that already existed and, in the eyes of the reformers, at least, corroborated their case.

It should, however, be emphasised that these general political circumstances in no way explain the emergence of the issue of *representation*, though they may well account for support for parliamentary reform. Fears of constitutional subversion, whether deeply felt or fabricated, customarily produced the demand for a purer House of Commons; intrinsically, there was no reason why they should be the harbinger of a reformed representation. Indeed, on the very numerous occasions when previous oppositions had raised the spectre of a plot to undermine the constitution, they had often offered the panacea of a pristine lower House. This, however, had rarely, if ever, included the suggestion of a changed representation; when such suggestions were made, it was usually for an increase in the number of county seats, rather than for the representation of new or emergent interests.

There had been some few occasions earlier in the century when the idea of representing new interests had been aired with approval. Swift, for example, had advocated the enfranchisement of populous towns, as had a number of Real Whig thinkers and pamphleteers. Even that pillar of eighteenth-century conservative constitutionalism, Sir William Blackstone, supported a measure of reform, or at least regretted the anomalies in the existing system, though this did not stop him siding with the government against the Middlesex electors in 1768. Others, such as Hume (a political maverick if ever there was one), William Beckford, and the author of *Political Disquisitions proper for public Consideration*, could be added to the list.[25] But in none of these instances can it be maintained that the question of representation was a matter of serious public debate, or that it was supported by more than a few isolated individuals. No fully-fledged organisation or political group took it up until the SSBR made advocacy of a more equal representation a condition of their endorsement of parliamentary candidates, and no systematic or sustained debate about representation occurred before the Stamp Act crisis of 1765–6.

By the summer of 1765 the colonists who opposed taxation and the apologists for Grenville's Stamp Act had already joined battle on the issue of representation in a pamphlet war that was to continue until the end of the decade. As every schoolboy knows, the starting point of the debate was the contention by the Americans that they were not directly represented in the British parliament (though they were British subjects), and that it was one of 'the *noble principles* of English liberty'[26] that a man could not be taxed unless he had consented to such an impost through his duly elected representatives.

In response to this challenge almost every defendant of the government's determination to obtain revenue in North America took up the same argument in reply. Both Englishmen and Americans who were unenfranchised legitimately paid taxes because they were 'virtually represented'. Why, scoffed Soame Jenyns, 'every *Englishman* is taxed, but not one in twenty is [directly] represented'.[27] The actual franchise was confined to a few; vast and considerable interests in the nation did not enjoy the right to cast a vote. Thomas Whately, in what was virtually an official government apologia,[28] listed the dispossessed with remarkable gusto:

all landed Property in short, that is not Freehold, and all monied Property whatsoever are excluded: the Possessors of these have no Votes in the Election of Members of Parliament; Women and Persons under Age be their Property ever so large, and all of it Freehold, have none. The Merchants of *London*, a numerous and respectable Body of Men, whose Opulence exceeds all that America could collect; the Proprietors of that Vast Accumulation of Wealth, the public Funds; the Inhabitants of *Leeds*, of *Halifax*, of *Manchester*, Towns that are each of them larger than the largest in the Plantations; many of less Note that are yet unincorporated; and that great Corporation the East India Company, whose Rights over Countries they possess, fall little short of Sovereignty, and whose Trades and whose Fleets are sufficient to constitute them a maritime Power, are all in the same Circumstances.[29]

Yet, it was maintained, they rightly paid taxes, for though unenfranchised they were represented, not actually but *virtually*. Members of Parliament were not merely or primarily the representatives of their constituency or locality, but of the entire nation. Hence the lower House was, as George Grenville pointed out, 'the *Commons in Parlia-*

ment assembled and not the *Representatives of the Commons*'.[30] This did not, however, mean that the affairs of the unenfranchised were disregarded. Such was the varied social composition of the House that, even though certain areas or interest groups were not directly represented, they would be protected by MPs who were naturally allied or sympathetic to their cause. At the same time, and in accordance with a view of the constitution and polity that saw it as an organic whole, it was assumed that particular interests would always be tempered and mediated by an MP's awareness that he was primarily concerned with the public good.[31]

In other words, though a member of parliament might be elected by a few, once he took his seat he represented all, even the unenfranchised. The conclusion, then, was obvious: 'This...being the case, it therefore follows, that our Birminghams, Manchesters, Leeds, Halifaxes etc and *your* Bostons, New-Yorks, and Philadelphias are all as *really*, though not so nominally represented, as any Part whatsoever of the British Empire.'[32] Americans were represented, and could therefore be taxed.[33]

This argument which, as one of its critics pointed out, was 'the only method that has been tried, to reconcile their assertion, that "the British parliament has a right to tax the Colonies", with the concession, "that the Colonists have the privileges of Britons, and are a free people"',[34] provoked two responses from those who defended the colonists. The first distinguished the state of representation in England from that in North America; it therefore played little or no part in developing English political arguments about representation. But the second view, put most vehemently by James Otis and supported by many others, equated the misfortunes of America with the ills of Britain; the arbitrary claims for taxation made against the colonists, they argued, were in no way excused by the sorry state of representation in England. It was this view that English radicals were to take up and incorporate within their schemes of parliamentary reform.

Emphasis on the difference between the situation of non-electors in Britain and in North America was based on the accurate observation that an affinity, a kinship or bond of political interest existed between MPs, the electors and the unenfranchised in England, but was absent in the thirteen colonies.[35] In England the chain of connection, as Richard Champion described it,[36] ensured the protection of non-electors' constitutional rights:

The Non-electors of *Great-Britain* are virtually secure, in having their property granted (for taxation) by the House of Commons; because both the members of that House, and their constituents, share in the burden of that grant. This dispenses liberty and security to every individual; and from thence arises that universal confidence, which is essentially necessary to the subsistence of a free Government.[37]

When MPs taxed other Englishmen they also taxed themselves, and would therefore naturally be inclined to caution and prudence; their action was 'general' not 'partial'.[38] This, however, was not the case in America – 'the whole people of *America* are virtually insecure, because there is not only no participation with them by the givers or their constituents, but an absolute saving to both'.[39]

This general principle was enforced by a number of other *ad hoc* objections to the contention that the situation of English and colonial non-electors was the same. An English non-elector, it was pointed out, could always, through acquisition of wealth or by changing his residence, acquire the necessary freehold property or borough qualification to exercise a vote.[40] No such possibility was open to a resident of North America. Besides, electoral influence in Britain was not simply confined to the unenfranchised:

There is not a Man in this Kingdom, be his condition ever so low in Life, who may not be said to have an Influence in the Choice of our Representatives, though not worth a single Shilling. He can at least make Part of the Mob, and huzza for the Man he likes. But if he has Property, his Influence rises in Proportion. There are People in this Capital, who are neither Freemen, nor Freeholders. Yet have it in their Power greatly to affect the Choice of Representation in this City, as well as in many Parts of the Nation.[41]

Again, the analogy between Birmingham and Boston was not a fair one. Freeholders in the unrepresented English towns, unlike their American counterparts, could at least vote in the county elections.[42] Moreover, if one needed a further explanation of why the enfranchised in England should pay taxes while colonists should not, one could always have recourse to Locke. One of the very few arguments that George Grenville and his colonial opponents held in common was the contention, based on the *Two Treatises*, that residence in a society constituted a tacit agreement to be bound by its laws, obligations and penalties.[43]

Though many apologists for the American cause did their utmost to distinguish the state of representation in the colonies from that of the mother country, there were others who drew analogies between the inadequate and inequitable distribution of seats in England, and the plight of the completely unrepresented colonists. To a very large extent the defenders of colonial taxation *invited* them to use such arguments. One cannot but be impressed by the relish with which the chief protagonists of the Stamp Act exposed the incongruities of the British electoral system. It is almost as if they savoured the irony of using such arguments against their colonial brothers. Deeply committed to the debate about American taxation, and in their desire to vindicate the general notion of virtual representation, they drove home the extremely limited nature of immediate or actual representation in Britain.

Such arguments made an effective *ad hoc* case but, as John Cannon has remarked,[44] they were dangerous because they linked England and America. Very little was required, in the face of this provocation, for first Americans and then Englishmen to point out that the inadequate state of representation at home was not an argument for making the situation worse in America. 'The representation of the people of Great Britain is very unequal', one pamphleteer mocked, 'therefore those in America shall not be represented at all: This inequality in England is already a great evil; therefore it is high time to make it worse.' This mode of argument, as many were quick to point out, confused descriptive and normative views: 'No man will contest with him the practices from whence he draws his inferences; but should they ask, Why is it so practised? the only answer they can collect...will be "Because it is".'[45] Two wrongs do not make a right.[46] If English representation was inequitable it ought to be reformed. James Otis, with the plaudits of the English *Monthly Review*,[47] boldly spelt out the reformers' case:

Right reason and the spirit of a free constitution require that the representation of the whole people should be as equal as possible...No good reason ...can be given in any country why every man of sound mind should not have his vote in the election of a representative...To what purpose is it to ring everlasting changes to colonists on the cases of Manchester, Birmingham and Sheffield, who return no members? If those now considerable places are not represented, they ought to be.[48]

By their defence of the government's right of taxation, supporters of the Stamp Act had unwittingly let a very radical cat out of the bag. In a mood of jocose desperation they drew attention to the dangers of rejecting virtual representation and of applying colonial claims of tax exemption to their native England:

Why then tax me? says the Copyholder; and me? says the monied Man; and us? say the Farmer, Labourer, Manufacturer of exhausted Britain...Will the Patriot of England plead only for America? No;...a more noble Fabric...[will] be reared on the broad Base of universal Representation: For he who is taxed without being represented is a Slave...This Doctrine of universal Representation utterly overthrows the present happy Constitution of Great Britain, destroys all Order, Degree and Subordination in the State, and makes the Fabric of Society a Ruin and a heap of Rubbish.[49]

Virtual representation, it rapidly came to be appreciated, stood as the only barrier between the existing constitutional arrangements and the spectre of major electoral reform. Small wonder that it was described as being 'interwoven with the first principles of government in England', and as 'the key basis on which our constitution stands'.[50]

But the process of ideological contamination had already taken place, and by 1766 a number of Englishmen were developing the case for a reformed representation. Starting from the premise granted them by such men as Whately and Knox the reformers proceeded to construct an explanation of why representation had become so unequal. The original 'Mode of Representation', it was claimed, had been 'established in those Ages when Land was almost the only species of Local Property in England'. Naturally social change had rendered such a system obsolete; it was 'necessarily...unequal, at a Time when Arts, Manufactures, and Commerce, have derived a Flow of Wealth of a different Species'.[51] As, however, the original purpose of the scheme of representation was 'to give every man, as near as possible, an influence in the publick deliberations proportioned to his interest in them',[52] it was time for parliamentary reform. This would not be an innovation, but a restoration of the constitution's original purpose and purity.

The actual proposals put forward in order to remedy what Richard Bland called 'this putrid part of the constitution'[53] were many and varied, at times exhibiting a breadth of imagination that refused to be fettered by the basic requirements of political pragmatism. There was open discussion, for instance, of the notion that there should be an imperial parliament based on an 'equal representation' which ought to include representatives not only from North America, but from the West and East Indies.[54] Even those who were not prepared to ascend to the giddy heights offered by this imperial design were ready and eager to welcome Americans into the British parliament once an appropriate measure of reform had been accomplished.[55] On the domestic front, the debate on reform produced those who wanted wholesale, one might almost say indiscriminate political reformation. Take, for example, the scheme offered to the readers of the *Gazetteer* in February 1766. Its proposals included

Whether reforming or abolishing corrupt boroughs; enlarging the whole number of representatives, by dividing the counties and great cities into districts, each to return two members; admitting no freehold votes under ten pounds a year; granting to considerable towns the election of members, suitable to the extent and trade of the inhabitants; making bribery treason; punishing Peers and Officers of the Crown who violate the Constitution by interfering in elections; introducing a ballot; limiting the creation of Peers, a creation of late years threatening the ballance of the Commons; forfeiting to the real discoverer all fraudulent qualification lands...and disqualifying

from all places of trust and profit, all parties concerned in fallacious qualifica-
tions...; registering the men of sufficient qualification properly in every
county, and sending them to parliament in rotation, or by casting losts [*sic*];
...the most solemn oaths to be taken by candidate and voters at the time of
polling. That no money, promise, gratuity or other consideration whatsoever,
has been given or accepted, or is intended to be given or accepted in trust,
or otherwise, on account of that election. Every member, at taking his seat,
to repeat the oath publicly in the House of Commons.[56]

Such schemes were a hotchpotch of old country-party ideas together
with some of the more novel views that had emerged in the Stamp
Act debate; they were in no way coherent or rounded proposals.

More considered schemes were, however, put forward. Of these the
two most important were *Reflexions on Representation* published in 1766,
and the scheme advocated by 'REGULUS' which appeared in the
Political Register in 1768 as part of a general campaign in favour of
electoral reform. Both of these schemes advocated what they called
a 'more equal representation', by which they meant one in which the
people's power of choosing their representatives was to be 'equally
diffused according to *property*'.[57] As long as the two schemes dealt with
landed property they were not, in the context of the Stamp Act debate,
especially radical. Both, however, argued for a redistribution of seats
on the grounds that electoral distribution and the contribution that
different regions made to the nation's revenue were (unjustifiably)
incongruous. The *Reflexions* even wanted the introduction of a system
which varied the number of MPs from a particular locality according
to the fiscal contribution made during any particular parliament by
the community or constituency.[58] The less speculative scheme in
the *Political Register* argued for a redistribution of seats on similar
grounds:

London, Westminster, and Southwark, pay eighty parts in five hundred and
thirteen of the land-tax, and of the subsidy, one hundred and thirty-five; while
they send only eight members to the house of commons. Cornwall and Devon,
pay twenty-nine parts land-tax, and twenty-four subsidy, while they send no
less than seventy members. In one view, two hundred sixty-five are represented by eight; while fifty-three are represented by *seventy*.[59]

If, as some Americans had so forcibly argued, taxation and representation went hand in hand, was it really just for some to be paying so
much for so little? Was not the situation of the metropolis and the
manufacturing towns remarkably similar to that of the Americans?

As these schemes show, the notions of *property* and *taxation* had, as
a result of the Stamp Act debate, become so closely associated that they
were almost treated as synonymous terms. Electoral distribution, based
on property, was tantamount to electoral distribution based on taxable

213

goods. A similar conflation can be observed in the discussion of the franchise. It is in this area of debate that the most radical steps were taken. The author of the *Reflexions*, for instance, drew directly on arguments hammered out in the Stamp Act polemic to argue the case for wide-scale enfranchisement:

Every man, in these Kingdoms, is taxed; that is a part of his property is taken from him; if this too is done without his consent, which is taking also a part of his liberty, in what sense can he be called free? If property intitles one man to representation, the title must be extended to all who are possessed of it.[60]

This conception of property is not confined to landed wealth or freehold. It is of any sort provided that the 'property is sufficient to render them [the electors] independent, and secure them, if they please, from undue influence'.[61] As such it was certainly intended to include monied and commercial wealth, and to obtain the enfranchisement of every independent householder.[62]

The emergence of this case is crucial; for the reformers it proved a *passe-partout*, a means of opening up and extending the debate about parliamentary reform far beyond its previous confines. James Burgh, for instance, in his classic exposition of the reformers' case, *Political Disquisitions*, pointed to the contradictions made apparent by the taxation/representation equation. Having established, as conventional wisdom, the idea that those who give up their property in the form of taxation ought to have some say in the election of those who dispose of their wealth, he goes on to point out the plight of the poor:

what is particularly hard upon the poor in this case is, that though they have no share in determining who shall be the law-givers of their country, they have a very heavy share in raising the taxes which support government. The taxes on malt, on beer, leather, soap, candles, and other articles, which are paid chiefly by the poor, who are allowed *no votes* for members of parliament, amount to as much as a heavy land-tax.[63]

On these grounds, he argued, not only independent householders, but all men ought to be entitled to vote. Adult male suffrage is being let in by the back door, ostensibly based on a concept of property, but in practice entailing the enfranchisement of men as men. Possibly the fact that the debate about taxation and representation centred upon the Stamp Act, a levy on *moveable* goods rather than land, is important here. For it was the association of a tax with moveable property that enabled such radicals as Burgh to draw their startling (and Leveller-like) conclusions. This same strategy was repeated by Cartwright in *Take Your Choice!* and other of his reformist works, though primarily, one suspects, for pragmatic reasons.[64] It was a way of leading a propertied conservative to rather more radical conclusions than he might, at first, wish to contemplate. With the subsequent emergence of attacks on 'Old Corruption', it also proved a razor-sharp weapon for reformers. It provided both a critique of government and an explanation of its inadequacies. Why should men pay for incompetent, extravagant administration when they were unrepresented, particularly when the reason why it was incompetent and extravagant was *because* it was not representative? No wonder the slogan 'No Taxation without Representation' was so enduring. It made as much sense to the demonstrators at Peterloo whose banners carried the motto[65] as it did to the unenfranchised of the American revolutionary period.

Both the advocacy of a more extensive suffrage and the support for a more equal representation take as their starting point the indisputable fact that owners of all sorts of property paid some kind of tax, and concluded that those who are taxed ought to be represented. The link between taxation and the surrender of property was a connection that the English reformers learnt from or, at least, had very strongly reinforced by the opponents of the Stamp Act. They were not, in fact, reluctant to acknowledge their debt to such colonial polemicists as James Otis.

The American contribution to the debate about parliamentary reform was even greater than this. For the Americans not only strengthened the case for reform, they acted as an ideological midwife, bringing into the political world a qualitatively different sort of reform. Beckford, it is true, had used the question of inequitable tax distribution as a case for parliamentary reform in his mayoroyalty speech of 1761.[66] Such an argument, however, was highly uncharacteristic, if not unique. Prior to the 1760s parliamentary reform had meant, in effect, country-party measures designed, either by the removal of placemen or by holding more frequent general elections, to obtain an independent, politically pure lower House. The American debate, however, gave those urban and mercantile interests which had begun to resent the difference between their financial power and their political impotence both the opportunity and the arguments with which to present a case for their greater participation in the political process. Thus in 1769 we find the Middlesex electors trying to organise a tax strike because, as they claimed, they were not properly represented.[67]

It is not fortuitous that English reformers such as the publisher, John Almon, and the members of the Society of the Supporters of the Bill of Rights should have had strong American connections. (Almon, indeed, was responsible for publishing a number of American tracts, including Otis's *A Vindication of the British Colonists*, not, as one might expect, during the Stamp Act crisis itself, but in 1769 when observations on representation were applicable to the reforming efforts of the supporters of Wilkes.) The urban, primarily metropolitan advocates of reform had borne the brunt of American propaganda in 1765–6; in their capacity as merchants, manufacturers and businessmen they had read the colonists' complaints in personal correspondence as well as in the pages of the London and provincial newspapers, worked for the repeal of the offending legislation, and absorbed, as often as not through personal contact, the strident arguments against 'virtual representation'. Not unnaturally, once they saw the advantages that could accrue, they marshalled their forces behind the American cause. By 1770, radicals on both sides of the Atlantic were urging upon each other the necessity for unity, mutual solidarity and strength.[68] English reformers had a further reason to feel kinship with their American brothers; it was the colonists who had provided them with the key with which to unlock the fetters imposed by an unreformed representation.

Part V

Two political nations

11. The politicians, the press and the public

꧁꧂

> I thank you from the bottom of my heart for the kind marks of your confidence communicated by Mr. Jenkinson and . . will exert my utmost efforts to deserve them. I wrote a paper, my Lord, the moment he left me upon the hints he gave me which I hope will appear in the Chronicle this evening. I send your Lordship a paper enclosed which is gone to the Gazetteer. I will pursue these steps daily with the warmest zeal and the most indefatigible diligence. (John Campbell to Lord Bute, 4 September 1762, Bute Mss.)

Up to this point we have examined the press from the point of view of the audience; our perspective has been that of a London club-man or of a provincial coffee-house newsreader. But the press was not merely the vehicle for news; it was an institution that politicians treated with respect, and attempted to manipulate for their own ends. Although most attempts by politicians to control the press were remarkably unsuccessful, it was not for want of trying; besides, they had a great many means, some coercive, some more subtle, by which they could bully and cajole the producers and distributors of the nation's news.

Doubtless the most direct means of control was through taxation. Throughout the century ministers, partly to increase revenue, but primarily as a means of constraint, taxed papers, pamphlets and advertisements. This affected both the format and quantity of newspapers. The proprietors of many papers, especially of those evanescent journals which relied upon a political crisis or furore to maintain their solvency, walked a financial tightrope. It needed only the gentlest of pushes, such as an alteration in the stamp revenue, to topple them off. Immediately after the Act of 1712, for instance, seven provincial papers ended their parlous existence. Papers vanished at a stroke. The results of such legislation were not always so predictable. A loophole in the Act of 1757 unintentionally encouraged the newspaper press, and led proprietors to increase the size of individual papers, thereby providing more room for advertisements and political commentary.[1] This act was, however, an idiosyncratic aberration; taxation was intended to keep the press down to a manageable size, and in most cases it enjoyed some success. It is therefore not surprising to find new legislation passed at times of political tension or conflict. A new stamp act, raising the costs of newspaper production, was used as a means of swatting a number of particularly irritating political gadflies. Yet this never removed the pest of the press, it merely decelerated its progress. In fact the long-term impact of taxation was limited; as a government employee who surveyed the tax situation in 1764 remarked, newspaper circulations were far more subject to the laws of supply and demand than to those of His Majesty the King.[2]

Press prosecutions were also used by politicians to define the parameters of political debate. There was a remarkable degree of consensus amongst parliamentary politicians about what it was permissible for the press to say. Although government and opposition might fight bitterly over the procedures involved in prosecution (general warrants being a particularly conspicuous example of this legal logic-chopping), they usually concurred with one another when it came to deciding whether or not a paper or pamphlet was libellous. Hence the contrast between the passionate attack on general warrants and the readiness to concede that the *North Briton no. 45* was a libel. No one wanted to support Wilkes's claim that his notorious periodical could not be libellous because it happened to be true.[3] All that was required, as far as the opposition was concerned, was that the appropriate political mileage be gained from the issues of parliamentary privilege and arbitrary arrest.[4] A similar attitude was evinced in the case of the *Whisperer*, a weekly paper that appeared at the end of the 1760s. The author took a tough, radical line: the administration was not just malevolently intended; the whole system was rotten – House of Commons, constitution and all.[5] In consequence, the paper received almost universal disapprobation; opposition politicians, supposedly the defenders of the liberty of the press, were the first to implement legal proceedings.

The employment of this kind of constraint became more difficult during the 1760s. Wilkes's successes in Entick *v.* Carrington and Leach *v.* Money and the unwillingness of juries to convict, all made prosecution a difficult, sometimes even a financially dangerous task. Prosecutions had a hope of success only against the most flagrant offences, and could no longer be undertaken lightly.

Perhaps this was one of the reasons why politicians increasingly used the methods of the carrot rather than those of the stick. They began, in other words, to exploit the press for their own ends. MPs were in a strong position to do this. Through their franking privilege they could distribute newspapers and political propaganda free of charge to their constituents and supporters. In the week 6–13 March 1764, for instance, the franking of newspapers for MPs cost the Post Office

£465 5s. 6d., a sum which, if Cranfield's calculations are correct, would imply that members had distributed some 10,000 copies of newspapers in a seven-day period.[6] This practice was increased by an act of 1764 which changed the administrative procedure for members' franking of newspapers. Before the act

Peers and Members of Parliament wrote their Names on the Covers of News Papers to pass them free, the rest of the Superscription being written by the Persons who made them up for the Country. Afterwards the practice changed, when the Members put their Names to a Letter Addressed to the Secretary of the Post Office requesting that News Papers might pass free to the Persons therein described.[7]

The opportunities available under this new system were not realised until 1768, when an act restricting newspaper franking for members to the parliamentary session drew MPs' attention to the loophole. Thereafter members – especially those in opposition – used their privilege to name printers, booksellers and dealers, thereby helping them distribute papers directly to their customers without paying postage. By 1771 the number of those listed as enjoying this privilege had risen to 1149.[8] The practice is well illustrated in a constituent's letter to Sir Roger Newdigate: 'Mr. Shuttleworth having declined the resuming his Seat in Parliament,' he wrote, 'I will take this Opportunity to request you to send my Name to the Post-Master in the List of those whom you permit to have Newspapers directed with your Name.'[9] Thus, by the end of the 1760s, the Post Office was circulating large quantities of newspapers for MPs free of charge. Ironically a government institution was helping such opposition members as Richard Oliver, Sir Robert Bernard, Sir Joseph Mawbey and Brass Crosby to distribute anti-government propaganda.

Access to a system of distribution encouraged politicians, both in and out of office, to supply the propaganda themselves. For some it was a much easier task than for others: those who knew booksellers, printers and publishers – and they were almost invariably the most radical parliamentary politicians – had little trouble getting into print or persuading others to write for them; but the novices in this field were forced to recruit support where they could.

Bute provides a singularly apt example of this latter case. It was, perhaps, one of the greatest ironies of the 1760s that the man who suffered most of the hands of the grub-street pamphleteers, journalists and cartoonists, Lord Bute, should also be the politician who, more than any other, made covert attempts to shape public opinion by using the press. In this enterprise he was urged on by his two allies at the beginning of the reign, Bubb Dodington and Henry Fox. Both of them, despite a professed contempt for the public,[10] knew from experience the political advantages to be gained from engaging in a paper war.

Early in the new reign Dodington had urged Bute to set up a newspaper, to employ coffee-house spies and to ensure that his position was fully stated to the public. In doing so, the future Lord Melcombe outlined the strategy that Bute was to pursue until his retirement from public politics in 1763. Although the idea of establishing a newspaper did not reach fruition until the summer of 1762, Bute had clearly been considering the scheme for some time. In December 1761 James Ralph had been commissioned to produce a number of projected weekly papers; three of these were sent to Bute for his personal scrutiny. Ralph, however, was reluctant to start a regular publication. He felt that 'Christmas...and the Adjournment attendant on it are apt to make such a Gap in the public Attention' that the papers ought to be deferred; he also refused, in view of his own ill-health, to produce regular papers without an assistant.[11] Thus it was not until the end of the following May and during the first week of June that Bute's papers finally appeared as the *Briton* and the *Auditor*. Quite possibly this delay was because of the opposition to their publication expressed by Bute's old friend and chief propagandist, Dr John Campbell. As he pointed out:

I have had my Lord much experience in these things and from that experience I speak. There is no doubt that you will receive many provocations. Papers will be set up to libel your measures. But, my Lord, that signifies little if you set up no paper to defend them, for in that case a paper war would commence and as in all wars those who live by [them] will study to continue them. In the state you are in an occasional paper now and then in those very vehicles of scandal in which you are abused will do the work effectually because truth is on your side and malice only on theirs.[12]

As it transpired Campbell's apprehensions were correct. Within a very short time the *Briton* and *Auditor* were in difficulties. William Guthrie had to be called in to help Smollett produce the *Briton*, and Jenkinson, in an attempt to improve the quality of the administration's journalism, approached another hack, Shebbeare, shortly afterwards. Shebbeare, however, was too well aware of the difficulties involved to be willing to commit himself to support the government's plans.[13] Neither of the two papers, therefore, was very successful. Indeed, by provoking the foundation of the *North Briton* they proved, as Campbell had predicted, an actual hindrance to Lord Bute's cause.

Bute also took up Dodington's suggestion of employing coffee-house spies. They were hired to sound out London opinion and, where necessary, write papers and pamphlets to counter objections to the Favourite voiced in the city. The two most important of their number were Hugh Baillie and Edward Richardson. The former made regular reports to Bute and conveyed suggestions from groups of merchants to Charles Jenkinson, the Favourite's secretary.[14] On 8 August 1762, for example, Baillie sent a full-length report of the views of members of the Half Moon Club in Cheapside, conveying their apprehensions about Bute's capacity to make a strong peace.[15] In the following October he was again hard at work, producing a pamphlet critical of Pitt and in favour of the peace preliminaries, and visiting the taverns and coffee houses in the city to gauge its reception. 'I have spent a good part of my time these two days past in the city', he informed Bute, 'in order to find out the sentiments of people concerning the Letter to the Lord Mayor, aldermen &c – published last Monday, which I had the better opportunity of knowing as they had no Suspicion I was the author.'[16]

Richardson, Baillie's chief colleague, was equally active. Urging the government to respond to the public, he wrote to Charles Jenkinson:

Your friends have hitherto, indeed, my dear Sir, but too much contemned popularity, which you know in this free country has ever been the scaffolding to ministerial buildings. We have seen a fair lay'd foundation but shall never behold its progress without the aid of your citizens poles, scurvy as they are, to raise it.[17]

In accordance with these views Richardson was assiduous in cultivating connections in the City. He was Bute's chief contact with the Common Council and Aldermanic body of London. (It was he who arranged the notorious meeting between the Favourite and Sir James Hodges over the cider tax in 1763.) Like Baillie he sent schemes, information and suggestions to Bute, while simultaneously acting as a propagandist.[18] Richardson, indeed, was responsible for one of the most successful pieces of government propaganda, the *Letter to a Gentleman in the City*, or the so-called Wandsworth Letter. This appeared in September 1762 and, according to the *Monitor*, 'was printed on a *half-sheet*; dispersed with great diligence on the Royal Exchange, and in all the places of public resort, in and about the metropolis, and franked by post all over the kingdom'.[19]

The coffee-house spies and the production of two newspapers were only a small part of Bute's efforts to win over the public to his cause. A whole bevy of pensioners and literary hacks – men like Campbell, Philip Francis, Richardson, Guthrie, Murphy and Ralph – were kept on the Favourite's payroll simply to write pamphlets and letters to the newspapers.[20] Bute first mobilised these men in October 1761 after Pitt's resignation. Although he had not wished the Secretary of State to resign, once Pitt had gone Bute set out to portray the former minister's action in the worst possible light. All of Pitt's former inconstancies were marshalled as evidence against him:

his [Pitt's] conduct is placed in such lights as may best explain it to Men of common Understandings. It is shewn from principle no Man can espouse his Interest as he has at different Times maintained and rejected every Principle by which hitherto any Party has been distinguished. It is next shewn that no hopes can be derived from personal attachment to him as he has been equally a cool Friend and an Inveterate Enemy without much respect to the Merits of either Side. Lastly it is proved that the reinvesting him with power or pleasing him while out of power is equally impracticable and all this from Facts of Public Notoriety as well as indisputable Authority.[21]

Though the attack on Pitt had common themes, it was produced in a variety of forms. Francis wrote the acerbic *Mr. Pitt's Letter Versified* and this was quickly followed by another piece of political poetry, the *Letter from a Right Honourable Person and the Answer to it, Translated into Verse* by Arthur Murphy.[22] Francis and James Ralph were told to attack the Pittite *Monitor* in the newspapers. Ralph, who received detailed instructions from Bute, promised that his writing should 'be accommodated to the best of my capacity to the idea now communicated to me by your Lordship'.[23] Campbell wrote a pamphlet critical of the Great Commoner, copies of which were sent to the Princess Dowager and the king. At the same time he peppered the London papers, especially the *London Chronicle*, with uncompromising attacks on Pitt. Two of his contributions were published on 27 October 1761, and three on 5 November; others appeared on 29 October, 25 and 27 November and 7 December. Campbell was clearly determined to overwhelm Pitt's supporters and block off every channel of reply.[24] As he wrote to Bute:

I have...my Lord very carefully watched all the Inflammatory Paragraphs that have appeared in the Papers and have encountered them by other Paragraphs better founded as well as of a better tendency. These I send to almost every Paper and as they cost them nothing they never fail to have a Place. I have cut out two from last Nights Chronicle and three from another Paper which was published the very night the King opened the Sessions by his Speech and I could in like manner send your Lordship a score every week. It is inconceivable how the Minds of the People are wrought on in this manner and therefore I flatter myself that as this is a useful it will be likewise an acceptable service.[25]

Once this first flurry of attacks upon Pitt had ended, Bute's writers settled down to the task – at which they were to achieve very little success – of defending the Favourite. Campbell, at once the most prolific propagandist amongst the group and probably the only one with a real sense of political purpose, formulated the stance from which Bute's apologists were to proceed:

The readers of public papers are chiefly of two sorts, those who are sensible and read for informaton and those who read from curiosity or because it is the fashion. To the first we must demonstrate that your Lordship's [Bute's] Administration is constitutional and that the preservation of the Constitution depends upon the support of it. We must convince the bulk of the people that your Lordship's Administration is built upon national principles and a resolution to act upon these in order to extricate it from those difficulties which have been created by an ambitious desire of continuing in Power. If these ends are steadily and effectually pursued, opposition will decline apace, the King's measures will be understood and approved and your Lordship will become a popular and a permanent Minister.[26]

In accordance with this overall plan, Campbell produced a pamphlet defending Bute which the Favourite later described as a work 'wrote in a candid manly manner & with great judgement & perpecuity [sic] sufficient to convince those who are open to conviction'.[27] This pamphlet, as Campbell's correspondence with Bute makes clear, was personally commissioned by the Favourite and written with Jenkinson's help:

The Day after I troubled your Lordship last I received from Mr. Jenkinson the Papers & the Heads of that Work which you had the Goodness to intrust to my Care and tho' I am extremely indisposed I will apply myself to it with all the fidelity & Diligence in my Power & hope by the Assistance of Mr. Jenkinson who is at once one of the modestest & most intelligent Persons I ever met with it may be brought to some degree of Perfection.[28]

Bute's only reservation about this official apologia was that it was too transparently the work of a hireling: 'the turn of the pamphlet, as well as the title carrys too much of the air of coming from Government itself. A few alterations would correct this, & by that means stamp the writer with more independency.'[29] The mask of impartiality was especially necessary for the man who wielded a prostituted pen.

Campbell seems to have enjoyed an unusual measure of confidence for a government propagandist. He was supplied with a copy of the 1762 peace preliminaries before they were made public, and enjoyed frequent consultations with Jenkinson who helped him sketch out potential articles for the press.[30] Between 1762 and 1763 Campbell was supplied with a mass of government information about the territorial acquisitions obtained at the Peace of Paris which, after considerable and painstaking labour and not a little prompting from Bute, finally appeared in the pamphlet shops as *Candid and Impartial Considerations on the Nature of the Sugar Trade*. This was intended by its author and his patron (despite its somewhat narrow title) as a major defence of Bute's diplomacy during the peace negotiations.[31]

Campbell's prodigious efforts were supported by several other authors. Richardson, the coffee-house spy, wrote letters to the *Gazetteer* under the *nom de plume* of 'Inquisitor'. Philip Francis produced his *Letter from the Cocoa Tree to the Country Gentleman,* a statement widely, and rightly, regarded as a full expression of Bute's position which, when it appeared, was 'the Discourse of Every Body at St. James's'.[32] 'Philo-Patriae', an anonymous newspaper letter writer, kept Bute supplied with information about hostile literature so that appropriate replies could be drafted. A former defender of Walpole in the old *Gazetteer,* Ralph Courteville, kept up his connection with the paper by writing letters defending the Favourite. He also produced an ambitious scheme for a weekly newspaper which was to have been widely distributed in the provinces with the aid of the Post Office. Even Dodington himself put pen to paper and attacked the opposition to the Favourite.[33]

The impression of Bute that emerges from this account of his press activities contrasts very forcibly with his traditional image of the court politician. There would be nothing particularly remarkable in finding Bute's more radical opponents in cahoots with some of the shadier characters in the seamy side of journalism; but to find the king's Favourite, a lofty not to say priggish man, rubbing shoulders with the inhabitants of the Grub Street garret, is truly remarkable. Nor can we explain Bute's contact with the literary *demi-monde* as a desperate course of last resort, forced upon him by the printed vituperation of others. For although, as I have demonstrated elsewhere,[34] he was subject to more malicious attacks than any other contemporary politician, he himself had started a press war against his opponents, even before they had begun their attack upon him. Perhaps Bute's concern for the press can be dismissed as yet another of the many errors of judgement that he made during his political career. Possibly so; but Bute's press activities stand as yet another example of the way in which he and the king were forced to utilise the weapons of party combat in order to counter party. Bute had to undermine Pitt because he represented an alternative to the patriot ruler; he also had to propagate the notion of a non-party reign of virtue, because he needed both the actual support of the financial and mercantile interests in the City of London, and the ostensible allegiance of the public at large to counteract his opponent's accusations of favouritism. The utilisation of the press was necessary for political survival.

This lesson was not lost on Newcastle and Rockingham, although it was only gradually learnt. The press never represented Newcastle's kind of politics. In the 1750s he retained, almost as a matter of course rather than for any specific motive, the services of William Guthrie, James Ralph and David Mallet through the auspices of the secret service fund;[35] but his actual understanding of the workings of the press was limited. His comments and ideas on the matter were usually confined to squeals of angry protest whenever he was the victim of the satirist's pen.[36] In 1762, after nearly forty years in government service and only a few months in opposition, he wrote to Hardwicke, 'I own, I don't understand any of those Prints, & Burlesques; I am too dull to taste them; And, if they are not decypher'd for Me, I could not in the least guess, very often, what they mean...*I detest the whole Thing.*' Yet, even in the same breath as he professed ignorance, Newcastle recognised the importance of the printed word: 'They [prints etc.] have their *real* Consequences, And there is an amazing Tameness, in not daring to take Notice of any of Them.'[37] Characteristically, Newcastle's timorousness was not without its perspicacity.

The rigours of opposition, the press activities of Bute and the parlous state of the party all combined to increase the Newcastle–Rockingham connection's sensitivity to press criticism. The publication of Francis's *Letter from the Cocoa Tree*, sponsored by Lord Bute, prompted Newcastle to turn to Henry Bilson Legge, one of the few members of the party versed in the arts of journalism.[38] The outcome was a riposte to Francis, the *Address to the Cocoa Tree from a Whig*, and the decision to reply in a fairly systematic way to government pamphlets as and when they appeared. Newcastle wrote to Legge:

Having reflected upon what you said of the Necessity of having some prudent Pamphlet wrote, which may set the Proceedings of the Ministers, & their Director behind the Curtain, in a true Light, & having read over cursorily a pamphlet lately published, and dispersed by the Administration, more to reflect upon us, than justify My Lord Bute, (and, I conclude, wrote by my Lord Bute,) I am of opinion, that a proper Representation of the Whole in Print, would be of great Service to the Publick...And I can think of no Person so able, & so proper, as the Author of the first Letter to the Cocoa Tree.[39]

Once realised, the importance of taking action through the press became a persistent theme amongst members of the party. Thus in April 1764, when Charles Townshend drew up an overall strategic plan for opposition, one of his main suggestions was that, 'To gain upon the minds of the people, a daily paper, upon the plan of the Prints, should be set up and circulated diligently, tho' quietly, and two good pens should be employed to write, from material suggested by men of knowledge and subject to their inspection.'[40] Though the plan never came to fruition, it was agreed, in principle at least, that a newspaper should be established, and Almon even asked Wilkes if he would like to be its editor.[41] Doubtless the scheme foundered on the same rock that sank Wildman's club. The idea of a party paper was not one that the whig grandees would have welcomed, for it might well have placed too much power in the hands of the enthusiastic young men of the party who would, inevitably, have been the driving force behind its publication.

The spectre of a misguided public continued to haunt the party after their return to power in 1765. They had not cultivated the press as they ought (though they cooperated with the merchants' and manufacturers' campaign for the repeal of the Stamp Act) and, in consequence, they suffered badly from public criticism from the supporters of both Grenville and Pitt. William, Count Bentinck, complained bitterly of the way in which the party neglected a gullible public. He wrote from the Hague:

I write today to the Duke of Grafton on a point which I have several times mentioned to your Grace [Portland] viz. the necessity of employing some good Pens to knock down your very insolent, impertinent and scurrilous, Pamphlet and Newspapers writers. This is, I assure you, an object of great importance, and of very serious attention in an Administration. I am very apt to believe that Mr. Pitt is greatly owing his Popularity at home, and his Reputation abroad to Pamphlets and News Papers wrote under his Direction, and that of his Admirers. The wisest and prudentest Ministers have always considered this as a very important affair, and acted in consequence. You have no notion of all the stuff and nonsense I have heard, in the eight days I have now been here, without being being [*sic*] able to make my self believed by People, who would know me, and would give entire credit to whatever I say, if they had not been intoxicated by the Pamphlets and News Papers. I beg your Grace to speak or to write to your Friends, and let the Public be amused and directed with Pamphlets and News, since they must have 'em, wrote in favour of the Present Administration. Believe me on my word. It is of the greatest importance. For the consequences extend over all Europe. Ridiculous as this may appear to you, it is nevertheless true.[42]

The frequency with which these sentiments were repeated by members of the party is indicative of the limited results that such exhortations actually produced.[43] As, by predilection and composition, the Rockingham–Newcastle connection was a highly patrician body, it had precious little of the experience of the Chathamites and city radicals in dealing with printers and publishers. In consequence, throughout the time that the party was in opposition, they had to contend with a group of colleagues whose political views were less cautious than their own, and who dominated the newspaper press.[44] There is remarkably little newspaper comment for the 1760s that can be clearly identified as distinctively Rockinghamite, and, where it can be found, it is usually swamped by a much greater volume of more radical criticism.

This partly explains why the party tended to give expression to its views in the less widely circulated medium of the pamphlet. This enabled them to exercise greater control over the finished product than would have been the case with a newspaper letter. Besides, a pamphlet was more likely to be read by the political elite than a less substantial work, and it permitted sustained expression – which might run to several hundred pages – of the party's views.

Throughout the decade, party supporters published a steady flow (it could never be called a stream) of political pamphlets. In the opposition before 1765, the most important contributions were Charles Townshend's *Defence of the Minority in the House of Commons, on the Question Relating to General Warrants*, and Hartley's *The Budget*. The former was widely circulated amongst the members of the party before its publication in August 1764. Newcastle was delighted with it;[45] he told the author, 'I read, with the greatest Pleasure, and Approbation, that most Excellent, & Unanswerable Pamphlet...I could not avoid ...giving it all the Praise it deserves...It is a great, a perfect, & a manly Work, & does great Honor to whoever wrote it.'[46] Rockingham was equally laudatory. 'I am most highly delighted with the defence of the Minority,' he wrote, simultaneously informing Newcastle that he had had copies of the work circulated in Yorkshire.[47] At the end of September Thomas Walpole estimated that the piece had sold at least 1500 copies.[48]

Yet the pamphlet was not an unmitigated success. Neither Pitt nor Wilkes liked it, and Horace Walpole believed the work did 'not sell much, as a notion prevails that it has been much altered and softened'.[49] The pamphlet certainly suffered from an excellent reply that appeared in September under the title of *Defence of the Majority*. Townshend petulantly refused to answer this riposte, claiming, rather unjustly, that his friends had neglected his work. Stating his case he wrote to Thomas Walpole:

I know not what the Author of the Defence will do, but, if I were that man, I should certainly take no notice of so frivolous an answer (as the *Defence of the Majority*), which comprehends no part of the question, understands not even the common proceedings of the Judicature, & touches not upon the delays by Privilege. I have been told that the Author of this work is the less inclined to move further in this matter from the strange negligence in circulating his work, & from the objections peevishly made, by the party it vindicates, to the temper and tendency of this pamphlet. Some have complained of its candor: others have wondered he would justify general warrants in cases even of treason; and no one man has received it with zeal enough to spread it in any distant Towns: An indifference which resembles little the activity & union with which the Majority espouse, maintain, & circulate every weak word which interest of authority obtains in their favour. Upon hearing this mentioned I enquired into the truth of it, & happening to have friends with me just come from Bristol, Bath and Liverpole, I found, upon asking them, that they had eagerly enquired after the Defence in these places, & could not hear of one which had been sent. It is the same at Oxford, where I could not get one; but where I bought a defence of the Majority one day before it was advertised. Lord T[emple]. tells me he has heard of the pamphlet in Norfolk, but could not get it at Norwich or Lynne or Yarmouth...no consideration should induce me to move one step further in the contest, but I would leave it to those, who diaspproved of...[my] temper, and find [my] argument imperfect, to merit more from the Minority by a fuller vindication, written with less temper, & upon a better plan.[50]

Ruffled by these criticisms, the party leaders decided to reply to the attack on Townshend. He himself would have nothing to do with it, and Sir William Meredith, a man of little legal knowledge, was persuaded to take his place. His *Answer to the Majority*, personally corrected by Newcastle, appeared at the end of 1764.[51]

Hartley's *Budget*, the other chief party pamphlet of this period, also had its difficulties. At the outset it was hard to find a printer, which led Legge to suggest that the party should employ one of its own.[52] Nevertheless the pamphlet was much more successful than Townshend's. According to Onslow, who sent bundles of the work to Newcastle, it was 'the best Pamphlet we have had'. Within a month of publication Newcastle was enthusing about its success: '*The Budget does great good*; I hope it will be dispersed Everywhere.'[53] By 1766 it had reached its eleventh edition and it was said that Grenville's budget speech of 1765 was an attempt to refute its assertions. It also launched the first salvo in what was to become a running battle between Grenville and the Newcastle–Rockingham connection on financial matters. *The Budget* was answered by Mauduit, the extremely successful author of *Considerations on the German War*, and by Whately, a junior member of the Treasury.[54] But Hartley remained undaunted. In March 1765 he brought out his *State of the Nation, with a Preliminary Defense of the Budget* which Onslow described as 'unanswerable' and which again delighted Newcastle.[55] 'This comes out just in the proper Moment,' wrote the ageing duke, 'to prepare all Unprejudiced People for Mr. Grenville's Budget, & to puzzle all the Supporters of the present Plan of Oeconomy, & Supplies.' His only reservation was that 'I am sorry to see, that it is dated Feb[ry] 28th, by which, I fear, the Plans agreed to, voted, and resolved, this Session of Parliament, will not be touched upon in it.'[56] But Hartley was soon hard at work producing a new edition designed to include the latest financial measures, as well as additional information supplied by Newcastle himself.[57] Again

Hartley's pamphlet quickly generated controversy. Grenville's accomplished hacks, Whately and Knox, replied, and this brought Dowdeswell and Burke to Hartley's defence.[58] *The Budget*, therefore, proved a tremendous success; it had all the attributes of a fine pamphlet: cogently argued, it had presented a coherent case which brought into question the entire fiscal and colonial policy of Grenville. It had sold well, been frequently reprinted, and generated a controversy that had spawned such fine works as Knox's *State of the Nation*, and Burke's famous reply, *Observations*. Much of this debate had been technical and, at times, almost arcane; even Burke, not one to shirk the arduous task of unravelling the twisted strands of government finance, had been forced to fall back on Dowdeswell's fiscal expertise. But the question of taxes was second only to the question of constitutionality in the minds of the land-tax paying squirearchy to whom much of this pamphlet literature was addressed. Though, from many points of view, Grenville's policies made at least as much sense as those of the followers of Rockingham, there can be little doubt that Hartley, Dowdeswell and Burke had the better of the pamphlet debate and, in consequence, increased the public credit of the party.

After the financial debate which, apart from Burke's *Short Account of a late Short Administration*, very much dominated the middle years of the decade, the party's journalism was concentrated on two issues, *Nullum Tempus* and the Middlesex election. Work on the former was supervised by the ever industrious Hartley. He provided papers on the Cumberland election, wrote a pamphlet that attacked Sir James Lowther, and acted as coordinator between Portland and Almon. It was also his task to fix the number of pamphlets to be printed and sent to the country, so that Portland could distribute the propaganda in the localities.[59]

In the party's history during the 1760s, one can see a progressive sophistication and rationalisation in the presentation of the party's opinions to the public. There is some evidence in the *Nullum Tempus* affair, for instance, of attempts to tailor the amount and type of propaganda to a specifically provincial audience. This represented the culmination of an increased sensitivity to provincial political sentiment which stemmed from the experiences of the Rockingham administration. Both the alarming rumours that the party had sold out to Lord Bute and the success of the campaign against the Stamp Act convinced the party leaders that opinion outside the metropolis had to be cultivated. No doubt this development is also explained by Rockingham's supersession of Newcastle. The duke, despite his Sussex home, never really had roots in any substantial locality, nor cared as deeply about the fate of the county as he did about the fortunes of court and treasury. Rockingham, however, took his task as Lord Lieutenant in the West Riding very seriously indeed. He spent as much time as he could in Yorkshire, and always interested himself in local affairs. Thus, when the Halifax coiners murdered an exciseman, he was one of the first to take action and bring the Mint Solicitor into the case. Similarly his enthusiasm for the repeal of the Stamp Act stemmed from his intimate acquaintance with the languishing state of the West Riding textile industry during the American embargo.

As the party looked more and more to the public, so it took its pamphleteering more seriously. Party manifestoes now had to be scrutinised by the party's senior members before they were published. Thus, in 1769, when Dowdeswell laboured long and hard over a pamphlet on the Middlesex election, it was circulated before publication to Burke and Rockingham. Dowdeswell, doubtful of the legal niceties of the matter, wanted a lawyer to criticise his work: 'I should wish Wedderburn to see it, and any confidential Friends, & wish they would put down in writing their remarks with reference to the pages they apply to, so that when I come to Wentworth I may avail myself of those remarks, and give this thing some more correction.'[60] This suggestion was followed, but it meant that the work was not sent to London until October, and not published until November when it appeared under the title of *The Sentiments of an English Freeholder, on the late Decision of the Middlesex Election.*[61]

A similar process of consultation was employed with the two pamphlets that Sir William Meredith wrote on the same subject in 1769. The first, his *The Question Stated...In a Letter from a Member of Parliament to one of his Constituents*, was put before a party meeting in May and subsequently circulated amongst those who had been absent on that occasion.[62] As Meredith informed Portland:

I take the Liberty to send your Grace a written Copy of a pamphlet for your looking over, if you think it worth while, before it is published.

I undertook it, because nobody else would; and found great difficulty in stating Law points with that precision that is necessary, & which I am used to. But, I believe, I am pretty accurate in the Facts & grounds, on which the Vote was supported.

Sr Geo. Savil[e], L^d Jo Cavendish, Bourke, Barwel's Legh & Wedderburn have all inspected, but I made very little alteration, except Sir Geo Savil[e], to whom I am indebted for Three Sentences.[63]

This same practice was used a few months later when Meredith had to reply to an attack on his original work. Rockingham, Portland and Wedderburn all scrutinised the new pamphlet.[64] Similarly during 1769 and early 1770, Burke's major synthesis of the Rockinghamites' party creed, the *Thoughts*, was read by Portland, Rockingham, Sir George Savile and Dowdeswell.[65]

Thus, by the end of the decade the party had developed a standard procedure for the publication of its propaganda, chiefly in the form of pamphlets. This marked a considerable improvement on the first years of opposition when Newcastle and the whig mandarinate had fumbled and hesitated in their dealings with the press. The connection's politics had, of necessity adapted itself to the ways of opposition: the public was more self-consciously wooed, and the process of decision-making within the party extended to include those outside the charmed circle of the great whig families. The party's willingness to engage in public debate, therefore, was symptomatic of the way in which it had changed during the 1760s. The party still retained vestiges of its old distaste for the press – it was reluctant, for instance, to become involved in any newspaper war – but it had come to see that journalism was not merely a threat but could be used to positive political advantage.

George Grenville had a somewhat similar and equally ambivalent attitude. Much of the press left him cold. He frequently commented on the mendacity of newspapers, was at great pains to avoid any personal involvement in public controversy, and had, after all, been instrumental in the prosecution of the *North Briton*.[66] Nevertheless, he employed his private secretary, Charles Lloyd, to write pamphlet attacks on the Rockingham administration, including *An Honest Man's Reasons for Declining to take Part in the New Administration* and his *Critical Review of the New Administration*. Lloyd also collected materials for the press, and wrote the occasional newspaper letter. His activities only ceased with the publication of the *History of the late Minority*. This pamphlet antagonised the King's Friends who felt that both Temple and Grenville had had a hand in its composition. In order to heal the wounds, therefore, Grenville persuaded Lloyd to stop writing.[67]

Whately and William Knox were the two other chief protagonists for Grenville and his policies. The former kept Grenville supplied with pamphlets which he thought his friend should see, as well as items from newspapers other than the *Public Advertiser*, which was the only journal to which Grenville subscribed. Throughout 1765 and 1766 he corresponded with John Temple in the North American colonies, sending pamphlets and information, and receiving American publications in return. Whately, in other words, acted as Grenville's press agent, as well as writing a number of pamphlets himself.[68]

Knox's cooperation with Grenville was even closer. He was systematically provided with information and opinion for his two pamphlets, the *Present State of the Nation* and *Controversy Between Great Britain and her Colonies Reviewed*. In long and painstaking letters Grenville outlined his views on taxation, sovereignty, the nature of the constitution and the causes of the current political crisis.[69] These were faithfully reproduced by Knox. Grenville was delighted:

They are written with so much temper and force with so much knowledge and Precision that I am persuaded they will do you great honor, if ever you shall think fit to avow yourself as the author of them. The general Principles laid down in them correspond so much with my declared opinions and are so favorable to the public Measures I have pursued, that to express my Approbation of them to you who are so perfectly acquainted with both would be unnecessary.[70]

Other members of the Grenville connection were no less reluctant than their leader to explore the labyrinthine complexities of the newspaper press. Lord Sandwich, 'Jemmy Twitcher', was responsible for employing Dr James Scott, a clergyman, whose letters of 'Anti-Sejanus' were an enormous success.[71] Scott had a very powerful prose style, full of metaphor and striking classical allusions: from a literary point of view his work was more successful than the often over-estimated writings of Junius. Anti-Sejanus's capacity to prick the bubble of pretension was especially useful in these letters, which concentrated on attacking Bute and stigmatising successive administrations as lackeys of the Favourite. Scott had a long and thriving career. Under the pseudonym of 'Old Sly Boots' he became one of the most effective defenders of the Grafton and North administrations, utilising in the cause of government those same talents which had had such effect in opposition.

One other Grenville party journalist deserves consideration. Augustus Hervey was one of the most prolific letter writers of the age. Using the columns of the *Gazetteer* and the *Public Advertiser*, he published letters under such pseudonyms as 'Simon Friendship', 'An Honest Man tho' no Weaver', 'Cominus', 'A True Englishman', 'An Independent, but loyal Country Squire', and 'A Briton', covering topics which ranged from taxation to the pay of the naval seaman.[72] His other works included such anti-Rockinghamite songs as 'Who's that with Bum and back so wide' (a reference to Cumberland), 'A New Sailors' Song', and a number of other ballads, some of which attacked Pitt. He was also responsible for planning a set of prints attacking the Great Commoner when he accepted a peerage in 1766.[73]

Hervey's greatest success, however, was a pamphlet that appeared in August 1765, entitled *A Letter to Lord Bute relative to the late Changes that have happened in A - - - - - - - - - - - - n*. Though written in rather casual circumstances, it was regarded as the chief apologia of the Grenvilles and, as such, was partly reprinted in the *Gentleman's*

Magazine. This had not been Hervey's original intention, but what began as a collection of random thoughts was transformed by circumstance into a timely attack on the system of favouritism:

This was first wrote with[t] any design to Print it, and merely for something to do in an hour or two, July 9th: at Sleaford in an Inn whilst I was waiting for my B[r] B[ll] who was just settling his Stewards Acc[t] & to whom I read it in his chaise, intending to [? illegible] it, as the Administration was then unfix'd – but on coming to Town the 14th: I found all My Friends Disgraced, and turn'd out by L[d] B - - - and in an Ill humour I revised & corrected this, & gave it to Mr. Grenvill[e] to read, & then to Lord Sandwich to do what he wd. wth. He published it – but a little diff[t] from this as he added some warmer Expressions – however very little so – as I had inserted no Scurrilous language.[74]

Ironically, a pamphlet tossed off in a couple of hours achieved more notoriety than any of the many letters that Hervey painstakingly composed and copied into his journal.

Our examination of three political groups in the 1760s – the followers of Bute, the Rockingham–Newcastle connection and the Grenvillites – reveals a fairly high level of press activity in every case. In many ways this is remarkable, for these three groups had no reason to feel charitably disposed towards the gentlemen of the press or their publishing activities. Bute, Grenville and Newcastle, if not Rockingham, all regarded the press with a mixture of fear, loathing and contempt. All of them, especially Bute, had come in for public castigation, and had seen themselves lampooned, libelled, satirised and insulted in cartoons, pamphlets and newspapers. Dealing with the press was no easy matter for them: none of the groups ever produced a polemicist to match Wilkes, and few of them knew how to present their material in a way that would spark their audience's imagination and appeal to their wit. They never realised that, at this level, politics had to be entertaining. Yet, for all their inadequacies, they stuck doggedly to the task of wooing the public, and plodded on with their appeal to the people.

But we should not be beguiled by this evidence into believing that men like Bute, Burke, Rockingham, Grenville and Sandwich saw the press as a 'fourth estate', in some way representative of a body of public opinion, nor should we assume that they envisaged the public as playing an enduring role in national politics. Although there was a good deal of talk about the people (as, for example, in Burke's *Thoughts* where one of the remedies to the current crisis was '*the interposition of the body of the people itself*'),[75] the term was not used as a synonym for the populace at large. Rather a clear distinction was made between 'the people' and 'the mob'. As a correspondent in the *Gazetteer* put it:

By the people I understand not the mob, but those who are able to make any judgement of public affairs. Among these I reckon the Nobility and Gentry, the Professions of Law, Physic, and Divinity, and the trading part of the kingdom.[76]

This view was echoed by Chase Price who defined the people for the Duke of Portland as 'the house of commons in general, and the opinion of the part of creation that runs about Town, and from whom the majority of the world imbibe their conceptions'.[77] Thus, when referring to 'the people', or 'public opinion' or to what the Rockinghams frequently called 'public credit', politicians excluded most of the population. The mob, i.e. most people, were 'Canaille', men who 'whatever they may pretend, howsoever they may talk of Liberty, and all that; are always bad men, bad husbands, bad fathers, and mean nothing less than to create confusion, and bring destruction on those that are so foolish as to listen to their advice'.[78] Membership of that auspicious body, the people, was, as far as most politicians were concerned, a privilege open only to those who were rightly qualified.

This attitude is not surprising when seen in context. Take, for instance, the Rockingham whigs. They wished to utilise the power of public opinion in their struggle against the Crown. Mindful of Burke's adage that 'if we mean to get *redress*, we must strengthen the hands of the minority within Doors by the accession of the publick opinion',[79] they tried to counterweigh royal strength with the force of public approval. But, as one would expect of such a patrician group, they did not wish to democratise politics or in any way jeopardise their own highly privileged social and economic position. Their attitude towards the public mirrored their ambivalent attitude towards the press. Horace Walpole put it well: 'I feel what every good man will feel in civil commotions, that there is nothing so difficult as to make the people go far enough, and to prevent their going too far.'[80]

According to this conception of politics the role of the people was rather like that of the deity in a Newtonian universe. Just as the clockwinder was chiefly necessary only to start the cosmological chronometer, so the body of the people was needed to make the contract that established civil society, and set up the much praised institutions of the British constitution; but thereafter the populace was largely banished from the political arena. The people's return was only permitted at times of crisis, and then with the proviso that expressions of public opinion be mediated and controlled by the leaders of political society. The role that such politicians wished to assign to public opinion, therefore, was essentially a *corroborative* one. Their conception of the public did not permit extra-parliamentary initiative or countenance political beliefs that in any way questioned existing political institutions. Even Burke who, more than any other member of Rockinghamite whigs, was responsible for cooperation and fraternisation with merchants and disgruntled gentry, saw the party's role as *custodial*.

This view represented an integral part of a conception of how political society ought to work. The exercise of politics was seen as a privilege necessarily confined to those who by virtue of their pedigree, wealth and experience, and occasionally, because of their skill, were peculiarly qualified in that arcane science. Politics was complex, readily open to distortion; men could easily be misguided. They should therefore place their trust in the presiding wisdom of their natural, patrician leaders. Hence, of course, a theory of representation that emphasised the deliberative capacity of the individual MP and that cushioned him against constituency pressure. Nothing must interfere with the individual conscience of the representative, not even instructions voted by his constituents.[81] One of Burke's remarks illuminates this view of politics with his characteristic perspicacity:

> As to popular instructions I take not the rule of my Conduct from their opinions, but I take indications from their Temper – As a Physician does not take his Idea of the remedy from the raving of his Patient; He judges however that when the Patient raves he distempers some way or other. When therefore I see addresses & instructions filled with Triennial, Biennial, annual Parlt[y] Elections by Ballot; exclusion of Eldest Sons of Peers, sons of Scotch Peers; Irish Peers; I gather this & this only that they are of opinion that things amongst us are not carried on just as they ought to be & that there is something amiss in the Constitution of the H. of Commons.[82]

The patient utters cries, complains of pain, may even offer radical and hysterical remedies, but it is the task of the all-knowing and sober physician to diagnose the patient's ills and prescribe an appropriate remedy. Politicians clung desperately, as the medical profession do today, to the idea that, because they had access to a special body of wisdom and learning, others should not be permitted to taste the fruit from that particular tree of knowledge. Just as it would have been gross presumption and folly for the patient to leap up from the table and diagnose his own case, so the public was a body that did not know its own best interests.

In the light of these views, the Rockinghams' extra-parliamentary activities have to be set in context. It is true that they wooed city interests in their opposition to Bute and Grenville,[83] applied opposition tactics when they returned to office to procure the repeal of the Stamp Act and the acceptance of their other American legislation, and used the political capital accumulated with the merchant classes to try to win seats in Lancashire in the 1768 general election.[84] They were also prepared, in conjunction with Grenville and Chatham, to organise the petitioning movement over the Middlesex election in 1769, and to support the City of London over the prosecution of the printers of Parliamentary debates in 1771.[85] Yet studied ambivalence towards the public prevailed. Even while Rockingham or, for that matter, Grenville were using the petitioning campaign to shake the foundations of a tottering administration, they tried to contain the movement, seeking to ensure that only the issue of the Middlesex election, and not those of parliamentary corruption and reform, were contained in the petitions and addresses.[86]

It is here that we arrive at the basic paradox. How was it possible for a patrician political party to maintain its own distinctive conception of politics, and simultaneously use popular support as a weapon against the king's administration? It could only succeed as long as the public accepted the apparatus and ideology of political distance; as long as men were content with the idea of 'politics from above' rather than 'from below'. The mystique of politics was essential to the Grenvilles and Rockinghams as well as the Butes. But the press, especially because it was dominated by a radical viewpoint, constantly undercut their position. It was simply not possible for party politicians successfully to limit the parameters of political debate, placing, as it were, a moratorium on such issues as parliamentary reform. This lesson came home, as it had not done for more than a generation, during the 1760s. The SSBR, which prompted such viperous comments from Burke, made quite clear that it cared little for the malcontented detritus of the old whig oligarchy, and was determined to follow its own political course.

This problem increased in severity as the century proceeded. The 1780s – especially the election of 1784 – and the pyrotechnics of the 1790s revealed the obsolescence of a view of politics based on aristocratic trust, a predominantly passive or politically excluded populace, and a parliamentary oligarchy.[87] The patient was beginning to diagnose his own ills. Once the mystique of politics was attacked, the traditional political leaders were forced to retrench their position. The radicalism of Paine – in *Common Sense* as much as *The Rights of Man* – was to demystify politics and debunk the social apparatus and rituals of power. He showed that common sense, the understanding of the ordinary citizen, enabled all to grasp the true (and simple) nature of politics; and to say that politics was simple was to say something very radical indeed. Small wonder that Burke, the most subtle and sophisticated apologist for trusteeship and the old regime, should spring to its defence, and evolve a justification for the existing political order, quite unlike most of those that had been employed in the political debates earlier in George III's reign.

The acrimonious quarrels of the 1790s may well seem very far removed from the different political debate of the 1760s. Yet even by the accession of George III, or certainly by 1770, it had become apparent that the press and the political groups with which it was most strongly associated were determined upon a degree of political independence. As a result it was difficult for members of the parliamentary factions either to utilise public opinion as they wished, or to conduct politics in the manner to which they were accustomed. Compared with the party conflicts of these years, this seemed a minor difficulty; but, in the long term, it was a development of far greater consequence than the patrician infighting that excited the attentions of most MPs. Already we can observe the 'cloud no bigger than a man's hand' that presages a major storm.

12. The present discontents; party ideology and public unrest

When I reflect on our constitution, I seem as it were to contemplate a game at chess, a recreation in which we both delight; For we have a king, whose dignity we strenuously defend, but whose power is very limited; the knights, and rooks, and other pieces, have some kind of resemblance to the orders of nobility, who are employed in war, and in the management of public affairs; but the principal strength is in the pawns or people; if these are firmly united they are sure of victory, but if divided and separated, the battle is lost. (William Jones to Reviczki, April 1768, in Teignmouth (ed.), *Memoirs of the Life, Writings and Correspondence of Sir William Jones* (1804), 60–1)

This Country, or the Inhabitants of it are become a disgrace to civil Society. Would to God! the Government of it was in such hands, as would risk any thing rather than permit the Mob to lord it over Us in this Manner.

When they have kicked both Houses of Parliament down Stairs, which we shall live to see happen, I suppose some Government will again be established in this Land. (Rigby to Bedford, 4 August 1769, Bedford Mss. LVIII, f. 126)

The combination of ministerial instability and public discontent made the 1760s one of the most volatile decades in the reign of George III. Seven ministries came and went, parliamentary opposition grew apace, the radical press burgeoned, and crowds became both more frequent and more prominent. It is therefore unsurprising to find politicians increasingly preoccupied by the problem of instability. Not only was there abundant evidence of this development, but it impinged directly and personally on many of the leading politicians of the day. The configuration of party politics and the quarrel with the Crown served to create unease and insecurity; the political landscape had been refashioned and men found themselves in unfamiliar surroundings. Simultaneously politicians were attacked by those outside the parliamentary classes. They were the victims of the press war, just as they were the men mobbed in the streets. Bute, as the most unpopular politician of the decade, was lampooned, burnt in effigy and physically manhandled.[1] But his experiences were not exceptional: Fox and Grenville were burnt in effigy,[2] Lord North had his coach destroyed, and narrowly escaped with his life at the very door of the House of Commons.[3] In 1765 an English Duke, Bedford, was besieged by mobs of weavers outside his London house, and had to be rescued by troops.[4]

Three years later he was set upon by a mob who used bulldogs to attack his horse.[5] During the celebration of Wilkes's election in 1768, roving bands of Wilkites smashed aristocrats' windows in the West End.[6] The leaders of the political nation could draw on personal experience to prove the existence of public discontent.

The reactions of MPs to this increased instability have to be seen in a *political* context. To a quite remarkable degree economic and social explanations of discontent were eschewed for those that sought to isolate the political determinants of unrest. At first sight this is surprising as there were good (and obtrusive) grounds for attributing discontent to the economic dislocation at the end of the Seven Years War, the American embargoes on English goods, and the bad state of the recent harvests. But we have to remember that what we are dealing with is a *political* debate, whose prime purpose was to connect a series of extra-parliamentary phenomena to the state of politics at Westminster. The intention of politicians on both sides of the House of Commons was not to adduce objective, scholarly explanations of why the nation was in turmoil, but to show why it was that their political opponents were reponsible for distress and instability.

To do this they had to refer to a set of conventions about political change, and although these norms were generally accepted they were used to produce (one is almost tempted to say, concoct) very different explanations of the situation. By examining these explanations, and the historical analyses on which they were based, we can see just how far political argument had progressed in the decade.

APOLITICAL NORM: BRITAIN'S MIXED BALANCED CONSTITUTION

Nearly every eighteenth-century politician agreed that the British constitution was 'the *best constitution* in the world'.[7] Praised in pamphlets, learned legal tomes, and even poetry,[8] this 'pure solar system of English government and English liberty' was held to be 'demonstrably far preferable to, and better formed for duration, than any of the most celebrated Republicks of antiquity'.[9] Despite their quarrels with the Crown, the politicians agreed with George in one respect: they concurred with his view that the British constitution was 'the most beautiful combination that ever was framed'.[10]

Why was the British constitution so lavishly praised? It was regarded as the best constitution because it embodied a mixed form of government, one composed 'of a due admixture of monarchy, aristocracy and democracy'.[11] According to contemporary notions of how political societies ought to work – notions based on the classical models of

Aristotle, Cicero, and Polybius, transmitted by such Italian humanists as Machiavelli, and embedded in English constitutional thought since the sixteenth century[12] – the virtues of a mixed constitution were twofold. First, it maximised the constraints upon political power, and therefore prevented its abuse; and secondly, as a concomitant of this, it ensured that a nation enjoyed as much liberty as was possible.

The way in which this was achieved by the British constitution is best explained in terms of the problem of power. For it was power, or more accurately, the abuse and growth of power, which dominated the political thinking of the eighteenth-century politician, polemicist and theoretician. Political man, it was assumed, was a malleable, self-interested creature, easily led into error and down the path of corruption. For

as every wise Man knows, that by the universal Laws and Principles of Nature, Selfishness is the fundamental primary ingredient in the Composition of every Being throughout the whole animal Creation, and in human Kind no less than in the rest; so unless a Man is a Fool himself, he will never go about to persuade any Body but a Fool, that he alone is exempt from that general Influence in his way of Acting.[13]

In these circumstances it was considered wise to presume 'that great powers *will be* abused', that power, especially when unconstrained, would tend to grow in the hands of self-interested men.[14] 'Most men', one pamphleteer wrote, 'have an insatiable Lust for Power', and, as another sagely added, 'it requires, I am sure, something more than modern virtue to stand against [its] intoxication'.[15] So 'bewitching' was this phenomenon that it was even able 'to change the Dispositions of the best Men'.[16] Indeed, once suborned, they entered upon a path that led inevitably to increased depravity and corruption:

Those who possess much, are desirous of obtaining more; they are solicitous to rise higher, and with this view court the favour of those above them; and are often too much enervated with luxury, to be influenced by any principles of patriotism... Wealth and Power give Opportunities for Indulgence; Indulgence naturally inflames Appetite – Flattery awakens Contempt; and Contempt weakens Fear of Offence and Shame.[17]

The rapaciousness of power was all the more alarming as it was always directed against liberty, whose preservation was one of the main objects of any constitution. 'It is an undoubted truth', wrote one contributor to the *Leeds Mercury*, 'that power, let it be lodged in what hands it will, is ever proceeding sometimes faster, sometimes slower, towards the suppression of liberty.'[18] The difficulty, therefore, in establishing a virtuous constitution was to constrain and check those who wielded power, and thereby to protect liberty.[19]

The present discontents

The problem was that every political society had to have an ultimate source of authority and power which, by virtue of being final, was also unconstrained.[20] This meant that the three 'pure' forms of government – monarchy, aristocracy, and democracy (i.e. the rule of one, the few, and the many) – were all likely to produce the abuse of power. They would, in other words, slowly but inexorably change from their pure to their corrupt forms: monarchy would become tyranny, aristocracy transform itself into oligarchy, and democracy transmute into ochlocracy or, as it was more usually referred to, anarchy. Such political societies were inherently unstable. They created a situation in which men were dependent for their rights and liberties upon the fickle whims of other men.[21]

Mixed government, however, seemed to provide an answer to the problem of unconstrained power. It combined all three pure forms of government into a single form which balanced the conflicting powers of all three, thereby creating a kind of political equilibrium. Each individual source of power was constrained by the others, but no two powers could combine to overthrow the remaining power. The special value of mixed government in checking power had long been recognised. Polybius, who was quoted with approval during the 1760s, had been fully aware of the values of mixed government. Mixed government, he argued,

united the peculiar excellencies of all the best Governments in one form, that neither of the three parts, by swelling beyond its just bounds, might ever be able to deviate into its original inborn defects: but that whilst each power was mutually drawn back by the opposite attraction of the other two, neither power might ever preponderate, but the balance of Government continue suspended in its true aequipoise.[22]

It was this balance that the British constitution had achieved, and it was for this reason that it was so highly praised. Of all the possible forms of government or types of constitution, that found in Britain was least liable to corruption or change. Moreover, unlike other nations, especially those in Asia, the British, thanks to their constitution, had been able to preserve their liberty from the encroachments of power. Liberty, indeed, was regarded as 'the Soul, the Spirit that animates this System'.[23] Although 'generally prevalent in human Nature', it was 'remarkably predominant in the Bosoms of free-born Britons'.[24] As the aptly named *Freeholder's Magazine* summarised the case:

The constitution of our English government (the best in the World) is no arbitrary tyranny, like the Turkish Grand Seignior's, or the French King's, whose wills (or rather lusts) dispose of the lives and fortunes of their unhappy subjects: Nor an Oligarchy, where the great one[s] (like fish in the ocean) prey upon, and live by devouring the lesser at their pleasure: Nor yet a democracy

243

or popular state, much less an anarchy, where all confusedly are hail fellows well met. But a most excellent mixt or qualified monarchy, where the king is vested with large prerogatives sufficient to support Majesty; and restrained only from power of doing himself and his people harm, (which would be contrary to the very end of all government, and is properly rather weakness than power) the nobility adorned with priviledges [*sic*] to be a screen to Majesty and a refreshing shade to their inferiors, and the commonalty too, so guarded in their persons and properties by the fence of the law, as renders them free-men, not slaves.[25]

The essential difference between Britain and other nations was that her constitution was a government of laws, not one contingent upon the fickle whims of some potentate or oligarchy.[26] All those who held power (except for the king who enjoyed a rather special and peculiar position)[27] were deemed subject to the law which also acted, because of the way in which it constrained power, as a barrier that protected liberty.[28] Moreover the whole nation was represented in the law-making process, for law could only be made by all three of the institutions – king, Lords and Commons – that correspond to the three pure forms of government. And because all three made law together, yet simul-taneously retained different roles and interests, they acted as checks upon each other, ensuring that the law embraced the interests of the whole community. 'What the elements of earth, air, fire, and water are to the natural body', the *Monitor* declared, 'the three different branches of the legislature are to the body politic in the British constitution.'[29] This 'common school-boy position', as Chatham called it,[30] was most frequently expressed in architectural terms. As De Grey put it to his colleagues in the House of Commons:

The three parts which compose the legislative power of England are equal, yet scarce ever contest, for their power has different objects: they are mutually checks upon each other yet are acknowledged to be perfectly independent: our constitution, then, being composed of three powers, each absolute in certain things within its own department, and by that means formidable to the other two, stands firm like a piece of skilful masonry, merely by the equipoise of its parts: take away ever so little weight from one, and the whole will immediately fall into ruins.[31]

The delicate balance of its constitutional mechanism gave Britain enormous advantages over other nations. A free constitution based on the rule of law guaranteed property and liberty; it provided the ideal circumstances for a flourishing community:

Wherever the true Principles of Liberty are best established, there Arts and Sciences, Trade and Commerce, refined Morality, pure Religion, wise and just Policy, all Social Virtues, and all that tends to make length of Days desirable, or to give a prospect to a happy Futurity, are most likely to flourish and abound.[32]

Hence the extraordinarily high regard in which both British and foreign commentators held the institutions, customs, conventions and spirit that made up the nation's constitution. It is even a permissible exaggeration to say that the *Anglomanie* that prevailed during the years of the high enlightenment was directly attributable to the island's mixed, balanced constitution.[33]

Yet, despite the fact that the British mixed constitution was held to be the best constitution, it was not entirely perfect. As *The Citizen* rather dolefully put it: 'Every condition of this life has its inconveniences; and a free government, though the best is not perfect.'[34] Indeed,

mixed systems have also their natural and certain bane, as well as simple forms: and as the latter carry in themselves the seeds of some congenial [*sic*] evil, which causes their destruction; so the former are brought to dissolution, by the change that is produced insensibly in the parts of which they are composed.[35]

The mixed constitution occupied, in Burke's felicitous phrase, an 'isthmus between arbitrary power and anarchy',[36] a delicate balance point from which it could be toppled if the strength and forces of any one of the elements of the constitution came to preponderate. 'This well guarded government', therefore, was 'exposed to three evils, a tyrannical king, an overbearing ministry, and an enraged populace.'[37] Once one of the three elements of the constitution found ways of circumventing the constraints imposed upon it – a process perfectly possible in the fluid situation of a free government[38] – a complete cycle of corruption would begin. The first signs of imbalance, regardless of their cause, would be the discontent and growing licentiousness of the people which, in turn, would produce anarchy, which ultimately would engender tyranny. The constitution would go full circle.[39]

THE PRESENT DISCONTENTS, 1768–70; PATHOLOGY AND CURE

This view of the British constitution and of the standard scenario of political change which accompanied it, was broadly accepted by those from every political camp. All recognised the dangers of incipient corruption. They acknowledged that growing popular discontent and political instability were the first symptoms of a political pathology which, unless remedial measures were taken, would inexorably lead to the demise of the free constitution, and with it the society whose values, properties and liberties it protected. Any discussion of popular unrest or public disorders, therefore, had to take place in this context. Clearly, if there was public unrest, constitutional equilibrium was threatened. But the question at issue was not *whether* it was threatened, but by whom, and why. To explain the discontents was to explain how the constitution was losing its delicate balance. It was to apportion blame, and locate responsibility for the situation. This was the focus of political debate in 1768–70. The problem for the supporter of government was to explain the 'present discontents' despite the workings of a benevolent and wise administration, and to answer the accusations of an opposition which attributed the public outcry to an incompetent, and even malevolently intended ministry. *Per contra*, the opposition sought to demonstrate that there was a link between administration and popular discontent, while simultaneously trying to counter a government case that attributed the situation to a factious, and therefore constitutionally subversive opposition. The problem for each side between 1768 and 1770, therefore, was to accommodate the events of the 1760s to a standard pathology in such a way as to justify their own position and place their opponents beyond the constitutional pale. Their arguments were not intended merely as descriptions or even as explanations of political discontent; they were legitimations of each side's political position: an apologia for administration or a justification for opposition.

The government case, which reached its culmination in the speeches made by Lord North in the House of Commons at the end of the decade, started from the premise that once a nation had reached its peak, there was a danger that its very success would create a climate of moral enervation.[40] The riches of empire, wealth and prosperity would make men grow venal and surrender to the 'Wantonness of Luxury'.[41] A concomitant of wealth (which was itself a consequence of a free constitution) was corruption. This, however, was not the corruption that stemmed from the abuse of the executive power. Rather it was a loss of virtue in the people as they became prodigal, ambitious and avaricious, turning away from good government and the rule of law in order to gratify their own desires:

The change of manners, that is introduced by time and prosperous events, the presumption that arises from success, and the vices that are spread among them [the people] by an overflow of wealth, soon render them alike incapable, of submitting to the authority which they have delegated to others, and of applying to the true ends of government that which they have retained. Obedience then becomes an intolerable constraint: the magistracies are suspected and opposed; and even the subordination, that was at first established by themselves, is judged to be injurious to the rights of liberty.[42]

In other words discontent among the people, that first sign of constitutional imbalance, was not attributable to poor government or the abuse of power. The enervating effects of a climate of luxury were responsible for the spread of avarice, licentiousness and a disregard for the constraints necessary to maintain a free constitution. It was all very well, as Jenkinson and others eagerly pointed out, for opposition to harp on the theme of the corrupting effects of power, but 'the lust of popular applause has no less power to corrupt the mind, than the lust of money'.[43]

But, of course, government apologists did not simply maintain that the growth of luxury and the development of 'irreligion, profaneness and sensuality of every kind'[44] was responsible for the kind of hostility and opposition that the administration faced. Rather they emphasised that this corruption created a situation favourable to those who wished to exploit the growing rejection of subordination in order to further their own ends. Since the beginning of the reign, or at least since Newcastle and Pitt had revealed their true colours by going into opposition in 1762, the constitution, it was maintained, had had to contend with those who sought to make an oligarchy or at least an aristocracy out of mixed monarchy. The politicians had tried to constrain the legitimate powers and prerogatives of the king for their own factious ends.[45] Some commentators even asserted that they wished to be rid of the king and establish a republic.[46] Such men, forced to resign when faced by a virtuous king, had rushed headlong into an unscrupulous opposition in order to force themselves into power upon their own terms. They were the representatives of 'the Power of Faction, trampling upon all Reverence to Principles and Characters', and assailing 'every Rampart of our Constitution'.[47] These were no high-principled patriots, but creatures willing to raise the factious cry of 'Despotism and the Increasing Power of the Crown' as a means of concealing their sole and true intention of forcing themselves into power.[48] Splenetic and ambitious, they were ready to see 'the Rancor and intoxication of Faction...sap the very Foundations of Government', rather than continue without political office.[49]

It had been easy, it was argued, for the opponents of government to gain the semblance of popular support by deliberately misleading the people. They had falsely described the cider tax as a general excise. They had distorted the issues of general warrants and the Middlesex election. The press had been used to whip up feeling against the ministers. Above all, by attributing the measures of the government and the nation's difficulties to a non-existent design or plot against the constitution formulated by Lord Bute and the so-called King's Friends, the factious politicians had succeeded in awakening, especially amongst the most ignorant and poorest sections of the population, a fear that their liberties were being subverted.[50] The opposition, moreover, had not simply told lies about the policies and intentions of the government. They had deliberately engaged in political agitation – notably in the solicitation of petitions in 1768–9 – in order to convey the false impression that the nation was up in arms. As North put it in one of his speeches to the lower House:

But, after all, what evidence have we that there are public grievances, which demand an enquiry: that a number of ignorant mechanics and rustics have been treated in one place with beer, and broken windows in another, is true: are these the grievances into which we are to enquire? That some persons whose share in the public interest, and rank in life should have taught them better, have treated these rustics and mechanics, and taught them in the jollity of their drunkenness, to cry out that they were undone, is also true: are these then the grievances into which we are to enquire?... The nation is quiet, and content, except where tumult and discontent are industriously excited.

The drunken and ignorant have been made dupes to the crafty and the factious, signed papers that they have never read, and determined questions that they do not know; roared against oppression and tyranny, with licentious-ness that makes liberty blush, and staggered home with impunity, swearing they were in danger of slavery, while every one they met, who did not join in their cry, was in danger of a broken head.[51]

By adopting these tactics, ascribing ills to the constitution that were only those of a 'Malade imaginaire',[52] the unscrupulous opposition had exaggerated even further the growing preponderance of the demo-cratical part of the constitution. They were spreading licentiousness (the obsession of every government politician and writer), and under-mining the constitution simply to obtain the rewards and riches of office.[53] So intoxicated with power were the opponents of the Crown that, although men of property, they were prepared to help destroy property's very basis.[54]

Adopting this interpretation of events, government supporters felt that the only way to end such a threat to good government and public order was to stand firm. They had a responsibility to defend the existing constitution against the wild encroachments of the embittered, factious and deluded forces which had allied themselves against both government and constitution. The growing 'spirit of anarchy', as one MP remarked, 'must be checked by acts of power'.[55] Only by teaching the people a due regard for the institutions of law and a respect for political order could the fabric of the constitution be preserved. Hence the deliberate pursuit, most notably by Grafton and North, but also by George Grenville,[56] of a firm policy towards 'licentiousness' whether it occurred in the Old World or the New.

The government case firmly placed the blame for the 'present discontents' upon the opposition. It established a clear causal connec-tion between the activities of the Crown's opponents and political instability both in parliament and out-of-doors. The activities of the people were treated as corroborative evidence for the malicious activities of those out of office.

The posture adopted by government was, however, primarily defensive, for they had to contend with a serious and carefully constructed indictment by their opponents. There is little doubt that the 'present discontents' aided opposition far more than they helped government, for they enabled the former to use public opinion as a counter-weight (and, indeed, a counter-argument) to the powers of the Crown. For all the ambiguity that, as we have seen, the politicians exhibited towards the public, they were never averse, when in opposition, to utilising discontent for their own pragmatic political purposes.

The opposition of 1768–70 began their argument from the premise that a free form of government such as the British constitution contained plentiful safeguards and barriers against a direct assault upon its people's liberties. The interlocking institutions of government ensured this. But, at the same time, they emphasised that this was far from guaranteeing immunity for the constitution. The forces of power were subtle and insidious. Finding it impossible to extend their boundaries by naked aggression, they would attempt to suborn the constitution, engaging in a covert and frequently conspiratorial attempt to subvert it from within. Hence (and this was as much an obsession with opposition apologists as was the fear of 'licentiousness' by government writers) the need for constant and unfailing vigilance, or what one pamphleteer referred to as 'the watchful eye of public spirit'.[57] Unless every act of government and every subtle change in the balance of the constitution was scrupulously watched, the nation's liberties might be lost by the almost imperceptible but ever-growing increase in the power of England's rulers. Thus those who were politically negligent were as remiss as those who were actually involved in subverting the constitution. In Burke's words: 'He trespasses against his duty who sleeps upon his watch, as well as he that goes over to the enemy.'[58]

The task of scrutinising those who held power was best fulfilled, it was maintained, by the House of Commons. The lower House, according to Dowdeswell, was 'the grand inquest of the nation',[59] and MPs were, if we are to believe a newspaper writer, 'the tutular guardians of her [England's] sacred constitution, the undaunted avengers of all opponents to lawful authority, the glorious assertors of the rights of mankind against the repeated efforts of despotism and tyranny'.[60] In this capacity, the people's representatives played a crucial part in the preservation of free government. They were '*the Salt of the* Constitution' which, 'Like the sword of Dionysius...suspended o'er the head

9-2

of Damocles' acted as a constant warning to those who felt inclined to abuse their power.[61] The House of Commons, in other words, was the 'Paladium [*sic*] of the constitution' and the preservative of British liberty.[62]

But the greatest danger to the Commons' fulfilment of their role as a constitutional guardian was that of spreading corruption. This corruption was not that found by government apologists in the moral enervation of the people, but the corruption of government itself. Growing wealth, frequent wars and the acquisition of an empire (those same phenomena isolated by government apologists) had created an enormous executive, and thereby enormous powers of patronage for the government. Sectarian and particular interests – notably those of financiers, merchant contractors and stock-jobbers – were tied to administration. Similarly placemen – Treasury officials, members of the diplomatic and colonial services – as well as pensioners, courtiers and members of the armed forces were dependent for at least part of their livelihood upon the good offices of the Crown.[63] These enormous resources could and indeed were put to work, it was asserted, to suborn the virtue of those from the highest government official to the lowliest tide-waiter. Corruption emanated from the centre of government: its source was the Treasury, but it flowed through every channel of society. Even the House of Commons, the body which above all others ought to contain virtuous men, was not immune from the noxious effect of its poisonous waters.[64] (Burke, indeed, thought it was also potentially 'the most corruptible part of the whole constitution'.)[65] The presence of placemen, pensioners and the members of the military, those 'reptiles that would have for ever remained in their caterpillar state, were it not for the sunshine of a court, which has given the insects wings, and taught them to flutter and fly in our faces',[66] provided government with a corrupt corps of supporters. More mindful of retaining their own sinecures and wealth than of the nation's best interests, they furnished government with a majority, regardless of the rights and wrongs of the case. The lower House, it was asserted, was increasingly filled with ministerial dependants, each of whose

Passions and Appetites must always be under command, and his Heart and his Tongue move only by direction. In short, he must be as mechanical as a Clock or a Puppet, acquiring that by Habit, which is necessary in them.[67]

This process eventually produced a House of Commons 'dependent on the Minister, and independent of the People'.[68]

This situation, it was maintained, was the very worst possible: one which to the untrained eye appeared 'fair and plausible',[69] because the basic relationship between the different institutions of government appeared not to have changed; but which in fact had engendered a covert tyranny. The forms of the constitution were retained, but it had lost its substance and spirit, becoming a hollow sham.[70] In its place the nation would find itself subject to the most restrictive tyranny possible:

with a corrupt Parliament there remains not only no security for our Liberties; but a House of Commons debauched into submissions to bad Ministers, or measures inconsistent with Liberty, must demonstrably be the surest pledge, and in the end, with the greatest ease, effect the firmest establishment of the worst sort of tyranny.[71]

Such a tyranny was not only difficult to detect, but hard to root out, for it occurred with the consent of all branches of the legislature. It was a disastrous situation.

Yet, according to the opposition, the growing discontent of the 1760s was the result of the emergence of such a tyranny. Bute had convinced the king, it was argued, that he should elevate his prerogative and disregard the wishes of the people. Adopting the 'declared profession of increasing the power of the Crown, by creating influence and dependencies upon it in both Houses of Parliament',[72] Bute had established his own power, and laid the foundations of a plan to subvert free government. This had been obvious from the so-called 'Massacre of the Pelhamite Innocents' which, according to the opposition, had shaken 'the great Pillar of this Noble Constitution'[73] and announced the renewal of whig/tory conflict. Additional evidence had been furnished by the imposition of the cider tax – a direct threat to the liberties and properties of the people. Thereafter more and more evidence had come to hand of a plot to destroy the constitution in accordance with a 'timetable of despotism'.[74] The employment of a general warrant in the apprehension of John Wilkes had shown how little regard the government had for the subject's personal liberties and property. Together with other newspaper prosecutions it demonstrated the determination to destroy the liberty of the press. The various attempts to impose taxes and duties on the Americans, despite the fact that they were unrepresented in parliament, reflected the same attitude towards subjects' rights and a similar plan of corruption, concocted by an administration 'who wanted to feed their dependents on the riches of America'.[75] Above all, the case of the Middlesex election when a majority of the House of Commons had, it was asserted, effectively disenfranchised (and therefore dispossessed of their property) the freeholders of Middlesex, seemed to prove conclusively that the constitution had been thoroughly corrupted. And, if further evidence was needed, it could be found in the growing use of military force, notably at the 'massacres' of St George's Fields and in Boston. Administration seemed bent not only on corrupting the House of Commons, but on establishing a standing army. The old spectre of military tyranny was raised.[76]

The opposition was quick to list the government's crimes:

the late arbitrary invasion of the rights of individuals; the attacks on the Liberty of the Press; the violation of the freedom of electors; the misapplication of the public treasure; the prevailing and open corruption; the employing of money collected from the people, in practices that tend to deprive them of their most valuable rights; the sanguinary and illegal use that has been made of military troops, who are maintained by the people to be their defenders, and not their murderers; the total disregard of the principles and spirit of the constitution, and the avowed contempt of the people by those in power.[77]

Each of these acts or forms of conduct, of course, was individually held to weaken free government, but, when considered together, they demonstrated conclusively that there was a plot to establish national despotism:

You know, that these apparently distinct and independent acts, are all under-parts of one and the same concerted plan of despotism, begun, contrived and now labouring towards completion, under the influence of one and the same evil spirit, whose malignant poison has almost destroyed the vitals of the constitution.[78]

This view of the conspiratorial intentions of government was adumbrated as early as 1762, but, as the decade proceeded, more and more corroborative detail was added, and more and more credence given to the plot. What was particularly remarked upon was the parallel development of oppression in the colonies and the mother country. A 'tyrannical' policy towards the colonies was deemed to show that the government was using them as a testing-ground for the subversion of liberty, and that England would soon be contaminated in a similar way.[79] Equally, acts of oppression in England – especially those against Wilkes and his supporters – appeared to affirm despotic intentions towards the thirteen colonies.[80] In this way a conspiratorial spiral was created, each new event building upon and affirming the meaning of the last. The more evidence that was accumulated, the less willing were opponents of the administration to attribute governmental actions to folly, misapprehension and ignorance. Malfeasance, the deliberate and intentional attempt to destroy the fabric of British liberty, explained the covert intrigue and depravity of the administration and the king's flunkeys.[81]

This indictment of government helped legitimise opposition, gave them a strong rallying cry for political unity, and also provided them with justifiable grounds on which to remedy the situation. If the Crown had suborned the virtue of the legislature, it was argued, only one hope remained. Although the vast resources of ministerial corruption might succeed in harnessing the House of Commons, it was far harder for them to corrupt a whole people. There would always be some who retained sufficient virtue to perceive the nation's political ills and to try to obtain redress. Customarily, it was argued, the people tended to be too submissive rather than too tumultuous. But, when really serious ills occurred, they were almost invariably sufficiently sensitive to perceive them. Their voice, if properly exerted and duly regarded, could bring the nation's leaders to their senses and preserve the constitution from its final dénouement.[82] Indeed, unless the government listened to the protests of the people, they would forfeit their right to govern the nation; the contract between the rulers and the ruled would be terminated, and open rebellion might ensue.

Of course, the way in which the people were to convince the government of its errors was a matter of contention. Most leaders of the parliamentary opposition felt that opinion out-of-doors should only act through their mediation, and meekly follow their advice. Although it was essential for the politicians to utilise the present discontents they had, simultaneously, to try to limit their impact and scope. Only Wilkes and his few radical fellow-travellers were willing to contemplate a more active role for the people. Nevertheless, all of the opposition agreed that the situation demanded '*the interposition of the body of the people itself*',[83] even if interpretations of the mode of this interposition differed.

This opposition argument appears to be remarkably similar to the country-party ideology of the first half of the century. Indeed many of the ideas discussed here have also been considered in the writings of Pocock and Kramnick on the opposition of Walpole.[84] But the case put forward during the 1760s cannot simply be accommodated to the country-party model. Apart from the familiar country-party case, two distinct solutions were offered by members of the opposition to the constitutional crisis, just as two different interpretations of English history and the history of the British constitution were put forward to sustain these respective cases.

The first of these arguments was that put forward by the radical wing of the opposition. Wilkes, the Society of Supporters of the Bill of Rights, much of the press, some parliamentary independents, such city radicals and commonwealthmen as Sawbridge, and many of the followers of Chatham, all supported this view. Their remedy for the nation's ills was concisely, if not completely accurately summarised by the tickets that some of the guests to the Mansion House banquet of

1770 wore in their hats declaring 'Annual Parliaments, Equal Representation and Pension Bill'.[85] The Middlesex election and its surround-
ing events, the disasters of colonial policy, and the growing power
of the Crown, all, it was argued, revealed that the nation could no
longer rely on the political virtue of its leaders. The existing political
situation demanded some substantive measure of reform which would
affect a structural change in government. The constitution, which had
in recent years become so palpably corrupt, urgently needed to be
restored to its first principles. A number of writers cited Machiavelli's
Discorsi in favour of such a course of action:

It is a maxim of Machiavel that governments should as often as possible be
brought back to their first principles; and though the general practice of
statesmen, disapproves this maxim, I have not known it overturned by
argument: it is certainly just when applied to well constituted governments,
and is in one sense applicable to the worst, that their defects are generally
fewest at the beginning; therefore, when they revert to their first principles,
I may safely say, that they come nearer to perfection.[86]

This meant, in the short run, that parliament should be immediately
dissolved, and a general election called. When members had to be
endorsed by their constituents, government returned to its source of
origin, the people. A temporary solution to the political crisis would
therefore be to hold an election and remove those politicians who were
a canker on the body politic. Yet this was not sufficient. In order to
preserve constitutional purity once it had been recovered, more
frequent elections, whether annual or triennial, would have to become
mandatory.

Secondly, an alteration in the state of representation was necessary
to ensure that MPs accurately reflected the interests and wishes of their
constituents, and remained primarily dependent upon the people,
rather than upon the Crown or the First Lord of the Treasury. This
would be obtained in a variety of ways. Possibly, in good country-party
fashion, the number of county MPs could be increased; alternatively,
the nature of representation could be altered to reflect the distribution
of taxable wealth, and new towns and manufacturing districts be
enfranchised in their own right.

Suggestions for electoral reform did not stop there. Schemes were
concocted in which MPs could be recalled if two thirds of their
electorate so wished, and quite a number of journals and debating
societies discussed the use of the ballot in order to remove patrician
pressure on the humble voter.[87]

The other major plank in the radicals' platform was the complete
separation of the court or executive from the parliament or legislature.
In the words of one correspondent in the *Gazetteer*: 'There is but *one*

thing needful for the redress of our national *grievances*, even for the final quieting of all our *fears* and *apprehensions*, viz. the breaking of all *connection* between the *Court* and the House of Commons.'[88] Only if the means of corrupting the lower House was removed would the possibility of a ministerial takeover of the body that guarded the nation's liberties be satisfactorily pre-empted.

The radicals, therefore, evolved a wide range of possible solutions to the crisis of 1768–71, all of which endeavoured to change the way in which politics was currently organised. They differed amongst themselves about the precise means by which to remove corruption, but they were all united in the belief that, 'a change of Ministers alone will not remedy the evil'.[89] Corruption and constitutional subversion were a product of the way in which the institutions of government had developed, and no amount of political virtue and independence could counteract the vast institutionalised forces which served to perpetuate degenerate and oligarchical rule. Somehow the props which supported this enclosed and irresponsible political system had to be knocked away, and the whole edifice brought tumbling down. Then the business of reconstructing the republic of virtue could commence.

Much of this radical case resembles country-party ideology in its purest form. This is very much as one would expect because the radicals were attacking the entire system of political stability, not merely those who immediately controlled it, and therefore had aims and aspirations not unlike many in the country-party opposition to George II. But the case for reform was now more coherent, and laid greater emphasis on the representation of new interests.

In certain other respects the radicals' case was a considerable advance on country-party ideology. The country-party case rested very strongly on the notion of an independent House of Commons; independent of the Crown, but also independent of other outside pressures. Its lynchpin was the independent MP: an individual of sufficient (landed) means to be capable of exercising his wisdom and judgement unconstrained by pecuniary dependence or obligation. A perfect House of Commons would have been composed almost entirely of such men. Country-party ideology was, in essence, the belief-system of a landed, gentry class, though it was used, on occasion, by urban, especially metropolitan interest-groups. As such, its conception of the public or political nation was relatively confined, and it rarely stressed the need for parliament to represent accurately the interests of those in society at large. Though mention was made of how power ultimately stemmed from the people, country-party ideology rarely went further than reminding the administration of this particular skeleton in the closet. Its view of politics was as *custodial* as that of the Rockinghamite whigs.

The radicals of the 1760s, however, entertained an altogether different conception of a pure House of Commons. For them, as for the country-party ideologues, it had to be independent of government, but it also had to represent those who had an interest in government, over and beyond the landed classes. Taxpayers should have appropriate representation in parliament, and unincorporated towns which were now of economic consequence should be permitted to elect their own borough members. In this way the legislature would more accurately reflect the interests of those 'out of doors'.[90] Some substance would be given to the notion that power emanated from the people.

Neither these solutions nor the political analysis on which they were based were acceptable to the Rockinghamite whigs. The reforming aspirations of the radicals were peremptorily dismissed as idealistic and impracticable, exhibiting no real awareness of the business and workings of government.[91] Shorter parliaments and the removal of placemen, for instance, would make effective administration impossible, and help create political chaos. What was needed to solve the crisis was a practical, pragmatic approach to the nation's ills. Thus William Baker, one of Rockingham's supporters in the City of London, refused to sign the SSBR engagement in favour of reform on the grounds that,

Truths, clear in the Abstract, are not always maintainable in Practice – the Generality and indefinite Extent of the Engagement for the Exclusion of Placemen and Pensioners must put a stop to all Parliamentary Business whatsoever, and must fatally discourage all Public Merit, of which Pensions have been the Honourable Reward.[92]

In the face of the practicalities of politics, substantial changes in the constitution were wishful and perhaps dangerous thinking. The point at issue was not how to reconstruct the fabric of the constitution, but how to succeed in replacing wicked by virtuous men. Government had been satisfactory before the present king's accession because the holders of power were politically experienced, understood free government (i.e. were good whigs), and enjoyed public credit. Under George III these men had suffered political annihilation at the hands of those who were incompetent, unpopular and (this being virtually an entailment of the two preceding characteristics) unconstitutional. Hence the divisions within the nation: the growing licentiousness on one side and growing tyranny on the other. If those who knew how to exert influence 'constitutionally' were returned to power, there would be no need for parliamentary reform. The problem, therefore, was not one of the inadequacy of the mechanisms designed to preserve the nation's liberties, but of the abuse of an otherwise perfectly adequate constitution by an incompetent and malevolently intended leadership.[93]

The difference between the Rockinghamites and the radicals is, therefore, quite clear. The radicals wanted an alteration in the nature of politics, while the party men were working within the existing political system, seeking to reacquire the influence and power of which they had been so recently deprived.

This is not to say, however, that the Rockinghams did not support certain limited reforms. Dowdeswell put forward the motion to disenfranchise revenue officers (perhaps the first glimmerings of economical reform), and the party wholeheartedly supported George Grenville's Election Committees Bill.[94] But these are secondary considerations when compared with the party's first priority of replacing the existing ministers in power. Hence the Rockinghamite manifesto of the era, Burke's *Thoughts on the Cause of the Present Discontents* (1770), although it adopted the standard analysis of the political pathology of the previous decade, rejected radical remedies in favour of organised party and a union to storm the closet. The Rockinghamites, therefore, did not see the present discontents as grounds for substantial political reform, but as the occasion for seizing power.

They justified this in ways which would have been incomprehensible to a country-party ideologue. Not only were their political solutions meliorist rather than reformist, they contained a view of party that represented all that country-party ideology had fought against. The Rockinghamite whigs were only interested in those aspects of country-party thought that served their immediate political purposes. Electoral reform and an end to party could not be included in their number; in fact, if they had been enacted, they would probably have hindered Rockinghamite political designs. Many of the old shibboleths were therefore deliberately rejected because the party's purposes were so particular. As Burke summarised it: it was 'Necessary often to destroy administration to support Government – remedy the disorders and confusions at the head'.[95]

THE HISTORICAL BASIS OF POLITICAL ARGUMENT

The Rockinghamite case, and those of the government and the radicals, were supported by historical expositions, each of which was intended to give greater credence to its respective view. This is hardly surprising. Few can have been more conscious of the value of history than the eighteenth-century Englishman. Because it was assumed that politics was a science like astronomy or mathematics, and that human nature was the same everywhere, the past was regarded as the repository of political examples which were *directly* applicable to the present. Statesmen were therefore obliged to study history as a guide to their immediate conduct:

The rise and fall of kingdoms and states, the establishment of liberty and laws, or the encroachments of slavery and despotism, the flourishing of arts and sciences, or the prevalence of ignorance and barbarity; the enervating effects of luxury and vice, or the happy influence of temperance and virtue: These ...are the contents of the historick page, and in these men of quality and fortune are deeply interested, as their conduct must necessarily have great influence in promoting the grandeur and happiness, or preventing the fall and misery of their country.[96]

Because of the wealth of historical literature available, the politician, according to the *Political Register*, 'stands in need only of an accurate judgement to enable him to cull the flowers, and shun the poisonous weeds that are to be found in the field of political science'.[97] He could readily learn political lessons from the past. It was for this reason, for instance, that Charles Townshend encouraged the young Buccleuch to study the history of England under Charles I:[98] no other reign provided such an excellent opportunity of distinguishing the forces of darkness from the forces of light, or of examining changes in the British constitution.

But the historical periods and constitutional circumstances that were most frequently invoked were those of the free constitutions of the ancient republics. It was not just that Pitt could be dubbed Tully, Bute Sejanus, and the Anglo-American situation compared to Tacitus's account of the pro-consuls in Africa,[99] but that the constitutions of Greece and especially Rome provided precise analogues with British political experience:

As the British State and the ancient free republics were founded upon the same principles, and their policy and constitution nearly similar; so, as like causes will ever produce like effects, it is impossible not to perceive an equal semblance between their and our manners, as they and we equally deviated from these first principles.[100]

Above all it was the history of the later Roman empire that political polemicists as different as Wilkes and Allan Ramsay drew upon to sustain their respective cases.[101] The comparisons were obvious: both nations had mixed constitutions; both had been highly successful in war; both had acquired extensive empires; each, because a free nation, was politically volatile; and, above all, each appeared to be the victim of growing luxury and corruption.[102] The lesson of fallen Rome was there for all to see, though, not surprisingly, interpretations of its decline varied with the political views of each commentator.

If the Roman example was the most frequently drawn historical parallel, the Asiatic states, and especially Turkey, were the contemporary societies invoked by all parties as a warning to free Britons. Just as history served as philosophy by example, so observation of the current state of other nations served to instruct the politician. Hence the importance of travel, whose purpose was 'to make observations upon the laws, customs, police, and manners of other countries, and to compare them with our own'.[103] To observe Turkey and the other Asiatic states was to observe tyranny. If Rome was the standard example of a corrupted mixed government, Turkey was the exemplar of arbitrary rule. All were agreed that such a nation – whether because of the climate, luxury, or superstition and theocracy – was a despotic state where the ruler's will was law. Deprived of liberty and kept in thrall by a standing army,[104] the people were slothful and effeminate. Thus, when the editor of the *Constitutional Guardian* wanted to condemn the arbitrary nature of the ministry in 1770, he produced a woodcut of George III with 'His arbitrary ministers endeavouring to put a turban on his head instead of his Crown'.[105]

But, far more important than the frequent appeals to these historical and contemporary examples were the different interpretations of English history, and *a fortiori* the history of the British constitution, that were employed to sustain the respective political arguments put forward by government and the two chief groups in opposition. The government case relied heavily on the basic assertion that the history of England was a history of the growth and progress of British liberty. It was nonsense, they maintained, to refer to some idealised ancient constitution in our Saxon or medieval past. The Saxons had been a primitive and barbaric people, conquered by the Normans and subjected to feudalism. The nation's liberties had only been won over a long period of time, and had only reached their consummation in recent years. The government supporter who wrote an *Essay on the Constitution* in 1766 therefore summarised his purpose in producing the work thus:

It means, then, to trace the actual progress of English liberty, from its lowest ebb to that glorious height to which it has arrived; to shew that this encrease was constant and gradual, not arising from any providential laws or contrivances of men; but from a certain tide of things which flowed, not only against the means that were contrived to prevent it, but sometimes flowed the faster by those very means. To shew that Magna Charta was not the cause, but the consequence of a degree of liberty, and that what was liberty then would be no better than slavery now.[106]

An almost identical approach was adopted by the government's leading apologist of the early 1760s, Dr John Campbell, in a 'Systematical History of our Constitution' which he completed in October 1761. 'The great Point I had in View', he wrote to his friend Baron Mure,

was to shew that after the Norman Conquest our Constitution was full of radical Inconveniences which were continually producing national convulsions that by degrees they were worked out and a new and better Regimen established the perfecting of which we might with a degree of Moral certainty expect under his Majesty's auspicious Reign.[107]

Quite naturally the defenders of government concluded from this argument that

the freedom of the subject in England is now arrived at the highest degree of perfection consistent with the nature of civil government, and that it is the duty of every good Englishman to cry, with a late ingenious author, ESTO PERPETUA, without adding any contradiction to this pious wish, by wishing for any innovation or pretence of improving it.[108]

This was a remarkably similar argument to those deployed by the defenders of Walpole a generation earlier. Equally the historical case presented by the opposition in the 1760s bore a more than partial resemblance to its country-party predecessors.[109] In essence their case was that of the ancient constitution. The fall of Rome, it was argued, had been achieved by that bold and virtuous race, the Goths, who had overrun an empire dulled by avarice, luxury and vice. The Goths, in their primitive purity, had established free governments embodying representative institutions all over Europe: 'in the north, diets; in Spain, cortes; in France, estates; and in Britain, parliaments'.[110] The Saxons, that peculiarly British group of Goths, had laid down the foundations of English liberty through the precursor of, if not the first parliament, the Witenagemot.[111] Saxon England was a paradigm of constitutional virtue. (It was therefore not surprising that an opposition pamphleteer should urge, during the crisis of the Middlesex election, that the forms of election employed by their Saxon forefathers should be investigated.)[112]

It might appear to follow from this argument that, if the Saxon constitution was praised as an instance of mixed government, on 'rational' rather than historical, prescriptive or customary grounds, then the opposition had little need to concern themselves with the subsequent history of the constitution. All that they needed to do was assess the degree to which the contemporary constitution conformed to its Saxon predecessor. If it failed to do so, their task was simply to take measures to ensure its restoration to its first principles and original balance.

But opposition writers were concerned to demonstrate something more than the freedom of Saxon England. They wished to show that, in contradiction to the government view that liberty was a recent development, England had been free until modern times. They therefore combined an argument based on custom with that of constitutional balance, maintaining that the ancient constitution was not only ancient but immemorial, and that the liberties of Britons, as guaranteed by the nation's institutions and especially the common law, had existed time out of mind.[113] This was both an argument for continuity, linking post-Conquest medieval institutions with Gothic government across the somewhat awkward gulf of the Norman Conquest, and the demonstration that Gothic freedom existed in post-Conquest England.[114] This freedom, it was maintained, had been epitomised in Magna Carta which had been based on Gothic principles,[115] and had been preserved from the assaults of the Crown by representative institutions until the advent of modern corruption.

This argument, moreover, was used, especially by the 'radical' wing of the opposition, to assert the existence of certain basic rights and privileges independent of the Crown, parliament or the House of Commons. Thus Pitt defended parliamentary privilege on the grounds that

no Privileges were concessions from the Crown, but derived to us of the Rights of our Saxon Ancestors, that those rights were the foundation of our liberties, and W^m the Conqueror either adopted them or ingrafted upon them.[116]

Similar arguments were used over the Middlesex election, when it was asserted that no one, not even the House of Commons or the three law-making bodies, could deprive men of such basic rights as that of the right of election.[117]

It was possible for all groups in opposition to agree that the current conduct of the Crown and of government was reminiscent of the worst excesses of the first two Stuarts, and of the persecution of such true whigs as Shaftesbury and Sidney under Charles II.[118] But they differed about their interpretation of British history since the Revolution. Nearly everyone (with the notable exception of Mrs Macaulay who, according to the *Political Register*, 'attacks the principles and system of government of the revolution, in so strange and unaccountable manner that her best friends are astonished at it')[119] agreed that the

Revolution of 1688 had seen the embodiment of the true principles of the constitution. But Rockinghamites disagreed fundamentally with their colleagues in opposition on the interpretation of subsequent years. The 'radicals', the Chathamites and those independents who had been in opposition before 1760, argued that ever since the Revolution the growth of the executive, army and administration had increased the prevalence of corruption. The crisis of the 1760s, they maintained, was the natural concomitant of an imbalance in the constitution that had persisted since the days of William III.[120]

In other words, their interpretation of recent British political history affirmed their determination to dismantle the entire system that maintained political stability. The continuities between this body of thought and the earlier 'politics of the dispossessed' are therefore obvious enough. The radicals and independents saw their efforts as the culmination of the attack on oligarchy and governmental corruption that had been in progress at least since the reign of George I.

The present discontents were therefore no accident but the logical consequence of excluding a substantial part of the political nation from the parliamentary process. The expulsion of Wilkes or the oppression of the American colonies was yet another in a long catalogue of crimes which included not only the heinous acts of Bute, Grenville and Grafton but also those of Walpole, Pelham and Newcastle. For the radicals it was the continuities of politics that were both revealing and depressing. The changes that the new king had promised had failed to materialise; his reign had ushered in the old oligarchy with (some) new faces. The only difference was that the leaders of the political nation were divided, and that the political situation was therefore more favourable to the dispossessed than it had been for more than a generation. Current circumstance, especially the Wilkes affair, made the possibility of some kind of structural, parliamentary reform more than a very distant chimera.

While the radicals, the independents and many Chathamites emphasised the historical parallels and continuities between the reign of George III and those of his two predecessors, the Rockinghams were concerned to highlight the differences between them. They were not in the least bit disapproving of the political developments that had occurred after the Revolutionary Settlement. Burke, for instance, even equated the ancient constitution with that under William III.[121] Nor did they disapprove of the growth of oligarchy under Walpole and the Pelhams. The increased strength and power of government was not a threat in itself as long as it was exercised by 'men of popular weight and character',[122] who looked to the public as much as they looked to the Court. As long as these virtuous whigs acted as an 'intermediate and independent' body between the king and his people, all would be well; 'influence' would not be abused as corruption but directed towards the public good.[123] Serious problems, it was claimed, only arose once this link between the monarch and the the public was severed, and the whig leadership replaced by those who looked exclusively to the Court for political power and influence. The inevitable concomitant of this situation would be a collapse in public confidence, and royal recourse to a system of irresponsible favouritism formally institutionalised in the 'double cabinet'.[124] Thus the Rockinghams' panacea for the crisis of the 1760s was their return to power.[125] The reacquisition of the right to rule, something they regarded as little short of their natural inheritance, would replace the misguided and malicious by those who were perspicacious and responsible. In consequence, influence would not be put to corrupt use, and there would therefore be no need for any kind of parliamentary reform.

This historical interpretation of Georgian politics emphasises the degree to which the Rockinghamite whigs were fighting their battles within a received and narrow conception of politics. Although there were conspicuous and important differences between them and their opponents in office, notably over party, the questions at issue were primarily to do with who should run the political machine, and not how the political mechanism ought to be changed. In sum, Rockinghamite politics was a matter of infighting within a political consensus.

The party's version of recent political history also highlights the continuities between their view of politics and the operative principles of Walpole and Pelham. Rockingham and his followers were just as committed to olig chy, as long as it was managed in the right way. Their conceptic of how it should be correctly run was, again, derived from th example of Walpole and, to an even greater extent, from that of Newcastle and Pelham. Pushed out of power, they did not reject their old party adages; rather, they were more strongly reinforced. Yet they were faced with the ineluctable paradox that, in order to reacquire control of the oligarchy, they had to work with those whose avowed intent was to bring the whole system of enclosed politics crashing to the ground.

By 1770, therefore, there were two views of politics – radical and Rockinghamite – both of which, although they embodied many of the ideas and precepts of country-party ideology, had moved beyond that corpus of thought to formulate distinctive conceptions of the political order. Each was to be an enduring feature of politics until the outbreak of the French Revolution and, to some extent, beyond it. Their evolution is very largely explained by the events of the 1760s: the breakdown of an existing political configuration, and the opportunity that that created, in propitious economic and social circumstances, for the emergence of an independent extra-parliamentary movement which, though heterogeneous in the extreme, was able to propagandise and spread its political message with remarkable proficiency.

Part VI

Conclusion

13. Afterword

The decade of the 1760s is one of the most important for us to examine if we are to understand the presuppositions that under-pinned eighteenth-century politics, and the ways in which the pattern of politics was being transformed during the century. The quarrels between the king and the politicians, and between the politicians and the public, led many to articulate explicitly the assumptions that they entertained about political behaviour, and the aspirations that they held for the political order. Thus we can observe in detail the complex arguments that were deployed during the infighting that occurred within the political elite. The accession of George III *did* make a very substantial difference to politics because the political realignments for which he was more than partially responsible produced new ideologies, especially in the sphere of party, and new and more substantial disagreements amongst the leaders of the political nation. Even this kind of face-to-face politics was ideological, and, as I have argued, cannot be understood without reference to the arguments that the protagonists employed.

Yet just as significant as the quarrel within the elite, and the ramifi-cations which that had for the history of party (a topic that, like the crocodile in the Punch and Judy, could justifiably claim to have been flogged to death on more than one occasion), was the realisation by members of that elite of the paradoxical and perilous position that they occupied towards the public. This was not a new perception, any more than the ideas about ministerial responsibility in the 1760s were novel, but it was one that was driven home more forcibly than ever before. The simultaneous emergence of a radical ideology, extra-parliamen-tary political organisation (the SSBR), and widespread popular protest was an alarming development for all members of the parliamentary classes. Although the elite had at its disposal certain customary ways of dealing with those out-of-doors, and despite the fact that these methods enjoyed some success during the 1760s, it was increasingly apparent that the structural and ideological barriers that the parlia-mentary politicians had erected for their own protection were being slowly eroded and, occasionally, were even under direct assault.

The direction and thrust of this attack was neither truly plebian nor exclusively political; rather it was predominantly bourgeois and char-

267

acteristically commercial. It is exemplified by the newspaper proprietor, the printer of cartoons, the producer of artifacts, the brewer,
the tavern proprietor, and the city merchant, all of whose conceptions
of politics differed substantially from that of the political elite. Thanks
to Wilkes, these men, who had been of little political significance before
1750, came into their own during the 1760s. It was not so much
that their politics differed from the conventional wisdom of the
parliamentary parties (though it certainly did), but that their whole
modus operandi was socially and politically different. They would not
tolerate patrician leadership, and their conception of social and
political relations was entrepreneurial rather than deferential. They
had a vested interest in opening up politics, just as they were concerned
to open up new markets for their products. It was they who helped
spread political consciousness through the English provinces.

It might well be argued that the *évènements* of the 1760s were
something of a flash in the pan. By the outbreak of the American war
the Wilkite movement seems to have fizzled to a halt, and the
parliamentary scene had acquired an almost Pelhamite serenity. From
this perspective it looks as if the accession of the new king, party
squabbles and economic discontent all combined to produce an out-
burst of popular feeling and an intensification of political debate that,
in the final analysis, were insubstantial and evanescent. If this is merely
to claim that there was less political activity between 1771 and 1776
directed towards the issues discussed in parliament, few would deny
its validity. There is no doubt that radicalism lost its focus, and that
Westminster was in the doldrums. (One gets the distinct impression
that certain historians of parliament, as well as the eighteenth-
century political elite, have breathed a sigh of relief as the spectre of
popular politics has receded below the horizon).

But this does not mean that we can write off the conflicts of the 1760s
as a fortuitous conflagration, or disregard the evidence of political
consciousness that is revealed by the activities of the press, the radicals
and Wilkes. Though the alternative political nation was less prominent
by the outbreak of the American war, it did not disappear altogether,
but only temporarily vanished from sight. The press, the local debating
societies, the coffee houses and tavern politicians all persisted.

Throughout the eighteenth century, whenever a political crisis
occurred, the scope and scale of this alternative political nation
increased. Each occasion on which the politically excluded were able
to focus on an issue, movement or controversy produced a brief
burgeoning of papers, pamphlets, clubs and crowds, followed by a
falling back to a new regular level of activity. But after each crisis the
extent of a popular indigenous political culture was greater than it had

been before the conflict occurred. By 1770 an alternative structure of politics was as much an enduring feature of the English political scene as the House of Commons itself.

This does not mean that those who worked within that structure were united by a common ideology. The vanguard of radicals who had moved beyond country-party ideology had yet to win any widespread support for their new views. The existence of an indigenous popular political culture, identifiably separate from (though connected with) the politics of Westminster is not evidence of radicalism *per se*, except in as much as any demand for participation by members of that culture threatened to subvert the existing order. But if we, as historians, can show that this political culture was not predominantly radical in that it often lacked the ideological coherence of a fully-fledged movement for parliamentary reform, this should not lead us to neglect popular politics, any more than the realisation that eighteenth-century parties were not the same as those of Dizzy and Mr Gladstone should induce us to disregard eighteenth-century party altogether.

The complexities of eighteenth-century popular politics have yet to be unravelled. Country-party ideology, parliamentary reform, very traditional modes of political behaviour as well as attempts to com-mercialise politics all combined to produce what can only be described as a political agglomeration. The gradual emancipation of this body from the constraints and control of the parliamentary politicians produced new leaders and gave new vigour. This development was the work of those who were rarely a substantial proportion of the indigenous culture, and who were sometimes renegade members of the political elite. Yet they exercised a political influence far in excess of their numbers. It was they who kept the tide of popular politics rising, even after it had fluctuated to a low ebb; and it was they who made the parliamentary politicians look ever more like the ill-fated King Canute.

Notes

Bibliography

Index

Notes

A NOTE ON REFERENCES

The place of publication in all notes is London, unless otherwise stated. All references to Additional Manuscripts are to those of the British Museum, unless there is indication to the contrary. I have tried to keep the notes as simple as possible. Full references to pamphlets are given in the bibliography.

The following abbreviations are used:

Add. Mss	Additional Manuscripts
AQC	*Ars Quatuorum Coronati*
Bedford Correspondence	Lord John Russell (ed.), *The Correspondence of John, Fourth Duke of Bedford* (3 vols., London, 1842–6)
BIHR	*Bulletin of the Institute of Historical Research*
Burke, *Correspondence*	T. W. Copeland *et al.* (eds.), *The Correspondence of Edmund Burke* (9 vols., Cambridge, 1958–70)
Burke, *Works*	*The Works of Edmund Burke* (8 vols., Bohn's British Classics, London, 1854–89)
Bute Mss	Bute Mss, Mount Stuart
Bute Mss (Cardiff)	Bute Mss, Cardiff City Library
Chatham Correspondence	W. Stanhope Taylor and J. H. Pringle (eds.), *The Correspondence of William Pitt, Earl of Chatham* (4 vols., London, 1838–40)
EHR	*English Historical Review*
GLB	Grenville Letter Book
Grenville Papers	W. J. Smith (ed.), *The Grenville Papers: being the correspondence of R. Grenville, Earl Temple, and the Rt. Hon. G. Grenville, their friends and contemporaries* (4 vols., London, 1852–3)
HJ	*Historical Journal*
Jenkinson Papers	Ninetta S. Jucker (ed.), *The Jenkinson Papers 1760–1766* (London, 1949)
Namier, *England*	Sir Lewis Namier, *England in the Age of the American Revolution* (2nd ed., London, 1961)
P & P	*Past and Present*
PRO	Public Record Office
Ren. & Mod. Stud.	*Renaissance and Modern Studies*
ScRO	Scottish Record Office
THSLC	*Transactions of the Historic Society of Lancashire and Cheshire*
TRHS	*Transactions of the Royal Historical Society*
Walpole, *Letters*	Paget Toynbee (ed.), *The Letters of Horace Walpole* (16 vols., Oxford, 1903–25)
Walpole, *Memoirs of George III*	Horace Walpole, *Memoirs of the Reign of King George III. Now first published from the original manuscript*, ed. Sir Denis Le Marchant (4 vols., London, 1845)
WMQ	*William and Mary Quarterly*

1. Hanoverian politics and the 1760s;
the historical perspective

1 J. H. Plumb, *The Growth of Political Stability in England 1675–1725* (1967), xviii.
2 *Ibid* 98–128.
3 John B. Owen, *The Rise of the Pelhams* (1957), 62.
4 Owen, 'Political Patronage in Eighteenth Century England', *The Triumph of Culture: Eighteenth Century Perspectives*, ed. Paul Fritz and David Williams (Toronto, 1972), 373.
5 These figures are taken from Namier, *England*, 225–8.
6 W. A. Speck, *Tory and Whig, the Struggle in the Constituencies 1701–1715* (1971), *passim*; J. H. Plumb, 'The Growth of the Electorate in England 1660–1715', *P & P* 45 (1969), 110–16.
7 Plumb, *Growth of Political Stability*, 173–5.
8 John Cannon, *Parliamentary Reform 1640–1832* (Cambridge, 1973), 36.
9 H. J. Habakkuk, 'Marriage Settlements in the Eighteenth Century', *TRHS* 4th Ser. XXXII (1950), 15–30.
10 These figures are arrived at by comparing the figures in Speck, *Tory and Whig*, Appendix E, with those given in L. B. Namier and John Brooke, *The History of Parliament. The House of Commons, 1754–1790* (3 vols., HMSO, 1964).
11 Barbara Whittingham-Jones, 'Liverpool's Political Clubs, 1812–1830', *THSLC* CXI (1959), 117.
12 Cannon, *Parliamentary Reform*, 42.
13 R. J. Robson, *The Oxfordshire Election of 1754; a study in the interplay of city, county and university politics* (Oxford, 1949), 144–6.
14 J. H. Plumb, 'Political Man', in James L. Clifford (ed.), *Man Versus Society in Eighteenth-Century Britain* (Cambridge, 1968), 1–21.
15 By this figure I mean that London was the workplace for one adult male in six at some time during his working life, not that one sixth of the adult males at any moment in time worked in London. (E. A. Wrigley, 'A Simple Model of London's Importance in Changing English Society and Economy, 1650–1750', *P & P* 37 (1967), 49.)
16 For which see George Rudé, *Hanoverian London 1714–1808* (1971), 120–7.
17 Figures in typescript, Cambridge Group for the Study of Population and Social Structure.
18 This can be readily seen from Herbert M. Atherton, *Political Prints in the Age of Hogarth* (Oxford, 1974), 1–24.
19 Bryant Lillywhite, *London Coffee Houses* (1963), 23.
20 Ian R. Christie, *Myth and Reality in Late-Eighteenth-Century British Politics* (1970), 314.
21 R. J. Allen, *The Clubs of Augustan London* (Cambridge, Mass., 1933), 129–36; Frederick A. Pottle (ed.), *Boswell's London Journal 1762–3 together with the Journal of my Jaunt. Harvest 1762* (1951), 322.
22 John Loftis, *The Politics of Drama in Augustan England* (Oxford, 1963), 1–2, 21, 54–5, 57–8, 65, 136, 151.
23 G. W. Stone (ed.), *The London Stage 1660–1800*, Part IV, *1747–1776* (3 vols., Carbondale, Ill., 1962), nos. 1276–482.
24 A. M. Ogilvie, *Ralph Allen's Bye, Way and Cross-Road Posts* (1898), *passim*. The same documents are printed in Adrian E. Hopkins (ed.), 'Ralph Allen's own narrative 1720–1761', *Postal History Society* Special Series no. 8 (1960), 15–35.
25 Aytoun Ellis, *The Penny Universities. A History of the Coffee Houses* (1956), 202, 206–13; A. H. Arkle, 'Early Coffee Houses in Liverpool', *THSLC* LXIV (1912), 1–16.
26 Arkle, 'Early Coffee Houses', *THSLC* LXIV (1912), 6; Paul Kaufman, *Libraries and their Users* (1969), 44.

27 Hilda M. Hamlyn, 'Eighteenth-Century Circulating Libraries in England', *Library* 5th Series 1 (1946), 197–222.
28 J. H. Plumb, 'Political Man', in Clifford, *Man Versus Society in Eighteenth-Century Britain*, 14.
29 Namier, *England*, 161.
30 Marie Peters, 'The *Monitor* on the Constitution, 1755–1765: new light on the ideological origins of English radicalism', *EHR* LXXXVI (1971), 706–25.
31 See the remarks in P. D. Langford, 'William Pitt and Public Opinion, 1757', *EHR* CCCXLVI (1973), 73–5.
32 Duchess of Newcastle to Newcastle, 14 November 1760, Newcastle (Clumber) Mss 19/74; Devonshire Diary, 5 April 1762, Devonshire Mss 260/370.
33 See, for instance, Namier, *England*, 159.
34 G. A. Cranfield, *The Development of the Provincial Newspaper 1700–1760* (Oxford, 1962), 21.
35 T. S. Ashton, *Economic Fluctuations in England 1700–1800* (Oxford, 1959), 22–3.
36 Walter James Shelton, *English Hunger and Industrial Disorders* (1973), 142.
37 Ashton, *Economic Fluctuations*, 151–4.
38 J. M. Beattie, 'The Pattern of Crime in England 1660–1800', *P & P* 62 (1974), 94–5.
39 George Rudé, *Wilkes and Liberty. A Social Study of 1763 to 1774* (Oxford, 1962), 90.
40 George Rudé, *The Crowd in History; a study in popular disturbances in France and England, 1730–1848* (1964), 37.
41 'Additional Brief. King v. James Murphy and others', PRO, T.S. 11/818/2096.
42 James Burgh, *Political Disquisitions: or an enquiry into public errors, defects and abuses* (3 vols., 1774–5), I, 37–8; *Parliamentary History* XVIII, 1295–6.
43 John Cartwright, *Take Your Choice!* (1776), 20–1.
44 E. P. Thompson, 'The Moral Economy of the English Crowd in the Eighteenth Century', *P & P* 50 (1971), 78–9.
45 Catharine Macaulay, *Observations on. . . Thoughts on the Cause of the Present Discontents* (1770), 15.
46 Memoirs of Thomas Hollis (2 vols., 1780), I, 98–9.
47 But see Isaac Kramnick, *Bolingbroke and his Circle. The Politics of Nostalgia* (Cambridge, Mass., 1968), 121–4.

2. Historiography and method

1 The most readily available discussion of the historiography is Herbert Butterfield, *George III and the Historians* (1957), *passim*. For more recent writings see Christie, *Myth and Reality*, 9–25.
2 Thomas Erskine May, *The Constitutional History of England Since the Accession of George III* (2 vols., 1861–3), I, 5–6, 12–13; W. R. Fryer, 'King George III: His Political Character and Conduct, 1760–84. A new Whig Interpretation', *Ren. & Mod. Stud.* VI (1962), 77; John Cannon, *The Fox–North Coalition. Crisis of the Constitution, 1782–4* (Cambridge, 1970), xii–xiii.
3 Fryer, 'George III', *Ren. & Mod. Stud.* VI (1962), 71, 80–4.
4 Namier, *England*, 47.
5 Namier, *England*, 47–51; Lewis Namier, *Crossroads of Power, Essays on Eighteenth-Century England* (1962), 83–6.
6 See Namier's strictures in *Crossroads of Power*, 77–8.
7 Namier, *Crossroads of Power*, 213–14; Romney Sedgwick (ed.), *Letters from George III to Bute 1756–1766* (1939), viii.
8 May, *Constitutional History of England*, II, 2.
9 G. O. Trevelyan, *The Early History of Charles James Fox* (1888), 33–4; G. M. Trevelyan, *The Two Party System in English Political History* (Oxford, 1926); T. B. Macaulay, *Critical and Historical Essays contributed to the Edinburgh Review* (1877),

775–6; D. A. Winstanley, *Personal and Party Government* (Cambridge, 1910); D. A. Winstanley, *Lord Chatham and the Whig Opposition* (Cambridge, 1912); G. H. Guttridge, *English Whiggism and the American Revolution* (Berkeley and Los Angeles, 1963).

10 Namier, *Crossroads of Power*, 220–1; Ian R. Christie, *The End of Lord North's Ministry 1780–1782* (1958), 188–9; John B. Owen, *The Pattern of Politics in Eighteenth-Century England* (Hist. Assoc., Aids to Teachers, no. 10, 1962), 4–6.

11 Fryer, 'King George III', *Ren. & Mod. Stud.* VI (1962), 82–5; May, *Constitutional History of England*, II, 9–12.

12 Namier, *England*, 84; Sedgwick, *Letters from George III to Bute*, lvi.

13 Namier, *England*, 52–3. But see John Owen, 'George II Reconsidered' in Anne Whiteman, J. S. Bromley and P. M. G. Dickson (eds.), *Statesmen, Scholars and Merchants* (Oxford, 1973), 113–34.

14 Almost every instance of pre-Namier whig historiography seems to contain these assumptions.

15 Lewis Namier, *Personalities and Powers* (1955), 2. See Quentin Skinner, 'The Principles and Practice of Opposition: the case of Bolingbroke versus Walpole' in Neil McKendrick (ed.), *Historical Perspectives. Studies in English Thought and Society in honour of J. H. Plumb* (1974), 100–2 for a summary of this and other tory historians' views.

16 Skinner, 'The Principles and Practice of Opposition', *Historical Perspectives*, 107.

17 Christie, *Myth and Reality*, esp. 27.

18 See my criticisms of Namier in 'The Misfortunes of Lord Bute: A Case-study in Eighteenth-century Political Argument and Public Opinion', *HJ* XVI, 1 (1973), 36–7.

19 Fryer, 'George III', *Ren. & Mod. Stud.* VI (1962), 78, and see Ian R. Christie's criticisms of Cannon's *Fox–North Coalition* in *Studies in Burke and His Time*, XIV, i (1972), 94.

20 See note 15 above.

21 The only work that seems to me to recognise adequately this problem in the period is B. W. Hill in his 'Executive Monarchy and the Challenge of Parties, 1689–1832', *HJ* XIII, 3 (1970), 379–401.

22 Christie, *Myth and Reality*, 28.

23 *Ibid* 36.

24 Cf. John Dunn, 'The Identity of the History of Ideas', *Philosophy* XLIII (1968), 87.

25 Quentin Skinner, 'Some Problems in the Analysis of Political Thought and Action', *Political Theory* II, 3 (1974), 279–303.

3. Whig and tory

1 Lewis Namier, 'Monarchy and the Party System', in *Personalities and Powers*, 13–15; G. M. Trevelyan, *The Two Party System*. John Brooke's remark that Namier was not primarily an historian of the eighteenth century but of parliament is interesting in this context. (Brooke, 'Namier and Namierism', *History and Theory*, III, 3 (1964), 334.)

2 Carl B. Cone, *Burke and the Nature of Politics. The Age of the American Revolution* (University of Kentucky, 1957), 193, 203.

3 I have criticised his view in 'Party and the Double Cabinet: Two Facets of Burke's *Thoughts*', *HJ* XIV, 3 (1971), 494–5.

4 See p. 28 above.

5 Lewis Namier, *The Structure of Politics at the Accession of George III* (2nd ed., 1963), xi.

6 [J. Palmer], *An Essay on the Constitution of England* (1765), 57; E. W. Montagu, *Reflections on the Rise and Fall of Ancient Republics* (2nd ed., 1760), 4. Compare *The Loyal or Revolutional Tory* (1733), 2; [Egmont], *Faction Detected by the Evidence of Facts. Containing an Impartial View of Parties at Home, and Affairs Abroad* (3rd ed., 1743),

6–7; 'THOUGHTS Political and Moral', *Universal Magazine* XLIII (1768), 175; *Considerations on the Times* (1769), 33; [J. Marriott], *Political Considerations*; (1762), 14–15; Burke, *Works*, i, 185. It was also widely held that nations grew more factious in proportion to their increasing wealth. (See, for example, *Ministerial Patriotism Detected* (1763), 9–10.)

7 Lord John Cavendish to Newcastle, 26 July 1766, Add. Mss 32976 f. 269; Newcastle to Lord John Cavendish, 26 July 1766, *ibid* f. 271.

8 Walpole, *Memoirs of George III*, i, 382; ii, 2–4.

9 See, *inter alia*, *Oxford Magazine* IV (1769), 136.

10 Johnson gives his definition thus: 'PARTY. I. A number of persons confederated by similarity of designs or opinions in opposition to others; a faction.' For examples of the distinction between a faction and a party made on the basis of members' intentions see pp. 71–2 above.

11 Romney Sedgwick (ed.), *The History of Parliament. The House of Commons 1715–54* (2 vols., HMSO, 1971), i, 19. These figures may be compared with those of W. A. Speck for the general elections of 1713 and 1715 in *Tory and Whig*, Appendix D.

12 Sedgwick, *History of Parliament*, i, 34, 42, 57; Owen, *The Rise of the Pelhams*, 66; Namier, *England*, 419–21.

13 Ian R. Christie in his analysis of the House of Commons in 1780 does not denote a category of tories (*The End of Lord North's Ministry*, 167–230), although Foord cites a few self-confessed tories of this period (Archibald S. Foord, *His Majesty's Opposition 1714–1830* (Oxford, 1964), 335–8), and Burke identified 'five or six Tories, who act on principle, such as it is' in 1782 (Burke to John Burgoyne, 24 December 1782, *Burke Correspondence*, v, 58).

14 This happened to such tory families as the Foxes, Winningtons, Chetwynds, Gowers, Finches and Legges. (Owen, *Rise of the Pelhams*, 69; Namier, 'Monarchy and the Party System' in *Personalities and Powers*, 33.)

15 The Duke of Newcastle, for example, in common with a great many other politicians of the 1760s treated the terms 'tory' and 'country-gentleman' as virtually synonymous. (Newcastle to Legge, 24 March 1764, Add. Mss 32957 f. 230.) Cf. *Annual Register* (1762), 47.

16 Walpole, *Memoirs of George III*, i, 244.

17 I use the epithet 'hard-headed' in view of Waldegrave's extraordinary suggestions to be found in the manuscript continuation of his published memoirs amongst the Holland House papers. There, in a political solution which would have flattered the cynicism of Henry Fox, he suggests that the way to obtain political stability is through a massive proliferation of patronage and government offices: 'The Addition of many Lords and Grooms to the royal Bedchamber was a masterly stroke of State Policy, and had a surprising Effect.

'A short Act of Parliament might be of extraordinary Benefit to the subject, by extending this salutary Measure to some more lucrative Employments. We might have nine Commissioners of the Treasury, thirteen of the Admiralty, as many of the Board of Trade: or if it should be necessary, any of the great Offices might be put into Commission, the present great Officer retaining the Rank and Salary, under the title of the First Commissioner.

'This will be a comfortable maintenance for many worthy Senators who are not yet provided for, every Party will have its Share, and we shall continue till Time, or Money shall be no more, a Rich, a Virtuous, and a United People.' (Add. Mss 51380 f. 104.) It has been suggested to me that this statement is perhaps ironic or satirical. This may be so, but I know of no evidence to support such an assertion, and the context of the remark implies that it was seriously intended.

18 Waldegrave, *Memoirs from 1754 to 1758* (1821), 20.

19 As Foord remarks, 'There were, among a host of others, Old Whigs and New Whigs, Court Whigs and Country Whigs, Zealous Whigs and Moderate Whigs, Staunch

Whigs and Independent Whigs, Constitution Whigs and Renegado Whigs, False Whigs and Rotten Whigs.' (A. S. Foord, 'Horace Walpole, the only unadulterated Whig', in W. H. Smith (ed.), *Horace Walpole, Writer, Politician and Connoisseur. Essays on the 250th Anniversary of Walpole's Birth* (1967), 25–6 and note.)

20 *An Address to the People of England* (1767), 40–1.

21 Macaulay, 'Essay on Chatham', in *Critical and Historical Essays*, 776.

22 *A Full and Free Inquiry into the Merits of the Peace* (1765), 141. Cf. *The Balance* (1753), 3. For a discussion of this development see David Thomson, *The Conception of Political Party in England, in the period 1740 to 1783* (Cambridge University, unpub. Ph.D., 1938), 77–8. It was a comment something like this that got Horace Walpole into such trouble with Princess Amelia in December 1762. She evidently thought it was a pro-administration remark – not a commonplace – and according to Walpole 'flew into the most outrageous passion, coloured like scarlet'. It was only later that he was able to explain exactly what he meant. (Walpole to Montagu, 20 December 1762, *Walpole Letters*, v, 281–3.)

23 *Parliamentary History* XVI, 46. Cf. the manuscript notes in *View of Internal Policy* (1764), 145. Horace Walpole, along with other contemporaries, thought Calvert a little mad, but in this case, at least, his words may be taken as representative. (Walpole, *Memoirs of George III*, i, 167; Rigby to Bedford, 26 November 1762, *Bedford Correspondence*, iii, 161; Burke to O'Hara, 25 November 1762, *Burke Correspondence*, i, 157.)

24 Henry Fielding, *The History of the Life of the late Mr Jonathan Wild the Great*, Ch. VI, 'Of Hats'.

25 Betty Kemp, *Sir Francis Dashwood. An Eighteenth-Century Independent* (1967), 8; Namier, *England*, 196–7.

26 This is apparent from the analysis of divisions made by Sedgwick in *History of Parliament*, i, 81, 86, 89, 104.

27 A. N. Newman (ed.), 'The Parliamentary Diary of Sir Edward Knatchbull 1722–1730', *Camden Society* 3rd Series, XCIV (1963), viii, 59, 67; Sir Richard Lodge (ed.), 'Private Correspondence of Chesterfield and Newcastle 1744–46', *ibid*, XLIV (1930), 40–1.

28 For an elaboration of these trends see Foord, *His Majesty's Opposition*, 332–8.

29 'A State of the Parties Sept 1 1762 to the D - - - of P - - - - - d', Hatfield House, Chase Price Mss A 10.

30 Walpole to Montagu, 11 December 1760, *Walpole Letters*, v, 11. Walpole implicitly recognises his plagiarism in *Memoirs of George III*, i, 115. Gascoigne made the comment on the afternoon before Walpole wrote his letter. (Devonshire Mss 260/357.)

31 Though not everyone went as far as Sir John Dalrymple who wanted to revive whigs and tories to restore stability. He wrote to Charles Yorke on 6 November 1769, 'the present distractions arise chiefly from this, that great partys are at an end, & an hundred little ones have come in their places. While Whig & tory tilted at each other in Charles the 2nd reign, the constitution was safe, because they only differed upon the mode of improving & preserving it. After the revolution it continued still safe, because one great party had an interest to support the crown, & another took up that of the country. But that at present the Mechanics of London make one party, the Transported felons of America make an other; the Irish a third, twenty others follow, none support the crown. All struggle who shall take something from it. Now an association of those who know not their own greatness, & consent to follow others in place of commanding them, would probably bring back the old great party's again. For all the little partys would join against it; the crown would naturally connect with it; & thus the two great & useful partys of Whig & Tory would take their ranks again in the nation.' (Stair Mss ScRO GD35/60/82; Add. Mss 35639 f. 144.)

32 Conway's comment in the lower House in December 1768, for example, was not just wishful thinking – though it might have been: 'Speaking of parties, the General said, there are so many great men in the world, and so many little ones belonging to them, that it is impossible for any party to set up a firm administration.' (J. Wright (ed.), *Sir Henry Cavendish's Debates of the House of Commons, during the Thirteenth Parliament of Great Britain, commonly called the Unreported Parliament* (2 vols., 1841), i, 109.)

33 *Craftsman*, XL (24 April 1727). Compare *Cato's Letters*, LXIX (10 March 1721/2); LXXX (9 June 1722); Bolingbroke, *Works* (4 vols., 1844), ii, 23–4; [Pulteney], *An Answer to One Part of a late Infamous Libel* (1731), 17; *The Loyal or Revolutionary Tory*, 2–4.

34 *Craftsman*, LXVI (7 October 1727); LXIX (28 October 1727); CCCLXVI (7 July 1733); CCCLXXIX (6 October 1733); Bolingbroke, *Works*, ii, 11–12; *The Protest* (1757), 27–9.

35 *Craftsman*, XVII (30 January 1726/7).

36 *A Defence of the People: or, Full Confutation of the Pretended Facts* (1744), 98.

37 See the division figures from Sedgwick, *History of Parliament* in note 26.

38 For the opposition's links with the Pretender see Sedgwick, *History of Parliament*, i, 68–73, 77. The break-up of the opposition at the fall of Walpole in 1742 naturally revived the distinction that the two groups in opposition had tried to bury. Thus Egmont, back in power in 1742, reversed his previous position and adopted the standard whig government posture of distinguishing whigs from tories. (*Faction Detected by the Evidence of Facts*, 42.)

39 Bolingbroke, *Works*, ii, 6; *The Craftsman by Caleb D'Anvers* (17 vols., collected ed., 1731–7), I, vi–ii; *Essay on Patriotism, and on the Character and Conduct of some late famous Pretenders to that Virtue* (1768), 26.

40 Kramnick, *Bolingbroke and his Circle*, 119–21. I appreciate that the politics of the Pelhams was that of accommodation rather than proscription, but it was accommodation on whig terms.

41 For the reality of a Jacobite threat, at least until 1731, see P. Fritz, *Jacobitism and the English Government, 1717–1731* (Cambridge University, unpub. Ph.D., 1967), Ch. v. And for party discrimination see *Craftsman*, LXIX (28 October 1727); *A Speech Without Doors, by a Lobby-Member* (1762), 13; *The Political Balance. In which the Principles and Conduct of the Two Parties are weighed* (1765), 8–9; *HMC Onslow*, 465. There was some attempt to continue this discrimination, in admittedly transmuted form, into the 1760s. See, for example, *North Briton* XXXIII (15 January 1763); *The History of the late Minority* (1766), 15.

42 *A Letter to the Whigs* (1748), 29. Compare [Pulteney], *An Humble Address to the Knights, Citizens and Burgesses* (1734), 7–8; *The True Whig Displayed* (1762), 10. As Bute remarked to George Grenville, one of Newcastle's strengths under George II, which he had lost under the new king, was the opportunity 'to tip the Rascal and the Jacobite to every man that opposed Him'. (Bute to George [Grenville], [13 October 1761], endorsed 'This Letter I directed Elliot to read to G. Grenville when fluctuating about taking the lead in the H. of Commons on Pitt's resignation'. Bute Mss 1761/738.)

43 *A Letter to the Right Honourable the Earl of B**** (1761), 66. Hence, of course, Horace Walpole's comment on the accession of George III that 'the extinction of parties had not waited for, but preceded the dawn of the reign'. (Walpole, *Memoirs of George III*, i, 5.)

44 'Memorandum' n.d. (1772?), Royal Archives, Windsor, RA 15672 printed in Herbert Butterfield, *George III, Lord North and the People 1779–80* (1949), 3. To some extent George's claim to be the creator of this situation looks like a deliberate attempt to disregard the work of Pitt in reconciling the tories to government in 1757. But in one sense George was right. Only a non-party monarch – not a politician – could admit tories to personal royal favour and to the court.

45 *The True Whig Displayed* (1762), 11. Cf. *A Letter from a Gentleman in Town* (1763), 10.

46 As is made clear by Devonshire in his political journal (Devonshire Mss 260/288). Pitt avowed the measure and said, 'he wou'd be judged by any candid man whether his Grace [Devonshire] ought or the Whigs cou'd take umbrage at a few of the principal Tories being taken into the King's service as supernuminaries'.

47 Some idea of the remarkable change can be obtained from Mordaunt's letter to Sir Roger Newdigate of 4 December 1760 (Warwick RO Newdigate Mss B18/1839a): 'This day at noon, I was surpris'd with the news yt. Ld Oxford & Ld Bruce were made Lords of the Bedchamber and George Pitt, Norborne Berkley, & Northey Grooms, the Three last are not to kiss hands till towards the end of the Session as you see the good things of this world are coming amongst us, I think you sh^d not be absent, & tho' you will be too late to make any Alteration in the Civil List, if you design'd any, you may yet be in Time to take some of it to your own Share.' Not surprisingly contemporaries were soon commenting on the extent to which the tories were 'almost to a Man for the Court'. (Rigby to Bedford, 24 November 1762, Bedford Mss XLVI f. 128.)

48 Fox to Bute, 23 November 1762, Bute Mss.

49 *London Evening Post*, 8 January 1761; *Political Controversy*, i, 164; *Briton*, 18 July 1762; *Auditor Extraordinary*, 4 December 1762.

50 *London Evening Post* 9 June 1761; *London Magazine* XXX (1761), 286–7. The original agreement between Prince Frederick and the Tories can be found printed in Aubrey N. Newman (ed.), 'Leicester House Politics, 1750–1760, from the Papers of John, Second Earl of Egmont', *Camden Miscellany* XXIII, 4th Series v. 7 (1969), 90–1. Hardwicke thought that this document was the basis of Bute's political plans. He told Newcastle that 'the plan was that which the late Prince of Wales sent by my Lord Talbot to the Tories, and that they governed themselves entirely by that; that he feared that Whiggism would not exist in this Kingdom long'. (Newcastle to Devonshire, 23 December 1762, Yorke, *Hardwicke*, iii, 446. Cf. *History of the late Minority*, 38.)

51 'CHARITAS, Oxford', *Gazetteer*, 1 June 1762.

52 Hugh Baillie to Bute, 8 August 1762, Bute Mss 1762/285. Cf. Rev. Charles Godwyn to Mr Hutchins, 18 April 1763, in John Nicols, *Literary Anecdotes of the Eighteenth Century; comprising the biographical memoirs of W. Bowyer* (9 vols., 1812–15), viji, 233.

53 'A view of the present political debates', *London Magazine* XXXI (1762), 291.

54 'Civicus', *St James's Chronicle*, 12 June 1762; *Auditor* 19 August 1762; 'INDEPENDENT WHIGG', *Gazetteer*, 28 April 1763; *Contrast* (1765), 2; 'W. M. PRYNNE', *St James's Chronicle*, 15 October 1761; Matthew Fetherstonehaugh to Newcastle, 14 August 1763, Add. Mss 32950 f. 129; Devonshire to Grafton, 7 November 1762, Devonshire Mss 260/375/395; Walpole, *Memoirs of George III*, i, 318–19; *Gentleman's Magazine* XXXII (1762), 269.

55 *A Parallel Drawn between the Administration In the Four Last Years of Queen Anne, and the Four First of George III. By a Country Gentleman* (1766), *passim*; Burke, *Works*, i, 374–5; *Essay on Patriotism*, 29; *Briton*, 21 July, 9 October 1762; *North Briton* XXV, 20 November 1762; *Political Register* v (1769), 38–9.

56 *A Review of Lord Bute's Administration* (1763), 76, 79–80. Compare the views of 'C. A.', *Lloyd's Evening Post*, 29 November 1762; [John Butler], *An Address to the Cocoa Tree from a Whig* (1762), 6–7; 'PLAIN SENSE', *Gazetteer*, 20 May 1763; *Contrast*, XIII (21 September 1763), 149–50; [Almon], *History of the late Minority*, 27; 'FRESNOY. to K***', *Middlesex Journal*, 5 May 1770; Legge to Newcastle, 25 April 1764, Add. Mss 32958 f. 206.

57 *Observations on Public Liberty* (1769), 15.

58 Devonshire Journal, 11 June 1761, Devonshire Mss 260/322. Devonshire issued a similar warning in April 1762 when Bute, at Lord Lichfield's request, wanted to create a number of tory justices for Denbighshire (*ibid* 260/370). That Devonshire was a moderate is apparent to anyone who has read his journal for these years.

Only with his very abrupt dismissal did he really join opposition. He persistently sought to mediate between the king and the Old Corps because he was apprehensive of a clash between a young king and the party. As he said to J. Grenville in December 1760, with what turned out to be a good deal of foresight: 'I was much concern'd for the King & apprehensive yt Ld Bute thro' want of Judgement & aiming at a power which it was impossible for him to attain wd throw his Master into great difficulties. yt not content with being ye Favourite, he must be the Minister over the other Ministers wou'd inevitably bring on attempts to force him from the King, the thought of which I abhorr'd & the consequences I dreaded, as the impression it must naturally make on the mind of a Young King wou'd be such as to render his Reign uneasy to him & throw the greatest confusion into his Affairs, & yet if Ld Bute went on in the way he proceeds at present that stroke will inevitably come.' (*Ibid* 260/289.)

59 This point is well made by B. W. Hill in 'Executive Monarchy and the Challenge of the Parties, 1689–1832', *HJ* XIII, 3 (1970), 391–3. For a discussion of the content of the 'new toryism' and its relations with personal monarchy see Ch. 7 above.

60 Walpole, *Memoirs of George III*, i, 15.

61 Newcastle to Hardwicke, 31 July 1762, Add. Mss 32941 f. 129.

62 William Meredith to Burke, 26 June 1767, Sheffield Mss Burke 1–72.

63 Legge to Newcastle, 25 April 1764, Add. Mss 32958 f. 206 [emphasis added]; Col. G. Onslow to Newcastle, 19 July 1765, Add. Mss 32968 f. 92; Grenville Diary, 28 August 1763, *Grenville Papers*, ii, 199. Cf. Legge's bitter comments on 'Jacobite & Tory supporters of Scotch Tyranny & Oppression'. (Legge to Newcastle, 20 July 1764, Add. Mss 32960 f. 337.)

64 '*From the Earl of Or - - - d in the Shades, to the D - - - of G - - - - - -*', *Oxford Magazine* II (1769), 267.

65 Sir George Yonge to Newcastle, 18 October 1764, Add. Mss 32962 f. 341.

66 Newcastle to Devonshire, 11 August 1763, Add. Mss 32950 ff. 67, 73.

67 George Onslow to Newcastle, 5 May 1763, Add. Mss 32948 f. 234.

68 George Onslow to Newcastle, 3 October 1764, Add. Mss 32962 f. 197.

69 *Grenville Papers*, ii, 198–9; Sir H. Erskine to Bute, 19 May [1762], Bute Mss (Cardiff) 2/181.

70 See, *inter alia*, Add. Mss 32952 f. 36; 32956 f. 104; 32958 f. 237; 32965 f. 26; 32976 f. 79; 32977 f. 209; Sheffield Mss Rockingham 83–3.

71 'A Battle of the Whigs and Tories', *Oxford Magazine*, v (1770), 256.

72 *The Parliamentary Spy*, XIX, 3 April 1770.

73 [Philip Francis], *A Letter from the Cocoa Tree to the Country Gentlemen* (1762), 13. Though, as this rhetoric makes clear, there is some attempt even in this apologist to invoke traditional divisions.

74 For example *Auditor*, 25 December 1762; *True Whig Displayed* (1762), 4.

75 'A.Z.', *London Magazine* XXXII (1763), 25–6.

76 Thus the British Museum Catalogue lists this as one of Wilkes's works and D. H. Watson, 'The Rise of the Opposition at Wildman's Club', *BIHR* XLIV (May 1971), 67, treats the pamphlet as such. But it is clear from a full reading of the pamphlet and from Wilkes's own expressions of surprise that he should not be called the author of the pamphlet. ('I wish to hear what impudent catchpennies the letters are, which I am told are circulated in my name *to a Noble Lord*, to the *Minority Club* &c', Wilkes to Cotes, 5 April 1764, Add. Mss 30868 f. 66.)

77 *A Letter to a Noble Member of the Club in Albemarle-Street from John Wilkes, Esq; at Paris* (1764), 9.

78 *A Letter to a Noble Member of the Club* (1764), 12. Cf. [J. H. Stevenson], *A Pastoral Puke. A Second Sermon Preached before the People called Whigs. By an Independent* (1764), 20.

4. *Opposition and the proprietary parties*

1 Namier and Brooke (ed.), *History of Parliament*, ii, 137, 140; George Pitt to Bute, 30 November 1760, Bute Mss 1760/112; Fitzmaurice to Bute [March 1761], Bute Mss 1761/181; Shute Barrington, *The Political Life of William Wildman, Viscount Barrington, compiled from original papers* (1815), 105; Scarsdale to George III, 2 March 1764, Sir John Fortescue (ed.), *The Correspondence of King George III from 1760 to 1783* (6 vols., 1927–8), i, 66–7. Such examples could, of course, be considerably extended.

2 Bernard Bailyn, *The Origins of American Politics* (New York, 1968), 36.

3 'H', *St James's Chronicle*, 25 January 1763. Cf. *Universal Magazine* XLI (1765), 262; *Auditor*, 25 December 1762; *A Letter to his Grace the D - - - of N - - - - - - - e* (1757), 19; [Egmont], *Faction Detected* (1743), 174; [Pulteney], *A Proper Answer to the Bystander* (1742), 34–5; *Loyal or Revolutionary Tory*, 49; *Craftsman* CCXLIV, March 1730/1.

4 *Con-Test*, IV, 14 December 1756. Cf. [Gordon and Trenchard], *Cato's Letters* (4 vols., 6th ed., 1755), I, xxii.

5 'Anti-Sejanus' in *New and Impartial Collection of Letters* (1767), ii, 47–8; 'The Politician' no. 1, *The Political Controversy or Weekly Magazine of Ministerial and anti-Ministerial Essays*, ii, 227–8; *What Should be Done* (1766), 27; [John Brown], *Thoughts on Civil Liberty, on Licentiousness and Faction* (2nd ed., 1765), 117; Elliott to Molyneux, 10 April 1763, Norfolk RO, Molyneux Letter Book, f. 203.

6 Kinnoull to Newcastle, 26 July 1763, Add. Mss 32949 f. 420.

7 *A Defence of the People* (1744), 8; 'Y.Z.', *Gazetteer*, 8 July 1763; Egerton Mss 3711 f. 104; J. Douglas to Robertson, 21 April 1769, Nat. Lib. of Scot., Robertson-Macdonald Letters, Mss 3942 f. 92.

8 *HMC Onslow Mss*, 458.

9 Bamber Gascoigne to Strutt, 17 September 1769, Strutt Mss. Bolingbroke, of course, employed the two contending notions of the spirit of liberty and the spirit of faction to provide the framework for his 'Remarks on the History of England'. (Bolingbroke, *Works*, i, 297–8, 304.)

10 *A Mirror for the Multitude* (1769), 38; *Auditor*, 19 August 1762; *Loyal or Revolutionary Tory*, 2–4; George III to Pitt, 30 May 1767, *Chatham Correspondence*, iii, 264; 'Y.Z.', *Gazetteer*, 8 July 1763.

11 Bute to George Grenville, 10 October 1762, Add. Mss 38191 f. 9 [draft]; 36797 f. 13 [copy]. Cf. Bute to Sir James Lowther, 17 November 1762, *ibid* ff. 22–3 printed in *HMC Lonsdale 13th Report*, Part VII, 131 and *Jenkinson Papers*, 87. There is a more extensive discussion of this question in Ch. 7.

12 Namier and Brooke, *History of Parliament*, ii, 451–2; iii, 406–7. Even such a vigorous party man as William Baker could proclaim, 'My Political Religion has but few Tenets – perhaps they are rather unfashionable, but I am rather a Bigot to them – To consult those whom I believe honest, and my own heart – to attend to the advice of the one, but to follow implicitly the Dictates of the other. Acting thus, the best and generous may sometimes, that of a Young Man frequently, be deceived – I confess it. But it is a deception, which, if it brings me into outward Trouble, will never hurt my piece [*sic*] of mind.' (Baker to Talbot, 13 September 1770, Herts. RO, Baker Mss 1/41.)

13 Torrington to Portland, 8 January 1765 [should be 1766], University of Nottingham, Portland Mss PwF 2274. This letter was written, of course, when Portland was in office, but the point about Torrington's independency stands. For a particularly good example of independency in opposition see P. D. G. Thomas, *The House of Commons in the Eighteenth Century* (Oxford, 1971), 112–13.

14 Richard Pares, *King George III and the Politicians* (Oxford, 1953), 72–3; W. T. Laprade (ed.), 'Parliamentary Papers of John Robinson 1774–1784', *Camden Society* 3rd Series XXXIII (1922), xiv.

15 Denbigh to Rochford, 17 September 1770, Denbigh Letter Book, 263.
16 Rockingham to Newcastle, 1 May 1768, Add. Mss 32990 f. 4.
17 Newcastle to Richmond, October 1768, Alison Olson, *The Radical Duke. The Career and Correspondence of Charles Lennox, third Duke of Richmond* (Oxford, 1961), 25–6.
18 Onslow to Newcastle [25 April 1764], Add. Mss 32958 f. 208. This sort of situation seems to have occurred quite often. William Baker, for example, complained bitterly of the absence of his colleagues when he opposed the Quebec Bill: 'I fought it through every stage almost alone when most of the Opposition were attending the Newmarket meeting or other occupations equally to be preferred to that duty.' (Namier and Brooke, *History of Parliament*, ii, 42.)
19 Thomas, *House of Commons in the Eighteenth Century*, 98.
20 For the best description of these negotiations see Cumberland's recollections which he wrote down in a marbled notebook now in the Sheffield Mss. ('An Account of the Negotiacion for the intended Change of Ministers in April & May 1765: recollected some Days after the whole was over, by help of Lord Albemarle, whom I had entrusted in the whole Transaction & who had his Part also to act', Sheffield Mss Rockingham 13.) Other race meetings were put to political purposes. Rockingham, for example, used the York meeting to assess local feeling about Wilkes and a county meeting in 1769, and one of the earliest signals of Newcastle's intention of going into opposition in 1762 was a gathering of the whig clans at Lewes races. (Rockingham to Burke, 1, 3 September 1769, *Burke Correspondence*, ii, 62; Chase Price to Portland, 24 July 1762, Portland Mss PwF 7898; Campbell to Bute, 21 July 1762, Bute Mss.)
21 For which see D. E. Ginter, *Whig Organisation in the General Election of 1790; selections from the Blair Adam Papers* (Berkeley, California, 1967), xxi–xxxviii.
22 Foord, *His Majesty's Opposition*, 341–2; Portland Mss PwF 1641–2, 4850, 5556, 6067, 6573–616, 6699–700, 7930, 8417.
23 Albemarle, *Memoirs of the Marquess of Rockingham and his Friends* (2 vols., 1852), i, 219–20.
24 Thomas, *House of Commons in the Eighteenth Century*, 113.
25 Foord, *His Majesty's Opposition*, 339–44.
26 D. H. Watson, 'The Rise of the Opposition at Wildman's Club', *BIHR* XLIV (1971), 56–67.
27 *Memoirs of John Almon, Bookseller of Piccadilly* (1790), 16. For further information on the opposition's press activities, see Ch. 11 above.
28 C. Townshend to Newcastle [30 April 1764], Add. Mss 32958 f. 250.
29 I have not felt it necessary to elaborate any further on Wildman's or give more detailed annotation in view of Derek Watson's excellent discussion of these problems in 'The Rise of the Opposition at Wildman's Club', *BIHR* XLIV, 68–75.
30 Newcastle to Hardwicke, 19 June 1762, 19 June 1762, Add. Mss 32939 ff. 410–11.
31 Newcastle to Rutland, 14 November 1764, Add. Mss 32963 f. 389. Cf. similar sentiments in Newcastle to Rockingham, 4 January 1765, Add. Mss 32965 f. 40. Compare Pulteney's *bon mot* in 1741: 'dividing is not the way to multiply'. (Coxe, *Walpole*, iii, 581–2.)
32 Devonshire to Newcastle, 2 July 1762, Add. Mss 32940 f. 229.
33 'Substance of what pass'd with HRH the Duke of Cumberland at Windsor Lodge, Oct. 19, 1762', Claremont 20 October 1762, Add. Mss 32943 ff. 313–14; Newcastle to Hardwicke, 19 December 1762, Add. Mss 32945 f. 313; Hardwicke to Newcastle, 20 December 1762, *ibid* f. 323; Newcastle to Hardwicke, 27 December 1762, *ibid* f. 424; Hardwicke to Newcastle, 1 January 1763, Add. Mss 32946 f. 4; Namier, *England*, 345, 361, 372–3, 377, 391, 392, 395–6.
34 Newcastle to Charles Townshend, 25 February 1764. Add. Mss 32956 f. 104; Bessborough to Newcastle, 5 January 1765, Add. Mss 32965 f. 93. Cf. Hardwicke to Charles Yorke, 11 April 1764, Add. Mss 35361 f. 95.

35 See, *inter alia*, Add. Mss 32949 ff. 131, 191; 32957 ff. 119, 239; 32958 ff. 224, 308; 32960 f. 332; Sheffield Mss Rockingham 1–812; 1–858; Olson, *Radical Duke*, 141–2; Albemarle, *Memoirs of the Marquess of Rockingham*, ii, 193–5.
36 Lord Jersey to Newcastle, 19 December 1763, Add. Mss 32954 f. 90.
37 Winstanley, *Personal and Party Government*, 146–50, 164–9, 186–201, 206–14, 216–19.
38 Temple to Wilkes, 21 December 1764, *Grenville Correspondence*, ii, 476.
39 See above, pp. 89–90.
40 Denbigh to Camden, 19 September 1767, Denbigh Letter Book, 58–9.
41 West to Newcastle, 3 December 1767, Add. Mss 32987 f. 149.
42 Bedford to George Grenville, 5 November 1767, *Bedford Correspondence*, iii, 395.
43 Rockingham to Newcastle, 24 November 1767, Add. Mss 32987 ff. 87–8; Minto Mss M6 no. 15.
44 Rockingham to Dowdeswell, 9 September 1767, Sheffield Mss R1-857, part printed in Wright (ed.), *Cavendish's Debates*, i, 585.
45 Burke to Rockingham, 6 November 1769, *Burke Correspondence*, ii, 105.
46 Walpole, *Memoirs of the Reign of George III*, iv, 123, 175.
47 Kramnick, *Bolingbroke and his Circle*, 153–63; H. T. Dickinson, *Bolingbroke* (1970), 195–7, 200–2; Foord, *His Majesty's Opposition*, 146–51; Thomson, *The Conception of Political Party*, 79–82.
48 Owen's phrase in *Rise of the Pelhams*, 64.
49 Pat Rogers, 'Swift and Bolingbroke on Faction', *Journal of British Studies* IX (1970), 81.
50 'Remarks on the History of England', Bolingbroke, *Works*, i, 394.
51 Bolingbroke, *Works*, i, 428. Cf. *ibid*, i, 233. The argument that immediate and effective opposition would avoid the unpalatable choice between slavery and open resistance was also used by Burke in his *Thoughts*. (Burke, *Works*, i, 379.)
52 Foord, *His Majesty's Opposition*, 150.
53 Bolingbroke, *Works*, ii, 48.
54 Bolingbroke, *Works*, ii, 370.
55 *A Defence of the People* (1744), 98.
56 At least, this was Bolingbroke's view of it. (Foord, *His Majesty's Opposition*, 148–50.)
57 Foord, *His Majesty's Opposition*, 231–56; Thomson, *The Conception of Political Party*, 94–7. Augustus Hervey referred to the Chatham administration as 'broad bottom' in November 1766. (Burke to Charles O'Hara [*post* 11 November 1766]. *Burke Correspondence* i, 280.)
58 *Cn-Test* I, 23 November 1756. There is a further discussion of the idea of 'measures not men' and the associated notion of the patriot in Ch. 6.
59 *A Vindication of the Present Ministry* (1766), 50. Cf. *Briton*, 6 November 1762.
60 Foord, *His Majesty's Opposition*, 335–8; Christie, *The End of Lord North's Ministry*, 340–69.
61 [J. Shebbeare], *One More Letter to the People of England. By Their Old Friend* (1762), 34. Cf. [Marfolio], *An Historical view of the principal characters of the political writers in Great Britain* (1740), 45.
62 Walpole, *Memoirs of George III*, ii, 331; J. Dyson to Elliot, Minto Mss M11/4–5.
63 Walpole to T. Pitt, 5 June 1764, *Walpole Letters*, vi, 68–76; T. Pitt to George Grenville, 25 May 1764, *Grenville Papers*, ii, 325–7; [J. Shebbeare], *An Address to the Public on the late Dismission of a General Officer* (1764), *passim*; [Horace Walpole], *A Counter-Address to the Public, on the late Dismission of a General Officer* (1764), *passim*.
64 Waldegrave to [Cumberland?], [November 1762?], Add. Mss 51380 f. 107.
65 Newcastle to White, 19 June 1764, Add. Mss 32960 f. 17. Cf. Newcastle to Devonshire, 4 August 1764, Add. Mss 32961 f. 187; Foord, *His Majesty's Opposition*, 307–8.
66 George III to Chatham, 29 July, 28 November, [2 December] 1766, 30 May 1767, 14 October 1768, *Chatham Correspondence*, iii, 21, 134, 137, 264, 343; 'Memorandum' [July 1766], Fortescue, *Correspondence of George III*, i, 175.

67 'A Letter to the Earl of - - - - [Bute]', *Gentleman's Magazine* xxxv (1765), 351.
68 Burke, *Works*, i, 372.
69 Hardwicke to Newcastle, 13 May 1763, Add. Mss 32948 f. 276. Hardwicke expressed himself similarly in a further interview with Egremont in August. (Hardwicke to Royston, 5 August 1763, Yorke, *Hardwicke*, iii, 514.) Herbert Butterfield has discussed these ideas in 'Some Reflections on the Early Years of George III's Reign', *Journal of British Studies* iv (May 1965), esp. 83.
70 Wright (ed.), *Cavendish's Debates*, i, 276–7.
71 Burke to Rockingham, 29 October 1769, *Burke Correspondence*, ii, 101; Burke, *Works*, i, 373; Brewer, 'Party and the Double Cabinet', *HJ* xiv, 3 (1971), 491.
72 Wright (ed.), *Cavendish's Debates*, i, 17.
73 Burke, *Works*, i, 375; Brewer, 'Party and the Double Cabinet', *HJ* xiv, 491.
74 *The Detector Detected* (1743), 58. Cf. *Seventeen Forty Two* (1743), 43; [Gregory Sharpe], *A Short Dissertation upon Oligarchy* (1748), 5. For this trend see Thomson, *The Conception of Political Party*, 188–96.
75 Wright (ed.), *Cavendish's Debates*, i, 119.
76 Burke, *Works*, i, 374–5.
77 See Ch. 5 above.
78 Burke, *Works*, i, 376.
79 Burke to Rockingham, 29 October 1769, *Burke Correspondence*, ii, 101.
80 Burke, *Works*, i, 373–4.
81 I am aware that to a certain extent I am disagreeing with, or at least realigning my earlier views on the *Thoughts*. (Brewer, 'Party and the Double Cabinet', *HJ* xiv, esp. 491–2.) I would now wish to give greater emphasis to Burke's novelty, though *not* for the reasons given in the prevailing historiography described in the above article.
82 *Seventeen Forty Two*, 43. Cf. *Considerations on the Times* (1769), 34–5.
83 [Wilkes], *Letter to his Grace the Duke of Grafton* (1767), 4.
84 [J. Douglas], *A Letter addressed to two great men* (2nd ed., 1760), 2. At least one commentator was outraged at Douglas's suggestion: 'Surely it must surprise, and grieve every Lover of the *British* Constitution to hear, from such good Authority, that the Extinction of factious Opposition by the happy Unanimity of every Party, should have closed the Channel of parliamentary Instruction. Can Instruction then never reach the Ears of a Minister in Parliament, but from the Mouth of Opposition?... Instruction conveyed through such a Channel, can serve only to gratify Malignity on one hand, and mortify Pride on the other. It is like the application of a Caustick, which must torture the Patient, before it can operate to his Benefit.

'No one, Sir, can entertain a higher Notion of the Dignity of Parliaments than myself, or bear greater Respect to their Authority. For the Honour, therefore, of those august Assemblies, nay, for the Credit of human Nature, I am unwilling to believe, that nothing but Enmity to a Minister can open the Mouths of our Representatives, and that Senatorial Eloquence has its Root in Faction.' (*Reasons why the approaching Treaty of Peace should be debated in Parliament* (1760), 7–8.)
85 P. D. G. Thomas (ed.), 'Parliamentary Diaries of Nathaniel Ryder, 1764–7', *Camden Miscellany* xxiii (1969), 252. Cf. *Parliamentary Spy*, x, 6 March 1770.
86 'Legal Opposition recommended. SERTORIUS', *London Packet*, 20 December 1769. Cf. *Considerations on the Times* (1763), 32; 'CREON', *Gazetteer*, 30 January 1770; 'Opposition Considered. OBSERVATOR', *Public Ledger*, 4 December 1769; [Edward Spelman], *A Fragment out of the Sixth Book of Polybius. By a Gentleman* (1743), viii–ix. The whole of Spelman's very interesting preface is reproduced in Peter Campbell, 'An Early Defence of Party', *Political Studies* iii, 2 (1955), 166–7.
87 Walpole, *Memoirs of George III*, ii, 58 and note 85 above.

Notes to pp. 78–82

5. From Old Corps to Rockinghamite whigs: the emergence of a party

1 Devonshire Journal, 28 October 1760, Devonshire Mss 260/276.
2 Pitt to Newcastle, 13 October 1763, *Chatham Correspondence*, ii, 260.
3 Hardwicke to Charles Yorke, 11 April 1764, Add. Mss 35361 f. 95.
4 Newcastle to Rockingham, 19 June 1765, Add. Mss 32967 f. 70.
5 [West to Newcastle], 3/4 past 10 [7 February 1766], Add. Mss 32973 f. 377; Newcastle to Rockingham, Friday night [21 February 1766?], Sheffield Mss R1–579.
6 Richmond to Rockingham, 12 February 1771, Olson, *Radical Duke*, 141–2.
7 Sir William R. Anson (ed.), *The Autobiographical and Political Correspondence of Augustus Hervey, 3rd Duke of Grafton* (1898), 247.
8 Richmond to Rockingham, 12 February 1771, Olson, *Radical Duke*, 142.
9 Grenville Diary, 28 August 1763, *Grenville Papers*, ii, 198.
10 See, *inter alia*, Add. Mss 32920 ff. 166–70, 192, 381–2; Add. Mss 32922 f. 65.
11 Namier, *England*, 163–7. One gets the impression from Newcastle's memorandum on his conversation with Bute on the 10 March 1761 that the duke suspected that Bute knew more of Pitt's attitude than he was prepared to reveal; and that Bute knew that Pitt would not resign. (Namier, *England*, 166. And see above, pp. 103–4.)
12 Namier, *England*, 290–4.
13 Winstanley, *Personal and Party Government*, 165–9, 189–90, 211.
14 See above, pp. 81, 125.
15 Newcastle to Devonshire, 4 August 1764, Add. Mss 32961 f. 187; Newcastle to Lord John Cavendish, 22 August 1764, *ibid* f. 308.
16 Rigby to Bedford, 7, 20 December 1762, Bedford Mss XLVI ff. 160, 202.
17 Derek Watson, 'The Rise of the Opposition at Wildman's Club', *BIHR* XLIV, 58.
18 For which see 'An Account of the Negociation', Sheffield Mss R 13.
19 Albemarle, *The Marquess of Rockingham*, i, 219–20.
20 Anson (ed.), *Correspondence of Grafton*, 54. Cf. P. Langford, *The First Rockingham Administration 1765–1766* (Oxford, 1973), 11–12.
21 Newcastle to Grafton, 6 November 1765, Add. Mss 32971 f. 289; Newcastle to Rockingham, 26 November 1765, Add. Mss 32972 f. 60. Langford, *Rockingham Administration*, 104–5.
22 Onslow to Newcastle, Sunday morning [15 December 1765], Add. Mss 32972 f. 251.
23 Shelburne to Pitt, 21 December 1765, *Chatham Correspondence*, ii, 356.
24 Mary Bateson (ed.), 'A Narrative of the Changes in the Ministry, 1765–1767', *Camden Society* New Series LIX (1898), 43–4.
25 'Lord Rockingham's Account of his Conversation with Mr Pitt, Newcastle House, 23 January 1766', Add. Mss 32973 f. 237.
26 Add. Mss 32973 ff. 127–8; Bateson, *Narrative*, 44.
27 Newcastle to Page, 7 January 1766, Add. Mss 32973 ff. 56–7.
28 George III to Egmont, 11 January 1766, *Correspondence of George III*, ed. Fortescue, i, 220; Namier, *Additions and Corrections to Fortescue* (Manchester, 1937), 46; Bateson, *Narrative*, 44–5; Langford, *Rockingham Administration*, 138–9.
29 Shelburne to Pitt, 24 February 1766, in Lord Fitzmaurice, *Life of William Earl of Shelburne, afterwards First Marquess of Lansdowne, with extracts from his papers and correspondence* (2 vols., 1912), i, 377–80; 'Memorandum of a Conference with Lord Rockingham (Read by Mr. Nuthall to Mr. Pitt), Wednesday 26 February 1766', *Chatham Correspondence*, ii, 397–8; 'Message from Mr Pitt to Lord Rockingham, (Committed to writing by Mr Nuthall, from Mr Pitt's mouth)', 27 February 1766, *ibid* ii, 398–9; T. Nuthall to Pitt, 28 February [1766], *ibid* ii, 399–400; Pitt to T. Nuthall, 28 February 1766, *ibid* 400–1.
30 For which see pp. 85–6, 128 above.

286

31 See, for example, the messages that were conveyed to Conway and Gower. (John Brooke, *The Chatham Administration, 1766–1768* (1956), 12, 14; Bateson, *Narrative*, 58.)

32 Bateson, *Narrative*, 83.

33 George III to Chatham, 29 July 1766, *Chatham Correspondence*, iii, 21.

34 Newcastle to White, 20 July 1766, Add. Mss 32976 f. 76.

35 Bateson, *Narrative*, 56.

36 Brooke, *Chatham Administration*, 20–2.

37 Brooke, *Chatham Administration*, 38–42.

38 Newcastle to Onslow, 7 October 1766, Add. Mss 32977 f. 209.

39 For the whole of this episode see Brooke, *Chatham Administration*, 53–62.

40 Portland to Newcastle, 23 November 1766, Add. Mss 32978 f. 43.

41 Brooke, *Chatham Administration*, 62.

42 Brooke, *Chatham Administration*, 56–7.

43 Rockingham to Newcastle, 22 November 1766, Add. Mss 32978 ff. 23–4; 'Narrative 2nd', Claremont, 2 December 1766, *ibid* ff. 130–1; Burke to Charles O'Hara, [29] November [1766], *Burke Correspondence*, i, 282–3.

44 Portland to Newcastle, 8 September 1766, Add. Mss 32977 f. 58.

45 Namier and Brooke, *History of Parliament*, ii, 124.

46 This by no means comprehensive list is gleaned from the pages of Namier and Brooke, *History of Parliament*.

47 George Yonge to Newcastle, 17 October 1764, Add. Mss 32962 ff. 329–30; Yonge to Newcastle, 18 October 1766, *ibid* f. 341.

48 Newcastle to Albemarle, 19 October 1764, Add. Mss 32962 ff. 360–2; Newcastle to Cumberland, 20 October 1764, *ibid* ff. 366–8.

49 Newcastle to Hardwicke, 26 November 1762, Add. Mss 32945 f. 153. Cf. Namier, *England*, 389–90.

50 Albemarle to Newcastle, 24 October 1764, Add. Mss 32963 ff. 19–20; 'Substance of what passed with HRH the Duke of Cumberland at Cumberland House, Saturday, 10 November 1764', Claremont, 14 November 1764, *ibid* f. 364; Rockingham to Newcastle, 23 November 1764, Add. Mss 32964 f. 95; Beaumont Hotham to Portland, 22 November 1764, Portland Mss PwF 5219.

51 Charles Townshend to Newcastle [30 April 1764], Add. Mss 32958 f. 249; Newcastle to Cumberland, 5 May 1764, *ibid* f. 307.

52 Newcastle to Rockingham, 2 May 1766, Add. Mss 32975 f. 72; Bateson, *Narrative*, 60–2.

53 Newcastle to Portland, 1 July 1765, Add. Mss 32967 f. 187. Cumberland reported to Newcastle that 'I am to acquaint you, that His Majesty has declared to Me, That It is not his Intention, that the Earl of Bute should, either publickly or privately, interfere in the Management of Public Affairs, either at Home, or Abroad; Or recommend to any Employments either in England, or Scotland.

'And I was also to acquaint you, that I took the Liberty to let His Majesty know, that, if any Thing of that Kind should appear, you, and the other Ministers, who should now come into His Majesty's Service, would find yourselves Obliged, immediately to resign your Employments, And, that I could not disuade you from it.' (July 1765, Add. Mss 32968 f. 381.)

54 Egmont to George III, 1 [should be 2] May 1766, Fortescue, *Correspondence of George III*, i, 300.

55 Bateson, *Narrative*, 62. This is also apparent from Egmont's conversation with Mackenzie on 3 May when Egmont, at the king's request, asked the King's Friends to play along with the Rockinghams. 'I found', Egmont wrote, 'as I expected that neither Mr Mackenzie or any of his Friends are likely to engage with y. present Ministers upon the Narrow Bottom w' Lord Rockingham only means, and that (without the Precaution I had taken) Their Answers would have been not firm alone,

but rough and of a Nature to have given Advantage against them – But I hope what has passed with Mr. Mackenzie and afterwards with Lord Northumberland (for y. discourse was very nearly the same with both) Your Majesty will in some Measure avoid this Inconvenience, wth would not have been small in y. future Settlement of Your Affairs.' (Egmont to George III, 4 May 1766, Fortescue, *Correspondence of George III*, i, 305.) This is a nice example of John Cannon's point – that the supporters of the king's anti-party crusade were forced to adopt the techniques of party itself. (Cannon, *Fox–North Coalition*, 235.)

56 Egmont to George III, 4 May 1766; Fortescue, *Correspondence of George III*, i, 305–6.
57 Alison Olson, 'The Duke of Richmond's Memorandum, 1–7 July 1766', *EHR* LXXV (1960), 477–8.
58 Olson, 'Richmond's Memorandum', *EHR* LXXV (1960), 481.
59 Portland to Newcastle, 17 December 1766, Add. Mss 32978 ff. 378–9, extract in Sheffield Mss RI-736; Albemarle to Newcastle, 19 December 1766, Add. Mss 32978 f. 420.
60 Portland to Newcastle, 17 December 1766, *ibid* f. 378.
61 Newcastle to Mansfield, 24 May 1767, Add. Mss 32982 f. 112.
62 'An Account of what passed with the Duke of Bedford', Newcastle House, 14 April 1767, Add. Mss 32981 f. 157. Compare Bedford's view in Albemarle to Rockingham, 8 July 1767, Sheffield Mss RI-809; Bedford to Rockingham, *ibid* RI-823.
63 Newcastle to Portland, 27 May 1767, Add. Mss 32982 f. 146; Albemarle to Newcastle, 10 July 1767, Add. Mss 32983 f. 102; Bessborough to Newcastle, 10 July 1767, *ibid* f. 193; Frederick Montagu to Portland, 20 July [1767], Portland Mss PwF 6874; Frederick Montagu to Burke, 21 July [1767], Sheffield Mss BI-73a. After the negotiations of July 1767, Meredith, however, suffered a radical change of mind. When the Bedfords finally joined the Chatham administration he wrote to Rockingham: 'It gives me no concern that the Bedfords are at last settled. I had no Idea of your Negotiation succeeding with them last Summer. They have cast a Lot's Wife's Eye on Lord Bute ever since they left him. But had they come in with your Lordship, not as an incorporated body, but (what they affected to be) a detached Corps, on the first disagreement, or first prospect of better pay or better quarters they would [have] turned against you.' (Meredith to Rockingham, 7 January 1768, Sheffield Mss RI-928.)
64 Rockingham to Conway, 19 July 1767, Sheffield Mss RI-834; Rockingham to Hardwicke, 26 July 1767, *ibid* RI-539.
65 Newcastle to Rockingham, 8 July 1767, Sheffield Mss RI-812; Newcastle to Lord Frederick Cavendish, 25 September 1767, Add. Mss 32985 f. 215.
66 Rockingham to Dowdeswell, 8 January 1767, Sheffield Mss RI-743, printed in Wright (ed.), *Cavendish's Debates*, i, 581–2. For all the other occasions when Rockingham hammered home this theme see notes 68, 77, 78 below, and Rockingham to Newcastle, 15 August 1767, Add. Mss 32984 f. 288; Rockingham to Dowdeswell, 9 September 1767, Sheffield Mss RI-857, extract printed Wright (ed.), *Cavendish's Debates*, i, 504–5; Rockingham to Portland, 17 September 1767, Portland Mss PwF 8991; Rockingham to Newcastle, n.d., Sheffield Mss R9–18.
67 Brooke's suggestion that Rockingham was 'dazzled with the vision of the comprehensive Administration' is so much nonsense. If any politician was guilty of the charge it was Newcastle (see note 72).
68 Rockingham to Newcastle, 16 March 1767, Add. Mss 32980 ff. 296–7.
69 'Memorandum', Onslow's, 31 March 1767, Add. Mss 32980 f. 450.
70 Brooke, *Chatham Administration*, 203–10; Bateson, *Narrative*, 141–9.
71 Bateson, *Narrative*, 145. Bateson prints Grafton as the speaker but this is obviously a mistake for Bedford. It is not at all clear to what 'conduct' of Conway's Bedford is referring – if about General Warrants and America there was clearly very little common ground between the Duke and Rockingham.

72 See for example his views in Add. Mss 32985 ff. 39–40, 65, 72, 253.

73 Newcastle to Rockingham, 11 September 1767, Add. Mss 32985 f. 76 (copy); Sheffield Mss RI-858 (original).

74 Bateson, *Narrative*, 161.

75 Richmond to Rockingham, 4 October 1767, Sheffield Mss RI-863. Richmond, of course, as his queries make clear, was hostile towards Bedford and eager for an accommodation with Conway and the Ministry. He would not have minded if the Rockinghams had come in on their own bottom.

76 'I find the Duke of Bedford's Suspicions', Newcastle wrote angrily, 'that the Cavendishes, viz. Ld Frederick & Ld John do not even *Wish* a thorough Union with the Duke of Bedford and His Friends, are well founded.' (Newcastle to Mansfield, 14 September 1767, Add. Mss 32985 f. 88.) It was Lord John, of course, who in 1765 had 'said he wished the Opposition was reduced to six or seven, who could depend on one another'. (Walpole, *Memoirs of George III*, ii, 129.)

77 Rockingham to Newcastle, 1 October 1767, Add. Mss 32975 fol. 307.

78 Rockingham to Dowdeswell, 14 September 1767, Sheffield Mss RI-860.

79 See p. 64 above. There seems to be a note of relief in Rockingham's comment, expressed once the possibility of coalition was over, that 'We have nothing *now* to do, but to look to our *Own Friends, form* our own Plans for any Matters of Business which we may think proper to bring on – & need not Trouble our Thoughts about what may suit this or that Set of Men, as there are none, *as Sets*, with whom we can have any thing to do.' (Rockingham to Newcastle, 22 December 1767, Add. Mss 32987 ff. 394–5). Meredith seems to have reached similar conclusions to those of Rockingham. 'All I wish', he wrote, 'is, that your Friends may look to themselves & themselves only: that Eye which they have constantly kept on some body or other whose Object they were not, has been the bane of the Party, before they went into Office, whilst they were there, & since they came out.' (Meredith to Rockingham, 7 January 1768, Sheffield Mss RI-928.)

80 See note 69.

81 This I take to be Brooke's point. (*Chatham Administration*, 216.)

82 'Thoughts on the present state of publick affairs and the propriety of accepting or declining administration, Written the 23 and 24 of July 1767', Sheffield Mss RI-842.

83 Burke, *Works*, i, 295, 376.

84 'Thoughts on the present state of publick affairs, 23 and 24 July 1767', Sheffield Mss RI-842.

85 Sir George Savile to Portland, 12 January 1767, Portland Mss PwF 8202.

86 Burke, *Works*, i, 185–305.

87 Burke, *Works*, i, 365–9.

88 Burke, *Works*, i, 376.

89 Burke, *Works*, i, 377.

90 Portland to Rockingham, 3 December 1769, Sheffield Mss RI-1250, part printed in Albemarle, *Marquess of Rockingham*, ii, 145–7; Brewer, 'Party and the Double Cabinet', *HJ* xiv, 484–5.

91 Burke to Rockingham, 18 July 1768, *Burke Correspondence*, ii, 4.

92 I have discussed this concern with union in my 'Party and the Double Cabinet', *HJ* xiv, 485, 487–8, 492.

93 Burke, *Works*, i, 295.

94 Richmond to Rockingham, 12 February 1771, Olson, *Radical Duke*, 142.

95 D. Hamer, *From Grafton to North, 1768–1772* (Cambridge University, unpub. Ph.D., 1971), 279–80; Cannon, *Fox–North Coalition*, 241n.

96 Brooke, *Chatham Administration*, 291.

97 Christie, *Myth and Reality*, 116–26; Pares, *George III and The Politicians*, 85; Cannon, *Fox–North Coalition*, 76.

98 For a more detailed discussion of some of the issues involved see Ch. 7 above.

99 *Parliamentary History* xvi, 833–41.

6. Pitt and patriotism: a case study in political argument

1 But see Foord, *His Majesty's Opposition*, 124n.

2 [J. Douglas], *A Letter Addressed to two great men* (2nd ed., 1760), 50.

3 Pitt to Thomas Walpole, 5 November 1765, *Chatham Correspondence*, ii, 329; Chatham to Calcraft, 20 October 1770, *ibid*, iii, 475–6; Basil Williams, *The Life of William Pitt, Earl of Chatham* (2 vols., 1915), i, 137, 150, 230; Pitt to Mayor of Bath (draft), 1757, PRO 30/8/6/2.

4 Williams, *Pitt*, i, 116.

5 Albert von Ruville, *William Pitt, Earl of Chatham* (3 vols., 1907), i, 278–9.

6 [T. Hervey], *A Letter to William Pitt, Esq; concerning the Fifteen New REGIMENTS lately voted by PARLIAMENT* (1746), 22.

7 'True Patriot' and 'Patriot Minister' being the titles of two highly successful political cartoons of Pitt in the period. (*BM Catalogue of Prints and Drawings*, iii, nos. 3599, 3600.)

8 'A Character of Mr. Pitt', Sheffield Mss Rockingham 93–8.

9 See especially *Con-Test* I, 23 November 1756; *ibid* IV, 4 December 1756. Only one other attempt, to my knowledge, was made in George II's reign to justify administration employing patriot rhetoric. This was in Fielding's *True Patriot* (1745–6). This, however, imparts a slightly different perspective to patriotism in the light of the Rebellion – patriotism almost being a synonym for Hanoverian – and is not such a sustained defence as the *Con-Test*. After 1760, of course, patriot defences of government were much more common with George posing as the patriot king. (See, for example, *A Letter from a Gentleman in Town to his Friend in the Country* (1763), 9–10.)

10 [Egmont], *Faction Detected by the evidence of Facts* (3rd ed., 1743), 164–5. Cf. *An Essay on Patriotism, and on the Character and Conduct of some late famous Pretenders to that Virtue* (1768), 12–13.

11 [Samuel Johnson], *The Patriot. Addressed to the Electors of Great Britain* (1774), 3.

12 [Pulteney], *An Humble Address to the Knights, Citizens and Burgesses* (1734), 6; *Con-Test* I, 23 November 1756; *ibid* VI, 25 December 1756; *ibid* XVIII, 19 March 1757.

13 For 'measures not men' see pp. 68–9 above.

14 See, for example, Pitt to Newcastle, 19 October 1764, Add. Mss 32962 ff. 348–9 for a typical instance of such conduct.

15 Namier, *England*, 95–7.

16 Sedgwick, *Letters from George III to Bute*, 45, 49.

17 See Devonshire's remarks in his journal. ('Diary', 4 October 1761, Devonshire Mss 260/347.)

18 Namier, *England*, 128; Fitzmaurice, *Life of William Petty, Earl of Shelburne*, i, 33.

19 Talbot told Bute that 'the Speech has had a most pleasing effect & I have been this moment informed that many Cocoa Tree Gentlemen Violated their Sobriety last Night by Drinking felicity to his Majesty in pint Bumpers'. (Talbot to Bute, November 1760, Bute Mss 1760/118.)

20 Talbot to Bute, November 1760, Bute Mss 1760/119; Newdigate Diaries, 12, 14 November 1760; 11 November 1761; 27 January, 18 March 1762, Newdigate Mss CR 136/A.6, 7; Mordaunt to Newdigate, 4 December 1760, *ibid* B.19/1839a.

21 Fox to Bute, 23 November 1762, Bute Mss; Fox to Bute, 24 November, *ibid*; Temple to Pitt, Saturday night [26 February 1763?], PRO 30/8/61/172; Betty Kemp, *Sir Francis Dashwood*, 53–4, 64.

22 Harwicke to Newcastle, 17 October 1761, Add. Mss 32939 f. 332.

23 This is a reference to Selwyn's delight in executions. He never missed a hanging day and would always pay good money to have the best view at Tyburn.

24 Fox to Devonshire, 17 December 1761, Devonshire Mss 330/239. Cf. Campbell to Bute, 28 December 1761, Bute Mss 1761/713.

25 Denbigh to Temple, 8 October 1761, Denbigh Letter Book, 10.
26 'Diary', 14 November 1762, Devonshire Mss 260/394; Newcastle to Devonshire, 31 January 1763, Add. Mss 32946 f. 267.
27 Rockingham to Newcastle, 26 March 1763, Add. Mss 32946 ff. 317–18.
28 Rigby to Bedford, 10 March 1763, *Bedford Correspondence*, iii, 219.
29 Namier, *England*, 106.
30 Namier, *England*, 107, 120–1.
31 'Substance of what pass'd in my conversation with Lord Bute this day', 10 March 1761, Add. Mss 32920 ff. 67–8. Cf. Williams, *Pitt*, ii, 65–6; 'My Conversation with Mr. Pitt – His Ideas of the Terms of Peace ', 10 April 1761, Add. Mss 32921 f. 382; 'Acct. of the Death of George II and the circumstances of the early days of the reign', Minto Mss M 6/4/12.
32 Devonshire to Fox, 21 December 1761, Add. Mss 51382 f. 134; Temple to Pitt, 14 November 1762, PRO 30/8/61/79.
33 For the Yorke family's role in anti-Pittite propaganda see Royston to Hardwicke, 16 October 1761, Add. Mss 35352 ff. 199–200; Hardwicke to Royston, 17 October 1761, *ibid* ff. 202–3.
34 Walpole to Mann, 10 October 1761, *Walpole Letters*, v, 128. Cf. his letters to Montagu, the Countess of Ailsbury and Conway in the same week. (*Ibid*, v, 129–35.)
35 'Meeting of the Bankers', 8 October 1761, Add. Mss 32929 f. 113.
36 For further details of this see Ch. 11 above and Robert R. Rea, *The English Press in Politics, 1760–1774* (Lincoln, Neb., 1963), 19–21.
37 Conway to Devonshire, 17 December 1761, Devonshire Mss 416/73.
38 *The Right Hon. Annuitant Vindicated* (1761), 10. Cf. *A Speech Without Doors. By a Lobby-Member* (1762), 8; Campbell to Bute, 6 November 1761, Bute Mss 1761/629.
39 Dr Johnson's definition in the first edition of his *Dictionary of the English Language* (1755).
40 *Right Hon. Annuitant Vindicated*, 50.
41 *An Impartial Enquiry into the Conduct of a late Minister* (1761), 2–3.
42 [Francis], *A Letter from the Anonymous Author of the Letters Versified to the Anonymous Writer of the Monitor* (1761), 29; 'It hath been frequently and justly remarked', Bute Mss, Anonymous Bundle; 'An Answer to a Letter to a Friend in the Country', Bute Mss.
43 [Francis], *A Letter from a Right Honourable Person, And the Answer to it, Translated into Verse* (1761), 15.
44 *An Earnest Address to the People of Great Britain and Ireland: occasioned by the dismission of W. Pitt, Esq. from the office of Secretary of State* (Dublin, 1761), 39; *North Briton* XII, 21 August 1762; Temple to Denbigh, 13 October 1761, Denbigh Letter Book, 10–11.
45 See pp. 79–84 above.
46 'Substance of what passed with Mr Michel here, Yesterday, who came to take his leave. As he sets out the 28th Inst. for Berlin', Claremont, 12 August 1764, Add. Mss 32961 f. 187; Newcastle to Lord John Cavendish, 22 August 1764, *ibid* f. 308.
47 Williams, *Pitt*, ii, 174.
48 Walpole, *Memoirs of George III*, i, 269; Sackville to Irwin, 17 January 1766, HMC *Stopford-Sackville* I, 104; Sarah Osborn to John Osborn, 17 January 1766, E. F. D. Osborn (ed.), *The Political and Social Letters of a Lady of the Eighteenth Century, 1721–1771* (1890), 127; *Parliamentary History* XVI, 97–8; Rouet to Mure, 16 January 1766, Mure (ed.), *Selections from the Family Papers preserved at Caldwell. In two Parts* (Glasgow, 1854), Part II, ii, 59–60; Minto Mss M6/12.
49 Fox to Bute, 11 February [1766], Bute Mss.
50 George Sackville to Unwin, 11 March 1766, HMC *9th Report Appendix Part III*, 23. Cf. Walpole, *Memoirs of George III*, i, 305; [West to Newcastle], 3/4 past 11 [4 March 1766], Add. Mss 32974 f. 137.
51 William Baker to Talbot, 6 August 1766, Baker Mss 1/22. For the view that

Chatham had sold out to Bute see, *inter alia*, John Pringle to Walter Scott, 11 December 1766, *HMC Polwarth*, v, 365; *Walpole Letters*, vii, 76; Rockingham to Portland, 4 December 1766, Portland Mss PwF 8987; Bamber Gascoigne to Strutt, 5 December 1766, Strutt Mss.

52 Harcourt to Jenkinson, 8 August 1766, N. S. Jucker (ed.), *The Jenkinson Papers, 1760–1766* (1949), 422.

53 [Humphrey Cotes], *An Enquiry into the Conduct of a late Right Honourable Commoner* (3rd impression, 1766), *passim*; Rea, *English Press in Politics*, 127–30. Temple and his allies had levelled such accusations against Pitt during the negotiations of 1765, (Walpole, *Memoirs of George III*, ii, 188.)

54 *BM Catalogue of Prints and Drawings*, iv, nos. 4146–8, 4153–5, 4162; 'Notes 1743–1779', Hervey Mss 941/50/5/509–10.

55 *A genuine Collection of the several pieces of Political Intelligence Extraordinary, Epigrams, Poetry, &c that have appeared before the Public in Detached Pieces* (1766), 32. This together with *The New Foundling Hospital for Wit* (1766) is the best collection of items attacking Pitt/Chatham. There is a good summary of much of the literature in Rea, *English Press in Politics*, 127–31.

56 *A genuine Collection* (1766), 10–13, 18, 25, 27, 34, 87, 106; [Cotes], *Enquiry into the Conduct of a late Commoner* (1766), 22, 33, 54; [John Wilkes], *A Letter to his Grace the Duke of Grafton* (1767), 12; *A Free Appeal to the People of Great Britain, On the Conduct of the Present Administration* (2nd ed., 1767), 29; *Essay on Patriotism* (1768), 7, 11; Sarah Osborn to John Osborn, 12 August 1766, *Osborn Letters*, 146–7.

57 *A genuine Collection* (1766), 39.

58 'Substance of a late Conversation held by the E[arl] of C – – – – m', Claremont, 7 September 1766, Add. Mss 32977 f. 41.

59 '*No Contradiction in the Terms* of Patriot and Peer *being consistent with each other*', *Universal Magazine* xxxix (1766), 160.

60 *Parliamentary History* xvi, 841; Walpole, *Memoirs of George III*, iv. 94.

61 Samuel Johnson, *A Dictionary of the English Language* (4th ed., 1773).

62 Hatfield cites instances of this use of patriot as early as the seventeenth century. (Glenn W. Hatfield, *Henry Fielding and the Language of Irony* (Chicago, 1968), 95–6.)

63 'To Lord Mansfield', Add. Mss 36595 f. 317. Cf. Egerton Mss 3711 f. 26; [Johnson], *The Patriot* (1774), *passim*; 'Northerly', *London Evening Post*, 8 February 1770; 'A real account of the Earl of Chatham's principles in politics, TACITUS', *Public Advertiser*, 2 April 1770. For earlier examples of modern or false patriotism in the manner of Johnson's definition of 1773 see *Patriotism, A Mock-Heroic, in Six Cantos* (2nd ed., 1765), *passim*; *Political Controversy*, i, 125; *The Conduct of the late and the present Ministry Compared* (1742), 44; *The Constitution. With an Address to a Great Man* (1757), 7.

64 Namier, *England*, 159.

65 Namier, *England*, 158–60.

7. *Ministerial responsibility and the powers of the Crown*

1 Brewer, 'The Misfortunes of Lord Bute', *HJ* xvi (1973), 33–4, 36–7.

2 *A letter to a member of the Honourable House of Commons, on the present important crisis of national affairs* (1762), 4.

3 [Dowdeswell?], *The Sentiments of an English Freeholder, on the late decision of the Middlesex Election* (1769), 52–3.

4 'REVERIES', *Oxford Magazine* iii (1769), 65. For other general statements about the notion of ministerial responsibility see [Bolingbroke], *The Freeholder's Political Catechism* (1733), 6; [Walpole], *A Counter-Address to the Public* (1764), 30; [William Jones], *The Constitutional Criterion: By a Member of the University of Cambridge* (1768), 18–19; [Almon], *Biographical, Literary and Political Anecdotes* (1797), iii, 7–8; 'CON-

STITUTIONAL LIBERTY', *Gazetteer*, 25 May 1763; 'A LOVER OF TRUTH', *ibid*, 4 July 1763; *Weekly Amusement* I (1764), 218; 'On the Constitution of England', *Freeholders Magazine* I (1769), 62; R. J. Phillimore (ed.), *Memoirs and Correspondence of George, Lord Lyttelton* (2 vols., 1845), ii, 673.

5 See Clayton Roberts, *The Growth of Responsible Government in Stuart England* (Cambridge, 1966), *passim*.

6 Romney Sedgwick (ed.), *Letters from George III to Lord Bute, 1756–1766* (1939), 21; 'Conversation with Lord B - - - from the Attorney General', 9 April 1763, Add. Mss 32948 ff. 93–4.

7 Elliot to Bute [25 March 1761], Bute Mss 1761/161.

8 R. W. Chapman (ed.), *Boswell's Life of Johnson* (Oxford, 1970 ed.), 300. This conversation is also reported by Boswell in his *London Journal*. (Pottle (ed.), *Boswell's London Journal*, 292.)

9 [Kearsley], *Political Disquisitions* (1763), 43.

10 Namier, *Crossroads of Power*, 82–6; 'Memorandum', 10 August 1761, Add. Mss 32926 f. 353; Newcastle to John White, 19 June 1764, Add. Mss 32960 f. 17; 'Substance of what passed with Mr. Michel here, Yesterday, who came to take his leave, As he sets out the 28th inst. for Berlin', Claremont, 12 August 1764, Add. Mss 32961 f. 187. Early in 1761 even the city radical Beckford professed to wish to see the king his own minister, though Bute does not seem to have taken the comment very seriously. (*Dodington Diary*, 417.)

11 [Owen Ruffhead], *Considerations on the Present Dangerous Crisis* (2nd ed., 1763), 46. Cf. James Stewart (ed.), *Commentaries on the Laws of England, In Four Books by Sir William Blackstone* (20th ed., 4 vols., 1841), i, 256–8; *A Collection of Scarce and Interesting Tracts. Written by Persons of Eminence; upon the most important, political and commercial subjects, during the years 1763, 1764, 1765, 1766, 1767, 1768, 1769 and 1770* (4 vols., 1788), ii, 303; Newdigate Mss B 2548/6.

12 These, of course, were the questions at issue in the debate on 13 February 1741 over whether Walpole should be dismissed from the king's counsels for ever. (W. Coxe, *Memoirs of the Life and Administration of Sir Robert Walpole, Earl of Orford. With Original Correspondence and Authentic Papers, never before published (3 vols., 1798)*, iii, 653; *Parliamentary History* xi, 1224–387.)

13 For this problem see pp. 135–6 above.

14 *Ministerial Usurpation Displayed, and the Prerogatives of the Crown, with the Rights of Parliament and of the Privy Council, considered in an appeal to the people* (1760), 20.

15 *Briton*, 25 December 1762.

16 Bute to Sir James Lowther, 17 November 1762, Add. Mss 36797 ff. 22–3, printed in *HMC Lonsdale, 12th Report Part VII*, 131 and *Jenkinson Papers*, 86–7.

17 Walpole, *Memoirs of George III*, iii, 66; Denbigh to Wentworth, 28 May 1767, Denbigh Mss, Letter Book, 35; [J. Marriott], *Political Considerations; being a few Thoughts of a Candid Man at the present Crisis. In a Letter to a Noble Lord retired from Power* (1762), 36. Holland remarked to a friend how, when the Grenvilles went out in 1765, 'so little had the old Ministers repented their Folly, that I know one of them being advised to wiser and gentler measures reply'd, By God he shan't make a footman'. (Holland to George McCartney, 20 December 1765, Add. Mss 51389 f. 46.) This sounds very like Rigby, especially in view of Horace Walpole's record of a very similar remark of his. (Walpole, *Memoirs of George III*, ii, 176n.)

18 Sedgwick, *Letters from George III to Bute*, 220, 233.

19 *A Political Analysis of the War: the Principles of the present political Parties examined; and a just, natural and perfect Coalition propos'd between the Two Great Men, whose Conduct is particularly consider'd* (1762), 56.

20 *The Right Hon. Annuitant Vindicated. With a word or two in favour of the other GREAT MAN, in Case of his Resignation. In a LETTER to a FRIEND in the COUNTRY* (1761), 62–3.

21 *The True Whig Displayed. Comprehending Cursory* REMARKS *on the Address to the Cocoa Tree. By a* TORY (1762), 7; 'Queries of VERAX answered·by VERITAE', *Gazetteer,* 29 November 1762.

22 Dodington to Bute, 22 December 1760, Bute Mss 1760/206.

23 Sedgwick, *Letters from George III to Bute,* 203, 227; Bute to Denbigh, 13 October 1762, Add. Mss 36797 f. 14; Bute to George Townshend, 8 April 1763, *ibid* f. 43.

24 [Francis], *A Letter from the Cocoa Tree to the Country Gentlemen* (1762), 4.

25 *The True Whig Displayed* (1762), 18. For other references to George as the Doge see *The Appeal of Reason to the People of England, on the present state of* PARTIES *in the Nation* (1763), 38; 'March 1763 the Dining List of the Opposition and Remarks thereupon', Bute Mss (Cardiff) 9/126.

26 *An Impartial Enquiry into the Conduct of a late Minister* (1761), 30; [Francis], *A Letter from the Cocoa Tree* (1762), 5; *The Secret Springs of the late Changes in the Ministry Fairly Explained* (1766), 37–8; Fitzmaurice, *Life of William, Earl of Shelburne,* i, 168; Hume to [Strahan], 25 October 1769, J. Y. T. Greig (ed.), *The Letters of David Hume* (2 vols., Oxford, 1932), ii, 209; 'Some Seasonable Reflections on the state of ROYALTY in England', *Universal Magazine* XLV (1769), 350; George Townshend to Bute, 9 April 1763, Bute Mss 1763/247; Fox to [Shelburne], [8 October 1762], Add. Mss 51379 f. 215.

27 *A Second Letter to the Right Honourable the Earl of B***. By the Author of the First* (1761), 12–13.

28 Hardwicke to Newcastle, 15 October 1763, Add. Mss 32951 f. 430. Cf. Sedgwick, *Letters from George III to Bute,* 49.

29 Bute to George Grenville, 10 October 1762, Add. Mss 38191 f. 9 (draft); 36797 f. 13 (copy); Bristol to Countess of Chatham [2 March 1767], *Chatham Correspondence,* iii, 226; A. Hervey to George Grenville, 16 July 1767, *Grenville Papers,* iv, 56.

30 Fox to Devonshire, 12 October 1762, Add. Mss 51383 f. 18; Bedford to Fox, 20 October 1762, Add. Mss 51385 f. 51; Bute to Denbigh, 13 October 1762, Denbigh Mss, Letter Book, 14; Bute to George Grenville [1 April 1763], *Grenville Papers,* ii, 40–1; George III to Chatham, 29 July 1766, *Chatham Correspondence,* iii, 21; George III to Cumberland, 12 June 1765, Fortescue (ed.), *Correspondence of George III,* i, 118. It should perhaps be added that, despite all this talk of the possible enslavement of the king, Bute told George Grenville in October 1761 that he did not believe that Newcastle would try to fetter his master: 'To me the very idea seems both absurd and Impossible, & that for two Reasons first that I am convinced in my own opinion that the d. of Newcastle never formed so chimerical a Project, 2ndly that a Young Nobility & a numerous Body of Gentlemen both in Parliament and out of it would be Mad beyond the Cure of Hellefore to follow such a Project, of such a worn out Statesman against a Prince were it possible for him to have framed it.' (Bute to George [Grenville], [13 October 1761], endorsed 'This letter I directed Elliot to read to G. Grenville when fluctuating about taking the lead in the H. of Commons on Pitt's resignation', Bute Mss 1761/738.) This may just have been bravura on the part of Bute; at least, he had certainly changed his mind by 1762.

31 [Butler], *Address to the Cocoa Tree from a Whig* (1762), 2–3; [Kearsley], *Political Disquisitions* (1763), 43–4; Newcastle to Hardwicke, 1 January 1763, Add. Mss 32946 f. 12.

32 'A Letter to the Right Hon. George Grenville', *Gentleman's Magazine* XXXIII (1763), 327.

33 [Butler], *Letter to the Cocoa Tree from a Whig,* 7.

34 [Almon], *Biographical, Literary and Political Anecdotes,* iii, 32.

35 [Butler], *Letter to the Cocoa Tree from a Whig,* 9; 'W. PYM', *Gazetteer,* 11 January 1765. Some went further than this and pointed out that even the office of kingship was a public trust that could be withdrawn if necessary. ('Anon', *Gazetteer,* 16 June 1763; 'DECIUS', *Middlesex Journal,* 17 February 1770.)

36 'John Bull' in *A New and Impartial Collection of Interesting Letters* (1767), i, 23.
37 'Remarks on the British Government', *Political Register* I (1767), 8.
38 *Le Montagnard Parvenu: or, The New Highland Adventurer in England: His Accidental Rise from Obscurity; His glaring Progress to Power: the WAYS and MEANS* (1763), 32. And see the excellent survey of this argument as well as the royal counter-case probably written by Burke in *The Annual Register* (1763), 41–2.
39 Devonshire to Fox, 14 October 1762, Ilchester (ed.), *Letters to Henry Fox Lord Holland, with a few addressed to his brother Stephen, Earl of Ilchester* (1915), 163. Richard Pares (*George III and the Politicians*, 99) sees this as evidence that the Rockinghams, unlike the other politicians, 'aimed at limiting the king's choice from the first'. But Devonshire's point is simply a practical one, and both he and Newcastle were very eager in the first year of the reign to allow play to the king's choice by getting Bute into responsible office. (Devonshire Journal, 5 November 1760, Devonshire Mss 275/282; Newcastle to Mansfield, 14 March 1761, Add. Mss 32920 f. 295; Newcastle to White, Add. Mss 32921 f. 60.) Of course subsequently the party tried to constrain the king more severely than any other group had done – with the possible exception of George Grenville in 1765 – but they still couched their argument in terms of responsibility and did not explicitly avow the aim of 'forcing' the king.
40 Bute to Bedford, 10 October 1761, *Bedford Correspondence*, iii, 50. Compare Bute to George III [24 March 1761], Add. Mss 36797 f. 48.
41 'Anti-Sejanus' in *New and Impartial Collection of Letters* (1767), ii, 28. Cf. *An Application of some General Political Rules, to the Present State of Great Britain, Ireland and America. In a Letter to the Right Honourable Earl Temple* (1766), 28–9.
42 [Temple?], *Principles of the late Changes Impartially Examined* (1765), 35. All of the contemporary literature abounds with historical examples of favourites who created trouble or came to a sticky end. Bute was compared to Cromwell (*The Triumphs of Bute. A Poem* (1770), 12); Hubert de Burgh (*Monitor*, 24 July 1762); Sejanus, Wolsey, Fleury and Dymoche (*North Briton* I, 5 June 1762); 'Anti-Sejanus' in *New and Impartial Collection of Letters*, ii, 28; Carr (*BM Catalogue of Prints and Satires*, iv, no. 3845); Simon de Montfort, the earl of Essex (*ibid* no. 3867); the earl of Mar (*North Briton* II, 12 June 1762); William de la Pole (*ibid* 8, 24 July 1762); Tarquin (*ibid* 12, 21 August 1762) and Walpole (*Butiad*, p. 12). Especially popular were favourites or first ministers like Mortimer and Mazarin whose dalliance with the monarch's mother could be used to libel Bute and the Princess Dowager. [Cotes], *An Enquiry into the Conduct of a late Right Honourable Commoner* (1766), 48–9; *North Briton* v, 3 July 1762; *The Fall of Mortimer. An Historical Play. Revived from Montfort, with Alterations. Dedicated to the Right Honourable John, Earl of Bute* (Dublin, 1763), *passim*. The only favourite or first minister ever invoked by the supporters of Bute was Sully. (Foord, *His Majesty's Opposition*, 278–9.)
43 *A Parallel Drawn* (1766), 20; [Owen Ruffhead], *Considerations on the Present Dangerous Crisis* (1763), 11.
44 *North Briton* VIII, 24 July 1762; [Butler], *Address to the Cocoa Tree* (1762), 10; *Political Disquisitions proper for public consideration*, 4.
45 *Le Montagnard Parvenu* (1763), 32; [John Wilkes], *The Favourite, With a Dedication to my Lord B**** (1765), 6; *Political Register* II (1768) 399; Hervey Mss 50/5/318–19. Mss copy of *A Letter to Lord Bute relative to the late Changes that have happened in A- - - - - - - - - - - -n.*
46 Brewer, 'Misfortunes of Lord Bute', *HJ* XVI (1973), 5–12.
47 [Kearsley], *Political Disquisitions* (1763), 61; [John Almon], *A Review of Lord Bute's Administration* (1763), 9–10; 'Anti-Sejanus' in *A New and Impartial Collection of Letters* (1767), ii, 54–5; *The British Antidote to Caledonian Poison* (1763), i, 7; 'A Letter to the Earl of B - - -' in the *Gentleman's Magazine* (1765), 351–2; P. D. G. Thomas (ed.), 'Parliamentary Diaries of Nathaniel Ryder, 1764–7', *Camden Miscellany*

4th Series XXIII, 346; Crisp Molyneux to George Irvine, 13 November 1768, Molyneux Letter Book, f. 48.

48 [Butler], *Address to the Cocoa Tree* (1762), 5, 9.

49 'A Letter concerning libels, warrants, and the seizure of papers; with a view to some late proceedings, and the defence of them by the majority', *Gentleman's Magazine* XXXIV (1764), 618. Cf. 'CONSTITUTIONAL LIBERTY', *Gazetteer*, 25 May 1763; 'JOHN', *ibid* 14 July 1763.

50 'Answer to a series of Queries', *Gazetteer*, 28 May 1763. Cf. [Kearsley], *Political Disquisitions* (1763), 45–6.

51 'NO MATTER WHOM', *Gazetteer*, 13 June 1763. Cf. 'A Fragment. Containing many interesting and constitutional remarks on the case of Mr Wilkes. Written in the summer of 1763; and now first published', *Political Register* II (1768), 165–6. These arguments were used to defend Wilkes's *North Briton* no. 45. An attack on the King's Speech, it was argued, was *not* an attack on the king and a refusal to recognise this distinction would have been to flout a basic constitutional convention. ('Tacitus Britannicus', *Universal Magazine* XXXIII (1763), 36; [Almon], *Biographical, Literary and Political Anecdotes* (1797), ii, 18; Wright (ed.), *Cavendish's Debates*, i, 35–6; Wilkes to Cotes, 17 February 1764, Add. Mss 30868 f. 40; 'Proceedings in the Common Pleas', 3 May 1763, Add. Mss 32948 ff. 215, 221–2.) This was about the firmest ground on which Wilkes's case stood although, surprisingly enough, to my knowledge only one MP, Lord North, advanced the obvious objection when he said, 'Distinctions of K[ing] & [his] Ministers [was] established in Parlt but not for anonymous writers'. (Debate, 15 November 1763, Newdigate Mss B2543/5.)

52 Newcastle to Hardwicke, 3 October 1763, Add. Mss 23951 f. 267; Bute to Newcastle, 17 July 1761, Add. Mss 32925 f. 133; Wilkes to Cotes, 20 January 1764, Add. Mss 30868 f. 25. It should be added that on the question of royal interference in patronage Hardwicke blamed Bute for using the king's name to achieve his own ends. (Hardwicke to Newcastle, July 1761, Add. Mss 32925 f. 185.)

53 The Lord Strange incident is a complicated one. It would appear that, in view of George Grenville's motion on 7 February calling for the enforcement of the Stamp Act, George gave Rockingham a written memorandum, or at least permission to assure verbally the supporters of the administration, to the effect that the king was for repeal. ('Memorandum' [7 February 1766?], Fortescue, *Correspondence* of George III, i, 266; Namier, *Additions and Corrections*, 52.) The Rockinghams made sure that this was publicly known, and no doubt drew the attention of the King's Friends to it. Whether as a result of this or not, Lord Strange, the Chancellor of the Duchy of Lancaster and a friend of Bute, saw the king in his closet on 10 February and during this conversation – either at the request of Strange or without any prompting – George told him that he preferred modification to enforcement or repeal, although in a choice between the last two he would favour repeal. This angered Rockingham as it appeared as if he had misled others on the king's position, and threatened to destroy the possibility of repeal. The interpretation of this incident seems to hang on whether Strange was summoned, or had to see the king on official business, or requested to see the king, and the extent to which it was already known that the king was for modification, and whether Strange was actually 'authorised', as he claimed, to tell others of George's changed position. The comments of some of the King's Friends, especially Gilbert Elliot, seem to imply that the intimates of the king knew of his preferences, but this may just have been their interpretation of the speech that Bute had made in the Lords on the 6th when, although he had dissociated himself from the king's views, he had come out against repeal. The situation was so confused that even some of the King's Friends did not know what to think. (Fortescue, *Correspondence of George III*, i, 268–70; Mary Bateson (ed.), 'A Narrative of the Changes in the Ministry 1765–1767', *Camden Society* New Series LIX (1898), 51–2; Albemarle, *Memoirs of Rockingham*, i, 300–2;

Gilbert Elliot to Gilbert Elliot Snr, 18 February [1766], Minto Mss M3/29; *Caldwell Papers* Part II, ii, 71, 73; Rockingham to Newcastle, 8 February 1766, Add. Mss 32973 f. 384. See Langford, *First Rockingham Administration*, 163–7 for a balanced account of the incident.)

54 Wright (ed.), *Cavendish's Debates*, i, 63, 69; Egerton Mss 3711 ff. 6, 95–6.

55 Newcastle to Hardwicke, 3 January 1761, Add. Mss 32917 f. 92; Newcastle to Rockingham, 26 March 1765, Sheffield Mss. Rockingham I–447.

56 Brewer, 'Misfortunes of Lord Bute, *HJ* XVI (1973), 36.

57 J. Brewer, 'Lord Bute' in Hubert van Thal (ed.), *The Prime Ministers*, vol. I (1974), 112.

58 See, for example, Grenville's remarks in Grenville to Sandwich, 20 June 1765, *Bedford Correspondence*, iii, 296.

59 Hardwicke to Newcastle, 28 July 1762, Add. Mss 32941 f. 87.

60 Newcastle to Hardwicke, 29 July 1762, Add. Mss 32941 f. 109; 'Most Secret', 4 September 1762, Add. Mss 32942 f. 152; Newcastle to Granby, 14 September 1762, *ibid* f. 254.

61 Albemarle to Newcastle, 19 June 1765, Add. Mss 32967, f. 79.

62 Newcastle to Bishop of Oxford, 25 May 1765, Add. Mss 32966 f. 464.

63 'At a Meeting at Mr. Grenville's in Downing Street', 22 May 1765, *Grenville Papers*, iii, 41–4.

64 'An Account of the Negociation for the intended Change of Ministers in April and May 1765; recollected some Days after the whole was over, by help of Lord Albemarle, whom I had entrusted in the whole Transaction & who had his Part also to act', Sheffield Mss Rockingham 13/13.

65 Rockingham to Newcastle, 17 May 1765, Add. Mss 32966 f. 420.

66 'For His Royal Highness' Consideration', 21 May 1765, *ibid* f. 434.

67 [Cumberland] to [Newcastle], July 1765, Add. Mss 32968 f. 381. This may in fact simply be a record of the conversation that took place between Cumberland and the party leaders on 5 July as its wording bears a remarkable resemblance to that in Bateson, *Newcastle's Narrative*, 30–1.

68 These, at least, were the measures drawn up by Newcastle on 27 June ('Measures' [27 June 1765], Add. Mss 32967 ff. 124–5), and they tally in number with the three conditions mentioned in note 69. On the other hand Newcastle makes no mention of these conditions in his account of the meeting with Cumberland on 5 July and perhaps the two conditions refer to the removal of Lord Lichfield and the appointment of Portland, not Northumberland, as Lord of the Bedchamber.

69 'Minute of a Letter intended the Beginning of July 1765', Add. Mss 32967 f. 172.

70 Langford, *First Rockingham Administration*, 42–5, 70–5.

71 I would speculate that the stipulations were dropped *qua* conditions on the understanding that the king would not actually obstruct these measures.

72 Newcastle to Page, 7 January 1766, Add. Mss 32973 f. 55.

73 Typical examples would be Newcastle to Joseph Yorke, 14 November 1760, Add. Mss 32914 f. 320; Newcastle to Hardwicke, 17 August 1761, Add. Mss 32927 f. 73; Newcastle to Devonshire, 9 October 1761, Add. Mss 32929 ff. 140–1. Cf. Namier, *England*, 307–8.

74 'Considerations to be laid before My Lord Rockingham, only to be desired of His Lordship', 9 November 1765, Add. Mss 32971 f. 317. Cf. Langford, *First Rockingham Administration*, 35–6.

75 Royston to Charles Yorke, 8 March 1762, Add. Mss 35361 f. 4.

76 'Memds for My Lord Bute', 15 July 1761, Add. Mss 32925 f. 85.

77 Newcastle to Hardwicke, 30 December 1761, Add. Mss 32932 f. 409. Cf. Add. Mss 32929 ff. 407, 428.

78 Newcastle to Hardwicke, 10 April 1762, Add. Mss 32937 f. 14.

79 Namier does not seem to have fully grasped the grounds for Newcastle's resignation.

He did *not* resign because he was spied on by his colleagues through the Treasury's subordinates, but because his subordinates, on the orders of his colleagues, were actually drawing up policy papers in direct contradiction to Newcastle's known views. This is apparent even from the material quoted by Namier. (Newcastle to Joseph Yorke, 14 May 1762, Add. Mss 32938 f. 242; Namier, *England*, 316–18.)

80 Perhaps the most useful accounts of this negotiation are in Sandwich to Holland, 26 September 1763, Ilchester (ed.), *Letters to Fox*, 181, and Hardwicke to Royston, 4 September 1763, P. C. Yorke, *The Life and Correspondence of Philip Yorke, Earl of Hardwicke* (3 vols., Cambridge, 1913), iii, 525–9.

81 'Diary', 26 August 1763, *Grenville Papers*, ii, 195.

82 Gilbert Elliot to George Grenville, 31 August 1763, *Grenville Papers*, ii, 101; George Grenville to Lord Strange, 3 September 1763, *ibid*, ii, 104–7; Bute to Shelburne, 4 September 1763, Fitzmaurice, *Life of Shelburne*, i, 207–8.

83 'Diary', 6 September 1763, *Grenville Papers*, ii, 204.

84 'Diary', 26, 28, 30 September, 1 October 1763, *ibid*, ii, 208–11.

85 'Diary', 26 February, 10, 14, 23 March, 13 August 1764, *ibid*, ii, 492–3, 495, 496, 500, 512.

86 Jenkinson to George Grenville, 5 July 1764, *Grenville Papers*, ii, 382–4; Mackenzie to Grenville, 15 July 1764, *ibid*, ii, 388–90; 'Diary', 15 November, 19 December 1764, *ibid*, ii, 524, 535; 'Diary', 25, 27 January, 24 February, 18 March 1765, *ibid*, iii, 116–17, 119, 122–3; *Jenkinson Papers*, 318, 326, 393–400; Stuart Mackenzie to Bute, 3 June, 15, 18 July, 20 August 1764, Bute Mss 1764/49, 64, 68, 74.

87 Derek Jarrett, 'The Regency Crisis of 1765', *EHR* LXXXV (1970), 296–9.

88 See note 63 above.

89 Walpole, *Memoirs of George III*, ii, 154; *Chesterfield's Letters*, vi, 2657; 'Account of the Crisis May–June 1765', Minto Mss M6. no. 3.

90 Rockingham to George III, 5 June 1766, Fortescue (ed.), *Correspondence of George III*, i, 354–5; George III to Rockingham [5 June 1766], *ibid*, i, 355. Rockingham was right to look on the dismissal of Dyson as a mark of confidence. The Lord Chancellor advised the king that if he wished to keep his ministers he ought to remove Dyson, but if he did not intend to keep them long, he should retain him. (Northington to George III, 5 June [1766], *ibid*, i, 356.)

91 Bateson, 'A Narrative of the Changes in the Ministry', *Camden Society* New Series LIX (1898), 70–1. The king's reaction may have been so sharp because he had got wind of an idea of Newcastle's that the party 'insist upon Examples of some of Ld Bute's Friends, before either the present Ministers should engage, or undertake for the Princes' Establishment'. ('Memo', 16 April 1766, Add. Mss 32974 f. 389.) If Rockingham and Newcastle were pursuing such tactics it makes all the more intelligible George's anger and complete lack of patience in the matter. It was this issue, after all, that seems to have decided George to drop the administration. (George III to Egmont, 28 May 1766, Fortescue, *Correspondence of George III*, i, 347.)

92 Bateson, 'A Narrative of the Changes in the Ministry', *Camden Society* New Series LIX (1898), 72.

93 *Ibid*, 73–5.

94 *Ibid*, 79.

95 Newcastle to Page, 7 January 1766, Add. Mss 32973 ff. 56–7; Brooke, *The Chatham Administration*, 164, 194; Anson (ed.), *Autobiography of the Duke of Grafton*, 144.

96 Owen, *The Rise of the Pelhams*, Chs. VI–VIII.

97 Yorke, *Hardwicke*, i, 427.

98 A minute drawn up on 13 February 1746 puts the Pelhams' case perfectly: 'That, out of duty to the King, and regard to the public, it is apprehended that His Majesty's late servants cannot return into his service, without being honoured, with that degree of authority, confidence, and credit from His Majesty, which the ministers of the Crown have usually enjoy'd in this country, and which is

absolutely necessary for carrying on his service. That His Majesty will be pleased entirely to withdraw his confidence and countenance from those persons, who of late have, behind the curtain, suggested private councils, with the view of creating difficulties to his servants, who are responsible for everything, whilst those persons are responsible for nothing.' (Owen, *Rise of the Pelhams*, 298-9.) Throughout 1745-6 Newcastle was worried about the way in which he was accused of trying to force the king – which in practical terms, because of his control of the Commons, was exactly what he was doing – but Chesterfield was all for driving Granville from the closet by force. (Newcastle to Hardwicke, 5 January 1745, Yorke, *Hardwicke*, i, 391; Chesterfield to Newcastle, 10 March 1745, J. Lodge (ed.), 'The Private Correspondence of Chesterfield and Newcastle 1744-46', *Camden Society* XLIV (1930), 21-2.)

99 John B. Owen, 'George II Reconsidered', in Whiteman *et al.*, *Statesmen, Scholars and Merchants*, 118-27.

100 Owen, *Rise of the Pelhams*, 276-7; Williams, *Life of William Pitt*, i, 307.

101 Owen, *Rise of the Pelhams*, 281; Williams, *Pitt*, i, 311.

102 Yorke, *Hardwicke*, i, 347, 370, 382-3.

103 Owen, *Rise of the Pelhams*, 296-7; Williams, *Pitt*, i, 317, 321-2; Waldegrave, *Memoirs*, 108-34.

104 Walpole, *Memoirs of George III*, iv, 136-7; Richmond to Rockingham, 12 February 1771, Olson, *Radical Duke*, 141.

105 For these other components of George's thought see pp. 47–8, 51, 53.

106 Hardwicke to Newcastle, 3 January 1761, Add. Mss 32917 f. 96.

107 The politicians did not help themselves by playing on the king's fears of being forced. Thus Pitt told the king after his resignation in October 1761 that the Old Corps would end up forcing him. (Minto Mss M5/18. Cf. Pitt's earlier remark to Devonshire recorded in the latter's political diary, Devonshire Mss 260/277.) Devonshire was also always harping at court on the way in which, if George was not careful or failed to work with Newcastle, he would end up by being forced like his grandfather. (*Ibid* 260/289, 356, 384.) It would not surprise me if the king saw these remarks as threats, although Devonshire intended them to produce some prudence and flexibility from George and Bute in order to avoid the sort of confrontation from which the old king had emerged so badly.

108 Christie, *Myth and Reality*, 83.

109 Burke, *Works*, i, 376.

110 Pares, *George III and the Politicians*, 182.

8. The press in the 1760s

1 'THOUGHTS Political and Moral', *Universal Magazine* XLIII (1768), 175. Cf. E. W. Montagu, *Reflections on the Rise and Fall of the Ancient Republics* (1759), 4. For good examples of the role of the press in political education see O. M. Haberdasher in [Alexander Carlyle], *Plain Reasons for removing a certain Great Man from his M - - - - - y's presence and councils for ever* (1759), 4; *The Constitution Defended, and Pensioner exposed; in Remarks on the False Alarm* (1770), 25.

2 Jotting, n.d., Whitefoord Mss. Add. Mss 36595 f. 201.

3 *Northern Revolutions: or, the Principal Causes of the Declension and Dissolution of several once flourishing GOTHIC CONSTITUTIONS in EUROPE. In a Series of Letters from the GHOST of TRENCHARD, Once a FREE BRITON* (1757), 28.

4 This, of course, was the view of John Wilkes. See for example *North Briton* xx, 16 October 1762.

5 *Some Cool Thoughts on the present State of Affairs; with a Word to the Old Servant* (1762), 16.

6 *A Letter to her R - - - l H - - - - - - S THE P - - - - - - S D - w - g - r of W - - - - On the Approaching PEACE. With a few Words concerning the Right Honourable the Earl of B- - -, and the General Talk of the World* (1762), 49. Cf. *Idler* VII, 27 May 1758.

7 [Marriott], *Political Considerations* (1762), 55. Cf. *An Address to the People of England* (1763), 5; 'CANDIDUS', *St James's Chronicle*, 4 January 1763.

8 *Political Controversy*, i, 491; ii, 167–8, 238–9.

9 *A Letter to Her R - - - l H - - - - - - S THE P - - - - - - - S D - w - g - r* (1762), 46.

10 *An Appeal to the Facts: In a Letter to the Rt. Hon. Earl Temple* (1763), 3.

11 *An Apology for the Ministerial Life and Actions of a celebrated Favourite* (1766), 17–18.

12 *St James's Chronicle*, 19 August 1762. Cf. 'A Constitutional and Political English Catechism, Necessary for all Families', *London Magazine* xxxv (1766), 265.

13 *Remarks on the Importance of the Study of Political Pamphlets, Weekly Papers, Periodical Papers, Daily Papers, Political Music* (1765), 3–4.

14 Except on one occasion in 'A New Political Dictionary', where the mob is defined as 'The Dukes of *Devonshire, Grafton, Portland*, and *Newcastle*; the Marquis of *Rockingham*; the Earls *Temple, Hardwicke, Bessborough, Ashburnham*, &c; the Lords *Dudley, Monson, Sondes*, &c. Mr *William Pitt*, Mr. *Grenville*, Sir George *Savile*, Mr. *Beckford* &c.' (*The Scots Scourge: or Pridden's Supplement to the Antidote to Caledonian Poison* (2 vols., 1763), i, 33; *Gazetteer*, 1 July 1763; *Universal Magazine*, Supplement xxxii (1763), 356–8; *London Magazine* xxxii (1763), 378–9.)

15 R. S. Schofield, 'The Measurement of Literacy in Pre-Industrial England', in J. Goody (ed.), *Literacy in Traditional Societies* (Cambridge, 1968), 313–14, 323–4.

16 For the problems associated with employing these registers see Schofield, 'Measurement of Literacy', *Literacy in Traditional Societies*, 321–2; Lawrence Stone, 'Literacy and Education in England, 1640–1900', *P & P* 42 (1969), 103.

17 Stone, 'Literacy and Education', *P & P* 42 (1969), 102.

18 Stone, 'Literacy and Education', *P & P* 42 (1969), 109.

19 Burke, *Works*, v, 190. The figure of 80,000 referred to in R. D. Altick, *The English Common Reader: a social history of the mass reading public; 1800–1900* (Chicago, 1957), 49, is the figure for Jacobins, not for the British public.

20 *Commons Journals*, xxvii, 769; Christie, *Myth and Reality*, 313.

21 Christie, *Myth and Reality*, 314; A. Aspinall, 'Statistical Accounts of the London Newspapers during the Eighteenth Century', *EHR* LXIII (1948), 220–3.

22 P. D. G. Thomas, 'The Beginning of Parliamentary Reporting in Newspapers, 1768–1774', *EHR* LXXIV (1959), 624–5.

23 Cranfield, *Development of the Provincial Newspaper*, 21, 176; R. M. Wiles, *Freshest Advices* (Ohio State University Press, 1965), 26.

24 Donald Read, *Press and People, 1790–1850; Opinion in Three English Cities* (1961), 59.

25 Wiles, *Freshest Advices*, 26; Cranfield, *Provincial Newspaper*, 114–15.

26 Cranfield, *Provincial Newspaper*, 259; John Money, 'Taverns, Coffee Houses and Clubs: Local Politics and Popular Articulacy in the Birmingham Area in the Age of the American Revolution', *HJ* XIV, 1 (1971), 17; John Money, *Public Opinion in the West Midlands, 1760–1793* (Cambridge University, unpub. Ph.D., 1967), 85–93.

27 S. Lutnick, *The American Revolution and the British Press, 1775–1783* (Columbia, Mo., 1967), Appendix.

28 R. L. Haig, *The Gazetteer 1735–1797: A Study in the Eighteenth-Century English Newspaper* (Carbondale, Ill., 1968), 79.

29 Add. Mss 38169, *passim*.

30 Cranfield, *Provincial Newspaper*, 170, 172.

31 Wiles, *Freshest Advices*, 126–7.

32 Cranfield, *Provincial Newspaper*, 202–3.

33 *Cambridge Chronicle* (1758). This is printed on each issue beneath the date line.

34 Money, *Public Opinion in the West Midlands* (unpub. Ph.D.), 202–3.

35 *Leeds Mercury*, 11 July 1769.

36 Bowyer Paper Ledger, Bodley Mss Don.b.4.ff.165, 189; Strahan Ledgers, Add. Mss 48800 ff. 128, 142, 143; Add. Mss 48801 f. 49; Add. Mss 48803 A ff. 63, 69, 79. Imprints of 500 included *Letter to Dr. Shebbeare* (1758); *Ministerial Influence display'd*

(1760); *Genuine Debate on the Liberty of the Press* (1763); *The Constitution Vindicated* (*1763*); *Anatomy of a late Negotiation* (1763); *Letter to the Opposition* (1763); *Foundling Hospital for Wit* (1763); *Address to the Public on Conway's Dismission* (1764); Dickinson's *Speech Delivered in the House of Assembly* (1764); Bollan's *American Fishery* (1764); *The Political Balance* (1765); *Secret Springs of the late Changes* (1765); Franklin's *Considerations on Taxing America* (1766); *Regulations respecting the British Colonies* (1766); *The Case of Great Britain and America* (1768); *Thoughts on Government* (1768); Hartley's *The Case of the Petitioners* (1772).

37 Strahan Ledgers, Add. Mss 48800 ff. 129, 132; Add. Mss 48803 A ff. 51, 61, 63; Bowyer Ledger, Bodley, Don.b.4.f.31. For further evidence of high sales for party manifestoes, see Enclosure in Rockingham to Newcastle, 15 September 1764, Add. Mss 32962 f. 114; Thomas Walpole to Charles Townshend (copy), 27 September 1764, *ibid* f. 159.

38 Bowyer Ledger, Bodley Don.b.4.f.169; Strahan Ledgers Add. Mss 48800 f. 126; Add. Mss 48801 ff. 43–4.

39 *Cambridge Chronicle*, 2 April 1768; *English Liberty, or the British Lion roused; Containing the Sufferings of John Wilkes, Esq; from the First of his Persecution, Down to the Present Time* (2 vols., 1769), i, 279.

40 M. D. George, *English Political Caricature: A Study in Opinion and Propaganda* (2 vols., Oxford, 1959), i, 135.

41 Nicholas Rogers, 'Aristocratic Clientage, Trade and Independency: Popular Politics in Pre-Radical Westminster', *P & P* 61 (1973), 101.

42 'Printing', Strutt Mss, Terling Place.

43 This was also apparently the case in Norfolk and Norwich in 1768 for, although we do not have the circulation figures, a wealth of individual materials survive. (*The Lynn Magazine: or a collection of papers published during the contest in that town begun December 12, 1766* (1768); [R. Gardiner], *Remarks on the Letter to John Buxton Esq.* (Norwich, [1768]); *Miscellaneous Pieces in prose and verse; relative to the contested election for Members of Parliament for the County of Norfolk, and the City and County of Norwich A.D. 1768* (Norfolk, 1768); *A New Song, Address'd to Sir Edward Astley, Bart. and Wenham Coke, Esq; and to the Independent Electors, in the Interest of these Gentlemen*, Norfolk RO Bradfer-Lawrence Mss VIId.)

44 Election Accounts, 1741–85, Huntington Library, Stowe Mss T3 PP6.

45 *Spectator* x, 12 March 1711; Haig, *Gazetteer*, 11.

46 Lillywhite, *London Coffee Houses*, 23.

47 *The Countenance or Gregg's Ghost* (1711), 11.

48 'QUIDAM', *St James's Chronicle*, 3 March 1770.

49 *Test* xxx, 4 June 1757; 'W.E. Great Piazza Coffee House Convent Garden', *St James's Chronicle*, 18 January 1763; 'QUIDAM', *ibid*, 3 March 1770; Altick, *English Common Reader*, 40.

50 Pottle (ed.), *Boswell's London Journal*, 51, 74–6.

51 Thomas Willoughby to George III, 8 October 1768, Windsor, R.A. 820.

52 Lillywhite, *London Coffee Houses*, 273; John Lane, *Masonic Records, 1717–1894* (2nd ed., 1895), 105, 138, 170.

53 Lillywhite, *London Coffee Houses*, 370; Lane, *Masonic Records*, 34, 64.

54 Lillywhite, *London Coffee Houses*, 442–3, 503.

55 *Letter to a Noble Member of the Club* (1764), 4. For Friendly Societies discussing politics see 'VELLUM', *St James's Chronicle*, 22 February 1763, and for a satirical attack on a tradesmen's political club see 'THE LAMPLIGHTER OF COLEMAN-STREET', *Gazetteer*, 29 June 1763.

56 Sir H. Erskine to Bute, Saturday night [end November 1762], Bute Mss (Cardiff) 2/191.

57 Newcastle to Hardwicke, 1 January 1763, Add. Mss 32946 f. 11.

58 Rockingham to Newcastle, Wednesday M: 1 o'clock [3 December 1766], Add. Mss 32978 f. 147.

59 *The Miscellaneous Works of Edward Gibbon, Esq. With Memoirs of his Life and Writings* (5 vols., 2nd ed., 1814), i, 154.

60 Talbot to Bute [November 1760], Bute Mss 1760/118.

61 Denbigh to Dr Knight, 7 September 1762, Newdigate Mss B18/1627; Newdigate to ?, 20 November 1762, *ibid* B23/2311.

62 'Diary 1761', Newdigate Mss A6.

63 'Diaries 1760–1770', Newdigate Mss. On December 8, 1762, for example, Newdigate spent the evening reading pamphlets at the Cocoa Tree.

64 Diary 1770, 15 November 1770, Newdigate Mss.

65 Cranfield, *Provincial Newspaper*, 182–3.

66 *Williamson's Liverpool Advertiser*, 23 January 1767; A. H. Arkle, 'Early Coffee Houses in Liverpool', *THSLC* 64 (1912), 1–16.

67 *Newcastle Journal*, 14 April 1770; John Sykes, *Local Records; or, Historical Register of Remarkable Events...in Northumberland and Durham* (2 vols., Newcastle, 1833), I, 272.

68 George Middleton to Bute, 10 July 1763, Bute Mss (Cardiff) 10/161. This may well have been the coffee room advertised in the *York Courant*, 29 May 1764.

69 Money, 'Taverns, Coffee Houses and Clubs', *HJ* xiv, i, 24.

70 Money, 'Taverns, Coffee Houses and Clubs', *ibid* 24–5.

71 R. B. Sheridan, *The Rivals* Act I, Scene II.

72 A. D. McKillop, 'English Circulating Libraries, 1725–50', *Library* xiv (1934), 482–3.

73 J. H. Plumb, *The Commercialisation of Leisure* (University of Reading, 1973), 7.

74 Kaufman, *Libraries and their Users*, 192.

75 *Gentleman's Magazine* xxxiv (1764), 44.

76 Hamlyn, 'Eighteenth-Century Circulating Libraries in England', *Library* 5th Series i (1946), 221.

77 Paul Kaufman, 'The Community Library: a Chapter in English Social History', *Transactions of the American Philosophical Society* (1967), 16.

78 Kaufman, *Libraries and their Users*, 44.

79 Cranfield, *Provincial Newspaper*, 177; A. Aspinall, *Politics and the Press c. 1780–1850* (1949), 17.

80 George, *English Political Caricature*, i, 74, 115.

81 *Auditor*, 7 October 1762. For the use of prints and cartoons as political propaganda see 'Letter sent in French and translated for the Gazetteer', *Gazetteer*, 9 December 1762; *Test* xxvi, 7 May 1757; *Con-Test* xxxi, 18 June 1757; George, *English Political Caricature*, i, *passim*.

82 Beaumont Hotham to Portland, 10 May 1763, Portland Mss PwF 5204. Cf. [Owen Ruffhead], *Considerations on the Present Dangerous Crisis* (2nd ed., 1763), 40. For further information on opposition handbills see *Letter to a Noble Member of the Club* (1764), 2–3; *Gentleman's Magazine* xxxv (1765), 94; *The Contrast: with corrections and restorations. And an Introductory Dissertation on the Origin of Feuds and Animosities in the State* (collected ed., 1765), 57.

83 'Snap Dragon', *Lloyd's Evening Post*, 1 December 1762.

84 *Gazetteer*, 10 December 1762; *Universal Magazine* xxxviii (1762), 310–14.

85 Walpole, *Memoirs of George III*, i, 16, 191; *Walpole Letters*, iv, 454; *ibid*, v, 4; A. N. Newman (ed.), 'Leicester House Politics, 1750–60, from the papers of John, Second Earl of Egmont', *Camden Miscellany* xxiii 4th Series 7 (1969), 227.

86 *English Liberty, or the British Lion roused* (1769), i, 291.

87 *Cambridge Chronicle*, 21 May 1768; *Gentleman's Magazine* xxxviii (1768), 245.

88 *Cambridge Chronicle*, 7 April 1770; *Leeds Mercury*, 28 March 1769.

89 Wright (ed.), *Cavendish's Debates*, i, 100–1; *Cambridge Chronicle*, 17, 31 December 1768. The original single sheet, *The Speech that was spoken by Oliver Cromwell, when he dissolved the Long Parliament* can be seen in the British Museum.

90 Altick, *English Common Reader*, 52. Cf. Ian Watt, *The Rise of the Novel* (1957), 42–3.

91 *Gentleman's Magazine* XXXII (1762), 276–84, 303–4, 313–19, 325, 367–8, 377–9, 411–18, 435–7, 473–80, 491–3, 530–6, 578–86; *ibid* XXXIII (1763), 61–6, 132–4; *Universal Magazine* XXXIX (1763), 153–6, 187–8; *London Magazine* XXXI (1762), 293, 375–8, 517–18; *ibid* XXXII (1763), 3–6; *Weekly Amusement* I (1764), 8–9, 23.

92 See, *inter alia*, *St James's Chronicle*, 3 June 1763, 8 June 1762; *Lloyd's Evening Post*, 2 July 1762; *London Chronicle*, 9 September 1762; *Gazetteer*, 12 July 1762.

93 William B. Todd, *A Bibliography of Edmund Burke* (1964), 73–5.

94 Brewer, 'Party and the Double Cabinet', *HJ* XIV (1971), 493n.

95 Lutnick, *The American Revolution and the British Press*, Appendix.

96 Brewer, 'Party and the Double Cabinet', *HJ* XIV (1971), 493–4; *Oxford Magazine* IV (1770), 182–6.

97 Brewer, 'Party and the Double Cabinet', *HJ* XIV (1971), 496.

98 *The Repository or Treasury of Politics and Literature* (2 vols., 1770–1), i, 73–4.

99 Francesco Cordasco, *A Junius bibliography, with a preliminary essay on the political background, text and identity* (New York, 1949), 22–3, 25–6.

100 *Gentleman's Magazine* XXXIX (1769), 65–8, 71, 131–3, 138, 194, 228, 237, 293, 334, 435, 481, 485, 538, 563, 581; *Political Register* IV (1769), 111, 179, 185, 234, 245, 300, 302, 350; *ibid* V (1769), 81, 85, 108, 146, 221–2, 224, 285–7; *ibid* VI (1770), 15–16, 140, 201, 270, 332; *ibid* VII (1770), 148, 335; *Universal Magazine* XLV (1769), 155–8; *ibid* XLVI (1770), 83–5, 180–2; *London Magazine* XXXVIII (1769), 199–200, 316–19, 363–6, 390–2, 472–6, 520–3, 532–5, 610–11, 632–7; *ibid* XXXIX (1770), 98–100, 192–4; *Freeholder's Magazine* I (1769), 33–7, 40–1, 94–7, 138–9.

101 *Literary Register* I (1769), 85–7, 105–6, 134–6, 159–60, 166–8, 182–4, 195–7, 229–30, 245–50, 253–4, 289, 301, 307–11; *ibid* II (1770), 45–7, 73–4, 85–6, 127–8, 183, 212, 282–5.

102 Rea, *English Press in Politics*, 177.

103 *Cambridge Chronicle*, 27 December 1769, 17 February, 17, 24 March, 7 April, 2 June 1770; *Leeds Mercury*, 19, 26 December 1769.

104 Schofield, 'Measurement of Literacy' in Goody, *Literacy in Traditional Societies*, 312–13.

105 *London Magazine* XXXVIII (1769), 580.

106 *An Appeal to the Nation* (1757), 2.

107 Lucy S. Sutherland, 'The City of London and the Devonshire–Pitt Administration 1756–7', *Proceedings of the British Academy* XLVI (1960), 156; Cambridge University Library Madden Collection of Ballads 4/7, 10, 12. Cf. *Boh Peep-Peep Boh*, *Admiral Bing's Apology*; *Admiral Byng's LETTER to Secretary Cleveland OR Who will kick at a Coward*; *Capt. ANDREW's Ghost, to A - - - - - l B - - g as he lay at Anchor at Gibraltar* (Madden Ballads 4/8, 11, 13). At least one pro-Byng ballad appeared: *Admiral Byng's Complaint*, and was reprinted as *All is out - - or, ADMIRAL BYNG* (Madden Ballads 4/6, 9.)

108 *No Liberty! No Life! Proper Wages, and Down with Oppression. In a Letter to the Brave People of England. By John Englishman* (3rd ed., 1768), 18.

109 [Henry Howard], *The K - - - s A - -. A New Song Intended as a Companion to the Q - - - - s A - -* (1762); [Howard], *The Masquerade or the Political Bagpiper* (1762); [Howard], *The Pe**e Soup-Makers, Or, a new mess at the B - d - d Head* (1762). These and other songs by Howard can be found in BM 1850c. 10 nos. 73, 78, 79, 80, 82.

110 Royston to Hardwicke, 5 May 1763, Add. Mss 35352 f. 345.

111 Walpole, *Letters*, vii, 386.

112 Madden Ballads 5/1415; 6/1746, 1842, 1937–43.

113 Madden Ballads 5/1297; 6/1681; Boswell to Johnson, 9 July 1763, Ralph S. Walker (ed.), *The Correspondence of James Boswell and John Johnston of Grange* (1966), 86–7.

114 Altick, *English Common Reader*, 35; Haig, *The Gazetteer*, 24; Aspinall, *Politics and the Press*, 26–7; Cranfield, *Provincial Newspaper*, 188–9.

115 Walpole, *Memoirs of George III*, i, 313–14.

116 *Walpole Letters*, v, 421.
117 Mallet to Bute, 2 November 1762, Add. Mss 36796 f. 163; Talbot to Bute [July 1761], Bute Mss 1761/506.
118 *The Three Conjurers, a political interlude. Stolen from Shakespeare* [1764]; *The Fall of Mortimer* (1763); [Wilkes] *The Favourite, with a Dedication to my Lord B**** (1765). All these plays evidently fall under the sole head of printed propaganda.
119 Sutherland, 'The Circulation of Newspapers', *Library* 4th Series xv (1934), 111; Henry L. Snyder, 'The Circulation of newspapers in the reign of Queen Anne', *Library* 5th Series xxiii (1968), 210–11.
120 M. R. A. Harris, 'Figures relating to the Printing and Distribution of the *Craftsman* 1726 to 1730', *BIHR* xliii (1970), 236.
121 Christie, *Myth and Reality*, 315–21.
122 William Albert, *The Turnpike Road System in England 1663–1840* (Cambridge, 1972), 31, 42, 189.
123 Ogilvie, *Ralph Allen's Bye, Way and Cross-Road Posts*, 22–3.
124 Ogilvie, *Allen's Posts*, 23.
125 Cranfield, *Provincial Newspaper*, 23.
126 Alan Everitt, 'The English Urban Inn, 1560–1760', in Everitt (ed.), *Perspectives in English Urban History* (1973), 111, 116.
127 Plumb, *Commercialisation of Leisure*, 13–15; Everitt, 'Urban Inn', *Perspectives in Urban History*, 114–19.
128 Everitt, 'Urban Inn', *Perspectives in Urban History*, 112.
129 Money, 'Taverns, Coffee Houses and Clubs', *HJ* xiv (1971), 24–8, 32.

9. Personality, propaganda and ritual: Wilkes and the Wilkites

1 *A Serious and Friendly Address* (1768), 5.
2 *The Historical and Posthumous Memoirs of Sir Nathaniel Wraxall, 1772–1784*, ed. H. B. Wheatley (5 vols., 1884), ii, 48.
3 L. W. Hanson, *Government and the Press 1695–1763* (Oxford, 1936), 31–2; Rea, *English Press in Politics*, 59–69.
4 Cannon, *Parliamentary Reform*, 33–4; Plumb, 'The growth of the electorate in England from 1600 to 1715', *P & P* 45 (1969), 115–16.
5 'Address to the Gentlemen, Freeholders and Clergy in the County of Middlesex, 20 February 1769', *English Liberty* ii, 188.
6 'To the Worthy Inhabitants of the Ward of Farringdon Without' (1769), Single Sheet (S.S.) in *A Collection of contemporary papers relating to the City Elections 1768–1796*, Guildhall Library.
7 For the limitations after 1771 see A. Aspinall, 'The reporting and publishing of the House of Commons Debates, 1771–1834', Richard Pares and A. J. P. Taylor (eds.), *Essays presented to Sir Lewis Namier* (1956), 228–32.
8 For this whole incident see P. D. G. Thomas, 'John Wilkes and the Freedom of the Press', *BIHR* xxxiii (1960), 86–98; Thomas, 'Parliamentary Reporting', *EHR* lxxiv (1959), 623–36; Haig, *Gazetteer*, 102–18; Rea, *English Press in Politics*, 201–11.
9 *Walpole Letters*, vii, 178–9.
10 *English Liberty, or the British Lion roused* (1769), i, 117–20.
11 O. A. Sherrard, *A Life of John Wilkes* (1938), 99; Raymond Postgate, *That Devil Wilkes* (1930), 66; *A Narrative of the Proceedings against John Wilkes, Esq. From his Commitment in April 1763 to his Outlawry. With a full View of the Arguments used in Parliament and out of Doors in canvassing the various important Questions that arose from his Case* (1768), 13–14.
12 *The Correspondence of the late John Wilkes with his friends, printed from the original manuscripts, in which are introduced memoirs of his life, by John Almon* (5 vols., 1805),

iii, 234–7; Sherrard, *Life of John Wilkes*, 167–9; Almon to Wilkes 12 May 1767, Add. Mss 30869 f. 123.

13 *A Collection of all Mr. Wilkes's Addresses to the Gentlemen, Clergy, and Freeholders of the County of Middlesex* (1769), *passim*.

14 E.g. *Leeds Mercury*, 10 January, 4 April 1769; *Cambridge Chronicle*, 19 March, 26 March, 14 May, 25 June, 5 November 1768; *Norwich Mercury*, 19 March 1768, 7, 28 January, 11 February, 1, 22 April 1769; *English Liberty, or the British Lion roused* (1769), i, 352–6, 373–6; ii, 42–9, 71–3, 172–6, 180–3, 186–7; *English Liberty established* (1768), single sheet; *A Collection of Mr. Wilkes's Addresses* (1769), *passim*; *Gentleman's Magazine* XXXVIII (1768), 124; *ibid* XXXIX (1769), 182–6, 190–1; *ibid* XL (1770), 167–8.

15 George Nobbe, *The North Briton. A Study in Political Propaganda* (New York, 1939), 37. The *North Briton* did, however, contain fairly frequent references to the general principle of the freedom of the press.

16 Annotation in *A History of the late Minority*, 401 (Wilkes's pagination). This copy of the pamphlet is British Museum class mark G. 13453.

17 [John Wilkes], *Fragments and Anecdotes, proper to be read at the present crisis by every honest Englishman* (1764), 41.

18 *The Correspondence of Wilkes*, iv, 15. Cf. *English Liberty established* (1768) s.s.; *Letters between the Duke of GRAFTON, the Earls of HALIFAX, EGREMONT, CHATHAM, TEMPLE, and TALBOT, Baron BOTTETOURT, Rt. Hon. HENRY BILSON LEGGE, Rt. Hon. Sir JOHN CUST, Bart., Mr CHARLES CHURCHILL, Monsieur VOLTAIRE, Abbe WINCKLEMANN &c. AND JOHN WILKES, ESQ., With explanatory notes* (1769), 107–8, 129; *English Liberty: being a collection of Interesting Tracts, From the Year 1762 to 1769. Containing the Private Correspondence, Public Letters, Speeches and Addresses, of John Wilkes Esq. Humbly Dedicated to the King* (2 vols., 1769), i, iv–v.

19 *The Correspondence of Wilkes*, v, 285. Thus *An Ode on the Enlargement of Wilkes* (1770), s.s. chants: 'Each unvenal unvenal Eye can see/The Soul of Wilkes is Liberty'. (*BM Catalogue of Prints and Drawings*, no. 4385.)

20 *BM Catalogue of Prints and Drawings*, no. 4207, s.s. Guildhall Broadsides 29.3.

21 Thus in the broadside that included his Address to the Middlesex electors of 29 March 1768, there is also reprinted the vital lines of his speech of 6 May 1763, referring to his concern for 'the lower and intermediate class of people'. (Guildhall Broadsides 21.131.)

22 Though, of course, Wilkes's counsel, Serjeant Glynn, raised the question of parliamentary privilege, and it was on these grounds that Pratt had Wilkes released. (*Walpole Letters*, v, 322; Horace Bleackley, *Life of John Wilkes* (1917), 105–7.)

23 'To the Freeholders of the County of Middlesex, particularly to my Neighbours in Wapping. By a Freeholder of Wapping', Beauchamp Proctor Mss, Ealing Borough Reference Library.

24 *Old Bailey Proceedings* (1768), 207; *ibid* (1769–70), 42; Sutherland, *The City of London*, 15–16n.

25 Jane Blenkinsopp to Wilkes, 22 January 1769, Add. Mss 30870 f. 103; Taylor to Wilkes, 17 March 1769, *ibid* f. 127; Edward Slade to Wilkes, 20 Feb. 1769, *ibid* f. 113.

26 Bayley to Wilkes, 27 May 1770, Add. Mss 30871 f. 33.

27 See, for instance, *A New Song* [1769?], s.s.: 'Old *Farringdon's* Boys,/Will have Cause to rejoice,/For all *England* shall honour their Name'.

28 *A Collection of all Mr. Wilkes's Addresses* (1769), 3.

29 *Ibid*, 15.

30 William Purdie Treloar, *Wilkes and the City* (1917), 235.

31 Apart from the pamphlets that Wilkes wrote himself, there were many Wilkite defences of his position (see, for example, *A Letter on the Public Conduct of Mr. Wilkes* (1768)) in addition to those tracts written by sympathisers amongst the parliamen-

tary opposition. Almon's *Political Register* and the new *Freeholder's Magazine* were virtually Wilkite organs. For Wilkite newspaper letters see *The Repository or Treasury of Politics and Literature* (2 vols., 1770–1), especially the letters of 'An Independent Whig', i.e. Almon. For Wilkite handbills and ballads see pp. 152, 156 above; *Leeds Mercury*, 4 February 1769; *Cambridge Chronicle*, 23 March, 2 April 1768, *Norwich Mercury*, 7 January 1769; *The Battle of the Quills: or, Wilkes attacked and defended* (1768), 6–8; *Wilkes's Jest Book; or the Merry Patriot* (1770), 33–6. For verses see *The Crisis; an ode to John Wilkes, Esq.* (1763); [E. B. Greene], *The Tower: a Poetical epistle, inscribed to J. Wilkes, Esq.* (1763); *The Group, composed of the most shocking figures, though the greatest in the nation* (1763); *The Patriotic Miscellany; being a collection of interesting papers, jests, anecdotes, epigrams, &c. in the Case of John Wilkes Esq* (1769), 62 seq. For cartoons see George, *English Political Caricature*, i, 141–9.

32 These included *An Authentick account of the proceedings against John Wilkes Esq* (1763); *A Complete Collection of the Genuine Papers, Letters, &c. in the Case of John Wilkes, Esq.* (Paris and Berlin editions, 1767); *A Narrative of the Proceedings against John Wilkes, Esq.* (1768); *The whole account of John Wilkes, Esq.* (1768); *The Life and Political Writings of John Wilkes, Esq* (Birmingham, 1769); *English Liberty, or the British Lion roused* (1769); *English Liberty: being a collection of Interesting Tracts* (1769).

33 This work is Guildhall Library Wilkes Mss 3332/1–2.

34 *English Liberty, or the British Lion roused* (1769), ii, 177.

35 *Notes and Queries* 1st Series VIII (1853), 203.

36 John Money, 'Taverns, Coffee Houses and Clubs' *HJ* XIV, 1 (1971), 27.

37 *No. 45. A Comic Song* [1768?], s.s. Guildhall Broadsides 21.132.

38 Guildhall Broadsides 21.131.

39 Cf. *Original and Select Letters from J. Wilkes, Esq. to the Aldermen of London: likewise Oliver Cromwell's Speech, which he made when he dissolved the Long Parliament* (1769). This includes three letters, a portrait of Wilkes, and Cromwell's speech all in a single folio sheet.

40 *General Evening Post*, 17 April 1770; Pauline Maier, 'John Wilkes and American Disillusionment with Britain', *WMQ* 3rd Series XX (1963), 373.

41 Add. Mss 30870 f. 186; 30871 ff. 55, 60, 62; Rea, *English Press in Politics*, 207–8.

42 E.g. Almon to Wilkes, 3 July 1767, Add. Mss 30869 f. 139; Herbert Lawrence to Wilkes, 24 July 1769, Add. Mss 30870 f. 169; Shaw to Wilkes, 27 October 1769, *ibid* f. 215; R. Thompson to Wilkes, 18 January 1771, Add. Mss 30871 f. 55.

43 Rudé, *Wilkes and Liberty*, 172–6.

44 Cranfield, *Provincial Newspaper*, 84–5, 117–18.

45 This was especially true in local politics. In the Essex election of 1768, for example, the proprietor of the *Chelmsford Chronicle*, Mr Lobb, refused to print a particularly vituperative political letter. He wrote to its author, giving his reasons: 'As Printers of a public paper, we consider ourselves as public persons. The pieces that we admit into our paper may be divided into two classes, viz. 1. Whatever we insert by way of Entertainment or Intelligence, & 2ndly Advertisements, whether of a political or private nature. With respect to the first, we are like the Managers of a Theatre – accountable to the Public for whatever we select. But as to the Disputes (whether political or private) that are carried on by way of Advertisements, we have no manner of judgement with regard to the Argument. We lay the Sentiments & the *assertions* of different parties before the public, & we leave the public to judge for themselves. All that we assume, is just so much common sense, as is necessary to discern any particular passage wherein any one of the Combatants may exceed the Limits prescribed by *Law*, by Decency, & by good Manners.

'Whenever, then, we are apprehensive that the Writer of any Piece exceeds these essential Limits, it becomes our Interest, it becomes an absolute Regard to our Safety, to reject the piece in question, unless the writer will disclose his name, & assure us of an indemnification...

'We hope...that you will pardon us, if we cannot possibly deviate from the declaration that we made last week, viz. *that every Letter relative to County Affairs must be paid for as an Advertisement.* Because, by admitting any piece by way of Entertainment or Information, we become answerable for the Justness and Prioriety of the Argument, & subject ourselves to numberless Inconveniences, We are justified in this Declaration by the constant practice of the Ipswich Journal and the Norwich Mercury; the latter of which has every week some Address from the two contending parties, which are all paid for as Advertisements.' (Lobb to Peter Muilman, 3 January 1768, Strutt Mss.)

46 Cranfield, *Provincial Newspaper,* 75–81, 119, 137–40.

47 See, for instance, *Williamson's Liverpool Advertiser,* 16 October 1761.

48 The criterion employed by Christie in *Myth and Reality,* 244–60.

49 *Norwich Mercury,* 12 March 1768; 'PHILANTHROPOS', *Aris's Birmingham Gazette,* 7 December 1767; 'Several Independent Freeholders'; *ibid,* 25 September 1769; 'TRANQUILIUS', *Leeds Mercury,* 14 February 1769; *ibid,* 2, 21 March 1769; 'PLAIN TRUTH'; *ibid,* 1 August 1769; *Cambridge Chronicle,* 24 February 1770; 'Pro Patria', *Jopson's Coventry Mercury,* 4 April 1768; *Liverpool Chronicle,* 10, 17 March 1768. The *Liverpool Chronicle* by this time had sections of comment in the paper under the heading 'THE EDITORS'.

50 *Leeds Mercury,* 14 March 1769; Samuel Champion to Wilkes, 24 March 1769, Add. Mss 30870 f. 131; Henzell to Wilkes, 24 March 1769, *ibid* f. 132.

51 *Leeds Mercury,* 1 January 1769; 'Friend to Liberty' to Wilkes, 3 January 1770, Add. Mss 30871 f. 1.

52 *Leeds Mercury,* 14 March 1769; Hart to Wilkes, 23 November 1768, Add. Mss 30870 f. 81; Common Council of Richmond, Yorks. to Wilkes, 16 March 1769, *ibid* f. 125.

53 *Newcastle Journal,* 18 March 1769.

54 Jane Blenkinsopp to Wilkes, 22 January 1769, Add. Mss 30870 f. 103; *Leeds Mercury,* 21 February 1769.

55 Money, 'Taverns, Coffee Houses and Clubs', *HJ* XIV (1971), 26.

56 Taylor to Wilkes, 17 March 1769, Add. Mss 30870 f. 127; Edward Slade to Wilkes, 20 February 1769, *ibid* f. 113.

57 For which see Jack P. Greene (ed.), *The nature of Colony Constitutions* (Columbia, S.C., 1970), *passim.*

58 *The Correspondence of John Wilkes,* v, 42–4, 256–7; Peter Manigault *et al.* to Hankey and Partners, 9 December 1769, Add. Mss 30870 f. 237; Maier, 'Wilkes and American disillusionment', *WMQ* (1963), 391.

59 H. Dresser to Wilkes, 24 February 1770, Add. Mss 30871 f. 11.

60 *Norwich Mercury,* 18 November 1769.

61 Roger Lonsdale (ed.), *The Poems of Thomas Gray, William Collins, Oliver Goldsmith* (1969), 646.

62 *Cambridge Chronicle,* 1 November 1768.

63 *Northampton Mercury,* 23 April 1770. It might be argued that all of the following examples are unreliable because they stem primarily, and very often exclusively from newspaper reports. I accept that this is a very real difficulty. Many of the demonstrations, because comparatively orderly, do not supply the sort of judicial evidence that is available for some Wilkite riots. There is also only limited corroborative information available from other sources, usually of a very sketchy kind. In the case of the London demonstration on Wilkes's release, Horace Walpole, for instance, mentions the illuminations at Beckford's house described in the papers, but tends to underplay, by comparison with the press, such events as occurred (*Walpole Letters* VII, 375). No doubt the papers embellished their accounts, as they still do, but the accuracy of the reports about Wilkes's presents seems to imply that the broad outlines of the accounts of demonstrations are accurate enough. Accounts from local papers are more accurate, and often are easier to corroborate.

64 *Northampton Mercury*, 23 April 1770.
65 *Middlesex Journal*, 19 April 1770; *General Evening Post*, 21 April 1770.
66 *Cambridge Chronicle*, 28 April 1770.
67 *St James's Chronicle*, 17 April 1770; *London Evening Post*, 19 April 1770.
68 *London Evening Post*, 24 April 1770; *Public Advertiser*, 20 April 1770.
69 *Middlesex Journal*, 19 April 1770; *General Evening Post*, 21 April 1770; Rudé, *Wilkes and Liberty*, 149.
70 *Lloyd's Evening Post*, 20 April 1770; *London Evening Post*, 21, 24, 30 April 1770; *Gazetteer*, 23 April 1770; *Sherborne Mercury*, 16, 23, 30 April 1770. I am grateful to Diane Pearson for the last reference.
71 *Cambridge Chronicle*, 28 April 1770; *Northampton Mercury*, 30 April 1770.
72 Money, 'Taverns, Coffee Houses and Clubs', *HJ* XIV (1971), 28.
73 *London Evening Post*, 24 April 1770.
74 Sykes, *Local Records; or, Historical Register of Northumberland and Durham*, I, 271–2.
75 Sykes, *Local Records*, I, 272; *St James's Chronicle*, 24 April 1770; *Newcastle Journal*, 14, 21, 28 April 1770; *Lloyd's Evening Post*, 23 April 1770.
76 *York Courant*, 24 April 1770.
77 *Norwich Mercury*, 24 April 1770.
78 *Ibid.*
79 Rudé, *Wilkes and Liberty*, 149; Jack P. Greene (ed.), *The Nature of Colony Constitutions*, 14; *London Evening Post*, 28 April 1770.
80 *General Evening Post*, 21 April 1770.
81 Rudé, *Wilkes and Liberty*, 135.
82 Rudé, *Wilkes and Liberty*, 130–2; Money, *Public Opinion in the West Midlands* (unpub. Ph.D.), 289–92.
83 See, for instance, the numbers given in T. S. Willan, *An Eighteenth-Century Shopkeeper, Abraham Dent of Kirkby Stephen* (Manchester, 1970), 2–3. Reference can also be made for the composition of the professional and trading classes in a larger town to G. T. and I. Shaw, *Liverpool's Fifth Directory* (Liverpool, 1932), 95–106.
84 For some interesting criticisms of Rudé's concern see *Bulletin of the Society for the Study of Labour History* 25 (1972), 14, where Peter Linebaugh argues that the social composition of the criminal classes of eighteenth-century England was no different from the composition of Wilkite crowds.
85 Natalie Zemon Davis, 'The Rites of Violence: Religious Riot in Sixteenth-Century France', *P & P* 59 (1973), 54.
86 Rudé, *The Crowd in History*, 59; Rudé, *Paris and London in the Eighteenth Century* (1970), 295. I do not wish to imply that Rudé does not mention the more formal manifestations of Wilkite behaviour. He certainly does, but he fails to subject them to the type of analysis here employed.
87 It is difficult to see why chimney-sweeps were so important. Possibly they were regarded as 'liminal' people (for this notion see note 116), occupying a twilight world of their own. Both their appearance and their activities would reinforce this view. Hanway certainly thought of them as a group that operated outside the usual mechanisms of social control, but he had his reasons for wanting to exaggerate their unruly and supposedly callous nature. For obvious reasons they were difficult to identify, and this seems to have been a genuine cause for concern on the part of the London magistracy (e.g. *Old Bailey Proceedings* (1768), 360). Persons described as chimney sweeps may not have been sweeps at all, but simply those who dressed as sweeps, both for the purposes of disguise, and to emphasise the peculiarity of the situation.
88 Rudé, *Wilkes and Liberty*, 69; *Middlesex Journal*, 11 April 1769.
89 *Cambridge Chronicle*, 18 June 1769.
90 Problems of definition obviously arise here. In the case of symbols I follow the useful, workmanlike definition adopted by Raymond Firth. A symbol is where 'a

sign [he uses this as a generic term] has a complex series of associations, often of an emotional kind, and difficult (some would say, impossible) to describe in terms other than partial representation. The aspect of personal or social construction in meaning may be marked, so no sensory likeness of symbol to object may be apparent to the observer, and imputation of relationship may seem arbitrary'. (Raymond Firth, *Symbols, Public and Private* (1973), 75. Cf. 66, 67.) This is a view that, in a rather different context gains the concurrence of E. H. Gombrich. (*Symbolic Images. Studies in the art of the Renaissance* (1972), 1–5; 'The Use of Art for the Study of Symbols', *American Psychologist* xx, i (1965), 38.) The question of ritual is equally complex. Max Gluckman uses ceremony, in common with many other anthropologists, as a generic term 'to cover any complex organization of human activity which is not specifically technical or recreational and which involves the use of modes of behaviour which are expressive of social relationships'. Ritual, as a category within ceremony, is characterised by its reference to or association with external ideas or notions normally of a mystical or non-rational kind. (Max Gluckman (ed.), *Essays on the Ritual of Social Relationships* (Manchester, 1962), 20–3.)

Thus we can talk generally of Wilkite ceremonial, some, indeed much of which is also ritual. The difficulty here is one of explaining when a ceremony is not a ritual. Such an event with a minimum of reference points, perhaps a simple march of followers made in order to vote at Brentford, would fall into this category. But such a simple event very rarely occurred, and I have tended to use the two terms almost interchangeably. This may offend some anthropologists, but for the purposes of studying Wilkite crowd behaviour it does not seem to obfuscate meaning.

91 For similar criticisms see Davis, 'Rites of Violence', *P & P* 59 (1973), 54, 70–1; Thompson, 'The Moral Economy of the English Crowd in the Eighteenth Century', *P & P* 50 (1971), 78.
92 E. J. Hobsbawm, *Primitive Rebels* (New York, 1959), 152.
93 J. Prebble, *Culloden* (1961), 201–2.
94 Rudé, *Paris and London*, 236–7; idem, *Wilkes and Liberty*, 222. By Wilkite rioter I mean to refer here only to those who were involved in specifically political demonstrations. Coal-heavers and weavers, both of which included Wilkite supporters, suffered far more severely for their industrial actions.
95 *The whole Proceedings in the King's Commission of the Peace, Oyer and Terminer, and Gaol Delivery for the City of London and...for the County of Middlesex*, ed. J. Gurney (1767), 285–6; *Cambridge Chronicle*, 14 May 1768.
96 PRO State Papers Domestic Entry Books SP 44/142/88–9.
97 Donald Read, *Peterloo. The Massacre and its Background* (Manchester, 1958), 136.
98 For general comments on this subject see C. Wright Mills, *The Sociological Imagination* (New York, 1959), 36; A. Cohen, 'The Analysis of the Symbolism of Power Relations', *Man* IV (1969), 215–35.
99 J. Sykes, *An Account of the Rejoicings, Illuminations etc. That have taken place in Newcastle and Gateshead* (Newcastle, 1821).
100 Adam Ferguson, *An Essay on the History of Civil Society* (Edinburgh, 1767), 104. In France, of course, tradesmen were even required to wear badges, designating their *métier*. Socially appropriate dress was considered insufficient as a means of identifying an individual's place or *niveau*. (Richard Cobb, *The Police and the People* (Oxford, 1970), 25.) Social identification through external appearance and dress was such that the revolutionary group *par excellence*, the *sans-culottes*, have been sartorially so identified ever since.
101 For these price riots see Thompson, 'Moral Economy', *P & P* 50 (1971), esp. 107–20; Louise A. Tilly, 'The Food Riot as a Form of Political Conflict in France', *Journal of Interdisciplinary History* II, i (1971), 23–5.
102 Rudé, *Wilkes and Liberty*, 164. Perhaps the nicest example of this sort of symbolic justice occurred in Alnwick in April 1770: 'a big Fox, which had been kept some

Time for the Purpose, was set off in the Neighbourhood of Alnwick, with a Collar round his Neck, on which was engraved, in huge Characters, *A publick Defaulter.* He was soon run down, and made a poor Shift for his Life, which was imputed to the Weight of Metal he carried about him.' (*York Courant,* 1 May 1770.) The reference should be obvious.

103 J. T. Smith, *Book for a Rainy Day* (1845), 8n.; Bleakley, *Life of Wilkes,* facing 200. This list has been compiled after investigation in several museums.

104 Chandos to George Grenville, 23 March 1769. *Grenville Papers,* iv, 415–17; *Cambridge Chronicle,* 26 March 1768.

105 Rudé, *Paris and London,* 234; Cf. the following lines which appeared in the *Patriotic Miscellany* (1769), 73: 'Let slav'ry's sons on lavish measures dwell,/Our rights infringe, our patriot Wilkes expel;/He boasts a seat, in spite of all their art,/He sits enthron'd in ever'y Britons heart.'

106 See for instance Hitchcock's description of the public meeting in Holborn to celebrate Wilkes's birthday in 1769. (Guildhall Mss 3332/1 p. 391.)

107 J. Spiller to Proctor, 20 May 1769, Beauchamp Proctor Papers; *Cambridge Chronicle,* 17 September 1769; Gerald Miller, *English Inn Signs. Being a Revised and Modernised Version of the History of Signboards, by Jacob Larwood and J. C. Hotten* (1951), 48.

108 *Middlesex Journal,* 17 April 1770.

109 R. W. Malcolmson, *Popular Recreations in English Society 1700–1850* (Cambridge, 1973), 64.

110 Rudé, *Wilkes and Liberty,* 43–4. Thus John Green said to his lodger, 'let me have some candles, don't let me have my windows broke on the account of Mr. Wilkes or any one else'. (*Old Bailey Proceedings* (1768), 212.)

111 Rudé, *Wilkes and Liberty,* 43; *Leeds Mercury,* 7 February 1769; *Cambridge Chronicle,* 12 November 1768; *Norwich Mercury,* 26 March 1768.

112 [Mandtypo], *Britannia's Intercession for the Happy Deliverance of John Wilkes* (1768), no pagination.

113 *General Evening Post,* 17 April 1770. Compare the ceremony arranged for Wilkes's birthday in November 1768 (*Cambridge Chronicle,* 5 November 1768) and the occasion described in the Broadside, *Number Forty-Five; or, the Ghost of the North Briton, Lord Granby for Ever* (1769), s.s. For similar plays on the number 45 in North America see Pauline Maier, *From Resistance to Revolution* (New York, 1972), 170, 193, 205.

114 Thompson, 'Moral Economy', *P & P* 50 (1971), 95–7; Robert F. Wearmouth, *Methodism and the Common People of the Eighteenth Century* (1945), 143–4, 147–9. It is interesting to notice that the most common form of punishment inflicted on Methodist ministers was 'ducking', the same punishment as that for being a scold.

115 For 1760s examples see *Old Bailey Proceedings* (1770), 24; PRO Treasury Solicitors Papers 11/818/2696; SP 37/6/80/13. Other examples can be found in Rudé, *Crowd in History,* 160; F. Peel, *The Risings of the Luddites,* ed. E. P. Thompson (4th ed., 1968), 78; Gwyn Lewis, 'The White Terror of 1815 in the Department of the Gard', *P & P* 58 (1973), 130; Maier, *From Resistance to Revolution,* 7; E. J. Hobsbawm and George Rudé, *Captain Swing* (1973 ed.), 178; *Bulletin of the Society for the Study of Labour History* 25 (1972), 10–11.

116 This terminology needs some explanation. Developing the ideas of Van Gennep, Victor Turner has laid particular emphasis on the intermediate or liminal stage in the rites of passage. Van Gennep's three phases are separation, margin or transition (i.e. Turner's liminal), and aggregation. Turner cites the example of the installation of the Kanongesha of the Ndembu. This chief-elect is ceremonially humiliated and insulted, being treated in a worse manner than his fellow tribesmen, before being admitted to the exalted status of chief. This intermediate stage, being one when he is neither citizen nor chief, serves to emphasise the importance of the change in status. Furthermore, in the intermediate stage, Turner argues,

customary social distinctions of hierarchy and status cease to apply. But certain liminal characters – in this case those who humiliate the king – act the part of guardians of the community conscience and community values, expressing the values of *communitas*, of an egalitarian social order. (Victor W. Turner, *The Ritual Process. Structure and Anti-Structure* (1969), 95–102.) This sort of model, provided it is treated with appropriate caution, seems to me to be extremely useful when examining crowd behaviour. In a fairly obvious sense a crowd situation is a liminal one: customary social rules are suspended yet, as often as not, no separate and distinct set are there to replace them. Such rules and patterns of behaviour as do exist derive their meaning, form and significance from the symbiotic relationship that the crowd has with the existing social order. At the same time some crowds also clearly do seek to express *communitas*, or a set of values unencumbered by the pragmatic considerations of an established social order. *Communitas*, for instance, seems singularly appropriate as a designation of Thompson's 'moral economy', and the Wilkite notion of 'Liberty' could also be so described. Liminal hierarchies are also a feature common to crowds and other liminal groups. Not only Wilkites with their emphasis on Wilkite rule, but most crowds, Chicago street gangs, Chinese secret societies, and criminal and bandit groups all exhibit such characteristics. (Turner, *Ritual Process*, 192–4; Hobsbawm and Rudé, *Captain Swing*, 174; Geoffrey Parker, 'Mutiny and Discontent in the Spanish Army of Flanders, 1572–1607', *P & P* 58 (1973), 40; Hobsbawm, *Primitive Rebels*, 21, 27, 51; E. P. Thompson, *The Making of the English Working Class* (Penguin ed., 1968), 601, 620.) One difficulty with this approach is that it may overlook the thorny problem of how insurrectionary or revolutionary the crowd is. This, however, is a problem that can only be resolved by considering the relationship between the values and attitudes of particular crowds and dissident groups, and the ideas and attitudes of authority.

117 Elias Canetti, *Crowds and Power* (Penguin ed., 1973), 21–4, 32.
118 Rudé, *Paris and London*, 236–7.
119 *Wilkes's Jest Book; or the Merry Patriot* (1770), 2, 8.
120 For this incident see *Leeds Mercury*, 4 April 1769.
121 Sutherland, *City of London and the Opposition to Government*, 11–12.
122 Thompson, *The Making of the English Working Class*, 87.
123 Add. Mss 30884 f. 72.
124 See, for instance, *Wilkes and Loyalty*, Madden Ballad collection 6/1940.
125 Maier, *From Resistance to Revolution*, 5.
126 E.g. *Williamson's Liverpool Advertiser*, 8 April 1768; *Norwich Mercury*, 4 February, 20 May, 1 July 1769; *Cambridge Chronicle*, 19 November, 3 December 1768; *ibid*, 20 January, 31 March 1770.
127 *Leeds Mercury*, 28 February 1769.
128 For this idea see Malcolmson, *Popular Recreations in English Society*, 75–7.
129 This I infer from Enid Welsford, *The Fool. His Social and Literary History* (1935), 211–12.
130 For physiognomic distortion and sexual potency see William Willeford, *The Fool and his Sceptre* (1969), 10–15. For attacks on Wilkes's sexuality, and its connection with his political licentiousness see *A History of the Jack Wilks* [*sic*] (2 vols., 1769), *passim*, and 'A WHATS TO COME CHRONICLE' in *Battle of the Quills: or, Wilkes attacked and defended* (1768), 30–1, where Wilkes is described as an infidel and non-believer who wishes to introduce legislation to legalise rape and adultery. This relationship between domestic or personal conduct and notions of civil government was an eighteenth-century commonplace. It is well illustrated by the different treatment accorded Sophie by Squire Western and his sister. The former, a good Tory, tries force, arbitrary measures and confinement to keep her from Tom Jones; the latter, in good Hanoverian, courtly style, attempts to use subtlety and guile. (See esp. Book Six, Ch. 14 of Henry Fielding, *The History of Tom Jones*.)

131 See Welsford, *The Fool*, Ch. IV; Max Gluckman, *Politics, Law and Ritual in Tribal Society* (Oxford, 1965), 102–4.
132 Welsford, *The Fool*, 223.
133 Willeford, *Fool and his Sceptre*, 114.
134 *Walpole Letters* VII, 366–7.
135 *Town and Country Magazine* (1770), 265–6; *Gentleman's Magazine* (1770), 98.
136 *BM Catalogue of Prints and Drawings*, no. 4375. Hogarth's caricature of Wilkes makes him look like a fool, especially as the staff of maintenance looks like a fool's staff. There is some resemblance between this caricature and Quinten Massys' 'Allegory of Folly'.
137 Newspaper cutting interleaved in *The Correspondence of John Wilkes*, i, no pagination. This is in the Cambridge University Library copy. I have been unable to trace its source of origin.
138 *Norwich Mercury*, 7 January 1769.
139 *Cambridge Chronicle*, 2 April 1768; *Norwich Mercury*, 4 February 1769.
140 Rudé, *Wilkes and Liberty*, 151–5.
141 A. M. Broadley, *Brother John Wilkes as Freemason,'Buck','Leech' and Beefsteak* (1914), *passim*; *Leeds Mercury*, 21, 28 February, 14, 21 March 1769; *Norwich Mercury*, 4 March 1769; State Papers Entry Books 44/142/ff. 114–15; Lillywhite, *London Coffee Houses*, 88, 531.
142 John Amies to John Wilkes, 14 June 1764, Add. Mss 30868 f. 89; [Onslow to Newcastle], [30 April 1766], Add. Mss 32975 f. 58; Lillywhite, *Coffee Houses*, 256, 273, 440, 463; *Leeds Mercury*, 21 February 1769; Knox to George Grenville, 10 November 1769, *Grenville Papers*, iv, 479; Lane, *Masonic Records*, 43, 73, 105, 136, 138, 154, 170.
143 Lillywhite, *Coffee Houses*, 235–6; Lane, *Masonic Records*, 34.
144 Lillywhite, *Coffee Houses*, 91, 435; *Leeds Mercury* 28 February, 21 March, 18 April 1769; *Cambridge Chronicle*, 14 April 1770. *Connoisseur* XIX (6 June 1754) gives a good idea of the difference between the city taverns and coffee houses frequented by the merchant community, and those nearer the court where affluence and conspicuous consumption were more apparent.
145 *Newcastle Journal*, 1 April 1769.
146 *Leeds Mercury*, 18 April 1769.
147 *Cambridge Chronicle*, 28 April 1770.
148 The most readily available account of this complex problem is Bernard E. Jones, *Freemason's Guide and Compendium* (1956), 193–212.
149 H. de Strange, 'The Great Lodge, Swaffham, Norfolk 1764–1785', *AQC* XX (1907), 246–7.
150 F. W. Levander, 'The Jerusalem Sols and some other London Societies of the Eighteenth Century', *AQC* XXV (1912), 29–30.
151 Jones, *Freemason's Guide*, 163.
152 W. H. Rylands, 'A Forgotten Rival of Masonry: The Noble Order of Bucks', *AQC* II (1890), 140–9; William Hickey, *Memoirs 1749–1809* (4 vols., 1913–15), I, 119; *Connoisseur* LIV (8 February 1755).
153 *Leeds Mercury*, 25 April 1769.
154 Sutherland, *City of London and the Opposition to Government*, 13, 21.
155 Rudé, *Wilkes and Liberty*, 149–54.
156 Rudé, *Wilkes and Liberty*, 74–89.
157 PRO SP Dom. 37/6/80/13.
158 *Newcastle Journal*, 15 April 1769.
159 Rogers, 'Aristocratic Clientage, Trade and Independency' *P & P* 61 (1973), 70–106.
160 Sutherland, *City of London and the Opposition to Government*, 11.

10. American ideology and British radicalism

1 For this problem see Namier, *England*, 273–82; L. H. Gipson, *The British Empire Before the American Revolution* (15 vols., New York, 1936–70), vol. 9.

2 E. S. and H. M. Morgan, *The Stamp Act Crisis: Prologue to Revolution* (Chapel Hill, N.C., 1953), 67, 70.

3 *Political Debates* (Paris [i.e. London], 1766), *passim*; P. D. G. Thomas (ed.), 'The Parliamentary Diaries of Nathaniel Ryder, 1764–7', *Camden Miscellany* XXIII (1969), 254–6, 282–3, 287–9, 316–17; George Grenville to Thomas Whately, 12, 23 July 1767, GLB, vol. 2, no foliation, Huntington Library; Grenville to Clive, 19 July 1767, *ibid*; Grenville to Colden, 28 July 1768, *ibid*; George Grenville to Knox, 16 August 1768, *ibid*.

4 P. Langford, 'The Rockingham Whigs and America, 1767–1773' in Whiteman *et al.*, *Statesmen, Scholars and Merchants*, 135–52; Dowdeswell to Rockingham, 10 January 1767, Dowdeswell Mss; Ross Hoffman, *The Marquis. A Study of Lord Rockingham, 1730–1782* (New York, 1973), 109–10.

5 Thomas R. Adams, *American Independence, The Growth of an Idea* (Providence, R.I., 1965), 1–65; Charles Evans, *American Bibliography* (14 vols., New York, 1903–59), nos. 8584–5, 8751, 9489, 9542–4, 10112–13, 10273, 10300–3, 10402, 10462–3, 10663, 11119, 11191, 11305, 11310, 11471, 11532, 11693.

6 Maier, *From Resistance to Revolution*, 168–9; G. H. Guttridge (ed.), *The American Correspondence of a Bristol Merchant, 1766–1796. The Letters of Richard Champion* (Berkeley, Calif., 1934), 16–18; Charles Goore to R. H. Lee, 14 August 1766, *Lee Family Papers, 1742–1795*, ed. Paul P. Hoffmann (University of Virginia microfilm, Charlottesville, Va.), Roll 1; R. H. Lee, *The Life of Arthur Lee, Ll.D* (2 vols., Boston, 1829), I, 245; Charles Steuart to James Parker, 11 September, 15 November 1763, 29 January, 4 May 1764, 11 February, 18 April, 26 May 1770, Parker Mss 920/1/27/2, 3, 5, 6, 10, 28–30.

7 [Onslow to Newcastle], [30 April 1766], Add. Mss 32975 f. 58; Langford, *First Rockingham Administration*, 119–20.

8 M. G. Kammen, *A Rope of Sand: The Colonial Agents, British Politics and the American Revolution* (Ithica, N.Y., 1968), 85–7, 89; L. W. Labaree (ed.), *The Papers of Benjamin Franklin* (18 vols. to date, New Haven, Conn., 1959), XII, 184; XV, 37.

9 Kammen, *Rope of Sand*, 90; [William Bollan], *Continued Corruption, Standing Armies, and Popular Discontents Considered* (1768), *passim*.

10 [Arthur Lee], *The Political Detection; or, the Treachery and Tyranny of Administration, Both at Home and Abroad* (1770), 150.

11 Lee, *Life of Arthur Lee*, I, 245.

12 Arthur Lee to R. H. Lee, 3 December 1769, *Life of Lee*, I, 193.

13 R. H. Lee to Arthur Lee, 5 April 1770, *Lee Papers*, Roll 2; Adams, *American Independence*, 40–1; Strahan Ledgers, Add. Mss 48801 f. 40.

14 Bernard Bailyn, *Pamphlets of the American Revolution, vol. 1, 1750–1765* (Cambridge, Mass., 1965), 32.

15 Caroline Robbins, 'The Strenuous Whig, Thomas Hollis of Lincoln's Inn', *WMQ* 3rd Series 7 (1950), 433, 435, 437–40; Kammen, *Rope of Sand*, 91.

16 See, for example, *Annual Register*, 1765, 50–5; *Gazetteer*, 1 February 1766; *Political Register* III (1768), 87–93, 138–44, 354–75; IV (1769), 27–31; V (1769), 98–106; *Cambridge Chronicle*, 28 April 1770.

17 'E', *Public Advertiser*, 4 January 1766; Anon., *Gazetteer*, 22 January 1766; [Thomas Hollis], *The True Sentiments of America: Contained in a Collection of Letters* (1768), 141; [Lee], *Political Detection* (1770), 65–7; Junius Americanus to Chatham, n.d., Lee, *Life of Lee*, I, 21; Maier, *From Resistance to Revolution*, 381.

18 See pp. 251–3.

19 Cannon, *Parliamentary Reform*, 60.

20 J. R. Pole, *Political Representation in England and the Origins of the American Republic* (1966), 427.
21 Cannon, *Parliamentary Reform*, 45–6.
22 Christie, *Myth and Reality*, 245.
23 Lucy Sutherland, 'The City of London in Eighteenth-Century Politics' in Pares and Taylor (eds.), *Essays Presented to Sir Lewis Namier*, 49–74.
24 Cannon, *Parliamentary Reform*, 56–9.
25 The information for this paragraph is based on Pole, *Political Representation*, 414, 417–19; Cannon, *Parliamentary Reform*, 24–5; Caroline Robbins, *The Eighteenth-Century Commonwealthman* (Cambridge, Mass., 1959), 193, 357.
26 [William Knox], *The Controversy Between Great Britain and her Colonies Reviewed* (1769), 11.
27 [Soame Jenyns], *The Objections to the Taxation of our American Colonies by the Legislature of Great Britain, briefly considered* (1765), 6. Cf. *An Examination of the Rights of the Colonies, upon the Principles of Law. By A Gentleman at the Bar* (1766), 15.
28 Bailyn, *Pamphlets of the American Revolution*, 601. The wording of the pamphlet bears a marked resemblance to George Grenville's comments in the House of Commons (*Political Debates*, 9).
29 [Thomas Whately], *The Regulations lately made concerning the Colonies, and the Taxes imposed upon them, considered* (1765), 108.
30 George Grenville to William Knox, 16 August 1768, GLB, vol. 2.
31 Pole, *Political Representation*, 442–57.
32 [Josiah Tucker], *A Letter from a Merchant in London to his Nephew in North America* (1766), 20. Cf. [Jenyns], *Objections to Taxation* (1765), 8.
33 Further exposition of this view can be found in [Matthew Wheelock], *Reflections, Moral and Political on Great Britain and her Colonies* (1770), Preface; 'A.Z', *Public Advertiser*, 20 February 1766; 'VINDEX PATRIAE', *Gazetteer*, 23 December 1765, 3 January 1766; 'RECTUS', *ibid*, 4 February 1766. Bailyn, *Pamphlets of the American Revolution*, 599–603, provides a good summary of this view.
34 [George B. Butler], *The Case of Great Britain and America, Addressed to the King, and both Houses of Parliament* (Dublin, 1769), 6.
35 Bernard Bailyn, *The Ideological Origins of the American Revolution* (Cambridge, Mass., 1967), 167–8.
36 Champion to Caleb and John Lloyd, 12 May 1770, Guttridge (ed.), *American Correspondence*, 18.
37 [Lee], *Political Detection* (1770), 75.
38 *A Letter to the Right Honourable the Earl of Hilsborough* [*sic*], *on the present Situation of Affairs in America* (1769), 83. Cf. [John Dickinson], *Letters from a Farmer in Pennsylvania, to the Inhabitants of the British Colonies* (1768), 53–4; [Stephen Hopkins], *The Grievances of the American Colonies Candidly Examined* (1766), 33–4; [Edward Bancroft], *Remarks on the Review of the Controversy between Great Britain and her Colonies* (1769), 95; [Butler], *Case of Great Britain and America* (1769), 9; 'A FRIEND TO CIVIL LIBERTY', *Gazetteer*, 17 February 1766; Labaree (ed.), *Papers of Benjamin Franklin*, XV, 37.
39 [Lee], *Political Detection* (1770), 75.
40 [Butler], *Case of Great Britain and America* (1769), 7.
41 [John Fothergill], *Considerations relative to the North American Colonies* (1765), 27. Cf. 'AMOR PATRIAE', *Gazetteer*, 1 January 1766.
42 *The Mutual Interest of Great Britain and the American Colonies Considered* (1765), 4; 'Extract of a Letter from a Gentleman in Virginia to his Friend in this City', *Farley's Bristol Journal*, 10 August 1765.
43 George Grenville to William Knox, 16 August 1768, GLB, vol. 2; [Richard Bland], *An Enquiry into the Rights of the British Colonies* (1769), 9.
44 Cannon, *Parliamentary Reform*, 60.

45 *Reflexions on Representation in Parliament* (1766), 13.
46 [W. Bollan], *A Succinct View of our Colonies...Being an Extract from an Essay lately published, entitled, the Freedom of Speech and Writing* (1966), 25; [Bancroft], *Remarks on the Review* (1769), 93–4; [Butler], *Case of Great Britain and America* (1769), 23; [Langrische], *Considerations on the Dependencies of Great Britain. With Observations on a Pamphlet, intitled, The Present State of the Nation* (1769), 76; Labaree (ed.), *Papers of Benjamin Franklin* XII, 184; Frederick J. Hinkhouse, *The Preliminaries of the American Revolution as seen in the English Press, 1763–1775* (New York, 1926), 90.
47 *Monthly Review* XXXIII (1765), 398–9.
48 [James Otis], *Considerations on behalf of the Colonists. In a Letter to a Noble Lord* (2nd ed., 1765), 5–6.
49 'Anon', *Public Advertiser*, 3 February 1766. Cf. 'JOHN PLOUGHMAN', *ibid*, 17 February 1766.
50 'PACIFICUS', *Gazetteer*, 10 December 1765.
51 [Bancroft], *Remarks on the Review* (1769), 93. Cf. 'C', *Public Advertiser*, 4 February 1766.
52 *Reflexions on Representation* (1766), 4.
53 [Bland], *Enquiry into Rights* (1769), 10.
54 *Reflexions on Representation* (1766), 26–7; [Joshua Steele], *An Account of a late Conference on the Occurrences in America. In a Letter to a Friend* (1766), *passim*; 'FRIBOURG', *Public Advertiser*, 19 December 1765.
55 [F. Maseres], *Considerations on the Expediency of admitting representatives from the American Colonies into the British House of Commons* (1770), *passim*; 'AMOR PATRIAE', *Gazetteer*, 1 January 1766; 'RATIONALIS', *Owen's Weekly Chronicle*, 11 January 1766.
56 'ACHERLEY', *Gazetteer*, 20 February 1766.
57 'REGULUS', *Political Register* II (1768), 222.
58 *Reflexions on Representation* (1766), 16–17.
59 'REGULUS', *Political Register* II (1768), 225. Cf. 'A BRITON', *Public Advertiser*, 10 February 1766.
60 *Reflexions on Representation* (1766), 6.
61 *Ibid*, 5.
62 'REGULUS', *Political Register* II (1768), 225–6.
63 Burgh, *Political Disquisitions* (1774–5), I, 37–8.
64 John Cartwright, *Take Your Choice!* (1777), 20–1; *Give us our Rights!* [1782], 12, 17, 43.
65 Read, *Peterloo*, 129.
66 Sutherland, *The City of London and the Opposition to Government*, 10–11.
67 *Leeds Mercury*, 11 April 1769.
68 Maier, *From Resistance to Revolution*, 199–200.

11. The politicians, the press and the public

1 F. J. Siebert, *The Freedom of the Press in England, 1476–1776* (Urbana, Ill., 1952), 320–1; Cranfield, *Provincial Newspaper*, 17–18.
2 'State of the Revenue arising from Stamps (1764)', Add. Mss 38338 f. 128.
3 Walpole, *Memoirs of George III*, i, 316.
4 *Parliamentary History* XVI, 1360–71.
5 Rea, *English Press in Politics*, 168–70.
6 Post Office Records, Treasury Letter Book June 1760 to March 1771, Post 9/252; Cranfield, *Provincial Newspaper*, 179–80.
7 Daniel Stow Memorandum, 10 March 1832, Post Office Records Post 24/4.
8 Daniel Stow Memorandum, 10 March 1832, Post Office Records Post 24/4; Kenneth Ellis, *The Post Office in the Eighteenth Century: A Study in Administrative History* (1958), 52–3, 158–9.

9 T. Patten to Newdigate, 31 March 1768, Newdigate Mss B22/2212.
10 Holland to Sir George Macartney, 20 December 1765, Add. Mss 51389 f. 45; Memorandum, Hatfield House, Chase Price Mss D48; Dodington to Bute, 8 October 1761, J. Carswell and L. A. Dralle (eds.), *The Political Journal of Bubb Dodington, Lord Melcombe* (Oxford, 1965), 427.
11 James Ralph to Bute, 13 December 1761, Bute Mss 1761/695.
12 Campbell to Bute, 5 June 1762, Bute Mss.
13 Guthrie to Bute, 30 December 1762, Bute Mss (Cardiff), 3/44; J. Shebbeare to [Jenkinson], 30 July 1762, Bute Mss 1762/254.
14 Baillie to Bute, 13 November, 27 November, [6 December], 23 December 1762, Bute Mss (Cardiff) 1/44–7; Baillie to Bute, 3 September 1762, Bute Mss 1762/393.
15 Baillie to Bute, 8 August 1762, Bute Mss 1762/285.
16 Baillie to Bute, 21 October 1762, Bute Mss 1762/556.
17 Richardson to Jenkinson, Tuesday night [December 1763], *Jenkinson Papers*, 247.
18 Richardson to [Jenkinson], 17 March [1762], Bute Mss (Cardiff) 5/136; Richardson to [Jenkinson], [24 March], *ibid* 11/67; *Jenkinson Papers*, 69–70, 71, 145–6, 162–3.
19 Richardson to Jenkinson, 11 September 1762, Bute Mss 1762/420; *Monitor*, 18 September 1762.
20 For Bute's distribution of pensions see Bute to Campbell, Friday [30 October 1761], Bute Mss 1761/663; Campbell to Bute, 31 October 1761, Bute Mss (Cardiff) 1/164; Bute to Campbell, Wednesday [October 1761], Thursday [21 January 1762], Bute Mss; Campbell to Bute, 5 May 1761, Bute Mss; *Jenkinson Papers*, 69; Namier, *Structure of Politics*, 229; Rea, *English Press in Politics*, 23, 37, 102; 'Memorandum', 22 October 1761, Add. Mss 32929 f. 435.
21 Campbell to Bute, 28 November 1761, Bute Mss 1761/663; Add. Mss 36796 f. 121.
22 Rea, *English Press in Politics*, 21–4; Ilchester, *Henry Fox, First Lord Holland. His Family and Relations* (2 vols., 1920), ii, 154.
23 Fox to Francis [December 1761], Add. Mss 51405 f. 2; Ralph to Bute [early October 1761], 7 October [1761], 28 October [1761], Bute Mss (Cardiff) 5/125, 126, 127.
24 Bute to Campbell, Friday [30 October 1761], Bute Mss; Campbell to Bute, 28, 30, 31 October, 9 November, 26 December 1761, Bute Mss (Cardiff) 1/162, 163, 164, 166, 167; Jenkinson to Bute [December 1761], *ibid* 3/116.
25 Campbell to Bute, 28 November 1761, Bute Mss 1761/663.
26 Campbell to Bute, 16 June 1762, Bute Mss.
27 Bute to Campbell, Saturday night [10 April 1762], Bute Mss.
28 Campbell to Bute, 2 February 1762, Bute Mss (Cardiff) 1/172. Cf. Campbell to Bute, 6, 10 February 1762, *ibid* 1/173, 174.
29 Bute to Campbell, Friday [26 February 1762], Bute Mss.
30 Campbell to Bute, 17 July, 10, 16 August 1762, Bute Mss.
31 Campbell to Bute, 18 February, 18 March, 4 April, 4 April (*sic*), 20 July, 22 August, 11 November 1763, Bute Mss (Cardiff) 9/45, 47, 48, 49, 53, 55, 56.
32 Richardson to Jenkinson, 11 September 1762, Bute Mss 1762/420; Newcastle to Hardwicke, 29 November 1762, Add. Mss 32945 f. 199.
33 Philo-Patriae to Bute, 23 February 1763, Bute Mss; Dodington to Bute, 18 June, 10 July 1762, Bute Mss (Cardiff) 2/92, 93; *Bubb Dodington's Political Journal*, 438–9; Courteville to Bute, 11 February, 17 March 1763, Bute Mss (Cardiff) 9/84, 87; Courteville to Jenkinson, 15, 18 February 1763, *ibid* 9/85, 86; Dodington to Bute, 19 December 1760, Add. Mss 36796 f. 64.
34 Brewer, 'Misfortunes of Lord Bute', *HJ* xvi (1973), esp. 11–12, 16–18.
35 Namier, *Structure of Politics*, 229.
36 See, for example, Newcastle to Devonshire, 21 October 1761, Add. Mss 32929 f. 428; Newcastle to Devonshire, 22 October 1761, *ibid* f. 437; Newcastle to Devonshire, 6 July 1764, Add. Mss 32960 f. 194.

37 Newcastle to Hardwicke, 30 September 1762, Add. Mss 32942 f. 429.
38 Newcastle to Hardwicke, 26 November 1762, Add. Mss 32945 f. 153; Newcastle to Hardwicke, 27 November 1762, *ibid* f. 160; J. West to Newcastle, 28 November 1762, *ibid* f. 178; Newcastle to Hardwicke, 29 November 1762, *ibid* f. 199.
39 Newcastle to Legge, 18 May 1763, Add. Mss 32948 f. 314.
40 Charles Townshend to Newcastle [30 April 1764], Add. Mss 32958 f. 250.
41 Newcastle to Devonshire, 6 May 1764, Add. Mss 32958 f. 318; Fitzherbert to Wilkes, 19 July 1764, Add. Mss 30868 f. 96; Almon to Wilkes, 23 October 1764, *ibid* f. 137; Newcastle to Cumberland, 5 May 1764, Add. Mss 32958 f. 250.
42 Bentinck to Portland, 8 October 1765, Portland Mss PwF 1219.
43 See, for instance, Dowdeswell to Burke, 4 January 1766 [should be 1767], Dowdeswell Mss, William Clements Library; Rockingham to Burke, 15 October 1769, *Burke Correspondence*, ii, 92; Burke to Rockingham, 29 December 1770, *ibid*, ii, 175.
44 A good example of this problem occurred in 1764 with the publication of *An Enquiry into the Doctrine Lately Propagated Concerning Libels* (1764), which was probably written by the Chathamite Dunning. Because the pamphlet was critical of the late Lord Hardwicke as well as of the ministers, it never gained full approval from the Newcastle–Rockingham wing of the opposition, and to a certain extent helped divide those who opposed George Grenville. (T. Walpole to Newcastle, 5 December 1764, Add. Mss 32964 f. 202; Newcastle to T. Walpole, 8 December 1764, *ibid* f. 234; Grantham to Newcastle, 21 December 1764, *ibid* f. 353; Newcastle to Rockingham, 3 January 1765, Add. Mss 32965 f. 26; Charles Yorke to Hardwicke (2), 30 December 1764, Add. Mss 35361 f. 135.)
45 Newcastle to Powell, 9 July 1764, Add. Mss 32960 f. 227. The manuscript of the text of the pamphlet is in the Buccleuch muniments, ScRO GD 224/296/10.
46 Newcastle to Townshend, 25 August 1764, Add. Mss 32961 f. 358.
47 Rockingham to Newcastle, 15 September 1764, Add. Mss 32962 f. 114.
48 Thomas Walpole to Charles Townshend, 27 September 1764, *ibid* f. 158.
49 Rea, *English Press in Politics*, 108; *Walpole Letters*, vi, 111.
50 Charles Townshend to Thomas Walpole, 23 September 1764, Add. Mss 32962 ff. 146–7.
51 Rockingham to Newcastle, 23 November 1764, Add. Mss 32964 f. 94; Newcastle to Onslow, 24 November 1764, *ibid* f. 103; Onslow to Newcastle, Sunday morning [25 November 1764], *ibid* f. 114; Onslow to Newcastle, Wensday (*sic*) morning [12 December 1764], *ibid* f. 262; William Meredith to Portland, 1 November 1764, Portland Mss PwF 6709.
52 Legge to Newcastle, 25 April 1764, Add. Mss 32958 f. 207.
53 Onslow to Newcastle, 19 May 1764, Add. Mss 32958 f. 455; Newcastle to Rockingham, 23 May 1764, Add. Mss 32959 f. 43.
54 Rea, *English Press in Politics*, 95–7.
55 Onslow to Newcastle, 24 March 1765, Add. Mss 32966 f. 96.
56 Newcastle to Onslow, 26 March 1765, *ibid* f. 103.
57 Hartley to Newcastle, 11 April 1765, *ibid* f. 183.
58 Rea, *English Press in Politics*, 97; Dowdeswell to Burke, 4 January 1769, Dowdeswell Mss.
59 T. Fetherstonehaugh to Portland, 15 August 1768, Portland Mss PwF 3673; Hartley to Portland, 7 February, 9 March 1768; *ibid* PwF 4842, 4845; Joseph Hudson to Portland, 21 January 1768, *ibid* PwF 5556; Francis Warwick to Portland, 15 August 1768, *ibid* PwF 8966.
60 Dowdeswell to Burke, 20 July 1769, Sheffield Mss Burke 1–124; Dowdeswell to Rockingham, 5 September 1769, Dowdeswell Mss; Burke to Rockingham, 30 July 1769, *Burke Correspondence*, ii, 50; Dowdeswell to Burke, 5 September 1769, *ibid*, ii, 69–70.

61 Burke to Rockingham, [24] November 1769, *Burke Correspondence*, ii, 113–14n.; Dowdeswell to Rockingham, 24 October 1769, Sheffield Mss RI-1242.
62 Rockingham to Burke, 15 May 1769, *Burke Correspondence*, ii, 25.
63 Meredith to Portland, 9 June 1769, Portland Mss PwF 6731.
64 Meredith to Portland, 11 December 1769, *ibid* PwF 6736; Rockingham to Portland, 17 December 1769, *ibid* PwF 9024.
65 Brewer, 'Party and the Double Cabinet', *HJ* xiv (1971), 485–8.
66 George Grenville to Nugent, 13 August 1765, GLB, vol. 2; Grenville to Weston, 19 October 1769. GLB, vol. 2.
67 Rea, *English Press in Politics*, 122–3; [John Almon], *Biographical, Literary and Political Anecdotes... By the Author of the Anecdotes of the late Earl of Chatham* (3 vols., 1797), ii, 108–11; Whately to Grenville, 13 June 1766, *Grenville Papers*, iii, 247; Whately to Grenville, 25 June 1766, *ibid*, 251. Grenville to Simon Fraser, 11 June 1766, GLB, vol. 2; Grenville to Whately, 26 June 1766, GLB, vol. 2.
68 Grenville to Whately, 14 August 1768, 17 September 1769. GLB, vol. 2; Grenville to Augustus Hervey, 5 June 1769, GLB, vol. 2; Whately–Temple Letters, Stowe Mss STG Box 13 no. 6; [Almon], *Biographical Anecdotes* (1797), ii, 103–4.
69 Grenville to Knox, 27 June, 28 July, 16 August, 11, 19 September 1768, GLB, vol. 2.
70 Grenville to Knox, 9 October 1768, GLB, vol. 2.
71 Walpole, *Memoirs of George III*, ii, 269; Rea, *English Press in Politics*, 123.
72 'Notes 1743–1779', West Suffolk RO Hervey Mss 941/50/5/293–6, 311–14, 337–41, 343–6, 405–12; Hervey to Grenville, 21 July 1767, *Grenville Papers*, iv, 20.
73 'Notes 1743–1779', Hervey Mss 941/50/5/387, 389, 505, 509–10.
74 'Notes 1743–1779', Hervey Mss 941/50/5/336. The text of the pamphlet runs pp. 317–36.
75 Burke, *Works*, i, 369.
76 'R.C.', *Gazetteer*, 11 February 1763. Compare the slightly different views of Beckford quoted by Lucy Sutherland, 'The City of London in Eighteenth-Century Politics' in Pares and Taylor (eds.), *Essays Presented to Sir Lewis Namier*, 66.
77 Chase Price to Portland, 19 August 1762, Portland Mss PwF 7901. The rather eccentric Dr John Brown defined 'the *People* of this *Kingdom* in their *Collective* Body' as 'all Those who send Representatives from the Counties to Parliament. This Catalogue will include the landed *Gentry*, the beneficed County *Clergy*, many of the more considerable *Merchants* and Men in *Trade*, the substantial and industrious *Freeholders* or *Yeomen*: A collective Body of Men, with all their incidental Failings, as *different* in Character from the Populace of any great *City*, as the *Air* of RICHMOND HILL from that of BILLINGSGATE or WAPPING.' ([John Brown], *Thoughts on Civil Liberty, on Licentiousness and Faction* (2nd ed., 1765), 87–8.)
78 *No Liberty! No Life!* (1768), 26–7.
79 Burke to Rockingham, 30 July 1769, *Burke Correspondence*, ii, 51–2.
80 Walpole, *Memoirs of George III*, ii, 2.
81 Burke, *Works*, i, 447.
82 Draft speech, Sheffield Mss Burke 8B.
83 D. H. Watson, *The Duke of Newcastle, the Marquis of Rockingham, and Mercantile Interests in London and the Provinces, 1761–1768* (Sheffield University, unpub. Ph.D., 1968), 129–37.
84 Watson, *Newcastle, Rockingham and Mercantile Interests* (unpub. Ph.D.), 294–447; Lucy S. Sutherland, 'Edmund Burke and the first Rockingham Ministry', *EHR* XLVII (1932), 46–72; Sir William Meredith to Burke, 11 December 1765, Sheffield Mss Burke 1–39a; Rockingham to Dowdeswell, 9 November 1767, *ibid* Rockingham 1–869; West to Newcastle, 16 November 1767, *ibid* Rockingham 1–876; 'QUERIES Addressed to the Author of a Paper sign'd a Freeman, Lancaster 30 November 1767', Portland Mss PwF 6723.

85 Rudé, *Wilkes and Liberty*, 106–7.
86 Rudé, *Wilkes and Liberty*, 107–8, 111–12.
87 This theme is developed further in John Brewer, 'Rockingham, Burke and Whig Political Argument', *HJ* XVIII, 1 (1975), 196–7.

12. The present discontents

1 Brewer, 'Misfortunes of Lord Bute', *HJ* XVI (1973), 5–12.
2 *HMC Rutland*, iv, 235; Walpole, *Memoirs of George III*, iv, 307.
3 Bradshaw to Grafton [March 1771], West Suffolk RO Grafton Mss 423/634.
4 This incident can be followed in Bedford Mss LI, *passim*, and Walpole, *Memoirs of George III*, ii, 155–9.
5 Rigby to Bedford, 9 March 1769, Bedford Mss LVIII f. 8; *ibid* LXIV f. 113.
6 Rudé, *Wilkes and Liberty*, 43–4.
7 'Political Reflexions on Government: Politicus Scientificus', *London Magazine* XXXIX (1770), 132. Cf. 'On the Constitution', *Freeholder's Magazine* I (1769), 60.
8 Bailyn, *Origins of American Politics*, 17–19.
9 *A Speech in behalf of the Constitution, against the Suspending and Dispensing Prerogative* (1767), 6; Montagu, *Reflections on the Rise and Fall of the Ancient Republics* (1759), 375.
10 Pares, *George III and the Politicians*, 31.
11 Montagu, *Reflections on the Rise and Fall of the Ancient Republics* (1759), 361.
12 For which see the excellent studies of J. G. A. Pocock, *Politics, Language and Time. Essays on Political Thought and History* (London, 1972), Chs. 3 and 4.
13 [John Hervey], *Miscellaneous Thoughts on the present posture both of our Foreign and Domestic Affairs* (1742), 5. Cf. *A Fair Trial of the Important Question* (1769), 226; 'Discourse on Government', *Universal Magazine* XLIII (1768), 5.
14 [Dowdeswell], *The Sentiments of an English Freeholder, on the late Decision of the Middlesex Election* (1769), 52. Cf. [J. Hanway], *A Morning's Thoughts on Reading the Test and Con-Test* (1757), 23.
15 *Northern Revolutions: or, the Principle Causes of the Declension and Dissolution of several once flourishing GOTHIC CONSTITUTIONS in EUROPE* (1757), 29; *An Application of some General Political Rules* (1766), 29.
16 [Spelman], *A Fragment out of the Sixth Book of Polybius* (1743), xv; *Ministerial Usurpation Displayed* (1760), 16.
17 John Brown, *Thoughts on Civil Liberty, on Licentiousness and Faction* (2nd ed., 1765), 108; [J. Towers], *Observations on Public Liberty, Patriotism, Ministerial Despotism and National Grievances* (1769), 28.
18 'PLAIN TRUTH', *Leeds Mercury*, 1 August 1769. Cf. *Parliamentary Spy* x, 23 January 1770.
19 For a more detailed exposition of this problem see Bernard Bailyn, *Ideological Origins of the American Revolution*, Ch. 2 'Power and Liberty: A Theory of Politics'.
20 The importance of the idea of an autonomous final authority is brought out in Lyttelton's speech in *Parliamentary History* XVI, 166.
21 Bailyn, *Origins of American Politics*, 20. It is important to realise that the term 'corruption' is used in a specific and technical sense. As John Pocock has pointed out, 'the term "corruption" is used to mean three things: first, the degenerative tendency to which all particular forms of government are prone; second, the specific cause of that degeneration, which is the dependence of some men upon other men when they should be depending upon all and upon themselves; and third, the moral degeneration of the individual who, in these circumstances, is prevented from developing his virtue by identifying his particular good with the good of all'. (Pocock, *Politics, Language and Time*, 88).
22 Montagu, *Reflections on the Rise and Fall of the Ancient Republics* (1759), 361. The

extent to which Polybius was associated with the idea of mixed government seems to have increased during the 1760s. Before that time he was rarely mentioned in political tracts, though there were notable exceptions – Spelman's *Fragment* published in 1743 (for which see note 16 above) and James Hampton's *A Parallel between the Roman and British Constitution; comprehending Polybius's curious discourse of the Roman Senate. With a preface, wherein his principles are applied to our Government* (1747). Indeed when Hampton published the first volume of *The general history of Polybius* in 1756 and provided the first full English translation since that of Henry Skears and Dryden of 1693, the reviewers were enthusiastic about the new availability of what they called this 'little known' history (*Monthly Review* xv (1756), 334). Hampton published further extracts in 1764 along with a preface that made it clear that he supported government, and by 1770 readers of periodicals were requesting extracts from Polybius to illuminate the current state of Great Britain (*Court and City Magazine* I (1770), 260).

23 *The Constitution. With an Address to a Great Man* (1757), 33.
24 *A Critical Review of the Liberties of British Subjects. By a Gentleman of the Middle Temple* (2nd ed., 1750), 5, Cf. 'DISCOURSE *on the* Perpetuity *of* Freedom *in the* British Constitution', *Universal Magazine* xxxiv (1764), 3-8; 'Fragments and Anecdotes', London Guildhall Wilkes Mss.
25 'On the Constitution of England', *Freeholder's Magazine* I (1769), 60.
26 *Parliamentary History* xvi, 661; *The Principles of a Real Whig…Reprinted at the Request of the London Association. To which are added their Resolutions and Circular Letter* (1775), 8; [Wilkes, trans.], *The Origin and Progress of Despotism in the Oriental, and other Empires, of Africa, Europe and America* (Amsterdam, 1764), 2; 'LUCULLUS', *Public Ledger*, 16 April 1770.
27 For which see Ch. 7 above.
28 Liberty, of course, was defined in terms of dependence on the law to which all had (even if only virtually) consented. (*Gazetteer*, 24 February 1765; *Parliamentary History* xv, 1384.)
29 *Monitor*, 16 October 1762.
30 *Parliamentary History* xvi, 818.
31 *Parliamentary History* xvi, 796. Cf. 'On Legislature', *London Magazine* xxxviii (1769), 462. As Bailyn has pointed out (*Origins of American Politics*, 21-2) the idea of a mixed, balanced constitution should not be confused with the idea of the separation of the three functioning branches of government – legislative, executive and judicial. As far as English eighteenth-century political rhetoric was concerned, talk of separating powers almost invariably referred to the relations between the executive and the legislature, between Crown and parliament, and very little was said about the judicature – although Bolingbroke discussed it and George Grenville, in attacking the government over the Middlesex election, stressed the need for an independent judiciary and cited Montesquieu to support his case. (Wright (ed.), *Cavendish's Debates*, i, 170-1; W. B. Gwyn, *The Meaning of the Separation of Powers. Tulane Studies in Political Science IX* (New Orleans, 1965), 93-4.)
32 *A Critical Review of Liberties* (1750), 4. Cf. *The Constitution asserted and vindicated* (1763), 36-7; *Memoirs of Thomas Hollis* (1780), 98.
33 Peter Gay, *The Enlightenment: an Interpretation* (2 vols., 1967-70), i, 12; ii, 24-5.
34 *Citizen* I (1764), 7.
35 'Anti-Sejanus' in *A New and Impartial Collection of Interesting Letters* (1767), ii, 65.
36 Wright (ed.), *Cavendish's Debates*, i, 15-16.
37 *Contrast* xxiii, 7 December 1763.
38 'An Essay on the Balance of Power', *Oxford Magazine* iii (1769), 134-5. One writer in the *Leeds Mercury* of 5 September 1769, appropriately named GALLICUS, even argued that the British constitution was in a constant state of contention or flux; Burke put forward a similar point of view in a draft speech on the Middlesex

election: 'For every complicated constitution (& every free constitution is complicated), cases will arise, when the several orders of the state will clash with one
another, & disputes will arise about the Limits of their Several Rights and
privileges.' (Northampton RO Fitzwilliam Mss (M) A i. 39A.)

39 Montagu, *Reflections on the Rise and Fall of the Ancient Republics* (1759), 362;
*Ministerial Patriotism Detected; or the Present Opposition Proved to be founded on Truly,
just and laudable Principles, By the Evidence of Facts* (1763), 9–10; Strahan to David
Hall, 7 October 1769, Pomfret, 'Further Letters of William Strahan', *Pennsylvania
Magazine of History and Biography* LX (1936), 473; Minto Mss EFP 33/36.

40 Hampton, *Two Extracts from the sixth book of the general history of Polybius, translated
from the Greek* (1764), 3–3v.

41 Pomfret, 'Further Letters of William Strahan', *Pennsylvania Magazine of History and
Biography* LX (1936), 473.

42 Hampton, *Two Extracts from Polybius*, 3.

43 *Parliamentary History* XVI, 692. Cf. [Ruffhead], *Considerations on the Present Dangerous
Crisis* (1763), 37.

44 *The Memoirs of Sir John Eardley-Wilmot* (1802), 61.

45 'The Dining List of the Opposition and Remarks thereupon, March 1763', Bute
Mss (Cardiff) 9/126.

46 Strahan to Hall, 22 May 1769, 'Correspondence between William Strahan and
David Hall, 1763–1777', *Pennsylvania Magazine of History and Biography* XI (1887),
104.

47 Townshend to Bute, 9 July 1768, Bute Mss 1768/37.

48 John Campbell to Jenkinson, 1 February 1773, Add. Mss 38207 f. 223. Cf. *Letter
to a Noble Member of the Club* (1764), 10.

49 Northington to Grafton, 9 July 1767, Grafton Mss 423/10.

50 *Parliamentary History* XVI, 704–5.

51 *Parliamentary History* XVI, 759. Cf. *ibid* XVI, 717. Exactly the same model was used
to explain the discontents in America. Thus the Lords' Address of Thanks on 8
November 1768 stated: 'We feel the most sincere concern, that any of our fellow
subjects in North America, should be misled by factious amd designing men into
acts of violence and of resistance to the execution of the law, attended with
circumstances that manifest a disposition to throw off their dependence upon Great
Britain.' (*ibid* XVI, 471.)

52 *Parliamentary History* XVI, 1180.

53 *Parliamentary History* XV, 1343; XVI, 1117, 1164; John Pringle to William Scot, 8
November 1765, *HMC Polwarth* V, 361; Hooper to James Harris, 26 October 1765,
Malmesbury (ed.), *A Series of Letters of the First Earl of Malmesbury, His Family and
his Friends from 1748 to 1820* (2 vols., 1870), i, 131–2; [Ruffhead], *Considerations on
the Present Dangerous Crisis* (1763), 47.

54 Allan Ramsay to [?], 7 May 1768, Add. Mss 51389 ff. 80–1. Burke, in characteristic
style, brilliantly summarised the government's case at the beginning of his *Thoughts
on the Cause of the Present Discontents*: 'Our ministers, are of opinion, that the
increase of our trade and manufactures, that our growth by colonisation and by
conquest, have concurred to accumulate immense wealth in the hands of some
individuals; and this again being dispersed among the people, has rendered them
universally proud, ferocious, and ungovernable; that the insolence of some from
their enormous wealth, and the boldness of others from a guilty poverty, have
rendered them capable of the most atrocious attempts; so that they have trampled
upon all subordination, and violently borne down the unarmed laws of free
government; barriers too feeble against the fury of the populace so fierce and
licentious as ours. They contend, that no adequate provocation has been given for
so spreading a discontent; our affairs have been conducted throughout with
remarkable temper and consummate wisdom. The wicked industry of some

libellers, joined to the intrigues of a few disappointed politicians, have, in their opinion, been able to produce this unnatural ferment in the nation.' (Burke, *Works*, i, 308–9.)

55 Wright (ed.), *Cavendish's Debates*, i, 101. Cf. *ibid*, i, 150.

56 Grenville stuck to this view, and gave it frequent reiteration, even after he had gone into opposition. (Grenville to Whately, 12 July 1767; Grenville to Clive, 19 July 1767; Grenville to Colden, 28 July 1768; Grenville to Hood, 30 October 1768; Grenville to Trevor, 24 February 1769, all GLB, vol. 2.)

57 'SORANUS' in *The Repository or Treasury of Politics and Literature... Being a Complete Collection of the best Letters and Essays from the Daily Papers* (2 vols., 1770–1), i, 456. Cf. *Parliamentary History* XVI, 1212; 'DECIUS', *Middlesex Journal*, 17 February 1770; Wright (ed.), *Cavendish's Debates*, i, 274; 'Discourse on CORRUPTION, as it tends to Political SLAVERY', *Universal Magazine* XLI (1767), 57; *A Speech in behalf of the Constitution* (1767), 135–6.

58 Burke, *Works*, i, 379.

59 Thomas, *House of Commons in the Eighteenth Century*, 15. This, of course, was in no way an original comment. Cf. Pitt's remarks in 1741 quoted in Williams, *William Pitt, Earl of Chatham*, i, 90.

60 'MENTOR', *Independent Chronicle*, 17 January 1770.

61 *A Fair Trial of the Important Question* (1769), 225; *Parliamentary Spy* II, 28 November 1769.

62 Egerton Mss 3711 f. 120.

63 See Plumb, *Growth of Political Stability in England*, esp. Ch. 4.

64 Cf. the remark that 'while the fountain then is corrupt, we must not wonder if the streams do not run very clear'. (*The Honest Elector's Proposal for Rendering the Votes of all Constituents, throughout the Kingdom, Free and Independent. By C. W.* (1767), 24.)

65 Fitzwilliam Mss A. i, 39B.

66 *A Refutation of a Pamphlet, called Thoughts on the Late Transactions respecting Falkland's Islands; In a Letter Addressed to the Author, and Dedicated to Dr. Samuel Johnson* (1771), 25. Compare the image employed by Cartwright – 'That parliamentary corruption which, at the revolution was an imperceptible embryo, and next a *little insect*, is at length become a huge, filthy and gluttonous monster'. (John Cartwright, *Take Your Choice!* (1777), 42.)

67 'The Picture of a MINISTERIAL DEPENDENT', *Weekly Amusement* I (1764), 140.

68 [William Meredith], *A Letter to Dr. Blackstone, By the Author of the Question Stated. To which is prefixed, Dr. Blackstone's Letter to Sir William Meredith* (1770), 40.

69 'A Memorial of Family Occurrences from 1760 to 70 inclusive', January 1771, Add. Mss 35428 f. 2, printed in Yorke, *Hardwicke*, iii, 260.

70 Cf. the general remarks made in the *Annual Register* (1763), 41–2.

71 *Fair Trial of the Important Question* (1769), 227. Cf. [Dowdeswell], *Sentiments of an English Freeholder* (1769), 56; Egerton Mss 3711 f. 146.

72 [John Butler], *Serious Considerations on the Measures of the Present Administration* (1763), 4.

73 G. Armytage to Rockingham, 2 January 1763, Sheffield Mss Rockingham I-348.

74 'A Briton', *London Magazine* XXXIII (1764), 524.

75 *The Englishman Deceived; a Political Piece* (1768), 28.

76 'ANTIMARTIALUS', *St James's Chronicle*, 9 January 1770; William Baker to Sir William Baker, 18 May 1768, Hertford RO Baker Mss 1/30; West to Newcastle, 7 December 1767, Add. Mss 32987 f. 192; *Parliamentary History* XVI, 996; Wright (ed.), *Cavendish's Debates*, i, 149–50.

77 [Towers], *Observations on Public Liberty*, 30. Cf. *An Examination into the Conduct of Lord M --- F --- D, through the Affair of Mr. Wilkes* (1768), 3–4; [Joseph Priestley], *The Present State of Liberty in Great Britain and her Colonies. By an Englishman* (1769), 20–2.

78 'To the People of England. An ENGLISHMAN', *Middlesex Journal*, 29 March 1770.
79 Champion to Caleb and John Lloyd, 2 October 1769, Guttridge (ed.), *American Correspondence of a Bristol Merchant*, 16.
80 [Lee], *Political Detection* (1770), 36, 72–3.
81 Maier, *From Resistance to Revolution*, 170–1, 187–91.
82 Egerton Mss 3711 f. 63; 'DISCOURSE on the Causes of DISORDERS, TUMULTS, and SEDITIONS in a STATE', *Universal Magazine* XLV (1769), 2.
83 Burke, *Works*, i, 369.
84 Pocock, *Politics, Language and Time*, Ch. 4, esp. 124–5; Kramnick, *Bolingbroke and his Circle*, esp. Chs. 3, 6.
85 Sutherland, *The City of London, and the Opposition to Government, 1768–1774*, 11–12.
86 'The Constitutional Right of Annual Elections, MARCELLUS', *Freeholder's Magazine* I (1769), 129. Cf. Newdigate Mss 2548/2; 'PLAIN TRUTH', *Leeds Mercury*, 1 August 1769; 'A Sketch of our Political Constitution. CATO JUNIOR', *Independent Chronicle*, 18 December 1769; Egerton Mss 3711 f. 176; *Parliamentary History* XVI, 178–9.
87 'How to obtain an independent, honest H - - - e of C - - - s without d - - - - g the present P - - - - - - - t', *London Packet*, 25 December 1769; *Honest Elector's Proposal* (1767), 18–20; 'ANON', *Leeds Mercury*, 21 March 1769; J. H. Plumb, 'Political Man', in Clifford (ed.), *Man Versus Society*, 15.
88 'On the ill effects of Court Influence upon the House of Commons', *Gazetteer*, 27 December 1769.
89 Egerton Mss 3711 ff. 19–20.
90 See pp. 213–16 above.
91 These were the objections put forward by Burke in his *Thoughts*. (Burke, *Works*, i, 365–6.)
92 'To the worthy Liverymen of the City of London', 5 October 1774, Baker Mss I/48.
93 This argument can be most readily followed in Burke's *Thoughts* (esp. Burke, *Works*, i, 365–81), but can be found expressed in most of the speeches made by Rockinghamites in this period.
94 *Parliamentary History* XVI, 833–41.
95 Fitzwilliam Mss A. i. 39A.
96 'Letters to a young Nobleman', *London Magazine* XXXI (1762), 76.
97 'M. South Street, August 18, 1770', *Political Register* VII (1770), 131.
98 Charles Townshend to Buccleuch, 10 Ju[ne] 1764, ScRO Buccleuch Mss GD 224/296/1/4.
99 *A genuine Collection of the several pieces of Political Intelligence* (1766), 26; 'Anti-Sejanus' in *New and Impartial Collection of Letters* (1767), ii, 28; *Parliamentary History* XVI, 995.
100 *Universal Magazine* XLV (1769), 198.
101 *North Briton* XXXVII; Allan Ramsay to [?], 7 May 1768, Add. Mss 51389 f. 81.
102 *Fair Trial of the Important Question* (1769), 227–8; [Edward King], *An Essay on the English Constitution and Government* (1767), 14; *An Application of Political Rules to Great Britain, Ireland and America* (1766), 17–20.
103 'On Travelling, ATTICUS', *Middlesex Journal*, 27 January 1770.
104 [Wilkes, trans.], *The Origin and Progress of Despotism* (1764), *passim*, esp. 126–7, 148; *New and Impartial Collection of Interesting Letters from the Public Papers* (1767), i, 317–18; 'REVERIES', *Oxford Magazine* III (1769), 65.
105 *Constitutional Guardian* V, 13 November 1770.
106 *An Essay on the Constitution of England* (2nd ed., 1766), v–vi. Thus Northington, a stalwart government supporter, declared that 'I seek for liberty, and the constitution of this Kingdom no further back than the Revolution: there I make my stand'. (*Parliamentary History* XVI, 171.)
107 John Campbell to Baron Mure, 10 October 1761, Nat. Lib. of Scotland, Add. Mss 4942 f. 36. Cf. Campbell to Mure, 29 September 1761, *ibid* f. 32.
108 *An Essay on the Constitution of England* (1766), vii.

109 Kramnick, *Bolingbroke and his Circle*, 127–36, 177–81; Pocock, *Politics, Language and Time*, 134–43.
110 *A New and Complete Dictionary of Arts and Sciences... By a SOCIETY OF GENTLEMEN* (1754–5), 1475; *A Dissertation on the rise, progress, views, strength, interests and characters of the two parties of the WHIGS and TORIES* (Boston, 1773), 5; *The Principles of a Real Whig* (1775), 3.
111 Samuel Kliger, *The Goths in England* (Cambridge, Mass., 1952), 7–9, 14–15, 19, 21.
112 *Honest Elector's Proposal* (1767), 15–16.
113 Pocock, *Politics, Language and Time*, 132–3.
114 See for example Camden's comments, that could scarcely be more 'Cokean', during the discussion of the Declaratory Act: 'I am sure some histories, of late published, have done great mischief; to endeavour to fix the aera when the House of Commons began in this kingdom, is a most pernicious and destructive attempt to fix it in an Edward's or a Henry's reign, is owing to the idle dreams of some whimsical, ill-judging antiquarians: but, my Lords, this is a point too important to be left to such wrong-headed people. When did the House of Commons first begin? when, my Lords? it began with the Constitution, it grew up with the constitution.' (*Parliamentary History* XVI, 178–9.)
115 *A Dissertation on... the two parties of WHIGS and TORIES* (1773), 9; *The Court of Star Chamber, or seat of Oppression* (1768), 12. For a more general discussion of Magna Carta in the period see Anne Pallister, *Magna Carta* (Oxford, 1971), esp. Ch. 5.
116 Newdigate Mss 2543/13.
117 *Fair Trial of the Important Question* (1769), esp. 25, 75; *A Vindication of the Right of Election, against the disabling Power of the House of Commons* (1769), 14.
118 Egerton Mss 3711 f. 140; Baker to Talbot, 15 February 1765, Baker Mss 1/11; Wright (ed.), *Cavendish's Debates*, i, 8, 61–2, 152; *Speech in Behalf of the Constitution* (1767), 15; [Mulgrave], *A Letter from a Member of Parliament to One of his Constituents* (1769), 71.
119 *Political Register* VI (1770), 363; Christopher Hill, 'The Norman Yoke', *Puritanism and Revolution* (1958), 94. But cf. the comments in *Parliamentary Spy* III, 5 December 1769.
120 See William Temple's shrill manuscript note contradicting the view that the privileges of the people were established under William III in [R. Wallace], *A View of the Internal Policy of Great Britain. In Two Parts* (1764), 57. BM copy.
121 Wright (ed.), *Cavendish's Debates*, i, 104.
122 Burke, *Works*, i, 314.
123 Burke, *Works*, i, 314.
124 Burke, *Works*, i, 315–17.
125 Burke, *Works*, i, 379–81.

Bibliography

BIBLIOGRAPHIES AND WORKS OF REFERENCE

BIOGRAPHY

G. E. Cokayne, *The complete peerage of England, Scotland, Ireland, Great Britain and the United Kingdom, extant, extinct, or dormant* (14 vols., London, 1910–59).

Leslie Stephen and Sidney Lee (eds.), *The Dictionary of National Biography* (63 vols., London, 1885–1900).

DICTIONARIES

Samuel Johnson, *A Dictionary of the English Language: in which the words are deduced from their Originals, and Illustrated in their Different Signification by Examples from the best Writers. To which are prefixed, A History of the Language, and an English Grammar* (2 vols., London, 1755).

A New and Complete Dictionary of Arts and Sciences; comprehending all the Branches of Useful Knowledge. The Whole extracted from the Best AUTHORS in all Languages. By a SOCIETY OF GENTLEMEN (8 vols., London, 1754–5).

BIBLIOGRAPHY

Thomas R. Adams, *American Independence, The Growth of an Idea* (Providence, R.I., 1965).

Francesco Cordasco, *A Junius bibliography, with a preliminary essay on the political background, text and identity; a contribution to 18th century constitutional and literary history. With eight appendices* (New York, 1949).

R. S. Crane and F. B. Kaye, *A census of British newspapers and periodicals, 1620–1800* (Chapel Hill, N.C., 1927).

Charles Evans, *American Bibliography* (14 vols., New York, 1903–59).

J. Kennedy, W. A. Smith, A. F. Johnson *et al.* (eds.), *Dictionary of Anonymous and Pseudonymous English Literature (Samuel Halkett & John Laing)* (9 vols., Edinburgh, 1926–62).

John Lane, *Masonic Records, 1717–1894* (2nd ed., London, 1895).

R. T. Milford and D. M. Sutherland, *A catalogue of English newspapers and periodicals in the Bodleian library 1622–1800* (Oxford, 1936).

Stanley Pargellis and D. J. Medley, *Bibliography of British History. The Eighteenth Century 1714–1789* (Oxford, 1951).

G. W. Stone (ed.), *The London Stage 1660–1800. Part IV, 1747–1776* (3 vols., Carbondale, Ill., 1962).

The Times Tercentenary handlist of English and Welsh newspapers, magazines and reviews (new ed., London, 1933).

William B. Todd, *A Bibliography of Edmund Burke* (London, 1964).

Robert Watt, *Bibliotheca Britannica; or a General Index to British and Foreign Literature* (4 vols., Edinburgh, 1824).

Bibliography

MANUSCRIPT SOURCES

1. BRITISH MUSEUM

Almon Mss	Additional Mss 20733
Carteret-Webb Mss	Add. Mss 22131-2
Wilkes Mss	Add. Mss 30865-96
Newcastle Mss	Add. Mss 32913-3037
Hardwicke Mss	Add. Mss 35349-912
Whitefoord Mss	Add. Mss 36593-7
Bute Mss	Add. Mss 36796-7
Public Advertiser Ledger	Add. Mss 38169
Liverpool Mss	Add. Mss 38197-469
Martin Mss	Add. Mss 41348-57
Egmont Mss	Add. Mss 46920-7213
Strahan Mss	Add. Mss 48800-918
Holland House Mss	Add. Mss 51375-445
Cavendish's Debates	Egerton Mss 215-63, 3711
Dashwood Mss	Egerton Mss 2136

2. PUBLIC OFFICE RECORD

Chatham Mss	PRO 30/8/6-75
Granville Mss	PRO 30/29/1/14-16
State Papers Domestic	S.P. Dom 37/6
S.P. Dom., Entry Books	Entry Books, 44/142
Treasury Solicitors Papers	TS.11/433/1408; 11/818/2696; 11/946/3467; 11/1027/4317

3. BODLEIAN LIBRARY, OXFORD
Dashwood Mss
North Mss
Bowyer Ledger

4. NATIONAL LIBRARY OF SCOTLAND
Minto Mss
Mure Mss
Robertson-Macdonald Mss

5. SCOTTISH PUBLIC RECORD OFFICE
Townshend (Dalkeith) Mss
Stair Mss

6. NOTTINGHAM UNIVERSITY LIBRARY
Portland Mss
Newcastle (Clumber) Mss

7. GUILDHALL LIBRARY, LONDON
Wilkes Mss

Bibliography

8. NORFOLK RECORD OFFICE
Molyneux Letter Book
Walsingham Mss
Bradfer-Lawrence Mss

9. HERTFORDSHIRE RECORD OFFICE
Baker Mss

10. WEST SUFFOLK RECORD OFFICE
Grafton Mss
Hervey Mss

11. NORTHAMPTON RECORD OFFICE
Fitzwilliam (Milton) Mss

12. WARWICKSHIRE RECORD OFFICE
Newdigate Mss

13. SHEFFIELD CITY LIBRARY
Wentworth-Woodhouse Muniments:
Burke Mss
Rockingham Mss

14. LIVERPOOL RECORD OFFICE
Parker Mss

15. CARDIFF CITY LIBRARY
Bute Mss

16. POST OFFICE ARCHIVES
Post 9 Treasury Letter Books
Post 24 Newspapers

17. EALING BOROUGH REFERENCE LIBRARY
Beauchamp Proctor Mss

18. WILLIAM CLEMENTS LIBRARY, ANN ARBOR, MICHIGAN, USA
Dowdeswell Mss
Shelburne-Lacaita Mss

19. ROYAL ARCHIVES, WINDSOR CASTLE
Papers of George III

20. MOUNT STUART, ISLE OF BUTE
Bute Mss

21. CHATSWORTH HOUSE, DERBYSHIRE
Devonshire Mss

22. BEDFORD ESTATES OFFICE, LONDON
Bedford Mss

23. HATFIELD HOUSE, HERTFORDSHIRE
Chase Price Mss

24. TERLING PLACE, ESSEX
Strutt Mss

25. PAILTON HOUSE, RUGBY
Denbigh Mss

26. HUNTINGTON LIBRARY, SAN MARINO,
CALIFORNIA
Stowe Mss

NEWSPAPERS AND PERIODICALS

ANNUALS
Annual Register
Yearly Chronicle

PERIODICALS
Court and City Magazine
Critical Review
Freeholder's Magazine
Gentleman's Magazine
London Magazine
London Museum
Monthly Review
Oxford Magazine
Political Register
Town and Country Magazine
Universal Magazine

WEEKLY AND FORTNIGHTLY PAPERS
Auditor
Briton
Cato's Letters
Citizen
Connoisseur
Constitutional Guardian
Con-Test
Contrast
Craftsman
Idler
Monitor

Bibliography

North Briton
Parliamentary Spy
Political Controversy
Test
Weekly Amusement
Whisperer

LONDON PAPERS
Gazetteer
General Evening Post
Independent Chronicle
Lloyd's Evening Post
London Chronicle
London Evening Post
London Packet
Middlesex Journal
Public Advertiser
Public Ledger
St James's Chronicle

PROVINCIAL PAPERS
Aris's Birmingham Gazette
Cambridge Chronicle
Jopson's Coventry Mercury
Leeds Mercury
Liverpool Chronicle
Newcastle Journal
Northampton Mercury
Norwich Mercury
Sherborne Mercury
Williamson's Liverpool Advertiser
York Courant

PRINTED SOURCES

Historical Manuscripts Commission

Second Report Appendix – Dillon Mss
Fifth Report Appendix – Sutherland Mss
                        Lansdowne Mss
                        Shipley Mss
Ninth Report Appendix III – Stopford-Sackville Mss
Tenth Report Part I – Weston Mss
Eleventh Report Appendix IV – Townshend Mss
Twelfth Report Appendix Part V – Rutland Mss
Twelfth Report Appendix Part IX – Donoughmore Mss
Thirteenth Report Appendix Part VII – Lonsdale Mss
Fourteenth Report Appendix Part IX – Onslow Mss
Fifteenth Report Appendix I – Dartmouth Mss
Various VI

Bibliography

Various VIII
Lothian
Polwarth
Laing
Bathurst
Hastings
Savile Foljambe

Other printed sources arranged by subject

ALLEN
Adrian E. Hopkins (ed.), 'Ralph Allen's own narrative 1720–1761', *Postal History Society* Special Series no. 8 (1960).
A. M. Ogilvie, *Ralph Allen's Bye, Way and Cross-Road Posts* (London, 1898).
R. E. M. Peach, *The Life and Times of Ralph Allen* (London, 1895).

ALMON
Memoirs of John Almon, Bookseller of Piccadilly (London, 1790).

BARRINGTON
Shute Barrington, *The Political Life of William Wildman, Viscount Barrington, compiled from original papers* (London, 1815).

BEDFORD
Lord John Russell (ed.), *The Correspondence of John, Fourth Duke of Bedford* (3 vols., London, 1842–6).

DE BERDT
Albert Matthews (ed.), 'Letters of Dennys de Berdt, 1757–1770', *Publications of the Colonial Society of Massachusetts* XIII (1910–11).

BLACKSTONE
James Stewart (ed.), *Commentaries on the Laws of England, In Four Books by Sir William Blackstone* (20th ed., 4 vols., London, 1841).

BOLINGBROKE
The Works of Lord Bolingbroke (4 vols., 1844).

BOSWELL
James Boswell: *Private Papers, from Malahide Castle, in the Collection of R. H. Isham; prepared for the press by G. Scott (and F. A. Pottle), and now first printed* (18 vols., privately printed, 1928–34).
Frederick A. Pottle (ed.), *Boswell's London Journal 1762–63 together with the Journal of my Jaunt. Harvest 1762* (London, 1951).
Ralph S. Walker (ed.), *The Correspondence of James Boswell and John Johnston of Grange* (London, 1966).

330

BURKE

T. W. Copeland *et al.* (eds.), *The Correspondence of Edmund Burke* (9 vols., Cambridge, 1958–70).

The Works of Edmund Burke (8 vols., Bohn's British Classics, London, 1854–89).

BUTE

A Prime Minister and his Son, from the correspondence of the 3rd Earl of Bute and of the Hon. Sir C. Stuart; edited by the Hon. Mrs E. Wortley with an introduction by the Rt. Hon. Sir R. Rodd (London, 1925).

CALDWELL

Mure (ed.), *Selections from the Family Papers preserved at Caldwell. In Two Parts* (Glasgow, 1854).

CAVENDISH

J. Wright (ed.), *Sir Henry Cavendish's Debates of the House of Commons, during the Thirteenth Parliament of Great Britain, commonly called the Unreported Parliament* (2 vols., London, 1841).

CHAMPION

G. H. Guttridge (ed.), *The American Correspondence of a Bristol Merchant, 1766–1796. The Letters of Richard Champion* (Berkeley, Calif., 1934).

CHATHAM

[John Almon], *Anecdotes of the Life of the Rt. Hon. William Pitt, Earl of Chatham* (6th ed., 3 vols., London, 1797).

W. Stanhope Taylor and J. H. Pringle (eds.), *The Correspondence of William Pitt, Earl of Chatham* (4 vols., London, 1838–40).

CHESTERFIELD

B. Dobree (ed.), *Lord Chesterfield's Letters* (6 vols., London, 1932).

J. Lodge (ed.), 'The Private Correspondence of Chesterfield and Newcastle 1744–46', *Camden Society* XLIV (1930).

DEMPSTER

Sir James Ferguson (ed.), *Letters of George Dempster to Sir Adam Ferguson, 1756–1813* (London, 1934).

DODINGTON

J. Carswell and L. A. Dralle (eds.), *The Political Journal of Bubb Dodington, Lord Melcombe* (Oxford, 1965).

DUTENS

[Louis Dutens], *Memoirs of a Traveller now in Retirement, written by himself* (5 vols., London, 1866).

EARDLEY-WILMOT

The Memoirs of Sir John Eardley-Wilmot (London, 1802).

Bibliography

EGMONT

A. N. Newman (ed.), 'Leicester House Politics, 1750–60, from the papers of John, Second Earl of Egmont', *Camden Miscellany* XXIII 4th Series 7 (1969).

ELLIOT

G. F. S. Elliot, *The Border Elliots and the Family of Minto* (Edinburgh, 1897).
Countess of Minto, *Life and Letters of Sir Gilbert Elliott, 1st Earl of Minto* (3 vols., London, 1874).

FERGUSON

Adam Ferguson, *An Essay on the History of Civil Society* (Edinburgh, 1767).

FOX

Ilchester, *Henry Fox, First Lord Holland. His Family and Relations* (2 vols., London, 1920).
Ilchester (ed.), *Letters to Henry Fox, Lord Holland, with a few addressed to his brother Stephen, Earl of Ilchester* (London, 1915).

FRANCIS

B. Francis and E. Keary (eds.), *The Francis Letters* (4 vols., London, 1901).
J. Parkes and H. Merivale, *Memoirs of Sir Philip Francis* (2 vols., London, 1867).

FRANKLIN

L. W. Labaree (ed.), *The Papers of Benjamin Franklin* (18 vols. to date, New Haven, Conn., 1959).
A. H. Smith (ed.), *The Writings of Benjamin Franklin* (10 vols., New York, 1907).

GEORGE III

Sir John Fortescue (ed.), *The Correspondence of King George III from 1760 to 1783* (6 vols., London, 1927–8).
Sir Lewis Namier, *Additions and Corrections to Sir J. Fortescue's edition of the Correspondence of George III, vol. I* (Manchester, 1937).
Romney Sedgwick (ed.), *Letters from George III to Lord Bute 1756–1766* (London, 1939).

GIBBON

R. E. Prothero (ed.), *The Private Letters of Edward Gibbon (1753–94)* (2 vols., London, 1896).
The Miscellaneous Works of Edward Gibbon, Esq. With Memoirs of his Life and Writings (5 vols., 2nd ed., London, 1814).

GRAFTON

Sir William R. Anson (ed.), *The Autobiographical and Political Correspondence of Augustus Hervey, 3rd Duke of Grafton* (London, 1898).

GRAY

Roger Lonsdale (ed.), *The Poems of Thomas Gray, William Collins, Oliver Goldsmith* (London, 1969).

Bibliography

GRENVILLE

W. J. Smith (ed.), *The Grenville Papers: being the correspondence of R. Grenville, Earl Temple, and the Rt. Hon. G. Grenville, their friends and contemporaries* (4 vols., London, 1852–3).

John R. G. Tomlinson (ed.), *Additional Grenville Papers, 1763–1765* (Manchester, 1962).

HARDWICKE

P. C. Yorke, *The Life and Correspondence of Philip Yorke, Earl of Hardwicke* (3 vols., Cambridge, 1913).

HICKEY

William Hickey, *Memoirs 1749–1809* (4 vols., London, 1913–15).

HOLLIS

Memoirs of Thomas Hollis Esq., F. R. and A. S. S. Quique sui memores alios fecere merendo (London, 1780).

HOME

Henry Mackenzie (ed.), *John Home. Works* (3 vols., Edinburgh, 1822).

HUME

J. Y. T. Greig (ed.), *The Letters of David Hume* (2 vols., Oxford, 1932).

JENKINSON

Ninetta S. Jucker (ed.), *The Jenkinson Papers 1760–1766* (London, 1949).

JOHNSON

R. W. Chapman (ed.), *Boswell's Life of Johnson* (Oxford, 1970).

JONES

Teignmouth (ed.), *Memoirs of the Life, Writings and Correspondence of Sir William Jones* (London, 1804).

JUNIUS

C. W. Everett (ed.), *The Letters of Junius* (London, 1927).

KNATCHBULL

A. N. Newman (ed.), 'The Parliamentary Diary of Sir Edward Knatchbull 1722–1730', *Camden Society* 3rd Series XCIV (1963).

LEE

Lee Family Papers, 1742–1795, ed. Paul P. Hoffmann (University of Virginia microfilm, Charlottesville, Va.).

LENNOX

The Countess of Ilchester and Lord Stavordale (eds.), *The Life and Letters of Lady Sarah Lennox, 1745–1826* (2 vols., London, 1901).

LIVERPOOL

G. T. and I. Shaw, *Liverpool's Fifth Directory* (Liverpool, 1932).

Bibliography

LONDON
A collection of contemporary papers relating to the City Elections 1768–1796
(Guildhall Library, London).
*The whole Proceedings on the King's Commission of the Peace, Oyer and Terminer,
and Gaol Delivery for the City of London and...for the County of Middlesex,*
ed. J. Gurney (London, 1760–70).

LYTTELTON
R. J. Phillimore (ed.), *Memoirs and Correspondence of George, Lord Lyttelton* (2
vols., London, 1845).

MALMESBURY
Malmesbury (ed.), *A Series of Letters of the First Earl of Malmesbury, His Family
and his Friends from 1748 to 1820* (2 vols., London, 1870).

NEVILLE
B. Cozens-Hardy, *The Diary of Sylas Neville, 1767–88* (London, 1950).

NEWCASTLE
Mary Bateson (ed.), 'A Narrative of the Changes in the Ministry, 1765–1767',
Camden Society New Series LIX (1898).

NICHOLS
John Nichols, *Literary Anecdotes of the Eighteenth Century; comprising the biographical memoirs of W. Bowyer* (9 vols., London, 1812–15).

NORTHUMBERLAND
John Sykes, *Local Records; or, Historical Register of Remarkable Events which have
occurred in Northumberland and Durham, Newcastle-upon-Tyne, and Berwick-
upon-Tweed, from the earliest period of authentic Record to the present Time*
(2 vols., Newcastle, 1833).

OLDMIXON
J. Oldmixon, *The History of England during the reigns of William and Mary, Anne
and George I* (London, 1735).

OSBORN
E. F. D. Osborn (ed.), *Political and Social Letters of a Lady of the Eighteenth
Century (the Hon. Mrs. Osborn), 1721–1771* (London, 1890).

PARLIAMENT
William Cobbett (ed.), *Parliamentary History of England from the Norman
Conquest to the year 1803* (36 vols., London, 1806–20).

PELHAM
W. Coxe, *Memoirs of the Administration of the Rt. Hon. Henry Pelham, collected
from the family papers, and other authentic documents* (2 vols., London, 1829).

E. PYLE
Albert Hartshorne (ed.), *Memoirs of a Royal Chaplain, 1729–63* (London, 1915).

Bibliography

RICHMOND

Alison Olson, *The Radical Duke. The Career and Correspondence of Charles Lennox, third Duke of Richmond* (Oxford, 1961).

Alison Olson, 'The Duke of Richmond's Memorandum, 1–7 July 1766', *EHR* LXXV (1960).

ROBINSON

W. T. Laprade (ed.), 'Parliamentary Papers of John Robinson 1774–1784', *Camden Society* 3rd Series XXXIII (1922).

ROCKINGHAM

Albemarle, *Memoirs of the Marquess of Rockingham and his Friends* (2 vols., London, 1852).

RYDER

P. D. G. Thomas (ed.), 'The Parliamentary Diaries of Nathaniel Ryder, 1764–7', *Camden Miscellany* XXIII (1969).

SHELBURNE

Lord Fitzmaurice, *Life of William Earl of Shelburne, afterwards First Marquess of Lansdowne, with extracts from his papers and correspondence* (2 vols., 2nd ed., London, 1912).

SMOLLETT

Smollett, *Works* (12 vols., London, 1901).

STRAHAN

'Correspondence between William Strahan and David Hall, 1763–1777', *Pennsylvania Magazine of History and Biography* XI (1887).

Pomfret, 'Further Letters of William Strahan', *Pennsylvania Magazine of History and Biography* LX (1936).

TURNER

F. M. Turner (ed.), *The Diary of Thomas Turner of East Hoathley 1754–65* (London, 1925).

WALDEGRAVE

Memoirs from 1754 to 1758 by James Earl Waldegrave K.G. (London, 1821).

WALPOLE, HORACE

Horace Walpole, *Memoirs of the Reign of King George II. Edited from the original manuscript with a preface & notes by the late Lord Holland* (3 vols., London, 1846).

Horace Walpole, *Memoirs of the Reign of King George III. Now first published from the original manuscript*, ed. Sir Denis Le Marchant (4 vols., London, 1845).

Paget Toynbee (ed.), *The Letters of Horace Walpole* (16 vols., Oxford, 1903–25).

Bibliography

WALPOLE, ROBERT

W. Coxe, *Memoirs of the Life and Administration of Sir Robert Walpole, Earl of Orford. With Original Correspondence and Authentic Papers, never before published* (3 vols., London, 1798).

WHITEFOORD

W. A. J. Hewins (ed.), *The Whitefoord Papers being the Correspondence and other Manuscripts of Colonel Charles Whitefoord and Caleb Whitefoord from 1739 to 1810* (Oxford, 1898).

WILKES

The Correspondence of the late John Wilkes with his friends, printed from the original manuscripts, in which are introduced memoirs of his life, by John Almon (5 vols., London, 1805).

Weatherly (ed.), *Correspondence of John Wilkes and Charles Churchill* (New York, 1954).

WRAXALL

The Historical and Posthumous Memoirs of Sir Nathaniel Wraxall, 1772–1784, ed. H. B. Wheatley (5 vols., London, 1884).

PAMPHLETS
A. Pamphlets before 1760
Arranged alphabetically by author or by
title where author is unknown.

An Address of Thanks to the Broadbottoms (London, 1745).

An Address to the Great, recommending better ways and means of raising the necessary supplies than lotteries or taxes, with a word or two concerning an invasion (London [1756]).

An Appeal to the Nation (London, 1757).

The Balance; or the merits of Whig and Tory, exactly weigh'd and fairly determin'd (London, 1753).

[Bolingbroke], *A Final Answer to the Remarks on the Craftsman's Vindication; and to all the libels which have come, or may come from the same quarter against the person last mentioned in the Craftsman of the 22d of May* (London, 1731).

[Bolingbroke], *The Freeholder's Political Catechism* (London, 1733).

[John Brown], *An Estimate of the Manners and Principles of the Times. By the author of the Essays on the characteristics* (London, 1757).

[John Campbell], *The case of the opposition impartially stated. By a gentleman of the Inner Temple* (London, [1742]).

[Alexander Carlyle], *Plain Reasons for removing a certain Great Man from his M - - - - -y's presence and councils for ever; addressed to the people of England. By O. M. Haberdasher* (London, 1759).

The Character of Pericles; a Funeral Oration Sacred to the Memory of a Great Man (London, 1745).

The Conduct of the late and the present Ministry Compared; with an impartial review of public transactions since the resignation of the Right Honourable the Earl of Orford, and the causes that immediately effected the same. To which is added, remarks on a farther report of a certain committee, in a letter to a friend (London, 1742).

The Constitution. With an Address to a Great Man [I] (London, 1757).

The Constitution. With a Letter to the Author. Number II (London, 1757).

The Constitution. With some Account of a Bill lately rejected by the H - - - - of L - - - - [III] (London, 1757).

The Countenance or Gregg's Ghost (London, 1711).

A Craftsman Extraordinary. Or a full Answer to the Remarks upon the Craftsman's Vindication (London, 173–).

A Critical Review of the Liberties of British Subjects. By a Gentleman of the Middle Temple (2nd ed., London, 1750).

A Defence of the People: or, Full Confutation of the Pretended Facts, advanc'd in a late huge, angry pamphlet; call'd Faction Detected. In a Letter to the author of that weighty performance (London, 1744).

The Detector Detected: or, the Danger to which our Constitution now lies exposed, Set in a true and manifest Light (London, 1743).

[Egmont], *An Examination of the Principles, and an enquiry into the Conduct, of the Two B*****rs; in regard to the establishment of their power, and their prosecution of the War, 'till the signing of the preliminaries, In a letter to a Member of Parliament* (London, 1749).

[Egmont], *Faction Detected by the evidence of Facts: containing an impartial view of parties at home, and affairs abroad* (3rd ed., London, 1743).

[Egmont], *A Second Series of Facts and Arguments; Tending to Prove, that the Abilities of the Two B - - - - - rs are not more extraordinary than their Virtues. By the Author of an Examination of the Principles* (London, 1749).

The English Nation Vindicated from the Calumnies of Foreigners; In Answer to a late pamphlet intitled, Popular Prejudice concerning partiality to the Interests of Hanover (London, 1744).

An Essay on Liberty and Independency: being an Attempt to prove, that the People under a Popular Form of Government, may be as much Slaves, as those subject to the Arbitrary Will of one Man (London, 1747).

The Father of the City of Eutopia, or the Surest Road to Riches, Dedicated to the Rt. Honourable Wm. P - - -, Esq. (London, 1757).

[James Hampton], *A Parallel between the Roman and British Constitution; comprehending Polybius's curious discourse of the Roman Senate. With a preface, wherein his principles are applied to our Government* (London, 1747).

[J. Hanway], *A Morning's Thoughts on Reading the Test and the Con-Test* (London, 1757).

[John Hervey], *Miscellaneous Thoughts on the present posture both of our Foreign and Domestic Affairs. Humbly Offer'd to the Consideration of the Parliament and the People* (London, 1742).

[T. Hervey], *A Letter to William Pitt, Esq; concerning the Fifteen New REGIMENTS lately voted by PARLIAMENT: Wherein some of the general Arguments, together with his in particular, for Opposing the Motion to Address his MAJESTY, are fairly answered, and the Case itself is shortly and plainly stated* (London, 1746).

The Honest Grief of a Tory, expressed in a genuine Letter from a Burgess of - - - - -, in Wiltshire, to the Author of the Monitor, February 17, 1759 (London, 1759).

A Letter from a Merchant of London to a Member of Parliament: In Answer to a Letter From a Member of Parliament to his Friends in the Country, Concerning the Duties on Wine and Tobacco (London, 1733).

Bibliography

A Letter to a Noble Lord (London, 1742).

A Letter to a young Member of the House of C - m - - ns; where the question between PARTY *and* CONSCIENCE *is impartially stated; and which of these ought to be the invariable rule of conduct in P - rl - - - - t fully established* (London, 1745).

A Letter to his Grace the D - - - of N - - - - - - - E, on the Duty he owes himself, his King, his Country and his God (London, 1757).

A Letter to the People of England, upon the Militia, Continental Connections, Neutralities, and Secret Expeditions (London, 1757).

A Letter to the Secret Committee (London, 1742).

The Loyal or Revolutional Tory. Being Some Reflections on the Principles and Conduct of the Tories; shewing them true Friends to the present Establishment, one of the capital Pillars of the Constitution, and worthy of Royal Trust and Confidence. By a FRIEND *to the Church and Constitution* (London, 1733).

[Mansfield], *The Thistle; a dispassionate examine of the prejudice of Englishmen in general to the Scotch nation; and particularly of a late arrogant insult offered to all Scotchmen, by a modern English journalist. In a Letter to the author of Old England of December 27, 1746* (London, 1746).

[Marchmont], *A Serious Exhortation to the electors of Great Britain; wherein the importance of the approaching elections is particularly proved from our present situation both at home and abroad* (London, 1740).

[Marfolio], *An Historical view of the principal characters of the political writers in Great Britain* (London, 1740).

The Masque of Patriotism and Truth: or, the Court Fool. As it was presented before the ***'s Majesty in the Christmas Hollidays, at the Court of *** (London, 1743).

Miscellaneous Reflections upon the Peace, and its Consequences (London, 1749).

E. W. Montagu, *Reflections on the Rise and Fall of the Ancient Republics adapted to the Present State of Great Britain* (London, 1759).

[Sir J. Mordaunt], *An Appeal to the Nation: being a full and fair vindication of Mr. Mordaunt, and the other gentlemen employed in the conduct of the late secret expedition, in which the circumstances relating to the miscarriages of that affair are set in a just and satisfactory light* (London, 1757).

[Corbyn Morris], *A Letter from a By-Stander to a Member of Parliament* (London, 1741).

Northern Revolutions: or, the Principal Causes of the Declension and Dissolution of several once flourishing GOTHIC CONSTITUTIONS *in* EUROPE. *In a Series of Letters from the* GHOST *of* TRENCHARD, *Once a* FREE BRITON (London, 1757).

An Ode on the expedition. Inscribed to the Right Hon. W - - - - - - P - - -, Esquire (London, 1757).

[Oglethorpe], *The Naked Truth* (London, 1755).

Opposition not Faction: Or, the Rectitude of the Present Parliamentary Opposition to the Present Expensive Measures, Justified by Reason and Facts. In a Letter from Bath to a Member of Parliament (London, 1743).

The Opposition. To be published occasionally (London, 1755).

Party Spirit in time of Public Danger considered; wherein the National Debt, the Necessity of our Connections on the Continent, with the Nature of our Subsidiary Forces, and the ancient Mercenaries are fully discussed (London, 1758).

A Plain Answer to a Plain Reasoner. Wherein the present state of affairs is set, not in a new but a true light, in contradiction to the Reasoner (London, 1745).

338

Bibliography

The Protest (London, 1757).

[Pultency], *An Answer to One Part of a late Infamous Libel, Intitled, ' Remarks on the Craftsman's Vindication of his two honourable Patrons'; in which the character and conduct of Mr. P[ulteney] are fully vindicated: in a letter to the most noble author* (London, 1731).

[Pulteney], *The Budget Opened. Or, an Answer to a Pamphlet Intitled, a Letter from a Member of Parliament to his Friends in the Country, concerning the Duties on wine and tobacco* (London, 1733).

[Pulteney], *An Humble Address to the Knights, Citizens and Burgesses, Elected to represent the Commons of Great Britain in the Ensuing Parliament. By a Freeholder* (London, 1734).

[Pulteney?], *A Proper Answer to the Bystander; wherein is shewn that there is no necessity for, but infallible ruin in the maintenance of a large regular (or mercenary) land force in this island* (London, 1742).

[Pulteney?], *A Review of the Excise-Scheme; in Answer to a Pamphlet, intitled the Rise and Fall of the late Projected Excise, impartially considered, with some proper hints to the electors of Great Britain* (London, 1733).

[Pulteney?], *The second Part of an Argument against Excises; in answer to the objections of several writers; especially with regard to that part of the subject, which relates to the power and conduct of the commissioners and officers of excise. With some remarks on the present state of affairs. By Caleb D'Anvers of Gray's Inn, Esq.* (London, 1733).

P. Rapin de Thoyras, *The History of Whig and Tory; from the Conquest to the present Time* (London, 1723).

Review of the whole Political Conduct of a late Eminent Patriot, and his friends; for Twenty Years last past; in which is contained a history of the opposition and a full answer to a pamphlet entitled, Faction detected by the evidence of Facts (London, 1743).

A Seasonable Recapitulation of Enormous National Crimes and Grievances, to Help the Memory for the Use and Consideration of all Honest Men and True Britons (1749).

Seventeen Forty Two (London, 1743).

[Gregory Sharpe], *A Short Dissertation upon the species of mis-government called an Oligarchy* (London, 1748).

[Edward Spelman], *A Fragment out of the Sixth Book of Polybius, containing a dissertation upon Government translated with notes. To which is prefixed a preface, wherein the system of Polybius is applied to the government of England: and to the fragment concerning the powers of the Senate is annexed a dissertation upon the constitution of it. By a Gentleman* (London, 1743).

Some General Considerations Concerning the Alteration and Improvement of Public Revenues (London, 1733).

The Spirit and Principles of the Whigs and Jacobites compared: being the substance of a discourse delivered in Edinburgh, December 22d, 1745 (London, 1746).

The Thoughts of an Impartial Man upon the Present Temper of the Nation; Offer'd to the Consideration of the Freeholders of Great-Britain (London, 1733).

[Robert Walpole], *A Letter from a Member of Parliament to his Friends in the Country, Concerning the Duties on Wine and Tobacco* (London, 1733).

A Whig's Remarks on the Tory History of the Four Last Years of Queen Anne by Dr. Jonathan Swift (London, 1758).

339

Bibliography

B. Pamphlets, 1760–70
Arranged chronologically.

The place of publication and the name of the publisher and printer, where known, are given after the titles in parentheses. At least one library location, if known, is given. The following abbreviations for the libraries have been used:

BM   British Museum, London
Bod   Bodleian Library, Oxford
C.   Cambridge University Library
Hun.   Huntington Library, San Marino, California
W.   Widener Library, Harvard University
Wren   Wren Library, Trinity College, Cambridge

1760

An Answer to the Letter to Two Great Men (London). Hun.

A Candid and Fair Examination of the Remarks on the Letter to Two Great Men (London). Hun.

The Conduct of the Ministry Impartially examined. And the Pamphlet entitled Considerations on the present German War, Refuted from its own Principles (London, R. Griffiths). BM.

A consolatory letter to a noble Lord (London, S. Hooper). Bod., Hun.

The Court-Spy; or, Memoirs of St. J-m-s's. In a Letter from a Person of Distinction in Town, to his Friend in Wales (London, H. Carpenter). Hun.

[J. Douglas], *The Conduct of a late Noble Commander, Candidly Considered With a View to expose the Misrepresentations of an Anonymous Author of the Two Letters Addressed to his L - - - - - p* (London, R. Baldwin). Hun.

[J. Douglas], *A Letter addressed to two great men on the prospect of peace; and on the terms necessary to be insisted upon in the negotiation* (2nd ed., London, A. Millar). BM, C., W., Hun.

A Full and Candid Answer to a Pamphlet, entitled, Considerations on the Present German War (J. Pridden, J. Burd, J. Gretton). Hun.

A Letter from a commoner in town, to a noble Lord in the country (London). Bod.

[Israel Mauduit], *Considerations on the present German War* (London, J. Wilkie). BM, C., W., Hun.

Ministerial Usurpation Displayed, and the Prerogatives of the Crown, with the Rights of Parliament and of the Privy Council, considered in an appeal to the people (London). C.

An Ode Inscribed to William Pitt (London). Bod.

Political Thoughts ([London]). BM, Wren.

One Thousand Seven hundred and Fifty Nine: A Poem, inscribed to every BRITON who bore a part in the Service of that distinguished year (London, R. Baldwin). Hun.

Reflections without doors, on what passes within. Recommended to the perusal of all friends to the Militia: As well as those who wish to preserve Unanimity and Coalition between Administration and People, so Necessary at this critical conjuncture. By A Country Gentleman (London, R. Davis). Hun.

Remarks on a Pamphlet Entitled, Reasons why the Approaching Treaty of Peace should be debated in Parliament. In a Letter to the Author (London, M. Cooper). Hun.

[Ruffhead], *Ministerial Usurpation Displayed, and the Prerogatives of the Crown, with the Rights of Parliament and of the Privy Council, considered in an appeal to the people* (London, R. Griffiths). BM, Hun.

[Ruffhead], *Reasons why the approaching Treaty of Peace should be debated in Parliament: As a Method most Expedient and Constitutional. In a Letter addressed to a Great Man and Occasioned by the Perusal of a Letter addressed to Two Great Men* (London, R. Griffiths). BM.

A Vindication of the Conduct of the Present War, in a Letter to - - - - - (London, J. and R. Tonson). Hun.

1761

An Answer to a Letter to the Right Honourable the Earl of B***, In which the false Reasoning, and absurd Conclusions, in that Pamphlet, are fully detected and refuted: Addressed to the Right Hon. Earl T - mple (London, J. Wilkie). BM, Bod., Hun.

The Case of the late Resignation set in a true Light (London, J. Hinxman). BM, Hun.

The Conduct of a Rt. Hon Gentleman in resigning the Seals of his Office justified, by facts, and upon the principles of the British Constitution. By a Member of Parliament (London, J. Newbury). C., Hun.

Constitutional Queries, Humbly Addressed to the Admirers of a Late Minister (London, R. Davis). Hun.

[J. Douglas], *Seasonable Hints from an Honest Man On the Present Important Crisis of a New Reign and a New Parliament* (London, A. Millar). BM, W., Hun.

An Earnest Address to the People of Great Britain and Ireland: occasioned by the dismission of W. Pitt, Esq. from the office of Secretary of State (Dublin, S. Watson). C., Hun.

The Equilibrium: or Balance of Opinions, on a late Resignation. By a Citizen of the World, residing in London (London, W. Nicoll). C.

Faction detected; or Five in One (London, Cabe).

[Francis], *A Letter from the Anonymous Author of the Letters Versified to the Anonymous Writer of the Monitor* (London, W. Nicoll). BM, Hun.

[Francis], *A Letter from a Right Honourable Person. And the Answer to it, Translated into Verse, as nearly as the different Idioms of PROSE and POETRY will allow. With Notes Historical, Critical, Political* (London, W. Nicoll). BM, Bod., C., Hun.

An Impartial Enquiry into the Conduct of a late Minister (London, R. Davis). BM, Wren, Hun.

Impartial Reflections upon the Present State of Affairs. With Incidental Remarks upon certain Recent Transactions. In a Letter to a Friend (Dublin). C., Hun.

A Letter from a Patriot in Retirement to the Right Hon. Mr. William Pitt upon resigning his Employment (London, Woodfall). Wren, Hun.

A Letter to his Grace the Duke of N********, on the Present Crisis in the Affairs of Great Britain. Containing Reflections on a late Great Resignation (London, R. Griffiths). BM, Wren, Hun.

A Letter to the Right Honourable Author of a Letter to a Citizen, with Animadversion on the Answer thereto, And on the Behaviour of the Corporation of the City of London. In which his reasons for resigning; the Conduct, Success and Advantages of his Administration; his Fidelity to his Country; Capacity for Directing the

Transactions of War, Commerce and Pacification, are fairly stated and freely considered (London, J. Hinxman). Hun.

A Letter to the Right Honourable the Earl of B***, on a late important RESIGNATION, and its probable Consequences (London, W. Coote), BM, Bod., Hun.

[Melcombe], *Occasional Observations on a double-titled Paper, about the clear produce of the Civil List Revenue from the Mid-summer 1727, to Mid-summer last* (London). BM, W.

The Patriot Unmasked, or, A Word to his Defenders. By John Trott, Cheese-monger and Statesman (London, J. Pridden). BM, Hun.

A Peep through a Key-hole: Or, the secret History of Some People and some Things (London, J. Hall). W.

Public Clamours Traced to their Original Sources: And the Advantage of a Man's being born here, or there, discussed. By A Briton (G. Kearsley). Hun.

Reasons in support of the war in Germany, in answer to considerations on the present German War (London). BM, Bod., Hun.

Remarks upon a popular letter to - - - - - - by a citizen of London (London). BM (imperfect), Bod.

The Right Hon. Annuitant Vindicated. With a Word or two in favour of the other GREAT MAN, in Case of his Resignation. In a LETTER to a FRIEND in the COUNTRY (London, J. Morgan). C., Hun.

The Scotch Portmanteau opened at York (London, M. Thrush). Hun.

A Second Letter to the Right Honourable the Earl of B***. By the Author of the First (London, J. Coote). BM, Hun.

Truth in rhyme: addressed to a Noble Lord (London, A. Millar). BM, C.

A Word to a Right Honourable Commoner (London, J. Dixwell and M. Cooper). Hun.

1762

An Address to the City of London (London, R. Davis). Hun.

[John Almon], *A Review of Mr. Pitt's Administration* (London, J. Almon). Hun.

[John Almon], *Review of the reign of George the second, in which new light is thrown on the transactions, and the effects of ministerial influence are traced and laid open* (London, Almon). BM, Goldsmith's Library London University, Hun.

[John Butler], *An Address to the Cocoa Tree from a Whig* (London, G. Kearsley). BM, C., Hun.

The Coalition: or, an Historical Memorial of the Negotiation for Peace, between his High Mightiness of C - - - - m - - t and his Sublime Excellency of H - y - s. With the Vouchers. Published by the Authority of One of the Contracting Powers (London, J. Hinxman). Hun.

A Consolatory Epistle to the Members of the old Faction; occasioned by the Spanish War. By the Author of the Consolatory Letter to the noble Lord dismissed the Military Service (London, S. Williams). BM, Hun.

A Continuation of the Address to the City of London (London, R. Davis). Hun.

An Enquiry how far L*** B*** merits the exalted Character given him by the Briton; and the Politics and Principles of the Briton and Auditor exposed and refuted (London, Williams).

An epistle to his Grace the Duke of N - - - - - - - e, on his Resignation. By an Independent Whig (London, A. and C. Corbett). Hun.

An Epistle to Lord Bute, on the happy Prospect of Peace (London, Rawlings).

Bibliography

An Epistle to the King (London, T. Waller). Hun.

Fart-Inando, *The Asses of Great Britain, An Answer to Harry H - - - - d's Ass* (London). Hun.

[Philip Francis], *A Letter from the Cocoa Tree to the Country Gentlemen* (London, W. Nicoll). BM, C., Hun.

[G. Heathcote], *A Letter to the Right Honourable the Lord Mayor, the Worshipful Aldermen, and Common-Council; the merchants, Citizens and Inhabitants, of the City of London. From an Old Servant* (London, W. Owen, Baldwin and Pugh). Hun.

[Henry Howard], *The K - - - s A - -. A New Song Intended as a Companion to the Q - - - -'s A - -* (London). BM.

[Howard], *The Masquerade or the Political Bagpiper* (London). BM.

[Howard], *An Ode to Lord B***, on the Peace. By the Author of the Minister of State, a Satire* (London). BM, Bod.

[Howard], *The Pe**e Soup-Makers, Or, a new mess at the B - d - d Head* (London). BM.

Invincible Reasons for the Earl of Bute's immediate resignation of the Ministry. In a Letter to that Nobleman (London, R. Mariner). BM, Bod., Hun.

A Letter addressed to the Right Hon. William Beckford, Esq. Lord Mayor, concerning Lord B[ute] and a Peace (London, Scott).

A Letter from Arthur's to the Cocoa Tree, in ANSWER to the LETTER from thence to the COUNTRY GENTLEMEN (London, W. Morgan). C., Hun.

A Letter to a member of the Honourable House of Commons, on the present important crisis of national affairs (London). BM, Hun.

A Letter to Her R - - - L H - - - - - - S THE P - - - - - - S D - w - g - r of W - - - - On the Approaching PEACE. With a few Words concerning the Right Honourable the Earl of B - - -, and the General Talk of the WORLD (London, S. Williams). C., Hun.

A Letter to the author of the Epistle to Lord B[ute], on the present happy Prospect of a Peace (London, W. Nicoll).

A Letter to the Right Honourable the Earl of Bute, on the Preliminaries of Peace. From neither a NOBLE Lord; a CANDID Member of Parliament; an IMPARTIAL Briton, but an ENGLISHMAN (London, W. Nicoll). BM.

A Letter to the Whigs, with some Remarks on a Letter to the Tories (London, W. Nicoll). Hun.

A Letter upon the three great Objects of Public Attention, Peace, Parties, and Resignations (London).

Letters to a young Nobleman (London. Bod., Hun.

[J. Marriott], *Political Considerations; being a few Thoughts of a Candid Man at the present Crisis. In a Letter to a Noble Lord retired from Power* (London, J. Hinxman). BM, C., Hun.

The Minister of State. A Satire (London, Wilson and Fell). Hun.

The Palladium of Great Britain and Ireland, or Historical Strictures of Liberty, from before the Reformation down to the present Times (London, T. Becket and P. A. De Hondt). BM, Hun.

A Political Analysis of the War: the Principles of the present political Parties examined; and a just, natural and perfect Coalition propos'd between the Two Great Men, whose Conduct is particularly consider'd (London, T. Payne). W., Hun.

Punch's Politicks; in Several Dialogues between him and his Acquaintance (London, W. Nicoll). Hun.

Reasons why Lord **** should be made a public example (London). Goldsmith's Library, London University.

[Richardson], *A Letter to a Gentleman in the City* (London). BM.

The Royal Favourite (London, Pridden).

A Serious Address to the Vulgar. In which the Character and Abilities of a certain Nobleman, and the prejudice against the Place of his Birth, are impartially Considered (London, Hooper). W., Hun.

[J. Shebbeare], *One More Letter to the People of England. By Their Old Friend* (London, J. Pridden). BM, Hun.

Some Cool Thoughts on the present State of Affairs; with a Word to the Old Servant (London, J. Cooke), BM.

A Speech Without Doors, by a Lobby-Member (London, J. Williams). BM, C., Hun.

A Third Letter to the Right Honourable the Earl of B*** in which the Causes and Consequences of the War between Great Britain and Spain, are fully considered; AND the Conduct of a Certain Right Honourable Gentleman further examined (London, J. Coote). BM, Hun.

Thoughts on the Times. To be continued occasionally. No. I, containing, I. The Crisis, addressed to the members of Parliament. No. II. The First Letter from Count ****. No. III. The Second Letter to Count **** (London, Bristow). Hun.

The Three Conjurers, a political interlude. Stolen from Shakespeare. Dedicated to John Wilkes (London, E. Cabe). W., Hun.

The True Whig Displayed. Comprehending Cursory REMARKS on the Address to the Cocoa Tree. By a TORY (London, W. Nicoll). BM.

The Windsor Apparition, or the Knight of the Blazing Star (London). BM.

1763

An Address to Sir John Cust, Speaker of the House of Commons; on which the Characters of Lord Bute, Mr. Pitt, and Mr. Wilkes are set in a new Light. By the Author of the Letters signed Scipio Americanus in the Gazetteer (London, Gretton). BM.

An Address to the People of England (London, J. Payne). BM.

An Address to the People of England; shewing the advantages arising from the frequent changes of Ministers; with an address to the next Administration (London, J. Almon). BM.

[John Almon], *An Appendix to the Review of Mr. Pitt's Administration By the Author of the Review* (London, J. Almon). Hun.

[John Almon], *A Letter to J. Kidgell, containing a full answer to his narrative* (London). BM, Hun.

[John Almon], *A Review of Lord Bute's Administration* (London, J. Almon). BM, Bod., W., Hun.

The Appeal of Reason to the People of England, on the present state of PARTIES in the Nation (London, T. Becket). BM, Hun.

An Appeal to the Facts: In a Letter to the Rt. Hon. Earl Temple (London, A. Millar). BM, Hun.

An Authentick account of the proceedings against John Wilkes Esq; Member of Parliament for Aylesbury, and late Colonel of the Buckinghamshire Militia (London, J. Williams and J. Burd). BM.

[Richard Bentley], *Patriotism, a mock-heroic. In Five Cantos* (London, J. Hinxman). Hun.

Bibliography

The Blessings of P - -, and a Scotch Excise; or the Hasty Resignation. A Farce in two Acts, as it was lately performed at the New Theatre (London). BM, Hun.

The Blood Hounds; a Political Tale; inscribed to the E[arl] of B[ute] (London, Griffin).

The British Antidote to Caledonian Poison: Consisting of the most humorous Satirical Political Prints, for the year 1762 (2 vols., London, J. Sumpter). BM, Hun.

A Briton, *Letter to John Wilkes, Esq; Member of Parliament* (London). BM.

The Butiad, or Political Register; being a Supplement to the British Antidote to Caledonian Poison (London). BM, C.

[John Butler], *Serious Considerations on the Measures of the Present Administration* (London, G. Kearsley). BM, Hun.

The Cabal; as Acted at the Theatre in George-Street (London, R. Marriner). Hun.

[John Campbell], *Candid and Impartial Considerations on the Nature of the Sugar Trade* (London). BM, Hun.

The Case of the county of Devon, with respect to the consequences of the new excise duty on cyder and perry (London). Bod.

Considerations on the prevailing Spirit and Temper of the Present Times. In a Letter to the Scots Nation (London, W. Sandby). Bod.

The Constitution asserted and vindicated (London, W. Nicoll). BM, Bod., Hun.

The Crisis; an ode, to John Wilkes, Esq. (London). BM, C.

England's Constitutional Test for the Year 1763: In which are discussed, I. Authorship. II. Popularity. III. Liberty of the Press. IV. The Dignity of London Juries (London, J. Morgan). BM.

The Fall of Mortimer. An Historical Play. Revived from Montfort, with Alterations. Dedicated to the Right Honourable John, Earl of Bute (Dublin, Peter Wilson). BM, Hun.

[T. Farmer], *The plain truth: being a genuine narrative of the methods made use of to procure a copy of the Essay on Woman. With several extracts from the work itself* (London). BM, C.

The Favourite. A political Epistle. Humbly addressed to all Monarchs, Favourites and Ministers in the known World. By an ancient Briton (London, Burd).

French Lenisdors for English Bricks: and the kitchen in an uproar (London). BM.

A genuine Petition to the King, and likewise a Letter to the Right Hon. E[arl] of B[ute] (London).

Gisbal, an Hyperborean Tale: Translated from the Fragments of Ossian, the Son of Fingal (London, J. Pridden). W.

[E. B. Greene], *The Tower: a Poetical epistle, inscribed to J. Wilkes, Esq.* (London, J. Ridley). C.

The Group, composed of the most shocking figures, though the greatest in the nation. Inscribed to John Wilkes (who is above Title) and Charles Churchill. By Salvator Rosa Or, Rather the Real Friend of Mr. Wilkes (London, C. Moran). C., Hun.

[Jacob Henriques], *An Epistle to the dictator, in his retirement. Humbly addressed to him, by his constant admirer, and faithful coadjutor, Pro Bono Publico* (London, J. Wilkie). Hun.

The History of Prime Ministers and Favourites. In England; from the Conquest down to the present time; with Reflections on the Fatal Consequences of their Misconduct; and Political Deductions on the Perpetuity of Freedom in the English Constitution;

12-2

ascertained and vindicated from the Despotism affected by any of our Sovereigns (London, G. Kearsley). Hun.

In and Out and turn about, a satirical ballad (London). BM.

[Kearsley?], *Political Disquisitions proper for public Consideration, in the present State of Affairs. In a Letter to a Noble Duke* (London, Kearsley). BM, W., Hun.

[J. Kidgell], *A genuine and succinct narrative of a scandalous libel, entitled an Essay on Woman* (London). BM, Bod., Hun.

A Letter from a Gentleman in Town to his Friend in the Country. Occasioned by a late Resignation (London, T. Becket and P. A. De Hondt). BM, Bod.

A Letter from an M.P. in London to his Friend in Edinburgh, relative to the present critical state of affairs, and the dangerous antipathy between the people of England and Scotland (London, J. Hinxman). BM, Hun.

A Letter from a Member of the Opposition to Lord B - - - (London, G. Burnet). BM.

A Letter from Jonathan's to the Treasury (London, G. Burnet). Hun.

A Letter from Scots Sawney the Barber to Mr. Wilkes an English Parliamenter. Philo-Britannicus (London). BM.

A Letter from the Cocoa-tree to the chiefs of the opposition (London). Bod.

A Letter to the author of the North Briton in which the low scurrilities of that paper are detected, by a north Briton (London). Bod.

A Letter to the Right Honourable Earl Temple; upon the probable Motives and Consequences of his LORDSHIP's Conduct with regard to Mr. WILKES (London, W. Nicoll). BM, C., Hun.

[Charles Lloyd], *The Anatomy of a late Negotiation. Earnestly Addressed to the Serious Consideration of the People of Great Britain* (London, J. Wilkie). BM, Hun.

MacStuart, *England's Scotch Friend* (London). BM.

Magna Carta (London). BM.

Ministerial Patriotism Detected; or the Present Opposition Proved to be founded on Truly, just and laudable Principles, By the Evidence of Facts (London, J. Cooke). BM.

Le Montagnard Parvenu: or, The New Highland Adventurer in England: His Accidental Rise from Obscurity; his glaring Progress to Power: the WAYS and MEANS (London, W. Morgan). BM, Hun.

Observations upon the authority, manner and circumstances of the apprehension and confinement of Mr. Wilkes. Addressed to free-born Englishmen (London). BM, C.

The Opposition to the late Minister Vindicated from the aspersions of a Pamphlet, intitled, Considerations on the Present Dangerous Crisis (London, W. Bathoe). BM, Hun.

Patriotism, A Farce, as acted by His Majesty's Servants (London). BM, W., Hun.

The Royal Register: or a Chronological List of creations and promotions in Church and State, Civil and Military from the accession of George III, in which it will appear the extraordinary partiality towards the Scotch (London, J. Williams). BM.

[Owen Ruffhead], *Considerations on the Present Dangerous Crisis* (2nd ed., London, T. Becket and P. A. De Hondt). BM, C., Hun.

The Scots Scourge; or Pridden's Supplement to the Antidote to Caledonian Poison (2 vols., London, J. Pridden). BM.

A second letter to the author of the North Briton in which the wicked and opprobrious invectives contained in that production, are confuted, and the gross misrepresentations of facts and characters shewn (London, A. Henderson). BM.

Bibliography

A Select Collection of the Most Interesting Letters on Government, Liberty and the Constitution of England; which have appeared in the different Newspapers (3 vols., London, J. Almon). Hun.

Serious Thoughts on the Ingratitude and Injustice of the Opposition against Lord B[ute]; with an Attempt to prove that we never were so happy as during his Lordship's Administration (London, Flaxney).

The True Flower of Brimstone. Extracted from the Briton, North Briton and Auditor (London, Williams). Bod., W.

[P. C. Webb], Some Observations on the late determination for discharging Mr. Wilkes from his commitment to the Tower of London. For being the Author and Publisher of a Seditious Libel, called the North Briton no. XLV. By a Member of the House of Commons (London, A. Millar). BM, C.

[G. O. Wyndham], A Letter to the Earls of Egremont and Halifax, secretaries of state, on the seizure of papers (London). Bod.

1764

[John Almon], A Review of Mr. Pitt's Administration. By the Author of the Review of Lord Bute's (4th ed., London, G. Kearsley). C., Hun.

The British Coffee-House. A Poem (London). W., Hun.

A Candid examination of the legality of the Warrant issued by the Secretaries of State for apprehending the printers, publishers of a late interesting paper (London, J. Fletcher). BM, Hun.

The Conduct of the Administration, in the Prosecution of Mr. Wilkes (London, J. Wilkie). BM.

An Enquiry into the Doctrine Lately Propagated Concerning Libels (London). BM.

[David Hartley], The Budget, inscribed to the man who thinks himself minister (London, J. Almon). BM, C., Hun.

A Letter from Albemarle Street to the Cocoa Tree on some late Transactions (2nd ed., London, J. Almon). BM, Bod., Hun.

A Letter from Candor, to the Public Advertiser: containing a series of constitutional remarks on some late interesting trials, and other points, of the most essential consequences to civil liberty (London, J. Almon). BM, Bod., Hun.

A Letter to a Noble Member of the Club in Albemarle-Street from John Wilkes, Esq; at Paris (London, W. Nicoll). BM, W.

A Letter to the gentlemen in opposition; wherein their principles and their conduct are considered (London). Bod.

A Letter to the Right Honourable Charles Townshend (London, W. Nicoll). Hun.

[Charles Lloyd], A Defence of the majority in the House of Commons, on the question relating to General Warrants (London). BM, Hun.

[Sir William Meredith], A Reply to the Defence of the Majority on the Question relating to General Warrants (London, J. Almon). BM, Hun.

Philanthropos, A Dissection of the North Briton, Number XLV (London). BM.

The Political Theatre (London, J. Wilkie). Hun.

[J. Shebbeare], An Address to the Public on the late dismission of a General Officer (London). BM, C.

[J. H. Stevenson], A Pastoral Puke. A Second Sermon Preached before the People called Whigs. By an Independent (London, J. Hinxman). BM, Hun.

The Three Conjurers, a political interlude. Stolen from Shakespeare (London). BM.

[Joseph Towers], An Enquiry into the Question, whether juries are, or are not judges

347

of the law, as well as of fact, with particular reference to libels (London, J. Wilkie). Hun.

[Charles Townshend], *A Defence of the Minority in the House of Commons, On the Question Relating to General Warrants* (London, J. Almon). BM, Hun.

The True-Born Scot: Inscribed to John Earl of Bute (London, E. Sumpter). C., Hun.

[R. Wallace], *A View of the Internal Policy of Great Britain. In Two Parts* (London, A. Millar). BM, Hun.

[Horace Walpole], *A Counter-Address to the Public, on the late Dismission of a General Officer* (London, J. Almon). BM, C., Hun.

[John Wilkes], *Fragments and Anecdotes, proper to be read at the present crisis by every honest Englishman* (London, J. Williams and J. Almon). BM, C.

J. Wilkes, *A Letter to the Worthy Electors of the Borough of Aylesbury in the County of Bucks* (London, Stuart Donaldson). BM, Hun.

[J. Wilkes, trans.], *The Origin and Progress of Despotism in the Oriental, and other Empires, of Africa, Europe and America* (by N. A. Boulanger) (Amsterdam). BM, C., Hun.

1765

An Address to both Parties (London, Wilkie). BM, Hun.

An Address to the Remaining Members of the Coterie (London, Wilkie). BM, Hun.

[John Brown], *Thoughts on Civil Liberty, on Licentiousness and Faction* (2nd ed., London, R. Davis and C. Reymers). BM, C., W., Hun.

A Candid Refutation of the Charges Brought against the Present Ministers, In a late pamphlet, entitled the Principles of the late Changes impartially examined, In a letter to a supposed Author (London, F. Newberry). BM, W., Hun.

[Grey Cooper], *The Merits of the New Administration Truly Stated in Answer to the several pamphlets and papers published against them* (London, J. Williams). W., Hun.

[Grey Cooper], *A Pair of Spectacles for Short Sighted Politicians: or, A Candid Answer to a late extraordinary Pamphlet, entitled, An Honest Man's Reasons for declining to take any Part in the New Administration* (London, J. Williams). BM, W., Hun.

J. Dumner, *A Defence of the New-England Charters* (London). C., Hun.

[John Fothergill], *Considerations relative to the North American Colonies* (London, Henry Kent). C., Hun.

[John Free], *The Voluntary Exile; or, the English Poet's Sermon in Verse, written upon divers important Subjects, Before he embarked for France, and dedicated à La Coterie, or the Society of English Patriots. Part the first. With Variety of Notes, Religious, Historical and Political* (London, J. Almon). W.

A Free and Candid Address to the Right Hon. William Pitt on the Present Posture of Affairs, both at Home and Abroad (London, Cooke).

A Full and Free Inquiry into The Merits of Peace; with some Strictures on the Spirit of Party (London, T. Payne). BM, W., Hun.

Joseph Gee, *A Detection of gross Impositions on the Parliament with respect to two acts passed the last session* (London, Baldwin).

[David Hartley], *The State of the Nation, with a Preliminary Defence of the Budget* (London, J. Almon). Hun.

Bibliography

[Augustus Hervey], *A Letter to the Earl of B - - -, relative to the late Changes that have happened in the Administration* (Richardson and Urquhart). Bod.

[Soame Jenyns], *The Objections to the Taxation of our American Colonies by the Legislature of Great Britain, briefly considered* (London, J. Wilkie). C., Hun.

[William Knox], *The Claim of the Colonies to an exemption from Internal Taxes imposed by Authority of Parliament, examined: In a Letter from a Gentleman in London* (London, W. Johnson). C., Hun.

[William Knox?], *A Letter to a Member of Parliament wherein the power of the British Legislature, and the case of the Colonists are briefly and impartially considered* (London, W. Flexney). BM, Hun.

A Letter concerning Libels, Warrants, and the Seizure of Papers; with a view to some Proceedings, and the Defence of them by the Majority (London, J. Almon). BM, C., Hun.

A Letter to a member of Parliament, wherein the power of the British legislature and the case of the colonists are briefly and impartially considered (London). Bod., BM, Hun.

A Letter to the Earl of L - - - - - - n; concerning a regency. To which is prefixed, His Majesty's Speech to both Houses of Parliament, the whole interspersed with anecdotes and among others an account of the North Briton no. 45 (London, A. Henderson). BM.

[Charles Lloyd], *A Critical Review of the New Administration* (London, J. Wilkie). BM, C.

[Charles Lloyd], *An Honest Man's Reasons for Declining to take part in the new Administration, in a letter to the Marquis of - - - - - - - -* (London, Wilkie). BM, C., W., Hun.

[Israel Mauduit], *Some Trifling Thoughts on Serious Subjects Addressed to the Earl of Sandwich to which is added Liberty's Dream, with a description of modern Patriotism* (London, Newell).

The Mutual Interest of Great Britain and the American Colonies Considered (London, W. Nicoll). BM.

Oppression, A Poem by an American, with Notes by a North-Briton (London, C. Moran). W., Hun.

[James Otis], *Considerations on behalf of the Colonists. In a Letter to a Noble Lord* (2nd ed., London, J. Almon). C., Hun.

[J. Palmer], *An Essay on the Constitution of England* (London). BM.

Patriotism, A Mock-Heroic, in Six Cantos (2nd ed., London, J. Wilkie). Wren.

The Political Balance. In which the Principles and Conduct of the Two Parties are weighed (London, T. Becket and P. A. De Hondt). C., Hun.

Remarks on the Importance of the Study of Political Pamphlets, Weekly Papers, Periodical Papers, Daily Papers, Political Music (London, W. Nicoll). BM, Bod., W., Hun.

[Temple?], *The Principles of the late Changes Impartially Examined: In a Letter from a Son of Candor to the Public Advertiser* (London, J. Almon). BM, W., Hun.

A Vindication of the Whigs against the Clamours of a Tory Mob; with an Address to the City (London, C. Moran). Wren, Hun.

[Thomas Whately], *The Regulations lately made concerning the Colonies, and the Taxes imposed upon them, considered* (London, J. Wilkie). BM.

[John Wilkes], *The Favourite. With a dedication to my Lord B**** (London, J. Harrison). W.

349

1766

An Address to the People of England; showing the advantages arising from the frequent changes of Ministers; with an address to the next Administration (London, J. Almon). BM, Hun.

[John Almon], ed., *A Collection of the most interesting Tracts, Lately published in England and America, on the subjects of Taxing the American Colonies and Regulating their Trade* (2 vols., London, J. Almon). W.

An Apology for the Ministerial Life and Actions of a celebrated Favourite (London, J. Pridden). BM, Hun.

An Application of some General Political Rules, to the Present State of Great Britain, Ireland and America. In a Letter to the Right Honourable Earl Temple (London, J. Almon). BM, W., Hun.

[W. Bollan], *A Succinct View of our Colonies . . . Being an Extract from an Essay lately published, entitled, the Freedom of Speech and Writing upon Public Affairs Considered* (London). BM, C., Hun.

British Liberties, or the Free-Born Subject's Inheritance; Containing the Laws that form the Basis of those Liberties, with Observations thereon; also an Introductory Essay on Political Liberty and a Comprehensive View of the Constitution of Great Britain (London, H. Woodfall and W. Strahan). BM, Hun.

[Edmund Burke], *Short Account of a late Short Administration* (London, J. Wilkie). Hun.

Collection of all the remarkable passages in the Briton, North Briton and Auditor (London). W.

Considerations on the American Stamp Act and on the Conduct of the Minister who planned it (London, W. Nicoll). W., Hun.

Constitutional Considerations on the Power of Parliament to levy Taxes on the North American Colonies (London). Hun.

[Samuel Cooper], *The Crisis, or a Full Defence of the Colonies in which it is incontestably proved that the British Constitution has been flagrantly violated in the late Stamp Act* (London, W. Griffin). W., Hun.

[Humphrey Cotes], *An Enquiry into the Conduct of a late Right Honourable Commoner* (3rd impression, London, J. Almon). BM, C., W., Hun.

[Daniel Delany], *Considerations on the Propriety of Imposing Taxes in the British Colonies, For the Purpose of raising a Revenue, by Act of Parliament* (London, J. Almon). BM, W., Hun.

An Essay on the Constitution of England (2nd ed., London, T. Becket and P. A. De Hondt). BM.

An Examination of the Rights of the Colonies, upon the Principles of Law. By A Gentleman at the Bar (London, R. Dymott and J. Almon). BM, Hun.

A genuine Collection of the several pieces of Political Intelligence Extraordinary, Epigrams, Poetry, &c that have appeared before the Public in Detached Pieces; Now carefully selected together in one View, by an IMPARTIAL HAND (London, T. Butcher and John Russell). Wren, Hun.

Good Humour; Or, a Way with the Colonies. Wherein is Occasionally enquired into Mr. P - - t's Claim of Popularity; and the Principles of Virtuous Liberty As Taught in the School of Mr. Wilkes and other Peripatetics (London). W., Hun.

The History of the late Minority. Exhibiting the Conduct, Principles, and Views of that Party, during the years 1762, 1763, 1764 and 1765 (London, J. Almon). BM, C., W., Hun.

Bibliography

[Stephen Hopkins], *The Grievances of the American Colonies Candidly Examined* (London, J. Almon). C., Hun.

The Justice and Necessity of Taxing the American Colonies, Demonstrated. Together with a Vindication of the Authority of Parliament (London, J. Almon). C., Hun.

The Late Occurrences in North America, and Policy of Great Britain Considered (London, J. Almon). W., Hun.

A Letter from a Gentleman in London to His Friend in the Country relating to the American Stamp Act, With Mr. P - - t's and other speeches on the Occasion (London).

A Letter to the E - - - T - - - - - upon his conduct in a late negociation. To which is prefixed, A curious dialogue between a certain author and his bookseller (London). Bod.

A Letter to the Gentlemen of the Committee of London Merchants, trading to North-America; shewing in what manner the trade and Manufacturers of Britain may be affected by some late Restrictions on the American Commerce, and by the Operation of the Act for the Stamp Duty (London, Richardson and Urquart). W., Hun.

A Letter to Will Chat-em, Esq; of Turn-about-Hall, From his Sister (London, S. Bladon). Hun.

[Charles Lloyd], *An Examination of the Principles and Boasted Disinterestedness of a late Right Honourable Gentleman. In a Letter from an Old Man of Business to a Noble Lord* (London, J. Almon). BM, Hun.

[Charles Lloyd], *A True History of a late Short Administration* (London). BM, Hun.

A Man of Abilities for the Earl of B - - e, Or, Scotch Politics defeated in America (London, J. Williams). Hun.

The New Foundling Hospital for Wit (London). BM.

J. Otis, *The Rights of the British Colonies Asserted and Proved* (London, J. Almon). C.

A Parallel Drawn between the Administration In the Four Last Years of Queen Anne, and the Four First of George III. By a Country Gentleman (London, J. Almon). BM, Hun.

A Plain and Seasonable Address to the Freeholders of Great Britain, on the present posture of affairs in America (London, Richardson and Urquart). Hun.

Political Debates (Paris [i.e. London]). C.

Pride: a poem. Inscribed to John Wilkes, Esquire. By an Englishman (London, J. Almon). C., Hun.

Reflexions on Representation in Parliament: being an Attempt to shew the Equity and Practicability, not only of Establishing a more Equal Representation throughout Great Britain, but also of admitting the Americans to a share in the Legislature (London, J. Flexney). BM, Hun.

The Secret Springs of the late Changes in the Ministry Fairly Explained, By an Honest Man. In Answer to the Abuse and Misrepresentations of a pretended Son of Candor (London, T. Becket and P. A. De Hondt). BM, C., W., Hun.

A Short History of the Conduct of the Present Ministry, with Regard to the American Stamp Act (London, J. Almon). W., Hun.

A Short View of the Political Life and Transactions of a late Right Honourable Commoner (London, W. Griffin). Hun.

Some Considerations upon some late extraordinary grants. And other particulars of a late Patriot's conduct (London, J. Almon). Hun.

Bibliography

[*Joshua Steele*], *An Account of a late Conference on the Occurrences in America. In a Letter to a Friend* (London, J. Almon). Hun.

[Josiah Tucker], *A Letter from a Merchant in London to his Nephew in North America, relative to the present posture of Affairs in the Colonies* (London, J. Walter). C., Hun.

A Vindication of the Present Ministry, from the many Flagrant Calumnies, Gross Misrepresentations and even Evident Falsities, contained in a Book, intitled, The History of the late Minority, &c. In a Letter to the supposed Authors of that piece (London, J. Cooke). C., W.

What Should be Done: or, Remarks on the Political State of Things. Addressed to the present Administration, the Members of the House of Commons, and the good People of England (London, W. Flexney). C.

[T. Whately], *Consideration on the Trade and Finance of this Kingdom and on the Measures of Administration with Respect to Those Great National Objects since the Conclusion of the Peace* (London). C.

1767

A Complete Collection of the Genuine Papers, Letters, &c. in the Case of John Wilkes, Esq. (Paris and Berlin), BM, C.

A Free Appeal to the People of Great Britain, On the Conduct of the Present Administration, since the Thirteenth of July, 1766 (2nd ed., London, J. Almon). BM, Hun.

The Honest Elector's Proposal for Rendering the Votes of all Constituents, throughout the Kingdom, Free and Independent. By C. W. (London, J. Almon). W.

[Edward King], *An Essay on the English Constitution and Government* (London, B. White). BM.

Letter from a minister in the country to his friend in London (London). Bod.

A Letter to G[eorge] G[renville] (London, J. Williams). BM, W., Hun.

A Letter to the Earl of Bute, upon his Union with the Earl of Chatham, in Support of the Popular Measure of Four Shillings Land-Tax (London, J. Almon). Hun.

A New and Impartial Collection of Interesting Letters, from the Public Papers; many of them written by Persons of Eminence, On a great variety of important subjects, which have occasionally engaged the Public Attention: From the Accession of his present Majesty, in September 1760 [sic], *to May 1767* (2 vols., London, J. Almon). BM, W., Hun.

A Review of the Present State of the Nation, its Maladies and Means of Relief (London, Peat). BM.

[Shebbeare], *A Seventh Letter to the People of England. A Defence of the prerogative Royal, as it was exerted in his Majesty's Proclamation for prohibiting the Exportation of Corn* (London, J. Almon). BM, Hun.

A Speech in behalf of the Constitution, against the Suspending and Dispensing Prerogative (London, J. Almon). BM, Wren, Hun.

A View of the Several Changes made in the Administration of Government since the Accession of His Present Majesty (London, J. Almon). BM.

[John Wilkes], *A Letter to his Grace the Duke of Grafton, First Commissioner of his Majesty's Treasury* (London, J. Almon). BM, C., W., Hun.

1768

*The A*********n's Letter to the L - - d M - - - r relative to his polite treatment of Mr. Wilkes. Versified by another A********n* (London, S. Hooper). BM.

Bibliography

[Almon], Ed., *The New Foundling Hospital for Wit. A Collection of pieces in prose and verse by Lord Chesterfield and other eminent persons* (Pts. 1–4, London, J. Almon). BM.

The Battle of the Quills: or, Wilkes attacked and defended. An impartial selection of pieces in prose and verse, relative to John Wilkes (London, J. Williams). BM, Hun.

[William Bollan], *Continued Corruption, Standing Armies, and Popular Discontents Considered; and the establishment of the English Colonies in America* (London, J. Almon). W., Hun.

[G. Canning], *A Letter to the Right Hon. William Earl of Hillsborough, on the connection between Great Britain and her Colonies* (London). BM, Hun.

G. S. Carey, *Liberty Chastised: or Patriotism in Chains. A Tragi, comi, political farce, as it was performed by his M - - - - - y's S - - - - - ts, in the year 1268* (London, Staples Steare). Hun.

A Cautionary Address to the Electors of England. Being a Touchstone between the Constituents and Candidates. With a word touching J. Wilkes, Esq. (London, J. Williams). BM, Hun.

A comparative View of the conduct of John Wilkes, Esq; as contrasted with the opposite measures during the last six years (London, J. Williams). BM, Hun.

A complete collection of the genuine papers, Letters, &c. in the Case of John Wilkes, Esq. Elected Knight of the Shire for the County of Middlesex, March XXVIII, 1768 (Paris). BM, Hun.

The Court of Star Chamber, or seat of Oppression (London, Staples Steare). Wren.

A Defence of the R - - - - H - - - - - - the E - - L of B - - E, from the Imputations laid to his Charge. In a Letter to His L - - DS - - P. by Sir Archy Mac Sarcasm, Bart. (London, Staples Steare). Hun.

Dialogue between the Two Giants at Guildhall, humbly addressed to John Wilkes, Esq; to which is added, a versification of two of Mr. W - - - - 's election pieces (London, Staples Steares). BM.

[John Dickinson], *The late Regulations respecting the British Colonies on the Continent of America Considered. In a Letter from a Gentleman in Philadelphia to his Friend in London* (London, J. Almon). C.

[John Dickinson], *Letters from a Farmer in Pennsylvania, to the Inhabitants of the British Colonies* (London, J. Almon). C., BM, Hun.

English Liberty established; or, a mirrour for posterity: John Wilkes esqr the undaunted assertor of the liberty of the press, and the rights of Englishmen (London, J. Lee and Williams). BM.

The Englishman Deceived; a Political Piece (London). BM.

An Epistle to James Boswell, Esq. Occasioned by his having transmitted the Moral Writings of Dr. Samuel Johnson, to Pascal Paoli, General of the Corsicans. With a Postscript, containing Thoughts on Liberty; and a Parallel, after the manner of Plutarch, Between the celebrated Patriot of late, and John Wilkes Esq., Member of Parliament for Middlesex. By W. K., Esq. (London, Fletcher and Anderson). BM.

An Essay on Patriotism, and on the Character and Conduct of some late famous Pretenders to that Virtue. Particularly of the Present Popular Gentleman (London, Staples Steare). C., Hun.

An Examination into the Conduct of Lord M - - - F - - - D, through the Affair of Mr. Wilkes (London, Staples Steare). Wren.

13-2

Bibliography

The Foundation of British Liberty; proving the indisputable Right of every English-man to the Common Laws of the Land, for the Protection of his Person and Property: In a Letter from a Gentleman in the Country to his Friend in London (London, T. Peat). Hun.

[A. Henderson], *A Letter to the Right Honourable the Earl T - - - - e: or, the Case of J - - - W - - - - s, Esquire: With respect to the King, Parliament, Courts of Justice, Secretaries of State, and the Multitude* (London, A. Johnson). BM.

[A. Henderson], *A Second Letter to the Right Honourable the Earl T - - - - E. In which the Proceedings relative to J - - N W - - - - S, from March 28th to June 18th, are minutely considered; the Person clearly pointed out who was the Cause of the Present Distractions: and a Curious Anecdote with regard to Lord M - - - - - - - D's Family, Never published before* (London). BM.

[Thomas Hollis], *The True Sentiments of America: Contained in a Collection of Letters sent from the House of Representatives of the Province of Massachusetts* (London, J. Almon). Hun.

[William Jones], *The Constitutional Criterion: By a Member of the University of Cambridge* (London, J. Almon). W.

[William Knox], *The Present State of the Nation: Particularly with respect to its Trade, Finance &c. Addressed to the King and both Houses of Parliament* (London, J. Almon). BM, C., W., Hun.

A Letter on the Public Conduct of Mr. Wilkes (London). BM.

A Letter to the Man who thinks himself Minister (London, J. Almon). W.

A Letter to the Right Hon. Thomas Harley, Esq; Lord Mayor of the City of London. To which is added a serious expostulation with the Livery (London, W. Bingley). BM, Hun.

A Narrative of the Proceedings against John Wilkes, Esq. From his Commitment in April 1763 to his Outlawry. With a full View of the Arguments used in Parliament and out of Doors in canvassing the various important Questions that arose from his Case (London, Richardson and Urquart). BM, Hun.

A New Form of Prayer, and Thanksgiving for the Happy Deliverance of John Wilkes, Esq. (London). BM.

No Liberty! No Life! Proper Wages, and Down with Oppression. In a Letter to the Brave People of England. By John Englishman (3rd ed., London, W. Harris). Wren.

[Mandtypo], *Britannia's Intercession for the Happy Deliverance of John Wilkes* (London). BM.

The North-Country Poll; or, An Essay on the New Method of Appointing Members to serve in Parliament (London, Staples Steare). C.

An original camera obscura; or the court, city and country magic-lanthorn (London, J. Wilkie). BM, Hun.

A Perspective View of the Complexion of some late Elections, and of the Candidates, With a Conclusion deduced from Thence. In a Letter addressed to a Member of Parliament (London, Staples Steare). C.

Reflections on the Case of Mr. Wilkes, and on the right of the people to elect their own representatives. To which is added, the case of Mr. Walpole (London, J. Almon). BM, C., Hun.

[Stephen Sayre], *The Englishman Deceived; A Political Piece: wherein some very Important Secrets of State are briefly recited, And offered to the Consideration of the PUBLIC* (London, Kearsley). BM, W., Hun.

Bibliography

A Seasonable Admonition on an important occasion (London). Bod.

A Serious and Friendly Address (London). BM, Hun.

The whole account of John Wilkes, Esq., from the time of his being chosen a Member of Parliament of Aylesbury, till his departure to France. To which is added his speeches since his return to England (London, J. Millar). BM, C.

[Wilkes], *A celebrated Letter sent from John Wilkes, Esq. at Paris, to the Electors of Aylesbury, in the year 1764* (London, Staples Steare). BM, C., Hun.

[Wilkes], *The History of England from the Revolution to the Accession of the Brunswick Line, vol. I* (London, J. Almon). BM, Hun.

1769

[Edward Bancroft], *Remarks on the Review of the Controversy between Great Britain and her Colonies* (London, T. Becket and P. A. De Hondt). C., Hun.

[Richard Bland], *An Enquiry into the Rights of the British Colonies; Intended as an Answer to The Regulations lately made concerning the Colonies, and the Taxes imposed upon them considered* (London, J. Almon). C., Hun.

[William Bollan], *The Free Briton's Memorial, To all the Freeholders, Citizens and Burgesses, who Elect the Members of the British Parliament, Presented in Order to the Effectual Defence of their Injured Right of Election* (London, J. Williams). W., Hun.

British Essays in favour of the brave Corsicans: by several hands. Collected and published by James Boswell (London). C., Hun.

[Edmund Burke], *Observations on a late State of the Nation* (London, Dodsley). BM, Bod., C., W., Hun.

[George B. Butler], *The Case of Great Britain and America, Addressed to the King, and both Houses of Parliament* (London, T. Becket and P. A. De Hondt). C., W., Hun.

The Case of the late Election for the County of Middlesex, considered on the Principles of the Constitution and the Authorities of Law (London, T. Cadell). BM.

Alexander Cluny, *The American Traveller; Or, Observations on the Present State, Culture and Commerce of the British Colonies in America* (London, E. and C. Dilly). W., Hun.

A Collection of all Mr. Wilkes's Addresses to the Gentlemen, Clergy, and Freeholders of the County of Middlesex (London, J. Burd). BM, C.

A complete Collection of the genuine papers, letters, &c in the Case of John Wilkes (Berlin). C.

Considerations on the Times (London, J. Almon). C.

[Dowdeswell], *The Sentiments of an English Freeholder, on the late decision of the Middlesex Election* (London, J. Dodsley). BM, Wren, W.

[J. Dyson], *A Word in behalf of the House of Commons: or, Remarks upon a Speech supposed to have been delivered by a Right Honourable Gentleman, On the Motion for expelling Mr. Wilkes, On Friday, February 3, 1769* (London, J. Dodsley). BM.

English Liberty: being a collection of Interesting Tracts, From the Year 1762 to 1769. Containing the Private Correspondence, Public Letters, Speeches and Addresses, of John Wilkes Esq. Humbly Dedicated to the King (2 vols., London, T. Baldwin). BM.

English Liberty, or the British Lion roused; Containing the Sufferings of John Wilkes, Esq; from the First of his Persecution, Down to the Present Time (2 vols., London, T. Marsh). C.

Bibliography

A Fair Trial of the Important Question, or the Rights of Electors Asserted; against the Doctrine of Incapacity by Expulsion or Resolution, with some Occasional Strictures (London, J. Almon). BM, C., W.

[Nathaniel Forster], *An Answer to a pamphlet entitled, 'The Question Stated, whether the Freeholders of Middlesex forfeited their Right by Voting for Mr. Wilkes at the last Election? In a Letter from a Member of Parliament to one of his Constituents'. With a Postscript, occasioned by a Letter in the Public Papers subscribed JUNIUS* (London, Fletcher, Walker and Robson). BM, C., W.

Harlequin Premier: A Farce, as it is Daily Acted (Brentford). BM, Hun.

A History of Jack Wilks [sic], *a lover of liberty* (2 vols., London, H. Gardener). BM.

An Inquiry into the Causes of the Present Disputes between the British Colonies in America and their Mother Country (London, J. Wilkie). Hun., C.

[William Knox], *An Appendix to the Present State of the Nation. Containing a Reply to the Observations on that Pamphlet* (London, J. Almon). BM, W.

[Knox], *The Controversy Between Great Britain and her Colonies Reviewed* (London, J. Almon). C., Hun.

[Sir Hercules Langrische], *Considerations on the Dependencies of Great Britain. With Observations on a Pamphlet, intitled, The Present State of the Nation* (London, J. Almon). BM, C., Hun.

A Letter to the author of the Question Stated (London). BM, Hun.

A Letter to the Right Honourable the Earl of Hilsborough [sic], *on the present Situation of Affairs in America* (London, Kearsley). C., Hun.

Letters between the Duke of GRAFTON, the Earls of HALIFAX, EGREMONT, CHATHAM, TEMPLE, and TALBOT, Baron BOTTETOURT, Rt. Hon. HENRY BILSON LEGGE, Rt. Hon. Sir JOHN CUST, Bart. Mr. CHARLES CHURCHILL, Monsieur VOLTAIRE, the Abbé WINCKELMAN &c. And JOHN WILKES, ESQ., With explanatory notes (London). BM.

The Life and Political Writings of John Wilkes, Esq; Four Times Elected Knight of the Shire for the County of Middlesex, and Alderman Elect of the Ward of Farringdon Without, London (Birmingham, J. Sketchley). BM.

[William Meredith], *The Question Stated, Whether the Freeholders of Middlesex lost their Right, by voting for Mr. Wilkes at the last election? In a Letter from a Member of Parliament to one of his Constituents* (London, Woodfall, Richardson and Urquart). BM, C., W., Hun.

[Mulgrave], *A Letter from a Member of Parliament to One of his Constituents, on the late Proceedings of the House of Commons in the Middlesex Elections. With a Postscript, Containing some observations on a pamphlet entitled, 'The Case of the late Election for the County of Middlesex considered'* (London, M. Hingeston). BM, C., W., Hun.

Observations on the Review of the Controversy between Great Britain and Her Colonies (London, T. Becket and P. A. De Hondt). W.

Original and Select Letters from J. Wilkes Esq. to the Aldermen of London: likewise Oliver Cromwell's Speech, which he made when he dissolved the Long Parliament (London, S. Sharp). BM.

J. Otis, *A Vindication of the British Colonies* (J. Almon, London). C., Hun.

The Patriotic Miscellany; being a collection of interesting papers, jests, anecdotes, epigrams, &c. in the Case of John Wilkes Esq; containing likewise, A succinct

356

Bibliography

Account of the Persecutions inflicted on that Gentleman, an account of No. 45 of the North Briton, & the Essay on Woman (London and Norwich). BM.

[R. Phelps], *The Rights of the Colonies, and the Extent of the Legislative Authority of Great-Britain, briefly Stated and Considered* (London, J. Nourse). C., Hun.

The Political Conduct of the Earl of Chatham (London, T. Becket and P. A. De Hondt). BM, C., W., Hun.

[Joseph Priestley?], *The Present State of Liberty in Great Britain and her Colonies. By an Englishman* (London, Johnson and Payne). W.

[Allan Ramsay], *Thoughts on the Origin and Nature of Government. Occasioned by the late Disputes between Great Britain and her American Colonies. Written in the Year 1766* (London, T. Becket and P. A. De Hondt). BM, C., W., Hun.

[John Rayner], *An Inquiry into the doctrine lately propagated, concerning Attachments of contempt, the alteration of Records, and the Court of Star Chamber, upon the Principles of Law, and the constitution, particularly as they relate to prosecutions for libels* (London). BM.

Remarks on the Appendix to the Present State of the Nation (London, R. Davis). BM, W.

[John Scott], *The Constitution Defended, and Pensioner Exposed; in Remarks on the False Alarm* (London, E. and C. Dilly, and J. Ridley). BM, W.

Serious Considerations on a late very important Decision of the House of Commons (London). BM.

Some Considerations upon the late Decision of the House of Commons with regard to the Middlesex Election (London, J. Wilkie). BM.

[J. Towers], *Observations on Public Liberty, Patriotism, Ministerial Despotism, and National Grievances. With some Remarks on Riots, Petitions, Loyal Addresses, and Military Execution. In a Letter to the Freeholders of the County of Middlesex, and the Livery of London. By an Independent Citizen of London* (London, J. Towers). C., W., Hun.

The True Constitutional Means of putting an end to the disputes between Great-Britain and the American colonies (London). Bod., Hun.

A Vindication of the Right of Election, against the disabling Power of the House of Commons; shewing that Power to be Contrary to the Principles of the Constitution, inconsistent with the Rights of the Electors, and not warranted by the Law and Usage of Parliament, In which is included Observations on the Power of Expulsion (London, G. Woodfall, J. Wilkie, Richardson and Urquart). BM, W.

[John Wilkes], *A Letter to the Right Honourable George Grenville, Occasioned by his Publication of the Speech he made in the House of Commons on the motion for expelling Mr. Wilkes, Friday, February 3, 1769. To which is added, A Letter on the Public Conduct of Mr. Wilkes. First published November 1, 1768; with an Appendix* (London, Isaac Fell). BM, C., W., Hun.

J. J. Zubly, *An Humble Enquiry into the Nature of the Dependency of the American Colonies upon the Parliament of Great Britain* (London). Hun.

1770

[William Bollan], *The Free Briton's Supplemental Memorial To the Electors of the Members of the British Parliament; Wherein the Origin of Parliaments in Europe, and other interesting Matters are Considered* (London, J. Williams). W.

357

Bibliography

[Edmund Burke], *Thoughts on the Cause of the Present Discontents* (London, J. Dodsley). BM, Bod., C., W., Hun.

The Constitution Defended, and Pensioner exposed; in Remarks on the False Alarm (London). BM.

A Defence of the Proceedings of the House of Commons in the Middlesex Election. In which are considered Two late pamphlets, viz. 'The Sentiments of an English Freeholder on the late Decision of the Middlesex Election' and 'An Essay on the Middlesex Election'. By the Author of the Answer to the Question Stated (London, J. Wilkie). Wren.

The Drivers: a dialogue (London, Fletcher and Hodson). C.

An Enquiry into the nature and legality of press warrants (London). BM.

Extract of a Letter from the House of Representatives of the Massachusetts Bay to their agent Dennys De Berdt, Esq. With some remarks (London). C.

[Nathaniel Forster], *A Letter to the Author of an Essay on the Middlesex Election: in which his objections to the power of expulsion are considered: and the nature of representation in Parliament examined. By the author of A Defence of the Proceedings of the House of Commons* (London, J. Wilkie). BM.

[Samuel Johnson], *The False Alarm* (London, T. Cadell). BM, C., W.

[Arthur Lee], *The Political Detection; or, the Treachery and Tyranny of Administration, Both at Home and Abroad; Displayed in a Series of Letters, signed Junius Americanus* (London, J. and W. Oliver). W., BM.

Liberty deposed, or the Western Election. A Satirical Poem in three books (London, J. Almon). BM.

[Catherine Macaulay], *Observations on a Pamphlet entitled Thoughts on the Cause of the Present Discontents* (London, E. and C. Dilly). BM, C., W.

[R. Macfarlane], *The History of the Reign of George the Third* (London). C., Hun.

[F. Maseres], *Considerations on the Expediency of admitting representatives from the American Colonies into the British House of Commons* (London, White). BM, Hun.

[William Meredith], *A Letter to Dr. Blackstone, By the Author of the Question Stated. To which is prefixed, Dr. Blackstone's Letter to Sir William Meredith* (London, G. Woodfall, Richardson and Urquart). BM, C., W.

A Mirror for the Multitude: or, Wilkes and his abettors no patriots (Glasgow, J. Gilmour). BM.

Observations on several acts of Parliament passed in the 4th, 6th and 7th years of his present Majesty's Reign. Published by the merchants of Boston (London). Bod.

An Ode on the Enlargement of Wilkes (London). BM.

Opposition no proof of Patriotism; with some Advice concerning Party Writing (London). BM, C.

The Repository or Treasury of Politics and Literature (2 vols., London). BM.

[George Rous], *An Essay on the Middlesex Election: In which the Power of Expulsion is Particularly Considered* (London, B. White). BM, W.

[Thomas Rushton], *Party dissected; or, Plain Truth; a Poem by a Plain Dealer* (London, Bell). C.

[J. Shebbeare], *An Eighth Letter to the People of England* (London). BM.

The True Alarm (London). Bod.

The Triumphs of Bute, A Poem (London, J. Swan). W.

[Matthew Wheelock], *Reflections, Moral and Political on Great Britain and her Colonies* (London, T. Becket). BM, W., Hun.

Bibliography

Wilkes's Jest Book; or the Merry Patriot. Being a collection of all the choicest Bons-Mots, Songs and other Witticisms, said or written from the year 1764, to the present time, respecting J. Wilkes, Esq (London, T. Evans). BM.

[John Wilkes], *A Letter to Samuel Johnson, L.L.D.* (London, J. Almon). BM, C.

[John Wilkes], ed., *Majesty Misled: A Tragedy* (London, T. Jordan). Guildhall Library, London.

C. Pamphlets after 1770
Arranged by author or by title where author is unknown.

[John Almon], *An Address to the Interior Cabinet* (London, 1782).

[John Almon], ed., *Biographical, Literary and Political Anecdotes... By the Author of the Anecdotes of the late Earl of Chatham* (3 vols., London, 1797).

[John Almon], *A Letter to the Earl of Bute* (London, 1771).

[John Almon], *A Letter to the Right Honourable Charles Jenkinson* (London, 1781).

James Burgh, *Political Disquisitions: or an enquiry into public errors, defects and abuses* (3 vols., London, 1774–5).

John Cartwright, *The Legislative Rights of the Commonalty Vindicated; or, Take Your Choice! Representation and Respect's Imposition and Contempt. Annual Parliaments and Liberty: Long Parliaments and Slavery. Wherein it is contended, upon the Unalterable Principles of Law and the Constitution, that an Equal and Complete Representation in Parliament, and Annual Elections, are at this Day the undoubted R I G H T S of the Commonalty of this Realm; notwithstanding the supposed Validity of certain Acts of Parliament: And wherin is also shewn precisely how far (and it is to a most alarming Degree) the People are Absolutely Enslaved already, notwithstanding they vainly imagine themselves free* (London, 1st ed. 1776, 2nd ed. 1777).

Characters, Containing an Impartial Review of the Public Conduct and Abilities of the Most Important Personages in the Parliament of Great Britain, Revised and Corrected by the Author Since the Original Publication in the Gazetteer (London, 1777).

A Collection of letters and essays in favour of public liberty first published in the newspapers in the years 1764, 1765, 1766, 1767, 1768, 1769 and 1770 by an amicable band of wellwishers to the religious and civil rights of mankind (3 vols., London, 1774).

A Collection of Scarce and Interesting Tracts. Written by Persons of Eminence; upon the most important political and commercial subjects. During the years 1763, 1764, 1765, 1766, 1767, 1768, 1769 & 1770 (4 vols., London, 1788).

The Controversial Letters of John Wilkes, the Rev. John Horne, and their principal adherents. With a supplement, containing material anonymous pieces (London, 1771).

[J. Craddock], *The Life of John Wilkes, in the manner of Plutarch: being a specimen of a larger work* (London, 1773).

A Dissertation on the rise, progress, views, strength, interests and characters of the two parties of the W H I G S and T O R I E S (Boston, 1773).

The Favourite; a Character from the Life. Addressed to the Sovereign Minion of the Times, on the much lamented Death of the Patriotic Earl of Chatham (London, 1778).

The Humours of the Times (London, 1771).

Bibliography

An Inquiry into the Origin and Consequences of the Influence of the Crown over Parliament. Submitted to the Consideration of the Electors of Great Britain (London, 1780).

[Soame Jenyns], *A scheme for the Coalition of Parties. Humbly submitted to the Public* (London, 1772).

[Samuel Johnson], *The Patriot. Addressed to the Electors of Great Britain* (London, 1774).

[Samuel Johnson], *Taxation no Tyranny; an answer to the resolutions and address of the American Congress* (London, 1775).

Letters Concerning the Present State of England, particularly respecting the Politics, Arts, Manners and Literature of the Times (London, 1772).

A Letter from a Member of the Long Parliament to a Member of the Present (London, 1778).

[William Augustus Miles], *A Political Mirror; or, a Summary of the Present Reign* (London, 1779).

'*The MINISTRY in the Suds*' or '*Jack with the Golden Chain in the Parliament-House*'. *In which is presented to the Public the true State of the Case between Mr. WILKES and the MINISTRY. Together with an Original Picture of Modern Patriotism in my good LORD BARRINGTON* (London, 1774).

The Principles of a Real Whig; contained in a Preface to the Famous Hotman's Franco-Gallia, written by the late Lord Viscount Molesworth; and now Reprinted at the Request of the London Association. To which are added their Resolutions and Circular Letter (London, 1775).

The Pamphlet, entitled 'Taxation No Tyranny', Candidly Considered, and its Arguments, and Pernicious Doctrines, Exposed and Refuted (London, n.d.).

A Refutation of a Pamphlet, called thoughts on the Late Transactions respecting Falkland's Islands; In a Letter Addressed to the Author, and Dedicated to Dr. Samuel Johnson (London, 1771).

SECONDARY WORKS
Books, arranged by author

William Albert, *The Turnpike Road System in England 1663–1840* (Cambridge, 1972).

R. J. Allen, *The Clubs of Augustan London* (Cambridge, Mass., 1933).

R. D. Altick, *The English Common Reader: a social history of the mass reading public; 1800–1900* (Chicago, 1957).

Alexander Andrews, *The History of British Journalism, from the foundation of the newspaper press in England, to the repeal of the Stamp Act in 1855; with sketches of press celebrities* (2 vols., London, 1859).

T. S. Ashton, *Economic Fluctuations in England 1700–1800* (Oxford, 1959).

A. Aspinall, *Politics and the Press c. 1780–1850* (London, 1949).

Herbert M. Atherton, *Politics Prints in the Age of Hogarth* (Oxford, 1974).

Bernard Bailyn, *The Ideological Origins of the American Revolution* (Cambridge, Mass., 1967).

The Origins of American Politics (New York, 1968).

Pamphlets of the American Revolution, vol. 1, 1750–1765 (Cambridge, Mass., 1965).

Horace Bleackley, *Life of John Wilkes* (London, 1917).

Bibliography

J. T. Boulton, *The Language of Politics in the Age of Wilkes and Burke* (London, 1963).

A. M. Broadley, *Brother John Wilkes as Freemason, ' Buck ', ' Leech ' and Beefsteak* (London, 1914).

John Brooke, *The Chatham Administration, 1766–1768* (London, 1956).

Peter Brown, *The Chathamites. A Study in the relationship between Personalities and Ideas in the second half of the Eighteenth Century* (London, 1967).

Wallace Cable Brown, *Charles Churchill, Poet, Rake and Rebel* (Lawrence, Kansas, 1953).

Sir Herbert Butterfield, *George III and the Historians* (London, 1957).
George III, Lord North and the People 1779–80 (London, 1949).

Francis P. Canavan, *The Political Reason of Edmund Burke* (Durham, North Carolina, 1960).

Elias Canetti, *Crowds and Power* (Penguin ed., London, 1973).

John Cannon, *The Fox–North Coalition. Crisis of the Constitution, 1782–4* (Cambridge, 1970).
Parliamentary Reform 1640–1832 (Cambridge, 1973).

C. Lennart Carlson, *The First Magazine: A History of the ' Gentleman's Magazine '* (Providence, Rhode Island, 1938).

Ian R. Christie, *The End of Lord North's Ministry 1780–1782* (London, 1958).
Myth and Reality in Late-Eighteenth-Century British Politics (London, 1970).
Wilkes, Wyvill and Reform. The Parliamentary Reform Movement in British Politics, 1760–1785 (London, 1962).

Dora Mae Clark, *British Opinion and the American Revolution* (New Haven, 1930).

James L. Clifford (ed.), *Man Versus Society in Eighteenth-Century Britain* (Cambridge, 1968).

Richard Cobb, *The Police and the People* (Oxford, 1970).

A. S. Collins, *Authorship in the Days of Johnson* (London, 1927).

Carl B. Cone, *Burke and the Nature of Politics. The Age of the American Revolution* (University of Kentucky, 1957).

G. A. Cranfield, *The Development of the Provincial Newspaper 1700–1760* (Oxford, 1962).

Philip Davidson, *Propaganda and the American Revolution* (Chapel Hill, North Carolina, 1941).

H. T. Dickinson, *Bolingbroke* (London, 1970).

Aytoun Ellis, *The Penny Universities. A History of the Coffee Houses* (London, 1956).

Kenneth Ellis, *The Post Office in the Eighteenth Century: A Study in Administrative History* (London, 1958).

C. S. Emden, *The People and the Constitution: being a history of the development of the people's influence in British government* (Oxford, 1933).

Alan Everitt (ed.), *Perspectives in English Urban History* (London, 1973).

E. Eyck, *Pitt Versus Fox, Father and Son* (London, 1950).

Keith Feiling, *The Second Tory Party 1714–1832* (London, 1938).

Raymond Firth, *Symbols, Public and Private* (London, 1973).

Archibald S. Foord, *His Majesty's Opposition 1714–1830* (Oxford, 1964).

Paul Fritz and David Williams (ed.), *The Triumph of Culture: Eighteenth Century Perspectives* (Toronto, 1972).

Bibliography

Paul Fussell, *The Rhetorical World of Augustan Humanism* (Oxford, 1965).

Peter Gay, *The Enlightenment: an Interpretation* (2 vols., London, 1967–70).

M. D. George, *English Political Caricature: a Study in Opinion and Propaganda* (2 vols., Oxford, 1959).

London Life in the Eighteenth Century (London, 1925).

D. E. Ginter, *Whig Organisation in the General Election of 1790; selections from the Blair Adam Papers* (Berkeley, California, 1967).

L. H. Gipson, *The British Empire Before the American Revolution* (15 vols., New York, 1936–70).

Max Gluckman, *Politics, Law and Ritual in Tribal Society* (Oxford, 1965).

Max Gluckman (ed.), *Essays on the Ritual of Social Relationships* (Manchester, 1962).

E. H. Gombrich, *Symbolic Images. Studies in the art of the Renaissance* (London, 1972).

Jack Goody (ed.), *Literacy in Traditional Societies* (Cambridge, 1968).

Jack P. Greene (ed.), *The Nature of Colony Constitutions* (Columbia, S.C., 1970).

G. H. Guttridge, *English Whiggism and the American Revolution* (Berkeley and Los Angeles, 1963).

W. B. Gwyn, *The Meaning of the Separation of Powers. Tulane Studies in Political Science IX* (New Orleans, 1965).

R. L. Haig, *The Gazetteer 1735–1797: A Study in the Eighteenth-Century English Newspaper* (Carbondale, Ill., 1968).

L. W. Hanson, *Government and the Press, 1695–1763* (Oxford, 1936).

Glenn W. Hatfield, *Henry Fielding and the Language of Irony* (Chicago, 1968).

Frederick J. Hinkhouse, *The Preliminaries of the American Revolution as seen in the English Press, 1763–1775* (New York, 1926).

E. J. Hobsbawm, *Primitive Rebels* (New York, 1959).

E. J. Hobsbawm and George Rudé, *Captain Swing* (1973 ed., London).

Ross Hoffman, *The Marquis. A Study of Lord Rockingham, 1730–1782* (New York, 1973).

Sir William Holdsworth, *A History of the English Law* (16 vols., London, 1903–66).

Geoffrey S. Holmes, *British Politics in the Reign of Queen Anne* (London, 1967).

Bernard E. Jones, *Freemason's Guide and Compendium* (London, 1956).

M. G. Kammen, *A Rope of Sand: The Colonial Agents, British Politics and the American Revolution* (Ithica, N.Y., 1968).

Paul Kaufman, *Libraries and their Users* (London, 1969).

Betty Kemp, *King and Commons, 1660–1832* (London, 1957).

Sir Francis Dashwood. An Eighteenth-Century Independent (London, 1967).

Samuel Kliger, *The Goths in England* (Cambridge, Mass., 1952).

Isaac Kramnick, *Bolingbroke and his Circle. The Politics of Nostalgia* (Cambridge, Mass., 1968).

P. Langford, *The First Rockingham Administration 1765–1766* (Oxford, 1973).

R. H. Lee, *The Life of Arthur Lee, Ll.D* (2 vols., Boston, 1829).

Bryant Lillywhite, *London Coffee Houses* (London, 1963).

John Loftis, *The Politics of Drama in Augustan England* (Oxford, 1963).

J. A. Lovat-Fraser, *John Stuart, Earl of Bute* (Cambridge, 1912).

S. Lutnick, *The American Revolution and the British Press, 1775–1783* (Columbia, Mo., 1967).

Bibliography

T. B. Macaulay, *Critical and Historical Essays contributed to the Edinburgh Review* (London, 1877).

S. Maccoby, *English Radicalism 1762–1785* (London, 1955).

Pauline Maier, *From Resistance to Revolution, Colonial Radicals and the Development of American Opposition to Britain, 1765–1776* (New York, 1972).

R. W. Malcolmson, *Popular Recreations in English Society 1700–1850* (Cambridge, 1973).

Harvey C. Mansfield, *Statesmanship and Party Government. A Study of Burke and Bolingbroke* (Chicago, 1965).

Thomas Erskine May, *The Constitutional History of England Since the Accession of George III* (2 vols., 1861–3).

Neil McKendrick (ed.), *Historical Perspectives. Studies in English Thought and Society in honour of J. H. Plumb* (1974).

Gerald Miller, *English Inn Signs. Being a Revised and Modernised Version of the History of Signboards, by Jacob Larwood and J. C. Hoffen* (London, 1951).

C. Wright Mills, *The Sociological Imagination* (New York, 1959).

G. E. Mingay, *English Landed Society in the Eighteenth Century* (London, 1963).

E. S. and H. M. Morgan, *The Stamp Act Crisis: Prologue to Revolution* (Chapel Hill, N.C., 1953).

Sir Lewis Namier, *Crossroads of Power, Essays on Eighteenth-Century England* (London, 1962).

England in the Age of the American Revolution (2nd ed., London, 1963).

Personalities and Powers (London, 1955).

The Structure of Politics at the Accession of George III (2nd ed., London, 1957).

Sir Lewis Namier and John Brooke, *Charles Townshend* (London, 1964).

(eds.), *The History of Parliament. The House of Commons 1754–1790* (3 vols., HMSO, 1964).

A. Natan (ed.), *Silver Renaissance: Essays in Eighteenth-Century English History* (London, 1961).

George Nobbe, *The North Briton. A Study in Political Propaganda* (New York, 1939).

John B. Owen, *The Rise of the Pelhams* (London, 1957).

The Pattern of Politics in Eighteenth-Century England (Hist. Assoc., Aids to Teachers, no. 10, 1962).

Anne Pallister, *Magna Carta* (Oxford, 1971).

Richard Pares, *King George III and the Politicians* (Oxford, 1953).

Richard Pares and A. J. P. Taylor (eds.), *Essays presented to Sir Lewis Namier* (London, 1956).

F. Peel, *The Risings of the Luddites*, ed. E. P. Thompson (4th ed., London, 1968).

J. H. Plumb, *The Commercialisation of Leisure* (University of Reading, 1973).

The Growth of Political Stability in England 1675–1725 (London, 1967).

Sir Robert Walpole (2 vols., London, 1956–60).

J. G. A. Pocock, *Politics, Language and Time. Essays on Political Thought and History* (London, 1972).

J. R. Pole, *Political Representation in England and the Origins of the American Republic* (London, 1966).

Raymond Postgate, *That Devil Wilkes* (London, 1930).

J. Prebble, *Culloden* (London, 1961).

Bibliography

Robert R. Rea, *The English Press in Politics, 1760–1774* (Lincoln, Neb., 1963).

Conyers Read (ed.), *The Constitution Reconsidered* (New York, 1938).

Donald Read, *Peterloo. The Massacre and its Background* (Manchester, 1958).

Press and People, 1790–1850: Opinion in Three English Cities (London, 1961).

Caroline Robbins, *The Eighteenth-Century Commonwealthman* (Cambridge, Mass., 1959).

Clayton Roberts, *The Growth of Responsible Government in Stuart England* (Cambridge, 1966).

R. J. Robson, *The Oxfordshire Election of 1754; a study in the interplay of city, county and university politics* (Oxford, 1949).

George Rudé, *The Crowd in History; a study in popular disturbances in France and England, 1730–1848* (London, 1964).

Hanoverian London 1714–1808 (London, 1971).

Paris and London in the Eighteenth-Century. Studies in Popular Protest (London, 1970).

Wilkes and Liberty. A Social Study of 1763 to 1774 (Oxford, 1962).

Albert von Ruville, *William Pitt, Earl of Chatham* (3 vols., London, 1907).

Romney Sedgwick (ed.), *The History of Parliament. The House of Commons 1715–1754* (2 vols., HMSO, 1971).

Walter James Shelton, *English Hunger and Industrial Disorders* (London, 1973).

O. A. Sherrard, *A Life of John Wilkes* (London, 1938).

F. J. Siebert, *The Freedom of the Press in England, 1476–1776* (Urbana, Ill., 1952).

J. T. Smith, *Book for a Rainy Day* (London, 1845).

W. H. Smith (ed.), *Horace Walpole, Writer, Politician and Connoisseur. Essays on the 250th Anniversary of Walpole's Birth* (London, 1967).

J. M. Sosin, *Agents and Merchants, British Colonial Policy and the Origins of the American Revolution, 1763–1775* (Lincoln, Neb., 1965).

W. A. Speck, *Tory and Whig, the Struggle in the Constituencies 1701–1715* (London, 1971).

M. M. Spector, *The American Department of the British Government, 1768–1782* (New York, 1940).

Lucy S. Sutherland, *The City of London, and the Opposition to Government, 1768–1774. A Study in the Rise of Metropolitan Radicalism* (Creighton Lecture, London, 1959).

The East India Company in Eighteenth-Century Politics (Oxford, 1952).

P. D. G. Thomas, *The House of Commons in the Eighteenth Century* (Oxford, 1971).

E. P. Thompson, *The Making of the English Working Class* (Penguin ed., London, 1968).

M. A. Thomson, *A Constitutional History of England, 1642–1801* (London, 1938).

William Purdie Treloar, *Wilkes and the City* (London, 1917).

G. M. Trevelyan, *The Two Party System in English Political History* (Oxford, 1926).

G. O. Trevelyan, *The Early History of Charles James Fox* (London, 1888).

A. S. Turberville, *The House of Lords in the Eighteenth Century* (London, 1924).

(ed.), *Johnson's England* (2 vols., Oxford, 1933).

Bibliography

Victor W. Turner, *The Ritual Process. Structure and Anti-Structure* (London, 1969).

Hubert van Thal (ed.), *The Prime Ministers* (London, 1974).

G. S. Veitch, *The Genesis of Parliamentary Reform* (London, 1913).

M. J. C. Vile, *Constitutionalism and the Separation of Powers* (Oxford, 1963).

J. Steven Watson, *The Reign of George III* (Oxford, 1960).

Ian Watt, *The Rise of the Novel* (London, 1957).

Robert F. Wearmouth, *Methodism and the Common People of the Eighteenth Century* (London, 1945).

Enid Welsford, *The Fool. His Social and Literary History* (London, 1935).

Corinne Comstock Weston, *English Constitutional Theory and the House of Lords, 1556–1832* (London, 1965).

Anne Whiteman, J. S. Bromley and P. M. G. Dickson (eds.), *Statesmen, Scholars and Merchants* (Oxford, 1973).

R. M. Wiles, *Freshest Advices* (Ohio State University Press, 1965).

J. W. Wilkes, *A Whig in Power; the political career of Henry Pelham* (Evanston, Ill., 1964).

T. S. Willan, *An Eighteenth-Century Shopkeeper, Abraham Dent of Kirkby Stephen* (Manchester, 1970).

William Willeford, *The Fool and his Sceptre* (London, 1969).

Basil Williams, *The Life of William Pitt, Earl of Chatham* (2 vols., London, 1915).

D. A. Winstanley, *Lord Chatham and the Whig Opposition* (Cambridge, 1912). *Personal and Party Government* (Cambridge, 1910).

Articles, arranged by author

The first reference to a periodical contains its title in full; thereafter it is given in abbreviation.

Douglas Adair, 'The Stamp Act in contemporary British Cartoons', *William and Mary Quarterly* x (1953).

A. H. Arkle 'Early Coffee Houses in Liverpool', *Transactions of the Historic Society of Lancashire and Cheshire* LXIV (1912).

A. Aspinall, 'Statistical Accounts of the London Newspapers during the Eighteenth Century', *English Historical Review* LXIII (1948).

J. M. Beattie, 'The Pattern of Crime in England 1660–1800', *Past and Present* 62 (1974).

J. M. Beatty, 'The Political Satires of Charles Churchill', *Studies in Philology* XVI (1919).

Frank Beckwith, 'The Eighteenth-Century Proprietary Library in England', *Journal of Documentation* III (1948).

John Brewer, 'Party and the Double Cabinet: Two Facets of Burke's *Thoughts*', *Historical Journal* XIV, 3 (1971).

'The Faces of Lord Bute: a visual contribution to Anglo-American political ideology', *Perspectives in American History* VI (1972).

'The Misfortunes of Lord Bute: A Case-study in Eighteenth-century Political Argument and Public Opinion', *HJ* XVI, 1 (1973).

'Rockingham, Burke and Whig Political Argument', *HJ* XVIII, 1 (1975).

John Brooke, 'Namier and Namierism', *History and Theory* III, 3 (1964).

Bibliography

Herbert Butterfield, 'George III and the Constitution', *History* XLIII (1958).

  'Some Reflections on the Early Years of George III's Reign', *Journal of British Studies* IV (1965).

M. H. Cable, '*The Idea of a Patriot King* in the propaganda of the Opposition to Walpole, 1735–39', *Philological Quarterly* XVIII (1939).

Peter Campbell, 'An Early Defence of Party', *Political Studies* III, 2 (1955).

D. E. Clark, 'News and Opinion concerning America in English newspapers 1754–1763', *Pacific Historical Review* X (1941).

A. Cohen, 'The Analysis of the Symbolism of Power Relations', *Man* IV (1969).

A. S. Collins, 'Growth of the Reading Public during the Eighteenth Century', *Review of English Studies* II (1926).

C. Collyer, 'The Rockingham connection and County Opinion in the early years of George III', *Proceedings of the Leeds Philosophical Society* VII (1955).

Natalie Zemon Davis, 'The Rites of Violence: Religious Riot in Sixteenth-Century France', *P & P* 59 (1973).

John Dunn, 'The Identity of the History of Ideas', *Philosophy* XLIII (1968).

W. R. Fryer, 'King George III: His Political Character and Conduct, 1760–84. A new Whig Interpretation', *Renaissance and Modern Studies* VI (1962).

Donald E. Ginter, 'The Financing of Whig Party Organisation, 1783–1793', *American Historical Review* LXXI (1966).

E. H. Gombrich, 'The Use of Art for the Study of Symbols', *American Psychologist* XX, i (1965).

H. J. Habakkuk, 'Marriage Settlements in the Eighteenth Century', TRHS 4th ser. XXXII (1950).

Halsey, '"Impolitical Prints"; the American Revolution as Pictured by Contemporary English Caricaturists', *Bulletin of the New York Library* (1939).

Hilda M. Hamlyn, 'Eighteenth-Century Circulating Libraries in England', *Library* 5th Series I (1946).

R. D. Harlan, 'Some Additional Figures of distribution of eighteenth-century books', *Papers of the Bibliographical Society of America* LIX (1965).

M. R. A. Harris, 'Figures relating to the Printing and Distribution of the *Craftsman* 1726 to 1730', *Bulletin of the Institute of Historical Research* XLIII (1970).

W. J. Hayes, 'Scottish Officers in the British Army', *Scottish Historical Review* XXXVII (1958).

B. W. Hill, 'Executive Monarchy and the Challenge of Parties, 1689–1832: Two Concepts of Government and Two Historiographical Interpretations', *HJ* XIII, 3 (1970).

Christopher Hill, 'The Norman Yoke', *Puritanism and Revolution* (London, 1955).

W. Holdsworth, 'The Conventions of the Eighteenth-Century Constitution', *Iowa Law Review* XVII (1931–2).

W. Hunt and H. W. Temperley, 'Pitt's retirement from office 5 October 1761', *EHR* XXI (1906).

G. M. Imlach, 'Earl Temple and the Ministry of 1765', *EHR* XXX (1915).

Derek Jarrett, 'The Regency Crisis of 1765', *EHR* LXXXV (1970).

Paul Kaufman, 'The Community Library: a Chapter in English Social History', *Transactions of the American Philosophical Society* (1967).

Bibliography

D. L. Keir, 'Economical Reform, 1779–87', *Law Quarterly Review* L (1934).

P. D. Langford, 'William Pitt and Public Opinion, 1757', *EHR* CCCXLVI (1973).

F. W. Levander, 'The Jerusalem Sols and some other London Societies of the Eighteenth Century', *Ars quatuorum coronati* XX (1907).

Gwyn Lewis, 'The White Terror of 1815 in the Department of the Gard', *P & P* 58 (1973).

Pauline Maier, 'John Wilkes and American Disillusionment with Britain', *William and Mary Quarterly* 3rd Series XX (1963).

A. D. McKillop, 'English Circulating Libraries, 1725–50', *Library* XIV (1934).

John Money, 'Taverns, Coffee Houses and Clubs: Local Politics and Popular Articulacy in the Birmingham Area in the Age of the American Revolution', *HJ* XIV, 1 (1971).

F. O'Gorman, 'Edmund Burke and the Idea of Party', *Studies in Burke and his Time* XI, 2 (1969).

'Party and Burke: The Rockingham Whigs', *Government and Opposition* III, i (1968).

R. Pares, 'George III and the Politicians', *Transactions of the Royal Historical Society* 5th Series I (1951).

Geoffrey Parker, 'Mutiny and Discontent in the Spanish Army of Flanders, 1572–1607', *P & P* 58 (1973).

Marie Peters, 'The *Monitor* on the Constitution, 1755–1765: new light on the ideological origins of English radicalism', *EHR* LXXXVI (1971).

J. H. Plumb, 'The Growth of the Electorate in England 1660–1715', *P & P* 45 (1969).

Caroline Robbins, '"Discordant Parties". A Study of the Acceptance of Party by Englishmen', *Political Science Quarterly* LXXIII (1958).

'The Strenuous Whig, Thomas Hollis of Lincoln's Inn', *WMQ* 3rd series 7 (1950).

Nicholas Rogers, 'Aristocratic Clientage, Trade and Independency: Popular Politics in Pre-Radical Westminster', *P & P* 61 (1973).

Pat Rogers, 'Swift and Bolingbroke on Faction', *JBS* IX (1970).

George Rudé, 'The Anti-Wilkite Merchants of 1769', *Guildhall Miscellany* II (1965).

W. H. Rylands, 'A Forgotten Rival of Masonry: the Noble Order of Bucks', *AQC* II (1890).

Quentin Skinner, 'History and Ideology in the English Revolution', *HJ* VIII, 2 (1965).

'The Limits of Historical Explanation', *Philosophy* XLI (1966).

'Meaning and Understanding in the History of Ideas', *History and Theory* VIII, i (1969).

'Some Problems in the Analysis of Political Thought and Action', *Political Theory* II, 3 (1974).

E. A. Smith, 'The Electoral Agent in English politics, 1734–1832', *EHR* LXXXIV (1969).

Henry L. Snyder, 'The Circulation of newspapers in the reign of Queen Anne', *Library* 5th Series XXIII (1968).

Lawrence Stone, 'Literacy and Education in England, 1640–1900', *P & P* 42 (1969).

Bibliography

H. de Strange, 'The Great Lodge, Swaffham, Norfolk 1764–1785', *AQC* xx (1907).

James R. Sutherland, 'The Circulation of Newspapers and Literary Publications, 1700–1730', *Library* 4th Series xv (1934).

Lucy S. Sutherland, 'The City of London and the Devonshire–Pitt Administration 1756–7', *Proceedings of the British Academy* xLVI (1960).

'Edmund Burke and the first Rockingham Ministry', *EHR* xLVII (1932).

P. D. G. Thomas, 'The Beginning of Parliamentary Reporting in Newspapers, 1768–1774', *EHR* LXXIV (1959).

'Check List of M.P.s speaking in the House of Commons, 1768–1774', *Bulletin of the Institute of Historical Research* xxxv (1962).

'John Wilkes and the Freedom of the Press', *BIHR* xxxIII (1960).

E. P. Thompson, 'The Moral Economy of the English Crowd in the Eighteenth Century', *P & P* 50 (1971).

Louise A. Tilly, 'The Food Riot as a Form of Political Conflict in France', *Journal of Interdisciplinary History* II, i (1971).

D. H. Watson, 'The Rise of the Opposition at Wildman's Club', *BIHR* xLIV (1971).

Barbara Whittingham-Jones, 'Liverpool's Political Clubs, 1812–1830', *Transactions of the Historic Society of Lancashire and Cheshire* cxi (1959).

E. A. Wrigley, 'A Simple Model of London's Importance in Changing English Society and Economy, 1650–1750', *P & P* 37 (1967).

Unpublished dissertations

P. Fritz, *Jacobitism and the English Government, 1717–1731* (Cambridge University, Ph.D., 1967).

D. Hamer, *From Grafton to North, 1768–1772* (Cambridge University, Ph.D., 1971).

A. Hardy, *The Duke of Newcastle and his friends in Opposition, 1762–1765* (Manchester University, M.A., 1956).

John Money, *Public Opinion in the West Midlands, 1760–1793* (Cambridge University, Ph.D., 1967).

W. A. Smith, *Anglo-Colonial Society and the Mob, 1740–1775* (Claremont Graduate School and University Center, Ph.D., 1965).

David Thomson, *The Conception of Political Party in England, in the period 1740 to 1783* (Cambridge University, Ph.D., 1938).

D. H. Watson, *The Duke of Newcastle, the Marquis of Rockingham, and Mercantile Interests in London and the Provinces, 1761–1768* (Sheffield University, Ph.D., 1968).

Index

Adam, William, 60
affiches, 152–3
Albemarle, George, 3rd Earl of, 80, 87, 90, 283 n.20
Allen, Ralph, 7, 159
Almon, John, 167, 174, 204, 227, 231, 306 n.31; as 'Independent Whig', 48; press agent for Wildman's, 61; publishes American tracts, 215; on Wilkes, 169, 171
Alnwick, 178, 309 n.102
Amelia, H.R.H. Princess, 278 n.22
American colonies, 15, 17, 20, 44, 50, 86, 89, 94, 128, 160, 201, 203, 204, 209, 232, 233, 241, 262; administrative and financial problem 201–2; contaminate Britain, 207; divided opposition, 64, 288 n.71; as geo-political problem, 201; links between Britain and, 205, 211; parliamentary sovereignty over, 202, 209; share complaints of English, 203, 209, 210, 252; taxation of, 202–3; *see also* American colonists; representation; parliamentary reform
American colonists, 205, 208, 210, 211, 213, 215, 251; agents, 203; defence of, 209–10; factious, 321 n.51; as ideological midwife, 215; and imperial parliament, 212; merchants, 203; propaganda of (1765–6), 216; should pay for themselves, 202, 209; on Stamp Act, 208, 216; *see also* American colonies; representation; parliamentary reform
Anne, Queen, 6, 42, 148, 157; reign compared with George III, 48, 72
Annual Register, 112, 147, 158
Antigallicans, 194, 195
'Anti-Sejanus', 56, 234; *see also* Scott, Dr James
Aris's Birmingham Gazette, 143, 145
Aristotle, 242
Arthur's Coffee House, 149–50
Ashburnham, John, 2nd Earl of, 80
Auditor, 48, 142, 154, 222
Augusta, Princess Dowager of Wales, 123, 152, 153, 156, 182, 184, 224, 295 n.42

Baillie, Hugh, 223

Bailyn, Bernard, 55, 204, 320 n.31
Baker, William, 256, 282 n.12, 283 n.18
Baldwin, Henry, 194
ballads and songs, 7, 35, 234, 303 n.109; on Byng, 156; circulation, 147; political importance of, 155–6; Wilkite and anti-Bute, 156, 169, 172, 190, 306 n.31
ballad singers, 7, 155–6
Banbury, 178
Barnsley, 146
Barnstaple, 178
Barré, Isaac, 75, 81, 102, 204
Barrington, William Wildman, 2nd Viscount, 55, 184
Barton, George, 151
Baskerville, John, 172
Bath, 151, 159, 178, 230
Bath, 1st Earl of, *see* Pulteney, William
Beckford, William, 102, 293 n.10, 307 n.63, 318 n.76; backs *Monitor*, 9; and parliamentary reform, 207, 215; and Wilkes, 171, 197, 198
Bedale, 178
Bedford, John Russell, 4th Duke of, 13, 64, 86, 87, 88, 89, 90, 91, 92, 95, 124, 149, 240–1, 288 n.71, 289 n.75, n.76
Bedford whigs, 40, 42, 58, 73, 82, 86; in 1767, 64, 87–8, 89, 90, 288 n.63, 289 n.76
Bedfordshire, 6, 145
Bentinck, William Count, 228
Berkeley, Norborne (Baron Botetourt), 280 n.47
Bernard, Sir Robert, 221
Berwick-on-Tweed, 145, 179
Bessborough, William Ponsonby, 2nd Earl of, 63, 80, 83, 87, 90
Betty's, 59
Birmingham, 172, 209, 210, 211; coffee houses and papers, 150–1, 158, 160; and Wilkes, 177, 178
Blackstone, Sir William, 6, 207
Bland, Richard, 212
Bolingbroke, Henry St John, 1st Viscount, 24, 284 n.56, 320 n.31; and Broadbottom, 67; on country party, 66–7, 72; on liberty and faction, 282 n.9; *Idea of a Patriot King* (1738), 99; *Letter on the Spirit of Patriotism* (1736), 99; and party distinctions, 46

369

373

Maryland, 177

masonic societies, 7, 149, 181, 194, 195, 196

Massacre of the Pelhamite Innocents, 44, 49, 84, 85, 149, 251; *see also* Old Corps

Mauduit, I., 146, 230

Mawbey, Sir Joseph, 221

May, Erskine, 27, 29

'measures not men', 65, 68–9, 70, 82, 284 n.58

Melcombe, Lord, *see* Dodington, George Bubb

Meredith, Sir William, 87, 289 n.79; *Answer to the Majority*, 230; on Bedfords, 288 n.63; *The Question Stated*, 232; and Wigan election, 60

Meynell, Hugo, 84

Middlesex elections (1768–9), 147, 152, 164–5, 167, 168, 170, 176, 179, 181, 186, 191, 198, 207, 210, 231, 238, 247, 251, 254, 260, 261, 320 n.31, n.38; and proposed tax strike, 215; *see also* petitions; Wilkes

Middlesex Journal, 142, 174, 195

Midlands, 142, 143, 172, 177

ministerial responsibility, 27, 35, 130, 267, 295 n.39; and claims of politicians, 123–5, 131; collective responsibility, 135–6; and demand for royal confidence, 126–9, 131; eighteenth-century definition of, 112–13, 292 n.39; Favourite abnegates, 120, 122; and impeachment, 114, 115, 117, 119, 136; inadequate definition of, 116; king not to act personally, 120–1; its limits, 135–6; ministers as public servants, 118–19; obtains redress, 114; and prerogative, 115; preserves monarchy, 113; threatens personal powers of Crown, 121; widely accepted, 114–15

Mitre Coffee House, 149

Molyneux, Crisp, 181, 197

Monitor, 9, 154, 223, 244

Montagu, Frederick, 87

Montesquieu, 320 n.31

Monthly Review, 16, 143, 147, 154, 158, 211

Mordaunt, Sir Charles, 102, 280 n.47

Morning Chronicle, 142, 150

Morning Post, 150

Morpeth, 179

Morton, John, 10

Murphy, Arthur, 48, 157, 223, 224

Namier, Sir Lewis, 4, 26, 27, 31, 276 n.1, n.14, n.18; on George III, 30; on ideas, 30; on king's right to choose ministers, 115; on ministerial responsibility, 32,

113; on Newcastle's resignation, 297 n.79; omits Newcastle's conditions, 132; and parliamentary government, 39, 113; and party labels, 39–40; on Pitt, 109

New Form of Prayer and Thanksgiving, 173

New York, 209

Newbury, 186

Newcastle, Thomas Pelham-Holles, 1st Duke of, 5, 11, 40, 43, 44, 49, 50, 53, 58, 59, 60, 62, 63, 68, 69, 80, 86, 97, 98, 106, 121, 123, 131, 132, 135, 156, 247, 262, 263, 280 n.50, 283 n.20, 286 n.11, 289 n.76, 294 n.30; on America, 202; attitudes towards press, 226–7, 229, 233; corrects pamphlets, 230; demands confidence, 126; desires coalition, 13, 78, 84, 87, 88, 89, 90, 95, 288 n.67; difference with Pitt, 64, 77, 79, 81, 101, 103, 104; on fate of whigs, 77, 82; loses supporters, 12–13, 54, 84; makes conditions, 123, 125, 287 n.53, 297 n.68, 298 n.91, 299 n.98; on ministerial appointments, 115; principles, 78; pro-party, 83; and provincial opinion, 231–2; and resignation (1762), 126, 297 n.79; and tories, 85, 277 n.15; and whigs and tories, 51; and Wildman's, 61–2; *see also* Newcastle-Rockingham whigs

Newcastle Journal, 145

Newcastle–Rockingham whigs, 42, 50, 60, 78, 85, 117, 123, 124, 149, 227, 230, 317 n.44; constrain king, 118; divided, 64; party meetings of, 60; problems of, 12, 79; relations with Pitt, 79–81, 82, 106; take office without Pitt, 60, 80; weakness of, 81; and Wildman's, 61–2

Newcastle-under-Lyme, 145

Newcastle-upon-Tyne, 143, 150, 155, 177, 178, 183

Newdigate, Sir Roger, 150, 221, 280 n.47, 302 n.63

Newgate Gaol, 178

Newmarket, *see* horse-racing

newspapers, 75, 104, 108, 139, 140, 147, 154, 160, 167, 171, 174, 177, 178, 183, 186, 189, 203, 204, 222, 224, 225, 227, 228, 229, 233, 234, 235, 268; and American colonies, 202, 205, 216; circulation, 16, 142–3, 143–5, 148, 157, 220; in circulating libraries, 151; in coffee houses, 148, 149, 150; franking of, 230–1; hired, 151; in London, 7, 142–4, 148–50, 158, 172, 176; provincial, 16, 35, 143–5, 158, 159, 174, 176, 179, 219; publicly read, 156; radical content, 8; reproduce Wilkes's addresses, 167; stim-

patriot, patriotism (*cont.*)
109–11; qualities of, 99–100; scepticism about, 100; in seventeenth century, 292 n.62; Wilkes as, 169
Patriotic Club, Newbury, 186
patronage, 57, 61, 62, 76, 83, 116, 120, 125, 127, 130, 250; control over, 131, 296 n.51
Peele's Coffee House, 149
Pelham, Henry, 5, 8, 24, 53, 54, 68, 98, 262, 263
Penton, Henry, 84
Penzance, 178
people, 248; assigned passive role, 237, 238, 255–6; definitions of, 235–6, 318 n.77; discontent of, first sign of constitutional imbalance, 245, 246–7; distinguished from mob, 235–6; like Newtonian clockwinder, 236; misled by opposition, 247; power comes from, 256; to remedy constitution's ills, 253
Percival, John, 182
periodicals, 16, 146–7, 154, 157, 171, 174, 183, 189; *see also individual periodical titles*
Peterloo, 182, 215
petitions, 194, 204, 238, 248
Philadelphia, 209
Phillips, Sir John, 102
Philo-Patriae, 226
Pitt, George, 55, 280 n.47
Pitt, William, the elder, 1st Earl of Chatham, 9, 10, 11, 13, 30, 35, 43, 47, 48, 49, 50, 51, 53, 60, 68, 69, 77, 78, 79, 81, 85, 91, 92, 93, 95, 99, 117, 122, 131, 135, 149, 186, 223, 229, 238, 244, 247, 258, 261, 279 n.44, 280 n.46, 286 n.11; administration of (1766), 69, 82, 84, 87, 118, 284 n.57, 288 n.63; on America, 202; on appointment of ministers, 115; attacked by Butist journalists, 233–4; and Bute, 106–7, 108, 223–4, 226, 292 n.51; difficulties in the 1760s, 12, 96, 101–3; early career, 96–7; and George II, 101, 131–2; hostility to connection, 79, 82–3; hostility to Newcastle–Rockingham whigs, 79, 80, 83, 107; hostility to Yorke, 64, 79–80; makes conditions, 124, 125, 129; as mock-patriot, 105, 108, 167; and Old Corps, 12, 77, 106; and peerage, 104, 107, 110, 234; and pension, 104–5, 108, 110; and press, 228, 291 n.33, 292 n.53, n.55; resignation (1761), 103–4, 299 n.107; support for (1756–7), 8, 46–7; waywardness, 11, 64, 100, 109; and Wilkes, 167, 197; *see also* Chathamites; George III; patriot
Pitt, William, the younger, 27

Plain Dealer, 142
Plumb, J. H., 3, 4, 5, 8
Plymouth, 6, 177, 178
Pocock, J. G. A., 253, 319 n.21
Pole, J. R., 206
Political Balance, 48
Political Controversy, 154
Political Disquisitions proper for public Consideration, 207
Political Register, 119, 142, 154, 167, 261, 306 n.31; on history, 258; on parliamentary reform, 213
Polybius, 242, 243, 320 n.22
Pontefract, 146
Popham, Edward, 84
Portland, William Henry Cavendish Bentinck, 3rd Duke of, 15, 44, 58, 60, 80, 83, 85, 87, 90, 228, 231, 232, 233, 236, 282 n.13, 297 n.68
Portsmouth, 178
Post Boy, 157
Post Man, 157
postal service, 7, 220–1, 226
Pratt, Sir Charles, *see* Camden, 1st Earl of
Pratt, Robert, 84
prerogative, 28, 29, 45, 47, 51, 57, 67, 112, 130, 131; defended in new way, 134; limited by Constitution, 119; of ministerial appointment, 115–16; needs constraint, 118; preserved by ministerial responsibility, 113; royal views on, 116, 129–30, 134; subverted by politicians, 247; unconstrained, 117, 133; *see also* Crown, powers of
press, 23, 139, 226, 240, 253, 268; availability, 157; attempts to control, 219–20; and 'bridging', 155, 157; changes in 1715–60, 158; and circulation, 141, 142–8; duplication, 154–5, 157, 158, 174; freedom of, 21, 164, 165–6, 251, 305 n.15; and Grenville, 233–5; independence of, 239; and literacy, 141–2; MPs exploit through franking, 220–1; national network, 16, 18; not a 'fourth' estate, 235; and political education, 140, 299 n.1; in provinces, 16, 158, 159, 174–5; and readership, 141, 148–53; and Rockingham whigs, 226–33, 235; and royal Favourite, 221–6, 227, 235; threat to politicians, 238; used by opposition, 247, 283 n.27; *see also* ballads; newspapers; pamphlets; periodicals
Price, Chase, 44, 236
Probus, 178
Proctor, Sir Beauchamp, 170
proprietary parties, 40, 42, 43, 54, 57, 63, 65, 68, 69, 72, 74, 84, 93, 149; lack

Index

Rockingham whigs, Rockinghamites (*cont.*)
262; extra-parliamentary activity,
237–8; and issue of confidence, 128–9;
and Lord Strange incident, 122, 296
n.53; narrow view of politics, 263; negotiation of 1767, 87–91; numbers, 94;
their pamphlets, 227–33; paradox of
principles, 91–2; and people, 236–7,
238, 256; and press, 228–33, 235; reject
radicalism and reform, 256, 261, 263;
solution to discontents, 256–7, 262–3;
support limited reform, 257; *see also*
Newcastle–Rockingham whigs
Rogers, Nicholas, 198
Rome, 258, 259, 260
Rotherhithe, 185
Rotterdam, 179
Royal Register, 149
Royal Society Club, 149
Rudé, George, 174, 180, 181, 198, 308
n.84, n.86
Rutland, 145

sailors, 18, 182
St George's Fields Massacre, 153, 185, 252
St Ives, 151, 185
St James's Chronicle, 48, 150, 154, 155
St James's Coffee House, 149
St James's Palace, 153
St Michael's Mount, 178
St Neots, 151
St Paul's Churchyard, 7
Salopian Coffee House, 150
Sandwich, John Montagu, 4th Earl of,
184, 234, 235; as 'Jemmy Twitcher',
156–7, 189; and Wilkite jests, 189
Saunders, Sir Charles, 90
Savile, Sir George, 58, 92, 232, 233
Sawbridge, John, 197, 198, 253
Saxons, 259, 260, 261
Sayre, Stephen, 203
Scarsdale, Lord, *see under* Curzon, Sir
Nathaniel
Schofield, Roger, 141, 155
Scott, Dr James, 234
Scudamore, Charles Fitzroy, 84
Selwyn, George, 102, 290 n.23
Septennial Act (1716), 6
Settle, 146
Shaftesbury, Antony Ashley Cooper, 1st
Earl of, 261
Shaw, Cuthbert, 174
Shebbeare, William, 222
Sheerness, 178
Sheffield, 16, 158, 211
Shelburne, William Fitzmaurice Petty,
2nd Earl of, 81, 197, 204

Sherborne, 178
Shields, 178
Shoreditch, 181, 185
Shrewsbury, 6, 145, 177
Shropshire, 159
Sidney, Algernon, 261
silk weavers, *see* weavers
Skipton, 146
Smollett, Tobias, 3, 151, 155, 222
Society of Antiquaries, 149
Society of Bucks, 194, 195, 196
Society of Old Souls, 194
Society of Supporters of the Bill of Rights
(SSBR), 21, 22, 23, 160, 176, 177, 180,
181, 190, 195, 196, 197, 204, 238, 253,
256, 267; American connections of,
215; demands for reform, 206, 208;
and election of 1774, 194; organises
petitioning, 194; as propagandist or-
ganisation, 194; schism in, 192, 194,
199
songs, *see* ballads
South Carolina, 177, 179
South Sea Bubble, 176
Southwark, 6, 181, 213
Speck, W. A., 5, 277, n.11
Spectator, 148
Stafford, 146, 159, 172
Staffordshire, 179
Stamford, 6
Stamp Act (1765), 20, 64, 68, 78, 122, 128,
147, 202, 203, 204, 208, 210, 211, 212,
213, 214, 215, 228, 231, 232, 237, 296
n.53
Steuart, Charles, 203
Stockton, 177
Strahan, William, 146, 203
Strange, Lord, 122, 128, 296 n.53
Stratford-on-Avon, 146
strikes, 18, 182
Stroud, 178
Suffolk, 6, 145
suffrage, 19, 208, 214; *see also* parliamen-
tary reform
Sunderland, 178–9
Surrey, 194
Sussex, 231
Sutherland, Dame Lucy, 197
Swaffham, 179
Swift, Jonathan, 207
symbols, symbolism, 22, 187–9; and au-
thority, 182–4; in broadsides, 169; of
Bute and the Princess Dowager, 182; in
crowds, 182; definition of, 308 n.90;
in gift-giving, 177–8; and the law, 183;
no.45 as, 177, 178, 179, 182, 186–7, 188;
see also ritual